Immanuel Kant

CRITIQUE OF JUDGMENT

Including the First Introduction

Translated, with an Introduction, by
Werner S. Pluhar

With a Foreword by
Mary J. Gregor

Hackett Publishing Company
INDIANAPOLIS/CAMBRIDGE

Immanuel Kant: 1724–1804

The *Critique of Judgment* was originally published in Prussia in 1790

Copyright © 1987 by Werner S. Pluhar
All rights reserved
Printed in the United States of America
24 23 22 21 20   8 9 10 11

Cover design by Listenberger & Associates
Interior design by Dan Kirklin

For further information, please address
 Hackett Publishing Company, Inc.
 P.O. Box 44937
 Indianapolis, Indiana 46244-0937

 www.hackettpublishing.com

Library of Congress Cataloging in Publication Data

Kant, Immanuel, 1724–1804.
     Critique of judgment.
     Translation of: Kritik der Urteilskraft.
     "Including the first introduction."
     Bibliography: p.
     Includes index.
1. Judgment (Logic)—Early works to 1800.
2. Aesthetics—Early works to 1800. 3. Teleology—
Early works to 1800. I. Pluhar, Werner S., 1940- .
II. Title.
B2783.E5P58 1986   121   87-14852
ISBN 0-87220-026-4
ISBN 0-87220-025-6 (pbk.)

ISBN-13: 978-0-87220-026-5 (cloth)
ISBN-13: 978-0-87220-025-8 (pbk.)

CRITIQUE
OF JUDGMENT

Critik

der

Urtheilskraft

von

Immanuel Kant.

Berlin und Libau,
bey Lagarde und Friederich
1790.

CONTENTS

CRITIQUE OF JUDGMENT

CONTENTS xiii

FOREWORD

By calling three of his works "critiques," Kant indicated their central role in the Critical Philosophy. The *Critique of Pure Reason,* which determines the limits of theoretical cognition for the human mind, is the foundation of Kant's mature philosophical thought, and the ideal approach to his philosophy would, I suppose, begin with the *Critique of Pure Reason* and work forward systematically. That is to say, as we found various kinds of judgments, we would first analyze the sort of claim to universal assent being made and then attempt to justify that kind of claim by tracing it to the necessary principles of our mental activity. But our philosophical development may not parallel Kant's. If we find ourselves drawn to Kant by an interest in, e.g., ethics or aesthetics, we can go only so far before we get into difficulties. For Kant's interest in any problem has two aspects, the substantive and the critical. The sort of claim we are making can be analyzed in a way that is intelligible to a wide audience. But the status of that claim remains problematic until we have investigated our competence to make it. To justify the principle implicit in our moral judgments, we shall have to undertake a *Critique of Practical Reason;* to justify the principle implicit in our judgments about beauty, we must resort to a *Critique of Judgment.* And our investigation inevitably leads back to the *Critique of Pure Reason.*

To the extent that Kant keeps his substantive and his critical interests more or less separate, some of his writings, or parts of them, will be widely read. What Kant has to say on substantive issues has proved to be of perennial interest. But the student who becomes

interested in Kant's analysis will be aware that he cannot stop short
with the analytic phase: Kant will have warned him repeatedly that
the validity of these claims is still very much in question. Two courses are open to the serious student. He can plunge into the *Critique
of Pure Reason* and work his way forward. In the process he will
probably become a Kant scholar, an affliction that generally proves
incurable. Or he can be content with a more general understanding
of Kant's solution to the critical phase of the problem, which will
leave him free to pursue his broader interests. One of the merits of
Professor Pluhar's work is that his translator's introduction provides
the sort of background for the *Critique of Judgment* that will guide
the student interested in aesthetics and philosophy of science through
the critical phases in Kant's discussion of aesthetic and teleological
judgments.

The combination of Kant's critical and substantive concerns, in
this highly complex work, may well account for the long-standing
neglect of the *Critique of Judgment* as a whole and the interest
recently shown in some of its parts. In his Introduction to the third
Critique, Kant's interest is primarily critical. On the basis of the first
two *Critiques* he acknowledges a "chasm" between nature and freedom that is not to be bridged by way of theoretical cognition. For
a post-Kantian philosopher bent on doing speculative metaphysics,
this acknowledgment indicates the failure of the Critical Philosophy. Not until nineteenth century idealism had run its course would
it seem worthwhile to consider the more modest task Kant had set
himself: that of making the transition, by way of reflective judgment
and its principle of teleology, from our way of thinking about nature
to our way of thinking about freedom. But even then, the connection
between the Introduction to the *Critique* and its two parts seemed so
tenuous as to raise doubts about the unity and coherence of the work.

In the meantime, developments in art criticism and aesthetic theory
focused attention on Kant's accessible and tightly structured analysis of our judgments of beauty, the "Analytic of the Beautiful," into
which we are plunged after the Introduction's prologue in heaven.
The emergence of formalism in art, the collapse of "expressionism"
as an aesthetic theory into a branch of psychology, and the perennial difficulties of assigning "objective" status to beauty suggest that
Kant's analysis of taste is relevant to contemporary problems. But,
after the analytic, Kant's critical concerns come to the foreground

and the course of the argument becomes puzzling. Kant is somehow, here as in the subsequent treatment of teleological judgments, carrying out the project outlined in the Introduction. But how? The second merit of Pluhar's introduction is that it attempts to explain how Kant is dealing with the problem posed in the Introduction to the *Critique*.

None of the periodic revivals of interest in Kant has, it seems to me, approached the magnitude of the present one. This is the appropriate time for an accurate translation into modern English of the work that has been called "the crowning phase of the critical philosophy." By including in his translation the original Introduction to the *Critique of Judgment* (which Kant replaced by a shorter one), and by adding his own helpful analysis of Kant's argument, Pluhar has taken an important step toward securing for the third *Critique* its rightful place in the Kantian corpus.

MARY J. GREGOR
San Diego State University

To my mother,

Irmgart Schrutka Pluhar

TRANSLATOR'S PREFACE

Because there seems to be general agreement that an accurate and readable translation of the *Critique of Judgment,* including the First Introduction, is needed, I shall not argue that point.

The translator's introduction which follows (and, to some extent, the bracketed footnotes accompanying the text of the translation itself) serves two main purposes. One of these is to supply important background materials to readers with only limited prior exposure to Kant's "critical philosophy": above all, summaries of the *Critique of Pure Reason* and the *Critique of Practical Reason,* including not only the views but also the terminology from these works which Kant presupposes in the *Critique of Judgment;* and summaries of other philosophers' views to which each of the three *Critiques,* but especially the *Critique of Judgment,* responds.[1] The other main purpose is to explain the many difficult passages in the work. In particular, the translator's introduction offers a new interpretation of key elements in the foundation of both Kant's teleology and his aesthetics and uses that same interpretation to make new and better sense not only of the link between these two parts of the work, but especially of Kant's claims as to how the *Critique of Judgment* unites the three *Critiques* in a system. The translator's introduction makes no attempt, apart from an occasional remark, to trace the development of Kant's thought.

---

[1] One excellent source of information on these views is Lewis White Beck's *Early German Philosophy: Kant and His Predecessors* (Cambridge: Belknap Press, Harvard University Press, 1969).

Any reader should of course feel free to skip those sections in the translator's introduction which contain material already familiar; and anyone who finds certain sections too difficult at first try should similarly feel free to set them aside for a while and return to them as needed to make sense of the Kantian passages they are intended to explain.

The translation of both the *Critique of Judgment* and the First Introduction is based on the standard edition of Kant's works, commonly referred to as the *Akademie* edition: *Kants gesammelte Schriften* (Berlin: Königlich Preußische Akademie der Wissenschaften, 1902–). The text of the *Akademie* edition of the *Critique of Judgment* comes from the work's second edition, which was published in 1793 (the first edition appeared in 1790); it was edited by Wilhelm Windelband and is contained in volume 5 of the *Akademie* edition. The First Introduction appears in volume 20 (193–251) of the *Akademie* edition; it was edited by Gerhard Lehmann. I have considered variant readings throughout but have indicated them only where I either adopted them or found them of special interest.

The translation generally follows the *Akademie* text in the use of parentheses, quotation marks, typographical emphasis, and paragraphing; occasional changes, all but the most trivial of which have been noted, were made in the interest of clarity. All material in brackets, whether in the text or in footnotes, is my own. German terms inserted in brackets are given in their modern spelling and (usually) in their standard form (e.g., verbs are given in the infinitive), to facilitate finding them in a modern German dictionary. All translations given in footnotes are my own, and this fact is not indicated in each such footnote individually.

The pagination along the margin of the text refers to the *Akademie* edition; the unprimed numbers refer to volume 5, the primed numbers to volume 20. All references to the work itself and to the First Introduction are to the *Akademie* edition; they are given as 'Ak.' followed by the page number and, as applicable, by the number of Kant's note ("n.") or of my bracketed note ("br. n."). (Because clarifying the text made it necessary to cut up Kant's inordinately long sentences and to rearrange some of them, as well as some of the more convoluted paragraphs, the correspondence between the numbers on the margins and the pages in the original is only approximate.) References to the translator's introduction are given in roman numerals.

References to works of Kant other than the *Critique of Judgment* and the *Critique of Pure Reason* are to the *Akademie* edition and are given as 'Ak.' followed by the volume number and the page number. References to the *Critique of Pure Reason* are to the first two editions of the work and are given in standard form, as 'A' and 'B' followed by the page number.

At the end of this work will be found a selected bibliography, a glossary of the most important German terms in the work along with their English equivalents, and an index.

I have consulted Bernard's and Meredith's translations of the *Critique of Judgment,* Cerf's translation of a portion of the first part of the work, and Haden's translation of the First Introduction.[2] Where my renderings of key terms break with tradition, I have indicated this in footnotes at the beginning of major portions of this translation, explaining my reasons for the change.

I would like to express my appreciation to Professor Lewis White Beck for having suggested initially that I undertake this massive translation project and for having given me early guidance pertaining to translation as well as publication. I am heavily indebted to Professors Mary J. Gregor and James W. Ellington for their careful reading of drafts of the entire manuscript, for their detailed and highly valuable criticism, for information concerning both the Kantian and the further background, and for their encouragement. I am grateful to Hackett Publishing Company for their sophisticated and considerate handling of the project. My warmest and deepest gratitude goes to my wife and colleague, Professor Evelyn Begley Pluhar, who has done vastly more to make this project possible than I could hope to express.

WERNER SCHRUTKA PLUHAR

The Pennsylvania State University

Fayette Campus, Uniontown

---

[2] J. H. Bernard's translation (New York: Hafner Publishing, 1951) first appeared in 1892, James Creed Meredith's in 1911 (first part of the *Critique*) and 1928 (second part) (Oxford: Oxford University Press), Walter Cerf's in 1963 (Indianapolis: Bobbs-Merrill), and James Haden's in 1965 (Indianapolis: Bobbs-Merrill). For an earlier translation of the First Introduction, see Immanuel Kant, *On Philosophy in General,* trans., with four introductory essays, by Humayun Kabir (Calcutta: The University Press, 1935).

Translator's Introduction

0.

Preliminary Note: The Scope of the *Critique of Judgment*

The *Critique of Judgment* contains Kant's mature views on aesthetics and teleology, and on their relation to each other as well as to the two earlier *Critiques,* the *Critique of Pure Reason* and the *Critique of Practical Reason.* It has two parts, the Critique of Aesthetic Judgment and the Critique of Teleological Judgment. The term 'judgment,' in these headings, means the same as 'power (or "faculty") of judgment' (*Urteilskraft*), which is simply our ability to make (individual) judgments (*Urteile*).[3]

The Critique of Aesthetic Judgment deals mainly with two kinds of aesthetic judgments: judgments of taste, i.e., judgments about the beautiful in nature and in art, and judgments about the sublime. Kant's main concern is with judgments of taste. The problem with

---

[3] For my use of 'power,' rather than 'faculty,' see below, Ak. 167 br. n. 3. On *Urteilskraft* and *Urteil,* cf. below, Ak. 167 br. n. 4.

these judgments is, roughly, the following. When we call something 'beautiful' we seem to do so on the basis of a certain liking, a certain feeling of pleasure; and pleasure is something very subjective. And yet it seems that in such a judgment we say more than 'I like the thing.' For in using the adjective 'beautiful' we talk as if beauty were some sort of *property* of the thing, and hence we imply that other people, too, should see that "property" and hence should agree with our judgment; in other words, we imply that the judgment is valid *not* merely for the judging subject but universally.

Kant's solution to this problem hinges on how he analyzes the special kind of feeling involved in judgments of taste. Specifically, the solution hinges on how Kant relates this feeling to, on the one hand, theoretical knowledge (i.e., knowledge of what is the case, as distinguished from knowledge of what ought to be done), and, on the other hand, to morality. The key concept (to be explained below: *lvi*) in Kant's analysis of judgments of taste is the concept of nature's subjective "purposiveness" (*Zweckmäßigkeit*), as judged aesthetically.

Kant analyzes this concept of nature's subjective purposiveness by reference to our mental powers, and much of Kant's theory of taste can indeed be understood in terms of that analysis. Yet Kant's main line of argument for the universal validity of judgments of taste brings in not only the concept of nature's subjective purposiveness but also the concept of something "supersensible" underlying that same purposiveness. In fact, as my new interpretation of abundant textual evidence will show, Kant *equates* (treats as equivalent) these two concepts. Because this equation seems very perplexing indeed, Kant should have made it thoroughly explicit and clear. Instead he just switches mysteriously from the one concept to the other, without informing the reader that the equivalence between them has been established, even if still not nearly as explicitly and clearly as it should have been, in the Critique of Teleological Judgment.

Kant goes on to apply his theory of taste to fine art. When we judge fine art by taste, we judge it as we do nature, viz., in terms of its beauty. But since, unlike nature, works of fine art are something created by man, we can judge them also by how much genius they manifest. Kant's main contribution to the theory of fine art is his analysis of genius.

The Critique of Teleological Judgment deals with our judgments of things in nature in terms of final causes, i.e., ends or purposes.

A purpose, for Kant, is an object or state of affairs insofar as it is, or is regarded as, the effect brought about by some cause through a concept that this cause has of it (cf. Ak. 180 and 408); thus a nightingale is a purpose insofar as we at least regard it as having been produced by some cause through the concept that this cause had of a nightingale. If the object or state of affairs was in fact produced through a concept that the cause had of it, then it is an intentional purpose; if we merely regard it as having been produced in this way, then it is an unintentional purpose. An intention (*Absicht*), it seems, is simply the cause's concept of the purpose it pursues, i.e., the concept of the object or state of affairs it seeks to bring about.[4] Sometimes Kant apparently forgets his definition of 'purpose' and uses the term, as indeed we often do in English, as synonymous with 'intention.'[5]

The Critique of Teleological Judgment argues that, while natural science cannot explain things without appealing to mechanism and hence to efficient causes, some things in nature, viz., organisms, are such that we cannot even adequately investigate them unless we judge them not only in mechanical terms but also in terms of final causes, i.e., unless we judge them at the same time as purposes. However, judgments of natural products as purposes do not seem to share the firm status and justification enjoyed by mechanistic explanations. Worst of all, such "teleological" judgments (from Greek τέλος [télos], 'end,' 'purpose') seem to involve us in contradiction. For in judging the object as a purpose we judge it as contingent, viz., contingent on ("conditioned by") the concept of a purpose; and yet, insofar as we judge and try to explain the same object as an object of nature, we judge that same object, even the same causal connections in it, at the same time as necessary.

Kant's solution to this problem hinges again on his analysis of the concept of nature's purposiveness (the "subjective" purposiveness with an "objective" one based on it), this time as judged teleologically rather than aesthetically. Here again Kant equates this concept with

---

[4] Although Kant does not define '*Absicht*,' this is how he seems to use the term most of the time. See, e.g., Ak. 383, 398, and 400 (line 19).

[5] See, e.g., Ak. 391, 393, and 397. Sometimes Kant seems to use '*Absicht*' to mean an intentional purpose, rather than the concept of such a purpose; in those cases I have rendered the term by 'aim.' See, e.g., Ak. 484.

the concept of the supersensible basis of that same purposiveness. Even here Kant does not make this equation nearly explicit and clear enough but leaves us to assemble laboriously the various things he says in different places. But the textual evidence that he does in fact make this equation is overwhelming. The argument from this interpretation of mine will proceed by pointing to that evidence and tying the pieces together gradually; it will not be complete until the end of this introduction.

That argument will connect with a second one. This second argument has to do with the relation of the Critique of Aesthetic Judgment to the Critique of Teleological Judgment and, above all, the relation of the entire work to Kant's critical philosophy as a systematic whole. Kant is greatly concerned to show that the *Critique of Judgment* is needed to complete the "critical system." Although this concern is not assigned a special part in the work, Kant brings it up again and again, especially in his two introductions. I shall devote the remainder of this preliminary note on the scope of the present (third) *Critique* to a rough sketch of that second argument of mine, the argument regarding the relation of the two parts of the *Critique of Judgment* to each other and to the critical system. Anyone not already familiar with the main views of the first two *Critiques* should, for now, feel free to skip the remainder of this note and proceed to the next section, with which this introduction actually begins.

The *Critique of Pure Reason,* as Section 2 of this introduction will explain, had argued that we need the concept of something supersensible as substrate of nature (of nature as it appears to us) if we are to solve four "antinomies" (seeming contradictions), into which our reason falls inevitably when it tries to make sense of nature. But this concept of the supersensible had to be left completely *indeterminate,* as merely the concept of "things as they may be in themselves" (rather than as they appear to us). In the *Critique of Practical Reason,* as will be explained in Section 3, another antinomy had arisen. This antinomy concerned the "final purpose" that the moral law of which we are conscious enjoins us to pursue, a purpose we must therefore regard as achievable although obstacles insuperable for us finite beings seem to stand in the way. Solving this antinomy required the assumption that we are immortal souls and that there is a "moral" God, a God the concept of whom (as, of course, something supersensible) is made *determinate* through attributes derived from the moral law (and from the final purpose that this law enjoins on us).

Now the Critique of Aesthetic Judgment and the Critique of Teleological Judgment each gives rise to another antinomy and, as I shall interpret these antinomies and Kant's solution to them, resolving these antinomies requires that we equate the concept of nature's (subjective and objective) purposiveness with the (indeterminate) concept of some supersensible basis of that purposiveness. Kant holds that this last concept of the supersensible, i.e., as the basis of nature's purposiveness, "mediates" between the other two concepts of the supersensible (respectively, as nature in itself, and as required by the moral law) so that the three concepts of the supersensible can for the first time be thought of as applying to the *same* (i.e., a united) supersensible. It is through this unification of the supersensible that the three *Critiques,* which give rise to the three concepts of the supersensible, are themselves united to form a whole having the coherence of a system. What allows the concept of nature's purposiveness to play this mediating role is, as I shall show, precisely Kant's equation of that concept with the concept of the supersensible basis of that same purposiveness, combined with the analysis he gives of the concept of that basis.

1.

Kant's Life and Works

Immanuel Kant was born at Königsberg, East Prussia, on April 22, 1724. His father was a master saddler of very modest means, his mother a woman without education but with considerable native intelligence. According to Kant's own account, his grandfather was an immigrant from Scotland. Kant was raised, both at home and at school (at the *Collegium Fridericianum* at Königsberg), in the tradition of Pietism, a Protestant movement with a strong ethical orientation and a de-emphasis of theological dogma.

Kant attended the University of Königsberg from 1740 to about

1746. After that he served as a tutor in several aristocratic families in different parts of East Prussia, earning a very modest income. Having kept up his studies in the meantime, he returned, in 1755, to the University of Königsberg, employed as an instructor. He continued in this position for fifteen years, lecturing in several natural sciences, in mathematics, and in philosophy. In 1770 he was appointed professor of logic and metaphysics at the University of Königsberg. He remained active in this position until a few years before his death, at Königsberg, on February 12, 1804.

Kant's first publication (on a topic in Leibnizian physics) appeared in 1747, when he was still a student. For the next fifteen years, most of his writings were in the natural sciences, but some were in philosophy. Two of these philosophical works were (roughly) in the philosophy of religion (the more important of these is *The Only Possible Basis of Proof for Demonstrating the Existence of God,* 1763); another was the *Observations on the Feeling of the Beautiful and Sublime,* 1764, Kant's only publication, apart from the *Critique of Judgment,* that touches on aesthetics. (It discusses the subject from the point of view of social psychology; not until a few years before publication of the third *Critique* did Kant believe that an aesthetic judgment about the beautiful or sublime had validity for persons other than the subject making it.) The Inaugural Dissertation of 1770 (which was written in Latin), *On the Form and Principles of the Sensible and Intelligible World,* marks the beginning of Kant's so-called "critical period" (as distinguished from the "precritical period"), because here for the first time Kant treats space and time as he does in the first *Critique:* as forms of sensibility (forms of "intuition"), i.e., as something that the subject contributes to the world of experience, which is therefore only a phenomenal world. (Kant does not yet assign such a contributory role to any concepts.)

By then Kant's publications had already won him a considerable reputation in learned circles in Germany; and the publication of Kant's most important work, the *Critique of Pure Reason,* was eagerly anticipated. It took Kant about a decade to complete the work. When it finally appeared, in 1781, it was met with enthusiasm by some, by others with consternation. Kant rewrote portions of the work for the second edition, of 1787; but first he published, in 1783, the *Prolegomena to Any Future Metaphysics,* a greatly simplified and shortened restatement of the main positions and arguments of the first *Critique*. Kant reversed this procedure in publishing his practical philosophy: the *Foundations of the Metaphysics of Morals,* a simplified introduction to the subject, appeared in 1785, the *Critique of Practical Reason* in 1788. Between the two, in 1786, appeared the *Metaphysical Foundations of Natural Science.*

The third *Critique,* the *Critique of Judgment,* was published in 1790. An essay pertaining to teleology, *On Using Teleological Principles in Philosophy,* had appeared in 1788, but teleology as well as theology were of great concern to Kant throughout his life and are discussed in many of his works, in some extensively (see the bracketed footnotes in the text). While Kant was preparing the third *Critique* for publication, he wrote (late in 1789 or early in 1790) an introduction, which later he decided was too long. He replaced it with a shorter introduction, and this was published with the first edition, with the second edition of 1793, and with later editions as well as translations ever since. The First Introduction was not published in its entirety until 1914, when it appeared in the Cassirer edition (vol. 5) of Kant's works.

In 1793 Kant published *Religion Within the Bounds of Reason Alone.* In the following year, the Prussian authorities informed Kant that the king, Frederick William II, had been displeased for some time with Kant's teachings and writings on religion, which the authorities found too rationalistic and unorthodox. Kant was ordered to desist from disseminating his views on the subject, and he did not return to it until the king died in 1797. In 1795 appeared *Perpetual Peace,* in 1797 the *Metaphysics of Morals,* and in 1798 Kant's last major work, the *Anthropology from a Pragmatic Point of View.*

Kant's style in these many works varies greatly, from the easy flow and almost conversational tone in some of his early works to the ponderous and scholastic presentation, with its often artificial structure, in the works he saw as most scientific. But the breadth of Kant's interests and learning, intellectual and cultural generally, is evident throughout his works.

As regards Kant's personality, what is most familiar to the general public is the caricature of Kant as a pedantic and puritanical Prussian, by whose regular afternoon walks the housewives of Königsberg would set their clocks, and so on. But some persons, persons who knew him, described him as sprightly (even as an old man), as witty, cheerful, and entertaining, even in his lectures. He had a circle of friends, with whom he dined regularly. Kant never married. Physically, he was never robust. Just over five feet tall and hollow-chested, he was able to avoid major illnesses until his final years. Although Kant was greatly interested in the rest of the world (he greeted the French Revolution with enthusiasm and listened to and read with eagerness the accounts of other people's journeys), he himself never traveled outside East Prussia.

2.

The *Critique of Pure Reason*

'Critique,' in Kant's sense of the term, consists in examining the scope and limits of our cognitive powers ('reason,' in the broadest sense in which Kant uses this term) in order to decide to what extent, if any, metaphysics is possible for us human beings. Metaphysics consists in the discovery of truths (true propositions) about the world that are not empirical (dependent on experience), in which case they would be contingent, but are necessary and hence a priori (knowable independently of experience). If such propositions not only are a priori but do not involve even an empirical *concept* (e.g., the concept of change, or of matter), then Kant calls them "pure."[6] Hence the *Critique of Pure Reason* tries to decide to what extent, if any, our cognitive powers permit us to discover a priori (and especially pure) truths about the world: about objects, space and time, the order in nature, ourselves, freedom of the will and the possibility of morality, and perhaps a God. (The first *Critique* discusses all of these to some extent.) Without such prior critique of our cognitive powers, Kant maintains, either affirming or denying the possibility of metaphysics is sheer dogmatism: dogmatic rationalism assumes that our reason is capable of metaphysics, and dogmatic empiricism assumes the opposite.

Kant himself had been trained in the rationalistic metaphysical

---

[6] See the *Critique of Pure Reason*, B 3, and cf. Konrad Cramer, "Non-Pure Synthetic A Priori Judgments in the 'Critique of Pure Reason,'" *Proceedings of the Third International Kant Congress* (Dordrecht: D. Reidel, 1972), 246–54.

tradition of Gottfried Wilhelm Leibniz (1646–1716) and his disciple, Christian Wolff (1679–1754). Leibniz (especially in his earlier years) and Wolff regarded the world as, in principle, knowable a priori. They held, moreover, that all a priori truths must, at least in principle, be "truths of reason," i.e., derivable from logic.

But Kant came to doubt that the assertions made a priori by these philosophers about the world could be justified. Worst of all, it seemed that the rationalistic principles of Leibniz and Wolff inevitably led reason into antinomies, i.e., pairs of propositions that seemed to contradict each other and yet were "provable": on these principles, Kant argues in the *Critique of Pure Reason,* one can "prove" that the world is limited in space and time and that it is not; that composites consist of simple (irreducible) parts and that they do not; that there are first causes (causes that initiate a causal series) and that there are not; that there is a necessary being and that there is not. Clearly, then, dogmatic rationalism had failed to secure metaphysics, and along with it whatever presupposes it: natural science, morality, and religion.

Kant's doubts about dogmatic rationalism arose in good part through his exposure to (German translations of) some of the works of the empiricist David Hume (1711–76), whom he credits with having awakened him from his "dogmatic slumber."[7] Hume (in the *Enquiry Concerning Human Understanding,* which Kant read[8]) agreed with the rationalists that a priori truths must be derivable from logic; they must be "analytic" truths, to use Kant's term. But logic, Hume went on, has to do only with the relations among our ideas (i.e., with analysis of our concepts) and can tell us nothing about the world. Our only access to the world is not a priori but a posteriori (empirical), i.e., through experience. It follows that whatever we discover about the world is contingent rather than necessary, and that even such modest metaphysical propositions about the world as 'Every event *must* have a cause,' or 'All properties *must* inhere in some substance,' cannot be justified in any way at all. Because in the strict sense of the term 'know' we can know only whatever is necessary, we do not (in this sense) know nature at all, let alone anything beyond nature. (Indeed, in view of the problem of induction, we do not even know it

---

[7] *Prolegomena*, Ak. IV, 260.

[8] Kant did not know Hume's *Treatise of Human Nature.*

in the weaker sense of the term, which implies mere probability rather than necessity.)

Although Kant agreed with Hume that dogmatic rationalism had failed to establish a metaphysics, Hume's skepticism (denial of knowledge) seemed to him equally dogmatic, and utterly implausible as well. Newton undeniably had discovered some basic laws of nature. These laws were clearly not analytic, not derived from reason alone, but were discovered through experience. On the other hand, if they were *laws* then they could not be wholly contingent but must imply something with necessity. But how, Kant asked, can there be propositions that are not analytic—Kant called such propositions "synthetic"— but that nevertheless imply something with necessity, and hence a priori? As Kant puts it: How are synthetic judgments possible a priori?[9] *That* they were possible a priori was suggested strongly by Newton's success in natural science. But the decisive evidence seemed to lie in mathematics, above all in geometry. Geometry, Kant argued, describes the space of nature and does not just spell out "relations of ideas," as Hume assumed. For example, Kant argued that no analysis of the mere concept of a triangle can teach us that the angles of every triangle must add up to two right angles; hence this proposition must be synthetic. Yet no experience could possibly falsify this proposition; it is not contingent but necessary, and therefore a priori. Hence at least in geometry we have judgments that describe the world we experience but that are nevertheless a priori. How is that possible?

Kant's answer is that there is only one way in which we can have a priori knowledge of spatial relations that is nevertheless not knowledge of the relations of our mere concepts: it must be knowledge of relations involving something else that we have in the mind and that we use in experiencing the world: intuition (i.e., roughly, visualization), sensibility. In other words, space must be a *form* of our intuition: we experience the world *in terms of* space, we structure it in terms of space, by contributing space to experience. That is why the spatial relations asserted by the principles of geometry apply a priori and necessarily to whatever experience we can have of the world, and why we can intuit and know these relations a priori. On the other hand, by the same token, that spatial world is only phenomenal, is only appearance: the world as we experience it. Hence, in order to

---

[9] *Critique of Pure Reason*, B 19.

account for the possibility of synthetic a priori propositions we must deny that they tell us anything about the world as it is *in itself.*[10] Kant's treatment of time is roughly similar: time is also a form of intuition, and hence is present in any experience. Hence, like space, time can also be intuited and known a priori as a necessary feature of the world as appearance.

Kant goes on to offer comparable arguments that there are, similarly, a priori concepts (categories), forms of thought that we have in our understanding and that we "build," as it were, into the world. They are twelve in number and make up four groups (of three categories each) under the headings of quantity, quality, relation, and modality. For example, two of the three categories under the heading of "relation" are substance (and accident, i.e., roughly, property inhering in a substance) and causality, i.e., (efficient) cause and effect. These two categories, just like our forms of intuition, also allow us to make synthetic a priori judgments. They allow us to judge and know a priori, and hence with necessity, such universal principles as that all properties in nature (i.e., in the world as it appears to us) must inhere in substances, and that every event in nature must have its cause. These principles are "universally valid" (hold for everything) in the phenomenal world (the world as it appears), i.e., in nature, simply because our understanding makes it so. The remaining categories give rise to more such a priori principles of nature. Hence we can have a "metaphysics" in the sense of a science of the a priori principles of all possible objects of experience. On the other hand, as with space and time, no such synthetic a priori judgments are possible (i.e., justifiable) as regards the world as it may be in itself, i.e., the world considered as supersensible (or "intelligible" or "noumenal," i.e., merely thinkable).

However, only some of our synthetic judgments about nature are a priori; the rest are empirical. In order to make an empirical judgment we must have an empirical intuition. Whereas a priori intuition involves no sensation but consists in visualizing purely in terms of space

---

[10] The distinction between a phenomenal world and a world in itself was already used by Leibniz and Wolff. But for them the phenomenal world was simply the world in itself as perceived through sensation, which they construed as being merely a confused, rather than distinct, kind of thought. Kant insists that sensibility is not reducible to thought at all but is different in kind, but this view does have the consequence that we have not even a confused perception of the world in itself.

and time, empirical intuition does involve sensation. Through sensation we discover in an object what further features it may have beyond those imposed on it by our forms of intuition and our categories. Those features of an object of our intuition which are "given" to us (i.e., are "data") in *sensation* are what Kant calls the 'matter' of intuition. As these data are received, they are structured—automatically, as it were—in terms of space and time by the forms of intuition. The result is an empirical intuition, or "perception."

But making an empirical judgment about the world as we experience it involves more than merely an empirical intuition with its structure in terms of space and time: in making such a judgment we also connect that empirical intuition with the thought of a certain object. An empirical judgment consists in our awareness that an empirical intuition we are having *matches* a certain concept. (Kant uses the generic term 'presentation' [*Vorstellung,* traditionally rendered as 'representation': see below, Ak. 175 br. n. 17] to stand for both intuitions and concepts, as well as for still further objects of our direct awareness: see below, Ak. 203 br. n. 4.) For example, when we make the judgment, 'This is a dog,' this judgment consists in our being conscious that our empirical intuition matches a concept we already have in our understanding, viz., the concept of "dog." Our judgment thus makes our empirical intuition determinate, by turning it into the *experience* of a dog, or, which comes to the same, a dog as experienced (a dog as "appearance"). The judgment is therefore called 'determinative' (or 'constitutive'); for it determines (or "constitutes") the dog.

Now suppose that we are intuiting a dog but that we do not already have the concept of "dog" but have only the concept of "animal." In that case we can acquire the concept of "dog" by *expanding* the concept of "animal": we do this by matching the empirical intuition with the concept of "animal," so that we are experiencing an animal, while also taking note of whatever further particular features in this experienced animal distinguish it from other animals. (We can take note of such further features even if we do not already know the *word* 'dog.') Such a judgment will determine not only an animal, but, more specifically, a dog, because in taking note of those distinguishing features we abstract them from our experience of the animal and add them to the concept of "animal," thus expanding that concept. This newly acquired empirical concept ("dog") is more determinate, has more "determinations" (predicates describing attributes). Similarly, we acquired the (empirical) concept of "animal" by expanding some other concept we already had in our understanding; and so on. In this way all empirical concepts are the result of our expanding concepts already present in our understanding.

Now the only concepts present in our understanding before *all* experience (from which new empirical concepts are acquired by abstraction) are the categories. Hence the categories form part of (enter into) all empirical concepts. This holds not only for the concepts of individual objects but also for the concepts of causal relations. For example, in judging the swelling of some brook as caused by a heavy rain that preceded it, we may be matching the empirical intuition of this sequence of events with a concept we already have of a causal relation between events of this kind; but we may, alternatively, be expanding a more general concept which will in turn have resulted from our expanding a still earlier one, and so on, until we get to the category of causality, i.e., cause and effect.

If an empirical judgment consists in the awareness that an empirical intuition matches some concept, how did that match come about? The data we receive passively through sensation are structured in terms of space and time and thus become an empirical intuition. If this intuition is to match a concept, we must have an active power or ability to structure the particular features of that intuition in accordance with the structure of the concept; this power is what Kant calls our 'imagination.' The imagination "apprehends" (takes up) what is given in intuition and then puts together or "combines" this diversity (or "manifold") so that it matches the concept. In this way the imagination "exhibits" (*darstellen,* traditionally rendered as "to present"[11]) the concept, i.e., provides it with a matching or "corresponding" intuition.

Some concepts, e.g., those of geometry, can be exhibited in a priori intuition, i.e., in intuition that includes no sensation. A priori exhibition of a concept is called the concept's 'construction.'[12] A priori exhibition, like exhibition in empirical intuition, can result in the expansion of the concept exhibited, viz., if we abstract from that

---

[11] "My reasons for abandoning 'to present' as translating '*darstellen*' and for reusing it to render '*vorstellen*' are given at Ak. 175 br. n. 17.

[12] Cf. below, Ak. 232 br. n. 51.

exhibition, and add to the concept, whatever further features we discover in intuiting the object (e.g., a triangle) a priori. When we are aware that our imagination is exhibiting a concept by means of a matching a priori intuition, this awareness is what constitutes a (theoretical and synthetic) a priori judgment. (A theoretical judgment is a judgment about what is the case, as distinguished from a judgment about what ought to be done. This distinction will be discussed more fully in the next section.)

However, something further is still needed to make it possible for any intuition to match a concept. A concept groups together many instances (of things or events) in terms of the attributes they share as instances of the same kind. It does not include all the attributes of the instances that fall (i.e., can be "subsumed") under it, but omits the particular attributes with reference to which the instances may still differ from one another. In other words, all concepts abstract from some of the particular; the categories are the most abstract concepts of all: they are universal and they abstract from everything particular. An intuition, by contrast, is concrete in the sense that it contains the particular omitted in the concept. How, then, can an intuition possibly be turned into an image that will match a concept, let alone our a priori concepts, the categories? Something is needed to *mediate* between intuition in general and the categories, viz., a rule or "schema" that stipulates what conditions the intuition must meet so that it *can* match a category. In the case of causal relation, the schema is the rule that *the effect must follow the cause in time.* Indeed, all schemata connect the categories with time; the reason for this is that time is the only form of intuition that applies to any intuition whatsoever, even to the inner intuition we have of ourselves, whereas space applies merely to all outer intuitions. Strictly speaking, the category of causality is already a temporalized, "schematized," category; for if the time condition is removed, the relation of cause and effect is nothing but the logical relation of ground and consequent. The same holds for the category of substance, which is not merely the thought of a thing, but the schematized thought of a thing that endures in time.

It is in fact these schematized categories which give rise to such principles as 'Every event must have its cause' and 'All substances have permanence.' Now since these principles, like the categories on which they are based, apply to any experience we can have of the world, they are *universal laws of nature* (of nature as appearance).

As such they form part of the mechanism studied by natural science, insofar as that mechanism (which deals with efficient causes) is a priori and hence necessary. Since these laws are based on the categories which our understanding contributes to nature, they are laws that are "given" to nature, i.e., prescribed or legislated to nature, by our understanding. These universal laws in turn have certain applications, viz., the (also mechanistic) laws of motion discovered by Newton. These laws are only "applications" of the former laws because, unlike them, they are not pure: they involve some empirical concepts (e.g., the concept of matter); yet they too hold—to the extent to which they are mathematical—for all possible experience and hence are themselves still a priori and universal.[13]

Any regularity or "lawfulness" in nature that is not based on the categories or their universal applications must, consequently, pertain to what is particular (rather than universal) in nature. Since such lawfulness is not the result of our understanding's legislation to nature, it can become known to us only empirically. Hence such lawfulness must always be contingent, i.e., lacking the strict necessity ("apodeictic" necessity, as found in a demonstration) that characterizes both the categorial principles (the principles based on the categories themselves) and the universal applications of these principles.

Kant calls the universal applications of the categorial principles *metaphysical* principles. The categorial (and pure) principles themselves, which involve no empirical concept and hence are presupposed by any experience whatsoever, he calls *transcendental*. On the other hand, if we use these transcendental principles to make judgments about something supersensible, something beyond all possible experience, then our use of them is *transcendent;* as so used, they cannot give rise to knowledge, but remain nothing more than mere thought. The distinction between the transcendental and the transcendent marks the boundary between theoretical knowledge (i.e., knowledge of what is the case) and mere thought, as the *Critique of*

---

[13] The distinction between these two kinds of universal laws is not drawn explicitly in the *Critique of Pure Reason* (see, e.g., A 691 = B 719, A 273 = B 329); but we do find it so drawn in the *Critique of Judgment* (Ak. 181), as well as in the *Metaphysical Foundations of Natural Science* (Ak. IV, 469–70). See also James W. Ellington's translation of the latter work, in conjunction with the *Prolegomena*, as Immanuel Kant, *Philosophy of Material Nature* (Indianapolis: Hackett Publishing, 1985), Translator's Introduction to the *Prolegomena*, xi–xvi.

Pure Reason draws it by deciding what our mental powers can and cannot do: our understanding is able to know a priori in nature whatever laws it prescribes to nature. Beyond all possible experience, we cannot have theoretical knowledge but can only think.

The concepts we use in thinking about what may lie beyond nature, beyond our understanding, are called by Kant 'rational ideas' or 'ideas of reason' (or simply 'ideas'). 'Reason' here no longer means our cognitive power as a whole, as it does in the title of the first *Critique,* but is used in a narrower sense. In this sense of the term, reason is the power that tries, using its ideas, to do *more* such structuring as understanding does by supplying the concepts that turn mere intuitions into experiences. Reason tries to combine these experiences themselves and the laws they contain into larger unified wholes, ultimately into a unity that includes everything, a totality. For example, reason seeks to unify various dog experiences by regarding them as appearances of some one thing underlying all these appearances, some (supersensible) thing in itself, whatever it may be, a thing that we cannot know because we cannot get beyond the appearance. In the same way, the general idea of a world in itself is the idea of something supersensible that unites *all* our experiences of nature. But since the structure that reason seeks to introduce by means of these ideas is a supersensible structure, a structure beyond all possible experience, reason can do no more than try: it can use these ideas only to *regulate* our experience of objects; it cannot use these ideas to *constitute* objects and so give rise to what would be a theoretical knowledge by *reason.* The world considered (theoretically) as it may be in itself, i.e., as supersensible rather than phenomenal, is for us a world of mere *noumena,* things we can only think. Our rational desire to unify our diverse experiences is so great that reason easily strays beyond the bounds within which theoretical knowledge is possible for us and consequently involves itself in seeming contradictions (the "antinomies" mentioned above). If we are to avoid such straying by reason, we must let our own critique remind us of the limits of our cognitive powers. We must let it remind us that the transcendent metaphysics of dogmatic rationalism is impossible, and hence we must restrict ourselves to *immanent* metaphysics; in other words, we must settle for a metaphysics that confines itself to the synthetic a priori principles (along with their universal applications) that are presupposed by, and hence stay within the range of, what experience is possible for us.

Hence immanent metaphysics, which the *Critique of Pure Reason* shows us to be capable of, will be a metaphysics of nature. Such a metaphysics cannot tell us anything about the supersensible: about objects in themselves, about a God, or even about ourselves as subjects in themselves (souls), as distinguished from how we appear to ourselves through our "inner sense"; in particular, it cannot tell us whether, despite the necessity inherent in nature's universal laws (the mechanistic laws regarding efficient causes), our will has the kind of freedom that is needed for morality. All we can do, as far as the *Critique of Pure Reason* goes, is *think* a "nature in itself," a God, and such freedom. For by regarding all of these as supersensible, we eliminate not only the need to provide theoretical justification (e.g., in the case of God, by means of the alleged theoretical "proofs" for God's existence), but we eliminate the antinomy between freedom and the necessity in nature by attributing the necessity to nature as appearance while thinking of freedom as pertaining to a supersensible (noumenal) self, a self of which we can know only the appearance.

Thus the *Critique of Pure Reason* pays the price of renouncing claims to theoretical knowledge where it was sought most eagerly, but it does at least rescue immanent metaphysics, and with it natural science, from dogmatic rationalism with its unjustifiable and contradictory claims, and from the skepticism of dogmatic empiricism.

3.

The *Critique of Practical Reason*

The second *Critique* examines again what reason can do, this time not in relation to theoretical knowledge, but in relation to action, i.e., as *practical* reason. It argues that reason not only enables us to achieve some particular purpose we happen to be pursuing, or satisfy some natural inclination; rather, the *Critique* argues, reason can be practical on its own, as completely independent from nature, i.e., as pure. In this role, reason is able to impose obligations (a moral law) on us, and to carry them out in freedom from natural necessity. Kant argues that we can "cognize" as well as "know" both this moral law and that freedom, although only "from a practical point of view." Let us pause here for an explanation of this terminology.[14]

Knowledge (*Wissen*), for Kant, is assent (*Fürwahrhalten*[15]) that is adequate not just subjectively but objectively, i.e., adequate to convince not just oneself but everyone.[16] Theoretical knowledge, discussed in the preceding section, is knowledge of what is the case (rather than knowledge of what ought to be done). Such knowledge arises from "theoretical cognition."

Theoretical cognition consists in determining (making determinate) an object[17] in the sense of establishing what the object's attributes are. If we take these attributes merely from the analysis of some concept, such cognition is conceptual,[18] or analytic; otherwise it is synthetic.[19] In synthetic cognition, the attributes determining the object are taken not from a concept but from intuition. If that intuition is a priori, then the cognition is a priori as well; if the intuition is empirical (i.e., if it is perception, which includes sensation), then the cognition too is empirical.[20] Empirical cognition is the same thing as experience.[21] As we saw in the preceding section, experience consists in turning empirical intuitions into determinate objects (as appearances) by means of concepts; if such experience results in our acquiring a new empirical concept by "expanding" some concept (or concepts) we already had, then our cognition provides us with new knowledge.

Just as theoretical knowledge is knowledge of what is the case, the

[14] For further details and references, see below, Ak. 467 incl. br. n. 75, and 475 incl. br. n. 96; and cf. Ak. 174–76.

[15] Literally, 'considering true.'

[16] See the *Critique of Pure Reason*, A 822 = B 850.

[17] Cf. *ibid.*, B 166.

[18] Cf. *ibid.*, A 320 = B 377–78.

[19] *Ibid.*, A 151–52 = B 191.

[20] *Ibid.*, A 176 = B218.

[21] *Ibid.*, B 147, 165–66, 234, 277.

theoretical cognition yielding this knowledge is cognition of what is the case, as distinguished from cognition of what ought to be done, which is called 'practical cognition.'[22] Only theoretical cognition is "insight."[23] (Cf. the etymology of 'theoretical.') Kant also uses the term 'cognition' in a second sense, according to which theoretical cognition *is* knowledge, rather than the process that yields it.

Let us turn now to practical cognition, i.e., cognition of what ought to be done. In practical cognition, or "cognition from a practical point of view," we again determine an "object," but here we do so by means of *practical* determinations taken from our moral consciousness. That is why practical cognition, like morality itself, involves "oughts," i.e., commands or "imperatives."[24] As we shall see in a moment, one such "object" of our practical cognition is the moral law itself; another is the freedom of the will that this law presupposes. As we shall also see, our cognition of these "objects" holds for everyone; as such, it yields (or, in the second sense of 'cognition,' is) objectively adequate assent, i.e., (practical) knowledge. But, because this cognition or knowledge is practical, it is not insight.

Our practical cognition is not limited to the moral law itself and what this law *presupposes,* viz., our freedom; we also cognize practically what this moral law *commands.* As I shall spell out more fully in a moment, the moral law commands that we try to achieve the "final purpose," and achieving the final purpose presupposes two things that we must, therefore, assume as "postulates": that there is a God and that we are immortal souls. According to Kant, we have practical cognition of the final purpose, of God, and of the immortality of the soul inasmuch as these three "objects" of our thought are made (practically) determinate by what the moral law commands. On the

---

[22] *Ibid.,* A 633 = B661.

[23] See the *Critique of Practical Reason,* Ak. V, 4. When Kant speaks simply of "cognition," he ordinarily means theoretical cognition, rather than both it and practical cognition (which I am about to discuss). Sometimes the omission of 'theoretical' gives rise to seeming contradictions. See, e.g., the *Critique of Practical Reason,* Ak. V, 4, where '*theoretisch*' appears in line 19 but is omitted in line 15, so that line 15 seems to contradict what Kant says at Ak. V, 137 concerning our cognition of God. Correcting for the omission removes the seeming contradiction, provided we use different terms to render '*erkennen*' (cognize) and '*wissen*' (know); rendering them by the same term results in another seeming contradiction between Ak. V, 4 and 137.

[24] See the *Logic,* Ak. IX, 86.

other hand, as these (supersensible) objects, unlike our freedom, are presupposed not by the moral law itself but only by what it commands, our practical cognition of them is not knowledge (as our practical cognition of the moral law itself and of freedom is). Rather, it is a rational faith, which is assent that is adequate not objectively but only subjectively, i.e., adequate only to convince oneself.[25]

With these distinctions in mind, we can now return to the task of the second *Critique*. The *Critique of Pure Reason* had indeed established that we can *think* the previously mentioned supersensible things, i.e., it had established that they are logically possible; but the *Critique of Practical Reason* argues that we can *cognize* them, even if only practically. Thus the second *Critique* rescues morality and religion, not only from the restrictive conclusions drawn by the first *Critique,* but above all—once again—from the much more damaging views that made the *Critique* necessary: dogmatic rationalism and dogmatic empiricism.

The dogmatic rationalism of Leibniz and Wolff had tried to derive moral obligation from our alleged knowledge of the supersensible: from God's will as manifested in the perfection of the world, a perfection that we can know through reason although not through the senses. Moral obligation lies in working toward this perfection by striving away from the confusion (indistinctness) inherent in our senses and toward the distinct intellectual "knowledge" of the supersensible world as it not only ought to be but in fact is. To have the will to act in this way is, for Wolff, nothing more than a somewhat more distinct awareness of this perfection that our senses present to us only indistinctly. We already know Kant's objection to these rationalistic claims to knowledge of the supersensible. But Kant, following (the Pietist) Christian August Crusius, also disagreed with the view that to know the good is the same as to will it. Above all, however, neither Leibniz nor Wolff could adequately explain how the world could already be perfect, through God's choice, and yet have room for human freedom.

Dogmatic empiricism restricted itself to the observations of empirical psychology about human motivation. Accordingly, Hume construed ethical judgments as seeking merely to influence people's motivation. One of Kant's objections to this approach was that these

---

[25] *Critique of Pure Reason,* A 822 = B 850.

empirical observations could yield only contingent judgments, whereas genuine moral obligation must be absolute, not conditioned by this or that particular purpose we happen to be pursuing. But his main objection was that empirical observations can tell us only what is the case, never (as Hume in fact acknowledged) what ought to be done, as a moral judgment must.

The key premise for Kant's own position is that we do, as a fact of reason revealed to us a priori, have a moral consciousness.[26] We are conscious of ourselves as obligated by an a priori moral law. That law commands us to fulfill our duty even where doing so requires that we struggle against circumstances in nature or against our natural inclinations. Hence the law commands absolutely or "categorically," rather than hypothetically, i.e., rather than with an if-clause specifying the condition ("hypothesis"), such as this or that natural circumstance or inclination, under which we ought to act in a certain way. This moral law is thus a "categorical imperative." The categorical imperative puts a restriction on the kind of "maxim," i.e., subjective rule devised by ourselves, that we may follow in our acts. It says: "Act in such a way that the maxim of your will [could] always hold at the same time as a principle laying down universal law."[27] In other words, we ought to act only on maxims that are universalizable and as such do not cater to this or that inclination or excuse us from our duty when circumstances make it difficult for us to perform it. What we know practically, this fact of reason, is the moral law itself,[28] a synthetic a priori proposition, and not merely that we are conscious of such a law: for if I think of this law as obligating me then it *is* obligating me.[29] Hence what makes *this* synthetic proposition "possible" a priori is that it describes a fact of reason: it is not derived from experience, yet it applies to all experience, has "objective reality,"

---

[26] *Critique of Practical Reason*, Ak. V, 31.

[27] *Ibid.*, Ak. V, 30.

[28] Cf. *ibid.*, Ak. V, 31 and 42. Cf. also the *Foundation of the Metaphysics of Morals*, Ak. IV, 448n.

[29] This claim hinges on the fact that the moral law demands of our maxims only that they be universalizable, and hence is a purely formal law. In the case of a more specific rule, such as 'Keep your promise to X,' my mere consciousness of the rule would not establish that the rule obligates me, for I could be mistaken in believing that I had made such a promise.

as we can discover through our own acts as manifested in experience (below, Ak. 468).

This fact of reason presupposes another: that we have a will that is free in the sense that it can indeed act independently of natural influences. Hence, because we have both practical cognition and knowledge of the moral law, we also have practical cognition and knowledge of what this law presupposes: our supersensible freedom, the freedom that the first *Critique* had established only as logically possible. But the will's freedom as presupposed by the moral law must be more than mere independence from the efficient causes of nature; for such mere independence would leave our "acts" random, not *our* acts at all. This freedom must be, rather, an ability of the will to give laws to itself (be "autonomous") and to obey (or disobey) such laws independently of nature. The will considered as autonomous, as giving its own law, is called simply (pure) practical reason; the same will (practical reason) considered as the ability to choose freely between obeying or disobeying this law is called the *power of choice*. As free from nature's efficient causes, this will can, through its choice, act "spontaneously"; i.e., it can initiate (be the "first cause" in) a new series of efficient causes in nature. Hence freedom, as we cognize and know it practically through the moral law, is itself a special causality.

Respect for the moral law, together with our awareness that we have the freedom to obey or disobey it, is what Kant calls 'moral feeling' (cf. below, Ak. 267).

We saw that the moral law commands us to act only on universalizable maxims. Hence in obeying that law our reason imposes on nature a universality, and this universality is a form that is supersensible inasmuch as nature as object of our sensibility (i.e., nature as appearance) does not already have it. But our reason imposes this form on nature not theoretically, as our understanding, by its legislation, imposes on nature the form of the categories, but imposes it practically, i.e., by prescribing a moral law and initiating in nature a causal series that will add that supersensible form to the categorial form through free action. In this way, once the moral law, when obeyed, has "determined" the will (i.e., has induced it to act as it does), the will's action "determines" practically something in the world, i.e., gives it additional formal attributes.

How can the categorical imperative, which is a purely formal law (it commands only that our maxims be universalizable), have (practical) *application* in nature with all the particular that nature includes? Something like a schema is needed, as it was for the categories, that will "mediate" between the universal moral law and the particular effects which, in conformity with it, we produce in nature. This mediator cannot *be* a schema, for a schema mediates the imagination's exhibition of a concept and the categorical imperative, which is a rational idea, cannot be exhibited, i.e., cannot structure a *given* intuition to make it match the idea. The only possible mediator between this moral law and those particular effects (which we bring about through reason as helped by understanding) is what Kant calls the *typus* of the moral law: the same law regarded as a law of nature.[30] The only cognition we can have of the moral law is practical, but the *typus* can be cognized theoretically, can be understood; hence the *typus* mediates between reason and (not imagination but) understanding.

As free, i.e., as determinable by its own moral law, the will is our "higher power of desire" (the lower being merely the will's ability to be influenced by incentives of sense, "inclinations").[31] Any object of such higher desire is a purpose, in the sense given above.[32] Now if we consider together all the purposes we could pursue under all the maxims that would satisfy the categorical imperative, they will form a kind of hierarchy, some of them being pursued for other purposes, these for others still, and so on. At the very top of this hierarchy is the "final purpose"; this is the one purpose that is unconditioned, i.e., not a means to (or "condition" of) any further purpose. The final purpose at which, as the moral law commands, all our acts are to aim is the highest good in the world: our own virtue (which lies in the will's obedience to the moral law), and happiness for everyone to the extent that he or she is virtuous and thus worthy of such happiness.

This final purpose, as enjoined on us by the moral law, is not something we can achieve in this life, because we are beings encumbered by sensibility, by certain obstacles which nature outside us and especially nature within us puts in our way and to which we too easily

---

[30] *Critique of Practical Reason*, Ak. V, 69.

[31] Cf. *Ibid.*, Ak. V, 9n and esp. 22–25.

[32] See above, *xxv*, and cf. the *Metaphysics of Morals*, Ak. VI, 384–85.

succumb. Therefore the final purpose can never be manifested in experience, and hence cannot be known, even practically. Yet the final purpose can be cognized practically; for the concept of it does have "practical reality" (is not empty): the final purpose is achievable in principle, because the moral law commands it and the moral law is a matter of fact (fact of reason). Because, with our weak wills, we can only *approach* this final purpose by an infinite progression, while yet we must conceive of it as achievable because the moral law commands us to pursue it, we are forced to make two assumptions ("postulates"), which are thus also based on the moral law. One of these is that we are not temporally finite, but are immortal souls. The other assumption is that there is a God who has the infinite knowledge, power, and benevolence required to make nature cooperate with our infinite endeavor: for if the final purpose is to be achieved, nature within us must cooperate with our endeavor to be virtuous, and nature in general must cooperate with our endeavor to bring about happiness for everyone in proportion to his or her virtue. As prerequisites ("conditions") of the final purpose, which the known moral law establishes as not illusory, the immortality of the soul and the existence of such a moral God can thus also be cognized practically; but, like the final purpose of which they are the conditions, they cannot be known, even practically; they are not matters of fact, but are matters of faith, of a rational faith that is justified a priori by the moral law.

Thus the *Critique of Practical Reason* establishes what neither dogmatic rationalism nor dogmatic empiricism had been able to establish: we can have rational cognition, although practical rather than theoretical, of all the important things that the *Critique of Pure Reason* had to relegate to the merely regulative ideas. It establishes that we can have practical knowledge of the moral law as obligating us a priori, from which we can then derive a "metaphysics of morals," i.e., a system of all a priori maxims satisfying the categorical imperative, and establishes that we can have practical knowledge of our will as a supersensible causality free from the necessity of natural causation. It also establishes that we can have practical cognition of the final purpose with its presuppositions of immortality and God. The first *Critique* had established these features of the supersensible as logically possible, by construing the world of nature as mere appearance, but it had to leave the idea of this supersensible completely indeterminate. The second *Critique,* as Kant puts it, makes the idea of the supersensible *determinate* (and hence makes the supersensible cognizable practically): through the final purpose as enjoined on us by the known moral law, the concept of the supersensible is determined as the concept of a nature in itself, including ourselves as immortal souls, as created by a moral God in terms of the final purpose.

Kant restates much of this when, in the Critique of Teleological Judgment, he discusses how teleology relates to theology, and how the *Critique of Judgment* "mediates" between the first two *Critiques* and so unites the three in a system.

4.

The Critique of Aesthetic Judgment: Background

As did the first two *Critiques,* the *Critique of Judgment* again examines our cognitive powers, this time in order to decide what justification, if any, is possible for aesthetic judgments, above all judgments of taste, and for teleological judgments. As regards judgments of taste, the problem is this: How, if at all, is it possible to judge something in nature (or in art) as beautiful on the basis of something very subjective, a feeling of pleasure, and yet demand for our judgment a universal assent? That we do demand such assent is implicit in the very fact that we use the predicate 'beautiful,' as if beauty were a *property* of things (which everyone ought to see). If these judgments do have some kind of universal validity, they must "contain some necessity" (claim something with necessity) and hence must be to some extent a priori. And yet they are clearly not analytic but synthetic. How then, if at all, are *these* synthetic propositions possible a priori, despite their dependence on pleasure? Here again Kant's answer can best be understood as a reaction against the views of the dogmatic rationalists and dogmatic empiricists. I have selected the key figures, and shall now set out their views somewhat more elaborately than I did for the background to the first two *Critiques*.

Leibniz and Wolff maintained that we have two ways of knowing or cognizing the world, a lower and a higher cognitive power. (In Leibniz and Wolff 'cognize' means "know" or "come to know.") The lower cognitive power is sense perception, the higher is thought. Yet the distinction they drew between thought and perception by the senses made the two different not in kind but only in degree. Using Descartes's terminology, as refined by Leibniz, of "clear" and "distinct" ideas, Leibniz and Wolff held that the sole difference between sensation and thought is that thought is distinct, while sensation is confused, though both can be clear (rather than obscure). An idea is clear if we can (without doubt) distinguish it from all other ideas, though we may not know by what characteristics we do so. An idea is distinct if it is clear in all its parts (characteristics) and their combination, so that it can be distinguished from all other ideas explicitly, by abstraction (from the sensible detail) and definition. Sense perception cannot be made distinct without turning it into thought; lower cognition is only a preliminary stage of the same knowledge. By the same token, sense perception can have no perfection of its own, and hence no rules of its own to govern such perfection. The rules that apply to it are simply the rules of all thought: the principle of contradiction, and the principle of sufficient reason (which is the principle that God followed in making this the best of all possible worlds).

Moreover, just as Wolff construed willing the good as mere knowledge of the good, Leibniz and Wolff construed beauty and the pleasure we take in it in cognitive terms: beauty is perfection as cognized through sense perception, and hence indistinctly; and the pleasure we take in it is, at bottom, identical with that perception of the perfection. Art too is construed in cognitive terms: Art presupposes this cognition and makes it possible through its creations; art "imitates nature" in the sense that it produces the best examples of perfection of which nature (the world as phenomenon, i.e., as perceived by the senses) is, ideally, capable. Art pleases to the extent that it teaches us through such examples.

The first major innovation in this view concerning beauty and art comes from Alexander Gottlieb Baumgarten (1714–62), the disciple of Wolff to whom we owe the term 'aesthetic' in a sense close to the current one. Baumgarten collaborated in his work with his former student, Georg Friedrich Meier (1718–77). Although the two differ on certain points, it is not always easy to determine which of the two contributed what to their published works. However, their views are similar enough to be left undistinguished here.

Baumgarten and Meier[33] took over from Leibniz and Wolff the view that sense perception and thought are, respectively, lower and higher cognition, and the view that sense perception is confused while thought is distinct. But they denied that sense perception can be perfected only by making it distinct and thereby turning it into thought. Sense perception, they maintained, can have a perfection of its own, a perfection whose standard is not that of logic (although it is analogous to that standard). Moreover, it is this standard peculiar to sense perception which must be met if we are to perceive beauty. Hence there are two different kinds, rather than just stages, of cognition (knowledge), and two kinds of theory (or "science") of knowledge: logic and aesthetics. Aesthetics in the *broad* sense is the science of sense knowledge. (This is how Kant uses the term in the first *Critique,* when he speaks of the "transcendental aesthetic": A 19–49 = B 33–73.) Aesthetics in the *narrow* sense (the modern sense, which we find in Kant's third *Critique*) deals with the standards of perfection that sense perception must meet in order for us to perceive beauty; it is the science (or art) of the beautiful and of taste, i.e., of the power to cognize beauty.

Perfecting sense perception in order to turn it into *thought* requires that we make it more distinct, which we do by *abstracting* from the individuality and singularity (i.e., from the detail and concreteness) it presents to us. On the other hand, giving sense perception the perfection *peculiar* to it involves *emphasizing* what individuality and singularity it presents to us in an example. The standard of this perfection is richness and vividness of detail in the singular perception; here the perception *must* be indistinct, confused (i.e., fused with others, rather than explicitly distinguished from them). This richness and vividness of an image or idea is called its "extensive" clarity, as distinguished

---

[33] The following sketch has been distilled mainly from Baumgarten's *Aesthetica* (*Aesthetics*) of 1750–58 (Hildesheim: Georg Holms Verlagsbuchhandlung, 1961) and Meier's *Anfangsgründe aller schönen Wissenschaften* (*Foundations of all Fine Sciences*) of 1754 (Hildesheim and New York: Georg Holms Verlag, 1976).

from the clarity, now called "intensive" clarity, of Descartes, Leibniz, and Wolff.

According to Baumgarten and Meier, when our sense perception has this perfection peculiar to it, this perfected perception allows us to perceive perfection *in the world* (all perfection is multiplicity in unity): the perfection of things, but above all the moral perfection of persons. To perceive beauty is to perceive such perfection by sense (as itself perfected by being made extensively clear); beauty is perfection insofar as we cognize this perfection not rationally and hence distinctly, but by taste, i.e., extensively clear sense perception. Aesthetic pleasure is the result of cognizing perfection by sense as perfected by being made extensively clear.

Because perfection (goodness) implies a standard, there are rules of perfection; hence, there are also rules of beauty, which can be derived from the rules of perfection in general. Thus we have two kinds of rules for "beautiful cognition" in general: rules about the cognition itself, and rules about the perfection of the objects we can cognize in this way.

In addition to these rules, there are the practical rules that apply those other rules to art. The aim of art is not simply to imitate nature, not even by selecting the most perfect examples of which nature is ideally capable, but to create a perfect whole out of indistinct images (or, in the case of poetry, indistinct ideas) made extensively clear, a whole that can then be judged in the same way as beauty in general can. Hence the fine arts, as informed by such rules, are at the same time "fine sciences"; and aesthetics, which is itself an art, similarly becomes a science, the science of the beautiful, to the extent that it offers higher-order rules (principles) for those other rules.

Kant accepted and defended the major innovation offered by Baumgarten and Meier: their insistence that sense perception is not the same as thought and can be perfected without turning it into thought. But Kant objected to the *cognitive* analysis that Baumgarten and Meier offered for our perception of beauty (Ak. 207–09). He objected to it because the analysis turns beauty into a property, viz., a perfection that something has by reference to a *purpose* as expressed by some *concept,* and because the analysis treats the perfection of the sense perception itself ("extensive clarity") as merely a prereq-uisite for perceiving the perfection of *something else* by means of sense. If judgments about beauty were conceptual, Kant argued, they could be proved by rules (just such rules as Baumgarten and Meier had tried to devise); yet this cannot be done (Ak. 284–85). By the same token, there can be no "fine science" but only fine art, and aesthetics cannot be a "science" of the beautiful but only critique.[34]

Hence, while the dogmatic rationalists had indeed offered an account of the universality of aesthetic judgments, viz., by construing them as conceptual and as cognitive judgments about a property, this very account assimilated judgments about beauty to judgments about the good (Ak. 346) and hence failed to explain their aesthetic and therefore subjective character. Some analysis of aesthetic judgments must be found that would preserve their universality without assimilating them to judgments of cognition, theoretical or practical. Such an analysis is just what the empiricists tried to provide.

Kant's own *Observations on the Feeling of the Beautiful and Sublime* of 1764 were empirical, but they were not empiricist: they offered no theory, as Kant did not yet think that an aesthetic theory was possible. Instead the work consists of amateur social psychology; it discusses beauty and sublimity in relation to the differences between people, ages, sexes, nationalities, temperaments. Even in the *Critique of Pure Reason* (both first and second editions) Kant says that Baumgarten's attempt to bring the rules for judging the beautiful under rational principles is futile, because these rules are merely empirical. (A 21n = B 35n.)

As for the theories of beauty and art of the British empiricists, a number of them were available in German translation by the time Kant wrote the third *Critique*. Kant was probably familiar with the *Inquiry into the Original of Our Ideas of Beauty and Virtue* (1725) of Francis Hutcheson (1694–1747);[35] he was in general familiar with Hume's views, although it is not clear that he had read "Of the Standard of Taste" (1757);[36] and he was clearly familiar with the *Philosophical Enquiry into the Origin of Our Ideas of the Sublime*

---

[34] See Ak. 304 and 355. That critique, on the other hand, *can* be scientific: Ak. 286.

[35] See, e.g., Francis Hutcheson, A*n Inquiry Concerning Beauty, Order, Harmony, Design*, ed. Peter Kivy (The Hague: Martinus Nijhoff, 1973).

[36] See, e.g., David Hume, *Of the Standard of Taste and Other Essays*, ed. John W. Lenz (Indianapolis: Bobbs-Merrill, 1965).

and Beautiful (1757) of Edmund Burke (1729–97),[37] to whom he responds by name.[38]

According to Hutcheson, beauty is not a quality of things; the term 'beauty' stands for the idea that certain qualities of things evoke in the mind. Our natural power to receive the idea of beauty when confronted by such qualities is analogous to perception: it is a "sense" of beauty. Perceiving such qualities by this sense produces an immediate (i.e., direct) delight. One such quality is formal: the compound ratio of uniformity in variety; if either of these is kept constant, "beauty" varies with the other. Art imitates, but its "beauty" is not that of the original; it is based on the unity found in the conformity of the work with the original. Another quality that arouses the idea of beauty is moral virtue. Moral virtue can be perceived by the *moral* "sense," but it can also produce aesthetic delight. (Vice can be represented beautifully as well, but only insofar as the representation manifests unity in its conformity with the original.) The standard of taste, the standard for judging beauty, is empirical: it is our common human nature, the sensibility we have for appreciating uniformity in variety; if we do not find universal agreement regarding judgments of taste, it is only because we become prejudiced by making irrelevant associations.

Hume, treating judgments of taste as he does moral judgments, also denies that beauty is a quality of things, and speaks of a "sense" or "feeling" of beauty, an ability to receive pleasure from the perception of certain qualities of things, or from association with such qualities. Hume is not specific about what these qualities are; they involve structural relations between parts and whole, or a thing's utility as it appears to us. The standard of taste is again human nature, but as subject to more qualifications than Hutcheson had spelled out. A qualified perceiver must not only be impartial (unprejudiced): the perceiver must be calm, as well as experienced in judging beauty, especially beauty in art. By abstracting the common features of objects that have pleased the sense of beauty of such qualified persons over the ages, we may be able to tell what qualities in general (e.g., what formal properties of objects) are capable of producing this pleasure. If we fail in this attempt, we can still use such persons

[37] A modern edition is that edited by James T. Boulton (London: Routledge & Kegan Paul, 1958).

[38] Ak. 277. The following sketch is distilled mainly from the works just mentioned.

(including ourselves, insofar as we fulfill the same criteria) as our standard for judging. Human nature does not vary so much that such persons would greatly disagree, even though perhaps some disagreement, e.g., that due to differences in temperament, cannot be resolved.

Burke again holds that all there is, as far as beauty is concerned, is our idea of it. We have a "feeling" of beauty, and we call an object beautiful if it evokes a certain idea, a certain feeling: love without interest. To this account Burke adds an explanation, in terms of the physiology of the day, as to how the object evokes this feeling (cf. Ak. 277 incl. br. n. 51). Burke does not say much as to what qualities in objects arouse the idea of beauty. As for a standard of taste, Burke seems to have assumed that taste is the same in all human beings.

The empiricist analysis of beauty by reference to a kind of "sense" or "feeling," as combined with the denial that beauty is a property of things, accounted well for the aesthetic and subjective character of judgments of taste. Kant's complaint against the empiricist analysis is that it fails to account for the fact that judgments of taste demand everyone's assent and hence claim a universality and necessity (Ak. 237), which presupposes some necessary and hence a priori principle. "Scouting about for empirical laws about mental changes" cannot yield this necessity (Ak. 278), nor can "gathering votes and asking other people what kind of sensation they are having" when facing a beautiful object (Ak. 281), even if as a matter of empirical fact many people happen to agree on a judgment of taste because "there is a contingent uniformity in the organization of [different] subjects" (Ak. 345–46). Hence the empiricist analysis cannot adequately distinguish between judgments of taste and judgments about the merely agreeable (Ak. 346), which are also subjective but imply no universality.

5.

Kant's Account of
Judgments of Taste as
Aesthetic Judgments
of Reflection

Kant's main concern in the Critique of Aesthetic Judgment is judgments of taste, i.e., judgments about the beautiful,[39] above all about the beautiful in nature.[40] A paradigm would be the judgment, 'The rose at which I am looking is beautiful' (cf. Ak. 215), provided that this judgment is made without using the *concept* (or "thought") of the rose, but is made, rather, with the mere *intuition,* i.e., with the rose as "given" (Ak. 230). Although the fact that in such a judgment we use the adjective 'beautiful' *suggests* that beauty is a property, beauty is not a property: "apart from a relation to the subject's feeling, beauty is nothing by itself" (Ak. 218). Hence it is this "feeling" that must be analyzed in such a way as to account for the judgment's claim to universality (universal validity). Because even judgments of taste have reference to the understanding (Ak. 203 n.1), the categories play some role in them. Accordingly, Kant explicates these judgments by reference to four "moments," which are based on the four category headings: quality, quantity, relation, and modality. (I shall not follow Kant's order here.)

"*Beautiful* is what, without a concept [such as the concept of the good], is liked universally" (Ak. 219). This universality is the aesthetic quantity of a judgment of taste (second moment) and is what distinguishes it from judgments about the agreeable. (In *logical* quantity, a judgment of taste is *singular:* Ak. 215.) But this universality is only "subjective": the judgment demands that all subjects give their assent to the judgment. By the same token, the judgment's "necessity" (fourth moment, as to modality) is not apodeictic (as the necessity in

---

[39] Judgments about the sublime will be discussed below. See Section 9.

[40] In sketching Kant's account, I shall largely disregard his own artificial and unhelpful division of the Critique of Aesthetic Judgment into an "Analytic" and a "Dialectic."

a demonstration) but only "exemplary" (Ak. 237): we demand universal assent to a judgment that we make as an example of a certain unstatable universal rule (Ak. 237). To make this demand is to claim that we speak with a "universal voice" (Ak. 216) and to presuppose a priori that taste and the feeling by which it judges is common to everyone and hence is a *sensus communis,* a "common sense" (Ak. 238). To justify this claim and presupposition is therefore to justify the claim to subjective universality. Before we turn to this justification, we must complete the analysis of judgments of taste.

Judgments about the agreeable and judgments about the beautiful are both aesthetic judgments. But the former are aesthetic judgments of sense: the pleasure (or "liking") we feel in a judgment about the agreeable is interested, viz., interested in the existence of some object as related to sense. In judgments of taste, on the other hand, the liking is "disinterested" (first moment, as to quality): *"beautiful is what we like in merely judging it"* (Ak. 306). Judgments of taste are aesthetic judgments not of sense but of "reflection."[41]

Reflective judgments in general, aesthetic as well as teleological,[42] are judgments that are not "determinative," i.e., they do not determine objects. We saw above (*xxxiv*) that the judgment, 'This is a dog,' determines the dog (as appearance) by having the imagination structure a matching empirical intuition in terms of the concept of "dog," i.e., by subsuming the intuition under that concept. Hence determinative judgments subsume a particular under some universal. We also saw (*xliv*) that judgments about the good (practical judgments) are determinative as well: they too use a concept to determine (give attributes to) experience; but here the determination is not performed simply by the understanding's legislation, but instead practically, by the will and its action. (The concept may be empirical, as when we produce some object, or may be a priori, as in morality.) On the other hand, reflective judgments, including aesthetic ones, do not give attributes to objects and hence are not determinative. Though Kant will talk about *judgments* as being "determined" by a feeling or a concept (Ak. 221) and will even say such things as "a judgment of

---

[41] Judgments about the sublime are the other kind of aesthetic judgments of reflection. They will be discussed in Section 9 below.

[42] Teleological reflective judgments will be discussed in later sections of the Translator's Introduction. See esp. Sections 10–13.

taste determines the object . . . with regard to liking and the predicate of beauty" (Ak. 219), and so on, yet in the strict and relevant sense of 'determinative' judgments of taste are not determinative. For they do not determine an object in the sense of giving it an attribute, because beauty is not an attribute (not a property), even though grammatically the term 'beauty' functions as a predicate. Moreover, judgments of taste do not use a *determinate* concept, as do cognitive judgments, theoretical or practical. The reason for this is that reflective judgments, including aesthetic ones, have no determinate concept available to them, no universal under which to subsume the particular that is given to us in intuition; rather, they try to *find* such a universal.

If this search for a universal is to succeed, it must be pursued not haphazardly but on some principle; and since in this case the power of judgment has no determinate concept available that could serve it as such a principle, it must *itself* have a concept, though only an indeterminate one, that can serve it as such a principle (Ak. 180–81, and cf. Ak. 340–41).

This indeterminate concept is the concept of nature's "subjective purposiveness," i.e., nature's purposiveness for our (the subject's) power of judgment; and the principle of judgment to which this concept gives rise is simply the assumption that nature in its particular (as we find it in empirical intuition) is "subjectively purposive," i.e., purposive for our power of judgment in the sense of *lending* itself to being judged by us (Ak. 193). (Since judgment is a function of understanding, Kant will also speak of nature's purposiveness for our understanding or for our cognitive power: Ak. 187; 184, 186.)

The difference between the concept of such subjective purposiveness and the concept of a purpose (see above, *xxv*) is precisely that the first concept is indeterminate, the second determinate. In order for nature's particular to be purposive for our power of judgment it must manifest a certain regularity (order, lawfulness). This regularity is not determinate, like the regularity that an intuition must have in order to match a determinate concept; rather, it is an indeterminate regularity, viz., the regularity that we need *in general* in order to match an empirical intuition with a concept so as to give rise to empirical cognition. Since the particular in nature is contingent (because not subject to our understanding's legislation), nature's subjective purposiveness consists in the regularity or "lawfulness" that the contingent must have (Ak. 404, 217′) in order for us to cognize it. Accordingly, the principle of judgment is the assumption that nature manifests a cognizable order not only in its (transcendental and metaphysical) universal laws (which are based on the categories) but in terms of its particular (and contingent) laws as well: *Nature makes its universal laws specific* (Ak. 186) in such a way that the particular laws will not be too "heterogeneous" (Ak. 188) for us to have coherent experience even in terms of them (Ak. 180). Thus judgment assumes that nature forms a hierarchy (Ak. 213′, 185) of genera and species (each genus and species representing a grouping and hence a "law"), and of empirical laws in general (including particular causal laws), and hence manifests simplicity and parsimony.[43] On this assumption, it is "as if" nature's order had been given it (legislated to it) "by some understanding, even if not ours" (Ak. 180). This assumed lawfulness, though indeterminate, is one that matches *understanding as such,* i.e., understanding considered indeterminately, apart from any specific concept. Hence it is also one that matches the form that *imagination* as such must have (as it apprehends, in general, something in empirical intuition) in order to harmonize with understanding as such so that cognition may arise. By the same token, the same assumed indeterminate lawfulness is one that matches the form of the power of judgment as such, i.e., it matches the *harmony* (which itself has that form) between imagination as such and understanding as such that is required for all (empirical: Ak. 190–91) judgment and cognition.

This principle of the power of judgment, that the power of judgment presupposes for its reflection, is itself a reflective judgment. Insofar as we only think this principle (rather than apply it directly to intuition), it is a logical judgment: the indeterminate principle of reflection as such. The two kinds of reflection, aesthetic and teleological, are both *based* on that principle.[44] Teleological judgments are indeed reflective and presuppose judgment's principle; yet in them the subjective purposiveness merely underlies an objective and "material" purposiveness, because teleological judgments are made

---

[43] Ak. 182. The *Critique of Pure Reason* discusses reflection in fairly similar terms (A 260–92 = B 316–49), but attributes the concern and search for this unity of the particular to reason (A 648–62 = B 676–90).

[44] The principle is not really a *third kind* of reflective judgment, as Paul Guyer seems to consider it: *Kant and the Claims of Taste* (Cambridge: Harvard University Press, 1979), 61–64. It is simply judgment's *principle itself* which *underlies* both aesthetic and teleological reflective judgments.

by reference to a determinate concept of a purpose (the "matter" of purposiveness), so that there the purposiveness is a purposiveness *with* a purpose. By contrast, in aesthetic reflective judgments the purposiveness is not based on a concept (Ak. 220) and hence also not on the concept of a purpose; so it is *merely* subjective, a "purposiveness without a purpose" (third moment, in terms of the relation "of the purposes we take into consideration").[45]

We saw that in aesthetic reflective judgments we judge the subjective purposiveness that nature displays in the empirical intuition (of something apprehended by the imagination) and that we judge this purposiveness without a determinate concept. Hence in such judgments, imagination and understanding harmonize without the constraint that a determinate concept would introduce and thus are in "free play." Moreover, since the apprehended form is not compared (matched) with a determinate concept, its purposiveness is not cognized but can only be felt. This feeling (of pleasure) is nothing more than our nonconceptual awareness (awareness without a [determinate] concept) of the form's purposiveness for our cognitive power as such, i.e., purposiveness for the harmony of imagination as such with understanding as such. (Ak. 222.) Anything in nature, as long as our imagination can apprehend it in an intuition, can be judged aesthetically: it could be a rose, or it might be some larger part of nature, such as a certain order among species and genera; but in the first case we must judge without the concept of a rose, in the second case without a (single determinate) concept of such order among species and genera. Judgment's principle of nature's purposiveness embodies a constant expectation in accordance with an "aim" we have (Ak. 187), viz., our aim (or "endeavor," as at Ak. 187) to cognize nature in an experience that coheres even in the particular. Hence when we actually find such order in nature, whether in the rose or in some larger but still intuitable part, then we feel a pleasure, as equated by Kant with our nonconceptual awareness of that purposiveness for our cognitive power as such (Ak. 184). This is why the natural scientist will frequently feel such pleasure upon discovering, and when judging aesthetically (i.e., without as yet having and using a [single determinate] concept for this), an *indeterminate* (subjectively) purposive

---

[45] Ak. 219. The purposiveness as we merely think it in judgment's principle itself is (a subjective purposiveness) neither with nor without a purpose but covers both possibilities.

order in parts of nature that he had, until then, conceptualized only in terms of a multiplicity of determinate concepts of species and genera.[46] If the scientist ceases to notice the pleasure, this is only because he is concerned mainly with cognition of such purposive order and therefore tends to focus on that cognition and hence to make no attempt to distinguish from it his *nonconceptual* awareness of such order (Ak. 187).

It is precisely this analysis of judgments of taste by reference to cognition as such (though not by reference to determinate cognitions, since then the judgments would be cognitive rather than aesthetic), which enables Kant to provide a "deduction," i.e., a justification, for them and their claim to universality and hence for their presupposition of a "common sense" (*sensus communis*).

6.

The Deduction of Judgments of Taste

In a judgment of taste we connect a noncognitive "predicate," a feeling, with the mere intuition of an object (Ak. 288), and to this extent the judgment is (singular and) empirical (Ak. 289). What needs a justification ("deduction") is only the a priori claim of the judgment, the claim that the pleasure (and to this extent the judgment as well) has universal validity (Ak. 289). Since a judgment of taste obviously is not analytic but synthetic,[47] what the deduction tries to show is that and how this kind of synthetic judgment is possible a priori (Ak. 289). It does this as follows (Ak. 289–90).

In a judgment of taste the liking is not connected with the sensation (through which the "matter" of intuition would be given us: see

---

[46] Cf. the connection Kant makes between beauty and "orienting" oneself in the immense diversity of nature at Ak. 193.

[47] "We can readily see that judgments of taste are synthetic; for they go beyond the concept of the object, and even beyond the intuition of the object, and add as a predicate to this intuition something that is not even cognition: namely, [a] feeling of pleasure (or displeasure)": Ak. 288.

above, *xxxiv*) as it is when we judge something (e.g., ice cream) to be
agreeable; nor is it connected with a concept as it is in judgments
about the good. In other words, in a judgment of taste the liking
involves no interest in an object's existence, whether as related to
sense (as in the case of something agreeable) or in terms of some
purpose (as in the case of the good). Rather, in a judgment of taste the
liking is disinterested: it is connected with the mere judging of the
form of the object. Hence this liking can be nothing but (our awareness of) the form's purposiveness for the power of judgment.[48] As the
power of judgment is not directed to the sensation or to a concept, it
can be directed only to the subjective conditions of (empirical) judgment as such: the harmony of imagination and understanding that is
needed for all (empirical) cognition. These subjective conditions of
(empirical) judgment as such, i.e., the harmony of the cognitive powers, can be assumed to be the same in everyone. Hence the liking is
nothing but (our consciousness of) the form's purposiveness for that
harmony, a harmony that can be assumed to be the same in everyone.
Therefore the liking has universal subjective validity, i.e., it is indeed
a *sensus communis* (a "common sense"), viz., taste, by which we
can judge given forms as to whether they have such purposiveness
without a purpose.

Kant's key premise in this deduction is that the subjective conditions of (empirical) judgment as such (the harmony of the cognitive
powers) can be assumed to be the same in everyone. He does not
argue for that premise in the deduction, because he has already done
so elsewhere: provided merely that (in accordance with the first *Critique*) we reject skepticism, we can assume that our ordinary (empirical) cognitions and judgments are universally communicable (Ak.
238–39); in other words, we can assume that what we call 'common
understanding' (not the *sensus communis* but what we *ordinarily* call
'common sense,' viz., sound judgment in everyday matters) is indeed
"common," i.e., shared by everyone, and hence can assume that the
cognitive powers presupposed by this common understanding are
shared universally as well (Ak. 292–93).

What makes it possible for this harmony to serve as a *standard* of

---

[48] I am inserting in parentheses what Kant often omits but regards as understood. He
clearly does identify this pleasure with the consciousness of the purposiveness (of
the form of an object) in the play of the cognitive powers: Ak. 222.

taste, i.e., a standard for judging form (as to its beauty), is that, although in any particular cognition the harmony varies (according to the concept and intuition involved), the same does not hold for the indeterminate harmony as such (which, like the purposiveness it matches, cannot be cognized but can only be felt [Ak. 219]): since understanding as such has whatever structure it has, and imagination can harmonize with that structure only by adopting it, there must be a harmony (having that same structure), an "attunement," that is *optimal* for empirical cognition as such (Ak. 238–39). On the other hand, we must still make sure that we use that standard correctly. We must be certain that our judgment is indeed disinterested, a judgment of reflection rather than a judgment based on a concept or on a mere sensation (cf. Ak. 216, 290–93). In other words, we must be certain that the pleasure is indeed based on nothing but the (indeterminate) subsumption of our imagination as such (as it apprehends a form in intuition) under our understanding as such (Ak. 287).

7.

Beyond the Deduction: Linking Beauty to Morality

Extensive debates have been carried on among scholars as to whether the deduction, as just sketched in accordance with Kant's presentation of it in § 38 (Ak. 289–90), is complete: some (e.g., Crawford) have argued that linking beauty to morality is still part of the deduction, whereas others (e.g., Guyer) have argued that it is not.[49]

On the one hand, Kant's *presentation* certainly suggests that the deduction is completed in § 38, even before the Comment that starts just after it. The section is entitled simply 'Deduction of Judgments of Taste'; the beginning of the Comment, 'What makes this deduction so easy . . .' (Ak. 290), clearly implies that the deduction is finished;

---

[49] Donald W. Crawford, Kant's *Aesthetic Theory* (Madison: University of Wisconsin Press, 1974), 142–59. Guyer, *Kant and the Claims of Taste*, 373–89.

and the explanation that the Comment offers for that remark, as to why the deduction is "so easy," is entirely in terms of the material in § 38. Moreover, the point of the deduction was to justify the demand of judgments of taste for universal assent; and establishing that we do have a "common sense" (*sensus communis*), a taste that all subjects must have (and can use correctly), is indeed sufficient to justify us in demanding that anyone else who judges the same object *reflectively* should agree with our judgment. This is why Kant says explicitly,

> ... [S]omeone who feels pleasure in the mere reflection on the form of an object ... rightly lays claim to everyone's assent, even though this judgment is empirical and a singular judgment. For the basis of this pleasure is found in the universal, though subjective, condition of reflective judgments, namely, the purposive harmony of an object ... with the mutual relation of the cognitive powers (imagination and understanding) that are required for every cognition (Ak. 191).

In other words, the conflict between the subjectivity of judgments of taste and their claim to universality is solved by means of the indeterminate concept of nature's purposiveness for our cognitive power.

On the other hand, when Kant presents the same conflict again, as the "antinomy concerning the principle of taste" (Ak. 338–39), he seems to have changed his mind. He now claims that the only way to solve the antinomy and "save [the] claim [of a judgment of taste] to universal validity" is by means of the indeterminate concept *of the supersensible* (Ak. 340). Similarly, Kant says that "our liking for [the beautiful] include[s] a claim to everyone else's assent . . . only because we refer the beautiful to . . . the *intelligible*" (Ak. 353), i.e., to the supersensible. Now, the concept of the supersensible which according to Kant will make the (seeming) contradiction in the antinomy "disappear" and which "make[s] the judgment of taste valid for everyone" is the indeterminate concept of the supersensible that *underlies nature's purposiveness for our cognitive power* (Ak. 340). Hence it seems that Kant, by switching to *this* indeterminate concept, is suddenly *equating* (treating as equivalent) the indeterminate concept of nature's purposiveness for our cognitive power with the indeterminate concept of the *supersensible basis* of that same (subjective) purposiveness. I shall argue, from textual evidence, that this is just what Kant is doing. Kant does not explain the equation at this point. The explanation can be found in the Critique of Teleological Judgment, where the same equation is made. Although Kant does not offer a clear explanation even there, the evidence that he is making the equation is overwhelming. I must delay my argument concerning this point until the last section of this introduction. I shall refer to this problem as 'Problem I.' In the meantime, I shall simply anticipate the conclusion and ask the reader to *assume* that, however perplexing it may seem, the two concepts are indeed equivalent.

However, the way in which Kant introduces the supersensible at this point raises a further difficulty. Just before he calls it the supersensible underlying nature's purposiveness for our cognitive power, he says that it is the supersensible "underlying the object (as well as underlying the judging subject) as an object of sense and hence as appearance" (Ak. 340). Moreover, Kant also says that the "intelligible" (i.e., supersensible) which "taste has in view" and by reference to which we demand universal assent to our judgments of taste is the "morally good" (Ak. 353), and "the pleasure that taste declares valid for mankind as such . . . must indeed derive from this [link to moral ideas] and from the resulting increase in our receptivity for the feeling that arises from moral ideas (and is called moral feeling)" (Ak. 356). This last supersensible is the one that "the concept of freedom [and hence the moral law] contains practically" (Ak. 176), viz., "the final purpose . . . the appearance of which in the world of sense . . . ought to exist";[50] in other words, it is our supersensible freedom and a supersensible substrate of nature that will make nature as appearance (especially the appearance of what nature we have *within* us: Ak. 196, 340), cooperate, through the agency of a moral God, with our endeavor to achieve the final purpose.

This difficulty, the fact that Kant seems to introduce, in order to solve the antinomy of taste, *three* supersensibles rather than just one, has an easy solution: what we have here are three *ideas* of the supersensible, but they are all ideas of the *same* supersensible. (Ak. 346.) The *idea* of the supersensible as required to solve the antinomy of taste is the idea of the supersensible as underlying nature's

---

[50] Ak. 195–96. Actually, Kant says, 'the final purpose which (or the appearance of which in the world of sense),' but in order for the morally good (the highest good) to be supersensible, we need the second disjunct, 'the appearance of which.'

purposiveness for our judgment; but the *supersensible* to which this idea refers is all of this: the substrate of objects and of ourselves as subjects,[51] the substrate of nature's purposiveness for our judgment, and the supersensible that "the concept of freedom contains practically."

What, however, justifies regarding the "three" supersensibles as one? Kant's answer is this: it is the way in which the supersensible as underlying nature's subjective purposiveness "mediates" the "transition" between the other "two" and hence between the domains of nature and of freedom (Ak. 176, 196–97). The idea of the supersensible as mere substrate of nature was left wholly indeterminate by the *Critique of Pure Reason;* the *Critique of Practical Reason,* on the other hand, made the idea of the supersensible as contained practically in the concept of freedom *determinate* (and hence made it possible for us to cognize this supersensible); and it is the idea that the *Critique of Judgment* provides of the supersensible underlying nature's subjective purposiveness which, although itself indeterminate and incapable of giving rise to cognition, nevertheless makes the idea of the supersensible *determinable* (Ak. 196). *How* the indeterminate idea of the supersensible basis of nature's subjective purposiveness can make the idea of the supersensible determinable (capable of being determined by practical reason) is a problem—I shall call it 'Problem II'—whose solution hinges on the solution of Problem I and hence must also wait until the last section of this introduction.

But while the indeterminate concept that unites the "three" supersensibles, and thus also unites the three *Critiques* in a system, is the concept of reflective judgment in general, i.e., aesthetic as well as teleological, Kant singles out *aesthetic* reflective judgment as special (even) for this mediation role: the concept of nature's subjective purposiveness is made "suitable" for that mediation role by the "spontaneity in the play of the cognitive powers, whose harmony with each other contains the basis of [the] pleasure [that we feel in judging the beautiful]" (Ak. 197). *How* the spontaneity makes the concept "suitable" for this is what I shall call 'Problem III,' and this problem too must be left for the last section of this introduction.

We are now in a position to resolve the seeming conflict between those of Kant's comments implying that the deduction is complete

---

[51] Sometimes Kant calls it simply 'the supersensible in us' (e.g., Ak. 341). I shall have more to say about this in n. 101 below.

and those that suggest otherwise. First, a correct analysis of judgments of taste, i.e., an analysis of them that avoids the antinomy of
taste, must indeed link beauty to the supersensible—to the supersensible as basis of the subjective purposiveness of nature. The concept
of *this* supersensible is indeed needed to "save [the] claim [of judgments of taste] to universal validity," i.e., this link is needed for the
justification of these judgments. But this link does not take us beyond
the deduction; it is already implicit in the deduction, because—as the
solution of Problem I will show—a fuller analysis of the concept of
the subjective purposiveness of nature reveals it to be equivalent to
the concept of the supersensible basis of that same purposiveness.
Second, beauty is linked to the supersensible as substrate of objects
and of ourselves only indirectly, viz., only insofar as the three ideas
of the supersensible all refer to the same supersensible; the idea of
the supersensible as mere substrate of objects and of ourselves is as
yet utterly indeterminate and hence could not *justify* judgments of
taste at all. The idea of the supersensible as underlying the subjective
purposiveness of nature, although still indeterminate as well, is—as
we shall see in the last section of this introduction—not *utterly* indeterminate but has just enough content to justify a claim to universal
subjective validity, by the same token that it can make the concept of
the supersensible determinable (by practical reason). Third, the link
of beauty to the supersensible as thus determined, and hence cognized, by practical reason not only is again indirect but *must* be indirect. For otherwise, despite Kant's repeated and express insistence to
the contrary, his account of judgments of taste would become cognitive after all and judgments of taste could be established a priori, viz.,
practically. It is because the link of beauty to this last supersensible
is only indirect that Kant, in discussing the link between beauty and
morality, no longer speaks of justification or deduction. Instead he
speaks of "explanation" (Ak. 296) and "interpretation" (Ak. 301).
Moreover, this explanation or interpretation comes about in a way
in which justification of what these judgments claim would never be
possible, viz., through the mere *analogy* between beauty and morality, i.e., through the mere fact that beauty is the "symbol" of morality
(Ak. 353, cf. 301). This explanatory or interpretive link can at most
provide our taste with "guidance" (Ak. 297–98). Hence beauty as
such does not "gain" from morality, nor the other way round (Ak.
231). By the same token, although we do tend to take an interest in

the existence and judging of the beautiful, an interest which is moral "in terms of its kinship" (Ak. 300), our *liking* for the beautiful remains nonetheless independent of all interest (Ak. 300); and even the interest itself that we take in beauty is due not to the link between beauty and morality but to "beauty's own characteristic of qualifying for such a link, which therefore belongs to it intrinsically" (Ak. 302). Only in this limited sense do we "refer" the beautiful to "the intelligible" that "the concept of freedom contains practically," i.e., the supersensible as made determinate practically; and only in this limited sense is aesthetic reflective pleasure "derived" from the link of beauty to morality; hence it is still "not practical in any way" (Ak. 222), as of course it *would* be if the link were justificatory rather than merely explanatory or interpretive.

Therefore, while the link of beauty to an as yet indeterminate "supersensible" is part of, but is also already implicit in, the deduction of judgments of taste as given in § 38, the link of beauty to morality is not needed for the deduction and would in fact take the deduction *too far* by making beauty cognizable. Taste, according to Kant, is not based on the supersensible as determined (practically), but only "has it in view" (Ak. 353), viz., insofar as both nature's subjective purposiveness and the supersensible basis of that purposiveness are analogous to that supersensible and thus capable of making it determinable.

8.

Beauty and Fine Art

There is "free" or "vague" beauty, Kant says, and "accessory" or "fixed" beauty, beauty fixed by the concept of the thing's purpose, the concept of what the thing is (meant) to be (Ak. 229–32). Judgments of taste about free beauty are pure, those about fixed beauty are applied judgments of taste and are partly conceptual, partly "intellectual" (Ak. 229–32). For example, beauty of which there can be an "ideal" (Ak. 231–36) must involve a concept of the purpose of the beautiful thing; Kant argues that only man is capable of an ideal of beauty, and this ideal involves the concept of man's moral purpose.

Since all fine art[52] (indeed, all art in general[53]) involves the concept of a purpose,[54] all beauty in fine art is fixed beauty, and hence judgments about this beauty are "logically conditioned" (Ak. 312), because we are also judging how *perfect* the object is in terms of that purpose (Ak. 311). But although the artist is thus proceeding by an intention (the intention to produce an object in accordance with the concept he has of it), the intention must not show in the work: the work must look like nature even though we are aware that it is art (Ak. 306–07). In other words, beauty in art is the same beauty as beauty in nature, except that it is restricted to the concept of the thing's purpose. By the same token, *nature* is beautiful if it also looks like *art;* the beauty of nature is not fixed, however, because nature, as judged in aesthetic reflective judgments, only "looks like" art, and we do not judge that it *is* art.[55]

Producing fine art, as distinguished from merely judging it by means of taste, requires genius (Ak. 307), although taste is needed as well: taste is needed to discipline genius, make it civilized by holding it within determinate rules (which we need in order to achieve a purpose: Ak. 310), and so keep it from producing nonsense (Ak. 319). But genius is a talent that does not simply *follow* rules but is original (Ak. 307–08); i.e., genius gives its own rule to art and hence produces works that are models and therefore exemplary (Ak. 308). But even the artist himself does not know what this rule is by which he connects his ideas (Ak. 308), and by which he then hits on a way of expressing them that communicates the "mental attunement" produced by these ideas (Ak. 317). This latter talent (of hitting on the right expression) Kant calls 'spirit' (Ak. 317). Spirit in an aesthetic

[52] 'Fine' in this sense and 'beautiful' are the same term in German (*schön*), which is used in both the classificatory and the laudatory senses.

[53] Kant distinguishes fine art from art in various other senses of the term at Ak. 303–04.

[54] Since "otherwise the product cannot be ascribed to any art at all, but would be a mere product of chance": Ak. 310.

[55] Crawford's "paradox" about this reciprocal relation between nature and art seems to arise mainly because, in both cases, he quotes Kant as saying 'is like' rather than 'looks like': *Kant's Aesthetic Theory,* 134.

sense of the term is the "animating principle of the mind" (Ak. 313), and is the ability to exhibit (*darstellen*, traditionally rendered as 'to present'[56]) *aesthetic ideas* (Ak. 313–14). An aesthetic idea is an intuition[57] that "prompts much thought" (Ak. 314); it is the "counterpart" of a rational idea: Just as no intuition can be adequate to an idea of reason, so there is no (determinate) concept that would be adequate to an aesthetic idea (Ak. 314).

Kant goes on to offer a classification of the various fine arts, and to discuss their similarities, differences, interrelations, and relative "aesthetic value" (Ak. 320–36).

9.

Judgments about the Sublime

Judgments about the sublime are the other kind of aesthetic reflective judgments. In analyzing them, Kant focuses on the sublime in nature, "since the sublime in art is always confined to the conditions that [art] must meet to be in harmony with nature" (Ak. 245). All sublimity involves vast magnitude; and nature, Kant says, is most sublime in its "chaos," in its "wildest and most ruleless disarray and devastation" (Ak. 246).

In Baumgarten and Meier, the notion that is closest to Kant's "sublimity" is "aesthetic magnitude," in a sense that includes largeness as well as greatness. But for Baumgarten and Meier this aesthetic magnitude is one of the necessary *ingredients in beauty* (another is aesthetic richness, and both of these are needed to convey "truth" aesthetically, i.e., needed for aesthetic "cognition"). A species of aesthetic magnitude is indeed called 'sublimity,' but in a rather older and narrower sense, as meaning 'grandeur,' 'splendor,' 'loftiness.' Hence both this "sublimity" and that "aesthetic magnitude" are treated cognitively, as beauty is. Kant rejects this cognitive analysis (Ak. 268)

---

[56] See above, *xxxv*.

[57] Actually, Kant says 'presentation' (*Vorstellung*, traditionally rendered as 'representation': see below, Ak. 175 br. n. 17.)

as he did in the case of beauty, offering instead an analysis of the sublime in terms of reflection and a universally valid feeling.

Kant had discussed the sublime, along with the beautiful, empirically in his *Observations on the Feeling of the Beautiful and Sublime* of 1764, but only, as I have already mentioned, in terms of amateur social psychology. The most important *empiricist* account of the sublime is that of Edmund Burke, with which Kant was familiar.[58] Burke analyzes the sublime along the same lines as the beautiful. We merely *call* objects sublime; we do so if they evoke a certain idea, a certain feeling. Here the feeling is one of "astonishment," a certain degree of "horror," but a horror that we feel only as we contemplate, without being in any actual danger. To this psychological account Burke again adds a physiological explanation as to how objects evoke this feeling. Kant quotes parts of Burke's analysis (see Ak. 277 incl. br. ns. 48 and 50), but rejects all such empiricist accounts of the sublime for the same reason he rejected empiricist accounts of the beautiful: judgments about the sublime claim universal validity and necessity, and this "lifts them out of [the reach of] empirical psychology" (Ak. 266), which can never provide us with more than contingent propositions about what is (rather than ought to be) the case.

According to Kant, the sublime, like the beautiful, is an object of our liking (feeling of pleasure), and a judgment about the sublime is again an aesthetic judgment that is reflective and disinterested (we like the sublime, too, for its own sake: Ak. 244) and claims universal validity and necessity. But in the case of the sublime the pleasure is indirect and negative (Ak. 245): it presupposes a displeasure (Ak. 260). In other words, the pleasure we take in the sublime is (an awareness of) a (subjective) purposiveness that presupposes (an awareness of) a (subjective) contrapurposiveness (Ak. 245) or "unpurposiveness" (Ak. 260).

Kant distinguishes two kinds of sublimity: mathematical and dynamical. In the mathematically sublime the vast magnitude is

---

[58] He must also have known the account given by his friend, Moses Mendelssohn: *Über das Erhabene und Naïve in den schönen Wissenschaften* (*On the Sublime and Naive in the Fine Sciences*), 1758; in Moses Mendelssohn, *Ästhetische Schriften in Auswahl* (*Selected Writings on Aesthetics*), ed. Otto F. Best (Darmstadt: Wissenschaftliche Buchgesellschaft, 1974). Mendelssohn's account has some similarity to Burke's. Mendelssohn did in fact read Burke, but not until after his own theory had been formulated: see Lewis White Beck, *Early German Philosophy*, 324–26.

above all one of size (largeness), as in the case of "shapeless moun-tain masses" (Ak. 256). (Greatness is also included, but I shall set it aside here.) In the dynamically sublime the vast magnitude is one of might, as in the case of the "boundless ocean heaved up" (Ak. 261).

The sublime is (subjectively) contrapurposive because our imagi-nation tries to apprehend the object of vast magnitude (in size or might) but fails. When we judge such an object, "this judging strains the imagination [as it tries to exhibit the object] to its limits, whether of expansion (mathematically) or of its might over the mind (dynam-ically)" (Ak. 268). Any attempt to exhibit something vast brings in reason, and reason (in accordance with its idea of totality) demands that imagination exhibit the object as an absolute whole (Ak. 257), an absolute magnitude (Ak. 268), i.e., a magnitude beyond all com-parison (Ak. 250). Yet nature as appearance can never have more than comparative magnitude (Ak. 250); in other words, imagination (which must structure empirical intuition so that it can become nature as appearance) can exhibit only comparative magnitude. Therefore, imagination cannot fulfill reason's demand, and hence we feel a dis-pleasure, i.e., we are aware of the object's contrapurposiveness for the imagination and hence for our cognitive power.

On the other hand, this very failure makes the sublime (subjectively) purposive at the same time. For, "finding that every standard of sen-sibility [i.e., imagination] is inadequate to the ideas of reason is [sub-jectively] purposive and hence pleasurable" (Ak. 258), because this discovery "arouses in us the feeling of our supersensible [moral] voca-tion" (Ak. 258) and of a "supersensible power" we have (viz., free-dom as causality) for pursuing it (Ak. 250), in other words, the feeling of our "superiority over nature" (Ak. 261), our ability to cross (with a moral aim) "the barriers of sensibility" (Ak. 255). Hence the sub-lime is judged subjectively purposive with regard to moral feeling.[59]

By the same token, "when we speak of the sublime in nature we speak improperly" (Ak. 280); properly speaking, only the mind is sublime (Ak. 245). More specifically, what is sublime is the mind's "attunement" in judging the sublime (Ak. 256). In speaking of the sublime "in nature" we merely *attribute* this sublimity of the mind to certain objects in nature (Ak. 247), viz., those which make us aware of the mind's sublimity (Ak. 280). The mind, insofar as it is

---

[59] Ak. 268. For "moral feeling," see above, *xliv.*

superior to nature, is reason. Hence judgments about the beautiful and judgments about the sublime both refer the imagination to our "power [i.e., faculty] of concepts" (Ak. 244). In the case of the beautiful this power is understanding; in the case of the sublime, reason (Ak. 256).

Because in judgments about the sublime "it is not the object *itself* that is judged to be purposive[60] . . . [but what is purposive is the] relation of the cognitive powers" (Ak. 280), i.e., imagination in relation to reason and our moral vocation, the exposition (analysis) of these judgments is at the same time their deduction (Ak. 280). For the will (which we know a priori through our moral consciousness) *presupposes* a priori this harmonious relation (Ak. 280), because the will is our "power of [carrying out] purposes [in nature]" (Ak. 280). Hence in the case of the sublime the link to morality is not, as it is in the case of the beautiful, merely explanatory or interpretive. Here this link justifies the claim of judgments about the sublime to universal validity, on the (legitimate) presupposition that man does in fact have moral feeling (Ak. 266).

10.

The Critique of Teleological Judgment: Background

It was generally accepted in Kant's time that natural science had to include, or be supplemented by, judgments in terms of purposes,[61] "final causes," i.e., teleological judgments; only then could natural science make sense of the striking order found in nature, above all in organisms. On the other hand, natural scientists since the Renaissance had come to de-emphasize teleology, partly because it did not seem empirical enough and partly because Aristotle's physics, which

---

[60] This fact "turns the theory of the sublime into a mere appendix to our judging of the purposiveness of nature": Ak. 246.

[61] For this term, as used by Kant, see above, *xxv.*

was teleological, had turned out to contain serious errors.[62] They emphasized, instead, observation and experimentation, careful measurement and the search for discoverable regularities that would allow prediction and explanation in terms of mechanical laws governing the sizes and shapes of particles (ultimately, atoms) and the forces of these particles that made them move in certain ways. On the other hand, it was generally agreed that all attempts to explain the purposelike things in the world (above all, organisms) mechanistically had met with little success: mechanistic causal relations were indeed found in these things, but they were not nearly sufficient to explain such things as wholes. In addition, it was commonly held that even if the physical universe were entirely mechanistic, this universe as a whole still required explanation, which therefore had to be sought beyond nature. For both of these reasons, explanation in terms of final causes seemed indispensable.

Kant shared all of these concerns throughout his career. Even in his earliest works we find him stressing the importance of investigating nature in terms of mechanism but also the need to go beyond mechanism and to teleology.[63] Hence the questions arose for Kant: How much can teleology do? Can it explain? Can it give us knowledge? Answering these questions requires a critique that will examine the scope and limits of our cognitive powers once again, this time in regard to teleological judgments. As happened in the case of all the critiques already discussed, Kant's Critique of Teleological Judgment again leads him to a position between dogmatic rationalism and dogmatic empiricism. Hence it will again be informative to discuss representative examples of these positions.[64]

Leibniz and Wolff (and Baumgarten, too) used the Cartesian version of the ontological argument in an attempt to establish the existence of a God with all, and hence also the moral, perfections. This God then served as the basis of their teleology as well: such a God must have created the best possible world, a world of rich detail

---

[62] For some examples, see Andrew Woodfield, *Teleology* (Cambridge: Cambridge University Press, 1976), 3–9.

[63] See, e.g., *Dreams of a Spirit-Seer* (1766), Ak. II, 331. For a passage in the *Critique of Pure Reason* which emphasizes the purposiveness in the world, see A 622 = B 650.

[64] I shall set aside here the views that expressly deny that there are in nature final causes distinct from matter and the efficient causes governing it (see Ak. 390–93).

harmoniously ordered to form a unity. The order of the world is one in terms of final causes. The material world, as governed by efficient causes, is simply that same world as it appears to us, i.e., as it is cognized through the indistinct perception of our senses. Hence whatever order we find in the world, including the purposelike order in organisms, can be "explained" by saying that God must have had a "sufficient reason" for choosing this order.

Kant has various objections against this kind of teleology. First, we cannot *explain* the purposelike order in the world by reference to causes that act intentionally unless we have insight into (i.e., theoretical cognition of) such causes (Ak. 394). But we do not have such insight (Ak. 459–60). All the arguments that traditionally have been offered as bases for such insight are inadequate. For his refutation of the ontological argument in its Cartesian form and of the cosmological argument, Kant refers us (Ak. 476) to the *Critique of Pure Reason*.[65] The teleological argument[66] is criticized in the third *Critique* as well. For one thing, Kant says, this argument would establish, at best, the existence of an "artistic understanding" that could provide us with "sporadic purposes"; it cannot establish the existence of a wisdom that would order these and all of nature in terms of a final purpose (Ak. 441). Moreover, the argument can "establish" even that much only subjectively, for our limited power of judgment; it cannot do so objectively ("dogmatically"), because then it would have to prove what it cannot prove: that mechanism *cannot* account for the purposelike order in the world (Ak. 395). Such dogmatic claims have no place in physics (Ak. 383): not only will they make reason too slothful[67] to try to explain this order in *natural* terms (Ak. 382), but, worst of all, reason moves in a vicious circle if it tries to explain this order in the world by reference to a God whose existence it tries to prove from this very order (Ak. 381).

Another rationalist, Baruch (Benedict) Spinoza (1632–77), construed God not as cause of the world but as the sole and simple substance (with its two attributes, thought and extension) in which everything *in* the universe (which this substance is), including organisms,

[65] See A 583–620 = B 611–48.

[66] In the *Critique of Pure Reason*, see A 620–30 = B 648–58.

[67] *Critique of Pure Reason*, A 689–92 = B 717–20.

"inheres" as accident. Hence Spinoza had no need to argue for the existence of a God *apart* from the universe, although he did argue for the *necessary* existence of the universe (i.e., God) by appealing to the nature of "substance." Kant's objection to this view (Ak. 393–94), as regards teleology, is that, though inherence in one substance does amount to a kind of unity (order), this sort of unity is not sufficient to account for the *purposive* unity found in organisms.

On the empiricist side, Kant was closer to Hume than to Locke. John Locke (1632–1704) argued[68] for the existence of a perfect God on the ground that the self-evident existence of oneself, as a mind capable of perception and knowledge (which cannot arise from mere matter), presupposes such a God. For "whatsoever is first of all things must necessarily contain in it, and actually have, at least, all the perfections that can ever after exist. . . ." Moreover, because God made this mind, he made also the "less excellent pieces of the universe."[69] Locke compared some of these, organisms, to watches (although he regarded them as superior to watches in certain ways), whose organization allows them to serve a "certain end."[70]

Kant agreed that one's own existence, as given in self-consciousness, requires that something or other exists *necessarily* (Ak. 476), but he argued that the step from this something or other to a supreme being[71] presupposes the (fallacious) ontological argument.[72] Moreover, Kant added, it is inconsistent for Locke, as an empiricist, to argue to the existence of something beyond the bounds of all experience.[73]

Hume, on the other hand, rejected all arguments for the existence of God (as he rejected, in contrast to Locke, claims about the existence of substances in general, even in the case of objects and of oneself as subject): existence is a matter of fact and hence is not derivable a priori from the relations among our ideas. Hume's objec-

---

[68] *An Essay Concerning Human Understanding.* Bk. IV, ch. x.

[69] *Ibid.*, 12.

[70] *Ibid.*, Bk. II, ch. xxvii, 5.

[71] I am refraining from capitalizing this expression. For my reasons, see below, Ak. 273 br. n. 43.

[72] *Critique of Pure Reason*, A 605–09 = B 633–37.

[73] *Ibid.*, A 854–55 = B 882–83.

tions against the teleological argument, which is a posteriori, are similar to Kant's own (Ak. 438 incl. br. ns. 32 and 33, and 455 br. n. 49). As for teleology in general, Hume held that there is no basis for distinguishing final causes from efficient causes: our idea of causal "efficacy" is derived from the constant conjunction of two objects, and hence it is already the idea of an *efficient* cause.[74] Moreover, there is not even a (legitimate) basis for the idea of any causal efficacy or "power": all (legitimate) ideas are derived from impressions and we have no impression of causal efficacy and hence no (legitimate) idea of causal efficacy.[75] The idea of a necessary causal link between two objects (and similarly for causal necessity in general) comes from my mind's habit of expecting an object because I have come to associate it with another object.[76] On Hume's view, then, our teleological judgments cannot give us genuine explanations of any kind.

Kant agrees that teleological judgments do not explain objectively. He argues, however, that they do explain "for us." Although this view is largely compatible with Hume's position, Kant seems to have thought that Hume denied it, and he criticizes Hume accordingly.[77] On the other hand, Hume would have denied that teleological judgments involve any kind of a priori principle or that they could yield cognition.

[74] *A Treatise of Human Nature*, Bk. I, Part III, Section xiv.

[75] *Ibid.* The parenthetical insertions are my own. Hume does hold, as the other paraphrases show, that we have *some* sort of idea of causal efficacy, an idea that is based on a mere mental habit (and hence is not legitimate).

[76] *Ibid.*

[77] Ak. 420–21. Hume's *Dialogues Concerning Natural Religion* appeared in German translation in 1780. Evidence that Kant had read the work can be found in the *Critique of Pure Reason* (see, e.g., A 745–46 = B 773–74), but in the *Prolegomena* of 1783 Kant refers to the work explicitly: Ak. IV, 358. It is not clear, however, to what extent Kant was *influenced* by Hume in this area of philosophy.

11.

Kant's Account of Teleological Judgments[78]: Why They Are Needed

If our investigation of nature is to be scientific, and thus capable of providing explanation (i.e., "distinct and determinate derivation from a principle": Ak. 412), then it must—so reason requires—consist of a *system* of cognitions, not a mere "rhapsody" of them; it must (ideally) be just as systematic as *organisms* are, e.g., an animal body.[79]

Now the a priori concepts (categories) of the understanding do provide nature with its universal laws (Ak. 186, 187), transcendental as well as metaphysical, and thus with a certain (minimal) systematicity (Ak. 203', 208'). As these laws are universal, there can be no natural science *without* this systematicity. But the legislation of the understanding does not extend to nature's particular (*as* particular: Ak. 404), which must be given empirically; hence in terms of nature's universal laws, any order in the particular, as particular, is contingent, as far as we can see.[80] For example, the universal principle of cause and effect tells us a priori that every event must have its cause, but it leaves contingent *what causes what.*

Yet the principles based on the categories, and the concept of nature we form by means of them, do imply that nature *as a whole,* which includes the particular, is systematic. For they imply that all of nature can be cognized and that, consequently, it has an order that permits us to acquire empirical concepts (Ak. 180, 359, 208'). On the other hand, those principles and the concept of nature tell us nothing further about the systematicity of nature as a whole.

Now a *demand* (of reason) for a cognizable order of nature as a

---

[78] I shall largely disregard Kant's own artificial and unhelpful division of the Critique of Teleological Judgment into an "Analytic," a "Dialectic," and a "Methodology."

[79] *Critique of Pure Reason,* A 832–33 = B 860–61.

[80] Ak. 183, 406. In the *Metaphysical Foundations of Natural Science,* of 1786, Kant does say that "science *proper*" must have *apodeictic* certainty, and hence must be a priori (i.e., transcendental or metaphysical): Ak. IV, 468.

whole (including the particular) is indeed embodied in the principle of the power of judgment (cf. Ak. 185). For this principle presupposes that nature is lawful even in the contingent (Ak. 404, 217′) and hence is purposive subjectively, i.e., for our cognitive power: judgment's principle presupposes that nature forms a hierarchy (Ak. 213′, 185) of genera and species and of empirical laws in general (including particular causal laws).

But this principle is still not sufficient for natural science. It is reflective and based on an indeterminate concept (the concept of nature's subjective purposiveness); hence it cannot itself provide cognition, much less explanation. It is a heuristic maxim by which we merely *presuppose* parsimony and simplicity in the particular in nature. Even if we do find such order in nature and form empirical concepts accordingly, the order in the particular (as particular) will still be contingent (as far as we can see: Ak. 184), and so will be the order of nature considered as a whole. Above all, the principle of judgment by itself does not allow us to cognize, let alone explain, an organism, even a mere blade of grass (Ak. 400, 409), any more than does the concept of nature (Ak. 194, 359), or the universal laws of nature. Rather, the principle of judgment permits and prepares us to make judgments that go beyond that principle (Ak. 218′, 193–94): teleological judgments, which use the (determinate) concept of purposes (Ak. 193), "final causes" (Ak. 380).

12.

Teleological Judgments about Organisms

Teleological judgments use the determinate concept of a purpose. They are logical reflective judgments about a purposiveness that is objective and material: objective as opposed to subjective, as is the purposiveness in aesthetic reflective judgments as well as in the principle of judgment itself; material as opposed to objective and *formal,* as is the purposiveness of geometric objects (Ak. 362–66).

In other words, teleological judgments are logically reflective judgments about a purposiveness that is based on a purpose.[81] Although the principle of judgment (of nature's subjective purposiveness) permits and prepares us to make teleological judgments, these judgments themselves do not use (but only presuppose) the power of judgment's own indeterminate concept of nature's subjective purposiveness but use only (reason's) determinate concept of a purpose (cf. Ak. 243'–44'). By the same token, the teleological power of judgment, unlike the aesthetic power of judgment, is not a special power but only the reflective power of judgment as such (Ak. 194). The *Critique of Judgment* includes it only in order to determine what the full range of the principle of judgment is (Ak. 244').

Natural science needs teleological judgments above all for organisms, beings that are "organized" in the sense that the idea of the whole is what allows us to judge and cognize all the parts in their systematic combination (Ak. 373), and hence to judge and cognize the "inner possibility"[82] of this being. An organism has a purposiveness that is not only objective and material but also intrinsic, as distinguished from the extrinsic (or "relative") purposiveness (which is also objective and material) that a thing has insofar as it is a means to something else (Ak. 425, and cf. 366–69). Since organisms are judged as purposes but also as products of nature, Kant calls them *natural purposes* (Ak. 374), as distinguished from "purposes of nature," which implies an (intentional) final purpose for nature as a whole (Ak. 378).

These judgments, though reflective, are cognitive (Ak. 221'). In the first place, we cognize the organism, a material whole, in mechanical terms, as the product of its parts and their forces and powers for combining on their own (Ak. 408); this is ordinary theoretical cognition and involves only our understanding. But since the matter in an organism is organized (Ak. 378) and forms a whole that is a natural purpose (Ak. 408), its form is *contingent* in terms of mechanism and hence cannot be judged by understanding alone, on which mechanism is based: a concept of reason (the concept of a purpose)

---

[81] Ak. 364. Sometimes Kant *equates* objective material purposiveness simply with *purpose*: Ak. 366.

[82] Ak. 408. Even though 'intrinsic' renders the German term '*inner*' better in most contexts dealing with natural purposes, it cannot be used to modify 'possibility' here, because 'intrinsic possibility' means something else, viz., 'possibility *in principle*.'

must come in as well (Ak. 370). The idea of reason restricts the object to a *particular* form for which "nature itself" (mechanism) contains no basis whatsoever (Ak. 422). This particular form is the form of a system: in an organism the parts produce one another (are cause and effect of one another) and thereby produce a whole the *idea* of which (as the idea of this whole as a purpose) *could* in turn, in a being capable of acting on ideas, be the cause of such a whole (Ak. 373). Only if we use reason's concept of a purpose can we judge and cognize, even empirically, the form of an organism in all its causal relations (Ak. 370), because only through elaborate observation, as guided by this concept, can we cognize the object's objective purposiveness (Ak. 194, and cf. 221', 192, 383, 398, 400). Hence teleological judgments are made by understanding and reason combined (Ak. 193, 233', 243', and cf. 386).

Our teleological judgments about organisms, then, use a determinate concept. However, they are reflective rather than determinative, for a determinative teleological judgment about organisms would construe natural purposes as purposes of nature, i.e., as intentional, and hence would be a transcendent judgment of reason (Ak. 236'). As a consequence, these judgments do not explain objectively, but explain only *for us,* subjectively,[83] i.e., only according to the character of our understanding and reason (Ak. 413, and cf. 388). Hence they give us no insight into how organisms are produced (Ak. 418, and cf. 411); rather, they belong merely to the description of nature (Ak. 417). Teleological judgments are therefore mere maxims that reason imposes on judgment (Ak. 398, and cf. 379), maxims by which reason tells judgment how it must think about organisms (Ak. 389). Hence reason's idea of a purpose is used *regulatively* by the power of judgment in its concept of a natural purpose (Ak. 375, 237').

Although we think natural purposes by a *remote analogy* with technically practical reason (Ak. 383), i.e., our causality in terms of purposes (Ak. 375), teleological judgments of reflection must be distinguished from judgments about *practical* purposiveness (Ak. 243'). For natural purposes are products of nature (Ak. 376), and we

[83] Ak. 379 and 413. Sometimes Kant omits the qualification 'subjective' and does speak simply of *explanation*: Ak. 383, 412, 414, 236'. Similarly, instead of saying that mechanism cannot explain organisms for us (cf. Ak. 413, and cf. 389), he sometimes says or implies that mechanism *cannot* account for them: Ak. 369, 411.

observe no intention as underlying them (Ak. 399); hence we must look for the purposive causality in nature itself (Ak. 382) rather than outside it, as we would if nature were more than remotely analogous to art (Ak. 374). On the other hand, even *thinking* of organisms by analogy (even by remote analogy) with practical reason involves the use of the *concept* of an intention (Ak. 398); but although we thus speak of nature *as if* the purposiveness in it were intentional (Ak. 383), we are not *attributing* an intention to nature (Ak. 236'). Similarly, when Kant calls nature's causality in terms of purposes an "intentional" technic and equates an "unintentional technic" with *mechanism* (Ak. 390–91), all he means is that, although in mechanism we do not even *think* an intention, in nature's causality in terms of purposes we do. But although teleological reflective judgments about organisms do not attribute an intention to nature, they also do not *deny* that the objective purposiveness in organisms is intentional. If these judgments either attributed or denied an intention to nature, they would be determinative and transcendent (Ak. 236'–37').

The only *objective* explanation of which we are capable is in terms of mechanical laws (Ak. 218'), above all the laws of motion (Ak. 390). If we are to have insight (theoretical cognition) into something, we must gain it through mechanism (Ak. 387, 410), because we ourselves use mechanism when we produce things and hence have complete insight only into mechanical production (Ak. 384). Now it may indeed be possible (noncontradictory) for organisms to be produced in terms of mechanism alone and hence possible for *some* understanding (a superhuman understanding) to explain organisms in terms of mechanism alone (Ak. 408). But for us, given the (unchangeable) character of our cognitive power, explaining organisms in terms of mechanism alone, or even getting to know them in terms of their inner possibility, is completely impossible and will forever remain so (Ak. 400), even though we should nevertheless *try* to explain all natural products mechanically as long as there is some probability of success (Ak. 418).

Hence objective explanation of organisms is impossible for us on mechanical as well as teleological principles, even though we do *judge* organisms in terms of both. Hence both principles are to this extent, i.e., *as applied to organisms,* mere maxims and hence merely regulative.[84] We judge the connection among an organism's parts in terms of efficient causes and then judge this same connection as causation through final causes (Ak. 373), trying to gain as much insight as we can in terms of mechanism, while using the teleological principle heuristically in order to discover all the characteristics of the organism and what forms it has that (as far as we can see) go beyond mechanism (Ak. 389, 400). *How* it is possible to judge the same connections both in terms of the principle of mechanism (which implies necessity) and in terms of the principle of final causes (which implies a contingency) is the problem addressed by the Dialectic, which will be discussed in Section 15.

13.

Is Nature as a Whole a Teleological System?

Once we judge organisms teleologically, Kant says, the concept of a natural purpose leads us necessarily to the idea of all of nature as a system in terms of the rule of purposes (Ak. 378–79), a "teleological system" (Ak. 429). We then express that systematicity in the maxim: Everything in the world is good for something or other; nothing in it is gratuitous; [everything] is purposive in [relation to] the whole (Ak. 379). What prompts us (Ak. 414) to think nature as a whole as such a system is the "example" of organisms (Ak. 379), because this example shows that nature has the *ability* to produce organisms (Ak. 380). Hence the idea of nature as a system in terms of purposes is reasonable (Ak. 427) and justified (Ak. 380).

How systematic is nature as a whole? If nothing in nature were gratuitous and everything in it were purposive in relation to the whole, nature would have the same systematicity that an organism has. If nature had that degree of systematicity, we could judge it, too,

---

[84] Ak. 386, 387. It is not mechanism *as such* that is regulative. I shall return to this point in the context of the antinomy of teleological judgment: see Section 15.

as a natural purpose and look for the purposive causality within nature (although, as we shall see in the next section, the purpose of the *existence* of nature as a whole would still have to lie outside nature). But it is simply not true for nature *as a whole,* as it is for an organism, that its parts "produce one another." It seems that all we have (beyond the categories) for nature as a whole is the principle of judgment, the maxim according to which nature must be thought as purposive *subjectively,* i.e., purposive for our cognitive power, and that the higher degree of systematicity we find in organisms is not present in other parts of the universe.

Kant does in fact acknowledge that the products of nature do not all have the same degree of (objective) purposiveness (Ak. 415). Only *organized* matter must be judged by means of the concept of a purpose (Ak. 378); mechanical laws (and what can be accounted for in terms of them alone) do not (Ak. 414). Hence as applied to the whole of nature the teleological maxim of judgment is "not indispensable," as it is for organisms, because "nature as a whole is not given us as organized (in the strictest sense of *organized* . . .)" (Ak. 398).

What, then, entitles us to judge everything in nature as belonging to a teleological system, even those products that do not have to be judged in terms of purposes? (Ak. 380–81.) We are *entitled* to do this because nature's ability to produce organisms already leads us to the idea of the supersensible (Ak. 381): the mere thought of an intention, as an intention in some cause beyond nature, is implicit in the concept of a purpose even as that concept is used to cognize natural purposes as natural. (This point will be spelled out somewhat more fully below.) Moreover, we *must* judge nature as a whole as a system of purposes because this maxim "may well allow us to discover many further laws of nature that would otherwise remain hidden from us" (Ak. 398). In other words, we must do so because reason demands that our cognitions form, not a mere "rhapsody," but a system (see above, *lxxvi*).

14.

Moving Beyond Teleological Cognition of Nature[85]

We have seen that there are two kinds of objective material purposiveness in nature: the intrinsic purposiveness of organisms, and the extrinsic or "relative" purposiveness that something has insofar as it is a means to something else. Now in order for us to judge some natural thing as a means, we must judge it as serving (at least mediately, i.e., indirectly) an (intrinsic natural) purpose, an organized being (Ak. 425). Moreover, once we think of a natural product as a natural purpose (which involves the thought of an intention), we must also think of the natural product's *existence* as (having) a purpose (Ak. 426). For example, we may judge that plants (a kind of organized being) exist for the sake of herbivores, these for the sake of predators, and predators for the sake of man (Ak. 426), so that we arrive at a chain of purposes (Ak. 435). If this chain is not to go on forever but is to be complete (Ak. 435), then there must be some purpose that does not have yet another purpose as its condition, i.e., there must be a final purpose (Ak. 434). But this final purpose cannot be in nature, because everything in nature is always conditioned in turn (Ak. 435, 426). The last *natural* member in the chain of purposes Kant calls the "ultimate" purpose (Ak. 426). That ultimate purpose of nature, Kant argues, is man (Ak. 426–27). But man is this ultimate purpose subject to a condition: he must "have the understanding and the will" to pursue the final purpose (Ak. 431) enjoined by the moral law, i.e., the highest good in the world; this highest good is man's virtue, and man's happiness to the extent that he is virtuous (cf. above, *xlv*). Subject to the condition that we pursue this final purpose, nature's *ultimate*

---

[85] This move is the task of the "methodology" of teleological judgment (Ak. 416), as distinguished from the "elementology." Whereas the elementology (cf. Ak. 354) provides the materials for the edifice (system) of cognitions, the methodology provides the plan for it (*Critique of Pure Reason*, A 707–08 = B 735–36). Hence the methodology of teleological judgment has the task of deciding how the science of teleology relates to natural science and to theology. (There can be no methodology of *aesthetic* reflective judgment because there can be no *science* of the beautiful: Ak. 354–55.)

purpose is to cooperate and make it possible for man to pursue the final purpose, viz., through the cultivation of man's nature, the cultivation (or "culture") of skill and discipline (Ak. 431–34).

Because all purposes in nature, including this ultimate purpose, are thought of as intentional, they are thought of as purposes pursued by an understanding as cause of that nature. Thus our teleological *cognition* of the purposes in nature leads us to the *thought* of an intelligent cause of the world (a cause of the world which has understanding) and to the thought of a final purpose. It does not enable us to cognize this cause, nor that final purpose (Ak. 378); it does not even allow us to *inquire* into the final purpose (Ak. 437).

Teleology as taken *beyond* the cognition of nature becomes *moral* teleology (Ak. 455), teleology from a practical point of view (Ak. 460). Indeed, once we think of an intelligent cause of all that objective purposiveness, we cannot help asking what objective basis in this cause *determines* it to create those purposes, and that basis would be the (idea of) the final purpose (Ak. 434–35). Although natural purposes prompt the idea of this final purpose (Ak. 485), only reason can have and use this idea (Ak. 454–55). One use of this idea is as the highest point in the chain of causes (Ak. 390). But the most important use of the idea of the final purpose is the one already outlined in the sketch of the *Critique of Practical Reason* (above, Section 3): since the moral law (and freedom) is a matter of fact and is known practically, the idea of the final purpose enjoined on us by the moral law is also determinate, and hence we have practical cognition of this final purpose and its achievability as a matter of rational faith. As a consequence, we also have practical cognition of the two matters of faith whose idea is in turn made determinate by the idea of the final purpose: immortality of the soul and the existence of a God as moral author of the world in itself, i.e., the world as substrate of objects and of ourselves as free subjects. This "moral proof" of the existence of God does not give us theoretical cognition, and knowledge,[86] of God as he is *in himself* (Ak. 456, 457). But what it does give us is fully adequate for theology (Ak. 484–85) and for religion (Ak. 474, 481). For it gives us *practical* cognition of God, as a matter of rational faith, in terms of an idea of this supersensible being[87] that the idea

---

[86] For this terminology, see above, *xl–xlii.*

[87] Cf. above, n. 71.

of our own freedom (as a supersensible causality) can, by analogy (Ak. 484–85), make determinate: the idea of God *as he relates* (practically) to the final purpose, the object of our practical reason (Ak. 457), in other words, as a moral being who makes this final purpose achievable (Ak. 457). Teleology alone, on the other hand, could establish only the existence of some understanding as cause of the world but would be unable to make this concept any more determinate, especially in moral terms (Ak. 477). Hence teleology can serve only as a propaedeutic to theology proper (Ak. 485); and to base religion on this indeterminate concept of God would be to pervert religion (Ak. 460, 481).

Yet teleology does help. For it shows that from a theoretical point of view the idea of God has some determination, some "reality" (more than the completely *empty* idea of the supersensible as mere possible substrate of nature), viz., the attribute 'some understanding as cause of the world.' By showing that the idea of God has some theoretical reality, teleology *supports* the reality that the idea of God has, through the analogy with our own practical reason, from a *practical* point of view (Ak. 456) and thereby confirms the moral argument (Ak. 479). (Teleology similarly confirms our practical cognition of the final purpose, by leading at least to the thought of such a purpose.) As I have indicated before, it is the power of judgment that mediates the transition from the completely indeterminate supersensible as substrate of nature to the morally determined supersensible, and hence from the realm of nature of the first *Critique* to the realm of freedom of the second *Critique* (Problem II: see above, *lxiv*). The power of judgment, especially the *aesthetic* power of judgment (Problem III: *lxiv*), performs this mediation by means of its indeterminate concept of nature's subjective purposiveness, as equivalent to the indeterminate concept of the supersensible basis of this purposiveness (Problem I: *lxii–lxiii*). It thereby unites the three *Critiques* in a *system.* I shall now address these three outstanding problems.

15.

How the *Critique of Judgment* Completes the Critical System

As regards aesthetic and teleological judgments (of reflection) as analyzed by the two parts of the *Critique of Judgment*, two points are beyond dispute: these judgments are indeed made, and they do make certain claims that call for such analysis. Kant can take these two points for granted and hence does not have to argue that the third *Critique* is in fact needed. On the other hand, the *justification* that Kant offers for these judgments involves assertions that he does not expect to be accepted so readily: assertions about specific mental powers and their interrelations, and, above all, assertions about at least our *ideas* of the "supersensible." Yet all of these assertions are to be as scientific as the subject matter permits. Hence Kant must establish that they are indeed far from arbitrary. He does so by showing that everything these assertions claim is required as part of a system and cannot be removed without destroying that system (cf. Ak. 168); and he shows that something is required as part of a system by pointing to already familiar parts of the system and showing how the less familiar part is required as a "mediator" between them. We have in fact already encountered, in the summaries of the first two *Critiques* (Sections 2 and 3 above), two examples of this sort of justification procedure. In the first *Critique,* Kant introduces the schema by arguing that it is needed to mediate between the pure concepts of the understanding and imagination (intuition). In the second *Critique,* Kant similarly introduces the *typus* as needed to mediate between reason's moral law and understanding.

In the *Critique of Judgment,* the same justification procedure appears again. Kant justifies his treatment of judgment as (to some extent) a cognitive power in its own right partly by showing how it mediates between the other two higher cognitive powers, understanding and reason (Ak. 168, 179): in a syllogism the power of judgment subsumes the particular under some universal (i.e., under some principle) supplied by *understanding* and thereby enables *reason* to make an inference from that universal to the particular (Ak. 201'). In the same way *feeling* must, according to Kant, be considered an independent member among the three *general* mental powers because it mediates between the cognitive power (in general) and the power of desire (Ak. 178); feeling mediates between the other two mental powers insofar as both the lower power of desire (the will as influenced by sense) and the higher (the will as determinable by its own moral law)[88] connect a pleasure with nature: the lower connects this pleasure with nature cognized as it already is; the higher, with nature cognized as it (morally) ought to be (Ak. 178–79). Thus Kant establishes a twofold systematicity: among the higher cognitive powers and among the mental powers in general. Moreover, because understanding legislates in the domain of the concept of nature (i.e., in the domain of the [theoretical] cognitive power) and reason legislates in the domain of the concept of freedom (i.e., in the domain of the power of desire), Kant can enhance that twofold systematicity further if he can establish that judgment, the mediator of the higher cognitive powers, similarly legislates to feeling, the mediator of the mental powers in general (Ak. 168, 177–79).

Now Kant's "deduction" of judgments of taste (Section 6) established the universal subjective validity of the feeling of pleasure in these judgments, i.e., the universal subjective validity of the state of awareness in which we are when we are judging, without a determinate concept, nature's purposiveness for our power of judgment, for, Kant argued, this feeling cannot be directed to anything but the conditions of (empirical) judgment as such (harmony of imagination and understanding), and these conditions can be presupposed to be the same in everyone. To this extent, then, Kant has already established that the power of judgment, with its indeterminate concept of nature's subjective purposiveness, governs, or "legislates to," feeling; hence to this extent he has already enhanced the mentioned twofold systematicity among the mental powers. On the other hand, such systematicity among the mental powers, including the higher cognitive (and legislative) powers, would mean very little if there were no similar systematicity among the "worlds" with which these powers deal; and as Kant's account of aesthetic and teleological judgments (of reflection) involves claims about the supersensible, Kant cannot complete the (full) justification of that account by pointing to such

[88] Cf. above, *xlv*.

systematicity unless he can show that there is such systematicity among those "worlds" even as they are in themselves, i.e., as
supersensible. Now understanding and the (theoretical) cognitive
power deal with the "world" of appearance as it is but tell us nothing
about the "world" underlying it, the supersensible "world" in itself,
except that it is logically possible. Reason and the (higher) power
of desire deal with the "world" of appearance as it ought to be and
also tell us about the supersensible conditions of making it so: supersensible freedom, immortality of the soul, and God. As Kant sees it,
he has not (fully) justified his claims about the supersensible, and
the three *Critiques* cannot form a system (and thus be scientific),
unless not only the mental powers but also those "worlds," especially as they are in themselves, are shown to form a system. That
is why it is especially important for Kant to show not only that the
power of judgment, just like understanding and reason, also points
to a supersensible, viz., the supersensible basis of nature's subjective
purposiveness, but also that this supersensible *mediates* between the
other "two" supersensibles and thus unites the "three" supersensibles
in one.

The key to this mediation among the supersensibles lies in the
solution to Problem I (see above, *lxii–lxiii*), concerning Kant's
equating (treating as equivalent) judgment's indeterminate concept
of nature's subjective purposiveness and the indeterminate concept
of the supersensible basis of that same purposiveness. I shall now
show how, in the Dialectic of teleological judgment, this equation
arises from the antinomy of teleological judgment, how this equation
(as well as the antinomy itself) applies not only to teleological judgments but to judgments of taste as well, and hence to the principle of
judgment as such.

As Kant presents the antinomy of teleological judgment initially,
it is a (seeming) conflict between these two maxims: the thesis that
all production of material things and their forms must be judged
possible in terms of merely mechanical laws, and the antithesis that
some products of material nature cannot be judged possible in terms
of merely mechanical laws but that judging them requires a quite
different causal law, that of final causes (Ak. 387). It then *seems* as if
this "conflict," which (as becomes clear from the way Kant addresses
it throughout the remainder of the Dialectic) actually turns out to be a
conflict between judging the *same* object in terms of both a necessary

mechanism and a contingent purposiveness,[89] is resolved by Kant's pointing out that the two principles are indeed only maxims, i.e., only regulative: they regulate our judgments of reflection and do not assert, for determinative judgment, that all objects are, or that they are not, possible on mechanism alone (Ak. 387–89). This has led a number of commentators to suppose that Kant solves the antinomy by construing both mechanism and the principle of final causes as regulative principles.[90] But, first, Kant is by no means revoking the

[89] Kant seems to have thought that the conflict must be stated in a form that at least *looks* propositional. In the third antinomy of the first *Critique* (cf. also the second and fourth antinomies) he states the conflict between causal necessity and freedom in terms of propositions that are interestingly similar to the ones under consideration here. See A 444–45 = B 472–73.

[90] For a list of such commentators and their works, along with the specific references, see John D. McFarland, *Kant's Concept of Teleology* (Edinburgh: Edinburgh University Press, 1970), the n. on 120–21. More recently, this view has been defended by Robert E. Butts in his *Kant and the Double Government Methodology* (Dordrecht: D. Reidel, 1984), 272–73. As Butts puts it, "regulative principles, . . . [u]nlike . . . declarative sentences, . . . cannot logically oppose one another. . . ." "They [can conflict] only . . . in the sense that it would be irrational to adopt both for the same purpose," i.e., in the same "context." (*Ibid.*, 262, as applied to 272.) It is true that in the strict sense of 'contradiction' two principles can contradict each other only if they are declarative. It is also true that Kant must have this strict sense of 'contradiction' in mind when he says that the thesis and antithesis contradict each other only if taken as determinative but not if taken as regulative (§ 70, Ak. 387). Moreover, he presumably means such a *contradiction* again when, near the end of §71 (Ak. 389), he says, roughly, that any semblance of an "antinomy" arises only when we forget that the two principles are only maxims. That Kant's use of the term 'antinomy' in this remark must be a slip is clear not only from what he does in the (sizable) remainder of the Dialectic, but also from the fact that the remark is still part of the "preliminary" to the solution of the antinomy. Now the antinomy itself, i.e., the conflict between judging the same object in terms of both a necessary mechanism and a contingent purposiveness, does indeed not involve a contradiction in that strict sense; if it did, it could not be solved. What it does involve, however, as I am about to show, is the *threat* of a contradiction, even if not one involving declarative sentences, between our judging both mechanistically and teleologically in the *very same* "context." Judging in contradictory terms would indeed be "irrational," but in so serious a sense of this term that neither Kant nor we could accept such "irrationality": our "judgments" would cancel each other; i.e., we would in fact not be judging at all. Hence we must reject, as McFarland does, the kind of interpretation put forward by Butts and by the commentators McFarland lists, according to which Kant "solves" the antinomy of teleological judgment by making both mechanism and the teleological principle regulative. As for McFarland's own interpretation of how Kant "solves" the antinomy of teleological judgment, it also seems to me untenable, as I shall explain below: *xcix–c.*

central doctrine of the first *Critique,* according to which the universal laws of nature—in particular, the principle of necessary efficient
(mechanical) causality—are legislated to nature by our understanding
and hence are constitutive and determinative, not regulative.[91] Rather,
the maxims involving mechanism that are here said to be regulative concern merely the *sufficiency or insufficiency* of mechanism for
judging objects in general (including organisms). Second, the fact
that the section that comes *after* the presentation of the antinomy
offers a "preliminary" to its solution (Ak. 388) makes it clear that
the solution *has not* yet been given.[92] Above all, third, the conflict
between a necessary mechanism and a contingent teleological principle, as I shall now explain, *cannot* be resolved by turning the two
into maxims, and Kant will in fact come up with a quite different[93]
and rather sophisticated solution.

When we judge an object (an organism) as a natural purpose, we
are judging it in terms of both mechanism and final causes: in terms
of mechanism insofar as the object is a product of nature, in terms
of final causes insofar as it is a purpose. Now mechanism involves
the necessity implicit in the principle of causality which is based on
the categories; on the other hand, we cannot think of an object as a
purpose without thinking of it as contingent, viz., contingent in terms
of the universal natural laws (Ak. 398). Hence it seems that we are
judging as both necessary and contingent "one and the same product"
(Ak. 413), indeed, even the same causal *connections* within that product (Ak. 373, and cf. 372–73). Hence we are *contradicting* ourselves
(Ak. 396) *unless we can reconcile the two principles* (Ak. 414). Only
if we reconcile the two principles can we actually judge an object
in terms of both of them, i.e., only then is the concept of a natural
purpose a possible concept (Ak. 405) rather than a contradiction in
terms. The fact that we are using these principles as mere maxims, as

---

[91] Butts argues that actually Kant *does*, even in the first *Critique*, revoke that doctrine
and construe the categories as regulative. I shall offer some brief comments on this
view below, n. 107.

[92] The single piece of counterevidence is a remark at the end of § 71 (Ak. 389) which
I just mentioned in n. 90. All the remainder of the evidence, including the title of
that section and everything else Kant does in the rest of the Dialectic, seems to me to
require that we discount this one remark rather than all that other evidence.

[93] The solution differs both from the one just rejected and from the one suggested by
McFarland: see below, *xcix–c.*

merely regulative, does not resolve this conflict at all: if the concepts that the two maxims use contradict each other, then we have not even a concept of a natural purpose; for the concepts and maxims will cancel each other, so that we shall not be "judging" at all. This is precisely why Kant himself points out that in order for the "conflict" between the two principles to be merely a *seeming* conflict we must have assurance that the two principles can be reconciled *objectively too*.[94] (It is mechanism and the causality in terms of purposes that must be reconcilable objectively; the determinative versions of the thesis and antithesis as Kant states them initially are not reconciled by Kant's solution of the antinomy and could not be reconciled by anything whatsoever, as Kant himself points out at Ak. 387.)

Kant solves the antinomy between the necessary mechanism and the contingent teleological principle as he solves all his antinomies: by invoking the supersensible (cf. Ak. 344–46). In the present case the supersensible is introduced as follows. Our understanding, Kant argues (see Section 2 above), has the peculiarity of being discursive, conceptual; and all concepts abstract (to some extent) from the particular: hence our understanding does not determine (legislate) the particular but determines only the universal, leaving the particular contingent (Ak. 406). As for our a priori intuitions, they too cannot determine all the particular that understanding leaves contingent. If they could, then the form (or "unity") of mere space (our a priori intuition which applies to all appearances in nature outside us) would be able, in conjunction with the categories, to determine completely and thus constitute (and in that sense give rise to) an organism; yet clearly the form of space is not sufficient for this (Ak. 409).[95] On the other hand, the very awareness that our human understanding has the *peculiarity* of determining the universal while leaving the particular contingent

---

[94] Ak. 413. In other words, it must be at least possible that the "necessity" is not in fact a necessity or that the "contingency" is not in fact a contingency. Kant says 'objectively,' rather than 'determinatively,' because for the same object or the same causal connections to be *determined* as both necessary and contingent would imply that they in fact *are* both necessary and contingent, which would indeed be contradictory and hence *would not* be possible.

[95] As Kant puts it, space with its unity "is not a basis [responsible] for the reality of products but is only their formal condition. . . ." The determination being denied here would not involve the concept of a purpose; this determination would be theoretical rather than practical.

implies the idea of a possible *different* understanding (Ak. 405), viz., an understanding that *is not* discursive (i.e., does not omit the particular in its legislation) but is intuitive (Ak. 406). Such an understanding would legislate a "synthetic" universal, i.e., a universal in the sense of a whole that includes determination of the particular in that whole (Ak. 407). An intuitive understanding would thus be an understanding that simply *determines,* and hence would be an understanding "in the most general sense" (Ak. 406); for, while any understanding requires intuition (to supply the particular needed for cognition: Ak. 406), we are not entitled to assume that any understanding must have, as ours does, an intuition which is *separate* from it and through which the particular is merely *given* (empirically) rather than legislated along with the universal (Ak. 402–03).

Such an understanding's intuition would thus not be a mere receptivity (which is passive), and hence not a sensibility as our intuition is, but would be an *intellectual* intuition, a complete *spontaneity* (i.e., it would be completely active): it would determine objects completely. It would not require for this determination (and cognition) a harmony between itself and some other, separate cognitive power (an imagination dealing with a passive intuition), but would determine objects in terms of the harmony within this understanding itself.

Moreover, because an intuitive understanding would not require that the particular be supplied from elsewhere but would itself supply the particular along with the universal, it would constitute its objects as complete, *as things in themselves,* not as mere appearances. It would constitute these objects through its *theoretical legislation* rather than "produce" (or "create") them, for it would not bring objects about practically and hence as contingent, i.e., conditioned by the concept of a purpose (i.e., by an intention) (Ak. 407), but would bring them about without an idea as producing cause (Ak. 408): nature in itself would simply *be* the intellectual (supersensible) intuition of this intuitive understanding, just as our world of experience simply is the experience that consists of our empirical intuition as structured in harmony with our categories. By the same token, such a supersensible understanding with its supersensible intuitions cannot be called a God; rather, the idea of it is utterly indeterminate, negative, the mere idea of an understanding that "is not discursive" (Ak. 406).

With this mere idea of an "intuitive understanding," Kant can now solve the antinomy of teleological judgment. As an intuitive understanding would *necessitate* even the particular, the mere idea of such an understanding permits us to *think* of the "contingency" of the particular as being only a *seeming* contingency, a "contingency for" our understanding with its peculiarity, but as in fact being a *necessity*. A merely seeming contingency that is in fact a necessity does not conflict with the necessity implicit in *mechanism*. Hence "objectively too" it is at least possible to reconcile the mechanistic principle with the teleological (Ak. 413), for it is at least possible that the causal connections that we have to judge in terms of purposes and hence as contingent are in fact legislated theoretically and are therefore necessary. The laws covering those necessary but yet particular causal connections would then either have the same *basis* as mechanism (viz., the intellectual intuition of that intuitive understanding) or would perhaps even be *identical* with the mechanism familiar to us—identical in the sense of forming part, along with the mechanism familiar to us, of some broader, ideal mechanism (Ak. 390), in which case even organisms would be possible on this (ideal) mechanism alone. Since we human beings do not have insight into the basis of the mechanism familiar to us (Ak. 395, 398)—that basis might be such a supersensible intuition, or it might not—we cannot tell if it forms part of such an ideal mechanism, and hence we are incapable of establishing whether organisms (can or) cannot come about mechanically (Ak. 395); a higher understanding, on the other hand, might be able to account for organisms in mechanistic terms (Ak. 406, 418).

Now although this antinomy is called the antinomy of "teleological" judgment, both it and its solution (as just sketched) actually apply to reflection in general. Kant does indeed discuss the antinomy mainly by reference to organisms, i.e., natural purposes, and hence by reference to objective purposiveness, i.e., purposiveness with a purpose. Yet the antinomy of "teleological" judgment and its solution apply just as much to the *subjective* purposiveness of nature which is claimed in the principle of reflective judgment itself, for this purposiveness too is clearly contingent in terms of mechanism and yet is a purposiveness *of nature* and as such is subject to nature's necessity. Hence it too can be thought without contradiction only if we think of the "contingency" it implies as in fact being a necessity legislated by an intuitive understanding with its intellectual intuition. Indeed, when Kant introduces the antinomy of teleological judgment, the purposiveness he first mentions *is the subjective* purposiveness of nature (Ak. 386). Similarly, although Kant does of course apply the solution of this antinomy to organisms and the contingency we find in them, he does not confine it to organisms; rather, he clearly applies it (Ak. 406, 407) to all the contingency in all the particular in nature (even though nature as a whole does not have the same high degree of systematicity that organisms have and hence is not itself a natural purpose: cf. Section 13 above): "[S]ince universal natural laws have their basis in our understanding, . . . the particular empirical laws must . . . be viewed in terms of such a unity as [they would have] if they too had been given by an understanding (even though not ours) so as to assist our cognitive powers . . ." (Ak. 180, 181, and cf. 184). Moreover, Kant says (Ak. 345) that apart from the antinomies of the first and second *Critiques,* there is, in the *Critique of Judgment,* "an" (i.e., one) antinomy. In other words, he implies that the antinomy of aesthetic judgment and the antinomy of teleological judgment are merely two manifestations of the same antinomy.[96]

Furthermore, since the antinomy of teleological judgment, along with its solution, applies not only to objective but also to subjective purposiveness of nature, it clearly applies, a fortiori, to nature's subjective purposiveness as judged *aesthetically,* i.e., to nature's "purposiveness without a purpose."[97] For, this purposiveness too implies a contingency, while yet, as a purposiveness of nature, it also implies necessity; hence it too can be thought without contradiction only if we have recourse to the idea of a supersensible intuition as necessitating the particular. Indeed, when Kant implies that the antinomy of aesthetic judgment and the antinomy of teleological judgment are merely manifestations of one antinomy, he calls that one antinomy an antinomy of reason concerning *aesthetic* judgment (Ak. 345).

We are now ready to solve Problem I (see above, *lxii–lxiii*), which concerns the mysterious switch that Kant, in solving the antinomy of aesthetic judgment, makes from the concept of nature's subjective

---

[96] The four antinomies of the first *Critique* are similarly referred to collectively as 'the antinomy' of pure reason: A 405 = B 432. See also the headings of § 69 (Ak. 385) and § 70 (Ak. 386), which refer to the antinomy of teleological judgment simply as 'antinomy of judgment.'

[97] See also above, n. 45.

purposiveness to the concept of the *supersensible basis* of that same
purposiveness. Nature's subjective purposiveness is the indeterminate
form (or "lawfulness," i.e., regularity or order: see *lvi*) that nature has
in the particular; and the indeterminate *concept* of this purposiveness
is the indeterminate concept of that form of the particular. But this
concept is *contradictory* (because of the antinomy) unless we think
of this purposive form as *necessitated* (a priori) by an intellectual
intuition. Moreover, just as our a priori concepts and intuitions *are*
the forms that we give to all objects of appearance, so the purposive
form that would be necessitated by this intellectual intuition would
simply *be* that intuition. (As this form already includes all the particular, the particular would not be attributable to any "matter," whereas
in *our* intuition the particular is found in the matter that is given to us
in sensation.) Hence, according to our indeterminate concept of this
supersensible intuition, the world in itself would *be* the completely
determinate form which that intellectual intuition is.[98] (The intuitive
understanding, which is merely the power of legislating the form that
this intuition is, would not itself be but would only "have" that form,
just as our understanding has, rather than is, the form consisting of
all the categories taken together.) Because, then, in order to think
of nature's subjective purposiveness without contradicting ourselves
we must think of this form as being *identical* with the form that such
an intellectual intuition would be, and because this intellectual intuition is thought of as the supersensible basis of nature's subjective
purposiveness, we can see how the concept of nature's subjective
purposiveness is indeed equivalent to the concept of the supersensible basis of that same purposiveness: although the two concepts
are not synonymous, because the one refers to the purposiveness and
the other to the "basis" of that purposiveness, the "two" forms to
which the two concepts refer "are" strictly identical. Now this

[98] Actually, the purposive form of nature's particular might be only part of the form
that the intellectual intuition is; the intuitive understanding might through the same
intuition legislate, in addition, in terms of the mechanism familiar to us, or in terms of
laws pertaining to *both* the purposive and the mechanistic forms in nature, in nature
outside and within us, and perhaps pertaining to our cognitive powers themselves
which are responsible (in part) for nature's appearing to us as it does. But even if the
purposive form of nature's particular were only *part* of the form that the intellectual
intuition is, it would still be necessitated by, and hence would still be based on and (in
that part) *be*, that intellectual intuition.

equivalence between the two concepts would already suffice to give *some* justification to Kant's switch from the one concept to the other; but the *full* justification lies in the fact that the concept of nature's subjectively purposive form is *contradictory* unless the switch is made.[99] Thus Kant's solution of the antinomy of aesthetic judgment includes the solution of the antinomy of teleological judgment. Accordingly, in order for us to judge, without contradiction, an object as beautiful, this judgment must be taken to imply (noncognitively) that the object has the kind of form that only a supersensible understanding could have given it through its intellectual intuition.

Because the concept of nature's subjective purposiveness is indeterminate, it can be equated with the concept of the supersensible basis of that purposiveness only if the latter concept is indeterminate as well. Now in certain ways the concept that we human beings can form of such an intellectual intuition must indeed be indeterminate,[100] despite the fact that we think of this intuition as one that would determine objects "completely." For we have no cognition of what all these determinations in their completeness are. (The concept of an intuitive understanding with its intellectual intuition is indeterminate in other ways as well: e.g., it tells us nothing whatsoever about a "being" that might "have" that understanding.) Hence *our* concept of the form that such an intellectual intuition would be and that such an intuitive understanding would have is indeed indeterminate.[101]

[99] "We may well ask why Kant does not explain this equation in the Critique of Aesthetic Judgment, but simply takes it for granted when he mysteriously switches from the indeterminate concept of nature's subjective purposiveness to the indeterminate concept of the supersensible basis of that purposiveness. If he considered the explanation too long, he could at least have referred us to the antinomy of teleological judgment. Such a referral would not have made Kant's aesthetics dependent on his teleology; but perhaps it would somehow have offended against his idea of what the proper structure of the *Critique of Judgment* should be.

[100] Even if not in all its details, as I shall explain in a moment.

[101] As we have already seen in the context of Problem II (*lxiv*), for which I am about to offer a solution, Kant considers the supersensible basis of nature's subjective purposiveness to be *the same* supersensible as the supersensible substrate of both objects and subjects and the supersensible that "the concept of freedom contains practically"; this "same" supersensible is referred to in all these ways in the context of the solution to the antinomy of aesthetic judgment. Sometimes, however, still in that same context, Kant refers to it simply as the supersensible "within us" (see esp. Ak. 341). Now Kant does indeed

On the other hand, even though this concept is indeterminate as a whole (as one concept), some *details* (specific determinations) in it must be determinate. For most of the reasoning just used concerning nature's subjective purposiveness applies to nature's objective purposiveness as well. For we saw that both the antinomy of teleological judgment and its solution apply not only to subjective but also to objective purposiveness in nature (the purposiveness found in natural purposes, organisms). Therefore, if the concept of nature's objective purposiveness is not to be contradictory, then this purposiveness also must be thought of as based on an intellectual intuition, and hence the concept of this purposiveness must likewise be equated with the concept of an intellectual intuition as basis of that purposiveness. And since objective purposiveness, despite presupposing judgment's general and indeterminate concept of nature's subjective purposiveness, does also involve determinate concepts of purposes, such concepts of determinate purposes must be included as details in the otherwise indeterminate concept of that intellectual intuition.

The solution just offered for Problem I can now be used to solve Problem II (see above, *lxiv):* how can the concept of the supersensible basis of nature's subjective purposiveness *make determinable* the concept of the supersensible that is contained practically in the idea of freedom, and thus help make the supersensible *cognizable* practically, even though the concept of the supersensible as basis of nature's subjective purposiveness is indeterminate, indeed, "intrinsically indeterminable and inadequate for cognition" (Ak. 340), even practical cognition (Ak. 176)? How can *this* supersensible mediate between the other "two" so that the "three" supersensibles turn out to be one and the same?

---

identify this supersensible also with the "others." Does he emphasize "within us" because this is where "the" supersensible is somehow "closest" to us? Or does he do so because he considers the indeterminate harmony between imagination and understanding as such to be itself based on, and identical with, parts of that same intellectual intuition? If the form in a beautiful object of nature must be thought of as identical both with the form of that harmony and with the form that an intellectual intuition would be, it would indeed follow (even if our cognitive powers *were not* based on an intuitive understanding's intellectual intuition) that the form of the harmony between our imagination and understanding as such is (not in origin, but simply as that form) supersensible as well (despite the fact that these powers themselves are not supersensible any more than the beautiful object is).

The key to this mediation role of the concept of the supersensible basis of nature's subjective purposiveness lies in the following three points: (1) by the solution of Problem I, this concept is equivalent to the concept of nature's subjective purposiveness; (2) the concept of nature's subjective purposiveness belongs to the power of judgment; and (3) the power of judgment is a function of understanding. From these three points it follows that our understanding must be able to think not only the concept of nature's subjective purposiveness but also the concept of the supersensible basis of that purposiveness. Indeed, since even the concept of nature's *objective* purposiveness must be thought as equivalent to (at least to certain details in) such a supersensible basis, our understanding must be able to think the concept of such a basis whenever it exercises its function of judging either kind of purposiveness in nature. Yet the concept of the supersensible basis we have been discussing, i.e., the concept of an intuitive understanding with its intellectual intuition, is a concept that only reason can think. For the very fact that our own understanding is not intuitive but discursive keeps it from being able to conceive of an intuitive understanding, i.e., an understanding that could legislate not merely the universal but the particular as well; in other words, our discursive understanding is incapable of conceiving of an understanding that legislates a "synthetic" universal, a whole that *makes possible* the character and combination of the parts (rather than the other way round, viz., a whole that *is made* possible by the character and combination of the parts, and hence made possible mechanically, as our understanding must conceive of wholes). (Ak. 407.) The best that our understanding can do in this regard is to conceive of the *idea* of a whole as making possible the character and combination of the parts (and hence the whole itself); in other words, the best our understanding can do is to conceive of this whole as produced, i.e., a *purpose* brought about by means of an intention, i.e., by means of an idea of the purpose (Ak. 407–08). Hence our understanding, because of its own peculiarity, can indeed think of another understanding as *causing* the particular (and its form), i.e., as determining it *practically;* but it cannot think of another understanding as *legislating* the particular, i.e., as determining it *theoretically.* Hence our understanding must think of the (subjectively or objectively) purposive form of the particular in nature by *analogy* with our own technically practical ability, i.e., our ability to produce objects through art[102] (Ak. 397) by means of understanding and reason. Thus our understanding too thinks, in judgment's concept of the (subjective or objective) purposiveness that nature has in its particular, a supersensible understanding; but it thinks this understanding as an intelligent cause of the world in terms of purposes. This (i.e., our understanding's) concept of the supersensible basis of nature's purposiveness is *still* indeterminate[103] (and inadequate for cognition); yet, through the analogy with our technically practical ability, this concept is somewhat more determinate (has more content) than the concept of the intuitive understanding.

Because what enables our understanding to give some content (determination) to the concept of the supersensible basis of nature's (subjective or objective) purposiveness is the analogy with our own technically practical ability, our understanding can go on to make further use of the same analogy. It can use this analogy to make *some* sense of the relation between mechanism and causation in terms of purposes, viz., by *subordinating* mechanism to that causality (Ak. 379, 422): once our understanding has conceived of the world with all its purposiveness as caused by some intelligence, it can go on to conceive of this intelligent cause as using mechanism, just as we human beings do, as the *means* to the purposes it pursues (Ak. 414, 390), "as an instrument, as it were" (Ak. 422). Moreover, our understanding can do this in different ways: in terms of occasionalism, in terms of the theory of preestablished harmony, and so on (Ak. 422–24).

It is important to realize, however, that in thus subordinating the principle of mechanism to the principle of (subjective or objective) purposiveness, understanding *does not itself resolve the antinomy* between mechanistic necessity and the contingency in the purposive form of the particular. When Kant says that no conflict arises if our power of judgment (and hence our understanding) uses both the mechanistic and the teleological principles because these two ways of explaining *do not contradict each other* (Ak. 409), he takes as

---

[102] In the broad sense of this term, which includes craft.

[103] E.g., the concept in no way implies that the "intelligent cause" has the properties, esp. the moral properties, that would qualify it as a "God."

understood the addition: *subject to the solution of the antinomy* of teleological judgment by which the "contingency" in the form of the particular is thought of as merely a seeming contingency; Kant *is not* saying that merely *subordinating* the principle of mechanism to the principle of purposiveness would *itself* remove the conflict between the two, as plainly it would not. Hence this subordination cannot possibly be, as McFarland takes it to be, Kant's solution to the antinomy of teleological judgment.[104] Our understanding and power of judgment can without contradiction use the two principles (even in the very same contexts), not because the two principles can be subordinated to each other, nor because they are regulative (see above, *lxxxviii–xc*), but because our understanding and power of judgment are *aware that reason* has solved the antinomy by means of the idea of an intuitive understanding with its intellectual intuition. Understanding and judgment themselves are incapable of thinking of the order in nature's particular, which to them seems purposive, as in fact involving necessity; hence as far as they are concerned the particular laws covering that order *do not* have genuine (i.e., apodeictic) necessity, but are only "rules" (Ak. 391, 360). Such rules, though "lawful" (Ak. 359), are still contingent; the only necessity they can involve would be a *practical* necessity (cf. Ak. 172, 450).[105]

Now, we saw a moment ago that our understanding's concept of an intelligent cause of the world is somewhat more determinate than the concept of an intuitive understanding as legislator of the purposive form of nature. But it is *also* somewhat more determinate than the concept of the supersensible as it was left by the *Critique of Pure Reason,* viz., the concept of the supersensible as mere "basis" (substrate) of nature; for this latter concept says nothing whatsoever as to what this supersensible substrate includes. Does it include only a nature in itself, or also an "intelligence" (understanding) as "cause"

---

[104] *Kant's Concept of Teleology,* 127–29.

[105] And they can involve even a practical "necessity" only after the supersensible causality has been determined further as a *moral* cause that acts in terms of the moral law (which is a necessary law). Such a supersensible moral cause, a God, would have a "holy" will, a will incapable of acting on maxims that conflict with the moral law (*Critique of Practical Reason*, Ak. V, 32). Perhaps this is the necessity Kant has in mind when, occasionally (e.g., at Ak. 183), he speaks of particular laws as "necessary" even as a result of causation rather than theoretical legislation.

of that nature in itself in terms of "purposes"? It is true that even the addition of these further predicates leaves the concept of the supersensible *indeterminate: How much* understanding should we conceive that cause of nature in itself as having? *How* great should we conceive its might to be (to affect that nature in itself)? Should we even conceive of this understanding as a *single* being rather than several? (Ak. 480.) Yet those further predicates do suffice to make that completely indeterminate concept of the "supersensible" *determinable:* the concept can now be determined *practically,* morally, by reason. For while we could not intelligibly have described a mere (utterly indeterminate) "supersensible basis of nature" in moral terms, viz., as being a "nature in itself created, in terms of the final purpose, by a God having all the divine perfections," we certainly can intelligibly describe in such terms a nature in itself created, as an intentional purpose, by an intelligent cause. In other words, we can now think of this cause as *moral author* of the world by reference to the *final* purpose, and hence we can also think of nature as being forced by this moral author to cooperate with our attempt to achieve the final purpose. The moral argument for the existence of God was indeed sufficient to determine the concept of the supersensible in this way; but it is judgment's concept, as thought by reason but then adapted by understanding, of the supersensible basis of nature's purposive order which made that determination possible and thus prepared us for that moral argument.

The solution to Problem II is therefore this. The antinomy of teleological judgment (which applies to aesthetic judgment and its antinomy as well) gives rise, in its solution, to the concept of the supersensible basis of nature's (subjective or objective) purposiveness. The concept of the supersensible basis of nature's purposiveness is the concept of an intuitive understanding with its intellectual intuition; but our understanding, unable to think the concept of an intuitive understanding, instead thinks of the supersensible basis of nature's purposiveness as an intelligent cause of the world in terms of purposes. The concept of an intelligent cause of the world in terms of purposes makes determinable the concept of the supersensible as mere basis of nature (as this latter concept arises from the antinomies of the *Critique of Pure Reason*), and thus "mediates" between this latter concept and the concept of the supersensible which is determined practically and contained in the idea of freedom (this concept arises from the antinomy of the *Critique of Practical Reason*). Through this mediation judgment's concept of the supersensible basis of nature's (subjective as well as objective) purposiveness (as equivalent to the concept of that purposiveness itself) *unites* the "three" supersensibles in one. For the substrate of nature was merely made determinate enough *to be* nature in itself as the "purpose" brought about by an intelligent cause, and then to be nature in itself as caused by a *moral author,* a God. Hence, in this way, the *Critique of Judgment* mediates between the other two *Critiques* and thus unites the three *Critiques* in the critical *system.*

We are now in a position to solve Problem III (see above, *lxiv*). This problem was Kant's assertion that what makes the concept of nature's purposiveness "suitable" for its mediation role is "the spontaneity in the play of the cognitive powers, whose harmony with each other contains the basis of [the] pleasure [that we feel in judging the beautiful]" (Ak. 197). Kant also claims, similarly, that in the *Critique of Judgment* the "essential" part is the Critique of *Aesthetic* Judgment (Ak. 193). He makes this claim because, whereas teleological judgments go beyond the power of judgment and also bring in reason with its determinate concepts of purposes, judgments of taste are based solely on reflection and hence solely on the power of judgment (Ak. 193–94). By the same token, Kant says that only the power of aesthetic judgment is a "special" power (Ak. 194); this is why, when Kant says that apart from the antinomies of the first and second *Critiques* there is, in the *Critique of Judgment,* "an" (i.e., one) antinomy, he calls that one antinomy (as I have already indicated) an antinomy of reason *"for the feeling of pleasure and displeasure,"* an antinomy "concerning the aesthetic use of judgment" (Ak. 345).

None of these claims imply that teleological judgment plays no role in the mediation. Not only are teleological judgments reflective and hence based, as judgments of taste are, on judgment's indeterminate concept of nature's subjective purposiveness, but—as we have seen— even the determinate concept used in a teleological judgment, viz., the concept of objective natural purposiveness (in natural purposes) must, if it is not to be contradictory, be equated with the concept of the supersensible basis of this purposiveness; and this latter concept can then be adapted by our understanding, as discussed above, and thus play its mediation role. Why, then, does the fact that teleological judgments bring in reason with its determinate concepts of purposes make them less "suitable" for the mediation than judgments of taste are?

First of all, although this mediation is a mediation among the "supersensibles," it is just as much—as we saw (*lxxxvi–lxxxvii*)—a mediation among our mental powers, including the higher cognitive (and legislative) powers. The mediation in its entirety is a mediation among these powers and among the "worlds" of appearance with which these powers deal along with the supersensible substrates of these "worlds." Specifically, the power of judgment is to mediate between the realm of nature and the realm of freedom. But judgment's concept of nature's subjective purposiveness is especially "suitable" for mediating between these two realms only if no *objective* purposiveness (purposiveness with a purpose) has been based on it, i.e., only if the subjective purposiveness is merely subjective, a purposiveness *without* a purpose, and hence a purposiveness as judged aesthetically. For only such purposiveness without a purpose is "analogous" to or "symbolic" of the supersensible form that the moral law enjoins us to impose on nature (see Ak. 353, 356, and above, *xliv*). What makes this purposiveness analogous to supersensible (moral) form is that, since it involves no determinate concept of a natural purpose with its objective (and material: see *lxxvii*) purposiveness, it is a purely *formal* and *free* purposiveness. It is formal, as the moral law is formal; it is free, as our will is free to obey or disobey the moral law (cf. Ak. 354). Moreover, the "play" in which our cognitive powers are when we judge subjective purposiveness aesthetically is "spontaneous"; i.e., this play is "active" inasmuch as it sustains itself (Ak. 313, 222, and cf. 220), and in this respect it is again similar to our will's freedom, which is active by being a special causality.

This same special mediation role of *aesthetic* reflective judgment manifests itself in our consciousness. In judgments of taste we are conscious nonconceptually (i.e., without a [determinate] concept) of the free harmonious play of imagination and understanding; this nonconceptual consciousness is the feeling of pleasure we have in a judgment of taste. Because of the link, just described, between this play and the moral law as well as our freedom, our nonconceptual consciousness of this play is linked to *moral* feeling (see *xliv*), i.e., respect for the moral law together with our awareness that we have the freedom we need in order to carry it out. This is why the spontaneity in the play of the cognitive powers, as accompanied by our awareness of it, can lead to moral feeling and thus can "promote" the mind's "receptivity" for moral feeling (Ak. 197, 356).

In conclusion, then, it is indeed the power of judgment, but above all the *aesthetic* power of judgment, i.e., the power of judgment as unaided by reason, that is responsible for the mediation between the "world" of the first *Critique* and the "world" of the second *Critique* by which the three *Critiques* come to form a system.

In this introduction, on the whole, I have had to limit myself to an *explanation* of the *Critique of Judgment* and to leave aside criticism. I must now make an exception and raise one problem beyond the three already discussed. This is a problem for which I can see no solution that does not create other serious trouble for Kant's doctrines. I must raise the problem because it concerns the key concept of the *Critique of Judgment,* viz., the concept of nature's (subjective or objective) purposiveness, as we must think this concept in accordance with the solution to the antinomy of teleological judgment.

There is, I am afraid, a conflict between the antinomy of teleological judgment and the third antinomy of the *Critique of Pure Reason;* the two give rise, as it were, to an "antinomy between antinomies."

In order for the antinomy of teleological judgment to work, i.e., to be an antinomy at all, the necessity in nature must be so strict as to *contradict* the contingency in the form of nature's particular *unless we remove* the contingency by *solving* the antinomy. For if the necessity were less strict than that, then we would not need, as solution of the antinomy, the idea of an intuitive understanding that *legislates* the form of the particular and thus makes it, too, strictly necessary; rather, we could then interpret the form of the particular (as our mere understanding with its "peculiarity" is forced to do: see *xcviii–xcix*) in *practical* terms, and hence as having only the lawfulness of a "rule" that is still contingent (*c*).

Now the conflict that Kant presents in the third antinomy of the *Critique of Pure Reason* is a very similar conflict, viz., a conflict between the necessity in nature and our freedom (which again implies contingency in terms of natural laws) to affect nature in alternative ways. Yet Kant does not solve that antinomy as he solves the antinomy of ideological judgment: he does not say that we must think of our practical freedom as being only a seeming freedom and as in fact being a theoretical *necessity* due to the legislation of some higher and intuitive understanding with its intellectual intuition. Instead, his solution of that antinomy consists in pointing out that we can attribute the necessity to nature as mere *appearance* and still also think of our freedom as a *supersensible* (noumenal) causality, although a supersensible causality that can nevertheless affect nature as appearance in alternative ways. If the necessity in nature is strict enough for the antinomy of teleological judgment to arise at all, and if our freedom with its contingency can be reconciled, as just described, with that strict necessity despite having to manifest itself in that nature as appearance with its necessity, why should the antinomy of teleological judgment require a solution that is so different? Why could we not solve it by thinking, not a supersensible understanding that is intuitive and hence removes the contingency in the particular, but a supersensible understanding that determines things only practically and hence leaves the contingency intact? We could then go on to claim, as Kant does in the case of freedom, that such a supersensible contingency, even as affecting the world as appearance, "does not conflict" with the mentioned strict necessity. The trouble with such an alternative "solution" to the antinomy of teleological judgment is, of course, that it does not seem to work; for if the world as appearance can be affected in alternative ways, how can it still involve strict necessity? By the same token, Kant's solution to the third antinomy of the first *Critique* is in the same trouble if our freedom, as something to be manifested in the world as appearance, must indeed be reconciled with such a strict necessity.[106] It seems, therefore, that if the third antinomy is to be capable of being solved, and if our freedom is not to be denied, then the necessity in nature cannot be allowed to be a strict necessity but must be weakened in some way.

One way to weaken the necessity in nature is to make regulative, rather than constitutive, not only the idea of freedom (which from the theoretical point of view taken by the first *Critique* is already regulative) but the categories as well, since it is on them that nature's mechanism

---

[106] See, e.g., Lewis White Beck, *A Commentary on Kant's Critique of Practical Reason* (Chicago: University of Chicago Press, 1960), 191–92.

with its necessity is based.[107] One serious problem with such a move is that it would undermine the first *Critique,* which could no longer support any claim to propositions that are synthetic and yet a priori and necessary (cf. n. 107). But a far worse problem is that such a

---

[107] This is how Beck proposes to remove the difficulty with Kant's solution to the third antinomy. (*Ibid.,* 192–94.) Beck's suggestion has been developed further by Butts. Butts argues that Kant himself makes the categories regulative in the first *Critique.* (*Kant and the Double Government Methodology,* esp. 261–63.) It seems to me, however, that this view involves at least the following four major difficulties. First, it flies in the face of Kant's entire immanent metaphysics as developed in the Analytic. (Butts emphasizes Kant's epistemology, but acknowledges that it entails an immanent or "local" ontology: *ibid.,* 243, 225.) Second, it undermines Kant's epistemology, which tries to show that there are (theoretical) synthetic judgments that are indeed a priori and necessary, and are not merely considered to be so. Third, the evidence Butts offers for his view can easily be interpreted in a different way, one that does not involve any of the difficulties I am mentioning here: as far as I can see, none of the citations given by Butts show that Kant is making regulative anything but the ideas of reason. That holds even for the passage that Butts seems to consider (*ibid.,* 261) his most important piece of evidence (viz., A 561–62 = B 589–90): In discussing the fourth antinomy, Kant does indeed include, as the initial part of the *regulative* principle of reason, a brief characterization of the phenomenal world in *categorial* terms. Yet the principle then continues in nothing but the *familiar* regulative terms: it seeks to regulate our investigation of nature, by telling us (as Kant tells us so often), roughly, that we should try to account for things in mechanical terms as far as we can and not appeal too hastily to causes beyond nature. Why, then, should we assume that the initial instruction to regard the phenomenal world first of all in categorial terms is more than a reminder not to forget that the phenomenal world is indeed mechanistic? After all, a methodology ("regulation") *can* be based on an ontology, as Butts himself points out (*ibid.,* 226, and cf. 241). The fourth difficulty with Butts' view strikes me as even more serious than the mentioned three: making the categories regulative does not in fact solve the third antinomy. For even if both the idea of freedom and the concept of causal necessity are regulative, I still cannot without contradiction think them together, i.e., in the same context. And yet I *must* think them together; for though I can study nature without thinking of freedom, I cannot think about freedom without bringing in nature, because it is *in nature* that my free will is to make a difference, as Kant points out again and again (e.g., in the *Critique of Judgment,* at Ak. 176 and 196). (We can of course choose to think of only one half of the antinomy at a time; but that holds even for all genuine contradictions and does not begin to remove the contradiction.) I find it interesting that after Butts construes Kant's solution of the antinomy of *teleological judgment* along the same lines as he does the third antinomy of the first *Critique* (see above, n. 90), he himself attributes to Kant the view that adopting even the *maxims* of mechanism and teleology would not be "consistent" (*ibid.,* 279) unless we invoke the supersensible (which, like McFarland [see above, *xcix–c*], he takes to be an intelligent cause of the world). Yet all that Butts says about this remaining conflict between the two regulative principles, along with Kant's alleged solution of it, is that it "does no harm" to Kant's "essential position on teleology" (*ibid.,* 278), as Butts has interpreted that position.

sacrifice would not even help. For just as construing the principle of mechanism and the teleological principle as regulative does not resolve the conflict between them and hence cannot solve the antinomy of teleological judgment (see *lxxxviii–xc*), so making the categories regulative would still leave them in conflict with a regulative principle of freedom. For we cannot even *think* of (categorial) necessity together with the contingency implied in the concept of freedom (cf. n. 107), since the two thoughts still contradict and hence cancel each other.

A less radical way to weaken the necessity in nature's mechanism would be the following. We might leave the categories constitutive, determinative, and strictly necessary, including the category on which mechanism is based above all, viz., the category of cause and effect; we might then go on to weaken just what the principle of causality, as based on that category, says with that strict necessity. According to that principle, every event must have "its" (efficient) cause (Ak. 183), though the principle does not determine what that cause is. We could weaken that principle to this: Every event has *some* (efficient) cause, and not only does the principle not determine what that cause is, but the cause need not even be the *same* in each otherwise similar event. It is at least possible that Kant has in mind this weak version of the causal principle (rather than merely the denial that the causal principle determines what causes what) when he says such things as that understanding does not determine the particular (Ak. 179, 185, 407), or that "nature, considered as mere mechanism, could have structured itself differently in a thousand ways" (Ak. 360).[108]

Weakening the principle of causality in this way (or construing Kant as defending only this weaker principle) has a twofold major advantage: allowing individual links in (unbroken) chains of efficient causes to *vary* leaves some contingency; hence it leaves room for freedom as well as for nature's purposiveness. It would allow us to think of nature's purposiveness as produced by an intelligent cause of the world; and it would allow us to think of our will as a free causality. Indeed, this free causality could, in obedience to the moral law, produce purposive order in nature in precisely those contexts where

---

[108] Henry E. Allison has argued, on the basis of more such textual evidence, that Kant does indeed intend his causal principle to say no more than this: *Kant's Transcendental Idealism* (New Haven, Conn.: Yale University Press, 1983), 216–34, esp. 216 and 229. Cf. also Lewis White Beck's "A Prussian Hume and a Scottish Kant," in his *Essays on Kant and Hume* (New Haven: Yale University Press, 1978), 111–29.

nature, including nature within ourselves, does not already have it but is seriously defective in ways that go against the moral law. Hence we could think of nature as governed practically in two ways: as governed by a moral God and as governed by human beings in those respects in which that God has chosen to leave the world imperfect and improvable by us. Moreover, even apart from such divine and human action directed toward making the world more "purposive" (orderly), the described variability that the weakened causal principle would permit would not make nature chaotic. For the variations among the efficient causes could still be (as, on Kant's view, particular causes already are) governed by particular *laws;* the variations would be *regularities* involving *some* contingency (Ak. 404). Hence we can still, on this view, predict eclipses, or human behavior, with a "certainty"[109] proportionate to this "lawfulness." Where regularities are already present, we could ascribe them to God; we would do so especially in the case of organisms, less so in the case of nature as a whole, and least in the case of "contrapurposive" arrangements in nature, i.e., whatever manifests least order and is most in conflict with the idea of nature as a system of purposes subordinated to the final purpose. Where such regularities are absent but are required morally, our free will could "initiate" causal series in nature in the sense of determining *what sort* of efficient cause is to appear in this or that position in certain chains of efficient causes.

Unfortunately, weakening the causal principle in this way has at least three major *disadvantages* as well. First, it does more than "solve" Kant's third antinomy: it destroys it. Kant could indeed suggest a seeming contradiction between categorial necessity and freedom and then point out that the causal principle is weak enough to allow for freedom; but he could no longer use the antinomy to get to anything supersensible (he then would have to rely on other routes). Second, weakening the causal principle as described would also destroy the antinomy of teleological judgment and with it another route to the supersensible: to the supersensible as an intuitive understanding with its intellectual intuition (the contingency in the particular would remain rather than be considered as merely a "seeming" one); to the supersensible as an intelligent cause of the world; and to

---

[109] *Critique of Practical Reason*, Ak. V, 99; and cf. the *Critique of Pure Reason*, A 549–50 = B 577–78.

the supersensible basis of nature's purposiveness as mediator between other "supersensibles" (if indeed there would be any supersensibles left between which to mediate) and as "needed" to solve the antinomy of *aesthetic* judgment. By the same token, if we say that Kant already considers his causal principle to be of this weaker sort, we saddle him with the difficulty of having set up "antinomies" where none can arise and of having introduced supersensibles without any justification. Moreover, third, the "antinomy between antinomies," i.e., the *conflict between* the antinomy of teleological judgment and the third antinomy of the first *Critique,* as Kant presents and handles these antinomies, would also remain a problem.

CRITIQUE
OF JUDGMENT

Immanuel Kant

PREFACE

TO THE
FIRST EDITION, 1790[1]

Our ability to cognize from a priori principles may be called *pure reason,* and the general inquiry into the possibility and bounds of such cognition[2] may be called critique of pure reason. These terms are appropriate even if, as I did in my *Critique of Pure Reason,* we mean by this power[3] [*Vermögen*] only reason in its theoretical use, without yet seeking to investigate what ability [*Vermögen*] and what special principles it may have as practical reason. A critique of pure reason, in this narrow sense, is concerned merely with our ability to

---

[1] [This is the full title of the Preface as it appeared in the second edition (1793), on which the *Akademie* edition is based.]

[2] [*Erkenntnis.* In Kant's philosophy, 'cognition' *most often* refers to the process of acquiring knowledge or to the product of this process; but there is also a *practical* (as opposed to theoretical) cognition, and most practical cognition (e.g., that of the existence of God), is not (and does not yield) *Wissen* (knowledge). See Ak. 475. Cf. also Ak. 174–76. See also the Translator's Introduction, *xl–xlii.*]

[3] [I am using 'power,' rather than 'faculty,' in order to disassociate Kant's theory (of cognition, desire, etc.) from the traditional *faculty psychology*; i.e., I am trying to avoid *reifying* the Kantian powers (which are mere abilities), in other words, avoid turning them into psychological entities such as compartments, sources, or agencies "in" the mind. Hence, in this translation, expressions like 'the power of judgment,' 'the power of thought,' 'the power of concepts,' 'the power of desire,' and so on, always refer to an ability (a "faculty" in *that* sense). In such expressions, 'power' is never used to mean anything like *strength or forcefulness* (of concepts, desire, and so on).]

3

cognize things a priori. Hence it deals only with the [theoretical] *cognitive power,* to the exclusion of the feeling of pleasure and displeasure and of the power of desire; and among the cognitive powers it deals with the *understanding* as governed by its a priori principles, to the exclusion of *judgment*[4] as well as *reason* (both of which are also powers involved in theoretical cognition). The understanding is singled out in this way because, as that critique discovers, it is the only one among the cognitive powers capable of providing principles of cognition that are constitutive [rather than merely regulative] a priori. The critique [discovers this as it] inspects every one of the cognitive powers to decide what each has [in fact] contributed from its own roots to the cognition we actually possess, [as distinguished from] whatever it might pretend to have contributed to it. Nothing, it turns out, [passes this inspection] except what the *understanding* [through its a priori concepts] prescribes a priori as a law to nature, as the sum total of appearances (whose form is also given a priori). All other pure concepts the critique relegates to the ideas, which are transcendent for our theoretical cognitive power, though that certainly does not make them useless or dispensable, since they serve as regulative principles: they serve, in part, to restrain the understanding's arrogant claims, namely, that (since it can state a priori the conditions for the possibility of all things it can cognize) it has thereby circumscribed the area within which all things in general are possible; in part, they serve to guide the understanding, in its contemplation of nature, by a principle of completeness—though the understanding cannot attain this completeness—and so further the final aim of all cognition.[5]

168

---

[4] [*Urteilskraft,* literally 'power of judgment.' Since this "power" is nothing more than our ability *to judge* (cf. Kant's translation of '*Urteilskraft*' with Latin '*iudicium*': *Anthropology from a Pragmatic Point of View,* Ak. VII, 199), 'power of' will be omitted where it may be regarded as understood and where there is no confusing reference to an *individual* judgment in the same context. ('*Urteil*' by itself, unlike 'judgment,' can refer only to an individual judgment.) This is one of several cases where I have revised the opinions on translation which I expressed in a paper whose main purpose was to defend my rendering of one key term: "How to Render *Zweckmäßigkeit* in Kant's Third Critique," in *Interpreting Kant,* ed. Moltke S. Gram (Iowa City: University of Iowa Press, 1982).]

[5] [Concerning the "regulative use of the ideas of pure reason," see the *Critique of Pure Reason,* A 642–68 = B 670–96.]

So it was actually the *understanding,* which has its own domain as a *cognitive power* insofar as it contains principles of cognition that are constitutive a priori, which the critique that we all call the critique of pure reason was to make the secure and sole possessor [of that domain] against all other competitors. Similarly *reason,* which does not contain any constitutive a priori principles except [those] for the *power of desire,* was given possession [of its domain] by the critique of practical reason.

The present critique, the critique of *judgment,* will deal with the following questions: Does judgment, which in the order of our [specific] cognitive powers is a mediating link between understanding and reason,[6] also have a priori principles of its own? Are these principles constitutive, or are they merely regulative (in which case they would fail to prove [that judgment has] a domain of its own)? Does judgment give the rule a priori to the feeling of pleasure and displeasure, the mediating link between the cognitive power [in general] and the power of desire[7] (just as the understanding prescribes laws a priori to the cognitive power and reason to the power of desire)?

A critique of pure reason, i.e., of our ability to judge according to a priori principles, would be incomplete if it failed to include, as a special part, a treatment of judgment, which, since it is a cognitive power, also lays claim to a priori principles; judgment must be treated, in a special part of the critique, even if, in a system of pure philosophy, its principles are not such that they can form a special part between theoretical and practical philosophy, but may be annexed to one or the other as needed. For if a system of pure philosophy, under the general title metaphysics, is to be achieved some day (to accomplish this quite completely is both possible and of the utmost importance for our use of reason in all contexts), the critique must already have explored the terrain supporting this edifice, to the depth at which lies the first foundation of our power of principles independent of experience, so that no part of the edifice may give way, which would inevitably result in the collapse of the whole.

[6] [Cf. Ak. 177.]

[7] [Cf. Ak. 178.]

169   On the other hand, the nature of the power of judgment (whose correct use is so necessary and universally required that this power is just what we mean by sound understanding) is such that an attempt to discover a principle of its own must plainly be accompanied by great difficulties (and it must contain some principle a priori, since otherwise, despite being a distinct cognitive power, it would not be subject even to the most ordinary critique): for this principle must, nevertheless, not be derived from a priori concepts, since these belong to the understanding and judgment only applies them. So judgment itself must provide a concept, a concept through which we do not actually cognize anything but which only serves as a rule for the power of judgment itself—but not as an objective rule, to which it could adapt its judgment, since then we would need another power of judgment in order to decide whether or not the judgment is a case of that rule.[8]

This perplexity about a principle (whether subjective or objective) arises mainly in those judgments [*Beurteilungen*],[9] called aesthetic, which concern the beautiful and the sublime in nature or in art. And yet a critical inquiry [in search] of a principle of judgment in them is the most important part of a critique of this power. For though these judgments do not by themselves contribute anything whatever to our cognition of things, they still belong to the cognitive power alone and prove a direct relation of this power to the feeling of pleasure or displeasure according to some a priori principle, without there being any confusion of this principle with the one that can be the basis determining the power of desire, since that power has its a priori principles in concepts of reason. [The fact that this

---

[8] [Cf. *On the Saying: That May Be Correct in Theory but Is Inadequate for Practice* (1793), Ak. VIII, 275, and the *Anthropology*, Ak. VII, 199.]

[9] [In one place (Ak. 211'), Kant makes a distinction between *Beurteilung* and *Urteil* (judgment), using the first term to stand for a *reflective* judgment. But he does not repeat this distinction anywhere else, nor does he consistently adhere to it. The reason for this seems to be that in German grammar adding '*be-*' to the intransitive '*urteilen*' simply turns it into the transitive '*beurteilen*.' By the same token, it is misleading to use 'to judge' (which is both transitive and intransitive) for '*urteilen*' but a different term for '*beurteilen*,' especially such a term as 'to estimate,' or 'to assess,' or 'to appraise,' all of which tend to imply *evaluation* rather than just reflection. (The *context* tells us when the judging is reflective.)]

aesthetic judging is directly referred to the feeling of pleasure and displeasure distinguishes it from a certain kind of] logical judging of nature: when experience manifests in things a lawfulness that understanding's concept of the sensible is no longer adequate to [help us] understand or explain, judgment can find within itself a principle that refers the natural thing to the uncognizable super-sensible, though judgment must use this principle for cognizing nature only in relation to itself. In these cases such an a priori principle can and must indeed be employed if we are to *cognize* the beings in the world, and it also opens up prospects advantageous to practical reason. Yet here the principle has no direct relation to the feeling of pleasure and displeasure, while it is precisely this relation which gives rise to that puzzle regarding judgment's principle, which necessitates a special division for this power in the critique: for the [mentioned kind of] logical judging according to concepts (from which no direct inference can ever be drawn to the feeling of pleasure and displeasure) could at most have formed an appendix, including a critical restriction on such judging, to the theoretical part of philosophy.

170

Since this inquiry into our power of taste, which is the aesthetic power of judgment, has a transcendental aim, rather than the aim to [help] form and cultivate taste (since this will continue to proceed, as it has in the past, even if no such investigations are made), I would like to think that it will be judged leniently as regards its deficiency for the latter purpose. As a transcendental inquiry, however, it must be prepared to face the strictest examination. Yet even here, given how difficult it is to solve a problem that nature has made so involved, I hope to be excused if my solution contains a certain amount of obscurity, not altogether avoidable, as long as I have established clearly enough that the principle has been stated correctly. [I say this because] the way in which I have derived from that principle this phenomenon, viz., judgment, may fall short of the clarity we are entitled to demand elsewhere, namely, where we deal with cognition according to concepts, and which I do believe I have achieved in the second part of this work.[10]

With this, then, I conclude my entire critical enterprise. I shall

[10] [That is, in the Critique of Teleological Judgment.]

proceed without delay to the doctrinal one, in order to snatch from my advancing years what time may yet be somewhat favorable to the task. It goes without saying that judgment will have no special part in doctrine, since in the case of this power critique takes the place of theory. Rather, in accordance with the division of philosophy, and of pure philosophy, into a theoretical and a practical part, the doctrinal enterprise will consist of the metaphysics of nature and that of morals.[11]

---

[11] [The *Metaphysics of Morals* appeared in 1797. The case of the metaphysics of nature is less clear. In 1786, four years *before* the publication of the *Critique of Judgment*, Kant had already published the *Metaphysical Foundations of Natural Science*. It is not clear in what respect he considered that work, as conjoined with the *Critique of Pure Reason*, as falling short of a metaphysics of nature. (Cf. the *Critique of Pure Reason*, B xliii.) Perhaps the missing part was the projected *Transition from the Metaphysical Foundations of Natural Science to Physics*, on which Kant worked until a year before his death and which appeared (in unfinished form) in what is now called the *Opus Postumum* (Ak. XXI and XXII). Cf. James W. Ellington, "The Unity of Kant's Thought in His Philosophy of Corporeal Nature," 135–219 (esp. 213–219) in Book II of his translation of the *Prolegomena* and the *Metaphysical Foundations of Natural Science:* Immanuel Kant, *Philosophy of Material Nature* (Indianapolis: Hackett Publishing Company, 1985).]

INTRODUCTION[12]

I

On the Division of Philosophy

Insofar as philosophy contains principles for the rational cognition of things through concepts (and not merely, as logic does, principles of the form of thought in general without distinction of objects[13]), it is usually divided into *theoretical* and *practical*. That division is entirely correct, provided there is also a difference in kind between the concepts that assign to the principles of this rational cognition their respective objects: otherwise the concepts would not justify a division, since a division presupposes that the principles of the rational cognition pertaining to the different parts of a science are opposed to one another.

There are, however, only two kinds of concepts, which [thus] allow for two different principles concerning the possibility of their respective objects. These are the *concepts of nature* and the *concept of freedom*. Concepts of nature make possible a *theoretical* cognition governed by a priori principles, whereas the very concept of freedom

---

[12] [This is the *second* introduction Kant wrote for the work. Cf. the Translator's Introduction, *xxix*. The (longer) First Introduction appears, as the Translator's Supplement, below, 383–441 (Ak. 193'–251')]

[13] [Cf. the *Logic*, Ak. IX, 12–13.]

carries with it, as far as nature is concerned, only a negative principle (namely, of mere opposition), but gives rise to expansive principles for the determination of the will, which are therefore called practical; hence we are right to divide philosophy into two parts that are quite different in their principles: theoretical or *natural philosophy,* and practical or *moral philosophy* (*morality* is the term we use for reason's practical legislation governed by the concept of freedom). In the past, however, these terms have been badly misused for dividing the different principles and along with them philosophy. For no distinction was made between the practical governed by concepts of nature and the practical governed by the concept of freedom, with the result that the same terms, theoretical and practical philosophy, were used to make a division that in fact did not divide anything (since the two parts might have the same kind of principles).

172

For the will, as the power of desire, is one of the many natural causes in the world, namely, the one that acts in accordance with concepts; and whatever we think of as possible (or necessary) through a will we call practically possible (or necessary), as distinguished from the physical possibility or necessity of an effect whose cause is not determined to [exercise] its causality through concepts (but through mechanism, as in the case of lifeless matter, or through instinct, as in the case of animals). It is here, concerning the practical, that people leave it undetermined whether the concept that gives the rule to the will's causality is a concept of nature or a concept of freedom.

Yet this distinction is essential. For if the concept that determines [the exercise of] the causality is a concept of nature, then the principles will be *technically*[14] *practical;* but if it is a concept of freedom, then the principles will be *morally practical.* And since the division of a rational science [-*wissenschaft*] depends entirely on that difference between the respective objects which requires different principles for [their] cognition, the technically practical principles will belong to theoretical philosophy (natural science [-*lehre*]), while the morally practical ones alone

---

[14] [In the sense derived from the Greek τέχνη (téchnē), i.e., 'art' in the sense that includes craft.]

will form the second part, practical philosophy (moral theory [-*lehre*[15]]).

All technically practical rules (i.e., those of art and of skill in general, or for that matter of prudence, i.e., skill in influencing people's volition), insofar as their principles rest on concepts, must be included only in theoretical philosophy, as corollaries. For they concern nothing but the possibility of things according to concepts of nature; and this includes not only the means we find in nature for producing them, but even the will (as power of desire and hence as a natural power), as far as it can be determined, in conformity with the mentioned rules, by natural incentives. However, such practical rules are not called laws (as are, e.g., physical laws), but only precepts. This is because the will is subject not merely to the concept of nature, but also to the concept of freedom; and it is in relation to the latter that the will's principles are called laws. Only these latter principles, along with what follows from them, form the second, i.e., the practical, part of philosophy.

The point is this: Solving the problems of pure geometry does not belong to a special part of geometry, nor does the art of land surveying deserve the name of practical geometry (as distinct from pure), as a second part of geometry in general. But it would be equally wrong, even more so, to consider the art of experimentation or observation in mechanics or chemistry to be a practical part of natural science, or, finally, to include any of the following in practical philosophy, let alone regard them as constituting the second part of philosophy in general: domestic, agricultural, or political economy, the art of social relations, the precepts of hygiene, or even the general theory [*Lehre*] of [how to attain] happiness, indeed not even—with that goal in mind—the taming of our inclinations and the subjugation of our affects. For all of these arts contain only rules of skill, which are therefore only technically practical, for producing an effect that is possible according to concepts of nature about causes and effects; and since these concepts belong to theoretical philosophy, they are subject to those precepts as mere corollaries of theoretical philosophy (i.e., of natural science), and so cannot claim a place in a special

173

[15] [For *Lehre* as *Theorie*, see *Perpetual Peace*, Ak. VIII, 370; for the term '*Theorie*' as applied to the *practical* (not just the theoretical), see *ibid.*, but especially *On the Saying: That May Be Correct in Theory*, Ak. VIII, 275–89.]

philosophy called practical. Morally practical precepts, on the other hand, which are based entirely on the concept of freedom, all natural bases determining the will being excluded, form a very special kind of precepts. Just as the rules that nature obeys are called laws simply, so too are these; but, unlike laws of nature, practical laws do not rest on sensible conditions but rest on a supersensible principle; [hence] they require just for themselves another part of philosophy, alongside the theoretical one, to be called practical philosophy.

What the above shows is that a set of practical precepts provided by philosophy cannot form a special part of philosophy, placed along-side the theoretical part, merely because they are practical; for they could be practical even if their principles (as technically practical rules) were taken entirely from our theoretical cognition of nature. Rather, they form such a special part when and if their principle is in no way borrowed from the concept of nature, which is always conditioned by the sensible, but rests on the supersensible that the concept of freedom alone enables us to know [*kennbar*] through for-mal laws, so that these precepts are morally practical, i.e., they are not just precepts and rules for achieving this or that intention, but are laws that do not refer to any purposes or intentions we already have.

174

II

On the Domain of Philosophy in General

The range within which we can use our power of cognition according to principles, and hence do philosophy, is the range within which a priori concepts have application.

We refer these concepts to objects, in order to bring about cogni-tion of these objects where this is possible. Now the sum total of all these objects can be divided in accordance with how adequate or inadequate our powers are for this aim.

Insofar as we refer concepts to objects without considering whether or not cognition of these objects is possible, they have their realm; and this realm is determined merely by the relation that the object of these concepts has to our cognitive power in general. The part of this realm in which cognition is possible for us is a territory (*territorium*) for these concepts and the cognitive power we need for such cognition. That part of the territory over which these concepts legislate is the domain (*ditio*) of these concepts and the cognitive powers pertaining to them. Hence empirical concepts do have their territory in nature, as the sum total of all objects of sense, but they have no *domain* in it (but only residence, *domicilium*); for though they are produced according to law, they do not legislate; rather, the rules that are based on them are empirical and hence contingent.

Our cognitive power as a whole has two domains, that of the concepts of nature and that of the concept of freedom, because it legislates a priori by means of both kinds of concept. Now philosophy too divides, according to these legislations, into theoretical and practical. And yet the territory on which its domain is set up and on which it *exercises* its legislation is still always confined to the sum total of the objects of all possible experience, insofar as they are considered nothing more than mere appearances, since otherwise it would be inconceivable that the understanding could legislate with regard to them.

Legislation through concepts of nature is performed by the understanding and is theoretical. Legislation through the concept of freedom is performed by reason and is merely practical. Only in the practical sphere can reason legislate; with regard to theoretical cognition (of nature), all it can do (given the familiarity with laws that it has attained by means of the understanding) is to use given laws to infer consequences from them, which however remain always within nature. But the reverse does not hold: if rules are practical, that does not yet make reason *legislative,* since they might only be technically practical.

Hence understanding and reason have two different legislations on one and the same territory of experience. Yet neither of these legislations is to interfere with the other. For just as the concept of nature has no influence on the legislation through the concept of freedom, so the latter does not interfere with the legislation of nature. That it is possible at least to think, without contradiction, of these two legislations and the powers pertaining to them as coexisting in the same subject was proved by the *Critique of Pure Reason,* for it exposed the

175

dialectical illusion in the objections against this possibility and thus destroyed them.[16]

Now although these two different domains do not restrict each other in their legislation, they do restrict each other incessantly in the effects that their legislation has in the world of sense. Why do these two domains not form *one* domain? This is because the concept of nature does indeed allow us to present[17] its objects in intuition, but as mere appearances rather than as things in themselves, whereas the concept of freedom does indeed allow us to present its object as a thing in itself, but not in intuition; and so neither concept can provide us with theoretical cognition of its object (or even of the thinking subject) as things in themselves, which would be the supersensible. We do need the idea of the supersensible in order to base on it the possibility of all those objects of experience, but the idea itself can never be raised up and expanded into a cognition.

Hence there is a realm that is unbounded, but that is also inaccessible to our entire cognitive power: the realm of the supersensible. In this realm we cannot find for ourselves a territory on which to set up a domain of theoretical cognition, whether for the concepts of the understanding or for those of reason. It is a realm that we must indeed occupy with ideas that will assist us in both the theoretical and the practical use of reason; but the only reality we can provide for these ideas, by reference to the laws [arising] from the concept of freedom, is practical reality, which consequently does not in the least expand our theoretical cognition to the supersensible.

Hence an immense gulf is fixed between the domain of the concept of nature, the sensible, and the domain of the concept of freedom, the supersensible, so that no transition from the sensible to the

176

---

[16] [See the Third Antinomy (A 444–51 = B 472–79) and its solution (A 532–58 = B 560–86).]

[17] [*Vorstellen.* The traditional rendering of this term as 'to *re*present' (similarly for the noun) suggests that Kant's theory of perception (etc.) is representational, which, however, it is not (despite the fact that Kant sometimes adds the Latin *repraesentatio*). Since 'to present' too is awkward, it will be replaced by a more specific term where clarity requires and no risk of distortion arises for Kant's point or his other views. The German term '*darstellen*' (similarly for the noun) has traditionally been translated as 'to present' but will here be rendered as 'to exhibit,' which seems both closer to Kant's meaning and less misleading. On the meaning of 'presentation,' see below, Ak. 203 br. n. 4.]

supersensible (and hence by means of the theoretical use of reason) is possible, just as if they were two different worlds, the first of which cannot have any influence on the second; and yet the second *is* to have an influence on the first, i.e., the concept of freedom is to actualize in the world of sense the purpose enjoined by its laws. Hence it must be possible to think of nature as being such that the lawfulness in its form will harmonize with at least the possibility of [achieving] the purposes that we are to achieve in nature according to laws of freedom. So there must after all be a basis *uniting* the supersensible that underlies nature and the supersensible that the concept of freedom contains practically, even though the concept of this basis does not reach cognition of it either theoretically or practically and hence does not have a domain of its own, though it does make possible the transition from our way of thinking in terms of principles of nature to our way of thinking in terms of principles of freedom.

III

On the Critique of Judgment as Mediating the Connection of the Two Parts of Philosophy to [Form] a Whole

A critique that assesses what our cognitive powers can accomplish a priori does not actually have a domain as regards objects. For it is not a doctrine: its only task is to investigate whether and how our powers allow us (when given their situation) to produce a doctrine. The realm of this critique extends to all the claims that these powers make, in order to place these powers within the boundaries of their rightful [use]. But if something [for lack of a domain] cannot have a place in the division of philosophy, it may still enter as a main part into the critique of our pure cognitive power in general, namely, if it contains principles that by themselves are not fit for either theoretical or practical use.

The concepts of nature, which contain a priori the basis for all theoretical cognition, were found to rest on the legislation of the understanding. The concept of freedom was found to contain a priori the basis for all practical precepts that are unconditioned by the sensible, and to rest on the legislation of reason. Therefore, both these powers, apart from being applicable in terms of logical form to principles of whatever origin, have in addition a legislation of their own in terms of content which is not subject to any other (a priori) legislation, and hence this justifies the division of philosophy into theoretical and practical.

And yet the family of our higher cognitive powers also includes a mediating link between understanding and reason. This is *judgment,* about which we have cause to suppose, by analogy, that it too may contain a priori, if not a legislation of its own, then at least a principle of its own, perhaps a merely subjective one, by which to search for laws. Even though such a principle would lack a realm of objects as its own domain, it might still have some territory; and this territory might be of such a character that none but this very principle might hold in it.

But there is also (judging by analogy) another basis, namely, for linking judgment with a different ordering of our presentational powers, an ordering that seems even more important than the one involving judgment's kinship with the family of cognitive powers. For all of the soul's powers or capacities can be reduced to three that cannot be derived further from a common basis: the *cognitive power,* the *feeling of pleasure and displeasure,* and the *power of desire.*[18] The under-

---

[18] If concepts are used as empirical principles and there is cause to suppose that there is a kinship between them and the pure a priori cognitive power, then it is useful to attempt, on account of that relation, to give a transcendental definition of them, i.e., a definition by means of pure categories, insofar as these suffice by themselves to indicate how the concept at hand differs from others. This procedure follows the example of the mathematician, who leaves the empirical data in his problem undetermined and only brings the relation they have in their pure synthesis under the concepts of pure arithmetic, thereby universalizing his solution of the problem. I have been reproached for following a similar procedure (*Preface to the Kritik der praktischen Vernunft,* p. 16[19]), namely, for defining the power of desire as the *power of being the cause, through one's presentations, of the actuality of the objects of these presentations.* The

[19] [Of the first edition (1788) of the *Critique of Practical Reason,* Ak. V, 9n.]

standing alone legislates for the cognitive power when this power is
referred to nature, namely, as a power of *theoretical cognition,* (as
indeed it must be when it is considered by itself, without being confused
with the power of desire); for only with respect to nature (as appearance) is it possible for us to give laws by means of a priori concepts
of nature, which are actually pure concepts of the understanding. For
the power of desire, considered as a higher power governed by the
concept of freedom, only reason (which alone contains that concept)
legislates a priori. Now between the cognitive power and the power of
desire lies the feeling of pleasure, just as judgment lies between understanding and reason. Hence we must suppose, at least provisionally,

---

criticism was that, after all, mere wishes are desires too, and yet we all know that
they alone do not enable us to produce their object. That, however, proves nothing
more than that some of man's desires involve him in self-contradiction, inasmuch as
he uses the presentation by itself to strive to produce the object, while yet he cannot
expect success from it. Such is the case because he is aware that his mechanical forces
(if I may call the nonpsychological ones that), which would have to be determined by
that presentation in order to bring the object about (hence to be the means for it) are
either insufficient, or perhaps even directed to something impossible, such as to undo
what is done (*O mihi praeteritos*, etc.[20]), or as being able, as one is waiting impatiently
for some wished-for moment, to destroy what time remains. In such fanciful desires we
are indeed aware that our presentations are insufficient (or even unfit) to be the *cause*
of their objects. Still their causal relation, and hence the thought of their *causality*, is
contained in every *wish* and is especially noticeable [*sichtbar*] when that wish is an
affect, namely, *longing.* For since these desires [alternately] expand the heart and
make it languid, thus exhausting its forces, they prove that these forces are repeatedly
tensed by presentations, but that they allow the mind each time to relapse into
weariness as it considers again the impossibility. Even prayers that ask for the
deflection of some great and, as far as we can see, unavoidable evil, and also various
superstitious means aimed at achieving purposes unattainable through nature prove
the causal relation of these presentations to their objects; and this relation is such that
even an awareness of its insufficiency for producing the effect cannot keep it from
striving for the effect. But why our nature was given a propensity toward desires of
whose futility we are aware is an anthropological-teleological question. It seems that
if we had to assure ourselves that we can in fact produce the object, before we could
be determined [by the presentation] to apply our forces, then our forces would remain
largely unused. For usually we do not come to know what forces we have in the first
place except by trying them out. Hence the deception contained in vain wishes is only
the result of a beneficent arrangement in our nature.[21]

[20] [Vergil's *Aeneid*, viii, 560: *O mihi praeteritos referat si Iuppiter annos*; i.e., If Jupiter
would only restore to me those bygone years. (All translations given in footnotes are my
own, and this fact is not indicated in each such footnote individually.)]

[21] [On defining the power of desire, cf. also the *Metaphysics of Morals*, Ak.
VI, 356–57.]

that judgment also contains an a priori principle of its own, and also suppose that since the power of desire is necessarily connected with pleasure or displeasure (whether this precedes the principle of this power, as in the case of the lower power of desire, or, as in the case of the higher one, only follows from the determination of this power by the moral law),[22] judgment will bring about a transition from the pure cognitive power, i.e., from the domain of the concepts of nature, to the domain of the concept of freedom, just as in its logical use it makes possible the transition from understanding to reason.

Hence, even if philosophy can be divided into only two main parts, theoretical and practical, and even if everything we might need to say about judgment's own principles must be included in the theoretical part of philosophy, i.e., in rational cognition governed by concepts of nature, yet the critique of pure reason, which must decide all of this before we attempt to construct the mentioned system so as to inform us whether this system is possible, still consists of three parts: the critiques, respectively, of pure understanding, of pure judgment, and of pure reason, which are called pure because they legislate a priori.

IV[23]

On Judgment as a Power That Legislates A Priori

Judgment in general is the ability to think the particular as contained under the universal. If the universal (the rule, principle, law) is given, then judgment, which subsumes the particular under it, is *determinative* (even though [in its role] as transcendental judgment it states a priori the conditions that must be met for subsumption under that universal to be possible).[24] But if only the particular

---

[22] [Cf. *ibid.*, Ak. VI, 212–13 and 377–78.]

[23] [On this and the next section, cf. the *Critique of Pure Reason*, A 650–68 = B 678–96.]

[24] [Cf. *ibid.*, A 131–36 = B 170–75.]

is given and judgment has to find the universal for it, then this power is merely *reflective*.

Determinative judgment, [which operates] under universal transcendental laws given by the understanding, is only subsumptive. The law is marked out for it a priori, and hence it does not need to devise a law of its own so that it can subsume the particular in nature under the universal. On the other hand, since the laws that pure understanding gives a priori concern only the possibility of a nature as such (as object of sense), there are such diverse forms of nature, so many modifications as it were of the universal transcendental concepts of nature, which are left undetermined by these laws, that surely there must be laws for these forms too. Since these laws are empirical, they may indeed be contingent as far as *our* understanding can see; still, if they are to be called laws (as the concept of a nature does require), then they must be regarded as necessary by virtue of some principle of the unity of what is diverse, even though we do not know this principle. Hence reflective judgment, which is obliged to ascend from the particular in nature to the universal, requires a principle, which it cannot borrow from experience, precisely because it is to be the basis for the unity of all empirical principles under higher though still empirical principles, and hence is to be the basis that makes it possible to subordinate empirical principles to one another in a systematic way. So this transcendental principle must be one that reflective judgment gives as a law, but only to itself: it cannot take it from somewhere else (since judgment would then be determinative); nor can it prescribe it to nature, because our reflection on the laws of nature is governed by nature, not nature by the conditions under which we try to obtain a concept of it that in view of these conditions is quite contingent.

Now this principle can only be the following: since universal natural laws have their basis in our understanding, which prescribes them to nature (though only according to the universal concept of it as a nature), the particular empirical laws must, as regards what the universal laws have left undetermined in them, be viewed in terms of such a unity as [they would have] if they too had been given by an understanding (even though not ours) so as to assist our cognitive powers by making possible a system of experience in terms of particular natural laws. That does not mean that we must actually assume such an understanding (for it is only reflective judgment that uses this idea as a principle, for reflection rather than determination); rather,

180

in using this principle judgment gives a law only to itself, not to nature.

Now insofar as the concept of an object also contains the basis for the object's actuality, the concept is called the thing's *purpose,* and a thing's harmony with that character of things which is possible only through purposes is called the *purposiveness* of its form. Accordingly, judgment's principle concerning the form that things of nature have in terms of empirical laws in general is the *purposiveness of nature* in its diversity. In other words, through this concept we present nature as if an understanding contained the basis of the unity of what is diverse in nature's empirical laws.

181

Hence the purposiveness of nature is a special a priori concept that has its origin solely in reflective judgment. For we cannot attribute to natural products anything like nature's referring them to purposes, but can only use this concept in order to reflect on nature as regards that connection among nature's appearances which is given to us in terms of empirical laws. This concept is also quite distinct from practical purposiveness (in human art or in morality), though we do think it by analogy with practical purposiveness.

V

The Principle of the Formal Purposiveness of Nature Is a Transcendental Principle of Judgment

A transcendental principle is one by which we think the universal a priori condition under which alone things can become objects of our cognition in general; on the other hand, a principle is called metaphysical if it is one [by] which [we] think the a priori condition under which alone objects whose concept must be given empirically can be further determined a priori.[25] Thus the principle by which we cognize bodies as substances and as changeable substances is transcendental if it says that a change in them must have a cause; but it is metaphysical if it says that a change in them must have an *external* cause. For in order for us to cognize the proposition a priori in the first case, we must think the body only through ontological predicates (pure concepts of the understanding), e.g., as a substance; but in the second case we must base the proposition on the empirical concept of a body (as a movable thing in space), after which we can, however, see completely a priori that the latter predicate (of motion that must have an external cause) applies to the body. Accordingly, as I will show in a moment, the principle of the purposiveness of nature (in the diversity of its empirical laws) is a *transcendental* principle. For the concept of objects, insofar as they are thought as subject to this principle, is only the pure concept of objects of possible empirical cognition in general and contains nothing empirical. On the other hand, the principle of practical purposiveness, the purposiveness that must be thought in the idea of the *determination* of a free *will,* is a metaphysical principle, because the concept of a power of desire, considered as a will, does have to be given empirically (i.e., it does not belong to the transcendental predicates).[26] Still, both principles are a priori rather than empirical, because in such judgments we need no further experience in order to connect the predicate with the empirical concept of the subject, but can see this connection completely a priori.

182

That the concept of a purposiveness of nature belongs to the transcendental principles is sufficiently evident from the maxims of judgment which we use as an a priori basis for our investigation of nature but which yet concern no more than the possibility of experience and hence of our cognition of nature, though not merely of nature as such but of nature as determined by a diversity of particular laws. These maxims occur only sporadically but fairly frequently in the course of the science of metaphysics, as pronouncements of its wisdom, when it formulates certain rules whose necessity cannot be established from concepts: "Nature takes the shortest way (*lex parsimoniae*); yet it makes no leap, either in the sequence of its

[25] [Cf. the *Metaphysical Foundations of Natural Science,* Ak. IV, 469–70.]

[26] [Cf. the *Metaphysics of Morals,* Ak. VI, 216–17.]

changes or in the juxtaposition of forms that differ in kind (*lex continui in natura*); its great diversity in empirical laws is nonetheless a unity under few principles (*principia praeter necessitatem non sunt multiplicanda*),"[27] and so forth.

If we try to indicate the origin of these principles by following the psychological route, then we go wholly against their meaning. For they do not say what happens, i.e., by what rule our cognitive powers actually play their role [*ihr Spiel treiben*], and how we judge: they rather say how we ought to judge; and if these principles are merely empirical, they cannot yield this logical objective necessity. Hence the purposiveness of nature for our cognitive powers and their use, which manifestly shines forth from these principles, is a transcendental principle of judgments; and hence it too requires a transcendental deduction [i.e., justification], by means of which we must try to find the basis for such judging in the a priori sources of cognition.

It is true that we do initially find something necessary in the bases
183   of the possibility of experience, namely, the universal laws without which nature as such (as object of sense) cannot be thought. These laws rest on the categories, applied to the formal conditions of all intuition that is possible for us, as far as it too is given a priori. Under these laws judgment is determinative, for all it has to do is to subsume under given laws. For example, the understanding says: All change has its cause ([this is a] universal law of nature), and transcendental judgment need only state the condition for subsumption under the a priori concept of the understanding offered to it, and this condition is successiveness of states [*Bestimmungen*] of one and the same thing. Now for nature as such (as object of possible experience) we cognize that law as absolutely necessary. But apart from that formal temporal condition, objects of empirical cognition are still determined [*bestimmt*], or—if we confine ourselves to what we can judge a priori—determinable, in all sorts of additional ways. Therefore, specifically different natures, apart from what they have in common as belonging to nature as such, can still be causes in an infinite diversity of additional ways; and each of these ways must (in accordance with the concept of a cause as such) have its rule, a rule that is a law and hence carries necessity with it, even though the character and limits

[27] [Respectively, the principle of parsimony, the principle of continuity in nature, and (the principle that) principles must not be multiplied beyond necessity.]

of our cognitive powers bar us altogether from seeing that necessity. Hence we must think nature, as regards its merely empirical laws, as containing the possibility of an endless diversity of empirical laws that [despite being laws] are nonetheless contingent as far as we can see (i.e., we cannot cognize them a priori); and it is in view of this possibility that we judge the unity of nature in terms of empirical laws, as well as the possibility of the unity of experience (as a system in terms of empirical laws) to be contingent. And yet we must necessarily presuppose and assume this unity, since otherwise our empirical cognition could not thoroughly cohere to [form] a whole of experience;[28] for though the universal natural laws do make things cohere in terms of their genus, as natural things as such, they fail to provide them with specific coherence in terms of the particular natural beings they are. Hence judgment must assume, as an a priori principle for its own use, that what to human insight is contingent in the particular (empirical) natural laws does nevertheless contain a law-governed unity, unfathomable but still conceivable by us, in the combination of what is diverse in them to [form] an experience that is intrinsically [an sich] possible. Now when we find in such a combination a law-governed unity cognized by us as conforming to a necessary aim that we have (a need of our understanding), but at the same time as in itself [an sich] contingent, then we present this unity as a purposiveness of objects (of nature, in this case). Hence judgment, which with respect to things under possible (yet to be discovered) empirical laws is merely reflective, must think of nature with regard to these laws according to a *principle of purposiveness* for our cognitive power; and that principle is then expressed in the above maxims of judgment. Now this transcendental concept of a purposiveness of nature is neither a concept of nature nor a concept of freedom, since it attributes nothing whatsoever to the object (nature), but [through] this transcendental concept [we] only think of the one and only way in which we must proceed when reflecting on the objects of nature with the aim of having thoroughly coherent experience. Hence it is a subjective principle (maxim) of judgment. This is also why we rejoice (actually we are relieved of a need) when, just as if it were a lucky

184

---

[28] [Cf. Kant's response to Johann August Eberhard in *On a Discovery According to Which Any New Critique of Pure Reason Has Been Made Superfluous by an Earlier One* (1790, just before the *Critique of Judgment*), Ak. VIII, 250.]

chance favoring our aim, we do find such systematic unity among merely empirical laws, even though we necessarily had to assume that there is such unity even though we have no insight into this unity and cannot prove it.

To convince ourselves of the correctness of this deduction [i.e., justification] of the concept in question and of the necessity of assuming the concept as a transcendental cognitive principle, we need only consider the magnitude of the task, which lies a priori in our understanding, of making coherent experience out of given perceptions of nature even though this nature could contain an infinite diversity of empirical laws. It is true that the understanding is a priori in possession of universal laws of nature, without which nature could not be the object of experience at all. Yet there is required in addition that nature also have a certain order in its particular rules—rules that the understanding can come to know only empirically and that, as far as it is concerned, are contingent. [But since] without these rules there would be no way for us to proceed from the universal analogy of a possible experience as such to the particular one, the understanding must think of these rules as laws (i.e., as necessary)—even though it does not cognize, nor could ever see, their necessity—for otherwise such laws would not form an order of nature. Hence, though the understanding cannot determine anything a priori with regard to these (objects),[29] still it must, in order to investigate these empirical so-called laws, lay an a priori principle at the basis of all reflection on nature: the principle that a cognizable order of nature in terms of these laws is possible. A principle like this is expressed in the following propositions: that there is in nature a subordination graspable by us of species under genera; that genera in turn approach one another under some common principle so as to make possible a transition from one to another and so to a higher genus; that, while initially it seems to our understanding unavoidable to assume as many different kinds of causality as there are specific differences among natural effects, they may nevertheless fall under a small number of principles which it is our task to discover, etc. This harmony of nature with our cognitive power is presupposed a priori by judgment, as an aid in its reflection on nature in terms of empirical laws. For understanding acknowledges at the same time that this harmony is contingent objec-

185

---

[29] [Objects of experience insofar as their form is particular rather than universal.]

tively, and only judgment attributes it to nature as a transcendental purposiveness (in relation to the subject's cognitive power), since without presupposing this harmony we would have no order of nature in terms of empirical laws, and hence nothing to guide us in using empirical laws so as to experience and investigate nature in its diversity.

For it is quite conceivable that, regardless of all the uniformity of natural things in terms of the universal laws, without which the form of an empirical cognition in general would not occur at all, the specific differences in the empirical laws of nature, along with their effects, might still be so great that it would be impossible for our understanding to discover in nature an order it could grasp [*fassen*]— i.e., impossible for it to divide nature's products into genera and species, so as to use the principles by which we explain and understand one product in order to explain and grasp [*begreifen*] another as well, thereby making coherent experience out of material that to us is so full of confusion (though actually it is only infinitely diverse and beyond our ability to grasp [it]).

Hence judgment also possesses an a priori principle for the possibility of nature, but one that holds only for the subject, a principle by which judgment prescribes, not to nature (which would be autonomy) but to itself (which is heautonomy), a law for its reflection on nature. This law could be called the *law of the specification of nature* in terms of its empirical laws. It is a law that judgment does not cognize a priori in nature, but that, in dividing nature's universal laws, it assumes a priori when it seeks to subordinate to them a diversity of particular laws, so that the division will have an order that our understanding can cognize. So if we say that nature makes its universal laws specific in accordance with the principle of purposiveness for our cognitive power—i.e., in a way commensurate with the human understanding with its necessary task of finding the universal for the particular offered by perception, and of finding interconnection, under the unity of this principle, with regard to what is different [across species] (though universal within any one species)—then we are neither prescribing a law to nature, nor learning one from it by observation (although observation can confirm the mentioned principle). For it is a principle not of determinative but merely of reflective judgment. We insist only that, however nature may be arranged in terms of its universal laws, any search for its empirical laws should follow both this principle of purposiveness and the

186

maxims based on it, because only to the extent that this principle has application can we make progress in using our understanding in experience and arrive at cognition.

VI

On the Connection of the Feeling of Pleasure with the Concept of the Purposiveness of Nature

In thinking of nature as harmonizing, in the diversity of its particular laws, with our need to find universal principles [*Allgemeinheit der Prinzipien*] for them, we must, as far as our insight goes, judge this harmony as contingent, yet as also indispensable for the needs of our understanding—hence as a purposiveness by which nature harmonizes with our aim, though only insofar as this is directed to cognition. The universal laws of the understanding, which are at the same time laws of nature, are just as necessary for nature (even though they arise from spontaneity) as are the laws of motion regarding matter; and the generation of such natural laws does not presuppose [on nature's part] any aim concerning our cognitive powers, because only through such laws do we first get a concept of what a cognition of things (of nature) is, and because these laws belong necessarily to nature taken as object of our cognition in general. But it is contingent, as far as we can see, that the order of nature in terms of its particular laws should actually be commensurate with our ability to grasp [that order], despite all the diversity and heterogeneity by which such order at least might go beyond that ability. Moreover, the discovery of this order is an occupation of the understanding conducted with regard to a necessary purpose of its own—the unification of this order under principles. And hence it is judgment that must then attribute this purpose to nature, because the understanding cannot prescribe a law regarding this [unity] to nature.

187

The attainment of an aim [*Absicht*] is always connected with the feeling of pleasure; and if the condition of reaching the aim is an a priori presentation—as, in this case, it is a principle for reflective judgment as such—then [there is] a basis that determines the feeling of pleasure a priori and validly for everyone. And the feeling of pleasure is determined a priori and validly for everyone merely because we refer the object to the cognitive power; [for] in this case the concept of purposiveness does not in the least concern the power of desire and hence is quite distinct from any practical purposiveness of nature.

The facts bear out this connection. Now it is true that we do not find that the concurrence of our perceptions with the laws governed by universal concepts (the categories) has the slightest effect upon our feeling of pleasure; nor can there ever be any such effect, because the understanding proceeds with these [laws] unintentionally [*unabsichtlich*], by the necessity of its own nature. On the other hand, it is a fact that when we discover that two or more heterogeneous empirical laws of nature can be unified under one principle that comprises them both, the discovery does give rise to a quite noticeable pleasure, frequently even admiration, even an admiration that does not cease when we have become fairly familiar with its object. It is true that we no longer feel any noticeable pleasure resulting from our being able to grasp nature and the unity in its division into genera and species that alone makes possible the empirical concepts by means of which we cognize nature in terms of its particular laws. But this pleasure was no doubt there at one time, and it is only because even the commonest experience would be impossible without it that we have gradually come to mix it in with mere cognition and no longer take any special notice of it. So, if we are to feel pleasure in [response to] the harmony, which we regard as merely contingent, of nature's heterogeneous laws with our cognitive power, we need something that in our judging of nature makes us pay attention to this purposiveness of nature for our understanding—namely, an endeavor to bring, if possible, these heterogeneous laws under higher though still empirical laws, when this endeavor is met with success. By contrast, we would certainly dislike it if nature were presented in a way that told us in advance that if we investigated nature slightly beyond the commonest experience we would find its laws so heterogeneous that our understanding could not unify nature's particular laws

188

under universal empirical laws. For this would conflict with the principle of nature's subjectively purposive specification in its genera, and with the principle that our reflective judgment follows in dealing with nature.

Yet judgment's presupposition [about this unity] is so indeterminate regarding the extent of that ideal purposiveness of nature for our cognitive power that if we are told that a deeper or broadened knowledge of nature based on observation must ultimately meet with a diversity of laws that no human understanding can reduce to a single principle, then we will be content with that too. But we would still prefer to hear others offer hope that if we had deeper insight into nature, or could compare the nature [we know] more broadly with the parts of it we do not yet know, then we would find nature ever simpler as our experience progressed and ever more accordant despite the seeming heterogeneity in its empirical laws. For judgment bids us proceed in accordance with the principle of nature's being commensurate with our cognitive power, as far as that principle extends, without deciding whether this principle has any bounds (since that rule is not given us by a determinative power of judgment). For though we can determine what the bounds are for the rational use of our cognitive powers, we cannot do so in the empirical realm.

VII

On the Aesthetic Presentation of the Purposiveness of Nature

What is merely subjective in the presentation of an object, i.e., what constitutes its reference to the subject and not to the object, is its aesthetic[30] character; but whatever in it serves, or can be used, to determine the object (for cognition) is its logical validity. In the cognition of an object of sense these two references [to the subject and to the object] occur together. When the senses present things

189

---

[30] [From Greek αἰσθέσθαι (aisthésthai), 'to sense.']

outside me, the quality of the space in which these things are intuited is the merely subjective [feature] of my presentation of them (and because of this [feature] I cannot tell what such things may be as objects in themselves), and because of this subjective reference the object is moreover thought as merely appearance. But despite its merely subjective quality, space is still an element in our cognition of things as appearances. [Now the term] *sensation* (in this case, outer sensation) also stands for what is merely subjective in our presentations of things outside us, though in its proper meaning it stands for what is material (real) in them (that through which something existent is given),[31] just as [the term] space stands for the mere a priori form that enables us to intuit things; yet sensation is also required for cognition of objects outside us.

On the other hand, that subjective [feature] of a presentation *which cannot at all become an element of cognition* is the *pleasure* or *displeasure* connected with that presentation. For through this pleasure or displeasure I do not cognize anything in the object of the presentation, though it may certainly be the effect of some cognition. Now a thing's purposiveness, insofar as it is presented in the perception of the thing, is also not a characteristic of the object itself (for no such characteristic can be perceived), even though it can be inferred from a cognition of things. Therefore, the subjective [feature] of the presentation which cannot at all become an element of cognition is the purposiveness that precedes the cognition of an object[32] and that we connect directly with this presentation even if we are not seeking to use the presentation of the object for cognition. Therefore, in this case we call the object purposive only because its presentation is directly connected with the feeling of pleasure, and this presentation itself is an aesthetic presentation of purposiveness. The only question is whether there is such a presentation of purposiveness at all.

When pleasure is connected with mere apprehension (*apprehensio*) of the form of an object of intuition, and we do not refer the apprehension to a concept so as to give rise to determinate cognition, then we refer the presentation not to the object but solely to the subject; and the pleasure cannot express anything other than the object's being commensurate with the cognitive powers that are, and insofar

[31] [Cf. the *Metaphysical Foundations of Natural Science*, Ak. IV, 481.]

[32] [I.e., the purposiveness that we present in mere *intuition*.]

190   as they are, brought into play when we judge reflectively, and hence [expresses] merely a subjective formal purposiveness of the object. For this apprehension of forms by the imagination could never occur if reflective judgment did not compare them, even if unintentionally, at least with its ability [in general] to refer intuitions to concepts. Now if in this comparison a given presentation unintentionally brings the imagination (the power of a priori intuitions) into harmony with the understanding (the power of concepts), and this harmony arouses a feeling of pleasure, then the object must thereupon be regarded as purposive for the reflective power of judgment. A judgment of this sort is an aesthetic judgment about the object's purposiveness; it is not based on any concept we have of the object, nor does it provide such a concept. When the form of an object (rather than what is material in its presentation, viz., in sensation) is judged in mere reflection on it (without regard to a concept that is to be acquired from it) to be the basis of a pleasure in such an object's presentation, then the presentation of this object is also judged to be connected necessarily with this pleasure, and hence connected with it not merely for the subject apprehending this form but in general for everyone who judges [it]. The object is then called beautiful, and our ability to judge by such a pleasure (and hence also with universal validity) is called taste. For the basis of the pleasure is posited merely in the form of the object for reflection in general, and hence not in a sensation of the object, nor with a reference to any concept that might involve some intention or other. Therefore, the harmony we are dealing with is only a harmony in reflection, whose a priori conditions are valid universally, between the presentation of the object and the lawfulness [inherent] in the empirical use in general of the subject's power of judgment (this lawfulness being the unity between imagination and understanding). And since this harmony of the object with the powers of the subject is contingent, it brings about the presentation of a purposiveness of the object with regard to the subject's cognitive powers.

Here then is a pleasure that, like any pleasure or displeasure that is not brought about by the concept of freedom (i.e., by the prior determination of the higher power of desire by pure reason), we cannot possibly gain insight into by means of concepts, as necessarily connected with the presentation of an object, but is a pleasure that
191   must always be recognized only through a perception upon which we

reflect [and] that must be recognized as connected with the perception. Hence [a judgment of taste, which involves] this pleasure[,] is like any empirical judgment because it cannot proclaim objective necessity or lay claim to a priori validity; but, like any other empirical judgment, a judgment of taste claims only to be valid for everyone, and it is always possible for such a judgment to be valid for everyone despite its intrinsic contingency. What is strange and different about a judgment of taste is only this: that what is to be connected with the presentation of the object is not an empirical concept but a feeling of pleasure (hence no concept at all), though, just as if it were a predicate connected with cognition of the object, this feeling is nevertheless to be required of everyone.

A singular empirical judgment, e.g., the judgment made by someone who perceives a mobile drop of water in a rock crystal, rightly demands that anyone else must concur with its finding, because the judgment was made in accordance with the universal conditions of the determinative power of judgment under the laws of a possible experience in general. In the same way, someone who feels pleasure in the mere reflection on the form of an object, without any concern about a concept, rightly lays claim to everyone's assent, even though this judgment is empirical and a singular judgment. For the basis of this pleasure is found in the universal, though subjective, condition of reflective judgments, namely, the purposive harmony of an object (whether a product of nature or of art) with the mutual relation of the cognitive powers (imagination and understanding) that are required for every empirical cognition. Hence the pleasure in a judgment of taste is indeed dependent on an empirical presentation and cannot be connected a priori with any concept (we cannot determine a priori what object will or will not conform to taste; we must try it out); but the pleasure is still the basis determining this judgment, solely because we are aware that it rests merely on reflection and the universal though only subjective conditions of the harmony of that reflection with the cognition of objects generally, the harmony for which the form of the object is purposive.

That is why judgments of taste, since their possibility presupposes an a priori principle, are also subject to a critique concerning their possibility, even though that principle is neither a cognitive principle for the understanding, nor a practical one for the will, and hence is not at all determinative a priori.

192

But our receptivity to a pleasure arising from our reflection on the forms of things (both of nature and of art) does not always indicate a purposiveness of objects in relation to the subject's reflective power of judgment, in accordance with the concept of nature; sometimes, on the contrary, it indicates a purposiveness of the subject with regard to objects in terms of their form, or even their lack of form, in conformity with the concept of freedom. And this is why not all aesthetic judgments are judgments of taste, which as such refer to the beautiful; but some of them arise from an intellectual feeling and as such refer to the *sublime,* so that this Critique of Aesthetic Judgment must be divided into two main parts corresponding to these.

VIII

On the Logical Presentation of the Purposiveness of Nature

When an object is given in experience, there are two ways in which we can present purposiveness in it. We can present it on a merely subjective basis: as the harmony of the form of the object (the form that is [manifested] in the *apprehension* (*apprehensio*) of the object prior to any concept)[33] with the cognitive powers—i.e., the harmony required in general to unite an intuition with concepts so as to produce a cognition. But we can also present it on an objective basis: as the harmony of the form of the object with the possibility of the thing itself according to a prior concept of the thing that contains the basis of that form. We have seen that the presentation of the first kind of purposiveness rests on the pleasure we take directly in the form of the object when we merely reflect on it. Since the presentation of the second kind of purposiveness does not refer the object's form, in its apprehension, to the subject's cognitive powers, but instead to a determinate cognition of the object under a given concept, the presentation of this purposiveness has nothing to do with a feeling of

[33] [Outer parentheses added.]

pleasure in things but rather with the understanding in our judging of them. When the concept of an object is given and we use it for cognition, the task of judgment is to *exhibit* (*exhibere*) the concept, i.e., to place beside the concept an intuition corresponding to it.[34] Exhibition may occur by means of our own imagination, as happens in art, where a concept which we have already formed of an object that is a purpose for us is made real. Or it may come about by nature, through its technic[35] (as in the case of organized bodies), where we attribute to nature our concept of a purpose in order to judge its product; in that case we present not just a *purposiveness* of nature in the form of the thing, but present the product itself as a *natural purpose*. Although our concept of a subjective purposiveness [manifested] in nature's forms in terms of empirical laws is not at all a concept of the object, but is only a principle of judgment by which it provides itself with concepts in nature's immense diversity (so that judgment can orient itself in this diversity), we are still attributing to nature, on the analogy of a purpose, a concern, as it were, for our cognitive power. Hence we may regard *natural beauty* as the *exhibition* of the concept of formal (merely subjective) purposiveness, and may regard *natural purposes* as the exhibition of the concept of a real (objective) purposiveness, the first of which we judge by taste (aesthetically, by means of the feeling of pleasure), and the second by understanding and reason (logically, according to concepts).

This is the basis for dividing the critique of judgment into that of *aesthetic* and that of *teleological* judgment. By the first I mean the power to judge formal purposiveness (sometimes also called subjective purposiveness) by the feeling of pleasure or displeasure; by the second I mean the power to judge the real (objective) purposiveness of nature by understanding and reason.

In a critique of judgment, the part that deals with aesthetic judgment belongs to it essentially. For this power alone contains a principle that judgment lays completely a priori at the basis of its reflection on nature: the principle of a formal purposiveness of nature, in terms of its particular (empirical) laws, for our cognitive power, without

193

---

[34] [Cf. Ak. 232 br. n. 51.]

[35] [In §72, Kant characterizes the technic of nature as "nature's power to produce [things] in terms of purposes" (Ak. 390–91). The term is derived from the Greek τέχνη (téchnē), i.e., 'art' in the sense that includes craft.]

which principle the understanding could not find its way about in nature. By contrast, we cannot indicate any a priori basis whatever [for saying] that there must be objective purposes in nature, i.e., things possible only as natural purposes; indeed, the concept of nature as object of experience, whether in its universal or in its particular [aspects], does not tell us that such a basis is even possible. Rather, judgment, without containing a priori a principle for such [objective purposiveness], merely contains the rule for using the concept of purposes for the sake of reason when cases (certain products) occur, after the former transcendental principle [of the formal purposiveness of nature] has already prepared the understanding to apply the concept of a purpose (at least in terms of form) to nature.

194

But as a principle for judging the form of a thing, the transcendental principle of presenting in the form a purposiveness of nature, with regard to the subject and his cognitive power, leaves it wholly undetermined where and in what cases when judging a product I am [to regard the product as having arisen] in accordance with a principle of purposiveness rather than merely in accordance with universal natural laws; the principle leaves it to *aesthetic* judgment to ascertain by taste whether the thing (its form) is commensurate with our cognitive powers (as far as judgment decides by feeling rather than by a harmony with concepts). On the other hand, when judgment is used teleologically, it indicates determinately the conditions under which something (e.g., an organized body) is to be judged in terms of the idea of a purpose of nature; but judgment cannot adduce a principle [derived] from the concept of nature, taken as object of experience, authorizing it to assert a priori that nature [makes products] by reference to purposes, or authorizing it even to assume in an indeterminate way that actual experience will manifest anything of the sort in such products. The reason for this is that, in order for us to cognize only empirically that a certain object has objective purposiveness, we would have to engage in many particular experiences and examine them under the principle that unites them. Hence aesthetic judgment is a special power of judging things according to a rule, but not according to concepts. Teleological judgment is not a special power, but is only reflective judgment as such proceeding according to concepts (as it always does in theoretical cognition),[36]

---

[36] [Parentheses added.]

but proceeding, in the case of certain natural objects, according to special principles, namely, according to principles of a power of judgment that merely reflects upon but does not determine objects. Hence, as regards its application, teleological judgment belongs to the theoretical part of philosophy; because of its special principles, which are not determinative (as would be required in a doctrine),[37] it must also form a special part of the critique. Aesthetic judgment, on the other hand, contributes nothing to the cognition of its objects; hence it belongs *only* to the critique that is the propaedeutic to all philosophy—viz., to the critique of the judging subject and his cognitive powers insofar as these are capable of [having] a priori principles, no matter what their use may be (theoretical or practical).

IX

How Judgment Connects
the Legislations
of the Understanding
and of Reason

The understanding legislates a priori for nature, as object of sense, in order to give rise to theoretical cognition of nature in a possible experience. Reason legislates a priori for freedom and for freedom's own causality, in other words, for the supersensible in the subject, in order to give rise to unconditioned practical cognition. The great gulf that separates the supersensible from appearances completely cuts off the domain of the concept of nature under the one legislation, and the domain of the concept of freedom under the other legislation, from any influence that each (according to its own basic laws) might have had on the other. The concept of freedom determines nothing with regard to our theoretical cognition of nature, just as the concept of nature determines nothing with regard to the practical laws of

---

[37] [Parentheses added.]

freedom; and to this extent it is not possible to throw a bridge from one domain to the other. And yet, even though the bases that determine the causality governed by the concept of freedom (and by the practical rule contained in this concept) do not lie in nature, and even though the sensible cannot determine the supersensible in the subject, yet the reverse is possible (not, indeed, with regard to our cognition of nature, but still with regard to the consequences that the concept of freedom has in nature); and this possibility[38] is contained in the very concept of a causality through freedom, whose *effect* is to be brought about in the world [but] in conformity with formal laws of freedom. It is true that when we use the word *cause* with regard to the supersensible, we mean only the *basis* that determines natural things to exercise their causality to produce an effect in conformity with the natural laws proper to that causality, yet in accordance with the formal principle of the laws of reason as well. Though we have no insight into how this is possible, the objection that alleges a contradiction in it can be refuted adequately.[39] The effect [at which we are to aim] according to the concept of freedom is the final purpose which (or the appearance of which in the world of sense) ought to exist; and we [must] presuppose the condition under which it is possible [to achieve] this final purpose in nature (in the nature of the subject as a being of sense, namely, as a human being). It is judgment that presupposes this condition a priori, and without regard to the practical, [so that] this power provides us with the concept that mediates between the concepts of nature and the concept of freedom: the concept of a

196

[38] [Of the supersensible's (i.e., freedom's) determining the sensible (nature).]

196

[39] One of the various supposed contradictions in this complete distinction of natural causality from the causality through freedom is given in the following objection to it. It is held that when I talk about nature putting *obstacles* in the way of the causality governed by laws of freedom (moral laws), or about nature *furthering* it, I do after all grant that nature *influences* freedom. But this is a misinterpretation, which is easily avoided merely by understanding what I have said. The resistance or furtherance is not between nature and freedom, but between nature as appearance and the *effects* of freedom as appearances in the world of sense; and even the *causality* of freedom (of pure and practical reason) is the *causality* of a natural cause (the subject, regarded as a human being and hence as an appearance) subject to [the laws of] nature. It is this causality's *determination* whose basis is contained, in a way not otherwise explicable, in the intelligible that is thought of when we think freedom (just as in the case of the intelligible that is the supersensible substrate of nature).

purposiveness of nature, which makes possible the transition[40] from pure theoretical to pure practical lawfulness, from lawfulness in terms of nature to the final purpose set by the concept of freedom. For it is through this concept that we cognize the possibility of [achieving] the final purpose, which can be actualized only in nature and in accordance with its laws.

The understanding, inasmuch as it can give laws to nature a priori, proves that we cognize nature only as appearance, and hence at the same time points to a supersensible substrate of nature; but it leaves this substrate wholly *undetermined.* Judgment, through its a priori principle of judging nature in terms of possible particular laws of nature, provides nature's supersensible substrate (within as well as outside us) with *determinability*[41] *by the intellectual power.* But reason, through its a priori practical law, gives this same substrate *determination.* Thus judgment makes possible the transition from the domain of the concept of nature to that of the concept of freedom.

Regarding the powers of the soul in general, insofar as they are considered as higher ones, i.e., as powers that have autonomy, [the following can be said]: for the power of *cognition* (theoretical cognition of nature), the *constitutive* a priori principles lie in the understanding; for the *feeling of pleasure and displeasure,* they lie in judgment, [as far as it is] independent of concepts and sensations, which might have to do with determining the power of desire and hence be directly practical; for the *power of desire,* they lie in reason, which is practical without the mediation of any pleasure whatsoever, regardless of origin, and which determines for this power, insofar as it is the higher power of desire, the final purpose that also carries with it pure intellectual liking for its object. Judgment's concept of a purposiveness of nature still belongs to the concepts of nature, but only as a regulative principle of the cognitive power, even though the aesthetic judgment about certain objects (of nature or of art) that prompts this concept of purposiveness is a constitutive principle with regard to the feeling of pleasure or displeasure. The spontaneity in the play of the cognitive powers, whose harmony with each other

197

---

[40] [On this "transition" and "mediation," see the Translator's Introduction, *lxiv* and *xcvii–cii.*]

[41] [This point is closely related to the mediation and transition just mentioned. See the references in n. 40.]

contains the basis of this pleasure, makes that concept of purposiveness suitable[42] for mediating the connection of the domain of the concept of nature with that of the concept of freedom, as regards freedom's consequences, inasmuch as this harmony also promotes the mind's receptivity to moral feeling. The following table may facilitate an overview of all the higher powers in their systematic unity.[43]

198

All the Mental Powers	Cognitive Powers	A Priori Principles	Application to
cognitive power	understanding	lawfulness	nature
feeling of pleasure and displeasure	judgment	purposiveness	art
power of desire	reason	final purpose	freedom

[42] [On why this is so, see "Problem III" in the Translator's Introduction, *lxiv* and *cii–civ*.]

[43] That my divisions in pure philosophy almost always turn out tripartite has aroused suspicion. Yet that is in the nature of the case. If a division is to be made a priori, then it will be either *analytic* or *synthetic*. If it is analytic, then it is governed by the principle of contradiction and hence is always bipartite (*quodlibet ens est aut A aut non A*[44]). If it is synthetic, but is to be made on the basis of a priori *concepts* (rather than, as in mathematics, on the basis of the *intuition* corresponding a priori to the concept), then we must have what is required for a synthetic unity in general, namely, (1) a condition, (2) something conditioned, (3) the concept that arises from the union of the conditioned with its condition; hence the division must of necessity be a trichotomy.

[44] [Any entity is either A or not A.]

Division of the Entire Work   199

---

[45] [There can be no methodology concerning taste, and this appendix explains why that is so: § 60, Ak. 354–56.]

PART I

CRITIQUE OF
AESTHETIC JUDGMENT

DIVISION I

ANALYTIC OF
AESTHETIC JUDGMENT

BOOK I

ANALYTIC OF
THE BEAUTIFUL

First Moment
of a Judgment of Taste,[1]
As to Its Quality

---

[1] The definition of taste on which I am basing this [analysis] is that it is the ability to judge the beautiful. But we have to analyze judgments of taste in order to discover what is required for calling an object beautiful. I have used the logical functions of judging[2] to help me find the moments that judgment[3] takes into consideration when it reflects (since even a judgment of taste still has reference to the understanding). I have examined the moment of quality first, because an aesthetic judgment about the beautiful is concerned with it first.

[2] [They fall under four headings: quantity, quality, relation, modality. See the *Critique of Pure Reason*, A 70 = B 95.]

[3] [*Urteilskraft*, in this case. Cf. above, Ak. 167 br. n. 4.]

§ 1

A Judgment of
Taste Is Aesthetic

If we wish to decide whether something is beautiful or not, we do not use understanding to refer the presentation[4] to the object so as to give rise to cognition;[5] rather, we use imagination (perhaps in connection with understanding) to refer the presentation to the subject and his feeling of pleasure or displeasure. Hence a judgment of taste is not a cognitive judgment and so is not a logical judgment but an aesthetic one, by which we mean a judgment whose determining basis *cannot be other* than *subjective*. But any reference of presentations, even of sensations, can be objective (in which case it signifies what is real [rather than formal] in an empirical presentation); excepted is a reference to the feeling of pleasure and displeasure— this reference designates nothing whatsoever in the object, but here the subject feels himself, [namely] how he is affected by the presentation.

204

To apprehend a regular, purposive building with one's cognitive power[6] (whether the presentation is distinct or confused) is very different from being conscious of this presentation with a sensation of liking. Here the presentation is referred only to the subject, namely, to his feeling of life, under the name feeling of pleasure or displeasure, and this forms the basis of a very special power of discriminating and judging.[7] This power does not contribute anything to cognition, but merely compares the given presentation in the subject with the entire presentational power, of which the mind becomes conscious when it feels its own state. The presentations given in a judgment may be

---

[4] [*Vorstellung*, traditionally rendered as 'representation.' (See above, Ak. 175 br. n. 17.) 'Presentation' is a generic term referring to such objects of our direct awareness as sensations, intuitions, perceptions, concepts, cognitions, ideas, and schemata. Cf. the *Critique of Pure Reason,* A 320 = B 376–77 and A 140 = B 179.]

[5] [*Erkenntnis*. Cf. above, Ak. 167 br. n. 2.]

[6] [For my use of 'power,' rather than 'faculty,' see above, Ak. 167 br. n. 3.]

[7] [*Beurteilung*. On Kant's attempt to make a terminological distinction between '*beurteilen*' and '*urteilen*,' see above, Ak. 169 br. n. 9.]

empirical (and hence aesthetic[8]), but if we refer them to the object, the judgment we make by means of them is logical. On the other hand, even if the given presentations were rational, they would still be aesthetic if, and to the extent that, the subject referred them, in his judgment, solely to himself (to his feeling).

§ 2

The Liking That Determines a Judgment of Taste Is Devoid of All Interest

Interest is what we call the liking we connect with the presentation of an object's existence. Hence such a liking always refers at once to our power of desire, either as the basis that determines it, or at any rate as necessarily connected with that determining basis. But if the question is whether something is beautiful, what we want to know is not whether we or anyone cares, or so much as might care, in any way, about the thing's existence, but rather how we judge it in our mere contemplation of it (intuition or reflection). Suppose someone asks me whether I consider the palace I see before me beautiful. I might reply that I am not fond of things of that sort, made merely to be gaped at. Or I might reply like that Iroquois *sachem* who said that he liked nothing better in Paris than the eating-houses.[9] I might even

---

[8] [From Greek αἰσθέθαι (aisthésthai), 'to sense.']

[9] [Wilhelm Windelband, editor of the *Akademie* edition of the *Critique of Judgment*, notes (Ak. V, 527) that Kant's reference has been traced to (Pierre-Francois-Xavier de) Charlevoix (1682–1761, French Jesuit traveler and historian), *Histoire et déscription générale de la Nouvelle-France* (*History and General Description of New France* [in eastern Canada]) (Paris, 1744). Windelband quotes a passage (from III, 322) in French, which translates: "Some Iroquois went to Paris in 1666 and were shown all the royal mansions and all the beauties of that great city. But they did not admire anything in these, and would have preferred the villages to the capital of the most flourishing kingdom of Europe if they had not seen the *rue de la Huchette* where they were delighted with the rotisseries that they always found furnished with meats of all sorts." (All translations given in footnotes are my own, and this fact is not indicated in each such footnote individually.)]

205

go on, as *Rousseau* would, to rebuke the vanity of the great who spend the people's sweat on such superfluous things. I might, finally, quite easily convince myself that, if I were on some uninhabited island with no hope of ever again coming among people, and could conjure up such a splendid edifice by a mere wish, I would not even take that much trouble for it if I already had a sufficiently comfortable hut. The questioner may grant all this and approve of it; but it is not to the point. All he wants to know is whether my mere presentation of the object is accompanied by a liking, no matter how indifferent I may be about the existence of the object of this presentation. We can easily see that, in order for me to say that an object is *beautiful,* and to prove that I have taste, what matters is what I do with this presentation within myself, and not the [respect] in which I depend on the object's existence. Everyone has to admit that if a judgment about beauty is mingled with the least interest then it is very partial and not a pure judgment of taste. In order to play the judge in matters of taste, we must not be in the least biased in favor of the thing's existence but must be wholly indifferent about it.

There is no better way to elucidate this proposition, which is of prime importance, than by contrasting the pure disinterested[10] liking that occurs in a judgment of taste with a liking connected with interest, especially if we can also be certain that the kinds of interest I am about to mention are the only ones there are.

[10] A judgment we make about an object of our liking may be wholly *disinterested* but still very *interesting,* i.e., it is not based on any interest but it gives rise to an interest; all pure moral judgments are of this sort. But judgments of taste, of themselves, do not even give rise to any interest. Only in society does it become *interesting* to have taste; the reason for this will be indicated later.[11]

[11] [See esp. Ak. 275–76 and 296–98.]

§ 3

A Liking *for the Agreeable*
Is Connected with Interest

AGREEABLE *is what the senses like in sensation.* Here the opportunity arises at once to censure and call attention to a quite common confusion of the two meanings that the word sensation can have. All liking (so it is said or thought) is itself sensation (of a pleasure). Hence whatever is liked, precisely inasmuch as it is liked, is agreeable (and, depending on the varying degrees or on the relation to other agreeable sensations, it is *graceful, lovely, delightful, gladdening, etc.*). But if we concede this, then sense impressions that determine inclination, or principles of reason that determine the will, or mere forms of intuition that we reflect on [and] that determine the power of judgment, will all be one and the same insofar as their effect on the feeling of pleasure is concerned, since pleasure would be the agreeableness [found] in the sensation of one's state. And since, after all, everything we do with our powers must in the end aim at the practical and unite in it as its goal, we could not require them to estimate things and their value in any other way than by the gratification they promise; how they provided it would not matter at all in the end. And since all that could make a difference in that promised gratification would be what means we select, people could no longer blame one another for baseness and malice, but only for foolishness and ignorance, since all of them, each according to his own way of viewing things, would be pursuing one and the same goal: gratification.

206

When [something determines the feeling of pleasure or displeasure and this] determination of that feeling is called sensation, this term means something quite different from what it means when I apply it to the presentation of a thing (through the senses, a receptivity that belongs to the cognitive power). For in the second case the presentation is referred to the object, but in the first it is referred solely to the subject and is not used for cognition at all, not even for that by which the subject *cognizes* himself.

As I have just explicated it [i.e., for the second case], the word sensation means an objective presentation of sense; and, to avoid constantly running the risk of being misinterpreted, let us call what must always remain merely subjective, and cannot possibly be the presentation of an object, by its other customary name: feeling.[12] The green color of meadows belongs to *objective* sensation, i.e., to the perception of an object of sense; but the color's agreeableness belongs to *subjective* sensation, to feeling, through which no object is presented, but through which the object is regarded as an object of our liking (which is not a cognition of it).

207

Now, that a judgment by which I declare an object to be agreeable expresses an interest in that object is already obvious from the fact that, by means of sensation, the judgment arouses a desire for objects of that kind, so that the liking presupposes something other than my mere judgment about the object: it presupposes that I have referred the existence of the object to my state insofar as that state is affected by such an object. This is why we say of the agreeable not merely that we *like* it but that it *gratifies* us. When I speak of the agreeable, I am not granting mere approval: the agreeable produces an inclination. Indeed, what is agreeable in the liveliest way requires no judgment at all about the character of the object, as we can see in people who aim at nothing but enjoyment (this is the word we use to mark the intensity of the gratification): they like to dispense with all judging.

§ 4

A Liking *for the Good* Is Connected with Interest[13]

Good is what, by means of reason, we like through its mere concept. We call something (viz., if it is something useful) *good for* [this or that] if we like it only as a means. But we call something *intrinsically good* if we like it for its own sake. In both senses of the term, the good always

---

[12] [Kant does not, however, consistently adhere to this stipulation, and the inconsistency has been left intact in the translation.]

[13] [Cf., in this section, the *Critique of Practical Reason,* Ak. V, 22–26.]

contains the concept of a purpose, consequently a relation of reason to a volition (that is at least possible), and hence a liking for the existence of an object or action. In other words, it contains some interest or other.

In order to consider something good, I must always know what sort of thing the object is [meant] to be, i.e., I must have a [determinate] concept of it. But I do not need this in order to find beauty in something. Flowers, free designs, lines aimlessly intertwined and called foliage: these have no significance, depend on no determinate concept, and yet we like [*gefallen*] them. A liking [*Wohlgefallen*[14]] for the beautiful must depend on the reflection, regarding an object, that leads to some concept or other (but it is indeterminate which concept this is). This dependence on reflection also distinguishes the liking for the beautiful from [that for] the agreeable, which rests entirely on sensation.

It is true that in many cases it seems as if the agreeable and the good are one and the same. Thus people commonly say that all gratification (especially if it lasts) is intrinsically good, which means roughly the same as to be (lastingly) agreeable and to be good are one and the same. Yet it is easy to see that in talking this way they are merely substituting one word for another by mistake, since the concepts that belong to these terms are in no way interchangeable. Insofar as we present an object as agreeable, we present it solely in relation to sense; but if we are to call the object good [as well], and hence an object of the will, we must first bring it under principles of reason, using the concept of a purpose. [So] if something that gratifies us is also called *good,* it has a very different relation to our liking. This is [also] evident from the fact that in the case of the good there is always the question whether it is good merely indirectly or good directly[15] (i.e., useful, or intrinsically good), whereas in the case of the agreeable

208

---

[14] [The only noun Kant had for the verb '*gefallen*' ('to be liked') was '*Wohlgefallen*,' and '*wohl*' does not add anything. Grammar aside, Kant uses the two interchangeably. Moreover, he uses them just as much concerning the good and the agreeable as concerning the beautiful, and what is special about the liking for the beautiful lies in what else Kant says about it, not in the word '*Wohlgefallen*' itself.]

[15] ['*Mittelbar*,' '*unmittelbar*.' The more literal rendering of these as 'mediately' and 'immediately' has been avoided in this translation because 'immediately' has also its temporal sense, which would frequently be misleading.]

this question cannot even arise, since this word always signifies something that we like directly. (What we call beautiful is also liked directly.)

Even in our most ordinary speech we distinguish the agreeable from the good. If a dish stimulates [*erheben*] our tasting by its spices and other condiments, we will not hesitate to call it agreeable while granting at the same time that it is not good; for while the dish is directly *appealing* to our senses, we dislike it indirectly, i.e., as considered by reason, which looks ahead to the consequences. Even when we judge health, this difference is still noticeable. To anyone who has it, health is directly agreeable (at least negatively, as the absence of all bodily pain). But in order to say that health is good, we must also use reason and direct this health toward purposes: we must say that health is a state that disposes us to [attend to] all our tasks. [Perhaps in the case of happiness, at least, the agreeable and the good are the same?] Surely everyone believes that happiness, the greatest sum (in number as well as duration) of what is agreeable in life, may be called a true good, indeed the highest good[?] And yet reason balks at this too. Agreeableness is enjoyment. But if our sole aim were enjoyment, it would be foolish to be scrupulous about the means for getting it, [i.e.,] about whether we got it passively, from nature's bounty, or through our own activity and our own doing. But reason can never be persuaded that there is any intrinsic value in the existence of a human being who lives merely for *enjoyment* (no matter how industrious he may be in pursuing that aim), even if he served others, all likewise aiming only at enjoyment, as a most efficient means to it because he participated in their gratification by enjoying it through sympathy. Only by what he does without concern for enjoyment, in complete freedom and independently of whatever he could also receive passively from nature, does he give his existence [*Dasein*] an absolute value, as the existence [*Existenz*[16]] of a person. Happiness, with all its abundance of agreeableness, is far from being an unconditioned good.[17]

209

[16] [In the *Critique of Judgment* Kant uses '*Dasein*' and '*Existenz*' synonymously, and they will both be rendered as 'existence.' Moreover, rendering '*Dasein*' as '*being*' or *Being*' leads to serious trouble in the contexts where Kant also refers to the original being (*Wesen*); see esp. Ak. 475.]

[17] An obligation to enjoy oneself is a manifest absurdity. So, consequently, must be an alleged obligation to any acts that aim merely at enjoyment, no matter how intellectually subtle (or veiled) that enjoyment may be, indeed, even if it were a mystical, so-called heavenly, enjoyment.

But despite all this difference between the agreeable and the good, they do agree in this: they are always connected with an interest in their object. This holds not only for the agreeable—see § 3—and for what is good indirectly (useful), which we like as the means to something or other that is agreeable, but also for what is good absolutely and in every respect, i.e., the moral good, which carries with it the highest interest. For the good is the object of the will (a power of desire that is determined by reason). But to will something and to have a liking for its existence, i.e., to take an interest in it, are identical.

§ 5

Comparison of the Three Sorts of Liking, Which Differ in Kind

Both the agreeable and the good refer to our power of desire and hence carry a liking with them, the agreeable a liking that is conditioned pathologically by stimuli (*stimuli*), the good a pure practical liking that is determined not just by the presentation of the object but also by the presentation of the subject's connection with the existence of the object; i.e., what we like is not just the object but its existence as well. A judgment of taste, on the other hand, is merely *contemplative,* i.e., it is a judgment that is indifferent to the existence of the object:[18] it [considers] the character of the object only by holding it up to[19] our feeling of pleasure and displeasure. Nor is this contemplation, as such, directed to concepts, for a judgment of taste is not a cognitive judgment (whether theoretical or practical) and hence is neither *based* on concepts, nor directed to them as *purposes*.

---

[18] [Cf. the *Metaphysics of Morals*, Ak. VI, 212.]

[19] [For comparison: i.e., the feeling, as we shall see shortly (Ak. 222), is a nonconceptual awareness of a harmony (with a certain indeterminate form) between imagination and understanding; in an aesthetic judgment of reflection we hold, for comparison, a *given* form up to the form of that harmony.]

210

Hence the agreeable, the beautiful, and the good designate three different relations that presentations have to the feeling of pleasure and displeasure, the feeling by reference to which we distinguish between objects or between ways of presenting them. The terms of approbation which are appropriate to each of these three are also different. We call *agreeable* what GRATIFIES us, *beautiful* what we just LIKE, *good* what we ESTEEM, or *endorse* [*billigen*], i.e., that to which we attribute [*setzen*] an objective value. Agreeableness holds for nonrational animals too; beauty only for human beings, i.e., beings who are animal and yet rational, though it is not enough that they be rational (e.g., spirits) but they must be animal as well; the good, however, holds for every rational being as such, though I cannot fully justify and explain this proposition until later. We may say that, of all these three kinds of liking, only the liking involved in taste for the beautiful is disinterested and *free,* since we are not compelled to give our approval by any interest, whether of sense or of reason. So we might say that [the term] liking, in the three cases mentioned, refers to *inclination,* or to *favor,* or to *respect.* For FAVOR is the only free liking. Neither an object of inclination, nor one that a law of reason enjoins on us as an object of desire, leaves us the freedom to make an object of pleasure for ourselves out of something or other. All interest either presupposes a need or gives rise to one; and, because interest is the basis that determines approval, it makes the judgment about the object unfree.

Consider, first, the interest of inclination, [which occurs] with the agreeable. Here everyone says: Hunger is the best sauce; and to people with a healthy appetite anything is tasty provided it is edible. Hence if people have a liking of this sort, that does not prove that they are selecting [*Wahl*] by taste. Only when their need has been satisfied can we tell who in a multitude of people has taste and who does not. In the same way, second, one can find manners (*conduite*) without virtue, politeness without benevolence, propriety without integrity, and so on.[20] For where the moral law speaks we are objectively no longer free to select what we must do; and to show taste in our conduct (or in judging other people's conduct) is very

[20] [I.e., taste, which is free, can manifest itself in manners, politeness, and propriety only where virtue, benevolence, and integrity, with the moral interest they involve, are absent.]

different from expressing our moral way of thinking. For this contains a command and gives rise to a need, whereas moral taste[21] only plays with the objects of liking without committing itself to any of them.

Explication of the Beautiful
Inferred from
the First Moment

211

Taste is the ability to judge an object, or a way of presenting it, by means of a liking or disliking *devoid of all interest*. The object of such a liking is called *beautiful*.

Second Moment
of a Judgment of Taste,
As to Its Quantity

§ 6

The Beautiful Is
What Is Presented
without Concepts as the Object
of a *Universal* Liking

This explication of the beautiful can be inferred from the preceding explication of it as object of a liking devoid of all interest. For if

---

[21] [As displayed in one's conduct: in manners, politeness, or propriety.]

someone likes something and is conscious that he himself does so without any interest, then he cannot help judging that it must contain a basis for being liked [that holds] for everyone. He must believe that he is justified in requiring a similar liking from everyone because he cannot discover, underlying this liking, any private conditions, on which only he might be dependent, so that he must regard it as based on what he can presuppose in everyone else as well. He cannot discover such private conditions because his liking is not based on any inclination he has (nor on any other considered interest whatever): rather, the judging person feels completely *free* as regards the liking he accords the object. Hence he will talk about the beautiful as if beauty were a characteristic of the object and the judgment were logical (namely, a cognition of the object through concepts of it), even though in fact the judgment is only aesthetic and refers the object's presentation merely to the subject. He will talk in this way because the judgment does resemble a logical judgment inasmuch as we may presuppose it to be valid for everyone. On the other hand, this universality cannot arise from concepts. For from concepts there is no transition to the feeling of pleasure or displeasure (except in pure practical laws; but these carry an interest with them, while 212 none is connected with pure judgments of taste). It follows that, since a judgment of taste involves the consciousness that all interest is kept out of it, it must also involve a claim to being valid for everyone, but without having a universality based on concepts. In other words, a judgment of taste must involve a claim to subjective universality.

§ 7

Comparison of the Beautiful
with the Agreeable
and the Good
in Terms of the
Above Characteristic

As regards the *agreeable* everyone acknowledges that his judgment, which he bases on a private feeling and by which he says that he likes some object, is by the same token confined to his own person. Hence, if he says that canary wine is agreeable he is quite content if someone else corrects his terms and reminds him to say instead: It is agreeable to *me*. This holds moreover not only for the taste of the tongue, palate, and throat, but also for what may be agreeable to any one's eyes and ears. To one person the color violet is gentle and lovely, to another lifeless and faded. One person loves the sound of wind instruments, another that of string instruments.[22] It would be foolish if we disputed about such differences with the intention of censuring another's judgment as incorrect if it differs from ours, as if the two were opposed logically. Hence about the agreeable the following principle holds: *Everyone has his own taste* (of sense[23]).

It is quite different (exactly the other way round) with the beautiful. It would be ridiculous if someone who prided himself on his taste tried to justify [it] by saying: This object (the building we are looking at, the garment that man is wearing, the concert we are listening to, the poem put up to be judged) is beautiful *for me*. For he must not call it *beautiful* if [he means] only [that] *he*[24] likes it. Many things may be charming and agreeable to him; no one cares about that. But if he proclaims something to be beautiful, then he requires the same liking from others; he then judges not just for himself but for everyone,

---

[22] [For an elaborate discussion of our different senses, see the *Anthropology*, §§ 15–27, Ak. VII, 153–67.]

[23] [As distinguished from taste of reflection.]

[24] [Emphasis added.]

and speaks of beauty as if it were a property of things. That is why he says: The *thing* is beautiful, and does not count on other people to agree with his judgment of liking on the ground that he has repeatedly found them agreeing with him; rather, he *demands* that they agree. He reproaches them if they judge differently, and denies that they have taste, which he nevertheless demands of them, as something they ought to have. In view of this [*sofern*] we cannot say that everyone has his own particular taste. That would amount to saying that there is no such thing as taste at all, no aesthetic judgment that could rightfully lay claim to everyone's assent.

And yet, even about the agreeable we can find people standing in agreement, and because of this we do, after all, deny that some people have taste while granting it to others; in speaking of taste here we do not mean the sense of taste, which involves an organ, but an ability to judge the agreeable in general. Thus we will say that someone has taste if he knows how to entertain his guests [at a party] with agreeable things (that they can enjoy by all the senses) in such a way that everyone likes [the party]. But here it is understood that the universality is only comparative, so that the rules are only *general* (as all empirical rules are), not *universal,* as are the rules that a judgment about the beautiful presupposes [*sich unternehmen*] or lays claim to. Such a judgment of taste about the agreeable refers to sociability as far as that rests on empirical rules. It is true that judgments about the good also rightfully claim to be valid for everyone, but in presenting the good as the object of a universal liking we do so *by means of a concept,* whereas this is the case neither with the beautiful nor with the agreeable.

213

§ 8

In a Judgment of Taste
the Universality of the Liking
Is Presented Only as Subjective

This special characteristic of an aesthetic judgment [of reflection], the universality to be found in judgments of taste, is a remarkable feature, not indeed for the logician but certainly for the transcendental philosopher.[25] This universality requires a major effort on his part if he is to discover its origin, but it compensates him for this by revealing to him a property of our cognitive power which without this analysis would have remained unknown.

We must begin by fully convincing ourselves that in making a judgment of taste (about the beautiful) we require [*ansinnen*] everyone to like the object, yet without this liking's being based on a concept (since then it would be the good), and that this claim to universal validity belongs so essentially to a judgment by which we declare something to be *beautiful* that it would not occur to anyone to use this term without thinking of universal validity; instead, everything we like without a concept would then be included with the agreeable. For as to the agreeable we allow everyone to be of a mind of his own, no one requiring [*zumuten*[26]] others to agree with his judgment of taste. But in a judgment of taste about beauty we always require others to agree. Insofar as judgments about the agreeable are merely private, whereas judgments about the beautiful are put forward as having general validity (as being public), taste regarding the agreeable can be called taste of sense, and taste regarding the beauti-

214

[25] [The transcendental philosopher tries to discover what enables us to make a priori judgments, especially synthetic ones: judgments in which the predicate is not already contained in the subject, as it is in analytic judgments, but which are nonetheless (wholly or partly) a priori rather than empirical. (See also above, Ak. 181–82, and cf. the *Critique of Pure Reason*, A 298–302 = B 355–59.)]

[26] ['*Ansinnen*' and '*zumuten*' are used interchangeably by Kant. Both mean 'to expect' as in 'I expect you to do this,' but not in the sense of anticipation. Because of this ambiguity (found also in '*erwarten*,' 'to expect'), 'require' is to be preferred. (It also has just about the right force.)]

ful can be called taste of reflection, though the judgments of both are aesthetic (rather than practical) judgments about an object, [i.e.,] judgments merely about the relation that the presentation of the object has to the feeling of pleasure and displeasure. But surely there is something strange here. In the case of the taste of sense, not only does experience show that its judgment (of a pleasure or displeasure we take in something or other) does not hold universally, but people, of their own accord, are modest enough not even to require others to agree (even though there actually is, at times, very widespread agreement in these judgments too). Now, experience teaches us that the taste of reflection, with its claim that its judgment (about the beautiful) is universally valid for everyone, is also rejected often enough. What is strange is that the taste of reflection should nonetheless find itself able (as it actually does) to conceive of judgments that can demand such agreement, and that it does in fact require this agreement from everyone for each of its judgments. What the people who make these judgments dispute about is not whether such a claim is possible; they are merely unable to agree, in particular cases, on the correct way to apply this ability.

Here we must note, first of all, that a universality that does not rest on concepts of the object (not even on empirical ones) is not a logical universality at all, but an aesthetic one; i.e., the [universal] quantity of the judgment is not objective but only subjective. For this quantity I use the expression *general validity,* by which I mean the validity that a presentation's reference to the feeling of pleasure and displeasure [may] have for every subject, rather than the validity of a presentation's reference to the cognitive power. (We may, alternatively, use just one expression, universal validity, for both the aesthetic and the logical quantity of a judgment, provided we add *objective* for the logical universal validity, to distinguish it from the merely subjective one, which is always aesthetic.)

Now a judgment that is *universally valid objectively* is always subjectively so too, i.e., if the judgment is valid for everything contained under a given concept, then it is also valid for everyone who presents an object by means of this concept. But if a judgment has *subjective* —i.e., aesthetic—*universal validity,* which does not rest on a concept, we cannot infer that it also has logical universal validity, because such judgments do not deal with the object [itself] at all. That is precisely why the aesthetic universality we attribute to a

215

judgment must be of a special kind; for although it does not connect the predicate of beauty with the concept of the *object,* considered in its entire logical sphere, yet it extends that predicate over the entire sphere *of judging persons.*

In their logical quantity all judgments of taste are *singular* judgments.[27] For since I must hold the object directly up to[28] my feeling of pleasure and displeasure, but without using concepts, these judgments cannot have the quantity that judgments with objective general[29] validity have. On the other hand, once we have made a judgment of taste about an object, under the conditions characteristic for such judgments, we may then convert the singular presentation of the object into a concept by comparing it [with other presentations] and so arrive at a logically universal judgment. For example, I may look at a rose and make a judgment of taste declaring it to be beautiful. But if I compare many singular roses and so arrive at the judgment, Roses in general are beautiful, then my judgment is no longer merely aesthetic, but is a logical judgment based on an aesthetic one. Now the judgment, The rose is agreeable (in its smell), is also aesthetic and singular, but it is a judgment of sense, not of taste. For a judgment of taste carries with it an *aesthetic quantity* of universality, i.e., of validity for everyone, which a judgment about the agreeable does not have. Only judgments about the good, though they too determine our liking for an object, have logical rather than merely aesthetic universality; for they hold for the object, as cognitions of it, and hence for everyone.

If we judge objects merely in terms of concepts, then we lose all presentation of beauty. This is why there can be no rule by which someone could be compelled to acknowledge that something is beautiful. No one can use reasons or principles to talk us into a judgment on whether some garment, house, or flower is beautiful. We want to submit the object to our own eyes, just as if our liking of it depended on that sensation. And yet, if we then call the object beautiful, we believe we have a universal voice, and lay claim to the

216

---

[27] [In the *Logic*, Kant spells out the (familiar) distinctions between universal, particular, and singular judgments in terms of inclusion and exclusion, total or partial, of the spheres of subject and predicate concepts, and also distinguishes universal from general propositions: Ak. IX, 102–03.]

[28] [See above, Ak. 209 br. n. 19.]

[29] [Kant meant to say 'universal.']

agreement of everyone, whereas any private sensation would decide solely for the observer himself and his liking.

We can see, at this point, that nothing is postulated in a judgment of taste except such a *universal voice* about a liking unmediated by concepts. Hence all that is postulated is the *possibility* of a judgment that is aesthetic and yet can be considered valid for everyone. The judgment of taste itself does not *postulate* everyone's agreement (since only a logically universal judgment can do that, because it can adduce reasons); it merely *requires* this agreement from everyone, as an instance of the rule, an instance regarding which it expects confirmation not from concepts but from the agreement of others. Hence the universal voice is only an idea. (At this point we are not yet inquiring on what this idea rests.) Whether someone who believes he is making a judgment of taste is in fact judging in conformity with that idea may be uncertain; but by using the term beauty he indicates that he is at least referring his judging to that idea, and hence that he intends it to be a judgment of taste. For himself, however, he can attain certainty on this point,[30] by merely being conscious that he is separating whatever belongs to the agreeable and the good from the liking that remains to him after that. It is only for this that he counts on everyone's assent, and he would under these conditions [always] be justified in this claim, if only he did not on occasion fail to observe these conditions and so make an erroneous judgment of taste.

---

[30] [Presumably the point that in a given case "may be uncertain" (at the outset): whether he is in fact judging in conformity with the idea of the universal voice. For the sources of error about to be mentioned (in this sentence), cf. Ak. 290–91 incl. n. 15 at Ak. 290, as well as §39, Ak. 293, and §40, Ak. 293–94. See also Ted Cohen, "Why Beauty Is a Symbol of Morality," in *Essays in Kant's Aesthetics,* eds. Ted Cohen and Paul Guyer (Chicago: University of Chicago Press, 1982), 221–36.]

§ 9

Investigation of the Question Whether in a Judgment of Taste the Feeling of Pleasure Precedes the Judging of the Object or the Judging Precedes the Pleasure

The solution of this problem is the key to the critique of taste and hence deserves full attention.

If the pleasure in the given object came first, and our judgment of taste were to attribute only the pleasure's universal communicability to the presentation of the object, then this procedure would be self-contradictory. For that kind of pleasure would be none other than mere agreeableness in the sensation, so that by its very nature it could have only private validity, because it would depend directly on the presentation by which the object *is given.*

Hence it must be the universal communicability of the mental state, in the given presentation, which underlies the judgment of taste as its subjective condition, and the pleasure in the object must be its consequence. Nothing, however, can be communicated universally except cognition, as well as presentation insofar as it pertains to cognition; for presentation is objective only insofar as it pertains to cognition, and only through this does it have a universal reference point with which everyone's presentational power is compelled to harmonize. If, then, we are to think that the judgment about this universal communicability of the presentation has a merely subjective determining basis, i.e., one that does not involve a concept of the object, then this basis can be nothing other than the mental state that we find in the relation between the presentational powers [imagination and understanding] insofar as they refer a given presentation to *cognition in general.*

When this happens, the cognitive powers brought into play by this presentation are in free play, because no determinate concept restricts them to a particular rule of cognition. Hence the mental state in this presentation must be a feeling, accompanying the given presentation, of a free play of the presentational powers directed to cognition in general. Now if a presentation by which an object is given is, in general, to become cognition, we need *imagination* to combine the manifold of intuition, and *understanding* to provide the unity of the concept uniting the [component] presentations. This state of *free play* of the cognitive powers, accompanying a presentation by which an object is given, must be universally communicable; for cognition, the determination of the object with which given presentations are to harmonize (in any subject whatever) is the only way of presenting that holds for everyone.

But the way of presenting [which occurs] in a judgment of taste is to have subjective universal communicability without presupposing a determinate concept; hence this subjective universal communicability can be nothing but [that of] the mental state in which we are when imagination and understanding are in free play (insofar as they harmonize with each other as required for *cognition in general*). For we are conscious that this subjective relation suitable for cognition in general must hold just as much for everyone, and hence be just as universally communicable, as any determinate cognition, since cognition always rests on that relation as its subjective condition.

Now this merely subjective (aesthetic) judging of the object, or of the presentation by which it is given, precedes the pleasure in the object and is the basis of this pleasure, [a pleasure] in the harmony of the cognitive powers. But the universal subjective validity of this liking, the liking we connect with the presentation of the object we call beautiful, is based solely on the mentioned universality of the subjective conditions for judging objects.

That the ability to communicate one's mental state, even if this is only the state of one's cognitive powers, carries a pleasure with it, could easily be established (empirically and psychologically) from man's natural propensity to sociability. But that would not suffice for our aim here. When we make a judgment of taste, the pleasure we feel is something we require from everyone else as necessary, just as if, when we call something beautiful, we had to regard beauty as a characteristic of the object, determined in it according to concepts, even though in fact, apart from a reference to the subject's feeling, beauty is nothing by itself. We must, however, postpone discussion of this question until we have answered another one, namely, whether and how aesthetic judgments are possible a priori.

At present we still have to deal with a lesser question, namely, how we become conscious, in a judgment of taste, of a reciprocal subjective harmony between the cognitive powers: is it aesthetically, through mere inner sense and sensation? or is it intellectually, through consciousness of the intentional activity by which we bring these powers into play?

If the given presentation that prompts the judgment of taste were a concept which, in our judgment of the object, united understanding and imagination so as to give rise to cognition of the object, then the consciousness of this relation would be intellectual (as it is in the objective schematism of judgment, with which the *Critique* [*of Pure Reason*] deals[31]). But in that case the judgment would not have been made in reference to pleasure and displeasure and hence would not be a judgment of taste. But in fact a judgment of taste determines the object, independently of concepts, with regard to liking and the predicate of beauty. Hence that unity in the relation [between the cognitive powers] in the subject can reveal itself only through sensation. This sensation, whose universal communicability a judgment of taste postulates, is the quickening of the two powers (imagination and understanding) to an activity that is indeterminate but, as a result of the prompting of the given presentation, nonetheless accordant: the activity required for cognition in general. An objective relation can only be thought. Still, insofar as it has subjective conditions, it can nevertheless be sensed in the effect it has on the mind; and if the relation is not based on a concept (e.g., the relation that the presentational powers must have in order to give rise to a power of cognition in general), then the only way we can become conscious of it is through a sensation of this relation's effect: the facilitated play of the two mental powers (imagination and understanding) quickened by their reciprocal harmony. A presentation that, though singular and not compared with others, yet harmonizes with the conditions of the

219

---

[31] [See A 137–47 = B 176–87, and cf. below, Ak. 253 br. n. 17.]

universality that is the business of the understanding in general, brings the cognitive powers into that proportioned attunement which we require for all cognition and which, therefore, we also consider valid for everyone who is so constituted as to judge by means of understanding and the senses in combination (in other words, for all human beings).

Explication of the Beautiful Inferred from the Second Moment

Beautiful is what, without a concept, is liked universally.

Third Moment of Judgments of Taste, As to the *Relation* of Purposes That Is Taken into Consideration in Them

§ 10

On Purposiveness in General

What is a purpose? If we try to explicate it in terms of its transcendental attributes (without presupposing anything empirical, such as the feeling of pleasure), then a purpose is the object of a concept insofar as we regard this concept as the object's cause (the real basis of its

220

possibility); and the causality that a *concept* has with regard to its *object* is purposiveness (*forma finalis*[32]). Hence we think of a purpose if we think not merely, say, of our cognition of the object, but instead of the object itself (its form, or its existence), as an effect that is possible only through a concept of that effect. In that case the presentation of the effect is the basis that determines the effect's cause and precedes it. Consciousness of a presentation's causality directed at the subject's state so as to *keep* him in that state, may here designate generally what we call pleasure; whereas displeasure is that presentation which contains the basis that determines [the subject to change] the state [consisting] of [certain] presentations into their own opposite (i.e., to keep them away or remove them).

The power of desire, insofar as it can be determined to act only by concepts, i.e., in conformity with the presentation of a purpose, would be the will.[33] On the other hand, we do call objects, states of mind, or acts purposive even if their possibility does not necessarily presuppose the presentation of a purpose; we do this merely because we can explain and grasp them only if we assume that they are based on a causality [that operates] according to purposes, i.e., on a will that would have so arranged them in accordance with the presentation of a certain rule. Hence there can be purposiveness without a purpose, insofar as we do not posit the causes of this form in a will, and yet can grasp the explanation of its possibility only by deriving it from a will. Now what we observe we do not always need to have insight into by reason (as to how it is possible). Hence we can at least observe a purposiveness as to form and take note of it in objects—even if only by reflection—without basing it on a purpose (as the matter of the *nexus finalis*[34]).

[32] [Purposive form. Concerning the use of 'purposiveness' for '*Zweckmäßigkeit*,' see above, Ak. 167 br. n. 4.]

[33] [Cf. the *Critique of Practical Reason*, Ak. V, 58–59, and the *Metaphysics of Morals*, Ak. VI, 384–85.]

[34] [Purposive connection.]

§ 11

A Judgment of Taste
Is Based on Nothing
but the *Form of Purposiveness*
of an Object
(or of the Way of Presenting It)

Whenever a purpose is regarded as the basis of a liking, it always carries with it an interest, as the basis that determines the judgment about the object of the pleasure. Hence a judgment of taste cannot be based on a subjective purpose. But a judgment of taste also cannot be determined by a presentation of an objective purpose, i.e., a presentation of the object itself as possible according to principles of connection in terms of purposes, and hence it cannot be determined by a concept of the good. For it is an aesthetic and not a cognitive judgment, and hence does not involve a *concept* of the character and internal or external possibility of the object through this or that cause; rather, it involves merely the relation of the presentational powers to each other, insofar as they are determined by a presentation.

Now this relation, [present] when [judgment] determines an object as beautiful, is connected with the feeling of a pleasure, a pleasure that the judgment of taste at the same time declares to be valid for everyone. Hence neither an agreeableness accompanying the presentation, nor a presentation of the object's perfection and the concept of the good, can contain the basis that determines [such a judgment]. Therefore the liking that, without a concept, we judge to be universally communicable and hence to be the basis that determines a judgment of taste, can be nothing but the subjective purposiveness in the presentation of an object, without any purpose (whether objective or subjective), and hence the mere form of purposiveness, insofar as we are conscious of it, in the presentation by which an object is *given* us.

§ 12

A Judgment of Taste
Rests on A Priori Bases

We cannot possibly tell a priori that some presentation or other (sensation or concept) is connected, as cause, with the feeling of a pleasure or displeasure, as its effect. For that would be a causal relation, and a causal relation (among objects of experience) can never be cognized otherwise than a posteriori and by means of experience itself.[35] It is true that in the *Critique of Practical Reason* we did actually derive a priori from universal moral concepts the feeling of respect (a special and peculiar modification of the feeling of pleasure and displeasure which does seem to differ somehow from both the pleasure and the displeasure we get from empirical objects).[36] But there we were also able to go beyond the bounds of experience and appeal to a causality that rests on a supersensible characteristic of the subject, namely, freedom. And yet, even there, what we derived from the idea of the moral, as the cause, was actually not this *feeling,* but merely the determination of the will, except that the state of mind of a will determined by something or other is in itself already a feeling of pleasure and is identical with it. Hence the determination of the will [by the moral law] does not [in turn] come about as an effect from the feeling of pleasure, [with that feeling being produced by the concept of the moral]; this we would have to assume only if the concept of the moral, as a good [and so as giving rise to respect, the pleasure], preceded the will's determination by the law;[37] but in that case the concept of the moral would be a mere cognition, and so it would be futile to [try to] derive from it the pleasure connected with it.

222

---

[35] [We cognize a priori only that every event must have some cause; what causes produce what effects, we discover by observation.]

[36] [For this derivation, and for a comparison with this entire paragraph, see the *Critique of Practical Reason*, Ak. V, 71–89. Cf. also the *Metaphysics of Morals*, Ak. VI, 211–13.]

[37] [The feeling of pleasure would then mediate this determination.]

Now the situation is similar with the pleasure in an aesthetic judgment, except that here the pleasure is merely contemplative, and does not bring about an interest in the object, whereas in a moral judgment it is practical.[38] The very consciousness of a merely formal purposiveness in the play of the subject's cognitive powers, accompanying a presentation by which an object is given, is that pleasure. For this consciousness in an aesthetic judgment contains a basis for determining the subject's activity regarding the quickening of his cognitive powers, and hence an inner causality (which is purposive) concerning cognition in general, which however is not restricted to a determinate cognition. Hence it contains a mere form of the subjective purposiveness of a presentation. This pleasure is also not practical in any way, neither like the one arising from the pathological basis, agreeableness, nor like the one arising from the intellectual basis, the conceived good. Yet it does have a causality in it, namely, to *keep* [us in] the state of [having] the presentation itself, and [to keep] the cognitive powers engaged [in their occupation] without any further aim. We *linger* in our contemplation of the beautiful, because this contemplation reinforces and reproduces itself. This is analogous to (though not the same as) the way in which we linger over something charming that, as we present an object, repeatedly arouses our attention, [though here] the mind is passive.

§ 13

A Pure Judgment of Taste
Is Independent
of Charm and Emotion

All interest ruins a judgment of taste and deprives it of its impartiality, especially if, instead of making the purposiveness precede the feeling of pleasure as the interest of reason does, that interest bases the purposiveness on the feeling of pleasure; but this is what always

---

[38] [Cf. the *Metaphysics of Morals,* Ak. VI, 212.]

happens in an aesthetic judgment that we make about something insofar as it gratifies or pains us. Hence judgments affected in this way can make either no claim at all to a universally valid liking, or a claim that is diminished to the extent that sensations of that kind are included among the bases determining the taste. Any taste remains barbaric if its liking requires that *charms* and *emotions* be mingled in, let alone if it makes these the standard of its approval.

And yet, (though beauty should actually concern only form), charms are frequently not only included with beauty, as a contribution toward a universal aesthetic liking, but are even themselves passed off as beauties, so that the matter of the liking is passed off as the form. This is a misunderstanding that, like many others having yet some basis in truth, can be eliminated by carefully defining these concepts.

A *pure judgment of taste* is one that is not influenced by charm or emotion (though these may be connected with a liking for the beautiful), and whose determining basis is therefore merely the purposiveness of the form.

§ 14
Elucidation by Examples

Aesthetic judgments, just like theoretical (i.e., logical) ones, can be divided into empirical and pure. Aesthetic judgments are empirical if they assert that an object or a way of presenting it is agreeable or disagreeable; they are pure if they assert that it is beautiful. Empirical aesthetic judgments are judgments of sense (material aesthetic judgments); only pure aesthetic judgments (since they are formal) are properly judgments of taste.

Hence a judgment of taste is pure only insofar as no merely empirical liking is mingled in with the basis that determines it. But this is just what happens whenever charm or emotion have a share in a judgment by which something is to be declared beautiful.

Here again some will raise objections, trying to make out, not merely that charm is a necessary ingredient in beauty, but indeed that

224

it is sufficient all by itself to [deserve] being called beautiful. Most people will declare a mere color, such as the green color of a lawn, or a mere tone (as distinct from sound and noise), as for example that of a violin, to be beautiful in themselves, even though both seem to be based merely on the matter of presentations, i.e., solely on sensation, and hence deserve only to be called agreeable. And yet it will surely be noticed at the same time that sensations of color as well as of tone claim to deserve being considered beautiful only insofar as they are *pure*. And that is an attribute that already concerns form, and it is moreover all that can be universally communicated with certainty about these presentations; for we cannot assume that in all subjects the sensations themselves agree in quality, let alone that everyone will judge one color more agreeable than another, or judge the tone of one musical instrument more agreeable than that of another.

If, following *Euler,*[39] we assume that colors are vibrations (*pulsus*) of the aether in uniform temporal sequence, as, in the case of sound, tones are such vibrations of the air, and if we assume—what is most important (and which, after all, I do not doubt at all[40])—that the mind perceives not only, by sense, the effect that these vibrations have on the excitement of the organ, but also, by reflection, the

---

[39] [Leonhard Euler (1707–83), Swiss mathematician, physicist, and physiologist. He is the author of many works and became a member of the Academies of Science, respectively, of St. Petersburg, Berlin, and Paris.]

[40] [*'Woran ich doch gar nicht zweifle,'* incorporated into the *Akademie* text from the third edition. Both the first and the second edition had *'woran ich doch gar sehr zweifle,'* i.e., 'which, however, I doubt very much.' Wilhelm Windelband, in his notes to the *Akademie* edition of the *Critique of Judgment,* points out (Ak. V, 527–29) that Kant's treatment of color and sound in this *Critique* (as allowing reflection on their form) presupposes Euler's view, and that Kant also speaks very favorably of it in these other places: *Meditationum quarundam de igne succincta delineatio (Brief Outline of Some Reflections Concerning Fire* [1755]), Ak. I, 378; and *Metaphysical Foundations of Natural Science* (1786), Ak. IV, the n. on 519–20. On the other hand, in the *Anthropology* (Ak. VII, 156) Kant writes: "Sight too is a sense [involving] *indirect* [or *mediate:* '*mittelbar*'] sensation by means of [*durch*] a matter in motion, *light*, which only a certain organ (the *eyes*) can sense. Unlike sound, light is not merely a wavelike motion of a fluid element, which spreads in all directions in the surrounding space; rather, it is an emanation by which a point in space is determined for the object. . . ." But the 'not merely' at least can be read in a way that makes this passage compatible with Windelband's evidence *and* hence with the third edition reading adopted here. Cf., on this whole issue, Theodore E. Uehling, Jr., *The Notion of Form in Kant's Critique of Aesthetic Judgment* (The Hague: Mouton, 1971), 22–26.]

regular play of the impressions (and hence the form in the connection of different presentations), then color and tone would not be mere sensations but would already be the formal determination of the manifold in these, in which case they could even by themselves be considered beauties.

But what we call pure in a simple kind of sensation is its uniformity, undisturbed and uninterrupted by any alien sensation. It pertains only to form, because there we can abstract from the quality of the kind of sensation in question (as to which color or tone, if any, is presented). That is why all simple colors, insofar as they are pure, are considered beautiful; mixed colors do not enjoy this privilege, precisely because, since they are not simple, we lack a standard for judging whether we should call them pure or impure.

225

But the view that the beauty we attribute to an object on account of its form is actually capable of being heightened by charm is a vulgar error that is very prejudicial to genuine, uncorrupted, solid [gründlich] taste. It is true that charms may be added to beauty as a supplement: they may offer the mind more than that dry liking, by also making the presentation of the object interesting to it, and hence they may commend to us taste and its cultivation, above all if our taste is still crude and unpracticed. But charms do actually impair the judgment of taste if they draw attention to themselves as [if they were] bases for judging beauty. For the view that they contribute to beauty is so far off the mark that it is in fact only as aliens that they must, indulgently, be granted admittance when taste is still weak and unpracticed, and only insofar as they do not interfere with the beautiful form.

In painting, in sculpture, indeed in all the visual arts, including architecture and horticulture insofar as they are fine arts, *design* is what is essential; in design the basis for any involvement of taste is not what gratifies us in sensation, but merely what we like because of its form. The colors that illuminate the outline belong to charm. Though they can indeed make the object itself vivid to sense, they cannot make it beautiful and worthy of being beheld. Rather, usually the requirement of beautiful form severely restricts [what] colors [may be used], and even where the charm [of colors] is admitted it is still only the form that refines the colors.

All form of objects of the senses (the outer senses or, indirectly, the inner sense as well) is either *shape* or *play;* if the latter, it is either play of shapes (in space, namely, mimetic art and dance), or mere play of sensations (in time). The *charm* of colors or of the agreeable tone of an instrument may be added, but it is the *design* in the first case and the *composition* in the second that constitute the proper object of a pure judgment of taste; that the purity of the colors and of the tones, or for that matter their variety and contrast, seem to contribute to the beauty, does not mean that, because they themselves are agreeable, they furnish us, as it were, with a supplement to, and one of the same kind as, our liking for the form. For all they do is to make the form intuitable more precisely, determinately, and completely, while they also enliven the presentation by means of their charm, by arousing and sustaining the attention we direct toward the object itself.

226

Even what we call *ornaments* (*parerga*), i.e., what does not belong to the whole presentation of the object as an intrinsic constituent, but [is] only an extrinsic addition, does indeed increase our taste's liking, and yet it too does so only by its form, as in the case of picture frames, or drapery on statues, or colonnades around magnificent buildings. On the other hand, if the ornament itself does not consist in beautiful form but is merely attached, as a gold frame is to a painting so that its charm may commend the painting for our approval, then it impairs genuine beauty and is called *finery.*

Emotion, a sensation where agreeableness is brought about only by means of a momentary inhibition of the vital force followed by a stronger outpouring of it, does not belong to beauty at all. But sublimity (with which the feeling of emotion is connected) requires a different standard of judging from the one that taste uses as a basis. Hence a pure judgment of taste has as its determining basis neither charm nor emotion, in other words, no sensation, which is [merely] the matter of an aesthetic judgment.

§ 15

A Judgment of Taste
Is Wholly Independent
of the Concept of Perfection

Objective purposiveness can be cognized only by referring the manifold to a determinate purpose, and hence through a concept. Even from this it is already evident that the beautiful, which we judge on the basis of a merely formal purposiveness, i.e., a purposiveness without a purpose, is quite independent of the concept of the good. For the good presupposes an objective purposiveness, i.e., it presupposes that we refer the object to a determinate purpose.

Objective purposiveness may be extrinsic, in which case it is an object's *utility,* or intrinsic, in which case it is an object's *perfection.* If our liking for an object is one on account of which we call the object beautiful, then it cannot rest on a concept of the object's utility, as is sufficiently clear from the two preceding chapters;[41] for then it would not be a direct liking for the object, while that is the essential condition of a judgment about beauty. But perfection, which is an objective intrinsic purposiveness, is somewhat closer to the predicate beauty, and that is why some philosophers of repute have identified perfection with beauty, adding, however, that it is *perfection thought confusedly.*[42] It is of the utmost importance, in a critique of taste, to decide if indeed beauty can actually be analyzed into the concept of perfection.

In order to judge objective purposiveness, we always need the concept of a purpose, and (if the purposiveness is not to be extrinsic—utility—but intrinsic) it must be the concept of an intrinsic [*inner*] purpose that contains the basis for the object's inner[43] [*inner*] possi-

227

---

[41] [The chapters on the first two *moments* of a judgment of taste, Ak. 203–19.]

[42] [Kant is responding to aestheticians of the Leibnizian school, especially Alexander Gottlieb Baumgarten and Georg Friedrich Meier. See the Translator's Introduction, *xlviii–li.*]

[43] [The German '*inner*' is rendered as 'inner' when it modifies 'possibility,' because 'intrinsic possibility' means 'possibility in *principle.*']

bility. Now insofar as a purpose as such is something whose *concept* can be regarded as the basis of the possibility of the object itself, presenting objective purposiveness in a thing presupposes the concept of the thing, i.e., *what sort of thing it is [meant] to be;* and the harmony of the thing's manifold with this concept (which provides the rule for connecting this manifold) is the thing's *qualitative perfection.* Qualitative perfection is quite distinct from *quantitative* perfection.[44] The latter is the completeness that any thing [may] have as a thing of its kind. It is a mere concept of magnitude (of totality); in its case *what the thing is [meant] to be* is already thought in advance as determined, and the only question is whether the thing has *everything* that is required for being a thing of that kind. What is formal in the presentation of a thing, the harmony of its manifold to [form] a unity (where it is indeterminate what this unity is [meant] to be) does not by itself reveal any objective purposiveness whatsoever. For here we abstract from what this unity is *as a purpose* (what the thing is [meant] to be), so that nothing remains but the subjective purposiveness of the presentations in the mind of the beholder. Subjective purposiveness [is] merely a certain purposiveness of the subject's presentational state and, within that state, [an] appealingness [involved] in apprehending a given form by the imagination. Such purposiveness does not indicate any perfection of any object whatever, [since] no object is being thought through any concept of a purpose. Suppose, for example, that in a forest I come upon a lawn encircled by trees but that I do not connect with it the thought of any purpose, e.g., that it is [meant] (say) for a country dance. In that case no concept whatsoever of perfection is given me through the mere form. But the thought of a formal *objective* purposiveness that nevertheless lacks a purpose, i.e., the mere form of a *perfection* (without any matter and *concept* of what the harmony is directed to, not even the mere idea of a lawfulness as such) is a veritable contradiction.

228

Now a judgment of taste is an aesthetic judgment, i.e., a judgment that rests on subjective bases, and whose determining basis cannot be a concept and hence also cannot be the concept of a determinate purpose. Hence in thinking of beauty, a formal subjective purposiveness, we are not at all thinking of a perfection in the object, an allegedly formal and yet also objective purposiveness; and the distinction

---

[44] [Cf. the *Metaphysics of Morals*, Ak. VI, 386.]

between the concepts of the beautiful and of the good which alleges that the two differ only in their logical form, with the first merely being a confused and the second a distinct concept of perfection, while the two are otherwise the same in content and origin, is in error. For in that case there would be no difference *in kind* between them, but a judgment of taste would be just as much a cognitive judgment as is a judgment by which we declare something to be good. So, for example, the common man bases his judgment that deceit is wrong on confused rational principles, and the philosopher bases his on distinct ones, but both at bottom base their judgments on one and the same rational principles. In fact, however, as I have already pointed out, an aesthetic judgment is unique in kind and provides absolutely no cognition (not even a confused one) of the object; only a logical judgment does that. An aesthetic judgment instead refers the presentation, by which an object is given, solely to the subject; it brings to our notice no characteristic of the object, but only the purposive form in the [way] the presentational powers are determined in their engagement with the object. Indeed, the judgment is called aesthetic[45] precisely because the basis determining it is not a concept but the feeling (of the inner sense) of that accordance in the play of the mental powers insofar as it can only be sensed. If, on the other hand, we wished to call confused concepts and the objective judgment based on them aesthetic, then we would have an understanding that judges by sense [*sinnlich*], or a sense that presents its objects by means of concepts, both of which are contradictory. Our power of concepts, whether they are confused or distinct, is the understanding; and although understanding too is required (as it is for all judgments) for a judgment of taste, as an aesthetic judgment, yet it is required here not as an ability to cognize an object, but as an ability to determine (without a concept) the judgment and its presentation in accordance with the relation that this presentation has to the subject and his inner feeling, namely, so far as this judgment is possible in accordance with a universal rule.

229

---

[45] [From Greek αἰσθέσθαι (aisthésthai), 'to sense', in the broad meaning of this term, which includes feeling. The Greek term thus shares the ambiguity of 'to sense' and of '*empfinden.*' Cf. Ak. 205–06.]

§ 16

A Judgment of Taste
by Which We Declare
an Object Beautiful
under the Condition
of a Determinate Concept
Is Not Pure

There are two kinds of beauty, free beauty (*pulchritudo vaga*) and merely accessory beauty (*pulchritudo adhaerens*). Free beauty does not presuppose a concept of what the object is [meant] to be. Accessory beauty does presuppose such a concept, as well as the object's perfection in terms of that concept. The free kinds of beauty are called (self-subsistent) beauties of this or that thing. The other kind of beauty is accessory to a concept (i.e., it is conditioned beauty) and as such is attributed to objects that fall under the concept of a particular purpose.

Flowers are free natural beauties. Hardly anyone apart from the botanist knows what sort of thing a flower is [meant] to be; and even he, while recognizing it as the reproductive organ of a plant, pays no attention to this natural purpose when he judges the flower by taste. Hence the judgment is based on no perfection of any kind, no intrinsic purposiveness to which the combination of the manifold might refer. Many birds (the parrot, the humming-bird, the bird of paradise) and a lot of crustaceans in the sea are [free] beauties themselves [and] belong to no object determined by concepts as to its purpose, but we like them freely and on their own account. Thus designs *à la grecque*,[46] the foliage on borders or on wallpaper, etc.,

---

[46] [Walter Cerf notes: "The phrase *à la grecque* was apparently used in the eighteenth century—and is still used by some present-day French art historians—to characterize the classicism in what is now called the Louis XVI style. Stimulated by the excavations at Pompeii, which began around 1748, the style *à la grecque* put an end to the style *rocaille* or rococo (*rocaille*, rock or grotto work) of Louis XV and flourished from about 1760 to 1792. . . ." From Walter Cerf's translation of part of the *Critique of Judgment*, entitled *Analytic of the Beautiful* (Indianapolis: Bobbs-Merrill, 1963), 111.]

mean nothing on their own: they represent [*vorstellen*] nothing, no object under a determinate concept, and are free beauties. What we call fantasias in music (namely, music without a topic [*Thema*]), indeed all music not set to words, may also be included in the same class.

When we judge free beauty (according to mere form) then our judgment of taste is pure. Here we presuppose no concept of any purpose for which the manifold is to serve the given object, and hence no concept [as to] what the object is [meant] to represent; our imagination is playing, as it were, while it contemplates the shape, and such a concept would only restrict its freedom.

230

But the beauty of a human being (and, as kinds subordinate to a human being, the beauty of a man or woman or child), or the beauty of a horse or of a building (such as a church, palace, armory, or summer-house) does presuppose the concept of the purpose that determines what the thing is [meant] to be, and hence a concept of its perfection, and so it is merely adherent beauty. Now just as a connection of beauty, which properly concerns only form, with the agreeable (the sensation) prevented the judgment of taste from being pure, so does a connection of beauty with the good (i.e., as to how, in terms of the thing's purpose, the manifold is good for the thing itself) impair the purity of a judgment of taste.

Much that would be liked directly in intuition could be added to a building, if only the building were not [meant] to be a church. A figure could be embellished with all sorts of curlicues and light but regular lines, as the New Zealanders do with their tattoos, if only it were not the figure of a human being. And this human being might have had much more delicate features and a facial structure with a softer and more likable outline, if only he were not [meant] to represent a man, let alone a warlike one.

Now if a liking for the manifold in a thing refers to the intrinsic purpose that determines [how] the thing is possible, then it is a liking based on a concept, whereas a liking for beauty is one that presupposes no concept but is directly connected with the presentation by which the object is given (not by which it is thought). Now if a judgment of taste regarding the second liking is made to depend on, and hence is restricted by, the purpose involved in the first liking, it is a rational judgment, and so it is no longer a free and pure judgment of taste.

It is true that taste gains by such a connection of aesthetic with intellectual liking, for it becomes fixed and, though it is not universal, rules can be prescribed for it with regard to certain objects that are purposively determined. By the same token, however, these rules will not be rules of taste but will merely be rules for uniting taste with reason, i.e., the beautiful with the good, a union that enables us to use the beautiful as an instrument for our aim regarding the good, so that the mental attunement that sustains itself and has subjective universal validity may serve as a basis for that other way of thinking that can be sustained only by laborious resolve but that is universally valid objectively.[47] Actually, however, neither does perfection gain by beauty, nor beauty by perfection. Rather, because in using a concept in order to compare the presentation by which an object is given us with that object itself (with regard to what it is [meant] to be), we inevitably hold the presentation up to the sensation in the subject, it is the *complete power* of presentation that gains when the two states of mind harmonize.

231

A judgment of taste about an object that has a determinate intrinsic purpose would be pure only if the judging person either had no concept of this purpose, or if he abstracted from it in making his judgment. But although he would in that case have made a correct judgment of taste, by judging the object as a free beauty, another person who (looking only to the object's purpose) regarded the beauty in it as only an accessory characteristic, would still censure him and accuse him of having wrong taste, even though each is judging correctly in his own way, the one by what he has before his senses, the other by what he has in his thoughts. If we make this distinction we can settle many quarrels that judges of taste have about beauty, by showing them that the one is concerned with free and the other with accessory beauty, the one making a pure and the other an applied judgment of taste.

[47] [On the link between the beautiful and the good, cf. §42 (Ak. 298–303) and § 59 (Ak. 351–54), as well as the *Anthropology*, § § 69–70, Ak. VII, 244–45.]

§ 17

On the Ideal of Beauty

There can be no objective rule of taste, no rule of taste that determines by concepts what is beautiful. For any judgment from this source [i.e., taste] is aesthetic, i.e., the basis determining it is the subject's feeling and not the concept of an object. If we search for a principle of taste that states the universal criterion of the beautiful by means of determinate concepts, then we engage in a fruitless endeavor, because we search for something that is impossible and intrinsically contradictory. The universal communicability[48] of the sensation (of liking or disliking)—a universal communicability that is indeed not based on a concept—[I say that] the broadest possible agreement among all ages and peoples regarding this feeling that accompanies the presentation of certain objects is the empirical criterion [for what is beautiful]. This criterion, although weak and barely sufficient for a conjecture, [does suggest] that a taste so much confirmed by examples stems from [a] deeply hidden basis, common to all human beings, underlying their agreement in judging the forms under which objects are given them.

232

That is why we regard some products of taste as *exemplary.* This does not mean that taste can be acquired by imitating someone else's. For taste must be an ability one has oneself; and although someone who imitates a model may manifest skill insofar as he succeeds in this, he manifests taste only insofar as he can judge that model himself.[49] From this, however, it follows that the highest model, the archetype of taste, is a mere idea, an idea which everyone must generate within himself and by which he must judge any object of taste, any example of someone's judging by taste, and even the taste of everyone [else].

---

[48] [Cf. § § 20–21 (Ak. 237–39) and § § 39–40 (Ak. 291–96).]

[49] Models of taste in the arts of speech must be composed in a language both dead and scholarly; dead, so that it will not have to undergo the changes that inevitably affect living ones, whereby noble expressions become flat, familiar ones archaic, and newly created ones enter into circulation for only a short while; scholarly, so that it will have a grammar that is not subject to the whims of fashion but has its own unalterable rule.

Idea properly means a rational concept, and *ideal* the presentation of an individual being as adequate to an idea.[50] Hence that archetype of taste, which does indeed rest on reason's indeterminate idea of a maximum, but which still can be presented not through concepts but only in an individual exhibition,[51] may more appropriately be called the ideal of the beautiful. Though we do not have such an ideal in our possession, we do strive to produce it within us. But it will be merely an ideal of the imagination, precisely because it does not rest on concepts but rests on an exhibition, and the power of exhibition is the imagination. How, then, do we arrive at such an ideal of beauty? Do we do so a priori or empirically? Also, which type of the beautiful admits of an ideal?

We must be careful to note, first of all, that if we are to seek an ideal of beauty then the beauty must be *fixed* rather than *vague,* fixed by a concept of objective purposiveness. Hence this beauty must belong not to the object of an entirely pure judgment of taste, but to the object of a partly intellectual one. In other words, if an ideal is to be located in any kind of bases for judging, then there must be some underlying idea of reason, governed by determinate concepts, that determines a priori the purpose on which the object's inner possibility rests. An ideal of beautiful flowers, of beautiful furnishings, or of a beautiful view is unthinkable. But an ideal of a beauty that is accessory to determinate purposes is also inconceivable, e.g., an ideal

233

---

[50] [Cf. the *Critique of Pure Reason*, A 567–71 = B 595–99.]

[51] [Cf. Ak. 192, where 'to exhibit' ('*darstellen*') is defined as 'to place beside [a] concept an intuition corresponding to it.' In the *Critique of Pure Reason*, 'to construct a concept' is defined as 'to exhibit a priori the intuition corresponding to it' (A 713 = B 741). Apart from that context (A 713–21 = B 741–49), the term '*darstellen*' rarely occurs in the first *Critique*, even where construction of concepts is discussed. By the time of the *Critique of Judgment*, Kant uses it frequently, and broadens it to include not only *schematic* exhibition (as, e.g., in construction) but also *symbolic* exhibition. See esp. § 59, (Ak. 351–54) as well as br. n. 31 at Ak. 351. See also the *Logic*, Ak. IX, 23, and the *Metaphysical Foundations of Natural Science,* Ak. IV, 486, and cf. the *Anthropology*, Ak. VII, 167–97. See also Kant's response to Johann August Eberhard in *On a Discovery According to Which Any New Critique of Pure Reason Has Been Made Superfluous by an Earlier One*, Ak. VIII, 185–251. The traditional rendering of '*darstellen*' as 'to present' has been abandoned in this translation because 'to exhibit' seems both closer to Kant's meaning and less misleading. (Similarly for the noun.) 'To present' has been used instead to replace the traditional rendering of '*vorstellen*' as 'to represent,' which wrongly suggests that Kant's theory of perception (etc.) is representational. Cf. above, Ak. 175 br. n. 17.]

of a beautiful mansion, a beautiful tree, a beautiful garden, etc., presumably because the purposes are not sufficiently determined and fixed by their concept, so that the purposiveness is nearly as free as in the case of *vague* beauty. [This leaves] only that which has the purpose of its existence within itself—*man*. Man can himself determine his purposes by reason; or, where he has to take them from outer perception, he can still compare them with essential and universal purposes and then judge the former purposes' harmony with the latter ones aesthetically as well. It is *man*, alone among all objects in the world, who admits of an ideal of *beauty*, just as the humanity in his person, [i.e., in man considered] as an intelligence,[52] is the only [thing] in the world that admits of the ideal of *perfection*.

But this [ideal of beauty] has two components. The *first* is the aesthetic *standard idea*, which is an individual intuition (of the imagination) [by] which [we] present the standard for judging man as a thing belonging to a particular animal species. The *second* is the *rational idea*, which makes the purposes of humanity, insofar as they cannot be presented in sensibility, the principle for judging his figure, which reveals these purposes, as their effect in appearance.[53] The standard idea of the [figure or] shape of an animal of a particular kind has to take its elements from experience. But the greatest purposiveness in the structure of that shape resides merely in the judging person's idea; and it is this greatest purposiveness—the image on which nature's technic[54] was, as it were, intentionally based, and to which only the kind as a whole but no individual by itself is adequate—which would be suitable as the universal standard for judging each individual of that species aesthetically. And yet this idea and its proportions can be exhibited as an aesthetic idea fully *in concreto* in a model image. In order that we may grasp this [process] to some extent (for who can elicit nature's secret entirely?), let us attempt a psychological explanation.

---

[52] [I.e., as a free rational (and noumenal) being, rather than as a being of sense. Cf. the *Critique of Practical Reason*, Ak. V, 114, and the *Metaphysics of Morals*, Ak. VI, 418.]

[53] [Cf. the *Prolegomena to Any Future Metaphysics*, Ak. IV, 343–47; the *Critique of Practical Reason*, Ak. V, 114–15; and the *Foundations of the Metaphysics of Morals*, Ak. IV, 446–63.]

[54] [See above, Ak. 193 br. n. 35.]

234

Notice how in a manner wholly beyond our grasp our imagination is able on occasion not only to recall, even from the distant past, the signs that stand for concepts, but also to reproduce [an] object's image and shape from a vast number of objects of different kinds or even of one and the same kind. Moreover, all indications suggest that this power, when the mind wants to make comparisons, can actually proceed as follows, though this process does not reach consciousness: the imagination projects, as it were, one image onto another, and from the congruence of most images of the same kind it arrives at an average that serves as the common standard for all of them. For instance: Someone has seen a thousand adult men. If now he wishes to make a judgment about their standard size, to be estimated by way of a comparison, then (in my opinion) the imagination projects a large number of the images (perhaps the entire thousand) onto one another. If I may be permitted to illustrate this by an analogy from optics: in the space where most of the images are united, and within the outline where the area is illuminated by the color applied most heavily, there the *average size* emerges, equally distant in both height and breadth from the outermost bounds of the tallest and shortest stature; and that is the stature for a beautiful man. (The same result could be obtained mechanically, by measuring the entire thousand, adding up separately all their heights and their breadths (and thicknesses) by themselves and then dividing each sum by a thousand. And yet the imagination does just that by means of a dynamic effect arising from its multiple apprehension of such shapes on the organ of the inner sense.[55]) Now if in a similar way we try to find for this average man the average head, for it the average nose, etc., then it is this shape which underlies the standard idea of a beautiful man in the country where this comparison is made. That is why, given these empirical conditions, a Negro's standard idea of the beauty of the [human] figure necessarily differs from that of a white man, that of a Chinese from that of a European. The same would apply to the model of a beautiful horse or dog (of a certain breed). This *standard idea* is not derived from proportions that are taken from experience *as determi-*

---

[55] [In the *Anthropology* (Ak. VII, 161), Kant suggests that one "might say" that the soul is the organ of the inner sense. But in the *Critique of Pure Reason* no such organ is mentioned, and the soul is repeatedly called the *object* of the inner sense. (E.g., at A 342 = B 400 and A 846 = B 874.)]

nate rules. Rather, it is in accordance with this idea that rules for judging become possible in the first place. It is the image for the entire kind, hovering between all the singular and multiply varied intuitions of the individuals, the image that nature used as the archetype on which it based its productions within any one species, but which it does not seem to have attained completely in any individual. The standard idea is by no means the entire *archetype of beauty* within this kind, but is only the form that constitutes the indispensable condition of all beauty, and hence merely the *correctness* in the exhibition of the kind. It is the *rule,* just as the famous *Doryphorus of Polyclitus* was called the rule (*Myron's* Cow, within its kind, also allowed this use, as such a rule).[56] It is precisely because of this, too, that the standard idea cannot contain any specific characteristics, since then it would not be the *standard idea* for that kind. Nor is it because of its beauty that we like its exhibition, but merely because it does not contradict any of the conditions under which alone a thing of this kind can be beautiful. The exhibition is merely academically correct.[57]

But from this *standard idea* of the beautiful we must still distinguish the *ideal* of the beautiful, which for reasons already stated must be expected solely in the *human figure.* Now the ideal in this figure consists in the expression of the *moral;* apart from the moral the object would not be liked universally and moreover positively (rather than merely negatively, when it is exhibited in a way that is [merely]

235

[56] [Polyclitus (the Elder) and Myron are both Greek sculptors of the fifth century B.C.; the *Doryphorus* (Spearbearer) and the Cow are works of theirs.]

[57] It will be found that a perfectly regular face, such as a painter would like to have as a model, usually conveys nothing. This is because it contains nothing characteristic and hence expresses more the idea of the [human] kind than what is specific in one person; if what is characteristic in this way is exaggerated, Le., if it offends against the standard idea (of the purposiveness of the kind) itself, then it is called a *caricature.* Experience shows, moreover, that such wholly regular faces usually indicate that inwardly too the person is only mediocre.[58] I suppose (if we may assume that nature expresses in [our] outward (appearance] the proportions of what is inward) this is because, if none of the mental predispositions stands out beyond the proportion that is required for someone to constitute merely a person free from defects, then we must not expect in him any degree of what we call genius; in the case of genius[59] nature seems to depart from the proportions it usually imparts to our mental powers, instead favoring just one.

[58] [Cf. the *Anthropology,* Ak. VII, 298.]

[59] [Cf. §§ 46–50, Ak. 307–20.]

academically correct). Now it is true that this visible expression of moral ideas that govern man inwardly can be taken only from experience. Yet these moral ideas must be connected, in the idea of the highest purposiveness, with everything that our reason links with the morally good: goodness of soul, or purity, or fortitude, or serenity, etc.; and in order for this connection to be made visible, as it were, in bodily expression (as an effect of what is inward), pure ideas of reason must be united with a very strong imagination in someone who seeks so much as to judge, let alone exhibit, it. The correctness of such an ideal of beauty is proved by its not permitting any charm of sense to be mingled with the liking for its object, while yet making us take a great interest in it. This in turn proves that a judging by such a standard can never be purely aesthetic, and that a judging by an ideal of beauty is not a mere judgment of taste.

236

Explication of the Beautiful
Inferred from
the Third Moment

Beauty is an object's form of *purposiveness* insofar as it is perceived in the object *without the presentation of a purpose.*[60]

---

[60] It might be adduced as a counterinstance to this explication that there are things in which we see a purposive form without recognizing a purpose in them [but which we nevertheless do not consider beautiful]. Examples are the stone utensils sometimes excavated from ancient burial mounds, which are provided with a hole as if for a handle. Although these clearly betray in their shape a purposiveness whose purpose is unknown, we do not declare them beautiful on that account. And yet, the very fact that we regard them as work[s] of art already forces us to admit that we are referring their shape to some intention or other and to some determinate purpose. That is also why we have no direct liking whatever for their intuition. A flower, on the other hand, e.g., a tulip, is considered beautiful, because in our perception of it we encounter a certain purposiveness that, given how we are judging the flower, we do not refer to any purpose whatever.

Fourth Moment
of a Judgment of Taste,
As to the Modality of
the Liking for the Object

§ 18

What the Modality of a
Judgment of Taste Is

About any presentation I can say at least that there is a *possibility* for it (as a cognition) to be connected with a pleasure. About that which I call *agreeable* I say that it *actually* gives rise to pleasure in me. But we think of the *beautiful* as having a *necessary*[61] reference to liking. This necessity is of a special kind. It is not a theoretical objective necessity, allowing us to cognize a priori that everyone *will feel* this liking for the object I call beautiful. Nor is it a practical objective necessity, where, through concepts of a pure rational will that serves freely acting beings as a rule, this liking is the necessary consequence of an objective law and means nothing other than that one absolutely (without any further aim) ought to act in a certain way. Rather, as a necessity that is thought in an aesthetic judgment, it can only be called *exemplary*, i.e., a necessity of the assent of *everyone* to a judgment that is regarded as an example of a universal rule that we are unable to state. Since an aesthetic judgment is not an objective and cognitive one, this necessity cannot be derived from determinate concepts and hence is not apodeictic. Still less can it be inferred from the universality of experience (from a thorough agreement among judgments about the beauty of a certain object). For not only would experience hardly furnish a sufficient amount of evidence for this, but

237

---

[61] [Emphasis added. Cf., on modality, the *Critique of Pure Reason*, A 80 = B 106.]

a concept of the necessity of these judgments cannot be based on empirical judgments.

§ 19

The Subjective Necessity
That We Attribute
to a Judgment of Taste
Is Conditioned

A judgment of taste requires everyone to assent; and whoever declares something to be beautiful holds that everyone *ought* to give his approval to the object at hand and that he too should declare it beautiful. Hence the *ought* in an aesthetic judgment, even once we have [*nach*] all the data needed for judging, is still uttered only conditionally. We solicit everyone else's assent because we have a basis for it that is common to all. Indeed, we could count on that assent, if only we could always be sure that the instance had been subsumed correctly under that basis,[62] which is the rule for the approval.

---

[62] [Cf. Ak. 216 incl. br. n. 30.]

§ 20

The Condition for the Necessity Alleged by a Judgment of Taste Is the Idea of a Common Sense

If judgments of taste had (as cognitive judgments do) a determinate objective principle, then anyone making them in accordance with that principle would claim that his judgment is unconditionally necessary. If they had no principle at all, like judgments of the mere taste of sense, then the thought that they have a necessity would not occur to us at all. So they must have a subjective principle, which determines only by feeling rather than by concepts, though nonetheless with universal validity, what is liked or disliked. Such a principle, however, could only be regarded as a *common sense*. This common sense is essentially distinct from the common understanding that is sometimes also called common sense (*sensus communis*); for the latter judges not by feeling but always by concepts, even though these concepts are usually only principles conceived obscurely.

238

Only under the presupposition, therefore, that there is a common sense (by which, however, we [also] do not mean an outer sense, but mean the effect arising from the free play of our cognitive powers)— only under the presupposition of such a common sense, I maintain, can judgments of taste be made.

§ 21

Whether We Have a Basis for Presupposing a Common Sense

Cognitions and judgments, along with the conviction that accompanies them, must be universally communicable. For otherwise we could not attribute to them a harmony with the object, but they would one and all be a merely subjective play of the presentational powers, just as skepticism would have it. But if cognitions are to be communicated, then the mental state, i.e., the attunement of the cognitive powers that is required for cognition in general—namely, that proportion [between them which is] suitable for turning a presentation (by which an object is given us) into cognition—must also be universally communicable. For this attunement is the subjective condition of [the process of] cognition, and without it cognition [in the sense of] the effect [of this process][63] could not arise. And this [attunement] does actually take place whenever a given object, by means of the senses, induces the imagination to its activity of combining the manifold, the imagination in turn inducing the understanding to its activity of providing unity for this manifold in concepts. But this attunement of the cognitive powers varies in its proportion, depending on what difference there is among the objects that are given. And yet there must be one attunement in which this inner relation is most conducive to the (mutual) quickening of the two mental powers with a view to cognition (of given objects) in general; and the only way this attunement can be determined is by feeling (rather than by concepts). Moreover, this attunement itself, and hence also the feeling of it (when a presentation is given), must be universally communicable, while the universal communicability of a feeling presupposes a common sense. Hence it would seem that we do have a basis for assuming such a sense, and for assuming it without relying on psychological observations, but as the necessary condition of the universal communicability of our cognition, which must be presupposed in any logic and any principle of cognitions that is not skeptical.

[63] [Cf. Ak. 167 br. n. 2.]

§ 22

The Necessity of the Universal Assent That We Think in a Judgment of Taste Is a Subjective Necessity That We Present as Objective by Presupposing a Common Sense

Whenever we make a judgment declaring something to be beautiful, we permit no one to hold a different opinion, even though we base our judgment only on our feeling rather than on concepts; hence we regard this underlying feeling as a common rather than as a private feeling. But if we are to use this common sense in such a way, we cannot base it on experience; for it seeks to justify us in making judgments that contain an ought: it does not say that everyone *will* agree with my judgment, but that he *ought* to. Hence the common sense, of whose judgment I am at that point offering my judgment of taste as an example, attributing to it *exemplary* validity on that account, is a mere ideal standard. With this standard presupposed, we could rightly turn a judgment that agreed with it, as well as the liking that is expressed in it for some object, into a rule for everyone. For although the principle is only subjective, it would still be assumed as subjectively universal (an idea necessary for everyone); and so it could, like an objective principle, demand universal assent insofar as agreement among different judging persons is concerned, provided only we were certain that we had subsumed under it correctly.

That we do actually presuppose this indeterminate standard of a common sense is proved by the fact that we presume to make judgments of taste. But is there in fact such a common sense, as a constitutive principle of the possibility of experience, or is there a still higher principle of reason that makes it only a regulative principle for us, [in order] to bring forth in us, for higher purposes, a common sense in the first place? In other words, is taste an original and natural ability, or is taste only the idea of an ability yet to be acquired and [therefore] artificial, so that a judgment of taste with its requirement for universal assent is in fact only a demand of reason to produce such agreement in the way we sense? In the latter case the *ought*,[64] i.e., the objective necessity that everyone's feeling flow along with the particular feeling of each person, would signify only that there is a possibility of reaching such agreement; and the judgment of taste would only offer an example of the application of this principle. These questions we neither wish to nor can investigate at this point. For the present our task is only to analyze the power of taste into its elements, and to unite these ultimately in the idea of a common sense.

Explication of the Beautiful Inferred from the Fourth Moment

Beautiful is what without a concept is cognized as the object of a *necessary* liking.

---

[64] [Emphasis added.]

General Comment on the
First Division[65]
of the Analytic

If we take stock of the above analyses, we find that everything comes down to the concept of taste, namely, that taste is an ability to judge an object in reference to the *free lawfulness* of the imagination. Therefore, in a judgment of taste the imagination must be considered in its freedom. This implies, first of all, that this power is here not taken as reproductive, where it is subject to the laws of association, but as productive and spontaneous (as the originator of chosen forms of possible intuitions).[66] Moreover, [second,] although in apprehending a given object of sense the imagination is tied to a determinate form of this object and to that extent does not have free play (as it does [e.g.] in poetry), it is still conceivable that the object may offer it just the sort of form in the combination of its manifold as the imagination, if it were left to itself [and] free, would design in harmony with the *understanding's lawfulness* in general. And yet, to say that the *imagination* is *free* and yet *lawful of itself,* i.e., that it carries autonomy with it, is a contradiction. The understanding alone gives the law. But when the imagination is compelled to proceed according to a determinate law, then its product is determined by concepts (as far as its form is concerned);[67] but in that case the liking, as was shown above,[68] is a liking not for the beautiful but for the good (of perfection, at any rate, formal perfection), and the judgment is not a judgment

241

---

[65] [The first *Book*, actually.]

[66] [Cf. the *Anthropology*, Ak. VII, 167: "The imagination (*facultas imaginandi*), as a power to intuit even when the object is not present, is either *productive* or *reproductive*. As productive, it is a power of original exhibition of the object (*exhibitio originaria*), and hence of an exhibition that precedes experience. As reproductive, it is a power of derivative exhibition (*exhibitio derivativa*), an exhibition that brings back to the mind an empirical intuition we have had before." See also the *Critique of Pure Reason*, B 151–52.]

[67] [Parentheses added.]

[68] [See esp. § § 15 and 16, Ak. 226–31.]

made by taste. It seems, therefore, that only a lawfulness without a law, and a subjective harmony of the imagination with the understanding without an objective harmony—where the presentation is referred to a determinate concept of an object—is compatible with the free lawfulness of the understanding (which has also been called purposiveness without a purpose[69]) and with the peculiarity of a judgment of taste.

It is true that critics of taste commonly adduce geometrically regular figures, such as a circle, square, or cube, etc., as the simplest and most indubitable examples of beauty. And yet these are called regular precisely because the only way we can present them is by regarding them as mere exhibitions of a determinate concept that prescribes the rule for that figure (the rule under which alone the figure is possible). Hence one of these two must be erroneous: either that judgment by the critics which attributes beauty to such figures, or our judgment that beauty requires a purposiveness without a concept.

Probably no one would hold that a man of taste is required in order to like a circular figure better than a scrawled outline, an equilateral and equiangular quadrangle better than one that is scalene and lopsided, as it were, misshapen; for no taste at all is required for this, but only common understanding. When we pursue an aim, such as to judge the size of an area or, in a division, to enable ourselves to grasp the relation of the parts to one another and to the whole, we require regular figures, and those of the simplest kind; and here our liking does not rest directly on how the figure looks, but rests on its usefulness for all sorts of possible aims. A room whose walls form oblique angles, a garden plot of that kind, even any violation of symmetry in the figure of animals (such as being one-eyed) or of buildings or flower beds: all of these we dislike because they are contrapurposive, not only practically with regard to some definite use of them, but contrapurposive also for our [very] judging of them with all sorts of possible aims [in mind]. This is not the case in a judgment of taste; when such a judgment is pure, it connects liking or disliking directly with the mere *contemplation* of the object,[70] irrespective of its use or any purpose.

It is true that the regularity leading to the concept of an object is

[69] [See Ak. 226 and 236.]
[70] [Cf. Ak. 209 and 222.]

the indispensable condition (*conditio sine qua non*) for apprehending [*fassen*] the object in a single presentation and determining the manifold in the object's form; [and] this determination is a purpose [we pursue] with regard to cognition, and as so related to cognition it is indeed always connected with a liking (since achieving any aim [*Absicht*], even a problematic one, is accompanied by a liking). But here the liking is merely our approval of the solution satisfying a problem, and not a free and indeterminately purposive entertainment [*Unterhaltung*] of the mental powers regarding what we call beautiful, where the understanding serves the imagination rather than vice versa.

In a thing that is possible only through an intention [*Absicht*], such as a building or even an animal, that regularity which consists in the thing's symmetry must express the unity of the intuition that accompanies the concept of the [thing's] purpose, and is part of the cognition. But where only a free play of our presentational powers is to be sustained [*unterhalten*] (though under the condition that the understanding suffers no offense), as in the case of pleasure gardens, room decoration, all sorts of tasteful utensils, and so on, any regularity that has an air of constraint[71] is [to be] avoided as much as possible. That is why the English taste in gardens, or the baroque taste in furniture, carries the imagination's freedom very far, even to the verge of the grotesque, because it is precisely in this divorce from any constraint of a rule that the case is posited where taste can show its greatest perfection in designs made by the imagination.

Everything that [shows] stiff regularity (close to mathematical regularity) runs counter to taste because it does not allow us to be entertained for long by our contemplation of it; instead it bores us, unless it is expressly intended either for cognition or for a determinate practical purpose. On the other hand, whatever lends itself to unstudied and purposive play by the imagination is always new to us and we never tire of looking at it. *Marsden*,[72] in his description of

243

---

[71] [Cf. Ak. 306.]

[72] [William Marsden (1754–1836), English philologist and ethnologist. He spent a number of years in Sumatra and is the author of a *History of Sumatra* (1783) as well as a *Grammar and Dictionary of the Malay Language* (1812). He also translated the *Travels of Marco Polo* (1818).]

Sumatra, comments that the free beauties of nature there surround the beholder everywhere, so that there is little left in them to attract him; whereas, when in the midst of a forest he came upon a pepper garden, with the stakes that supported the climbing plants forming paths between them along parallel lines, it charmed him greatly. He concludes from this that we like wild and apparently ruleless beauty only as a change, when we have been satiated with the sight of regular beauty. And yet he need only have made the experiment of spending one day with his pepper garden to realize that, once regularity has [prompted] the understanding to put itself into attunement with order which it requires everywhere, the object ceases to entertain him and instead inflicts on his imagination an irksome constraint; whereas nature in those regions, extravagant in all its diversity to the point of opulence, subject to no constraint from artificial rules, can nourish his taste permanently. Even bird song, which we cannot bring under any rule of music, seems to contain more freedom and hence to offer more to taste than human song, even when this human song is performed according to all the rules of the art of music, because we tire much sooner of a human song if it is repeated often and for long periods. And yet in this case we probably confuse our participation in the cheerfulness of a favorite little animal with the beauty of its song, for when bird song is imitated very precisely by a human being (as is sometimes done with the nightingale's warble) it strikes our ear as quite tasteless.

Again, we must distinguish beautiful objects from beautiful views of objects (where their distance prevents us from recognizing them distinctly). In beautiful views of objects, taste seems to fasten not so much on what the imagination *apprehends* in that area, as on the occasion they provide for it to engage in *fiction* [*dichten*] i.e., on the actual fantasies with which the mind entertains itself as it is continually being aroused by the diversity that strikes the eye.[73] This is

---

[73] [Cf. the *Anthropology*, Ak. VII, 167–68: "The imagination, insofar as it produces imaginings involuntarily as well, is called *fantasy*. . . . [So] (in other words) the imagination either engages in *fiction* (i.e., it is productive), or in *recall* (i.e., it is reproductive). But this does not mean that the productive imagination is *creative*, i.e., capable of producing a presentation of sense that was never before given to our power of sense; rather, we can always show [from where the imagination took] its material." Cf. also, in the same work, § § 31–33, Ak. VII, 174–82.]

similar to what happens when we watch, say, the changing shapes of the flames in a fireplace or of a rippling brook: neither of these are beauties, but they still charm the imagination because they sustain its free play.

244

BOOK II

ANALYTIC OF
THE SUBLIME

§ 23

Transition from the Power of Judging[1] the Beautiful to That of Judging the Sublime[2]

The beautiful and the sublime are similar in some respects. We like both for their own sake, and both presuppose that we make a judgment of reflection rather than either a judgment of sense or a logically determinative one. Hence in neither of them does our liking depend on a sensation, such as that of the agreeable, nor on a determinate concept, as does our liking for the good; yet we do refer the liking to concepts, though it is indeterminate which concepts these are. Hence the liking is connected with the mere exhibition or power of exhibition, i.e., the imagination, with the result that we regard this power, when an intuition is given us, as harmonizing with the *power of concepts,* i.e., the understanding or reason, this harmony furthering [the aims of] these. That is also why both kinds of judgment are *singular* ones that nonetheless proclaim themselves universally valid for all subjects, though what they lay claim to

[1] [For my use of 'power,' rather than 'faculty,' see above, Ak. 167 br. n. 3.]

[2] [Cf. the *Anthropology,* § § 67–68, Ak. VII, 239–43.]

97

is merely the feeling of pleasure, and not any cognition of the object.

But some significant differences between the beautiful and the sublime are also readily apparent. The beautiful in nature concerns the form of the object, which consists in [the object's] being bounded. But the sublime can also be found in a formless object, insofar as we present *unboundedness,* either [as] in the object or because the object prompts us to present it, while yet we add to this unboundedness the thought of its totality. So it seems that we regard the beautiful as the exhibition of an indeterminate concept of the understanding, and the sublime as the exhibition of an indeterminate concept of reason. Hence in the case of the beautiful our liking is connected with the presentation of *quality,* but in the case of the sublime with the presentation of *quantity.* The two likings are also very different in kind. For the one liking ([that for] the beautiful) carries with it directly a feeling of life's being furthered, and hence is compatible with charms and with an imagination at play. But the other liking (the feeling of the sublime) is a pleasure that arises only indirectly: it is produced by the feeling of a momentary inhibition of the vital forces followed immediately by an outpouring of them that is all the stronger. Hence[3] it is an emotion,[4] and so it seems to be seriousness, rather than play, in the imagination's activity. Hence, too, this liking is incompatible with charms, and, since the mind is not just attracted by the object but is alternately always repelled as well, the liking for the sublime contains not so much a positive pleasure as rather admiration and respect, and so should be called a negative pleasure.[5]

But the intrinsic and most important distinction between the sublime and the beautiful is presumably the following. If, as is permissible, we start here by considering only the sublime in natural objects (since the sublime in art is always confined to the conditions that [art] must meet to be in harmony with nature), then the distinction in question comes to this: (Independent) natural beauty carries with it a purposiveness in its form, by which the object seems as it were pre-

[3] [Cf. Ak. 226.]

[4] [Cf. the *Observations on the Feeling of the Beautiful and Sublime* (1764), Ak. II, 209: "The sublime MOVES us, the beautiful CHARMS us."]

[5] [On admiration, respect, and positive and negative pleasure, cf. the *Critique of Practical Reason,* Ak. V, 71–89.]

determined for our power of judgment, so that this beauty constitutes in itself an object of our liking. On the other hand, if something arouses in us, merely in apprehension and without any reasoning on our part, a feeling of the sublime, then it may indeed appear, in its form, contrapurposive for our power of judgment, incommensurate with our power of exhibition, and as it were violent to our imagination, and yet we judge it all the more sublime for that.

We see from this at once that we express ourselves entirely incorrectly when we call this or that *object of nature* sublime, even though we may quite correctly call a great many natural objects beautiful; for how can we call something by a term of approval if we apprehend it as in itself contrapurposive? Instead, all we are entitled to say is that the object is suitable for exhibiting a sublimity that can be found in the mind. For what is sublime, in the proper meaning of the term, cannot be contained in any sensible form but concerns only ideas of reason, which, though they cannot be exhibited adequately, are aroused and called to mind by this very inadequacy, which can be exhibited in sensibility. Thus the vast ocean heaved up by storms cannot be called sublime. The sight of it is horrible; and one must already have filled one's mind with all sorts of ideas if such an intuition is to attune it to a feeling that is itself sublime, inasmuch as the mind is induced to abandon sensibility and occupy itself with ideas containing a higher purposiveness.

246

Independent natural beauty reveals to us a technic[6] of nature that allows us to present nature as a system in terms of laws whose principle we do not find anywhere in our understanding: the principle of a purposiveness directed to our use of judgment as regards appearances. Under this principle, appearances must be judged as belonging not merely to nature as governed by its purposeless mechanism, but also to [nature considered by] analogy with art. Hence even though this beauty does not actually expand our cognition of natural objects, it does expand our concept of nature, namely, from nature as mere mechanism to the concept of that same nature as art, and that invites us to profound investigations about [how] such a form is possible. However, in what we usually call sublime in nature there is such an utter lack of anything leading to particular objective principles and to forms of nature conforming to them, that it is rather in its chaos that nature most arouses our ideas of the sublime, or in its

[6] [See Ak. 193 br. n. 35.]

wildest and most ruleless disarray and devastation, provided it displays magnitude and might. This shows that the concept of the sublime in nature is not nearly as important and rich in implications as that of the beautiful in nature, and that this concept indicates nothing purposive whatever in nature itself but only in what *use* we can make of our intuitions of nature so that we can feel a purposiveness within ourselves entirely independent of nature. For the beautiful in nature we must seek a basis outside ourselves, but for the sublime a basis merely within ourselves and in the way of thinking that introduces sublimity into our presentation of nature. This is a crucial preliminary remark, which separates our ideas of the sublime completely from the idea of a purposiveness of *nature,* and turns the theory of the sublime into a mere appendix to our aesthetic judging of the purposiveness of nature. For through these ideas we do not present a particular form in nature, but only develop [the] purposive use that the imagination makes of the presentation of nature.

247

§ 24

On Dividing an Investigation of the Feeling of the Sublime

In dividing the moments that are involved when we judge objects aesthetically in relation to the feeling of the sublime, the analytic can go on under the same principle that it followed in analyzing judgments of taste. For, since judgments about the sublime are made by the aesthetic reflective power of judgment, [the analytic] must allow us to present the liking for the sublime, just as that for the beautiful, as follows: in terms of *quantity,* as universally valid; in terms of *quality,* as devoid of interest; in terms of *relation,* [as a] subjective purposiveness; and in terms of *modality,* as a necessary subjective purposiveness. So our method here will not deviate from the one used in the preceding [book], except for a [detail that is] of no account: since aesthetic judgments about the beautiful concerned the form of the object, we there started by investigating their quality, whereas here, since what we call sublime may be formless, we shall begin with the quantity as the first moment of an aesthetic judgment about the sublime. The reason for this is evident from the preceding section.

But we do have to make one division in analyzing the sublime that the analysis of the beautiful did not require: we must divide the sublime into the *mathematically* and the *dynamically* sublime.

For while taste for the beautiful presupposes and sustains the mind in *restful* contemplation, the feeling of the sublime carries with it, as its character, a mental *agitation* connected with our judging of the object. But (since we like the sublime) this agitation is to be judged subjectively purposive, and so the imagination will refer this agitation either to the *cognitive power* or to the *power of desire,* but in both cases the purposiveness of the given presentation will be judged only with regard to these *powers* (without any purpose or interest). The first kind of agitation is a *mathematical,* the second a *dynamical,* attunement of the mind. And so we attribute both these kinds of agitation to the object, and hence present the object as sublime in these two ways.

A

ON THE
MATHEMATICALLY
SUBLIME

§ 25
Explication of
the Term Sublime

We call *sublime* what is *absolutely* [*schlechthin*] *large*. To be large [*groß*] and to be a magnitude [*Größe*] are quite different concepts (*magnitudo* and *quantitas*). Also, *saying simply* [*schlechtweg*] (*simpliciter*) that something is large is quite different from saying that it is *absolutely large* (*absolute, non comparative magnum*[7]). The latter is *what is large beyond all comparison*. But what does it mean to say that something is large, or small, or medium-sized? Such a term does not stand for a pure concept of the understanding, let alone an intuition of sense. Nor does it stand for a rational concept, for it involves no cognitive principle whatsoever. Hence it must stand for a concept that belongs to the power of judgment or is derived from such a concept, and it must presuppose a subjective purposiveness of the presentation in relation to the power of judgment. That something is a magnitude (*quantum*) can be cognized from the thing itself without any comparison of it with others, namely, if a multiplicity of the homogeneous together constitutes a unity. On the other hand, [to

---

[7] [Large absolutely rather than by comparison.]

judge] *how large* something is we always need something else, which is also a magnitude, as its measure. But since what matters in judging magnitude is not just multiplicity (number) but also the magnitude of the unity[8] [used as the unit] (the measure), and since [to judge] the magnitude of this unity we always need something else in turn as a measure with which we can compare it, it is plain that no determination of the magnitude of appearances can possibly yield an absolute concept of a magnitude, but at most can yield only a comparative one.

Now if I say simply that something is large, it seems that I have no comparison in mind at all, at least no comparison with an objective measure, because in saying this I do not determine at all how large [*groß*] the object is. But though my standard of comparison is merely subjective, my judgment still lays claim to universal assent. Such judgments as, This man is beautiful, and, He is large, do not confine themselves to the judging subject, but demand everyone's assent, just as theoretical judgments do.

249

But in a judgment by which we describe something simply as large, we do not just mean that the object has some magnitude, but we also imply that this magnitude is superior to that of many other objects of the same kind, yet without indicating this superiority determinately. Hence we do base our judgment on a standard, which we assume we can presuppose to be the same for everyone; but it is a standard that will serve not for a logical (mathematically determinate) judging of magnitude, but only for an aesthetic one, because it is only a subjective standard underlying our reflective judgment about magnitude [*Größe*] Furthermore, the standard may be either empirical or one that is given a priori. An empirical one might be the average size [*Größe*] of the people we know, of animals of a certain kind, of trees, houses, mountains, and so on. One that is given a priori would be confined, because of the deficiencies of the judging subject, to subjective conditions of an exhibition *in concreto;* an example from the practical sphere is the magnitude [or degree] of a certain virtue, or of the civil liberty and justice in a country; from the theoretical sphere,

---

[8] ['*Einheit*' can mean 'unity' or 'unit.' Here it means both, but the concern is with the imagination's effort to perform its usual function of providing an intuition (including that of a unit, even a *basic* unit) with *unity*, by comprehending it in accordance with a concept. See § 26 (Ak. 251–57) as well as Ak. 259. Cf. also the *Critique of Pure Reason*, A 98–100.]

the magnitude [or degree] of the correctness or incorrectness of some observation or measurement that has been made, and so on.

It is noteworthy here that even if we have no interest whatsoever in the object, i.e., we are indifferent to its existence, still its mere magnitude, even if the object is regarded as formless, can yet carry with it a liking that is universally communicable and hence involves consciousness of a subjective purposiveness in the use of our cognitive powers. But—and in this it differs from [the liking for] the beautiful, where reflective judgment finds itself purposively attuned in relation to cognition in general—this liking is by no means a liking for the object (since that may be formless), but rather a liking for the expansion of the imagination itself.

If (under the above restriction[9]) we say simply of an object that it is large, then our judgment is not mathematically determinative; it is a mere judgment of reflection about our presentation of the object, a presentation that is subjectively purposive for a certain use we can make of our cognitive powers in estimating magnitude; and we then always connect with the presentation a kind of respect, as we connect a [kind of] contempt with what we simply call small. Furthermore, our judging of things as large or small [*groß oder klein*] applies to anything, even to any characteristics of things. That is why we call even beauty great or little [*groß oder klein*], because no matter what we exhibit in intuition (and hence present aesthetically) in accordance with the precept of judgment, it is always appearance, and hence also a quantum.[10]

250

But suppose we call something not only large, but large absolutely [*schlechthin, absolut*], in every respect (beyond all comparison), i.e., sublime. Clearly, in that case, we do not permit a standard adequate to it to be sought outside it, but only within it. It is a magnitude that is equal only to itself. It follows that the sublime must not be sought in things of nature, but must be sought solely in our ideas; but in which of these it resides [is a question that] must wait for the deduction.[11]

The above explication can also be put as follows: *That is sublime in comparison with which everything else is small.* We can easily see

[9] [On the kind of standard we are presupposing.]

[10] [Cf. the *Critique of Pure Reason*, Axioms of Intuition, A 162–66 = B 202–07.]

[11] [See below, §30, Ak. 279–80.]

here that nothing in nature can be given, however large we may judge it, that could not, when considered in a different relation, be degraded all the way to the infinitely small, nor conversely anything so small that it could not, when compared with still smaller standards, be expanded for our imagination all the way to the magnitude of a world; telescopes have provided us with a wealth of material in support of the first point,[12] microscopes in support of the second. Hence, considered on this basis, nothing that can be an object of the senses is to be called sublime. [What happens is that] our imagination strives to progress toward infinity, while our reason demands absolute totality as a real idea, and so [the imagination,] our power of estimating the magnitude of things in the world of sense, is inadequate to that idea. Yet this inadequacy itself is the arousal in us of the feeling that we have within us a supersensible power; and what is absolutely large is not an object of sense, but is the use that judgment makes naturally of certain objects so as to [arouse] this (feeling), and in contrast with that use any other use is small. Hence what is to be called sublime is not the object, but the attunement that the intellect [gets] through a certain presentation that occupies reflective judgment.

Hence we may supplement the formulas already given to explicate the sublime by another one: *Sublime is what even to be able to think proves that the mind has a power surpassing any standard of sense.*

---

[12] [Cf. the *Universal Natural History and Theory of the Heavens* (1755), Ak. I, 215–368.]

§ 26

On Estimating the
Magnitude of Natural Things,
as We Must for the
Idea of the Sublime

Estimation of magnitude by means of numerical concepts (or their signs in algebra) is mathematical; estimation of magnitudes in mere intuition (by the eye) is aesthetic. It is true that to get determinate concepts of *how large* something is we must use numbers (or, at any rate, approximations [expressed] by numerical series progressing to infinity), whose unity is [the unit we use as[13]] the measure; and to that extent all logical estimation of magnitude is mathematical. Yet the magnitude of the measure must be assumed to be known. Therefore, if we had to estimate this magnitude also mathematically, i.e., only by numbers, whose unity would have to be a different measure, then we could never have a first or basic measure, and hence also could have no determinate concept of a given magnitude. Hence our estimation of the magnitude of the basic measure must consist merely in our being able to take it in [*fassen*] directly in one intuition and to use it, by means of the imagination, for exhibiting numerical concepts. In other words, all estimation of the magnitude of objects of nature is ultimately aesthetic (i.e., determined subjectively rather than objectively).

Now even though there is no maximum [*Größtes*] for the mathematical estimation of magnitude (inasmuch as the power of numbers progresses to infinity), yet for the aesthetic estimation of magnitude there is indeed a maximum. And regarding this latter maximum I say that when it is judged as [the] absolute measure beyond which no larger is subjectively possible (i.e., possible for the judging subject), then it carries with it the idea of the sublime and gives rise to that emotion which no mathematical estimation of magnitude by means of numbers can produce (except to the extent that the basic aesthetic

[13] [Cf. Ak.248 incl. br. n. 8.]

measure is at the same time kept alive in the imagination). For a mathematical estimation of magnitude never exhibits more than relative magnitude, by a comparison with others of the same kind, whereas an aesthetic one exhibits absolute magnitude to the extent that the mind can take it in in one intuition.

In order for the imagination to take in a quantum intuitively, so that we can then use it as a measure or unity in estimating magnitude by numbers, the imagination must perform two acts: *apprehension* (*apprehensio*), and *comprehension*[14] (*comprehensio aesthetica*). Apprehension involves no problem, for it may progress to infinity. But comprehension becomes more and more difficult the farther apprehension progresses, and it soon reaches its maximum, namely, the aesthetically largest basic measure for an estimation of magnitude. For when apprehension has reached the point where the partial presentations of sensible intuition that were first apprehended are already beginning to be extinguished in the imagination, as it proceeds to apprehend further ones, the imagination then loses as much on the one side as it gains on the other; and so there is a maximum in comprehension that it cannot exceed.

This serves to explain a comment made by *Savary* in his report on Egypt:[15] that in order to get the full emotional effect from the magnitude of the pyramids one must neither get too close to them nor stay too far away. For if one stays too far away, then the apprehended parts (the stones on top of one another) are presented only obscurely, and hence their presentation has no effect on the subject's aesthetic judgment; and if one gets too close, then the eye needs some time to complete the apprehension from the base to the peak, but during that time some of the earlier parts are invariably extinguished in the imagination before it has apprehended the later ones, and hence the comprehension is never complete. Perhaps the same observation can explain the bewilderment or kind of perplexity that is said to seize the spectator who for the first time enters St. Peter's Basilica in Rome.

252

[14] [*Zusammenfassung*. 'Comprehension' and 'comprehend' are used in this translation only in this sense of 'collecting together and holding together' (cf. 'comprehensive'), never in the sense of 'understanding.']

[15] [*Lettres sur l'Égypte* (*Letters on Egypt*), 1787, by Anne Jean Marie René Savary, Duke of Rovigo, (1774–1833), French general, diplomat, and later minister of police (notorious for his severity) under Napoleon Bonaparte, but active even after the latter's banishment to St. Helena in 1815. Savary took part in Bonaparte's expedition to Egypt.]

For he has the feeling that his imagination is inadequate for exhibiting the idea of a whole, [a feeling] in which imagination reaches its maximum, and as it strives to expand that maximum, it sinks back into itself, but consequently comes to feel a liking [that amounts to an[16]] emotion [*rührendes Wohlgefallen*].

I shall say nothing for now regarding the basis of this liking, a liking connected with a presentation from which one would least expect it, namely, a presentation that makes us aware of its own inadequacy and hence also of its subjective unpurposiveness for the power of judgment in its estimation of magnitude. Here I shall only point out that if the aesthetic judgment in question is to be *pure* (*unmixed with any teleological* and hence rational judgment), and if we are to give an example of it that is fully appropriate for the critique of *aesthetic* judgment, then we must point to the sublime not in products of art (e.g., buildings, columns, etc.), where both the form and the magnitude are determined by a human purpose, nor in natural things *whose very concept carries with it a determinate purpose* (e.g., animals with a known determination in nature), but rather in crude nature (and even in it only insofar as it carries with it no charm, nor any emotion aroused by actual danger), that is, merely insofar as crude nature contains magnitude. For in such a presentation nature contains nothing monstrous (nor anything magnificent or horrid); it does not matter how far the apprehended magnitude has increased, just as long as our imagination can comprehend it within one whole. An object is *monstrous* if by its magnitude it nullifies the purpose that constitutes its concept. And *colossal* is what we call the mere exhibition of a concept if that concept is almost too large for any exhibition (i.e., if it borders on the relatively monstrous); for the purpose of exhibiting a concept is hampered if the intuition of the object is almost too large for our power of apprehension. A pure judgment about the sublime, on the other hand, must have no purpose whatsoever of the object as the basis determining it, if it is to be aesthetic and not mingled with some judgment of understanding or of reason.

253

Since the presentation of anything that our merely reflective power of judgment is to like without an interest must carry with it a

[16] [Cf. Ak. 245 and 226.]

purposiveness that is subjective and yet universally valid, but since in the sublime (unlike the beautiful) our judging is not based on a purposiveness of the *form* of the object, the following questions arise: What is this subjective purposiveness, and how does it come to be prescribed as a standard, thereby providing a basis for a universally valid liking accompanying the mere estimation of magnitude—an estimation that has been pushed to the point where the ability of our imagination is inadequate to exhibit the concept of magnitude?

When the imagination performs the combination [*Zusammensetzung*] that is required to present a magnitude, it encounters no obstacles and on its own progresses to infinity, while the understanding guides it by means of numerical concepts, for which the imagination must provide the schema;[17] and in this procedure, which is involved in the logical estimation of magnitude, there is indeed something objectively purposive under the concept of a purpose (since any measuring is a purpose). And yet there is nothing in it that is purposive for, and liked by, the aesthetic power of judgment. Nor is there anything in this intentional purposiveness that necessitates our pushing the magnitude of the measure, and hence of the *comprehension* of the many [elements] in one intuition, to the limit of the imagination's ability, and as far as it may extend in exhibiting. For in estimating magnitudes by the understanding (arithmetic) we get equally far whether we pursue the comprehension of the unities to the number 10 (as in the decadic system) or only to 4 (as in the tetradic system): the further generation of magnitudes—in the [process of] combination or, if the quantum is given in intuition, in apprehension—is done merely progressively (rather than comprehensively), under an assumed principle of progression. This mathematical estimation of magnitude serves and satisfies the understanding equally well, whether the imagination selects as the unity a magnitude that we can take in in one glance, such as a foot or a rod, or whether it selects a German

254

---

[17] [A schema is what mediates, and so makes possible, the subsumption of intuitions under concepts of the understanding (and so the application of these concepts to intuitions). It does so by sharing features of both a concept and an intuition. See the *Critique of Pure Reason*, A 137–47 = B 176–87, and cf. Ak. 351–52 and the Translator's Introduction, *xxxvi*.]

mile,[18] or even an earth diameter, which the imagination can apprehend but cannot comprehend in one intuition (by a *comprehensio aesthetica*, though it can comprehend it in a numerical concept by a *comprehensio logica*). In either case the logical estimation of magnitude progresses without hindrance to infinity.[19]

But the mind listens to the voice of reason within itself, which demands totality for all given magnitudes, even for those that we can never apprehend in their entirety but do (in presentation of sense) judge as given in their entirety. Hence reason demands comprehension in *one* intuition, and *exhibition* of all the members of a progressively increasing numerical series, and it exempts from this demand not even the infinite (space and past time). Rather, reason makes us unavoidably think of the infinite (in common reason's judgment) as *given in its entirety* (in its totality).

The infinite, however, is absolutely large (not merely large by comparison). Compared with it everything else (of the same kind of magnitudes[20]) is small. But—and this is most important—to be able even to think the infinite as *a whole* indicates a mental power that surpasses any standard of sense. For [thinking the infinite as a whole while using a standard of sense] would require a comprehension yielding as a unity a standard that would have a determinate relation to the infinite, one that could be stated in numbers; and this is impossible. If the human mind is nonetheless to *be able even to think* the given infinite without contradiction, it must have within itself a power that is supersensible, whose idea of a noumenon cannot be intuited but can yet be regarded as the substrate underlying what is mere appearance, namely, our intuition of the world. For only by means of this power and its idea do we, in a pure intellectual estima-

255

---

[18] [The Prussian rod equaled 3.7662 m (meters), the Saxon 4.2951 m, whereas the English rod equals 5.5 yds. or 5.029 m. The German mile was quite long: 7500 m; the English statute mile equals only 1609.35 m. There was also a "geographic" or "Bavarian" as well as a "*Badische*" mile.]

[19] ['*Das Unendliche*.' What this expression says *literally* is 'the infinite.' Yet here (and similarly in mathematics, where the same expression is used), the expression does not mean *something infinite* (to which the estimation of magnitude progresses), even though it does mean this in other contexts (e.g., in the next paragraph). '*Unendlichkeit*,' on the other hand, usually means 'infinity' only in the most abstract sense: 'infiniteness,' 'being infinite.']

[20] [In this case, magnitudes that are *given* (in intuition).]

tion of magnitude, comprehend the infinite in the world of sense *entirely under* a concept, even though in a mathematical estimation of magnitude *by means of numerical concepts* we can never think it in its entirety. Even a power that enables us to think the infinite of supersensible intuition as given (in our intelligible substrate) surpasses any standard of sensibility. It is large beyond any comparison even with the power of mathematical estimation—not, it is true, for [the pursuit of] a theoretical aim on behalf of our cognitive power, but still as an expansion of the mind that feels able to cross the barriers of sensibility with a different (a practical) aim.

Hence nature is sublime in those of its appearances whose intuition carries with it the idea of their infinity. But the only way for this to occur is through the inadequacy of even the greatest effort of our imagination to estimate an object's magnitude. In the mathematical estimation of magnitude, however, the imagination is equal to the task of providing, for any object, a measure that will suffice for this estimation, because the understanding's numerical concepts can be used in a progression and so can make any measure adequate to any given magnitude. Hence it must be the *aesthetic* estimation of magnitude where we feel that effort, our imagination's effort to perform a comprehension that surpasses its ability to encompass [*begreifen*] the progressive apprehension in a whole of intuition, and where at the same time we perceive the inadequacy of the imagination—unbounded though it is as far as progressing is concerned—for taking in and using, for the estimation of magnitude, a basic measure that is suitable for this with minimal expenditure on the part of the understanding. Now the proper unchangeable basic measure of nature is the absolute whole of nature, which, in the case of nature as appearance, is infinity comprehended. This basic measure, however, is a self-contradictory concept (because an absolute totality of an endless progression is impossible). Hence that magnitude of a natural object to which the imagination fruitlessly applies its entire ability to comprehend must lead the concept of nature to a supersensible substrate (which underlies both nature and our ability to think), a substrate that is large beyond any standard of sense and hence makes us judge as *sublime* not so much the object as the mental attunement in which we find ourselves when we estimate the object.

Therefore, just as the aesthetic power of judgment in judging the beautiful refers the imagination in its free play to the *understanding*

256

so that it will harmonize with the understanding's *concepts* in general (which concepts they are is left indeterminate), so in judging a thing sublime it refers the imagination to *reason* so that it will harmonize subjectively with reason's *ideas* (which ideas they are is indeterminate), i.e., so that it will produce a mental attunement that conforms to and is compatible with the one that an influence by determinate (practical) ideas would produce on feeling.

This also shows that true sublimity must be sought only in the mind of the judging person, not in the natural object the judging of which prompts this mental attunement. Indeed, who would want to call sublime such things as shapeless mountain masses piled on one another in wild disarray, with their pyramids of ice, or the gloomy raging sea? But the mind feels elevated in its own judgment of itself when it contemplates these without concern for their form and abandons itself to the imagination and to a reason that has come to be connected with it—though quite without a determinate purpose, and merely expanding it—and finds all the might of the imagination still inadequate to reason's ideas.

Nature offers examples of the mathematically sublime, in mere intuition, whenever our imagination is given, not so much a larger numerical concept, as a large unity for a measure (to shorten the numerical series). A tree that we estimate by a man's height will do as a standard for [estimating the height of] a mountain. If the mountain were to be about a mile high, it can serve as the unity for the number that expresses the earth's diameter, and so make that diameter intuitable. The earth's diameter can serve similarly for estimating the planetary system familiar to us, and that [in turn] for estimating the Milky Way system. And the immense multitude of such Milky Way systems, called nebulous stars, which presumably form another such system among themselves, do not lead us to expect any boundaries here.[21] Now when we judge such an immense whole aesthetically, the sublime lies not so much in the magnitude of the number as in the fact that, the farther we progress, the larger are the unities we reach. This is partly due to the systematic division in the structure of the world edifice; for this division always presents to us whatever is large in nature as being small in turn, though what it actually presents to us is

257

[21] [Cf. the *Universal Natural History and Theory of the Heavens* (1755), Ak. I, 247–58, but esp. Ak. I, 306–22.]

our imagination, in all its boundlessness, and along with it nature, as vanishing[ly small] in contrast to the ideas of reason, if the imagination is to provide an exhibition adequate to them.

§ 27

On the Quality of the Liking in Our Judging of the Sublime

The feeling that it is beyond our ability to attain to an idea *that is a law for us* is RESPECT. Now the idea of comprehending every appearance that may be given us in the intuition of a whole is an idea enjoined on us by a law of reason, which knows no other determinate measure that is valid for everyone and unchanging than the absolute whole. But our imagination, even in its greatest effort to do what is demanded of it and comprehend a given object in a whole of intuition (and hence to exhibit the idea of reason), proves its own limits and inadequacy, and yet at the same time proves its vocation to [obey] a law, namely, to make itself adequate to that idea. Hence the feeling of the sublime in nature is respect for our own vocation. But by a certain subreption[22] (in which respect for the object is substituted for respect for the idea of humanity within our[selves, as] subject[s]) this respect is accorded an object of nature that, as it were, makes intuitable for us the superiority of the rational vocation of our cognitive powers over the greatest power of sensibility.[23]

Hence the feeling of the sublime is a feeling of displeasure that arises from the imagination's inadequacy, in an aesthetic estimation

---

[22] [Cf. the Inaugural Dissertation (1770), *De mundi sensibilis atque intelligibilis forma et principiis* (*On the Form and Principles of the Sensible and Intelligible World*), § 24, Ak. II, 412: "... *praestigia intellectus, per subornationem conceptus sensitivi, tamquam notae intellectualis, dici potest (secundum analogiam significatus recepti) vitium subreptionis*," i.e., "We may call *fallacy of subreption* (by analogy with the accepted meaning) the intellect's trick of slipping in a concept of sense as if it were the concept of an intellectual characteristic."]

[23] [I.e., the imagination "in its greatest expansion": cf. Ak. 269.]

of magnitude, for an estimation by reason, but is at the same time also a pleasure, aroused by the fact that this very judgment, namely, that even the greatest power of sensibility is inadequate, is [itself] in harmony with rational ideas, insofar as striving toward them is still a law for us. For it is a law (of reason) for us, and part of our vocation, to estimate any sense object in nature that is large for us as being small when compared with ideas of reason; and whatever arouses in us the feeling of this supersensible vocation is in harmony with that law. Now the greatest effort of the imagination in exhibiting the unity [it needs] to estimate magnitude is [itself] a reference to something *large absolutely,* and hence also a reference to reason's law to adopt only this something as the supreme measure of magnitude. Hence our inner perception that every standard of sensibility is inadequate for an estimation of magnitude by reason is [itself] a harmony with laws of reason, as well as a displeasure that arouses in us the feeling of our supersensible vocation, according to which finding that every standard of sensibility is inadequate to the ideas of reason is purposive and hence pleasurable.

258

In presenting the sublime in nature the mind feels *agitated,*[24] while in an aesthetic judgment about the beautiful in nature it is in *restful* contemplation. This agitation (above all at its inception) can be compared with a vibration, i.e., with a rapid alternation of repulsion from, and attraction to, one and the same object. If a [thing] is excessive for the imagination (and the imagination is driven to [such excess] as it apprehends [the thing] in intuition), then [the thing] is, as it were, an abyss in which the imagination is afraid to lose itself. Yet, at the same time, for reason's idea of the supersensible [this same thing] is not excessive but conforms to reason's law to give rise to such striving by the imagination. Hence [the thing] is now attractive to the same degree to which [formerly] it was repulsive to mere sensibility. The judgment itself, however, always remains only aesthetic here. For it is not based on a determinate concept of the object, and presents merely the subjective play of the mental powers themselves (imagination and reason) as harmonious by virtue of their contrast. For just as, when we judge the beautiful, imagination and *understanding* give rise to a subjective purposiveness of the mental powers by their *accordance,* so do imagination and *reason* here give rise to such a purposiveness

---

[24] [Cf. Ak. 245 and 226.]

by their *conflict,* namely, to a feeling that we have a pure and independent reason, or a power for estimating magnitude, whose superiority cannot be made intuitable by anything other than the inadequacy of that power which in exhibiting magnitudes (of sensible objects) is itself unbounded.

Measuring (as [a way of] apprehending) a space is at the same time describing it, and hence it is an objective movement in the imagination and a progression. On the other hand, comprehending a multiplicity in a unity (of intuition rather than of thought),[25] and hence comprehending in one instant what is apprehended successively, is a regression that in turn cancels the condition of time in the imagination's progression and makes *simultaneity* intuitable.[26] Hence, (since temporal succession is a condition of the inner sense and of an intuition) it is a subjective movement of the imagination by which it does violence to the inner sense, and this violence must be the more significant the larger the quantum is that the imagination comprehends in one intuition. Hence the effort to take up into a single intuition a measure for magnitude requiring a significant time for apprehension is a way of presenting which subjectively considered is contrapurposive, but which objectively is needed to estimate magnitude and hence is purposive. And yet this same violence that the imagination inflicts on the subject is still judged purposive *for the whole vocation* of the mind.

The *quality* of the feeling of the sublime consists in its being a feeling, accompanying an object, of displeasure about our aesthetic power of judging, yet of a displeasure that we present at the same time as purposive. What makes this possible is that the subject's own inability uncovers in him the consciousness of an unlimited ability which is also his, and that the mind can judge this ability aesthetically only by that inability.

In the logical estimation of magnitude, the impossibility of ever arriving at absolute totality by measuring the things in the world of sense progressively, in time and space, was cognized as objective, as an impossibility of *thinking* the infinite as given, and not as merely subjective, as an inability to *take it in.* For there we are not at all

259

[25] [Parentheses added.]

[26] [Cf., for this portion of the paragraph, the *Critique of Pure Reason,* A 411–13 = B 438–40.]

concerned with the degree of the comprehension in one intuition, [to be used] as a measure, but everything hinges on a numerical concept. In an aesthetic estimation of magnitude, on the other hand, the numerical concept must drop out or be changed, and nothing is purposive for this estimation except the imagination's comprehension to [form] a unity [to be used as] a measure (so that the concepts of a law of the successive generation of concepts of magnitude are avoided). Now if a magnitude almost reaches the limit of our ability to comprehend [it] in one intuition, but the imagination is still called upon to perform, by means of numerical magnitudes (regarding which we are conscious of having an unbounded ability), an aesthetic comprehension in a larger unity; then we feel in our mind that we are aesthetically confined within bounds. Yet, in view of the necessary expansion of the imagination toward adequacy regarding what is unbounded in our power of reason, namely, the idea of the absolute whole, the displeasure is still presented as purposive for the rational ideas and their arousal, and hence so is the unpurposiveness of our imagination's ability. This is precisely what makes the aesthetic judgment itself subjectively purposive for reason, as the source of ideas, i.e., as the source of an intellectual comprehension [compared] to which all aesthetic comprehension is small, and the object is apprehended as sublime with a pleasure that is possible only by means of a displeasure.

260

B

ON THE
DYNAMICALLY
SUBLIME IN NATURE

§ 28
On Nature as a Might

Might is an ability that is superior to great obstacles. It is called *dominance* [*Gewalt*] if it is superior even to the resistance of something that itself possesses might. When in an aesthetic judgment we consider nature as a might that has no dominance over us, then it is *dynamically*[27] *sublime.*

If we are to judge nature as sublime dynamically, we must present it as arousing fear. (But the reverse does not hold: not every object that arouses fear is found sublime when we judge it aesthetically.) For when we judge [something] aesthetically (without a concept), the only way we can judge a superiority over obstacles is by the magnitude of the resistance. But whatever we strive to resist is an evil, and it is an object of fear if we find that our ability [to resist it] is no match for it. Hence nature can count as a might, and so as dynamically sublime, for aesthetic judgment only insofar as we consider it as an object of fear.

We can, however, consider an object *fearful* without being afraid *of* it, namely, if we judge it in such a way that we merely *think* of the

---

[27] [From Greek δύναμις (dýnamis), i.e. 'might,' 'power,' etc.]

119

case where we might possibly want to put up resistance against it, and that any resistance would in that case be utterly futile. Thus a virtuous person fears God without being afraid of him. For he does not think of wanting to resist God and his commandments as a possibility that should worry *him*. But for every such case, which he thinks of as not impossible intrinsically, he recognizes God as fearful.

Just as we cannot pass judgment on the beautiful if we are seized by inclination and appetite, so we cannot pass judgment at all on the sublime in nature if we are afraid. For we flee from the sight of an object that scares us, and it is impossible to like terror that we take seriously. That is why the agreeableness that arises from the cessation of a hardship is *gladness*. But since this gladness involves our liberation from a danger, it is accompanied by our resolve never to expose ourselves to that danger again. Indeed, we do not even like to think back on that sensation, let alone actively seek out an opportunity for it.

On the other hand, consider bold, overhanging and, as it were, threatening rocks, thunderclouds piling up in the sky and moving about accompanied by lightning and thunderclaps, volcanoes with all their destructive power, hurricanes with all the devastation they leave behind, the boundless ocean heaved up, the high waterfall of a mighty river, and so on. Compared to the might of any of these, our ability to resist becomes an insignificant trifle. Yet the sight of them becomes all the more attractive the more fearful it is, provided we are in a safe place. And we like to call these objects sublime because they raise the soul's fortitude above its usual middle range and allow us to discover in ourselves an ability to resist which is of a quite different kind, and which gives us the courage [to believe] that we could be a match for nature's seeming omnipotence.

For although we found our own limitation when we considered the immensity of nature and the inadequacy of our ability to adopt a standard proportionate to estimating aesthetically the magnitude of nature's *domain,* yet we also found, in our power of reason, a different and nonsensible standard that has this infinity itself under it as a unit; and since in contrast to this standard everything in nature is small, we found in our mind a superiority over nature itself in its immensity. In the same way, though the irresistibility of nature's might makes us, considered as natural beings, recognize our physical impotence, it reveals in us at the same time an ability to judge ourselves independent of nature, and reveals in us a superiority over nature that is the basis of a self-preservation quite different in kind from the one that can be assailed and endangered by nature outside us. This keeps the humanity in our person from being degraded, even though a human being would have to succumb to that dominance [of nature]. Hence if in judging nature aesthetically we call it sublime, we do so not because nature arouses fear, but because it calls forth our strength (which does not belong to nature [within us]), to regard as small the [objects] of our [natural] concerns: property, health, and life, and because of this we regard nature's might (to which we are indeed subjected in these [natural] concerns) as yet not having such dominance over us, as persons, that we should have to bow to it if our highest principles were at stake and we had to choose between upholding or abandoning them. Hence nature is here called sublime [erhaben] merely because it elevates [erhebt] our imagination, [making] it exhibit those cases where the mind can come to feel its own sublimity, which lies in its vocation and elevates it even above nature.

262

This self-estimation loses nothing from the fact that we must find ourselves safe in order to feel this exciting liking, so that (as it might seem), since the danger is not genuine, the sublimity of our intellectual ability might also not be genuine. For here the liking concerns only our ability's *vocation,* revealed in such cases, insofar as the predisposition to this ability is part of our nature, whereas it remains up to us, as our obligation, to develop and exercise this ability. And there is truth in this, no matter how conscious of his actual present impotence man may be when he extends his reflection thus far.

I admit that this principle seems farfetched and the result of some subtle reasoning, and hence high-flown [überschwenglich] for an aesthetic judgment. And yet our observation of man proves the opposite, and proves that even the commonest judging can be based on this principle, even though we are not always conscious of it. For what is it that is an object of the highest admiration even to the savage? It is a person who is not terrified, not afraid, and hence does not yield to danger but promptly sets to work with vigor and full deliberation. Even in a fully civilized society there remains this superior esteem for the warrior, except that we demand more of him: that he also demonstrate all the virtues of peace—gentleness, sympathy, and even appropriate care for his own person—precisely because they reveal to us that his mind cannot be subdued by danger. Hence,

263

no matter how much people may dispute, when they compare the statesman with the general, as to which one deserves the superior respect, an aesthetic judgment decides in favor of the general. Even war has something sublime about it if it is carried on in an orderly way and with respect for the sanctity of the citizens' rights. At the same time it makes the way of thinking of a people that carries it on in this way all the more sublime in proportion to the number of dangers in the face of which it courageously stood its ground. A prolonged peace, on the other hand, tends to make prevalent a mere[ly] commercial spirit,[28] and along with it base selfishness, cowardice, and softness, and to debase the way of thinking of that people.[29]

   This analysis of the concept of the sublime, insofar as [sublimity is] attributed to might, may seem to conflict with the fact that in certain situations—in tempests, storms, earthquakes, and so on—we usually present God as showing himself in his wrath but also in his sublimity, while yet it would be both foolish and sacrilegious to imagine that our mind is superior to the effects produced by such a might, and is superior apparently even to its intentions. It seems that here the mental attunement that befits the manifestation of such an object is not a feeling of the sublimity of our own nature, but rather submission, prostration, and a feeling of our utter impotence; and this mental attunement is in fact usually connected with the idea of this object when natural events of this sort occur. It seems that in religion in general the only fitting behavior in the presence of the deity is prostration, worship with bowed head and accompanied by contrite and timorous gestures and voice; and that is why most peoples have in fact adopted this behavior and still engage in it. But, by the same token, this mental attunement is far from being intrinsically and necessarily connected with the idea of the *sublimity* of a religion and its object. A person who is actually afraid and finds cause for this in himself because he is conscious that with his reprehensible attitude he offends against a might whose will is at once irresistible and just is not at all in the frame of mind [needed] to admire divine greatness, which requires that we be attuned to quiet contemplation and that our judgment be completely free. Only if he is conscious that his attitude is sincere and pleasing to God, will these effects of might

---

[28] [Cf. *Perpetual Peace*, Ak. VIII, 368.]
[29] [Cf. §83, Ak. 429–34.]

serve to arouse in him the idea of God's sublimity, insofar as he recognizes in his own attitude a sublimity that conforms to God's will,
and is thereby elevated above any fear of such natural effects, which
he does not regard as outbursts of God's wrath. Even humility, as
a strict judging of our own defects which, when we are conscious
that our own attitudes are good, could otherwise easily be cloaked
with the frailty of human nature [as an excuse], is a sublime mental
attunement, namely, voluntary subjection of ourselves to the pain of
self-reprimand so as gradually to eradicate the cause of these defects.
This alone is what intrinsically distinguishes religion from superstition. The latter establishes in the mind not a reverence for the sublime, but fear and dread of that being of superior might to whose will
the terrified person finds himself subjected but without holding him
in esteem; and this can obviously give rise to nothing but ingratiation
and fawning, never to a religion based on good conduct.[30]

Hence sublimity is contained not in any thing of nature, but only in
our mind, insofar as we can become conscious of our superiority to
nature within us, and thereby also to nature outside us (as far as it
influences us). Whatever arouses this feeling in us, and this includes
the *might* of nature that challenges our forces, is then (although
improperly) called sublime. And it is only by presupposing this idea
within us, and by referring to it, that we can arrive at the idea of the
sublimity of that being who arouses deep respect in us, not just by his
might as demonstrated in nature, but even more by the ability, with
which we have been endowed, to judge nature without fear and to
think of our vocation as being sublimely above nature.

264

---

[30] [Cf. *Religion within the Bounds of Reason Alone*, Ak. VI, 51: ". . . [A]ll religions
can be divided into two kinds: religion of *ingratiation* (mere worship), and *moral*
religion, i.e., religion based on *good conduct*."]

§ 29

On the Modality of a Judgment about the Sublime in Nature

Beautiful nature contains innumerable things about which we do not hesitate to require everyone's judgment to agree with our own, and can in fact expect such agreement without being wrong very often. But we cannot with the same readiness count on others to accept our judgment about the sublime in nature. For it seems that, if we are to pass judgment on that superiority of [such] natural objects, not only must our aesthetic power of judgment be far more cultivated, but also so must the cognitive powers on which it is based.

In order for the mind to be attuned to the feeling of the sublime, it must be receptive to ideas. For it is precisely nature's inadequacy to the ideas—and this presupposes both that the mind is receptive to ideas and that the imagination strains to treat nature as a schema[31] for them—that constitutes what both repels our sensibility and yet attracts us at the same time, because it is a dominance [*Gewalt*] that reason exerts over sensibility only for the sake of expanding it commensurately with reason's own domain (the practical one) and letting it look outward toward the infinite, which for sensibility is an abyss. It is a fact that what is called sublime by us, having been prepared through culture, comes across as merely repellent to a person who is uncultured and lacking in the development of moral ideas. In all the evidence of nature's destructive force [*Gewalt,*] and in the large scale of its might, in contrast to which his own is nonexistent, he will see only the hardship, danger, and misery that would confront anyone forced to live in such a place. Thus (as Mr. de Saussure relates[32]) the good and otherwise sensible Savoyard peasant did not hesitate to call anyone a fool who fancies glaciered mountains. He might even have had a point, if Saussure had acted merely from fancy,

[31] [See Ak. 253 br. n. 17.]

[32] [Horace Bénédict de Saussure (1740–99), Swiss geologist, geographer. and botanist. He traveled extensively in the Alps (he was only the third to climb Mont Blanc, in 1787), and recorded his observations in his *Voyages dans les Alpes* (1779, 1786).]

as most travelers tend to, in exposing himself to the dangers involved in his observations, or in order that he might some day be able to describe them with pathos. In fact, however, his intention was to instruct mankind, and that excellent man got, in addition, the soul-stirring sensation and gave it into the bargain to the readers of his travels.

But the fact that a judgment about the sublime in nature requires culture (more so than a judgment about the beautiful) still in no way implies that it was initially produced by culture and then introduced to society by way of (say) mere convention. Rather, it has its foundation in human nature: in something that, along with common sense, we may require and demand of everyone, namely, the predisposition to the feeling for (practical) ideas, i.e., to moral feeling.

This is what underlies the necessity—which we include in our judgment about the sublime—of the assent of other people's judgment to our own. For just as we charge someone with a lack of *taste* if he is indifferent when he judges an object of nature that we find beautiful, so we say that someone has no *feeling* if he remains unmoved in the presence of something we judge sublime. But we demand both taste and feeling of every person, and, if he has any culture at all, we presuppose that he has them. But we do so with this difference: taste we demand unhesitatingly from everyone, because here judgment refers the imagination merely to the understanding, our power of concepts; in the case of feeling, on the other hand, judgment refers the imagination to reason, our power of ideas, and so we demand feeling only under a subjective presupposition (though we believe we are justified and permitted to require [fulfillment of] this presupposition in everyone): we presuppose moral feeling in man. And so we attribute necessity to this [kind of] aesthetic judgment as well.

In this modality of aesthetic judgments—their presumed necessity—lies one principal moment for a critique of judgment. For it is this necessity that reveals an a priori principle in them and lifts them out of [the reach of] empirical psychology, in which they would otherwise remain buried among the feelings of gratification and pain (accompanied only by the empty epithet of being a *more refined* feeling). Instead this necessity places them, and by means of them our power of judgment, into the class of those judgments that have a priori

266

principles at their basis, and hence brings them into transcendental philosophy.

General Comment
on the Exposition
of Aesthetic
Reflective Judgments

In relation to the feeling of pleasure an object must be classed with either the *agreeable,* or the *beautiful,* or the *sublime,* or the (absolutely) *good (iucundum, pulchrum, sublime, honestum).*

The *agreeable,* as an incentive for desires, is always of the same kind, wherever it may come from and however different in kind may be the presentation (of sense, and of sensation regarded objectively[33]). That is why what matters in judging its influence on the mind is only the number of stimuli (simultaneous and successive), and, as it were, only the mass of the agreeable sensation, so that this sensation can be made intelligible only through its *quantity.* Nor does the agreeable contribute to culture, but it belongs to mere enjoyment. The *beautiful,* on the other hand, requires that we present a certain *quality* of the object, and a quality that can be made intelligible and brought to concepts (even though in an aesthetic judgment the beautiful is not brought to concepts). It also contributes to culture, for it teaches us at the same time to be mindful of purposiveness in the feeling of pleasure. The *sublime* consists merely in a *relation,* for here we judge the sensible [element] in the presentation of nature to be suitable for a possible supersensible use. The *absolutely good* (the object of moral feeling), as judged subjectively by the feeling it inspires, is the ability of the subject's powers to be determined by the conception of a law that *obligates absolutely.* It is distinguished above all by its *modality:*

267

---

[33] [I.e., in the meaning of the term 'sensation' where the sensation refers to an object, rather than being a *feeling* and so referring *only* to the subject, like the *agreeable sensation* about to be mentioned. Cf. § 3, Ak. 205–06. Cf. also Ak. 207 br. n. 12; Kant continues to use 'sensation' to mean 'feeling' as well.]

a necessity that rests on a priori concepts and contains not just a *claim* but also a *command* that everyone approve. Actually, the absolutely good belongs not to aesthetic but to pure intellectual judgment; by the same token, we attribute it to freedom rather than to nature, and in a determinative rather than in a merely reflective judgment. But the *determinability of the subject* by this idea—the determinability, indeed, of a subject who can sense within himself, as a *modification of his state, obstacles* in sensibility, but at the same time his superiority to sensibility in overcoming these obstacles, which determinability is moral feeling—is nevertheless akin to the aesthetic power of judgment and its *formal conditions* inasmuch as it allows us to present the lawfulness of an act done from duty as aesthetic also, i.e., as sublime or for that matter beautiful, without any loss in the feeling's purity, while such a loss would be unavoidable if we sought to bring the feeling into a natural connection with the feeling of the agreeable.

If we take the result from the exposition given so far of the two kinds of aesthetic judgments, we arrive at the following brief explications:

Beautiful is what we like when we merely judge it (and hence not through any sensation by means of sense in accordance with some concept of the understanding). From this it follows at once that we must like the beautiful without any interest.

Sublime is what, by its resistance to the interest of the senses, we like directly.

Both of these are explications of universally valid aesthetic judging and as such refer to subjective bases. In the case of the beautiful, the reference is to subjective bases of sensibility as they are purposive for the benefit of the contemplative understanding. In the case of the sublime, the reference is to subjective bases as they are purposive in relation to moral feeling, namely, against sensibility but at the same time, and within the very same subject, for the purposes of practical reason. The beautiful prepares us for loving something, even nature, without interest; the sublime, for esteeming it even against our interest (of sense).

The sublime can be described thus: it is an object (of nature) *the presentation of which determines the mind to think of nature's inability to attain to an exhibition of ideas.*

If we speak literally and consider the matter logically, ideas cannot

268

be exhibited. But when in intuiting nature we expand our empirical power of presentation (mathematically or dynamically), then reason, the ability to [think] an independent and absolute totality, never fails to step in and arouse the mind to an effort, although a futile one, to make the presentation of the senses adequate to this [idea of] totality. This effort, as well as the feeling that the imagination [as it synthesizes empirical nature] is unable to attain to that idea, is itself an exhibition of the subjective purposiveness of our mind, in the use of our imagination, for the mind's supersensible vocation. And we are compelled to subjectively *think* nature itself in its totality as the exhibition of something supersensible, without our being able to bring this exhibition about *objectively.*

For we soon come to realize that nature in space and time [i.e., phenomenal nature] entirely lacks the unconditioned, and hence lacks also that absolute magnitude [i.e., totality] which, after all, even the commonest reason demands. And this is precisely what reminds us that we are dealing only with nature as appearance, which must yet be considered in turn the mere exhibition of nature in itself (of which reason has the idea). We cannot determine this idea of the supersensible any further, and hence we cannot *cognize* but can only *think* nature as an exhibition of it. But it is this idea that is aroused in us when, as we judge an object aesthetically, this judging strains the imagination to its limit, whether of expansion (mathematically) or of its might over the mind (dynamically). The judging strains the imagination because it is based on a feeling that the mind has a vocation that wholly transcends the domain of nature (namely, moral feeling), and it is with regard to this feeling that we judge the presentation of the object subjectively purposive.

It is in fact difficult to think of a feeling for the sublime in nature without connecting with it a mental attunement similar to that for moral feeling. It is true that the pleasure we take directly in the beautiful in nature also presupposes, as well as cultivates, a certain *liberality* in our way of thinking, i.e., an independence of the liking from mere enjoyment of sense; but here the freedom is still presented more as in *play* than as subject to a law-governed *task.* But the latter is what genuinely characterizes man's morality, where reason must exert its dominance over sensibility, except that in an aesthetic judgment about the sublime we present this dominance as being exerted by the imagination itself, as an instrument of reason.

269

By the same token, a liking for the sublime in nature is only *negative* (whereas a liking for the beautiful is *positive*):[34] it is a feeling that the imagination by its own action is depriving itself of its freedom, in being determined purposively according to a law different from that of its empirical use. The imagination thereby acquires an expansion and a might that surpasses the one it sacrifices; but the basis of this might is concealed from it; instead the imagination *feels* the sacrifice or deprivation and at the same time the cause to which it is being subjugated. Thus any spectator who beholds massive mountains climbing skyward, deep gorges with raging streams in them, wastelands lying in deep shadow and inviting melancholy meditation, and so on is indeed seized by *amazement* bordering on terror, by horror and a sacred thrill; but, since he knows he is safe, this is not actual fear: it is merely our attempt to incur it with our imagination, in order that we may feel that very power's might and connect the mental agitation this arouses with the mind's state of rest. In this way we [feel] our superiority to nature within ourselves, and hence also to nature outside us insofar as it can influence our feeling of well-being. For the imagination, acting in accordance with the law of association, makes our state of contentment dependent on [something] physical; but the same power, acting in accordance with principles of the schematism of judgment (and hence, to that extent, in subordination to freedom), is an instrument of reason and its ideas. As such, however, it is a might [that allows us] to assert our independence of natural influences, to degrade as small what is large according to the imagination in its first [role], and so to posit the absolutely large [or great] only in his (the subject's) own vocation. In this reflection of the aesthetic power of judgment, by which it seeks to elevate itself to the point of being adequate to reason (though without having a determinate concept from reason), we present the object itself as subjectively

[34] [Cf. Edmund Burke (to whom Kant responds at Ak. 277–78), *Philosophical Enquiry Into the Origin of Our Ideas of the Sublime and Beautiful* (1757): "[Sublimity and beauty] are indeed ideas of a very different nature, one being founded on pain, the other on pleasure . . ." (Pt. III, Sect. xxvii). The pleasure on which beauty is founded is "actual" pleasure (Pt. IV, Sect. v), because it is *positive* pleasure (Pt. I, Sect. iv); the sublime gives rise only to "delight," which is not a positive pleasure but merely a "relative" pleasure (Pt. I, Sect. iv) because it "turns on pain." (Pt. I, Sect. xviii), in the sense that it is merely the cessation or diminution of pain (Pt. I, Sect. iv). There are many more parallels between Kant's and Burke's accounts of beauty and (especially) sublimity.]

purposive, precisely because objectively the imagination, [even] in its greatest expansion, is inadequate to reason (the power of ideas).

We must in all of this be mindful of the injunction given above, namely, that the transcendental aesthetic of judgment must be concerned solely with pure aesthetic judgments. Hence we must not take for our examples such beautiful or sublime objects of nature as presuppose the concept of a purpose. For then the purposiveness would be either teleological, and hence not aesthetic, or else be based on mere sensations of an object (gratification or pain) and hence not merely formal. Therefore, when we call the sight of the starry sky *sublime,* we must not base our judgment upon any concepts of worlds that are inhabited by rational beings,[35] and then [conceive of] the bright dots that we see occupying the space above us as being these worlds' suns, moved in orbits prescribed for them with great purposiveness; but we must base our judgment regarding it merely on how we see it, as a vast vault encompassing everything, and merely under this presentation may we posit the sublimity that a pure aesthetic judgment attributes to this object. In the same way, when we judge the sight of the ocean we must not do so on the basis of how we *think* it, enriched with all sorts of knowledge which we possess (but which is not contained in the direct intuition), e.g., as a vast realm of aquatic creatures, or as the great reservoir supplying the water for the vapors that impregnate the air with clouds for the benefit of the land, or again as an element that, while separating continents from one another, yet makes possible the greatest communication among them; for all such judgments will be teleological. Instead we must be able to view the ocean as poets do, merely in terms of what manifests itself to the eye—e.g., if we observe it while it is calm, as a clear mirror of water bounded only by the sky; or, if it is turbulent, as being like an abyss threatening to engulf everything— and yet find it sublime. The same applies to the sublime and beautiful in the human figure. Here, too, we must not have in mind [*zurücksehen auf*], as bases determining our judgment, concepts of the purposes *for which* man has all his limbs, letting the limbs' harmony with these purposes *influence* our aesthetic judgment (which would then cease to be pure), even though it is certainly a necessary condition of

270

[35] [Kant discusses the possibility of extraterrestrial life elaborately (and movingly) in his *Universal Natural History and Theory of the Heavens* (1755), Ak. I, 349–68.]

aesthetic liking as well that the limbs not conflict with those purposes. Aesthetic purposiveness is the lawfulness of the power of judgment in its *freedom*. [Whether we then] like the object depends on [how] we suppose [*setzen wollen*] the imagination to relate [to it]; but [for this liking to occur] the imagination must on its own sustain the mind in a free activity. If, on the other hand, the judgment is determined by anything else, whether a sensation proper [*Sinnesempfindung*][36] or a concept of the understanding, then the judgment is indeed lawful, but it is not one made by a *free* power of judgment.

271

Sometimes we speak of intellectual beauty or sublimity. But, *first,* these expressions are not quite correct. For beauty and sublimity are aesthetic ways of presenting [things], and if we were nothing but pure intelligences[37] (or, for that matter, if in thought we put ourselves in the place of such [beings]), we would not present [things] in this way at all. *Second,* even though these two [intellectual beauty and sublimity], as objects of an intellectual (moral) liking, are indeed compatible with an aesthetic liking inasmuch as they do not *rest* on any interest, it still remains difficult to make them compatible with it: for they are to *produce* an interest, and yet, on the assumption that the exhibition is to harmonize with the [kind of] liking involved in an aesthetic judgment, this interest would have to be an interest of sense connected with the exhibition; but that would impair the intellectual purposiveness and make it impure.

The object of a pure and unconditioned intellectual liking is the moral law in its might, the might that it exerts in us over any and all of those incentives of the mind *that precede it.* This might actually reveals itself aesthetically only through sacrifice (which is a deprivation—though one that serves our inner freedom—in return for which it reveals in us an unfathomable depth of this supersensible power, whose consequences extend beyond what we can foresee). Hence, considered from the aesthetic side (i.e., in reference to sensibility), the liking is negative, i.e., opposed to this interest, but considered from the intellectual side it is positive and connected with an interest.

[36] [As distinguished from 'sensation' as meaning feeling. Cf. Ak. 291 incl. br. n. 19. (If the aesthetic judgment [of liking, which is a feeling] were determined by sensation proper, it would be a judgment about the agreeable, [and "lawful" only empirically]. Cf. Ak. 205–06.)]

[37] [Cf. Ak. 233.]

It follows from this that if we judge aesthetically the good that is intellectual and intrinsically purposive (the moral good), we must present it not so much as beautiful but rather as sublime, so that it will arouse more a feeling of respect (which disdains charm) than one of love and familiar affection. For human nature does not of itself harmonize with that good; it [can be made to harmonize with it] only through the dominance that reason exerts over sensibility. Conversely, too, what we call sublime in nature outside us, or for that matter in nature within us (e.g., certain affects), becomes interesting only because we present it as a might of the mind to rise above *certain* obstacles of sensibility by means of moral principles.

Let me dwell a little on that last point. If the idea of the good is accompanied by affect [as its effect], this [affect] is called *enthusiasm*.[38] This mental state seems to be sublime, so much so that it is commonly alleged that nothing great can be accomplished without it. But in fact any affect[39] is blind, either in the selection of its purpose, or, if that were to have been given by reason, in [the manner of] achieving it. For an affect is an agitation of the mind that makes it unable to engage in free deliberation about principles with the aim of determining itself according to them. Hence there is no way it can deserve to be liked by reason. Yet enthusiasm is sublime aesthetically, because it is a straining of our forces by ideas that impart to the mind a momentum whose effects are mightier and more permanent than are those of an impulse produced by presentations of sense. But (strange though it seems) even [the state of] *being without affects* (*apatheia, phlegma in significatu bono*[41]) in a mind that vigorously

---

[38] [On enthusiasm as an affect, cf. (and contrast) the *Anthropology*, §75, Ak. VII, 253–54; cf. also the *Metaphysics of Morals*, Ak. VI, 408–09.]

[39] *Affects* differ in kind from *passions*. Affects relate merely to feeling, whereas passions belong to our power of desire and are inclinations that make it difficult or impossible for us to determine our power of choice through principles. Affects are impetuous and unpremeditated, passions persistent and deliberate. Thus resentment in the form of anger is an affect, in the form of hatred (vindictiveness) it is a passion. Passion can never be called sublime, no matter what the circumstances; for while in an affect the mind's freedom is impeded, in passion it is abolished.[40]

[40] [On these distinctions, cf. the *Anthropology*, Ak. VII, 251–75 (see also *ibid.*, 235), and the *Metaphysics of Morals*, Ak. VI, 407–08.]

[41] [In their favorable (namely, moral) senses. Cf. the *Anthropology*, Ak. VII, 252–54, and the *Metaphysics of Morals*, Ak. VI, 408.]

pursues its immutable principles is sublime, and sublime in a far superior way, because it also has pure reason's liking on its side. Only a cast of mind of that sort is called noble—[though] the term has since come to be applied to things as well, such as a building, a garment, a literary style, a person's bearing, and so on—namely, if it arouses not so much *amazement* [*Verwunderung*] (an affect [that occurs] when we present novelty that exceeds our expectation) as *admiration* [*Bewunderung*] (an amazement that does not cease once the novelty is gone),[42] which happens when ideas in their exhibition harmonize, unintentionally and without art, without our aesthetic liking.

Every affect of the VIGOROUS KIND (i.e., which makes us conscious that we have forces to overcome any resistance, i.e., makes us conscious of our *animus strenuus*) is *aesthetically sublime,* e.g., anger, even desperation (provided it is *indignant* rather than *despondent* desperation). But an affect of the LANGUID kind (which turns the very effort to resist into an object of displeasure, an *animus languidus*), has nothing *noble* about it, though it may be classed with the beautiful of the sensible kind. Hence emotions that can reach the strength of an affect are very diverse as well. We have *spirited* [*mutig*] emotions, and we have *tender* ones. When the latter increase to the level [i.e., strength] of an affect, they are utterly useless; and a propensity toward them is called *sentimentality.* A sympathetic grief that refuses to be consoled or that, if it concerns fictitious evils, is courted deliberately even to the point where fancy deceives us into regarding the evils as actual proves and creates a soul that is gentle but also weak and that shows a beautiful side; we can call such a soul fanciful, but not even so much as enthusiastic. None of the following are compatible with anything that could be classed with beauty, let alone sublimity, in a cast of mind: romances and maudlin plays; insipid moral precepts that dally with (falsely) so-called noble attitudes but that in fact make the heart languid and insensitive to the stern precept of duty, and that hence make the heart incapable of any respect for the dignity of the humanity in our own person and for human rights

273

---

[42] [On amazement and admiration, cf. below, Ak. 365. See also the *Anthropology*, Ak. VII, 243 and 255. In one place (*ibid.*, Ak. VII, 261), Kant gives the Latin '*admirari*' for '*verwundern*' rather than '*bewundern*,' but while the Latin term can in fact stand for either of these terms, the English 'to admire' means only '*bewundern*.']

(which are something quite different from human happiness) and thus make it incapable of any firm principles in general; even a religious discourse that recommends fawning and groveling and base ingratiation and the abandonment of all reliance on our own ability to resist the evil within us, instead of recommending a vigorous resolve for testing what forces are left us despite all our frailty and for trying to overcome our inclinations; the false humility that posits self-contempt, whining hypocritical repentance, and a merely passive frame of mind as the only way we can please the supreme being.[43]

But even impetuous agitations of the mind—whether they are connected with religious ideas and are called edification, or with ideas involving a social interest and pertain merely to culture—can by no means claim the distinction of being a *sublime* exhibition [of ideas], no matter how much they may strain the imagination, unless they leave us with a mental attunement that influences, at least indirectly, our consciousness of our fortitude and resolution concerning what carries with it pure intellectual purposiveness (namely, the supersensible). For otherwise all these emotions belong only to [inner] *motion,* which we welcome for the sake of our health. The agreeable lassitude we feel after being stirred up by the play of affects is our enjoyment of the well-being that results from the establishment of the equilibrium of our various vital forces. This enjoyment comes to no more in the end than what Oriental voluptuaries find so appealing when they have their bodies thoroughly kneaded, as it were, and have all their muscles and joints gently squeezed and bent—except that in the first case the moving principle is for the most part within us, whereas in the second it is wholly outside us. Thus many people believe they are edified by a sermon that in fact builds no edifice (no system of good maxims), or are improved by the performance of a tragedy when in fact they are merely glad at having succeeded in routing boredom. Hence the sublime must always have reference to

274

[43] [Apart from the word 'God,' which is a proper name, expressions referring to the deity are not capitalized in this translation. For although some of these, e.g., 'Supreme Being,' would normally be capitalized in English, many *other* expressions that Kant uses to refer to the deity would not (e.g., 'original basis of the universe' [Ak. 392], 'supreme understanding as cause of the world' [Ak. 395], or even 'original being' in the sense used by Spinoza [Ak. 393]). Capitalizing some but not others would have the effect of attributing to Kant distinctions that he did not make. No such problem arises in German, because there *all* nouns are capitalized.]

our *way of thinking,* i.e., to maxims directed to providing the intellectual [side in us] and our rational ideas with supremacy over sensibility.

We need not worry that the feeling of the sublime will lose [something] if it is exhibited in such an abstract way as this, which is wholly negative as regards the sensible. For though the imagination finds nothing beyond the sensible that could support it, this very removal of its barriers also makes it feel unbounded, so that its separation [from the sensible] is an exhibition of the infinite; and though an exhibition of the infinite can as such never be more than merely negative, it still expands the soul. Perhaps the most sublime passage in the Jewish Law is the commandment: Thou shalt not make unto thee any graven image, or any likeness of any thing that is in heaven or on earth, or under the earth, etc. This commandment alone can explain the enthusiasm that the Jewish people in its civilized era felt for its religion when it compared itself with other peoples, or can explain the pride that Islam inspires. The same holds also for our presentation of the moral law, and for the predisposition within us for morality. It is indeed a mistake to worry that depriving this presentation of whatever could commend it to the senses will result in its carrying with it no more than a cold and lifeless approval without any moving force or emotion. It is exactly the other way round. For once the senses no longer see anything before them, while yet the unmistakable and indelible idea of morality remains, one would sooner need to temper the momentum of an unbounded imagination so as to keep it from rising to the level of enthusiasm, than to seek to support these ideas with images and childish devices for fear that they would otherwise be powerless. That is also why governments have gladly permitted religion to be amply furnished with such accessories: they were trying to relieve every subject of the trouble, yet also of the ability, to expand his soul's forces beyond the barriers that one can choose to set for him so as to reduce him to mere passivity and so make him more pliable.

275

On the other hand, this pure, elevating, and merely negative exhibition of morality involves no danger of *fanaticism,* which is the *delusion* [*Wahn*] *of wanting to* SEE *something beyond all bounds of sensibility,* i.e., of dreaming according to principles (raving with reason). The exhibition avoids fanaticism precisely because it is merely negative. For *the idea of freedom is inscrutable* and thereby precludes all positive exhibition whatever; but the moral law in itself can sufficiently and originally determine us, so that it does not even permit us to cast about for some additional determining basis. If enthusiasm is comparable to *madness* [*Wahnsinn*], fanaticism is comparable to *mania* [*Wahnwitz*].[44] Of these the latter is least of all compatible with the sublime, because it is ridiculous in a somber [*grüblerisch*] way[; for[45]] in enthusiasm, an affect, the imagination is unbridled, but in fanaticism, a deep-seated and brooding passion, it is ruleless. Madness is a passing accident that presumably strikes even the soundest understanding on occasion; mania is a disease that deranges it.

Simplicity (artless purposiveness) is, as it were, nature's style in the sublime. Hence it is also the style of morality, which is a second (namely, a supersensible) nature, of which we know only the laws, without being able to reach, by means of intuition, the supersensible ability within ourselves that contains the basis of this legislation.

A further comment is needed. It is true that our liking both for the beautiful and for the sublime not only differs recognizably from other aesthetic judgments by being universally *communicable,* but by having this property it also acquires an interest in relation to society (where such communication may take place). Yet we also regard *isolation from all society* as something sublime, if it rests on ideas that look beyond all sensible interest. To be sufficient to oneself and hence have no need of society, yet without being unsociable, i.e., without shunning society, is something approaching the sublime, as is any case of setting aside our needs. On the other hand, to shun people either from *misanthropy* because we are hostile toward them or from *anthropophobia* (fear of people) because we are afraid they might be our enemies is partly odious and partly contemptible. There is, however, a different (very improperly so-called) misanthropy, the predisposition to which tends to appear in the minds of many well-meaning people as they grow older. This latter misanthropy is philanthropic enough as regards *benevolence* [*Wohlwollen*], but as the result of a

276

[44] [Cf. (and contrast) the *Anthropology,* Ak. VII, 215 (also 202).]

[45] [The insertion replaces a mere period, and its point is to bring out the continuity between the preceding sentence that brings in madness and mania, and the following one, where the demonstrative adjectives in the original text can refer only to madness and mania again, not to enthusiasm and fanaticism.]

long and sad experience it has veered far away from a *liking* [*Wohlge-fallen*] for people. We find evidence of this in a person's propensity toward reclusiveness, in his fanciful wish that he could spend the rest of his life on a remote country estate, or for that matter (in the case of young people) in their dream of happily spending their lives with a small family, on some island unknown to the rest of the world— all of which novelists and writers of Robinsonades use so cleverly. Falseness, ingratitude, injustice, whatever is childish in the purposes that we ourselves consider important and great and in the pursuit of which people inflict all conceivable evils on one another, these so contradict the idea of what people could be if they wanted to, and so conflict with our fervent wish to see them improved, that, given that we cannot love them, it seems but a slight sacrifice to forgo all social joys so as to avoid hating them. This sadness, which does not concern the evils that fate imposes on other people (in which case it would be caused by sympathy), but those that they inflict on themselves (a sadness that rests on an antipathy involving principles), is sublime, because it rests on ideas, whereas the sadness caused by sympathy can at most count as beautiful. *Saussure*,[46] as intelligent as he was thorough, in describing his Alpine travels says of *Bonhomme,* one of the Savoy mountains, "A certain *insipid sadness* reigns there." Thus clearly he also knew an *interesting* sadness, such as is inspired by a wasteland to which people would gladly transfer themselves so as to hear or find out no more about the world, which shows that such wastelands cannot, after all, be quite so inhospitable as to offer no more to human beings than a most troublesome abode. This comment is intended only as a reminder that even grief (but not a dejected kind of sadness) may be included among the *vigorous* affects, if it has its basis in moral ideas. If, on the other hand, it is based on sympathy, then it may indeed be lovable, but belongs merely to the *languid* affects. My point is to draw attention to the fact that only in the first case is the mental attunement *sublime.*

We can now also compare the transcendental exposition of aesthetic judgments we have just completed with the physiological

[46] [See Ak. 265.]

one, regarding which work has been done by someone like *Burke*[47] and many acute men among us, so that we may see where a merely empirical exposition of the sublime and of the beautiful may lead. *Burke*,[48] who deserves to be mentioned as the foremost author in this way of treating the subject,[49] discovers along this route (p. 223 of [the German translation of] his work) "that the feeling of the sublime is based on the impulse toward self-preservation and on *fear*, i.e., on a pain, a pain that, since it does not go so far as actually to disarrange the parts of the body, gives rise to agitations. And since these agitations clear the vessels, small or large, of dangerous and troublesome obstructions, they are able to arouse agreeable sensations. These do not indeed amount to a pleasure, but they still amount to a kind of pleasant thrill, a certain tranquility mingled with terror."[50] He attributes the beautiful, which he bases on love (while insisting that desire be kept apart from this love) "to the relaxing, slackening, and enervating of the body's fibres, and hence to a softening, dissolution,

---

[47] [Edmund Burke (1729–97), British statesman and political thinker. His *Philosophical Enquiry Into the Origin of Our Ideas of the Sublime and Beautiful* (1757) gained him a reputation in Britain. Abroad it was read with interest not only by Kant but, among others, by Lessing, Mendelssohn, Schiller, and Diderot.]

[48] According to the German translation [by Christian Garve (1742–98), German moralist] of his work entitled *A Philosophical Enquiry Into the Origin of Our Ideas of the Sublime and Beautiful* ([the translation:] Riga: Hartknoch, 1773).

[49] [Kant's own *Observations on the Feeling of the Beautiful and Sublime* (1764) (Ak. II, 205–56) had been mainly empirical. Cf. Donald W. Crawford, *Kant's Aesthetic Theory* (Madison: University of Wisconsin Press, 1974), pp. 8–11, 60. The same applies of course to Kant's own *Remarks on the Observations*, Ak. XX, 1–192.]

[50] [Burke, *Enquiry*, Pt. IV, Sect. vii: ". . . [I]f the pain and terror are so modified as not to be actually noxious; if the pain is not carried to violence, and the terror is not conversant about the present destruction of the person, as these emotions clear the parts, whether fine or gross, of a dangerous and troublesome encumbrance, they are capable of producing delight; not pleasure, but a sort of delightful horror, a sort of tranquility tinged with terror; which, as it belongs to self-preservation, is one of the strongest of all the passions. Its object is the sublime." Cf. also above, Ak. 269 br. n.34.]

exhaustion, a fainting, a dying and melting away with delight"
(pp. 251–52 [of the translation].)[51] To confirm this kind of explanation he points not only to those cases where the feeling of the
beautiful and of the sublime may be aroused in us by the imagination in connection with the understanding, but even to those where
it is aroused by the imagination in connection with sensation.[52] As
psychological observations these analyses of the phenomena involved
in our mind are exceedingly fine and provide rich material for the
favorite investigations of empirical anthropology. Nor can it be
denied that all presentations in us, no matter whether their object
is merely sensible or instead wholly intellectual, can in the subject
still be connected with gratification or pain, however unnoticeable
these may be (because all of them affect the feeling of life, and
none of them can be indifferent insofar as it is a modification of
the subject). It cannot even be denied that, as Epicurus maintained,
gratification and *pain* are ultimately always of the body,[53] whether
they come from imagination or even from presentations of the
understanding. He maintained this on the ground that, in the absence
of [some] feeling of the bodily organ, life is merely consciousness of
our existence, and not a feeling of being well or unwell, i.e., of the
furtherance or inhibition of the vital forces; for the mind taken by
itself is wholly life (the very principle of life), whereas any obstacles
or furtherance must be sought outside it and yet still within man
himself, and hence in the [mind's] connection with his body.

But if we suppose that our liking for the object consists entirely in
the object's gratifying us through charm or emotion, then we also
must not require anyone *else* to assent to an aesthetic judgment that
we make; for about that sort of liking each person rightly consults
only his private sense. But, if that is so, then all censure of taste will

278

---

[51] [*Ibid.*, Pt. IV, Sect. xix: ". . . [A] beautiful object presented to the sense, by causing
a relaxation of the body, produces the passion of love in the mind. . . ." And a little
earlier: ". . . [B]eauty acts by relaxing the solids of the whole system. There are all
the appearances of such a relaxation; and a relaxation somewhat below the natural
tone seems to me to be the cause of all positive pleasure. Who is a stranger to that
manner of expression so common in all times and in all countries, of being softened,
relaxed, enervated, dissolved, melted away by pleasure?"]

[52] [*Ibid.*; for example, smoothness (Part IV, Sect. xx) and sweetness (Part IV, Sect.
xxii).]

[53] [See the Letter to Herodotus, V, "The Soul."]

also cease, unless the example that other people give through the contingent harmony among their judgments were turned into a *command* that we [too] approve. At such a principle, however, we would presumably balk, appealing to our natural right to subject to our own sense, not to that of others, any judgment that rests on the direct feeling of our own well-being.

It seems, then, that we must not regard a judgment of taste as *egoistic;* rather, we must regard it necessarily as *pluralistic* by its inner nature, i.e., on account of itself rather than the examples that others give of their taste; we must acknowledge it to be a judgment that is entitled to claim that everyone else ought also to agree with it. But if that is so, then it must be based on some a priori principle (whether objective or subjective), and we can never arrive at such a principle by scouting about for empirical laws about mental changes. For these reveal only how we do judge; they do not give us a command as to how we ought to judge, let alone an *unconditioned* one. And yet judgments of taste presuppose such a command, because they insist that our liking be connected *directly* with a presentation. Hence, though we may certainly begin with an empirical exposition of aesthetic judgments, so as to provide the material for a higher investigation, still a transcendental discussion of taste is possible, and belongs essentially to a critique of this ability. For if taste did not have a priori principles, it could not possibly pronounce on the judgments of others and pass verdicts approving or repudiating them with even the slightest semblance of having the right to do so.

The remainder of the analytic of aesthetic judgment contains first of all the deduction of pure aesthetic judgments, to which we now turn.

DEDUCTION[1] OF PURE AESTHETIC JUDGMENTS

§ 30

The Deduction of Aesthetic Judgments about Objects of Nature Must Be Directed Not to What We Call Sublime in Nature but Only to the Beautiful

Since an aesthetic judgment lays claim to universal validity for every subject and hence must be based on some a priori principle or other, it requires a deduction (i.e., a legitimation of its pretension). Such a deduction is needed, in addition to an exposition of the judgment, if the judgment concerns a liking or disliking for the *form of the object.*

---

[1] [*Deduktion.* The term means 'justification' or 'legitimation.' Cf. the *Critique of Pure Reason,* A 84–92 = B 116–24. (What we call 'deduction' in formal logic is called by Kant *Ableitung,* 'derivation.' Cf. Ak. 412.) This justification of judgments of taste is needed in addition to their *exposition* (which has just been completed), i.e., their explication or examination (cf. *ibid.,* as well as the *Critique of Pure Reason,* A 23 = B 38 and A 729–30 = B 757–58).]

Judgments of taste about the beautiful in nature are of this sort. For in their case the purposiveness does have its basis in the object and its shape, even though it does not indicate that we are referring the object to other objects according to concepts (so as to give rise to a cognitive judgment), but merely concerns the apprehension as such of this form, insofar as that form manifests itself in the mind as conforming to the *power* of concepts [the understanding] and the power of their exhibition (which is the same as the power of apprehension [the imagination]). This is also why, concerning the beautiful in nature, we can raise all sorts of questions about what causes this purposiveness in nature's forms, e.g.: How are we to explain why nature has so extravagantly spread beauty everywhere, even at the bottom of the ocean, where the human eye (for which, after all, this beauty is alone purposive) rarely penetrates?—and so on.

But then consider the sublime in nature, when our judgment about it is purely aesthetic, unmixed with any concepts of perfection, i.e., of objective purposiveness, in which case it would be a teleological judgment. The sublime in nature can be regarded as entirely formless or unshapely and yet as the object of a pure liking, manifesting a subjective purposiveness in the given presentation. Hence the question arises whether this kind of aesthetic judgment also requires a deduction of its claim to some (subjective) a priori principle or other, in addition to an exposition of what we think in [making] the judgment.

280   We can answer this question adequately as follows. When we speak of the sublime in nature we speak improperly; properly speaking, sublimity can be attributed merely to our way of thinking, or, rather, to the foundation this has in human nature. What happens is merely that the apprehension of an otherwise formless and unpurposive object prompts us to become conscious of that foundation, so that what is subjectively purposive is the *use* we make of the object, and it is not the object *itself* that is judged to be purposive on account of its form. ([That is, what is subjectively purposive is,] as it were, *species finalis accepta, non data.*[2]) That is why the exposition we gave of judgments about the sublime in nature was also their deduction. For when we analyzed these judgments in order to see what reflection by the power of judgment they contain, we found that they contain a purposive relation of the cognitive powers, which we must lay a priori

[2] [Purposive appearance as received, not as given.]

at the basis of the power of purposes (the will) and which is therefore itself a priori purposive; and that already provides the deduction, i.e., the justification of the claim of these judgments to universally necessary validity.

Hence the only deduction we shall have to attempt is that of judgments of taste, i.e., judgments about the beauty in natural things; that will suffice for a complete solution of the problem for the whole aesthetic power of judgment.

§ 31

On the Method
of the Deduction
of Judgments of Taste

The obligation to provide a deduction for judgments of a [certain] kind, i.e., a guarantee of their legitimacy, arises only if the judgment lays claim to necessity; this it does even if the universality it demands is subjective universality, i.e., if it demands everyone's assent, even though it is not a cognitive judgment but only a judgment about the pleasure or displeasure we take in a given object, i.e., [a judgment] claiming [*Anmaßung*] a subjective purposiveness that is valid for everyone, without exception [*durchgängig*], but that is not to be based on any concepts of the thing, since the judgment is one of taste.

Therefore, in the case of a judgment that demands subjective universality, we are not dealing with a cognitive judgment, neither a theoretical one based on the concept of a *nature* as such, as given by the understanding, nor a (pure) practical one based on the idea of *freedom,* as given a priori by reason. Hence what we must justify as a priori valid is neither a judgment presenting what a [certain] thing is, nor a judgment which says that I ought to carry something out so as to produce a [certain] thing. So what we shall have to establish is merely the *universal validity,* for the power of judgment as such, of a *singular* judgment that expresses the subjective purposiveness of an empirical

281

presentation of the form of an object; establishing such validity will serve to explain how it is possible for us to like something when we merely judge it (without [the liking being determined by] sensation proper [*Sinnesempfindung*][3] or [by] concept), and how it is possible for everyone to be entitled to proclaim his liking as a rule for everyone else, just as our judging of an object for the sake of *cognition* always [*überhaupt*] has universal rules.

[Therefore,] since a judgment of taste is in fact of this sort, its universal validity is not to be established by gathering votes and asking other people what kind of sensation they are having; but it must rest, as it were, on an autonomy of the subject who is making a judgment about the feeling of pleasure (in the given presentation), i.e., it must rest on his own taste; and yet it is also not to be derived from concepts. Hence a judgment of taste has the following twofold peculiarity, which is moreover a logical one: *First,* it has a priori universal validity, which yet is not a logical universal validity governed by concepts, but the universality of a singular judgment; *second,* it has a necessity (which must always rest on a priori bases), and yet a necessity that does not depend on any a priori bases of proof by the presentation of which we could compel [people to give] the assent that a judgment of taste requires of everyone.

If we resolve these logical peculiarities, which distinguish a judgment of taste from all cognitive judgments, we shall have done all that is needed in order to deduce this strange ability we have, provided that at the outset we abstract from all content of the judgment, i.e., from the feeling of pleasure, and merely compare the aesthetic form with the form of objective judgments as prescribed by logic. Let us begin, then, by presenting these characteristic properties of taste, using examples to elucidate them.

---

[3] [As distinguished from 'sensation' as meaning feeling, which is involved here. Cf. Ak. 291 incl. br. n. 19. (If the [feeling of] liking were determined by sensation proper, it would be a liking for the agreeable. Cf. Ak. 205–06.)]

§ 32

First Peculiarity of a Judgment of Taste

A judgment of taste determines its object in respect of our liking (beauty) [but] makes a claim to *everyone's* assent, as if it were an objective judgment.

To say, This flower is beautiful, is tantamount to a mere repetition of the flower's own claim to everyone's liking. The agreeableness of its smell, on the other hand, gives it no claim whatever: its smell delights [*ergötzen*] one person, it makes another dizzy. In view of this [difference], must we not suppose that beauty has to be considered a property of the flower itself, which does not adapt itself to differences in people's heads and all their senses, but to which they must adapt themselves if they wish to pass judgment on it? Yet beauty is not a property of the flower itself. For a judgment of taste consists precisely in this, that it calls a thing beautiful only by virtue of that characteristic in which it adapts itself to the way we apprehend it.

Moreover, whenever a subject offers a judgment as proof of his taste [concerning some object], we demand that he judge for himself: he should not have to grope about among other people's judgments by means of experience, to gain instruction in advance from whether they like or dislike that object; so we demand that he pronounce his judgment a priori, that he not make it [by way of] imitation, (say) on the ground that a thing is actually liked universally. One would think, however, that an a priori judgment must contain a concept of the object, this concept containing the principle for cognizing the object. But a judgment of taste is not based on concepts at all, and is not at all a cognition but only an aesthetic judgment.

That is why a young poet cannot be brought to abandon his persuasion that his poem is beautiful, neither by the judgment of his audience nor by that of his friends; and if he listens to them, it is not because he now judges the poem differently, but because, even if (at least with regard to him) the whole audience were to have wrong taste, his desire for approval still causes him to accommodate himself (even against his judgment) to the common delusion. Only later on, when his power of judgment has been sharpened by practice, will he voluntarily depart from his earlier judgment, just as he does with those of his judgments which rest wholly on reason. Taste lays claim merely to autonomy; but to make other people's judgments the basis determining one's own would be heteronomy.

It is true that we extol, and rightly so, the works of the ancients as models, and call their authors classical, as if they form a certain noble class among writers which gives laws to people by the precedent it sets. This seems to point to a posteriori sources of taste and to refute the autonomy of every subject's taste. But we might just as well say: the fact that the ancient mathematicians are to this day considered to be virtually indispensable models of supreme thoroughness and elegance in the synthetic method[4] proves that our reason [only] imitates and is unable on its own to produce rigorous and highly intuitive proofs by constructing concepts.[5] The same holds for all uses, no matter how free, of our powers, including even reason (which must draw all its judgments from the common a priori source): if each subject always had to start from nothing but the crude predisposition given him by nature, [many] of his attempts would fail, if other people before him had not failed in theirs; they did not make these attempts in order to turn their successors into mere imitators, but so that, by their procedure, they might put others on a track whereby they could search for the principles within themselves and so adopt their own and often better course. In religion, everyone must surely find the rule for his conduct within himself, since he is also the one who remains responsible for his conduct and cannot put the blame for his offenses on others on the ground that they were his teachers and predecessors; yet even here an example of virtue and holiness will always accomplish more than any universal precepts we have received from priests or philosophers, or for that matter found within ourselves. Such an example, set for us in history, does not make dispensable the autonomy of virtue that arises from our own and original (a priori) idea of morality, nor does it transform this idea into a mechanism of imitation. *Following* by reference to a precedent, rather than imitating,

---

[4] [The synthetic method proceeds from principles to their consequences, the analytic method the other way. Cf. the *Logic*, Ak. IX, 149, and the *Prolegomena*, Ak. IV, 263, 275, 276n, 279, and 365.)

[5] [Cf. Ak. 232 br. n. 51.]

283

is the right term for any influence that products of an exemplary author may have on others; and this means no more than drawing on the same sources from which the predecessor himself drew, and learning from him only how to go about doing so. Among all our abilities and talents, taste is precisely what stands most in need of examples regarding what has enjoyed the longest-lasting approval in the course of cultural progress, in order that it will not become uncouth again and relapse into the crudeness of its first attempts; and taste needs this because its judgment cannot be determined by concepts and precepts.

§ 33

Second Peculiarity of a Judgment of Taste

284

A judgment of taste, just as if it were merely *subjective,* cannot be determined by bases of proof.

If someone does not find a building, a view, or a poem beautiful, then, *first,* he will refuse to let even a hundred voices, all praising it highly, prod him into approving of it inwardly. He may of course act as if he liked it too, so that people will not think that he lacks taste. He may even begin to doubt whether he has in fact done enough to mold his taste, by familiarizing himself with a sufficient number of objects of a certain kind (just as someone who thinks he recognizes a forest in some distant object that everyone else regards as a town will doubt the judgment of his own eyes). And yet he realizes clearly that other people's approval in no way provides him with a valid proof by which to judge beauty; even though others may perhaps see and observe for him, and even though what many have seen the same way may serve him, who believes he saw it differently, as a sufficient basis of proof for a theoretical and hence logical judgment, yet the fact that others have liked something can never serve him as a basis for an aesthetic judgment. If others make a judgment that is unfavorable to us, this may rightly make us wonder about our own judgment, but it can never convince us that ours is incorrect. Hence there is no empirical *basis of proof* that could compel anyone to make [some] judgment of taste.

Second, still less can a judgment about beauty be determined by an a priori proof, in accordance with determinate rules. If someone reads me his poem, or takes me to a play that in the end I simply cannot find to my taste, then let him adduce *Batteux* or *Lessing*[6] to prove that his poem is beautiful, or [bring in] still older and more famous critics of taste with all the rules they have laid down; moreover, let certain passages that I happen to dislike conform quite well to rules of beauty (as laid down by these critics and universally recognized): I shall stop my ears, shall refuse to listen to reasons and arguments, and shall sooner assume that those rules of the critics are false, or at least do not apply in the present case, than allow my judgment to be determined by a priori bases of proof; for it is meant to be a judgment of taste, and not one of the understanding or of reason.

285

It seems that this is one of the main reasons why this aesthetic power of judging was given that very name: taste. For even if someone lists all the ingredients of a dish, pointing out that I have always found each of them agreeable, and goes on to praise this food—and rightly so—as wholesome, I shall be deaf to all these reasons: I shall try the dish on *my* tongue and palate, and thereby (and not by universal principles) make my judgment.

It is a fact that any judgment of taste we make is always a singular judgment about the object. The understanding can, by comparing the object with other people's judgment about their liking of it, make a universal judgment, e.g.: All tulips are beautiful. But such a judgment is then not a judgment of taste; it is a logical judgment, which turns an object's reference to taste into a predicate of things of a certain general kind. Only a judgment by which I find a singular given tulip beautiful, i.e., in which I find that my liking for the tulip is universally valid, is a judgment of taste. Its peculiarity, however, consists in the fact that, even though it has merely subjective validity, it yet extends its claim to *all* subjects, just as it always could if it were an objective

---

[6] [Charles Batteux (1713–80), French philosopher and, in particular, aesthetician, and author of several works; Gotthold Ephraim Lessing (1729–81), German dramatist and aesthetician.]

judgment that rested on cognitive bases and that [we] could be compelled [to make] by a proof.

§ 34

An Objective Principle of Taste Is Impossible

By a principle of taste would be meant a principle under which, as condition, we could subsume the concept of an object and then infer that the object is beautiful. That, however, is absolutely impossible. For I must feel the pleasure directly in my presentation of the object, and I cannot be talked into that pleasure by means of any bases of proof. Hence, although, as *Hume* says, critics can reason more plausibly than cooks,[7] they still share the same fate. They cannot expect the determining basis of their judgment [to come] from the force of the bases of proof, but only from the subject's reflection on his own state (of pleasure or displeasure), all precepts and rules being rejected.

There is, however, something about which critics nonetheless can and should reason, since doing so may serve to correct and broaden our judgments of taste. I do not mean that they should set forth the determining basis of this kind of aesthetic judgments in a universal formula that we could [then] use. What they should do is investigate

286

[7] [*Essays, Moral and Political* (1741–42), Essay VIII, "The Sceptic": "There is something approaching to principles in mental taste, and critics can reason and dispute more plausibly than cooks or perfumers. We may observe, however, that this uniformity among human kind hinders not, but that there is a considerable diversity in the sentiments of beauty and worth, and that education, custom, prejudice, caprice, and humour frequently vary our taste of this kind. You will never convince a man who is not accustomed to Italian music and has not an ear to follow its intricacies that a Scots tune is not preferable. You have not even any single argument beyond your own taste which you can employ in your behalf; and to your antagonist his particular taste will always appear a more convincing argument to the contrary. If you be wise, each of you will allow that the other may be in the right, and, having many other instances of this diversity of taste, you will both confess that beauty and worth are merely of a relative nature and consist in an agreeable sentiment, produced by an object in a particular mind, according to the peculiar structure and constitution of that mind."]

our cognitive powers and what task these powers perform in these judgments, and they should clarify by examples the reciprocal subjective purposiveness about which it was shown above that its form in a given presentation is the beauty of the object of this presentation. Hence the critique of taste is itself only subjective as regards the presentation by which an object is given us: it is the art, or science, of finding rules for the reciprocal relation that understanding and imagination have in the given presentation (without reference to prior sensation or concept), and hence for their accordance or discordance, and of determining them as regards their conditions. The critique of taste is an *art* if it shows this only through examples; it is a *science* if it derives the possibility of such judging from the nature of these powers as cognitive powers as such. It is with the latter alone, with a transcendental critique, that we are here concerned throughout. Its aim is to set forth and justify the subjective principle of taste as an a priori principle of the power of judgment. The critique that is an art merely takes the physiological (in this case psychological) and hence empirical rules by which taste actually proceeds, and (without thinking about [how] they are possible) seeks to apply them to our judging of objects of taste; and it criticizes the products of fine art, just as the *transcendental* critique criticizes our very ability to judge them.

§ 35

The Principle of Taste
Is the Subjective Principle
of the Power of
Judgment as Such

A judgment of taste differs from a logical one in that a logical judgment subsumes a presentation under concepts of the object, whereas a judgment of taste does not subsume it under any concept at all, since otherwise the necessary universal approval could be [obtained] by compelling [people to give it]. But a judgment of taste does resemble a logical judgment inasmuch as it alleges a universality and necessity, though a universality and necessity that is not governed by concepts of the object and hence is merely subjective. Now since the concepts in a judgment constitute its content (what belongs to the cognition of the object), while a judgment of taste cannot be determined by concepts, its basis is only the subjective formal condition of a judgment as such. The subjective condition of all judgments is our very ability to judge, i.e., the power of judgment. When we use this power of judgment in regard to a presentation by which an object is given, then it requires that there be a harmony between two presentational powers, imagination (for the intuition and the combination of its manifold) and understanding (for the concept that is the presentation of the unity of this combination). Now since a judgment of taste is not based on a concept of the object (in the case of a presentation by which an object is given), it can consist only in the subsumption of the very imagination under the condition [which must be met] for the understanding to proceed in general from intuition to concepts. In other words, since the imagination's freedom consists precisely in its schematizing[8] without a concept, a judgment of taste must rest upon a mere sensation,[9] namely, our sensation of both the imagination in its *freedom* and the understanding with its *lawfulness,* as they reciprocally quicken each other; i.e., it must rest on a feeling that allows us to judge the object by the purposiveness that the presentation (by which an object is given) has insofar as it furthers the cognitive powers in their free play. Hence taste, as a subjective power of judgment, contains a principle of subsumption; however, this subsumption is not one of intuitions under *concepts,* but, rather, one of the *power* of intuitions or exhibitions (the imagination) under the *power* of concepts (the understanding), insofar as the imagination *in its freedom* harmonizes with the understanding *in its lawfulness.*

In attempting to discover this legitimating basis by means of a deduction of judgments of taste, we can use as our guide only the

---

[8] [I.e., creating a schema; cf. Ak. 253 br. n. 17. Kant is about to say that in a judgment of taste the imagination as such is subsumed under the *understanding* as such. Strictly speaking, however, the imagination is subsumed under the (indeterminate) *schema* of the understanding as such; and this indeterminate schema is the "condition" which Kant has just mentioned.]

[9] [In the sense of *feeling,* in this case.]

formal peculiarities of this kind of judgments, i.e., we must consider merely their logical form.

§ 36

On the Problem of a Deduction of Judgments of Taste

288

With the perception of an object we can directly connect the concept of an object as such, [for] which it contains the empirical predicates, in order to give rise to a cognitive judgment. This is how an empirical judgment is produced.[10] Now this judgment is based on a priori concepts of the systematic unity of the manifold of intuition; hence we can think this manifold as the determination of an object. These concepts (the categories) require a deduction, and this was indeed provided in the *Critique of Pure Reason,*[11] which thus made it possible to solve the problem: How are synthetic cognitive judgments possible a priori? That problem, then, concerned the pure under-standing's a priori principles and theoretical judgments.

But we can also directly connect with a perception a feeling of pleasure (or displeasure) and a liking that accompanies the object's presentation and serves it in the place of a predicate. This is how an aesthetic judgment arises, which is not a cognitive judgment. Now if an aesthetic judgment is not a mere judgment of sensation, but a formal judgment of reflection that requires this liking from everyone

---

[10] ["As far as *empirical judgments have universal validity* they are JUDGMENTS OF EXPERIENCE; but those *that are valid only subjectively* I call mere JUDGMENTS OF PERCEPTION. The latter require no pure concept of the understanding, but only the logical connection of the perceptions in a thinking subject. Judgments of experience, on the other hand, require, in addition to the presentations of sensible intuition, special *concepts produced originally in the understanding*, and it is these concepts that make the judgment of experience *valid objectively*": *Prolegomena*, Ak. IV, 298. Cf. the *Critique of Pure Reason,* A 120, A 374, B 422n.]

[11] [The *metaphysical* deduction (for this name, see B 159), A 65–83 = B 90–116, is to show what categories there are (in the understanding); the *transcendental* deduction, A 84–130 and B 116–69, is to prove that these categories are objectively valid.]

as necessary, then it must be based on something as its a priori principle. This principle may well be merely subjective (in case an objective one were to be impossible for judgments of this kind), but even then it requires a deduction, in order that we may grasp how an aesthetic judgment can lay claim to necessity. And that is the basis of the problem with which we are now dealing: How are judgments of taste possible? So this problem concerns the a priori principles that the pure power of judgment [uses when it makes] *aesthetic* judgments, i.e., judgments where it does not (as it does in theoretical judgments) merely have to subsume under objective concepts of the understanding, [so that] it is subject to a law,[12] but where it is, subjectively, object to itself as well as law to itself.

We can also think of this problem as follows: How is a judgment possible in which the subject, merely on the basis of his *own* feeling of pleasure in an object, independently of the object's concept, judges this pleasure as one attaching to the presentation of that same object *in all other subjects,* and does so a priori, i.e., without being allowed to wait for other people's assent?

We can readily see that judgments of taste are synthetic; for they go beyond the concept of the object, and even beyond the intuition of the object, and add as a predicate to this intuition something that is not even cognition: namely [a] feeling of pleasure (or displeasure). And yet, that these judgments are, or want to be considered, a priori judgments as regards the demand that *everyone* assent, a demand they make despite the fact that their predicate (of one's *own* pleasure [as] connected with the presentation) is empirical, is also already implicit in the expressions used to make that claim. Hence this problem of the critique of judgment is part of the general problem of transcendental philosophy: How are synthetic judgments possible a priori?[13]

289

---

[12] [Cf. the *Critique of Pure Reason*, A 137–47 = B 176–87, and below, Ak. 351–52.]

[13] [Cf. the *Critique of Pure Reason*, B 19. 'A priori' has here been construed adverbially, as modifying 'possible.' It can also be read as an adjective modifying 'judgments,' so that Kant's question reads, 'How are synthetic a priori judgments possible?' Either reading can be supported by quotes in which the ambiguity does not arise, since Kant switches frequently between these two ways of talking. See, e.g., the passage immediately following the question Kant just quoted, B 20.]

§ 37

What Is Actually Asserted A Priori about an Object in a Judgment of Taste?

That the presentation of an object is directly connected with a pleasure can only be perceived inwardly, and if we wished to indicate no more than this, the result would be a merely empirical judgment. For I cannot connect a priori a definite feeling (of pleasure or displeasure) with any presentation, except in the case where an underlying a priori principle in reason determines the will; but in that case the pleasure (in moral feeling) is the consequence of that principle, and that is precisely why it is not at all comparable to the pleasure in taste: for it requires a determinate concept of a law, whereas the pleasure in taste is to be connected directly with our mere judging, prior to any concept. That is also why all judgments of taste are singular judgments, because they do not connect their predicate, the liking, with a concept but connect it with a singular empirical presentation that is given.

Hence it is not the pleasure, but *the universal validity of this pleasure,* perceived as connected in the mind with our mere judging of an object, that we present a priori as [a] universal rule for the power of judgment, valid for everyone. That I am perceiving and judging an object with pleasure is an empirical judgment. But that I find the object beautiful, i.e., that I am entitled to require that liking from everyone as necessary, is an a priori judgment.

§ 38
Deduction of
Judgments of Taste[14]

If it is granted that in a pure judgment of taste our liking for the object is connected with our mere judging of the form of the object, then this liking is nothing but [our consciousness of] the form's subjective purposiveness for the power of judgment, which we feel as connected in the mind with the presentation of the object. Now, as far as the formal rules of judging [as such] are concerned, apart from any matter (whether sensation or concept), the power of judgment can be directed only to the subjective conditions for our employment of the power of judgment as such (where it is confined neither to the particular kind of sense involved nor to a[ny] particular concept of the understanding), and hence can be directed only to that subjective [condition] which we may presuppose in all people (as required for possible cognition as such). It follows that we must be entitled to assume a priori that a presentation's harmony with these conditions of the power of judgment is valid for everyone. In other words, it seems that when, in judging an object of sense in general, we feel this pleasure, or subjective purposiveness of the presentation for the relation between our cognitive powers, then we must be entitled to require this pleasure from everyone.[15]

290

[14] [On the problem as to where the deduction *ends* (specifically, the problem as to whether the link of beauty to *morality* is still part of the deduction), see the Translator's Introduction, *lxi–lxvi*.]

[15] To be justified in laying claim to universal assent to a judgment of the aesthetic power of judgment, which rests merely on subjective bases, one need grant only the following: (1) that in all people the subjective conditions of this power are the same as concerns the relation required for cognition as such between the cognitive powers that are activated in the power of judgment; and this must be true, for otherwise people could not communicate their presentations to one another, indeed they could not even communicate cognition; (2) that the judgment has taken into consideration merely this relation (and hence the *formal condition* of the power of judgment) and is pure, i.e., mingled neither with concepts of the object nor with sensations as the judgment's determining bases. But even if a mistake be made on the latter point,[16] this amounts to nothing but an incorrect application, in a particular case, of an authority given to us by a law, and in no way annuls the authority [itself].

[16] [Cf. Ak. 216 incl. br. n. 30, as well as the Comment Kant is about to make, but esp. § 39, Ak. 293, and § 40, Ak. 293–94.]

155

Comment

What makes this deduction so easy is that it does not need to justify the objective reality of a concept; for beauty is not a concept of an object, and a judgment of taste is not a cognitive judgment. All it asserts is that we are justified in presupposing universally in all people the same subjective conditions of the power of judgment that we find in ourselves; apart from this it asserts only that we have subsumed the given object correctly under these conditions.[17] It is true that this latter assertion involves unavoidable difficulties that do not attach to the logical power of judgment (since there we subsume under concepts, whereas in the aesthetic power of judgment we subsume under a relation of imagination and understanding, as they harmonize with each other in the presented form of an object, that can only be sensed, so that the subsumption may easily be illusory [*trügen*]). But this does not in any way detract from the legitimacy of the power of judgment's claim in counting on universal assent, a claim that amounts to no more than this: that the principle of judging validly for everyone from subjective bases is correct. For as far as the difficulty and doubt concerning the correctness of the subsumption under that principle is concerned, no more doubt is cast on the legitimacy of the claim that aesthetic judgments as such have this validity (and hence is cast on the principle itself), than is cast on the principle of the logical power of judgment (a principle that is objective) by the fact that [sometimes] (though not so often and so easily) this power's subsumption under its principle is faulty as well. But if the question were, How is it possible to assume a priori that nature is a sum [*Inbegriff*] of objects of taste? that problem would have to do with teleology. For if nature offered forms that are purposive for our power of judgment, then this would have to be regarded as a purpose of nature belonging essentially to its concept. But whether this assumption is correct is as yet very doubtful, while the actuality of natural beauties is patent to experience.

[17] [Cf. just above, n. 15 and br. n. 16.)

§ 39

On the Communicability
of a Sensation

Sensation, [construed] as what is real [i.e., material rather than formal][18] in perception and [hence as] referred to cognition, is called sensation proper.[19] The only way for it to be conceivable that what is specific in the quality of such a sensation should be universally [*durchgängig*] communicable in a uniform way is on the assumption that everyone's sense is like our own. This, however, we simply

---

[18] [Cf. Ak. 189.]

[19] [*Sinnesempfindung*, i.e., *Empfindung* (sensation) as involving a (genuine) *Sinn* (sense) and hence having to do with perception, rather than as meaning feeling. This is the very same distinction that Kant has made before, though he did not then use the term '*Sinnesempfindung*' to make it: see §3, Ak. 205–06, and cf. Ak. 203–04 and 266 incl. br. n. 33. Now although the literal meaning of this term is 'sensation of sense,' rendering it that way would make it perplexing, since the component terms are cognate in English. 'Sensation proper' avoids this difficulty and still captures Kant's meaning: feeling *is not* sensation proper, precisely because it does not have its own *sense*. It is true that Kant sometimes uses even 'sense' in talking about feeling, especially in talking about our "shared" or "common sense" (§ § 20–22, Ak. 237–40, and § 40, Ak. 293–96), which he calls "not an outer" sense (Ak. 238), thus *suggesting* that it is the inner sense. But in fact Kant does not consider it a (genuine) sense at all. Though he uses the term, he uses it *much* more rarely in the context of feeling than he does the term 'sensation,' and he uses it very reluctantly: see § 40, Ak. 293 and esp. 295, and cf. the *Metaphysics of Morals*, Ak. VI, 400. Moreover, in the *Anthropology* (Ak. VII, 153) he says expressly that, though we *might* (emphasis added) call feeling an *interior* sense, this is not to be equated with the *inner* sense (the sense through which we perceive and cognize, rather than merely feel, ourselves). And this view is consistent with the fact that Kant also says that feeling is a receptivity that "belongs to" or "is based on" inner sense (*Critique of Practical Reason*, Ak. V, respectively 58 and 80. Section VIII of the First Introduction to the *Critique of Judgment* can be interpreted similarly: see esp. Ak. 226′, just before the Comment) and in so far can be called "sensible" (cf. Ak. 335 br. n. 76) or a feeling "of" inner sense (as at Ak. 228): inner sense, and through it even the outer senses, *besides* engaging in sensation proper, are also to some extent involved in feeling. Cf. § 3, Ak. 205. The alternative of rendering '*Sinnesempfindung*' by some expression referring to an "organ" has the difficulty that inner sense does not, strictly speaking, *have* an organ (so that '*Sinnesempfindung*' would wrongly exclude inner sense, and the contrast with feeling would be lost): see Ak. 234 br. n. 55.]

cannot presuppose about such a sensation. Thus to a person who lacks the sense of smell we cannot communicate this kind of sensation; and even if he does not lack the sense, we still cannot be certain whether he is getting the very same sensation from a flower that we are getting. Yet people must be considered even more divergent concerning the *agreeableness* or *disagreeableness* [they feel] when sensing one and the same object of sense, and we simply cannot demand that everyone acknowledge [taking] in such objects the pleasure [that we take in them]. This kind of pleasure, since it enters the mind through sense, so that we are passive, may be called pleasure of *enjoyment.*

292

On the other hand, when we like an act for its moral character, this liking is not a pleasure of enjoyment, but one that arises from our spontaneous activity and its conformity with the idea of our vocation. But this feeling, called moral feeling, requires concepts and is the exhibition of a law-governed, rather than a free, purposiveness. By the same token, the only way it can be communicated universally is by means of reason, and, if the pleasure is to be of the same kind in everyone, it must be communicated through quite determinate practical concepts of reason.

It is true that the pleasure we take in the sublime in nature, since it is a pleasure involved in reasoning contemplation, also lays claim to universal participation; and yet the feeling it presupposes is already different again: it is a feeling of our supersensible vocation, a feeling which, however obscure it may be, has a moral foundation. But I have no justification for simply presupposing that other people will take account of this feeling of mine and feel a liking when they contemplate the crude magnitude of nature. (We certainly cannot attribute this liking to nature's aspect itself, since that is closer to being terrifying.) Nonetheless, inasmuch as we should on every suitable occasion take those moral predispositions into account, I may require that liking too from everyone, but only by means of the moral law, which is in turn based on concepts of reason.

On the other hand, the pleasure we take in the beautiful is a pleasure neither of enjoyment, nor of a law-governed activity, nor yet of a reasoning contemplation governed by ideas, but is a pleasure of mere reflection. Without being guided by any purpose or principle whatever, this pleasure accompanies our ordinary apprehension of an object by means of the imagination, our power of intuition, in relation to the understanding, our power of concepts. This apprehension occurs by means of a procedure that judgment has to carry out to give rise to even the most ordinary experience. The only difference is that in the case of ordinary experience the imagination has to engage in this procedure in order [for us] to [obtain] an empirical objective concept, whereas in the present case (in aesthetic judging) it has to do so merely in order to perceive that the presentation is adequate for [giving rise to a] harmonious (subjectively purposive) activity of the two cognitive powers in their freedom, i.e., in order [for us] to feel the presentational state with pleasure. This pleasure must of necessity rest on the same conditions in everyone, because they are subjective conditions for the possibility of cognition as such, and because the proportion between these cognitive powers that is required for taste is also required for the sound and common understanding that we may presuppose in everyone. That is precisely why someone who judges with taste (provided he is not mistaken in this consciousness and does not mistake the matter for the form, i.e., charm for beauty) is entitled to require the subjective purposiveness, i.e., his liking for the object, from everyone else as well, and is entitled to assume that his feeling is universally communicable, and this without any mediation by concepts.

293

§ 40

On Taste as a Kind of
Sensus Communis[20]

We often call the power of judgment a sense, when what we notice is not so much its reflection as merely its result. We then speak of a sense of truth, a sense of decency, of justice, etc. We do this even though we know, or at least properly ought to know, that a sense cannot contain these concepts, let alone have the slightest capacity to

[20] [Cf. §§ 20–22, Ak. 237–40.]

pronounce universal rules, but that a conception of truth, propriety, beauty, or justice could never enter our thoughts if we were not able to rise above the senses to higher cognitive powers. [This] *common human understanding,* which is merely man's sound ([but] not yet cultivated) understanding, is regarded as the very least that we are entitled to expect from anyone who lays claim to the name of human being; and this is also why it enjoys the unfortunate honor of being called common sense (*sensus communis*), and this, indeed, in such a way that the word common (not merely in our language, where it is actually ambiguous, but in various others as well) means the same as *vulgar*—i.e., something found everywhere, the possession of which involves no merit or superiority whatever.

Instead, we must [here] take *sensus communis* to mean the idea of a sense *shared* [by all of us], i.e., a power to judge that in reflecting takes account (a priori), in our thought, of everyone else's way of presenting [something], in order *as it were* to compare our own judgment with human reason in general and thus escape the illusion that arises from the ease of mistaking subjective and private conditions for objective ones, an illusion that would have a prejudicial influence on the judgment. Now we do this as follows: we compare our judgment not so much with the actual as rather with the merely possible judgments of others, and [thus] put ourselves in the position of everyone else, merely by abstracting from the limitations that [may] happen to attach to our own judging; and this in turn we accomplish by leaving out as much as possible whatever is matter, i.e., sensation, in the presentational state, and by paying attention solely to the formal features of our presentation or of our presentational state. Now perhaps this operation of reflection will seem rather too artful to be attributed to the ability we call *common* sense. But in fact it only looks this way when expressed in abstract formulas. Intrinsically nothing is more natural than abstracting from charm and emotion when we seek a judgment that is to serve as a universal rule.

[Let us compare with this *sensus communis*] the common human understanding, even though the latter is not being included here as a part of the critique of taste. The following maxims may serve to elucidate its principles: (1) to think for oneself; (2) to think from the standpoint of everyone else; and (3) to think always consistently. The first is the maxim of an *unprejudiced,* the second of a *broadened,* the

294

third of a *consistent* way of thinking.[21] The first is the maxim of a reason that is never *passive*. A propensity to a passive reason, and hence to a heteronomy of reason, is called *prejudice;* and the greatest prejudice of all is *superstition,* which consists in thinking of nature as not subject to rules which the understanding through its own essential law lays down as the basis of nature. Liberation from superstition is called *enlightenment;*[22] for although liberation from prejudices generally may also be called enlightenment, still superstition deserves to be called a prejudice preeminently (*in sensu eminenti*[23]), since the blindness that superstition creates in a person, which indeed it even seems to demand as an obligation, reveals especially well the person's need to be guided by others, and hence his state of a passive reason. As for the second maxim concerning [a person's] way of thinking, it seems that we usually [use a negative term and] call someone limited (of a *narrow* mind as opposed to a *broad* mind) if his talents are insufficient for a use of any magnitude (above all for intensive use). But we are talking here not about the power of cognition, but about the *way of thinking* [that involves] putting this power to a purposive use; and this, no matter how slight may be the range and the degree of a person's natural endowments, still indicates a man with a *broadened way of thinking* if he overrides the private subjective conditions of his judgment, into which so many others are locked, as it were, and reflects on his own judgment from a *universal standpoint* (which he can determine only by transferring himself to the standpoint of others). The third maxim, the one concerning a *consistent* way of thinking, is hardest to attain and can in fact be attained only after repeated

295

---

[21] [Cf. the *Logic*, Ak. IX, 57, and the *Anthropology*, Ak. VII, 200, where these maxims are said to be contained in the precept for attaining wisdom; see also *ibid.*, Ak. VII, 28–29.]

[22] We can readily see that, although enlightenment is easy as a thesis [*in thesi*], as a proposal [*in hypothesi*] it is a difficult matter that can only be carried out slowly. For although to be always self-legislative, rather than passive, in the use of one's reason, is a very easy matter for someone who wants only to measure up to his essential purpose and does not demand to know anything that is beyond his understanding; yet, since it is hard to avoid striving for such knowledge, and since there will never be a shortage of others who promise us with much assurance that they can satisfy our desire for it, it must be very difficult to preserve or instil in [someone's] way of thinking (especially in the public's) that merely negative [element] which constitutes enlightenment proper.

[23] [In the eminent sense of the term.]

compliance with a combination of the first two has become a skill. We may say that the first of these maxims is the maxim of the understanding, the second that of judgment, the third that of reason.

Resuming now the thread from which I just digressed, I maintain that taste can be called a *sensus communis* more legitimately than can sound understanding, and that the aesthetic power of judgment deserves to be called a shared sense[24] more than does the intellectual one, if indeed we wish to use the word *sense*[25] to stand for an effect that mere reflection has on the mind, even though we then mean by sense the feeling of pleasure. We could even define taste as the ability to judge something that makes our feeling in a given presentation *universally communicable* without mediation by a concept.

The aptitude that human beings have for communicating their thoughts to one another also requires that imagination and understanding be related in such a way that concepts can be provided with accompanying intuitions, and intuitions in turn with accompanying concepts, these intuitions and concepts joining to [form] cognition. But here the harmony of the two mental powers is *law-governed*, under the constraint of determinate concepts. Only where the imagination is free when it arouses the understanding, and the understanding, without using concepts, puts the imagination into a play that is regular [i.e., manifests regularity], does the presentation communicate itself not as a thought but as the inner feeling of a purposive state of mind.

296

Hence taste is our ability to judge a priori the communicability of the feelings that (without mediation by a concept) are connected with a given presentation.

If we could assume that the mere universal communicability as such of our feeling must already carry with it an interest for us (something we are, however, not justified in inferring from the character of a merely reflective power of judgment), then we could explain how it is that we require from everyone as a duty, as it were, the feeling [contained] in a judgment of taste.

[24] Taste could be called a sensus *communis aestheticus*, and common understanding a *sensus communis logicus*.

[25] [Emphasis added.]

§ 41

On Empirical Interest
in the Beautiful

That a judgment of taste by which we declare something to be beautiful must not have an interest *as its determining basis* has been established sufficiently above.[26] But it does not follow from this that, after the judgment has been made as a pure aesthetic one, an interest cannot be connected with it. This connection, however, must always be only indirect. In other words, we must think of taste as first of all connected with something else, so that with the liking of mere reflection on an object there can [then] be connected, in addition, a pleasure *in the existence* of the object (and all interest consists in pleasure in the existence of an object). For what we say in [the case of] cognitive judgments (about things in general) also holds for aesthetic judgments: *a posse ad esse non valet consequentia.*[27] This something else may be something empirical, viz., an inclination inherent in human nature, or something intellectual, viz., the will's property of being determinable a priori by reason. Both of these involve a liking for the existence of an object and hence can lay the foundation for an interest in something that we have already come to like on its own account and without regard to any interest whatever.

Only in *society* is the beautiful of empirical interest.[28] And if we grant that the urge to society is natural to man but that his fitness and propensity for it, i.e., *sociability,* is a requirement of man as a creature with a vocation for society and hence is a property pertaining to his *humanity,* then we must also inevitably regard taste as an ability to judge whatever allows us to communicate even our *feeling* to everyone else, and hence regard taste as a means of furthering something that everyone's natural inclination demands.

Someone abandoned on some desolate island would not, just for himself, adorn either his hut or himself; nor would he look for

297

[26] [See esp. the First Moment, Ak. 203–11.]

[27] [An inference from possible to actual is invalid.]

[28] [Cf. Ak. 205 n. 10.]

flowers, let alone grow them, to adorn himself with them. Only in society does it occur to him to be, not merely a human being, but one who is also refined in his own way (this is the beginning of civilization[29]). For we judge someone refined if he has the inclination and the skill to communicate his pleasure to others, and if he is not satisfied with an object unless he can feel his liking for it in community with others. Moreover, a concern for universal communication is something that everyone expects and demands from everyone else, on the basis, as it were, of an original contract dictated by [our] very humanity. Initially, it is true, only charms thus become important in society and become connected with great interest, e.g., the dyes people use to paint themselves (roucou among the Caribs and cinnabar among the Iroquois), or the flowers, sea shells, beautifully colored feathers, but eventually also beautiful forms (as in canoes, clothes, etc.) that involve no gratification whatsoever, i.e., no liking of enjoyment. But in the end, when civilization has reached its peak, it makes this communication almost the principal activity of refined inclination, and sensations are valued only to the extent that they are universally communicable. At that point, even if the pleasure that each person has in such an object is inconsiderable and of no significant interest of its own, still its value is increased almost infinitely by the idea of its universal communicability.

This interest, which we indirectly attach to the beautiful through our inclination to society and which is therefore empirical, is, however, of no importance for us here, since we must concern ourselves only with what may have reference a priori, even if only indirectly, to a judgment of taste. For if even in this [pure] form [of a judgment of taste] an interest were to reveal itself [as] connected with it, then taste would reveal [how] our ability to judge [provides] a transition from sense enjoyment to moral feeling. Moreover, not only would we then have better guidance in using taste purposively, but we would also be showing [that judgment is] a mediating link in the chain of man's a priori powers,[30] the powers on which all legislation must depend. This much we can surely say about empirical interest in objects of taste and in taste itself: in such an interest taste caters to inclination, and no matter how refined this inclination may be, still the interest

298

---

[29] [Cf. the *Anthropology*, § § 69–70, Ak. VII, 244–45.]
[30] [Cf. Ak. 177 and 196.]

will also easily fuse with all the [other] inclinations and passions that reach their greatest variety and highest degree in society; and if our interest in the beautiful is based on these, then it can provide only a very ambiguous transition from the agreeable to the good. But whether taste, if taken in its purity, may not still be able to further this transition—this we have cause to investigate.

§ 42

On Intellectual Interest in the Beautiful

There are those who would like to regard every activity of man to which his inner natural predisposition impels him as being directed to the ultimate purpose of humanity, the morally good. These people have, with the best intention, regarded it as a sign of a good moral character to take an interest in the beautiful generally. But others have, not without grounds, contradicted them by appealing to the [fact of] experience that virtuosi of taste, who not just occasionally but apparently as a rule are vain, obstinate, and given to ruinous passions, can perhaps even less than other people claim the distinction of being attached to moral principles. And hence it seems, not only that the feeling for the beautiful is distinct in kind from moral feeling (as indeed it actually is), but also that it is difficult to reconcile the interest which can be connected with the beautiful with the moral interest, and that it is impossible to do this by an [alleged] intrinsic affinity between the two.

Now I am indeed quite willing to concede that an interest in the *beautiful in art* (in which I include the artistic use of natural beauties for our adornment, and hence for vanity's sake) provides no proof whatever that [someone's] way of thinking is attached to the morally good, or even inclined toward it. On the other hand, I do maintain that to take a *direct interest* in the beauty of *nature* (not merely to have the taste needed to judge it) is always a mark of a good soul; and that, if this interest is habitual, if it readily associates itself with the

299

contemplation of nature, this [fact] indicates at least a mental attunement favorable to moral feeling. But we must carefully bear in mind that what I mean here is actually the beautiful *forms* of nature, while I continue to set aside the *charms* that nature tends to connect so plentifully with them; for an interest in these, though also direct, is yet empirical.

Consider someone who is all by himself (and has no intention of communicating his observations to others) and who contemplates the beautiful shape of a wild flower, a bird, an insect, etc., out of admiration and love for them, and would not want nature to be entirely without them even if they provided him no prospect of benefit but instead perhaps even some harm. Such a person is taking a direct interest in the beauty of nature, and this interest is intellectual. That is, not only does he like nature's product for its form, but he also likes its existence, even though no charm of sense is involved; and he also does not connect that existence with any purpose whatever.

One thing is worthy of note here, however. Suppose we had secretly played a trick on this lover of the beautiful, sticking in the ground artificial flowers (which can be manufactured to look very much like natural ones) or perching artfully carved birds on the branches of trees, and suppose he then discovered the deceit. The direct interest he previously took in these things would promptly vanish, though perhaps it would be replaced by a different interest, an interest of vanity, to use these things to decorate his room for the eyes of others. [What this example shows is that] the thought that the beauty in question was produced by nature must accompany the intuition and the reflection, and the direct interest we take in that beauty is based on that thought alone. Otherwise we are left either with a mere judgment of taste without all interest, or with one connected with only an indirect interest, viz., an interest which refers to society and which provides no safe indication of a morally good way of thinking.

This superiority of natural beauty over that of art, namely, that— even if art were to excel nature in form—it is the only beauty that arouses a direct interest, agrees with the refined and solid [*gründlich*] way of thinking of all people who have cultivated their moral feeling. A man who has taste enough to judge the products of fine art with the greatest correctness and refinement may still be glad to leave a room in which he finds those beauties that minister to vanity and perhaps to social joys, and to turn instead to the beautiful in nature, in order to find there, as it were, a voluptuousness for the mind in a train of thought that he can never fully unravel. If that is how he chooses, we shall ourselves regard this choice of his with esteem and assume that he has a beautiful soul, such as no connoisseur and lover of art can claim to have because of the interest he takes in his objects [of art]. What, then, is the distinction [that prompts] so different an estimation of two kinds of objects [the beautiful in nature and in art], even though in the judgment of mere taste neither would vie for superiority over the other?

We have a merely aesthetic power of judgment, an ability to judge forms without using concepts and to feel in the mere judging of these forms a liking that we also make a rule for everyone, though our judgment is not based on an interest and also gives rise to none. On the other hand, we also have an intellectual power of judgment, i.e., an ability for determining a priori with regard to mere forms of practical maxims (insofar as such maxims qualify of themselves for giving universal law) a liking that we make a law for everyone; this judgment [too] is not based on any interest, *yet it gives rise to one.* The pleasure or displeasure in the first judgment is called that of taste; [in] the latter, that of moral feeling.

But reason also has an interest in the objective reality of the ideas (for which, in moral feeling, it brings about a direct interest), i.e., an interest that nature should at least show a trace or give a hint that it contains some basis or other for us to assume in its products a lawful harmony with that liking of ours which is independent of all interest (a liking we recognize a priori as a law for everyone, though we cannot base this law on proofs). Hence reason must take an interest in any manifestation in nature of a harmony that resembles the mentioned [kind of] harmony, and hence the mind cannot meditate about the beauty of *nature* without at the same time finding its interest aroused. But in terms of its kinship this interest is moral, and whoever takes such an interest in the beautiful in nature can do so only to the extent that he has beforehand already solidly established an interest in the morally good. Hence if someone is directly interested in the beauty of nature, we have cause to suppose that he has at least a predisposition to a good moral attitude.[31]

It will be said that this construal of aesthetic judgments in terms of

301

---

[31] [Cf. the *Anthropology*, § 69, Ak. VII, 244.]

a kinship with moral feeling looks rather too studied to be considered as the true interpretation of that cipher through which nature speaks to us figuratively in its beautiful forms. But, first of all, this direct interest in the beautiful in nature is actually not common, but is peculiar to those whose way of thinking is either already trained to the good or exceptionally receptive to this training. But in view of the analogy between a pure judgment of taste, which depends on no interest whatever and [yet] makes us feel a liking that it also presents a priori as proper for mankind generally, on the one hand, and a moral judgment, which does the same from concepts, on the other hand, someone with that way of thinking does not need to engage in distinct, subtle, and deliberate meditation in order to be led by this analogy to an interest in the object of the pure judgment of taste which is just as strong and direct as his interest in the object of the moral judgment; the only difference is that the first interest is free while the second is based on objective laws. Consider, in addition, how we admire nature, which in its beautiful products displays itself as art, [i.e., as acting] not merely by chance but, as it were, intentionally, in terms of a lawful arrangement and as a purposiveness without a purpose; and since we do not find this purpose anywhere outside us, we naturally look for it in ourselves, namely, in what constitutes the ultimate purpose of our existence: our moral vocation. (The inquiry into the basis that makes such a natural purposiveness possible will, however, first come up in the teleology.)[32]

The fact that our liking for beautiful art in a pure judgment of taste is not connected with a direct interest, as the liking for beautiful nature is so connected, is also easily explained. For either art imitates nature to the point of deception, in which case it achieves its effect by being (regarded as) natural beauty. Or it is an art in which we can see that it intentionally aimed at our liking; but in that case, though our liking for the product would arise directly through taste, it would arouse only an indirect interest in the underlying cause, namely, an interest in an art that can interest us only by its purpose and never in itself. Perhaps it will be said that this is also the case if an object of nature interests us by its beauty only insofar as we link it to an accompanying moral idea. However, it is not this link that interests us

302

---

[32] [As to what this basis is, see the Translator's Introduction, xciii–cii.]

directly, but rather the beauty's own characteristic of qualifying for such a link, which therefore belongs to it intrinsically.

The charms in beautiful nature, which we so often find fused, as it were, with beautiful form, belong either to the modifications of light (in coloring) or of sound (in tones). For these are the only sensations that allow not merely for a feeling of sense, but also for reflection on the form of these modifications of the senses, so that they contain, as it were, a language in which nature speaks to us and which seems to have a higher meaning. Thus a lily's white color seems to attune the mind to ideas of innocence, and the seven colors [of the spectrum], from red to violet, [similarly seem to attune it, respectively, to the ideas of] (1) sublimity, (2) courage, (3) candor, (4) friendliness, (5) modesty, (6) constancy, and (7) tenderness.[33] A bird's song proclaims his joyfulness and contentment with his existence. At least that is how we interpret nature, whether or not it has such an intention. But in order for us to take this interest in beauty, this beauty must always be that of nature: our interest vanishes completely as soon as we notice that we have been deceived, that only art was involved; it vanishes so completely that at that point even taste can no longer find anything beautiful, nor sight anything charming. What do poets praise more highly than the nightingale's enchantingly beautiful song in a secluded thicket on a quiet summer evening by the soft light of the moon? And yet we have cases where some jovial innkeeper, unable to find such a songster, played a trick—received with greatest satisfaction [initially]—on the guests staying at his inn to enjoy the country air, by hiding in a bush some roguish youngster who (with a reed or rush in his mouth) knew how to copy that song in a way very similar to nature's. But as soon as one realizes that it was all deception, no one will long endure listening to this song that before he had considered so charming; and that is how it is with the song of any other bird. In order for us to be able to take a direct *interest* in the beautiful as such, it must be nature, or we must consider it so. This holds especially, however, if we can even require others to take a direct interest in it. And we do in fact require this; for we consider someone's way of thinking to be coarse and ignoble if he has no *feeling* for beautiful nature (which is

303

[33] [Newton showed that the white color of sunlight can not only be broken up into, but also recomposed from, "seven" spectral components: red, orange, yellow, green, blue, indigo, violet: *Opticks*, Bk. I, Pt. II.]

what we call the receptivity for an interest in contemplating nature) and sticks to the enjoyments of mere sense that he gets from meals or the bottle.

§ 43

On Art in General

(1) *Art* is distinguished from *nature* as doing (*facere*) is from acting or operating in general (*agere*); and the product or result of art is distinguished from that of nature, the first being a work (*opus*), the second an effect (*effectus*).

By right we should not call anything art except a production through freedom, i.e., through a power of choice that bases its acts on reason. For though we like to call the product that bees make (the regularly constructed honeycombs) a work of art, we do so only by virtue of an analogy with art; for as soon as we recall that their labor is not based on any rational deliberation on their part, we say at once that the product is a product of their nature (namely, of instinct), and it is only to their creator that we ascribe it as art.

[It is true that] if, as sometimes happens when we search through a bog, we come across a piece of hewn wood, we say that it is a product of art, rather than of nature, i.e., that the cause which produced it was thinking of a purpose to which this object owes its form. Elsewhere too, I suppose, we see art in everything that is of such a character that before it became actual its cause must have had a presentation of it (as even in the case of bees), yet precisely without the cause's having [in fact] *thought* of that effect. But if we simply call something a work of art in order to distinguish it from a natural effect, then we always mean by that a work of man.

(2) *Art,* as human skill, is also distinguished from *science* ([i.e., we distinguish] *can* from *know*), as practical from theoretical ability, as technic from theory (e.g., the art of surveying from geometry). That is exactly why we refrain from calling anything art that we *can* do the moment we *know* what is to be done, i.e., the moment we are

sufficiently acquainted with what the desired effect is. Only if something [is such that] even the most thorough acquaintance with it does
not immediately provide us with the skill to make it, then to that
extent it belongs to art. *Camper*[34] describes with great precision
what the best shoe would have to be like, yet he was certainly unable
to make one.[35]

(3) *Art* is likewise distinguished from *craft*. The first is also called
free art, the second could also be called *mercenary art.* We regard
free art [as an art] that could only turn out purposive (i.e., succeed) if
it is play, in other words, an occupation that is agreeable on its own
account; mercenary art we regard as labor, i.e., as an occupation that
on its own account is disagreeable (burdensome) and that attracts us
only through its effect (e.g., pay), so that people can be coerced into
it. To judge whether, in a ranking of the guilds, watchmakers should
be counted as artists but smiths as craftsmen, we would have to take a
viewpoint different from the one adopted here: we would have to
compare [*Proportion*] the talents that each of these occupations
presupposes. Whether even among the so-called seven free arts a few
may not have been included that should be numbered with the
sciences, as well as some that are comparable to crafts, I do not here
wish to discuss. It is advisable, however, to remind ourselves that
in all the free arts there is yet a need for something in the order of a
constraint, or, as it is called, a *mechanism.* (In poetry, for example, it
is correctness and richness of language, as well as prosody and
meter.) Without this the *spirit,*[36] which in art must *be free* and which
alone animates the work, would have no body at all and would
evaporate completely. This reminder is needed because some of the
more recent educators believe that they promote a free art best if
they remove all constraint from it and convert it from labor into mere
play.

[34] [Peter Camper (1722–89), Dutch anatomist and naturalist. He is the author of
numerous works, the most important of which are on comparative anatomy.]

[35] In my part of the country, if you confront the common man with a problem like that
of Columbus and his egg, he will say: *That is not an art, it is only a science.* That is, if
you know it *then you can do it*; and he says just the same about all the alleged arts of
the conjurer. That of the tightrope dancer, on the other hand, he will not at all decline
to call art.

[36] [*Geist*; cf. §49, Ak. 313.]

§ 44
On Fine Art

There is no science of the beautiful [*das Schöne*], but only critique; and there is no fine [*schön*] science,[37] but only fine art. For in a science of the beautiful, whether or not something should be considered beautiful would have to be decided scientifically, i.e., through bases of proof, so that if a judgment about beauty belonged to science then it would not be a judgment of taste. As for a fine science: a science that as a science is to be fine is an absurdity; for if, [treating it] as a science, we asked for reasons and proofs, we would be put off with tasteful phrases (*bons mots*). What has given rise to the familiar expression, *fine sciences,* is doubtless nothing more than the realization, which is quite correct, that fine art in its full perfection requires much science: e.g., we must know ancient languages, we must have read the authors considered classical, we must know history and be familiar with the antiquities, etc.; and this is why these historical sciences have, through a confusion of words, themselves come to be called fine sciences, because they constitute the foundation and preparation needed for fine art, and in part also because they have come to include even a familiarity with the products of fine art (as in oratory or poetry).

If art merely performs the acts that are required to make a possible object actual, adequately to our *cognition* of that object, then it is *mechanical* art; but if what it intends directly is [to arouse] the feeling of pleasure, then it is called *aesthetic* art. The latter is either *agreeable* or *fine* art. It is agreeable art if its purpose is that the pleasure should accompany presentations that are mere *sensations;* it is fine art if its purpose is that the pleasure should accompany presentations that are *ways of cognizing.*

Agreeable arts are those whose purpose is merely enjoyment. They include [the art of providing] all those charms that can gratify a party at table, such as telling stories entertainingly, animating the group to open and lively conversation, or using jest and laughter to induce a

---

[37] [Or "beautiful" science: Kant is responding, above all, to Alexander Gottlieb Baumgarten and Georg Friedrich Meier. Cf. the Translator's Introduction, *l–li.*]

certain cheerful tone among them[38]—a tone such that, as is said, there may be a lot of loose talk over the feast, and no one wants to be held responsible for what he says, because the whole point is the entertainment of the moment, not any material for future meditation or quotation. (Such arts also include the art of furnishing a table so that people will enjoy themselves, or include, at large banquets, presumably even the table-music—a strange thing which is meant to be only an agreeable noise serving to keep the minds in a cheerful mood, and which fosters the free flow of conversation between each person and his neighbor, without anyone's paying the slightest attention to the music's composition.) Also included in these arts are any games that involve no further interest than that of making time go by unnoticed.

306

Fine art, on the other hand, is a way of presenting that is purposive on its own and that furthers, even though without a purpose, the culture of our mental powers to [facilitate] social communication.

The very concept of the universal communicability of a pleasure carries with it [the requirement] that this pleasure must be a pleasure of reflection rather than one of enjoyment arising from mere sensation. Hence aesthetic art that is also fine art is one whose standard is the reflective power of judgment, rather than sensation proper.[39]

§ 45

Fine Art Is an Art Insofar as It Seems at the Same Time to Be Nature

In [dealing with] a product of fine art we must become conscious that it is art rather than nature, and yet the purposiveness in its form must seem as free from all constraint of chosen rules as if it were a product of mere nature. It is this feeling of freedom in the play of our

[38] [Cf. the *Anthropology*, Ak. VII, 280.]

[39] [*Sinnesempfindung*; see § 39, Ak. 291 incl. br. n. 19.]

cognitive powers, a play that yet must also be purposive, which underlies that pleasure which alone is universally communicable although not based on concepts. Nature, we say, is beautiful [*schön*] if it also looks like art; and art can be called fine [*schön*] art only if we are conscious that it is art while yet it looks to us like nature.

For we may say universally, whether it concerns beauty in nature or in art: *beautiful is what we like in merely judging it* (rather than either in sensation proper or through a concept). Now art always has a determinate intention to produce something. But if this something were mere sensation (something merely subjective), to be accompanied by pleasure, then we would [indeed] like this product in judging it, [but] only by means of the feeling of sense. If the intention were directed at producing a determinate object and were achieved by the art, then we would like the object only through concepts. In neither case, then, would we like the art in *merely judging it,* i.e., we would like it not as fine but only as mechanical art.

307

Therefore, even though the purposiveness in a product of fine art is intentional, it must still not seem intentional; i.e., fine art must have the *look* of nature even though we are conscious of it as art. And a product of art appears like nature if, though we find it to agree quite *punctiliously* with the rules that have to be followed for the product to become what it is intended to be, it does not do so *painstakingly.* In other words, the academic form must not show; there must be no hint that the rule was hovering before the artist's eyes and putting fetters on his mental powers.

§ 46

Fine Art Is the Art of Genius

Genius is the talent (natural endowment) that gives the rule to art. Since talent is an innate productive ability of the artist and as such belongs itself to nature, we could also put it this way: *Genius* is the innate mental predisposition (*ingenium*) *through which* nature gives the rule to art.

Whatever the status of this definition may be, and whether or not it is merely arbitrary, or rather adequate to the concept that we usually connect with the word *genius* (these questions will be discussed in the following section), still we can prove even now that, in terms of the meaning of the word genius adopted here, fine arts must necessarily be considered arts of *genius*.

For every art presupposes rules, which serve as the foundation on which a product, if it is to be called artistic, is thought of as possible in the first place. On the other hand, the concept of fine art does not permit a judgment about the beauty of its product to be derived from any rule whatsoever that has a *concept* as its determining basis, i.e., the judgment must not be based on a concept of the way in which the product is possible. Hence fine art cannot itself devise the rule by which it is to bring about its product. Since, however, a product can never be called art unless it is preceded by a rule, it must be nature in the subject (and through the attunement of his powers) that gives the rule to art; in other words, fine art is possible only as the product of genius.

What this shows is the following: (1) Genius is a *talent* for producing something for which no determinate rule can be given, not a predisposition consisting of a skill for something that can be learned by following some rule or other; hence the foremost property of genius must be *originality*. (2) Since nonsense too can be original, the products of genius must also be models, i.e., they must be *exemplary;* hence, though they do not themselves arise through imitation, still they must serve others for this, i.e., as a standard or rule by which to judge. (3) Genius itself cannot describe or indicate scientifically how it brings about its products, and it is rather as *nature* that it gives the rule. That is why, if an author owes a product to his genius, he himself does not know how he came by the ideas for it; nor is it in his power [*Gewalt*] to devise such products at his pleasure, or by following a plan, and to communicate [his procedure] to others in precepts that would enable them to bring about like products. (Indeed, that is presumably why the word genius is derived from [Latin] *genius,* [which means] the guardian and guiding spirit that each person is given as his own at birth,[40] and to whose inspiration [*Eingebung*] those original ideas are due.) (4) Nature, through genius, prescribes

308

[40] [Cf. the *Anthropology*, Ak. VII, 225.]

the rule not to science but to art, and this also only insofar as the art is to be fine art.

§ 47

Elucidation and Confirmation of the Above Explication of Genius

On this point everyone agrees: that genius must be considered the very opposite of a *spirit of imitation.* Now since learning is nothing but imitation, even the greatest competence, [i.e.,] teachability (capacity) *qua* teachability, can still not count as genius. But even if someone does not just take in what others have thought but thinks and writes on his own, or even makes all sorts of discoveries in art and science, still, even that is not yet the right basis for calling such a *mind* (in contrast to one who is called a *simpleton,* because he can never do more than just learn and imitate) a *genius* (great though such a mind often is). For all of this *could* in fact have been done through learning as well, and hence lies in the natural path of an investigation and meditation by rules and does not differ in kind from what a diligent person can acquire by means of imitation. Thus one can indeed learn everything that *Newton* has set forth in his immortal work on the principles of natural philosophy, however great a mind was needed to make such discoveries; but one cannot learn to write inspired[41] poetry, however elaborate all the precepts of this art may be, and however superb its models. The reason for this is that Newton could show how he took every one of the steps he had to take in order to get from the first elements of geometry to his great and profound discoveries; he could show this not only to himself but to everyone else as well, in an intuitive[ly clear] way, allowing others to follow. But

---

[41] [*Geistreich*: 'rich in spirit,' literally.]

no *Homer* or *Wieland*[42] can show how his ideas, rich in fancy and yet also in thought, arise and meet in his mind; the reason is that he himself does not know, and hence also cannot teach it to anyone else. In scientific matters, therefore, the greatest discoverer differs from the most arduous imitator and apprentice only in degree, whereas he differs in kind from someone whom nature has endowed for fine art. But saying this does not disparage those great men, to whom the human race owes so much, in contrast to those whom nature has favored with a talent for fine art. For the scientists' talent lies in continuing to increase the perfection of our cognitions and of all the benefits that depend on [these], as well as in imparting that same knowledge to others; and in these respects they are far superior to those who merit the honor of being called geniuses. For the latter's art stops at some point, because a boundary is set for it beyond which it cannot go and which probably has long since been reached and cannot be extended further. Moreover, the artist's skill cannot be communicated but must be conferred directly on each person by the hand of nature. And so it dies with him, until some day nature again endows someone else in the same way, someone who needs nothing but an example in order to put the talent of which he is conscious to work in a similar way.

Since, then, [the artist's] natural endowment must give the rule to (fine) art, what kind of rule is this? It cannot be couched in a formula and serve as a precept, for then a judgment about the beautiful could be determined according to concepts. Rather, the rule must be abstracted from what the artist has done, i.e., from the product, which others may use to test their own talent, letting it serve them as their model, not to be *copied* [*Nachmachung*] but to be *imitated* [*Nachahmung*].[43] How that is possible is difficult to explain. The artist's ideas arouse similar ideas in his apprentice if nature has provided the latter with a similar proportion in his mental powers. That is why the models of fine art are the only means of transmitting

310

[42] [Christoph Martin Wieland (1733–1813), German poet and man of letters.]

[43] [Karl Vorländer, editor of the *Critique of Judgment* in the *Philosophische Bibliothek* edition, notes (v. 39a, 163, n. b) that Kant's manuscript read '*Nachahmung . . . Nachahmung*' ('[not to be] imitated [but to be] imitated'), which was then "corrected" to the reading found here, but that Kant presumably meant to write '*Nachahmung . . . Nachfolge*' ('[not to be] imitated [but to be] followed'), in line with what he says elsewhere: see esp. Ak. 318 and 283.]

these ideas to posterity. Mere descriptions could not accomplish this (especially not in the area of the arts of speech), and even in these arts only those models can become classical which are written in the ancient, dead languages, now preserved only as scholarly languages.[44]

Even though mechanical and fine art are very different from each other, since the first is based merely on diligence and learning but the second on genius, yet there is no fine art that does not have as its essential condition something mechanical, which can be encompassed by rules and complied with, and hence has an element of *academic correctness*. For something must be thought, as purpose, since otherwise the product cannot be ascribed to any art at all, but would be a mere product of chance. But directing the work to a purpose requires determinate rules that one is not permitted to renounce. Now since originality of talent is one essential component (though not the only one) of the character of genius, shallow minds believe that the best way to show that they are geniuses in first bloom is by renouncing all rules of academic constraint, believing that they will cut a better figure on the back of an ill-tempered than of a training-horse. Genius can only provide rich *material* for products of fine art; processing this material and giving it *form* requires a talent that is academically trained, so that it may be used in a way that can stand the test of the power of judgment. But it is utterly ridiculous for someone to speak and decide like a genius even in matters that require the most careful rational investigation. One does not quite know whether to laugh harder at the charlatan who spreads all this haze, in which we can judge nothing distinctly but can imagine all the more, or rather laugh at the audience, which naively imagines that the reason why it cannot distinctly recognize and grasp this masterpiece of insight is that large masses of new truths are being hurled at it, whereas it regards the detail (which is based on carefully weighed explications and academically correct examination of the principles) as only the work of a bungler.

[44] [Cf. Ak. 232 n. 49.]

§ 48

On the Relation of
Genius to Taste

Judging beautiful objects to be such requires *taste;* but fine art itself, i.e., *production* of such objects, requires *genius.*

If we consider genius as the talent for fine art (and the proper meaning of the word implies this) and from this point of view wish to analyze it into the powers that must be combined in order to constitute such a talent, then we must begin by determining precisely how natural beauty, the judging of which requires only taste, differs from artistic beauty, whose possibility (which we must also bear in mind when we judge an object of this sort) requires genius.

A natural beauty is a *beautiful thing;* artistic beauty is a *beautiful presentation* of a thing.

In order to judge a natural beauty to be that, I need not have a prior concept of what kind of thing the object is [meant] to be; i.e., I do not have to know its material purposiveness (its purpose). Rather, I like the mere form of the object when I judge it, on its own account and without knowing the purpose. But if the object is given as a product of art, and as such is to be declared beautiful, then we must first base it on a concept of what the thing is [meant] to be, since art always presupposes a purpose in the cause (and its causality). And since the harmony of a thing's manifold with an intrinsic determination of the thing, i.e., with its purpose, is the thing's perfection, it follows that when we judge artistic beauty we shall have to assess the thing's perfection as well, whereas perfection is not at all at issue when we judge natural beauty (to be that). It is true that when we judge certain objects of nature, above all animate ones, such as a human being or a horse, we do commonly also take into account their objective purposiveness in order to judge their beauty. But then, by the same token, the judgment is no longer purely aesthetic, no longer a mere judgment of taste. We then judge nature no longer as it appears as art, but insofar as it actually *is* art (though superhuman art), and [so we make a] teleological judgment that serves the aesthetic one as a foundation and condition that it must take into account. Thus if we say, e.g., That is a beautiful woman, we do in fact think nothing other than that nature offers us in the woman's figure a beautiful presentation of the purposes [inherent] in the female build. For in order to think the object in this way, through a logically conditioned aesthetic judgment, we have to look beyond the mere form and toward a concept.

Fine art shows its superiority precisely in this, that it describes things beautifully that in nature we would dislike or find ugly.[45] The Furies, diseases, devastations of war, and so on are all harmful; and yet they can be described, or even presented in a painting, very beautifully. There is only one kind of ugliness that cannot be presented in conformity with nature without obliterating all aesthetic liking and hence artistic beauty: that ugliness which arouses *disgust*. For in that strange sensation, which rests on nothing but imagination, the object is presented as if it insisted, as it were, on our enjoying it even though that is just what we are forcefully resisting; and hence the artistic presentation of the object is no longer distinguished in our sensation from the nature of this object itself, so that it cannot possibly be considered beautiful. The art of sculpture, too, has excluded from its creations any direct presentation of ugly objects, since in its products art is almost confused with nature. Instead it has permitted [ugly objects] to be presented by an allegory—e.g., death ([by] a beautiful genius) or a warlike spirit ([by] Mars)—or by attributes that come across as likable, and hence has permitted them only to be presented indirectly and by means of an interpretation of reason rather than presented for a merely aesthetic power of judgment.

Let this suffice for the beautiful presentation of an object, which is actually only the form of a concept's exhibition, the form by which this concept is universally communicated. Now, giving this form to a product of fine art requires merely taste. The artist, having practiced and corrected his taste by a variety of examples from art or nature, holds his work up to it, and, after many and often laborious attempts to satisfy his taste, finds that form which is adequate to it. Hence this form is not, as it were, a matter of inspiration or of a free momentum of the mental powers; the artist is, instead, slowly and rather painstakingly touching the form up in an attempt to make it adequate to his

---

[45] [Cf. Aristotle, the *Poetics*, ch. iv, 1448b, and Edmund Burke, *Enquiry Into the Origin of Our Ideas of the Sublime and Beautiful*, Pt. I, Section xvi.]

thought while yet keeping it from interfering with the freedom in the   313
play of these powers.

But taste is merely an ability to judge, not to produce; and if
something conforms to it, that [fact] does not yet make the thing a
work of fine art: it may belong to useful and mechanical art, or
even to science, as a product made according to determinate rules
that can be learned and that must be complied with precisely. If
this product has been given a likable form, then this form is only
the vehicle of communication, and, as it were, a manner [adopted]
in displaying the product, so that one still retains a certain measure of freedom in this display even though it is otherwise tied to
a determinate purpose. Thus we demand that tableware, or, for
that matter, a moral treatise, or even a sermon should have this
form of fine art, yet without its seeming *studied,* but we do not on
that account call these things works of fine art. In fine art we
include, rather, a poem, a piece of music, a gallery of pictures,
and so on; and here we often find a would-be work of fine art that
manifests genius without taste, or another that manifests taste
without genius.

§ 49

On the Powers of the Mind
Which Constitute Genius

Of certain products that are expected to reveal themselves at least in
part to be fine art, we say that they have no *spirit,* even though we
find nothing to censure in them as far as taste is concerned. A poem
may be quite nice and elegant and yet have no spirit. A story may be
precise and orderly and yet have no spirit. An oration may be both
thorough and graceful and yet have no spirit. Many conversations
are entertaining, but they have no spirit. Even about some woman we
will say that she is pretty, communicative, and polite, but that she has
no spirit. Well, what do we mean here by spirit?

Spirit [*Geist*] in an aesthetic sense is the animating principle in the mind.[46] But what this principle uses to animate [or quicken] the soul, the material it employs for this, is what imparts to the mental powers a purposive momentum, i.e., imparts to them a play which is such that it sustains itself on its own and even strengthens the powers for such play.

314

Now I maintain that this principle is nothing but the ability to exhibit *aesthetic ideas;* and by an aesthetic idea I mean a presentation of the imagination which prompts much thought, but to which no determinate thought whatsoever, i.e., no [determinate] *concept,* can be adequate, so that no language can express it completely and allow us to grasp it.[47] It is easy to see that an aesthetic idea is the counterpart (pendant) of a *rational idea,* which is, conversely, a concept to which no *intuition* (presentation of the imagination) can be adequate.

For the imagination ([in its role] as a productive cognitive power) is very mighty when it creates,[48] as it were, another nature out of the material that actual nature gives it. We use it to entertain ourselves when experience strikes us as overly routine. We may even restructure experience; and though in doing so we continue to follow analogical laws, yet we also follow principles which reside higher up, namely, in reason (and which are just as natural to us as those which the understanding follows in apprehending empirical nature). In this process we feel our freedom from the law of association (which attaches to the empirical use of the imagination); for although it is under that law that nature lends us material, yet we can process that material into something quite different, namely, into something that surpasses nature.

Such presentations of the imagination we may call *ideas.* One reason for this is that they do at least strive toward something that lies beyond the bounds of experience, and hence try to approach an exhibition of rational concepts (intellectual ideas), and thus [these concepts] are given a semblance of objective reality. Another reason, indeed the main reason, for calling those presentations ideas is that they are inner intuitions to which no concept can be completely

[46] [Cf. the *Anthropology*, Ak. VII, 225 and 246. Cf. also above, § 46, Ak. 308.]

[47] [Cf. § 57, Comment I, Ak. 341–44.]

[48] [On the "productive" imagination, see Ak. 240 br. n. 66; and cf. Ak. 243 br. n. 73, where Kant tells us in what sense the imagination *is not* creative.]

adequate. A poet ventures to give sensible expression to rational ideas of invisible beings, the realm of the blessed, the realm of hell, eternity, creation, and so on. Or, again, he takes [things] that are indeed exemplified in experience, such as death, envy, and all the other vices, as well as love, fame, and so on; but then, by means of an imagination that emulates the example of reason in reaching [for] a maximum, he ventures to give these sensible expression in a way that goes beyond the limits of experience, namely, with a completeness for which no example can be found in nature. And it is actually in the art of poetry that the power [i.e., faculty] of aesthetic ideas can manifest itself to full extent. Considered by itself, however, this power is actually only a talent (of the imagination).

Now if a concept is provided with [*unterlegen*] a presentation of the imagination such that, even though this presentation belongs to the exhibition of the concept, yet it prompts, even by itself, so much thought as can never be comprehended within a determinate concept and thereby the presentation aesthetically expands the concept itself in an unlimited way, then the imagination is creative in [all of] this and sets the power of intellectual ideas (i.e., reason) in motion: it makes reason think more, when prompted by a [certain] presentation, than what can be apprehended and made distinct in the presentation (though the thought does pertain to the concept of the object [presented]).

315

If forms do not constitute the exhibition of a given concept itself, but are only supplementary [*Neben-*] presentations of the imagination, expressing the concept's implications and its kinship with other concepts, then they are called (aesthetic) *attributes* of an object, of an object whose concept is a rational idea and hence cannot be exhibited adequately. Thus Jupiter's eagle with the lightning in its claws is an attribute of the mighty king of heaven, and the peacock is an attribute of heaven's stately queen. [Through] these attributes, unlike [through] *logical attributes,* [we] do not present the content of our concepts of the sublimity and majesty of creation, but present something different, something that prompts the imagination to spread over a multitude of kindred presentations that arouse more thought than can be expressed in a concept determined by words. These aesthetic attributes yield an *aesthetic idea,* which serves the mentioned rational idea as a substitute for a logical exhibition, but its proper function is to quicken [*beleben*] the mind by opening up for it a view into an immense realm of kindred presentations. Fine art does this not only in painting or sculpture (where we usually speak of attributes); but poetry and oratory also take the spirit that animates [*beleben*] their works solely from the aesthetic attributes of the objects, attributes that accompany the logical ones and that give the imagination a momentum which makes it think more in response to these objects [*dabei*], though in an undeveloped way, than can be comprehended within one concept and hence in one determinate linguistic expression. Here are some examples, though for the sake of brevity I must confine myself to only a few.

The great king, in one of his poems, expresses himself thus:

> Let us part from life without grumbling or regrets,
> Leaving the world behind filled with our good deeds.
> Thus the sun, his daily course completed,
> Spreads one more soft light over the sky;
> And the last rays that he sends through the air
> Are the last sighs he gives the world for its well-being.[49]

316

The king is here animating his rational idea of a cosmopolitan attitude, even at the end of life, by means of an attribute which the imagination (in remembering all the pleasures of a completed beautiful summer day, which a serene evening calls to mind) conjoins with that presentation, and which arouses a multitude of sensations and supplementary presentations for which no expression can be found. On the other hand, even an intellectual concept may serve, conversely, as an attribute of a presentation of sense and thus animate that presentation by the idea of the supersensible; but [we] may use for this only the aesthetic [element] that attaches subjectively to our consciousness of the supersensible. Thus, for example, a certain poet, in describing a beautiful morning, says: "The sun flowed forth, as seren-

---

[49] [Kant is giving a German translation (probably his own) of the following lines written in French by Frederick the Great (*Oeuvres de Frédéric le Grand*, 1846 ff., x, 203):

> *Oui, finissons sans trouble, et mourons sans regrets,*
> *En laissant l'Univers comblé de nos bienfaits.*
> *Ainsi l'Astre du jour, au bout de sa carrière,*
> *Répand sur l'horizon une douce lumière,*
> *Et les derniers rayons qu'il darde dans les airs*
> *Sont ses derniers soupirs qu'il donne à l'Univers.*]

ity flows from virtue."⁵⁰ The consciousness of virtue, even if we only think of ourselves as in the position of a virtuous person, spreads in the mind a multitude of sublime and calming feelings and a boundless outlook toward a joyful future, such as no expression commensurate with a determinate concept completely attains.⁵¹

In a word, an aesthetic idea is a presentation of the imagination which is conjoined with a given concept and is connected, when we use imagination in its freedom, with such a multiplicity of partial presentations that no expression that stands for a determinate concept can be found for it. Hence it is a presentation that makes us add to a concept the thoughts of much that is ineffable, but the feeling of which quickens our cognitive powers and connects language, which otherwise would be mere letters, with spirit.

So the mental powers whose combination (in a certain relation) constitutes *genius* are imagination and understanding. One qualification is needed, however. When the imagination is used for cognition, then it is under the constraint of the understanding and is subject to the restriction of adequacy to the understanding's concept. But when the aim is aesthetic, then the imagination is free, so that, over and above that harmony with the concept, it may supply, in an unstudied way, a wealth of undeveloped material for the understanding which the latter disregarded in its concept. But the understanding employs this material not so much objectively, for cognition, as subjectively, namely, to quicken the cognitive powers, though indirectly this does serve cognition too. Hence genius actually consists in the happy relation—one that no science can teach and that cannot be learned by any diligence—allowing us, first, to discover ideas for a given

317

⁵⁰ [From *Akademische Gedichte* (*Academic Poems*) (1782), vol. i, p. 70, by J. Ph. L. Withof (1725–89), professor of morals, oratory, and medicine at Duisburg, Germany. The original poem had 'goodness' instead of 'virtue.']

⁵¹ Perhaps nothing more sublime has ever been said, or a thought ever been expressed more sublimely, than in that inscription above the temple of *Isis* (Mother Nature): "I am all that is, that was, and that will be, and no mortal has lifted my veil." *Segner*⁵² made use of this idea in an ingenious vignette prefixed to his *Naturlehre* [*Natural Science*], so as first to imbue the pupil, whom he was about to lead into this temple, with the sacred thrill that is meant to attune the mind to solemn attentiveness.

⁵² [Johann Andreas von Segner (1704–77), German physicist and mathematician at Jena, Göttingen, and Halle. He is the author of several significant scientific works. He introduced the concept of the surface tension of liquids.]

concept, and, second, to hit upon a way of *expressing* these ideas that enables us to communicate to others, as accompanying a concept, the mental attunement that those ideas produce. The second talent is properly the one we call spirit. For in order to express what is ineffable in the mental state accompanying a certain presentation and to make it universally communicable—whether the expression consists in language or painting or plastic art—we need an ability [viz., spirit] to apprehend the imagination's rapidly passing play and to unite it in a concept that can be communicated without the constraint of rules (a concept that on that very account is original, while at the same time it reveals a new rule that could not have been inferred from any earlier principles or examples).

If, after this analysis, we look back to the above explication of what we call *genius,* we find: *First,* genius is a talent for art, not for science, where we must start from distinctly known rules that determine the procedure we must use in it. *Second,* since it is an artistic talent, it presupposes a determinate concept of the product, namely, its purpose; hence genius presupposes understanding, but also a presentation (though an indeterminate one) of the material, i.e., of the intuition, needed to exhibit this concept, and hence presupposes a relation of imagination to understanding. *Third,* it manifests itself not so much in the fact that the proposed purpose is achieved in exhibiting a determinate concept, as, rather, in the way *aesthetic ideas,* which contain a wealth of material [suitable] for that intention, are offered or expressed; and hence it presents the imagination in its freedom from any instruction by rules, but still as purposive for exhibiting the given concept. Finally, *fourth,* the unstudied, unintentional subjective purposiveness in the imagination's free harmony with the understanding's lawfulness presupposes such a proportion and attunement of these powers as cannot be brought about by any compliance with rules, whether of science or of mechanical imitation, but can be brought about only by the subject's nature.

318

These presuppositions being given, genius is the exemplary originality of a subject's natural endowment in the *free* use of his cognitive powers. Accordingly, the product of a genius (as regards what is attributable to genius in it rather than to possible learning or academic instruction) is an example that is meant not to be imitated, but to be followed by another genius. (For in mere imitation the element of genius in the work—what constitutes its spirit—would be lost.) The other genius, who follows the example, is aroused by it to a feeling of his own originality, which allows him to exercise in art his freedom from the constraint of rules, and to do so in such a way that art itself acquires a new rule by this, thus showing that the talent is exemplary. But since a genius is nature's favorite and so must be regarded as a rare phenomenon, his example gives rise to a school for other good minds, i.e., a methodical instruction by means of whatever rules could be extracted from those products of spirit and their peculiarity; and for these [followers] fine art is to that extent imitation, for which nature, through a genius, gave the rule.

But this imitation becomes *aping* if the pupil *copies* everything, including even the deformities that the genius had to permit only because it would have been difficult to eliminate them without diminishing the force of the idea. This courage [to retain deformities] has merit only in a genius. A certain *boldness* of expression, and in general some deviation from the common rule, is entirely fitting for a genius; it is however not at all worthy of imitation, but in itself always remains a defect that [any]one must try to eliminate, though the genius has, as it were, a privilege to allow the defect to remain [anyway], because the inimitable [element] in the momentum of his spirit would be impaired by timorous caution. *Mannerism* is a different kind of aping; it consists in aping mere *peculiarity* (originality) as such, so as to distance oneself as far as at all possible from imitators, yet without possessing the talent needed to be *exemplary* as well. It is true that we use the term *manner*[53] in another way as well: Whenever we convey our thoughts, there are two ways (*modi*) of arranging them, and one of these is called *manner* (*modus aestheticus*), the other *method* (*modus logicus*);[54] the difference between these two is that the first has no standard other than the *feeling* that there is unity in the exhibition [of the thoughts], whereas the second follows in [all of] this determinate *principles;* hence only the first applies to fine art. But in art a product is called *mannered* only if the way the artist conveys his idea *aims* at singularity and is not adequate to the idea. Whatever is ostentatious (precious), stilted, and affected, with the

319

[53] [Emphasis added.]
[54] [Cf. Ak. 355 br. n.41.]

sole aim of differing from the ordinary (but without spirit), resembles the behavior of those who, as we say, listen to themselves talking, or who stand and walk as if they were on a stage so as to be gaped at, behavior that always betrays a bungler.

§ 50

On the Combination of Taste with Genius in Products of Fine Art

If we ask which is more important in objects [*Sachen*] of fine art, whether they show genius or taste, then this is equivalent to asking whether in fine art imagination is more important than judgment. Now insofar as art shows genius it does indeed deserve to be called *inspired* [*geistreich*], but it deserves to be called *fine* art only insofar as it shows taste. Hence what we must look to above all, when we judge art as fine art, is taste, at least as an indispensable condition (*conditio sine qua non*). In order [for a work] to be beautiful, it is not strictly necessary that [it] be rich and original in ideas, but it is necessary that the imagination in its freedom be commensurate with the lawfulness of the understanding. For if the imagination is left in lawless freedom, all its riches [in ideas] produce nothing but nonsense, and it is judgment that adapts the imagination to the understanding.

Taste, like the power of judgment in general, consists in disciplining (or training) genius. It severely clips its wings, and makes it civilized, or polished; but at the same time it gives it guidance as to how far and over what it may spread while still remaining purposive. It introduces clarity and order into a wealth of thought, and hence makes the ideas durable, fit for approval that is both lasting and universal, and [hence] fit for being followed by others and fit for an ever advancing culture. Therefore, if there is a conflict between these two properties in a product, and something has to be sacrificed, then it should rather be on the side of genius; and

320

judgment, which in matters [*Sachen*] of fine art bases its pronouncements on principles of its own, will sooner permit the imagination's
freedom and wealth to be impaired than that the understanding be
impaired.

Hence fine art would seem to require *imagination, understanding, spirit,* and *taste.*[55]

§ 51

On the Division
of the Fine Arts

We may in general call beauty (whether natural or artistic) the
expression of aesthetic ideas; the difference is that in the case of
beautiful [*schön*] art the aesthetic idea must be prompted by a
concept of the object, whereas in the case of beautiful nature, mere
reflection on a given intuition, without a concept of what the object is
[meant] to be, is sufficient for arousing and communicating the idea
of which that object is regarded as the *expression.*

Accordingly, if we wish to divide the fine [*schön*] arts, we can
choose for this, at least tentatively, no more convenient principle than
the analogy between the arts and the way people express themselves
in speech so as to communicate with one another as perfectly as
possible, namely, not merely as regards their concepts but also as

---

[55] The first three abilities are first *united* by the fourth. *Hume,* in his history[56]
informs the English that, although they are in their works second to no other
people in the world as regards evidence of the first three properties considered
separately, in the property that unifies them they yet must yield to their neighbors, the
French.[57]

[56] [*History of England* (1754–62).]

[57] [In the *Observations on the Feeling of the Beautiful and Sublime* (1764), Kant
says: "Among the peoples of this continent I think it is the *Italians* and the *French*
who distinguish themselves from the rest by their feeling of the *beautiful*, but the
Germans, English, and *Spanish* who do so by their feeling for the sublime." (Ak.
II, 243).]

regards their sensations.[58] Such expression consists in *word, gesture,* and *tone* (articulation, gesticulation, and modulation). Only when these three ways of expressing himself are combined does the speaker communicate completely. For in this way thought, intuition, and sensation are conveyed to others simultaneously and in unison.

Hence there are only three kinds of fine arts: the art *of speech, visual* art, and the art *of the play of sensations* (as outer sense impressions). This division could also be arranged as a dichotomy: we could divide fine art into the art of expressing thoughts and that of expressing intuitions, and then divide the latter according to whether it deals merely with form, or with matter (sensation). But in that case the division would look too abstract, and less in keeping with ordinary concepts.

(1) The arts OF SPEECH are *oratory* and *poetry. Oratory* is the art of engaging in a task of the understanding as [if it were] a free play of the imagination; *poetry* is the art of conducting a free play of the imagination as [if it were] a task of the understanding.

Thus the *orator* announces a task and, so as to entertain his audience, carries it out as if it were merely a *play* with ideas. The *poet* announces merely an entertaining *play* with ideas, and yet the understanding gets as much out of this as if he had intended merely to engage in its [own] task. Now although the two cognitive powers, sensibility and understanding, are indispensable to each other, still it is difficult to combine them without [using] constraint and without their impairing each other; and yet their combination and harmony must appear unintentional and spontaneous if the art is to be *fine* art. Hence anything studied and painstaking must be avoided in art. For fine art must be free art in a double sense: it must be free in the sense of not being a mercenary occupation and hence a kind of labor, whose magnitude can be judged, exacted, or paid for according to a determinate standard; but fine art must also be free in the sense that, though the mind is occupying itself, yet it feels satisfied and aroused (independently of any pay) without looking to some other purpose.

321

---

[58] The reader must not judge this sketch of a possible division of the fine arts as if it were intended as a theory. It is only one of a variety of attempts that can and should still be made.

So while the orator provides something that he does not promise, namely, an entertaining play of the imagination, yet he also takes something away from what he promises and what is after all his announced task, namely, that of occupying the understanding purposively. The poet, on the other hand, promises little and announces a mere play with ideas; but he accomplishes something worthy of [being called] a task, for in playing he provides food for the understanding and gives life to its concepts by means of his imagination. Hence basically the orator accomplishes less than he promises, the poet more.

(2) The VISUAL arts, i.e., the arts of expressing ideas in *sensible intuition* (not by presentations of mere imagination that are aroused by words), are those of *sensible truth* and those of *sensible illusion.* The first kind is called *plastic art,* the second *painting.* Both express ideas by making figures in space; plastic art offers figures to two senses, sight and touch (though it offers them to touch without regard to beauty), painting offers them only to sight. The aesthetic idea (the archetype, or original image) underlies both of these arts, in the imagination. But the figure that constitutes its expression (the ectype, or derivative image) is given [differently in the two arts]: either with corporeal extension (as the object itself exists), or as that extension is pictured in the eye (i.e., as it appears in a plane). Differently put: whatever the archetype is, [it] is referred—and this reference is made a condition for reflection—either to an actual purpose or only [to] the semblance of such a purpose.

322

To *plastic art,* the first kind of visual fine art, belong *sculpture* and *architecture. Sculpture* is the art that exhibits concepts of things corporeally, as they *might exist in nature* (though, as a fine art, it does so with a concern for aesthetic purposiveness). *Architecture* is the art of exhibiting concepts of things that are possible *only through art,* things whose form does not have nature as its determining basis but instead has a chosen purpose, and of doing so in order to carry out that aim and yet also with aesthetic purposiveness. In architecture the main concern is what *use* is to be made of the artistic object, and this use is a condition to which the aesthetic ideas are confined. In sculpture the main aim is the mere *expression* of aesthetic ideas. Thus statues of human beings, gods, animals, and so on belong to sculpture; on the other hand, temples, magnificent buildings for public gatherings, or again residences, triumphal arches, columns, cenotaphs, and so on, erected as honorary memorials, belong to architecture; we may even add to this all household furnishings (such as the work of the cabinet maker and other such things that are meant to be used). For what is essential in a *work of architecture* is the product's adequacy for a certain use. On the other hand, a mere *piece of sculpture,* made solely to be looked at, is meant to be liked on its own account; though [in] such a work [sculpture] exhibits [its idea] corporeally, yet the work is a mere imitation of nature—even though one that involves a concern for aesthetic ideas—and so the *sensible truth* in it must not be carried to the point where the work ceases to look like art and a product of choice.

323

Painting, the second kind of visual art, exhibits *sensible illusion* artistically connected with ideas. I would divide it into *painting proper,* which *renders nature* beautifully, and *landscape gardening,* which *arranges* nature's *products* beautifully. For painting proper provides only the illusion of corporeal extension; landscape gardening, while providing corporeal extension truthfully, provides only the illusion of the use and utility [the garden has] for purposes other than the mere play of the imagination in the contemplation of its forms.[59] Landscape gardening consists in nothing but decorating the ground with the same diversity [of things] (grasses, flowers, shrubs, and trees, even bodies of water, hills, and dales) with which nature exhibits it to our view, only arranged differently and commensurately with certain ideas. But, like painting, this beautiful arrangement of corporeal things is given only to the eye, because the sense of touch cannot

[59] It seems strange that landscape gardening could be regarded as a kind of painting despite the fact that it exhibits its forms corporeally. It does, however, actually take its forms from nature (at least at the very outset: the trees, shrubs, grasses, and flowers from forest and field), and to this extent it is not art—whereas (say) plastic art is, [though it also exhibits its forms corporeally]—and the arrangement it makes has as its condition no concept of the object and its purpose (unlike the case of, say, architecture), but merely the free play of the imagination in its contemplation. Hence to that extent it does agree with merely aesthetic painting, which has no determinate topic (but by means of light and shade makes an entertaining arrangement of air, land, and water). All of this the reader should judge only as an attempt to combine the fine arts under one principle—in this case the principle of the expression of aesthetic ideas (by analogy with a language)—rather than regard it as a decisive derivation.

provide a presentation of intuition of such a form. In painting in the broad sense I would also include the decoration of rooms with tapestries, bric-à-brac, and all beautiful furnishings whose sole function is to be *looked at,* as well as the art of dressing tastefully (with rings, snuff-boxes, etc.). For a *parterre* with all sorts of flowers, a room with all sorts of ornaments (including even ladies' attire) make a kind of painting at some luxurious party, which, like paintings properly so called (those that are not intended to *teach* us, e.g., history or natural science) are there merely to be looked at, using ideas to entertain the imagination in free play, and occupying the aesthetic power of judgment without a determinate purpose. No matter how much the workmanship in all this decoration may vary mechanically, requiring quite different artists, still any judgment of taste about what is beautiful in this art is determined in the same way to this extent: it judges only the forms (without regard for any purpose) as they offer themselves to the eye, singly or in their arrangement, according to the effect they have on the imagination. But how can we (by analogy) include visual art under gesture in speech? What justifies this is [the fact] that through these figures the artist's spirit gives corporeal expression to what and how he has thought, and makes the thing itself speak, as it were, by mime. This is a very common play of our fancy, whereby to lifeless things is attributed a spirit that corresponds to their form and speaks through them.

324

(3) The art of the BEAUTIFUL PLAY OF SENSATIONS (which are produced externally, while yet the play must be universally communicable) can be concerned only with the ratio in the varying degrees of attunement (tension) of the sense to which the sensations belong, i.e., with the sense's tone. And [given] this broad sense of the word [tone], we may divide this art into the artistic play of the sensations of hearing and of sight,[60] and hence into *music* and the *art of color.* It s worthy of note that these two senses, besides having whatever receptivity for impressions they require in order [for us] to obtain concepts of external objects by means of these [senses], are also capable of [having] a special sensation connected with that receptivity, a sensation about which it is difficult to decide whether it is based

---

[60] [On hearing (including a reference to music) and sight, cf. the *Anthropology,* §§ 18–19, Ak. VII, 155–57.]

on sense or on reflection; and yet the ability to be affected in this way may at times be lacking, even though the sense is not at all otherwise deficient concerning its use for cognizing objects, or is perhaps even exceptionally keen. In other words, we cannot say with certainty whether a color or a tone (sound) is merely an agreeable sensation or whether it is of itself already a beautiful play of [component] sensations and as such carries with it, as we judge it aesthetically, a liking for its form. Just consider the rapidity of the vibrations of light or, in the case of tones, of the air,[61] which probably far exceeds all our ability to judge directly in perception the ratio in the temporal division [produced] by these vibrations. This fact might well lead us to believe that we sense only the *effect* of these vibrations on the elastic parts of our body, but that the *temporal division* [produced] by them goes unnoticed and does not enter into our judging, so that we connect only agreeableness with colors and tones, not beauty in the composition of the colors and tones. We must consider two points here, however. *First,* there is the mathematical one that can be made about the ratio of these vibrations in music, and about our judging of this ratio; and it is plausible to judge color contrast by analogy with music. *Second,* we can consult the examples, rare though they are, of people who, with the best sight in the world, have been unable to distinguish colors, or who, with the keenest hearing, have been unable to distinguish tones. Moreover, for those people who do have this ability, there is a definite [limit regarding their ability] to perceive a qualitative change (rather than merely a change in the degree of the sensation) in the varying intensities along the scale of colors or tones, and there is a similar limit on the number of these varying intensities that can be distinguished *intelligibly.* If we consider all of this, we may feel compelled to regard sensation of color and tone not as mere sense impressions, but as the effect of our judging of the form we find in the play of many sensations. However, the difference that the one or the other opinion would make to our judging of the basis of music would affect the definition only in this: we would declare music either, as we did above, to be the *beautiful* [*schön*] play of sensations (of hearing), or [to be the play] of *agreeable* sensations. Only under the first kind of explication will music be presented wholly as fine

325

[61] [Cf. Ak. 224 incl. br. n. 40.]

[*schön*] art, while under the second it would be presented (at least in part[62]) as *agreeable* art.

§ 52

On the Combination
of the Fine Arts
in One and the Same Product

Oratory may be combined with a pictorial exhibition of its subjects and objects in a *drama;* poetry may be combined with music in *song,* and song at the same time with a pictorial (theatrical) exhibition in an *opera;* the play of sensations in a piece of music may be combined with the play of figures, [viz.,] in *dance;* etc. Moreover, the exhibition of the sublime may, insofar as it belongs to fine art, be combined with beauty in a *tragedy in verse,* in a *didactic poem,* or in an *oratorio;* and in these combinations fine [*schön*] art is even more artistic. But whether it is also more beautiful [*schön*] (given how great a variety of different kinds of liking cross one another) may in some of these cases be doubted. But what is essential in all fine art is the form that is purposive for our observation and judging, rather than the matter of sensation (i.e., charm or emotion). For the pleasure we take in purposive form is also culture, and it attunes the spirit to ideas, and so makes it receptive to more such pleasure and entertainment; in the case of the matter of

326

---

[62] [The point of this qualification (similarly for the word 'wholly,' earlier in the same sentence) seems to be this: If we could not directly perceive and "notice" the form that an *individual* tone or color has in the play of its (component) sensations (as discussed in the *first* half of the paragraph), then the form in a composition from "many" such tones or colors could be (fine art and) beautiful, rather than just agreeable, only "in part": namely, to the extent that this form consists of relations *other* than the ratios *between* the (not directly perceived) numbers of vibrations in the individual tones or colors. On the other hand, this leaves us with the difficulty that (in the *second* half of the paragraph, *up to* the last sentence) Kant seems to be saying that if we do not notice the form of an individual tone or color then we could not notice *any* form in a composition from many such tones or colors and hence could connect with this composition "only" agreeableness, "not beauty."]

sensation, however, the aim is merely enjoyment, which leaves nothing behind as an idea and makes the spirit dull, the object gradually disgusting, and the mind dissatisfied with itself and moody because it is conscious that in reason's judgment its attunement is contrapurposive.

Unless we connect the fine arts, closely or remotely, with moral ideas, which alone carry with them an independent liking, the second of the two alternatives just mentioned is their ultimate fate. They serve in that case only for our diversion, which we need all the more in proportion as we use it to dispel the mind's dissatisfaction with itself, with the result that we increase still further our uselessness and dissatisfaction with ourselves. For the first of the two alternatives [culture, and the spirit's attunement to ideas], it is generally the beauties of nature that are most beneficial, if we are habituated early to observe, judge, and admire them.

§ 53

Comparison of the
Aesthetic Value
of the Various Fine Arts

Among all the arts *poetry* holds the highest rank. (It owes its origin almost entirely to genius and is least open to guidance by precept or examples.) It expands the mind: for it sets the imagination free, and offers us, from among the unlimited variety of possible forms that harmonize with a given concept, though within that concept's limits, that form which links the exhibition of the concept with a wealth of thought to which no linguistic expression is completely adequate, and so poetry rises aesthetically to ideas. Poetry fortifies the mind: for it lets the mind feel its ability—free, spontaneous, and independent of natural determination—to contemplate and judge phenomenal nature as having [*nach*] aspects that nature does not on its own offer in experience either to sense or to the understanding, and hence poetry lets the mind feel its ability to use nature on behalf of and, as it were, as a schema of the supersensible. Poetry plays with illusion, which it produces at will, and yet without using illusion to deceive us, for poetry tells us itself that its pursuit is mere play, though this play can still be used purposively by the understanding for its business. Oratory [on the other hand], insofar as this is taken to mean the art of persuasion (*ars oratoria*), i.e., of deceiving by means of a beautiful illusion, rather than mere excellence of speech (eloquence and style), is a dialectic that borrows from poetry only as much as the speaker needs in order to win over people's minds for his own advantage before they judge for themselves, and so make their judgment unfree. Hence it cannot be recommended either for the bar or for the pulpit. For when civil laws or the rights of individual persons are at issue, or the enduring instruction and determination of minds to a correct knowledge and a conscientious observance of their duty are at issue, then it is beneath the dignity of so important a task to display even a trace of extravagant wit and imagination, let alone any trace of the art of persuading people and of biasing them for the advantage of someone or other. For although this art can at times be employed for aims that are legitimate and laudable intrinsically, it is still made reprehensible by the fact that [by dealing with those issues] in this way [it] corrupts the maxims and attitudes of the subjects, even if objectively the action [they are persuaded to perform] is lawful; for it is not enough that we do what is right, but we must also perform it solely on the ground that it is right. Moreover, the mere distinct concept of these kinds of human affairs has, even on its own, sufficient influence on human minds to obviate the need to bring in and apply the machinery of persuasion as well—it is enough if the concept is exhibited vividly in examples and if there is no offense against the rules of euphony of speech or the rules of propriety in the expression of ideas of reason (these two together constitute excellence of speech). Indeed, since the machinery of persuasion can be used equally well to palliate and cloak vice and error, it cannot quite eliminate our lurking suspicion that we are being artfully hoodwinked. In poetry [on the other hand] everything proceeds with honesty and sincerity. It informs us that it wishes to engage in mere entertaining play with the imagination, namely, one that harmonizes in form with the laws of the understanding; it does not seek

327

to sneak up on the understanding and ensnare it by a sensible exhibition.[63]

328

After poetry, *if our concern is with charm and mental agitation,*[65] I would place the art which is closer to it than any other art of speech, and which can also be combined with it very naturally: the *art of music.* For though it speaks through nothing but sensations without concepts, so that unlike poetry it leaves us with nothing to meditate about, it nevertheless does agitate the mind more diversely and intensely, even if merely temporarily. However, it is admittedly more a matter of enjoyment than of culture (the play of thought that it arouses incidentally is merely the effect of an association that is mechanical, as it were), and in reason's judgment it has less value than any other of the fine arts. That is why, like any enjoyment, it needs to be changed fairly often and cannot bear several repetitions without making us weary. Its charm, so generally [*allgemein*] communicable, seems to rest on this: Every linguistic expression has in its context a tone appropriate to its meaning. This tone indicates, more or less, an affect[66] of the speaker and in turn induces the same affect in the listener too, where it then conversely arouses the idea which in language we express in that tone [*Ton*]. And just as modulation is, as

328

[63] I must confess that a beautiful poem has always given me pure delight [*Vergnügen*], whereas reading the best speech of a Roman public orator, or of a contemporary parliamentary speaker or preacher, has always been mingled with the disagreeable feeling of disapproval of an insidious art, an art that knows how, in important matters, to move people like machines to a judgment that must lose all its weight with them when they meditate about it calmly. Rhetorical power and excellence of speech (which together constitute rhetoric) belong to fine art; but oratory (*ars oratoria*), the art of using people's weaknesses for one's own aims (no matter how good these may be in intention or even in fact), is unworthy of any *respect* whatsoever. Moreover, both in Athens and in Rome, it came to its peak only at a time when the state was hastening to its ruin, and any true patriotic way of thinking was extinct. Someone who sees the issues clearly and has a command of language in its richness and purity, as well as a fertile imagination proficient in exhibiting his ideas and a heart vividly involved in the true good, is the *vir bonus dicendi peritus* [the excellent man and expert speaker], the orator who speaks without art but with great force, as *Cicero* would have him,[64] even though he himself did not always remain faithful to this ideal.

[64] [Wilhelm Windelband notes (Ak. V, 529) that it was not Cicero who said this, but (Marcus Porcius) Cato (the Elder, "the Censor," 234–149 B.C.).]

[65] [Mental agitation (see Ak. 258, 334) is what emotion involves; cf. Ak. 245 and 226.]

[66] [Cf. Ak. 272 n. 39.]

it were, a universal [*allgemein*] language of sensations that every human being can understand, so the art of music [*Tonkunst*] employs this language all by itself in its full force, namely, as a language of affects; in this way it communicates to everyone [*allgemein*], according to the law of association, the aesthetic ideas that we naturally connect with such affects. But since these aesthetic ideas are not concepts, not determinate thoughts, the form of the arrangement of these sensations (harmony and melody), which takes the place of the form of a language, only serves to express, by means of [the] proportioned attunement of the sensations, the aesthetic idea of a coherent whole of an unspeakable wealth of thought, and to express it in conformity with a certain theme that is the prevalent affect in the piece. (Since in the case of tones this attunement rests on the numerical relation of air vibrations that occur in uniform intervals of time—inasmuch as the tones are combined simultaneously or successively [in harmony and melody, respectively]—it can be brought under certain rules mathematically.) Although we do not present this mathematical form through determinate concepts, to such form alone is attached the liking that, when we merely reflect on such a multitude of concomitant or consecutive sensations, is connected with their play, as a condition, valid for everyone, of this play's beauty; and it is with regard to this form alone that taste can claim the right to pronounce in advance upon the judgment of everyone.

329

But mathematics certainly does not play the slightest part in the charm and mental agitation that music produces. Rather, it is only the indispensable condition (*conditio sine qua non*) of that ratio of the impressions, in their combination as well as change, which enables us to comprehend[67] them; and thus they are kept from destroying one another, so that they harmonize in such a way as to produce, by means of affects consonant with [this ratio], a continuous agitation and quickening of the mind, and thus they produce an appealing self-enjoyment.

If, on the other hand, we assess the value of the fine arts by the culture [or cultivation] they provide for the mind, taking as our standard the expansion of those powers that have to come together in the power of judgment in order for cognition to arise, then music, since it merely plays with sensations, has the lowest place among the fine arts (just as it may have the highest among those [whose value]

[67] [*Zusammenfassen*; cf. Ak. 252 br. n. 14.]

we assess by their agreeableness as well). So in this regard the visual arts are far ahead of it; for by putting the imagination into a free play that yet is also commensurate with the understanding, they carry on a task at the same time: they bring about a product that serves the concepts of the understanding as an enduring vehicle, a vehicle that commends itself to these very concepts, for furthering their union with sensibility and thereby the urbanity, as it were, of the higher cognitive powers. The two kinds of art pursue quite different courses: music proceeds from sensations to indeterminate ideas; the visual arts from determinate ideas to sensations. The latter [arts] produce a *lasting* impression, the former only a *transitory* one. The imagination can recall the lasting [impressions] and agreeably entertain itself with them; but the transitory ones either are extinguished entirely or, if the imagination involuntarily repeats them, they are more likely to be irksome to us than agreeable. Moreover, music has a certain lack of urbanity about it. For, depending mainly on the character of its instruments, it extends its influence (on the neighborhood) farther than people wish, and so, as it were, imposes itself on others and hence impairs the freedom of those outside of the musical party. The arts that address themselves to the eye do not do this; for if we wish to keep out their impressions, we need merely turn our eyes away. The situation here is almost the same as with the enjoyment [*Ergötzung*] produced by an odor that spreads far. Some-one who pulls his perfumed handkerchief from his pocket gives all those next to and around him a treat whether they want it or not, and compels them, if they want to breathe, to enjoy [*genießen*] at the same time,[68] which is also why this habit has gone out of fashion.[69] Among the visual

330

----

[68] [Cf. the *Anthropology*, Ak. VII, 158.]

[69] Those who have recommended that the singing of hymns be included at family prayer have failed to consider that by such a noisy (and precisely because of this usually pharisaical) worship they impose great hardship on the public, since they compel their neighbors to either join in the singing or put aside whatever they were thinking about.[70]

[70] [Cf. William Wallace, *Kant* (Philadelphia: Lippincott, n.d.), p. 42: "Kant, whose house stood not far from the castle, was disturbed in his studies at one period by the noisy devotional exercises of the prisoners in the adjoining jail. In a letter to Hippel [Theodor Gottlieb von Hippel, 1741–96, German writer and head mayor of Königsberg], accordingly, he suggested the advantage of closing the windows during the hymn-singings, and added that the warders of the prison might probably be directed to accept less than sonorous and neighbor-annoying chants as evidence of the penitent spirit of their captives."]

arts I would give priority to *painting,* partly because it is the art of design and as such underlies all the remaining visual arts, partly because it can penetrate much further into the region of ideas, and in conformity with them can also expand the realm of intuition more than the other visual arts can do.

§ 54

Comment

As we have frequently shown, there is an essential difference between *what we like when we merely judge it,* and what *gratifies* us (i.e., what we like in sensation). The second is something that, unlike the first, we cannot require of everyone. Gratification (even if its cause happens to lie in ideas) seems always to consist in a feeling that a person's life is being furthered generally [*gesamt*], and [this feeling] thus includes furtherance of his bodily well-being, i.e., his health.[71] To this extent, then, when *Epicurus* claimed that all gratification is basically bodily sensation,[72] he was perhaps not mistaken but only misunderstood himself in including intellectual and even practical liking among the gratifications. If we bear this latter distinction in mind, we can explain how a gratification can be disliked by the very person who feels it (for example the joy felt by a needy but upright person at being made the heir of his loving but stingy father), or how profound grief may yet be liked by the person suffering it (as a widow's sadness over the death of her worthy husband[73]), or how

331

---

[71] [Health matters are discussed extensively in the *Anthropology,* Ak. VII; they are also discussed in the *Streit der Fakultäten* (*Dispute among the* [*University's*] *Schools* [*Fakultäten*]), Ak. VII, 95–116, and in Kant's speech, *De medicina corporis, quae philosophorum est* (*On Medicine of the Body, as far as This* [*Discipline*] *Belongs to Philosophy*) (1788), Ak. XV, 939–53.]

[72] [Cf. Ak. 266, end of br. n. 33.]

[73] [Cf. the *Anthropology,* Ak. VII, 262: ". . . [A] widow who, as we say, will not let anyone console her, i.e., stop the flow of her tears, is fostering her health, even though she does not know this and actually does not want to know it." Cf. also *ibid.,* Ak. VII, 237.]

a gratification may be liked in addition (as our gratification in the sciences we pursue), or how a pain (such as hatred, envy, or a thirst for revenge) may be disliked in addition. The liking or disliking in these cases is based on reason and is the same as *approval* or *disapproval*. Gratification and pain, on the other hand, can rest only on the feeling of *being well* or *unwell* (whatever the cause), or on the prospect of possibly being so.

Any changing free play of sensations (that are not based on an intention) gratifies us, because it furthers our feeling of health, and it does not matter whether in our rational judgment we like the object of this play, or like this gratification itself. Moreover, this gratification can increase to the level of an affect even though we are not taking an interest in the object itself, at least not one proportionate to the affect's degree. We may divide such play into the *play [or game] of chance,* the *play of tones* [in music], and the *play of thought [or of wit]*. The *first* of these requires an *interest,* whether in vanity or in our own profit, but one far less strong than the interest we take in the manner according to which we pursue it. The play of *tones* requires merely a change of *sensations,* each of which relates to affect, but without having the strength [*Grad*] of an affect, and arouses aesthetic ideas. The play of *thought* arises merely from the change of presentations in judgment; although it produces no thought that carries any interest with it, it does quicken the mind.

How gratifying such play must be, without our having to assume an underlying interested intention, is shown by all our evening parties; for without play almost none of them could keep itself entertained. But many affects are at play there—hope, fear, joy, anger, and scorn, alternating constantly—and are so lively that they amount to an inner motion that seems to further all the vital processes in the body, as is proved by how sprightly the mind becomes as a result, even though nothing has been won or learned. But since the play of chance is not beautiful play, we shall here set it aside. But music and something to laugh about are two kinds of play with aesthetic ideas, or for that matter with presentations of the understanding, by which in the end nothing is thought; it is merely the change they involve that still enables them to gratify us in a lively way. This shows rather clearly that in both of them the quickening is merely bodily, even though it is aroused by ideas of the mind, and shows that all the gratification [we find] at a lively party, extolled as being so refined and inspired, consists [merely] in the feeling of health that is produced by an

332

intestinal agitation corresponding to such play. It is not our judging of the harmony we find in tones or in flashes of wit—this harmony, with its beauty, merely serves as a necessary vehicle—but the furtherance of the vital processes in the body, the affect that agitates the intestines and the diaphragm, in a word the feeling of health (which we cannot feel without such prompting), which constitutes the gratification we find in the fact that we can reach the body through the soul as well, and use the soul as the physician of the body.

In music this play proceeds from bodily sensation to aesthetic ideas (of the objects of affects), and from these back again [to the body], but with the force exerted on the body concentrated [*vereinigt*]. In jest[74] (which, just as much as music, deserves to be considered more an agreeable than a fine art) the play starts from thoughts, all of which, as far as they seek sensible expression, engage the body also. In the exhibition involved in jest, the understanding, failing to find what it expected, suddenly relaxes, so that we feel the effect of this slackening in the body by the vibration of our organs, which helps restore their equilibrium and has a beneficial influence on our health.

Whatever is to arouse lively, convulsive laughter must contain something absurd (hence something that the understanding cannot like for its own sake). *Laughter is an affect that arises if a tense expectation is transformed into nothing.* This same transformation certainly does not gladden the understanding, but indirectly it still gladdens us in a very lively way for a moment. So the cause of this must consist both in the influence that the presentation has on the body and in the body's reciprocal effect on the mind—but not because the presentation is objectively an object of our gratification (for how could an expectation that turned out to be false gratify us?), but solely because it is a mere play of presentations which produces in the body an equilibrium of the vital forces.

333

Suppose someone tells us this story: An Indian at an Englishman's table in Surat saw a bottle of ale being opened, and all the beer, turned to froth, rushing out. The Indian, by repeated exclamations, showed his great amazement.—Well, what's so amazing in that? asked the Englishman.—Oh, but I'm not amazed at its coming out, replied the Indian, but at how you managed to get it all in.—This makes us laugh, and it gives us hearty pleasure. This is not because, say, we think we are smarter than this ignorant man, nor are we laughing at

[74] [Cf. the *Anthropology*, §79, Ak. VII, 261–65.]

anything else here that is to our liking and that we noticed through our understanding. It is rather that we had a tense expectation that suddenly vanished, [transformed] into nothing. Or suppose that the heir of a rich relative wants to arrange for him a very solemn funeral service, but complains that things are not quite working out: For (he says), the more money I give my mourners to look grieved, the more cheerful they look.—This evokes ringing laughter in us, and the reason is that we have an expectation that is suddenly transformed into nothing. We must be careful to note that it must be transformed into nothing, not into the positive opposite of an expected object, for that is always something and may frequently grieve us. For if someone tells us a story that arouses great expectation in us, but at the close we see immediately that it is untrue, this arouses our dislike. An example of this is the story about people whose hair is said to have turned grey overnight from great grief. Suppose, on the other hand, that in response to a story like this some rogue gives us a longwinded account of the grief of some merchant who, during his return trip from India to Europe, with all his fortune in merchandise, was forced by a heavy storm to throw everything overboard, and whose grief was such that it made his *wig* turn grey that very night.—This will make us laugh; and it gratifies us because we treat our own mistake in reaching for some object that is otherwise indifferent to us, or rather the idea we had been pursuing, as we might a ball: we continue to knock it back and forth for a while, even though all we mean to do is seize [it] and hold on to [it]. What arouses our gratification here is not that we are dismissing someone as a liar or a fool. For even on its own account the latter story, told with an assumed seriousness, would make a party roar with laughter, whereas dismissing someone as a liar or a fool would not ordinarily merit attention.

334

It is noteworthy that in all such cases the joke must contain something that can deceive us for a moment. That is why, when the illusion vanishes, [transformed] into nothing, the mind looks at the illusion once more in order to give it another try, and so by a rapid succession of tension and relaxation the mind is bounced back and forth and made to sway; and such swaying, since whatever was stretching the string, as it were, snapped suddenly (rather than by a gradual slackening), must cause a mental agitation and an inner bodily agitation in harmony with it, which continues involuntarily, and which gives rise to fatigue while yet also cheering us up (these are the effects of a[n inner] motion conducive to our health).

For if we assume that all our thoughts are, in addition, in a harmonious connection with some agitation in the body's organs, then we can pretty well grasp how, as the mind suddenly shifts alternately from one position to another in order to contemplate its object, there might be a corresponding alternating tension and relaxation of the elastic parts of our intestines that is communicated to the diaphragm (such as ticklish people feel). The lungs, meanwhile, rapidly and intermittently expel air, and so give rise to an agitation that is conducive to our health. It is this agitation alone, and not what goes on in the mind, that is the actual cause of our gratification in a thought [by] which [we] basically present nothing. Voltaire said that heaven has given us two things to counterbalance the many hardships in life: *hope* and *sleep*.[75] He might have added *laughter,* if only the means for arousing it in reasonable people were as easy to come by, and if the wit or whimsical originality needed for it were not just as rare, as the talent is common for people to write, as mystical ponderers do, things that *break your head,* or to write, as geniuses do, things that *break your neck,* or to write, as sentimental novelists do (also, I suppose, sentimental moralists), things that *break your heart.*

It seems to me, therefore, that Epicurus may certainly be granted that all gratification, even if it is prompted by concepts that arouse aesthetic ideas, is *animal* (i.e., bodily) sensation. For granting this does not in the least impair the *intellectual*[76] feeling of respect for moral

335

[75] [*Henriade*, chant 7.]

[76] [*Geistig.* The *Geist* here is obviously not the "spirit in an aesthetic sense," the "animating principle in the mind," our "ability to exhibit *aesthetic ideas*" (§ 49, Ak. 313). Since the qualification, 'in an aesthetic sense,' is not repeated anywhere as Kant goes on to discuss *that* kind of *Geist*, it would be misleading if 'spirit' were used again to render '*Geist*' in a *non* aesthetic sense (except where the context clarifies what is meant, as it does, e.g., at Ak. 466 and 467). 'Intellect' seems closest to what Kant has in mind here, in the broad sense in which Kant has been using the term '*intellektuell*' all along in this work. As for the present case of intellectual *feeling*, it is true that in one place (*Critique of Practical Reason*, Ak. V, 117) Kant says that 'intellectual [*intellektuell*] feeling' would be a contradiction; for "all feeling is sensible" (*ibid.*, Ak. V, 75). Yet elsewhere he does talk about intellectual feeling; he speaks of "intellectual [*intellektuell*] pleasure" (*Anthropology*, Ak. VII, 230), and of "intellectual [*intellektuell*] liking" (above, Ak. 271 and 230, and below, Ak. 366). This seeming inconsistency can be resolved as follows. In calling a feeling (the feeling of respect) intellectual, a qualification must be taken as understood: this feeling too, *qua* feeling, is sensible, a receptivity, though one that does not have its own sense (see the *Metaphysics of Morals*, Ak. VI, 400, and cf. above, Ak. 291 br. n. 19); but we may still call it intellectual insofar as *the basis that gives rise to it is* (rational and as such) intellectual rather than sensible (*Critique of Practical Reason*, Ak. V, 73).]

ideas, which is not gratification but self-esteem (of the humanity within us) elevating us above the need for gratification—and indeed does not impair even the less noble feeling of *taste.*

Something composed of both of these [the bodily and the intellectual feeling] is found in *naiveté,* which is the eruption of the sincerity that originally was natural to humanity and which is opposed to the art of dissimulation that has become our second nature. We laugh at such simplicity as does not yet know how to dissemble, and yet we also rejoice in the natural simplicity here thwarting that art of dissimulation. We were expecting the usual custom, the artificial utterance carefully aimed at creating a beautiful illusion—and lo! there is uncorrupted, innocent nature, which we did not at all expect to find, and which is displayed by someone who also had no intention of doing so. Here the beautiful but false illusion, which usually has great significance in our judgment, is suddenly transformed into nothing, so that, as it were, the rogue within ourselves is exposed; and this is what agitates the mind alternately in two opposite directions, and is what also gives the body a wholesome shaking. But [the fact] that something infinitely better than all accepted custom, viz., integrity and character [*Lauterkeit der Denkungsart*] (or at least the predisposition to it), is after all not wholly extinct in human nature does mingle seriousness and esteem with this play of the power of judgment. But since this phenomenon manifests itself only for a little while, and since the art of dissimulation soon draws its veil over it again, regret is mingled in at the same time. This regret is an emotion of tenderness which, since it is play, can readily be combined with this sort of goodnatured laughter, and usually is in fact so combined with it. At the same time, the person who provides the food for this laughter is usually compensated for his embarrassment at not yet being shrewd in the [usual] human fashion by means of the tenderness involved. An art of being *naive* is therefore a contradiction; but there is certainly the possibility of presenting naiveté in a fictional character, and then it is fine, though also rare, art. We must not confuse naiveté with homely simplicity, which refrains from covering nature over with artificiality only because it does not understand the art of social relations very well.

The *whimsical* manner may also be included with whatever is cheerful and closely akin to the gratification derived from laughter, and which belongs to originality of intellect, but which certainly does not

336

belong to the talent for fine art. For *whimsicality,* in its favorable sense, means the talent enabling us to put ourselves at will into a certain mental disposition, in which everything is judged in a way quite different from the usual one (even vice versa), but yet is judged in conformity with certain principles of reason [present] in such a mental attunement. A person who is subject to such changes involuntarily is *moody [launisch].* But someone who can adopt them at will and purposively (so as to enliven his description of something by means of a contrast arousing laughter) is called *whimsical [launig],*[77] as is also the way he conveys [his thoughts]. However, this manner belongs more to agreeable than to fine art, because the object of fine art must always show itself as having some dignity; and so an exhibition of it requires a certain seriousness, just as taste does when it judges the object.

---

[77] [On moodiness vs. whimsicality, cf. the *Anthropology,* § 62, Ak. VII, 235.]

DIVISION II

DIALECTIC OF AESTHETIC JUDGMENT

§ 55

If a power of judgment is to be dialectical, then it must first of all engage in reasoning, i.e., its judgments must claim universality and must do so a priori;[1] for a dialectic consists in the opposition of such judgments. So when aesthetic judgments of sense (about the agreeable and disagreeable) are incompatible, this incompatibility is not dialectical. Even a conflict between different people's judgments of taste does not constitute a dialectic insofar as each person appeals merely to his own taste, since [to that extent] no one seeks to make his judgment a universal rule. Hence we are left with only one concept of a dialectic that could pertain to taste: that of a dialectic of the *critique* of taste (rather than of taste itself) concerning the *principles* of this critique. For when we consider the basis that makes judgments

---

[1] We may designate a reasoning [*vernünftelnd*] judgment (*iudicium ratiocinans*) to be any judgment proclaiming itself to be universal, hence being capable of serving as the major premise of a syllogism. But a judgment may be called a rational judgment (*iudicium ratiocinatum*) only if we think it as the conclusion of a syllogism and hence as having an a priori basis.[2]

[2] [In the *Critique of Pure Reason* (A 311 = B 368), Kant distinguishes "*conceptus ratiocinati* (correctly inferred concepts)" from "*conceptus ratiocinantes* (reasoning [*vernünftelnde*] concepts)," which he characterizes (differently and rather more negatively than the reasoning judgments here) as concepts "obtained surreptitiously by the semblance [*Schein*] of an inference."]

of taste as such possible, we find that concerning this basis conflicting concepts arise naturally and inevitably. Hence there is only one way for a transcendental critique of taste to include a part that can be called a dialectic of the aesthetic power of judgment—namely, if we find that the principles of this power give rise to an antinomy making doubtful whether this power is lawful and hence also whether such a power is intrinsically possible.

338

§ 56

Presentation of the
Antinomy of Taste

There are two commonplaces about taste. The following proposition contains the first of these and is used by everyone who lacks taste but tries to escape censure: *Everyone has his own taste.* That amounts to saying that the basis determining a judgment of taste is merely subjective (gratification or pain), and that such judgments have no right to other people's necessary assent.

The second commonplace about taste, which is used even by those who grant judgments of taste the right to speak validly for everyone, is this: *There is no disputing about taste.* That amounts to saying that, even though the basis determining a judgment of taste may be objective, that basis still cannot be brought to determinate concepts; and hence even proofs do not allow us to *decide* anything about such a judgment, although we can certainly *quarrel* about it, and rightly so. For though *disputing* and *quarreling* are alike in that [we] try to produce agreement between judgments by means of the mutual resistance between them, disputing is different inasmuch as here we hope to produce this agreement according to determinate concepts, by basing a proof on them, so that we assume that the judgment is based on *objective concepts;* and in cases where we think that this cannot be done, we judge that disputing also is impossible.

It is easy to see that between these two commonplaces a proposition is missing. This proposition is not in common use as a proverb, but everyone still has it in mind. It is this: *One can quarrel about taste* (though one cannot dispute about it). This proposition, however, implies the opposite of the first proposition above [Everyone has his own taste]. For if it is granted that we can quarrel about something, then there must be some hope for us to arrive at agreement about it, and so we must be able to count on the judgment's having bases that do not have merely private validity and hence are not merely subjective. But the above principle, *Everyone has his own taste,* says the direct opposite.

Hence the following antinomy emerges concerning the principle of taste:

(1) *Thesis:* A judgment of taste is not based on concepts; for otherwise one could dispute about it (decide by means of proofs).

(2) *Antithesis:* A judgment of taste is based on concepts; for otherwise, regardless of the variation among [such judgments], one could not even so much as quarrel about them (lay claim to other people's necessary assent to one's judgment).

339

§ 57
Solution of the
Antinomy of Taste

There is only one way for us to eliminate the conflict between the mentioned principles,[3] on which we base all our judgments of taste (and which are nothing but the two peculiarities of a judgment of taste[4] that were set out in the analytic): We must show that the concept to which we refer the object in such judgments is understood in different senses in those two maxims [or principles] of the aesthetic power of judgment, and show that it is necessary for our transcendental power of judgment to adopt both these senses (or points of view in judging) but that even the illusion arising from our confusion of the two is natural and hence unavoidable.

---

[3] [The thesis and antithesis.]

[4] [See § 31, Ak. 281, and § § 32–33, Ak. 281–85.]

A judgment of taste must refer to some concept or other, for otherwise it could not possibly lay claim to necessary validity for everyone. And yet it must not be provable *from* a concept, because, while some concepts can be determined, others cannot, but are intrinsically both indeterminate and indeterminable. Concepts of the understanding are of the first kind: for them there can be a corresponding sensible intuition whose predicates determine them. On the other hand, reason has a concept of the second kind: the transcendental concept of the supersensible underlying all that intuition, so that we cannot determine this concept any further theoretically.

Now, on the other hand, a judgment of taste does deal with objects of sense—though not so as to determine a *concept* of these objects for the understanding, since it is not a cognitive judgment. Rather, this judgment is a singular intuitive presentation referred to the feeling of pleasure, and hence is only a private judgment; and to this extent its validity would be restricted to the judging individual: The object is an object of liking *for me*;[5] the same may not apply to others: Everyone has his own taste.

340

And yet there can be no doubt that in a judgment of taste the presentation of the object (and at the same time of the subject as well) is referred more broadly [i.e., beyond ourselves], and this broader reference is our basis for extending such judgments [and treating them] as necessary for everyone. Hence this extension must be based on some concept or other; but this concept must be one that no intuition can determine, that does not permit us to cognize anything and hence does not permit us *to prove* a judgment of taste; such a mere concept is reason's pure concept of the supersensible[6] underlying the object (as well as underlying the judging subject) as an object of sense and hence as appearance. For unless we assumed that a judgment of taste relies on some concept or other, we could not save its claim to universal validity. Alternatively, if a judgment of taste were based on a concept of the understanding, such as that of perfection, even though merely a confused concept of per-

[5] [Cf. § 7, Ak. 212–13.]

[6] [On Kant's mysterious *switch* from the indeterminate concept of nature's purposiveness (Ak. 180–92 and the third Moment, Ak. 219–36) to the (indeterminate) concept of the *supersensible* (specifically the supersensible as basis of that same purposiveness of nature), see "Problem I" in the Translator's Introduction, *lxii–lxiii* and *xciv–xcviii*.]

fection, to which we could add the sensible intuition of the beautiful as corresponding to it, then it would be possible at least intrinsically to base a judgment of taste on proofs; but that contradicts the thesis.

However, all contradiction disappears if I say this: A judgment of taste is based on a concept (the concept of a general basis of nature's subjective purposiveness for our power of judgment), but this concept does not allow us to cognize and prove anything concerning the object because it is intrinsically indeterminable and inadequate for cognition; and yet this same concept does make the judgment of taste valid for everyone, because (though each person's judgment is singular and directly accompanies his intuition) the basis that determines the judgment lies, perhaps, in the concept of what may be considered the supersensible substrate of humanity.

What is needed to solve an antinomy is only the possibility that two seemingly [*dent Scheine nach*] conflicting propositions are in fact not contradictory but are consistent, even though it would surpass our cognitive power to explain how the concept involved [i.e., how what the concept stands for] is possible. Showing this [consistency] will also allow us to grasp [the fact] that and [the reason] why this illusion [*Schein*] is natural and unavoidable for human reason, and why this illusion remains so even though it ceases to deceive us once we have resolved the seeming contradiction.

For what gives rise to this antinomy is [the fact] that we treat the concept presupposed by the universal validity of a judgment as if that concept had the same meaning in the two conflicting judgments, and yet two opposed predicates are asserted of it. Hence the thesis should instead read: A judgment of taste is not based on *determinate* concepts; but the antithesis should read: A judgment of taste is indeed based on a concept, but on an *indeterminate* one (namely, that of the supersensible substrate of appearances); and then there would be no conflict between the two.

Eliminating this conflict between the claims and counterclaims of taste is the best we can do. It is absolutely impossible to provide a determinate, objective principle of taste that would allow us to guide, to test, and to prove its judgments, because then they would not be judgments of taste.[7] As for the subjective principle—i.e., the inde-

341

---

[7] [Cf. §34, Ak. 285–86.]

terminate idea of the supersensible in us—as the sole key for solving the mystery of this ability [i.e., taste] concealed from us even as to its sources, we can do no more than point to it; but there is nothing we can do that would allow us to grasp it any further.

The antinomy I have set forth and settled here is based on the concept of taste in the proper sense, i.e., as an aesthetic power of judgment that merely reflects; and I reconciled the two seemingly conflicting principles [by showing] that *they may both be true,* and that is all we need. If, on the other hand, we assumed, as some do, that the basis determining taste is *agreeableness* (because the presentation underlying a judgment of taste is singular), or, as others would have it, that it is the principle of *perfection* (because the judgment is universally valid), with the definition of taste formulated accordingly, then the result would be an antinomy that we could not possibly settle except by showing that the two opposed (but opposed [as contraries,] not as mere contradictories) *propositions are both false;*[8] and that would prove the concept underlying both of them to be self-contradictory. So we see that the elimination of the antinomy of aesthetic judgment proceeds along lines similar to the solution of the antinomies of pure theoretical reason in the *Critique* [*of Pure Reason*],[9] and we see here too—as well as in the *Critique of Practical Reason*[10]—that the antinomies compel us against our will to look beyond the sensible to the supersensible as the point [where] all our a priori powers are reconciled, since that is the only alternative left to us for bringing reason into harmony with itself.

Comment I

Since we so frequently find occasion in transcendental philosophy to distinguish ideas from concepts of the understanding, it may be useful to introduce technical terms to mark the difference. I think there will be no objection if I propose a few. Ideas, in the broadest sense, are

---

[8] [Cf. the *Logic,* Ak. IX, 71.]

[9] [For these antinomies and their solution, see A 405–567 = B 432–595.]

[10] [Ak. V, 107–19.]

presentations referred to an object according to a certain principle (subjective or objective) but are such that they can still never become cognition of an object. There are two kinds of ideas. One of these is referred to an intuition, according to a merely subjective principle of the mutual harmony of the cognitive powers (imagination and under-standing); and these ideas are called *aesthetic*. The other kind is referred to a concept, according to an objective principle, but these ideas still can never yield cognition of the object; they are called *rational* ideas.[11] Rational ideas are *transcendent* concepts; they differ from concepts of the understanding, which are called *immanent* because they can always be supplied with an experience that ade-quately corresponds to them.

An *aesthetic idea* cannot become cognition because it is an *intuition* (of the imagination) for which an adequate concept can never be found. A *rational idea* can never become cognition because it con-tains a *concept* (of the supersensible) for which no adequate intuition can ever be given.

I think we may call aesthetic ideas *unexpoundable* presentations of the imagination, and rational ideas *indemonstrable* concepts of reason. [But in saying this] I am presupposing that certainly neither of them lacks a basis, but that (as I said above in explicating ideas generally) they are produced according to certain principles of the cognitive powers to which they belong (aesthetic ideas acc-ording to subjective principles, rational ideas according to objective ones).

Concepts of the understanding must, as such, always be demon-strable (if by demonstrating we mean merely *exhibiting,* as we do in anatomy [for example[12]]; i.e., it must always be possible for the object corresponding to such concepts to be given in intuition (pure or empirical), because only in this way can they become cognitions. The concept of *magnitude* can be given in the a priori intuition of space, such as that of a straight line, and so on; the concept of *cause* can be given in [an intuition of] impenetrability, or [of] the impact of bodies, etc. Hence both these concepts can be supported by an empirical intuition, i.e., the thought of them can be illustrated (demonstrated, displayed) in an example; and this possibility must

---

[11] [Or 'ideas of reason.' Emphasis added.]

[12] [Constructing a (pure) concept is also included. Cf. Ak. 232 br. n. 51.]

343   [always] be there, since otherwise we cannot be certain that the thought is not empty, i.e., devoid of any object.[13]

In logic the terms demonstrable and indemonstrable are usually applied only to *propositions.* But it would be better if there we talked instead about propositions that are only indirectly certain and propositions that are *directly certain.* For pure philosophy also has propositions of both kinds, if we understand by them true propositions that can be proved, or that cannot.[14] For, as philosophy, it can indeed prove [propositions] from a priori grounds, but cannot demonstrate them, unless we totally abandon the meaning of the word demonstrate (*ostendere, exhibere*), which means the same as to exhibit one's concept [not only discursively but] in intuition as well (whether in proving or merely in defining something). If this intuition is a priori, [the exhibition[15]] is called the construction of the concept;[16] but even if the intuition is empirical, [the exhibition] is still a display of the object, which serves to assure us that the concept has objective reality. For example, if an anatomist has set forth the concept of the human eye discursively and goes on to dissect the eye to make the concept intuitable, we say that he demonstrates this organ.

Accordingly, the rational concept of the supersensible substrate of all appearances generally, or the rational concept of the supersensible that must be regarded as underlying our power of choice in relation to moral laws, i.e., the rational concept of transcendental freedom, is an indemonstrable concept and a rational idea, simply because of the type of concept it is; virtue too is such a concept, but [only] in degree. For in the case of the concept of the supersensible, there is not even an intrinsic possibility for anything corresponding to it in quality to be given in experience, whereas in the case of virtue no empirical product of our causality of freedom reaches the degree that the rational idea of virtue prescribes to us as the rule.

Just as in the case of a rational idea the *imagination* with its intuitions does not reach the given concept, so in the case of an aesthetic idea the *understanding* with its concepts never reaches the

---

[13] [Cf. the *Critique of Pure Reason,* B 291–93.]

[14] [Cf. the *Logic.* Ak. IX, 71 and 110.]

[15] [Correcting '*welche*' to '*welcher,*' as Windelband rightly recommends: Ak. V, 529.]

[16] [Cf. Ak. 232 br. n. 51, and Ak. 351 br. n. 31.]

entire inner intuition that the imagination has and connects with a given presentation. And since bringing a presentation of the imagination to concepts is the same as *expounding* it, aesthetic ideas may be called *unexpoundable* presentations of the imagination (in its free play). Later on I shall have occasion to make some further points about aesthetic ideas.[17] Here I shall merely point out that both kinds of ideas, rational as well as aesthetic, must have their principles, and both must have them in reason: the principles of rational ideas must be objective principles of reason's employment, those of aesthetic ideas subjective ones.

344

Hence GENIUS can also be explicated as the ability to [exhibit] *aesthetic ideas*.[18] This [explication] indicates at the same time why it is that, in products of genius, art (i.e., production of the beautiful) receives its rule from nature (the nature of the subject) rather than from a deliberate purpose. For we must judge the beautiful not according to concepts, but according to the purposive attunement of the imagination that brings it into harmony with the power of concepts as such. Hence the subjective standard for that aesthetic but unconditioned purposiveness in fine art that is to lay rightful claim to everyone's necessary liking cannot be supplied by any rule or precept, but can be supplied only by that which is merely nature in the subject but which cannot be encompassed by rules or concepts—namely, the supersensible substrate (unattainable by any concept of the understanding) of all his powers; and hence the mentioned standard can be supplied only by [means of] that by reference to which we are to make all our cognitive powers harmonize, [doing] which is the ultimate purpose given us by the intelligible [element] of our nature. It is in this way alone, too, that this purposiveness, for which we cannot prescribe an objective principle, can be based a priori on a principle that is subjective and yet universally valid.

[17] [See § 58, Ak. 350–51, and § 60, Ak. 355.]
[18] [Cf. § 49, Ak. 313–14.]

Comment II

Here the following important point arises spontaneously: that there are *three kinds of antinomy* of pure reason, all of which are still alike inasmuch as they force reason to abandon the otherwise very natural presupposition that objects of sense are things in themselves and force reason to regard them instead as mere appearances that are based on an intelligible substrate (something supersensible, the concept of which is only an idea and precludes cognition proper). If there were no such antinomy, reason could never bring itself to accept such a principle that so greatly narrows the area in which it can speculate and could never bring itself to make sacrifices that have to involve the complete destruction of so many hopes that were so brilliant otherwise. For though reason's prospect of proportionately greater employment in a practical respect has come to compensate it for the mentioned loss, still it seems that reason cannot help being pained as it tries to part with those hopes and to sever its old attachment.

That there are three kinds of antinomy is due to this: There are three cognitive powers—viz., understanding, judgment, and reason. Each of these (as a higher cognitive power) must have its a priori principles. Hence, insofar as reason passes judgment on these principles themselves and their use, it unrelentingly demands, for all of them, the unconditioned for the given conditioned. And yet we can never find this unconditioned if we regard the sensible as belonging to things in themselves, instead of regarding the sensible as mere appearance, based on something supersensible (the intelligible substrate of nature outside and within us) taken as thing in itself. And so three antinomies arise: (1) *for the cognitive power,* an antinomy of reason concerning the theoretical use of the understanding when this use is extended up to the unconditioned; (2) *for the feeling of pleasure and displeasure,* an antinomy of reason concerning the aesthetic use of judgment; (3) *for the power of desire,* an antinomy [of reason] concerning the practical use of our intrinsically legislative reason. These antinomies arise insofar as all these powers must have their higher a priori principles and, in conformity with an inescapable demand of reason, must be able both to judge and to determine their object under these principles *unconditionally* as well.

Now regarding two of the antinomies of those higher cognitive powers, viz., the antinomies concerning their theoretical and practical use, we have already shown elsewhere[19] that they are *inevitable* if in our theoretical and practical judgments we do not rely on [the assumption of] a supersensible substrate for the given objects [and take the latter] as appearances, but have shown there also that these antinomies *can be solved* once we do so. As for the antinomy in our use of the power of judgment in conformity with reason's demand and as for the solution given for that antinomy here, there is no way it can be avoided unless we adopt one of the following two alternatives. *One* of these is to deny that an aesthetic judgment of taste is based on any a priori principle whatever, so that [we would hold that] all claim to necessary universal assent is a baseless, vain delusion and [hold that] a judgment of taste deserves to be considered correct only insofar as there *happen* to be many people agreeing on it; actually even this [we would hold] not because we *suspect* that there is an a priori principle behind this harmony, but because (as with the taste of the palate) there is a contingent uniformity in the organization of [different] subjects. The *other* alternative is to assume that a judgment of taste is actually a disguised rational judgment about the perfection we have discovered in a thing and [in[20]] the reference of its manifold to a purpose, so that basically the judgment is teleological, and we call it aesthetic only because of the confusion that here attaches to our reflection. On this alternative we could declare it unnecessary and idle to solve the antinomy by means of transcendental ideas, and so we could reconcile those laws of taste with objects of sense even if these were things in themselves rather than mere appearances. However, we have shown in several places[21] in the exposition of judgments of taste that neither of these attempts to escape the antinomy will work at all.

346

On the other hand, if it be granted that our deduction is at least on the right track, even if not yet sufficiently clarified in all details, then we are led to three ideas: *first,* the idea of the supersensible in

---

[19] [*Critique of Pure Reason*, A 405–567 = B 432–595; *Critique of Practical Reason*, Ak. V, 107–19.]

[20] [Reading '*der Beziehung*' for '*die Beziehung*,' thus connecting it with '*an,*' not with '*über.*']

[21] [See §§3–5 (Ak. 205–11), §7 (Ak. 212–13), § 11 (Ak. 221), §§ 13–15 (Ak. 223–29), § 18 (Ak. 236–37), as well as Ak. 266–67.]

general, not further determined, as the substrate of nature; *second,* the idea of the same[22] supersensible as the principle of nature's subjective purposiveness for our cognitive power; *third,* the idea of the same supersensible as the principle of the purposes of freedom and of the harmony of these purposes with nature in the moral sphere.

§ 58

On the Idealism Concerning the Purposiveness of Both Nature and Art as the Sole Principle of Aesthetic Judgment

Note, first of all, that the principle of taste can be interpreted in two basically different ways. We can say that taste always judges by determining bases that are empirical and hence can be given only a posteriori through our senses, or we can grant that taste judges on a basis that is a priori. The former critique of taste would be an *empiricist* one; the latter would be *rationalistic.* On the empiricist[23] critique of taste the object of our liking would not be distinct from the *agreeable;* on the rationalistic one, if the judgment rested on determinate concepts, the object of our liking would not be distinct from the *good;* and so [in either case] all the *beauty* we find in the world would be denied, and we would have nothing left in its place except a special term, which might perhaps refer to a certain blend of those two kinds of liking. But we have already shown that liking can have [not only empirical but] also a priori bases, which are therefore consistent with the adoption of

347

---

[22] [On the assertion that the "three" supersensibles are the *same*, see the Translator's Introduction, *lxiii–lxiv.*]

[23] [Emphasis removed.]

rationalism as one's principle, even though such bases cannot be encompassed by *determinate concepts.*

If we adopt the rationalistic interpretation of the principle of taste, we may then interpret purposiveness either *realistically* or *idealistically.* But we have seen that a judgment of taste is not a cognitive judgment and that beauty is not a characteristic of the object when taken in its own right. Hence the rationalistic interpretation of the principle of taste can never be [the view] that in this judgment we think of the purposiveness as objective, i.e., [the view] that the judgment is theoretical and hence is also a logical judgment (even with [the qualification that] our judging is confused) regarding the perfection of the object, but [can] only [be the view] that the judgment is an *aesthetic* one regarding the harmony, within the subject, of the imagination's presentation of the object with the essential principles of judgment as such. Hence even if we adopt rationalism as our principle, there is only one way we can construe a judgment of taste and the difference between a realistic and an idealistic interpretation of it: on the realistic interpretation we assume that this subjective purposiveness is an actual (intentional) *purpose* that nature (or art) pursues, namely, harmony with our power of judgment; on the idealistic interpretation we assume only that the subjective purposiveness is a purposive harmony—manifesting itself on its own, contingently and without a purpose—with the needs of our power of judgment in dealing with nature and those of its forms that are produced according to [its] particular laws.

The realistic interpretation of the aesthetic purposiveness of nature finds much support in the beautiful formations in the realm of organized nature, for it certainly seems as if anything beautiful must have been produced on the basis of an idea of it in the producing cause, namely, a *purpose* that this cause pursued for the benefit of our imagination. Consider flowers, blossoms, even the shapes of entire plants, or consider the grace we see in the structure of various types of animals, which is unnecessary for their own use but is selected, as it were, for our taste. Consider above all the variety and harmonious combination of colors, so likable and charming to our eyes (as in pheasants, crustaceans, insects, down to the commonest flowers): since these colors have to do merely with the surface, and even there have nothing to do with the figure [i.e., (visible) structure] of these creatures—which might be needed for these creatures' inner purposes after all—it seems that their sole purpose is to be beheld from the outside. All of this lends weighty support to the kind of explanation that relies on the assumption that nature pursues actual purposes directed to our aesthetic power of judgment.

And yet this assumption cannot be upheld. Reason resists it with its maxims to avoid, wherever possible, unnecessary multiplication of principles. Above all, however, nature shows in all of its free formations a great mechanical tendency to produce forms that seem made, as it were, for the aesthetic employment of our power of judgment; and nature gives us no grounds whatever for supposing that [the production of such forms] requires anything more than nature's mechanism—considered as nothing but nature[24]—since nature's mechanism can make these forms purposive for our judging of them even if they are not based on any idea. In speaking of *free formations* of nature, I mean *those* where, in *a fluid at rest,* one part (sometimes merely caloric[25]) evaporates or separates from the fluid, and this separation makes the remainder solidify and take on a definite shape or fabric (figure or texture) that varies in accordance with what difference in kind there is in the matter, but is exactly the same whenever the matter is the same. This process does presuppose, however, that we are dealing with what we call a true fluid, in other words, a fluid in which the matter is completely dissolved, and not with one that would have to be considered a mere mixture of a fluid and solid particles merely suspended in it.

Under the described circumstances, formation then takes place, not by a gradual transition from the fluid to the solid state, but as it were by a leap: a sudden solidification called *shooting;* this transition is also called *crystallization.* The commonest example of this type of formation occurs when water freezes: At first straight slivers of ice form in it; these join together at angles of sixty degrees, while others similarly attach themselves to them at every point until all the water

[24] [I.e., without bringing in the supersensible substrate of nature and of nature's mechanism.]

[25] [Before it was discovered that heat is reducible to motion, heat was explained as due to caloric (*materia caloris*), which was thought of as an unweighable elastic fluid that could penetrate, expand and dissolve bodies, or dissipate them in vapor. In the *De igne* (*Concerning Fire*) (1755), Ak. I, 377, Kant equates caloric with aether, the "matter (i.e., medium) of light." Cf. also the *Metaphysical Foundations of Natural Science*, Ak. IV, 530.]

has turned to ice. So during this time the water between the slivers of ice does not become more viscous gradually but is as perfectly fluid as it would be at a much higher temperature, and yet it is quite as cold as ice. The matter that separates, and at the moment of solidification suddenly escapes, is a considerable quantity of caloric; since it was required merely to preserve fluidity, its departure does not leave the present ice any colder than was the fluid water from which the ice just formed.

Many salts and rocks have a crystalline figure and are produced in the same way by some kind of earth that has been dissolved in water through some unknown mediation. The drusy configurations of many minerals, such as cubical galena, red silver ore, and so on, very probably form in the same way, i.e., also in water and by the shooting of their particles, some cause forcing these particles to leave that vehicle and to combine into definite external shapes.

But the same applies to the inside as well; any matter that was fluid merely as a result of being heated, and that solidifies as it cools, will show a definite texture when it is broken. This permits the judgment that, if the matter's own weight or its contact with air had not prevented it, then the shape peculiar to its kind would have shown on the outside as well. This has been observed in some metals that, after having been molten, had hardened on the outside but were still fluid on the inside: when the inner still fluid portion was drained off, the remaining inner portion would now quietly crystallize. Many such mineral crystallizations, e.g., spars, hematite, and aragonite, often result in exceedingly beautiful shapes, such shapes as art might invent; and the halo in the grotto of Antiparos[26] is merely the product of water seeping through layers of gypsum.

It certainly seems that generally fluids are more ancient than solids, and that both plants and animal bodies are made from fluid nutritive matter, insofar as it takes form undisturbed. It is true that in the case of nutritive matter this formation occurs above all in accordance with a certain original predisposition which is directed to purposes (and which, as I shall show in Part II, we must judge not aesthetically but teleologically, with realism as the principle). But, in view of the universal law of the affinity of all types of matter, perhaps this formation occurs, in addition, freely and by crystallizing. We

349

[26] [Small island in the Cyclades, in Greece, noted for a splendid stalactite cavern on the south coast.]

could compare this, e.g., with an atmosphere, a mixture of different types of air; when the watery fluids that are dissolved in it separate from it because the heat [the caloric] is leaving, they produce snow-figures that, depending on what the particular mixture of air is at the time, often have a shape that seems very artistic and is exceedingly beautiful. Now it is quite conceivable, and involves no infringement on the teleological principle by which we judge organization, that the beauty in both the shape and the color of flowers, plumage, and sea-shells can similarly be attributed to nature and its ability to structure itself with aesthetic purposiveness as well—freely, without following specific purposes but merely in accordance with chemical laws, by depositing the matter needed for this organization.

350

But there is one fact that virtually proves the principle that the purposiveness in the beautiful in nature is *ideal,* that we ourselves lay this principle at the basis of all our aesthetic judgments, and that it does not permit us to explain [natural beauty] on the basis of a real purpose pursued by nature for our presentational power—namely, the fact that whenever we judge any beauty at all we seek the standard for it a priori in ourselves, and that the aesthetic power of judgment itself legislates concerning the judgment as to whether something is beautiful or not. This could not be so if we adopted a realistic interpretation of the purposiveness of nature, because then we would have to learn from nature what to consider beautiful, and a judgment of taste would be subject to empirical principles. In fact, however, what counts in judging beauty is not what nature is, nor even what purpose it [has] for us, but how we receive it. If nature had created its forms for our liking, such a purposiveness of nature would always be objective; it would not be a subjective purposiveness, based on the play of the imagination in its freedom, where it is we who receive nature with favor, not nature that favors us. This property of nature—that when we judge certain of its products nature allows us to perceive in the relation of our mental powers an inner purposiveness, and one that is to be declared necessary and universally valid on the basis of something supersensible—cannot be a natural purpose, or, rather, we cannot judge it to be that. For if our judgment were determined by such a purpose, it would be based on heteronomy; it would not be free and based on autonomy, as a judgment of taste should be.

This principle of the idealism concerning purposiveness can be recognized even more distinctly in fine art. That the purposiveness in fine art cannot be interpreted by assuming an aesthetic realism, with the purposiveness [working] through sensations, (since then the art would be not fine but merely agreeable art)—this much fine art shares with beautiful nature. But in fine art it is obvious furthermore that even a rationalistic interpretation of the principle of purposiveness must presuppose that the purposes are ideal rather than real. For the liking that arises from aesthetic ideas must not depend on our achieving determinate purposes (since then the art would be mechanical as well as intentional); and yet fine art, as such, must be regarded as a product of genius rather than of understanding and science, and hence as getting its rule through *aesthetic* ideas, which are essentially distinct from rational ideas of determinate purposes.

351

Just as we must assume that objects of sense as appearances are *ideal* if we are to explain how we can determine their forms a priori, so we must presuppose an *idealistic* interpretation of purposiveness in judging the beautiful in nature and in art if the critique [of taste] is to explain how there can be judgments of taste that claim a priori validity for everyone (yet without basing on concepts the purposiveness presented in the object).

§ 59
On Beauty as the
Symbol of Morality

Establishing that our concepts have reality always requires intuitions. If the concepts are empirical, the intuitions are called *examples*.[27] If they are pure concepts of the understanding, the intuitions are called *schemata*.[28] But if anyone goes as far as to demand that we establish the objective reality of the rational concepts (i.e., the ideas) for the

---

[27] [Cf. *On the Progress of Metaphysics since Leibniz and Wolff* (published in the year of Kant's death, 1804), Ak. XX, 325.]

[28] [See Ak. 253 br. n. 17.]

sake of their theoretical cognition, then he asks for something impossible, because absolutely no intuition can be given that would be adequate to them.[29]

All *hypotyposis* (exhibition, *subiectio ad adspectum*[30]) consists in making [a concept] sensible, and is either *schematic* or *symbolic.*[31] In schematic hypotyposis there is a concept that the understanding has formed, and the intuition corresponding to it is given a priori. In symbolic hypotyposis there is a concept which only reason can think and to which no sensible intuition can be adequate, and this concept is supplied with an intuition that judgment treats in a way merely analogous to the procedure it follows in schematizing; i.e., the treatment agrees with this procedure merely in the rule followed rather than in terms of the intuition itself, and hence merely in terms of the form of the reflection rather than its content.

---

[29] [See the *Critique of Pure Reason*, A 310–40 = B 366–98.]

[30] [Submission to inspection.]

[31] [Cf. *On the Progress of Metaphysics since Leibniz and Wolff*, Ak. XX, 279–80: To provide a concept with objective reality, Kant says, i.e., to show that it is not empty but is adequate for cognition, we must exhibit the concept. He goes on: "If we provide the concept with objective reality straightforwardly [*geradezu*] (*directe*) by means of the intuition that corresponds to it, rather than [indirectly or] mediately, this act is called schematism. But if the concept can be exhibited only [indirectly or] mediately, in its implications [*Folgen*: cf. above, Ak. 315] (*indirecte*), this act may be called the symbolization of the concept. The first we do for concepts of the sensible, the second is an expedient we use for concepts of the supersensible, which as such cannot actually be exhibited, and given in any possible experience. . . . The symbol of an idea (or rational concept) is a presentation of the object by analogy: i.e., we present the object of the idea [e.g., God; cf. below, Ak. 484 br. n. 107] in terms of the relation [which some other object, e.g., man, has] to its [effects or] consequences [*Folgen*] and which is the same relation that we consider the object itself as having to its consequences, and we do this even though the [two] objects themselves are quite different in kind. For example, I may in this way present certain products of nature, e.g., organized things, such as animals or plants, in relation to their cause, by presenting them like a watch in its relation to man, as its author. The relation [I use here is] identical in the two [cases]: it is causality as such, as a category; but the subject that has this relation [to its effects] remains unknown to me in its intrinsic character, and hence I cannot exhibit it, but can exhibit only that relation." Cf. also *De mundi sensibilis atque intelligibilis forma et principiis* (*On the Form and Principles of the Sensible and Intelligible World*), Ak. II, 396; *On [the] Dignified Tone Recently Adopted in Philosophy*, Ak. VIII, the n. on 399–401; the *Prolegomena*, § § 57–59, Ak. IV, 357–62; the *Anthropology*, Ak. VII, 191; and contrast the "schematism of analogy," *Religion within the Bounds of Reason Alone*, Ak. VI, the n. on 64–65. See also the *Critique of Practical Reason*, Ak. V, 70–71.]

The more recent logicians have come to use the word *symbolic* in another sense that is wrong and runs counter to the meaning of the word. They use it to contrast symbolic with *intuitive* presentation, whereas in fact symbolic presentation is only a kind of intuitive presentation. For the latter (the intuitive) can be divided into *schematic* and *symbolic* presentation: both are hypotyposes, i.e., exhibitions (*exhibitiones*), not mere *characterizations,* i.e., designations of concepts by accompanying sensible signs. Such signs contain nothing whatever that belongs to the intuition of the object; their point is the subjective one of serving as a means for reproducing concepts in accordance with the imagination's law of association. They are either words, or visible (algebraic or even mimetic) signs, and they merely *express* concepts.[32]

352

Hence all intuitions supplied for a priori concepts are either *schemata*[33] or *symbols*. Schemata contain direct, symbols indirect, exhibitions of the concept. Schematic exhibition is demonstrative. Symbolic exhibition uses an analogy (for which we use empirical intuitions as well), in which judgment performs a double function: it applies the concept to the object of a sensible intuition; and then it applies the mere rule by which it reflects on that intuition to an entirely different object, of which the former object is only the symbol. Thus a monarchy ruled according to its own constitutional laws would be presented as an animate body, but a monarchy ruled by an individual absolute will would be presented as a mere machine (such as a hand mill); but in either case the presentation is only *symbolic.* For though there is no similarity between a despotic state and a hand mill, there certainly is one between the rules by which we reflect on the two and on how they operate [*Kausalität*] This function [of judgment] has not been analyzed much so far, even though it very much deserves fuller investigation; but this is not the place to pursue it. Our language is replete with such indirect exhibitions according to an analogy, where the expression does not contain the actual schema for the concept but contains merely a symbol for our reflection. Thus the words *foundation* (support, basis), to *depend* (to

---

[32] The intuitive [element] in cognition must be contrasted with the discursive [i.e., conceptual] (not the symbolic). The former is either *schematic* and proceeds by *demonstration*; or it is *symbolic,* a presentation in accordance with a mere *analogy.*

[33] [Cf. Ak. 253 br. n. 17.]

be held from above), to *flow* (instead of to follow) from something, *substance* (the support of accidents, as *Locke* puts it[34]), and countless others are not schematic but symbolic hypotyposes; they express concepts not by means of a direct intuition but only according to an analogy with one, i.e., a transfer of our reflection on an object of intuition to an entirely different concept, to which perhaps no intuition can ever directly correspond. If a mere way of presenting [something] may ever be called cognition (which I think is permissible if this cognition is a principle not for determining the object theoretically, as to what it is in itself, but for determining it practically, as to what the idea of the object ought to become for us and for our purposive employment of it), then all our cognition of God is merely symbolic.[35] Whoever regards it as schematic—while including in it the properties of understanding, will, etc., whose objective reality is proved only in worldly beings—falls into anthropomorphism,[36] just as anyone who omits everything intuitive falls into deism, which allows us to cognize nothing whatsoever, not even from a practical point of view.[37]

Now I maintain that the beautiful is the symbol of the morally good; and only because we refer [*Rücksicht*] the beautiful to the morally good (we all do so [*Beziehung*] naturally and require all others also to do so, as a duty) does our liking for it include a claim to everyone else's assent,[38] while the mind is also conscious of being ennobled, by this [reference], above a mere receptivity for pleasure derived from sense impressions, and it assesses the value of other people too on the basis of [their having] a similar maxim in their power of judgment. The morally good is the *intelligible* that taste has in view, as I indicated in the preceding section;[39] for it is with this intelligible that even our higher cognitive powers harmonize, and

[34] [*Essay Concerning Human Understanding*, Bk. II, ch. xiii, 19.]

[35] [I.e., cognition by analogy. See above, Ak. 351 br. n. 31.]

[36] [Cf. Ak.457.]

[37] [Cf. the *Critique of Pure Reason*, A 631–33 = B 659–61.]

[38] [On the force of this link of beauty to morality, see the Translator's Introduction, *lxi* and *lxv–lxvi*.]

[39] [See the reference to the supersensible in § 58, Ak. 350. As Windelband points out, however, (Ak. V, 529), Kant presumably meant § 57, Ak. 340–46.]

353

without this intelligible contradictions would continually arise from the contrast between the nature of these powers and the claims that taste makes. In this ability [taste], judgment does not find itself subjected to a heteronomy from empirical laws, as it does elsewhere in empirical judging—concerning objects of such a pure liking it legislates to itself, just as reason does regarding the power of desire. And because the subject has this possibility within him, while outside [him] there is also the possibility that nature will harmonize with it, judgment finds itself referred to something that is both in the subject himself and outside him, something that is neither nature nor freedom and yet is linked with the basis of freedom, the supersensible, in which the theoretical and the practical power are in an unknown manner combined and joined into a unity. I shall now bring up a few points of this analogy [between the beautiful and the morally good], noting at the same time what difference there is between them.

(1) The beautiful we like *directly* (but only in intuition reflect[ed upon], not in its concept, as we do morality). (2) We like it *without any interest.* (Our liking for the morally good is connected necessarily with an interest, but with an interest that does not precede our judgment about the liking but is produced by this judgment in the first place.) (3) In judging the beautiful, we present the *freedom* of the imagination (and hence [of] our power[40] [of] sensibility) as harmonizing with the lawfulness of the understanding. (In a moral judgment we think the freedom of the will as the will's harmony with itself according to universal laws of reason.) (4) We present the subjective principle for judging the beautiful as *universal,* i.e., as valid for everyone, but as unknowable through any universal concept. (The objective principle of morality we also declare to be universal[ly valid], i.e., [valid] for all subjects, as well as for all acts of the same subject, but also declare to be knowable through a universal concept.) Hence not only is a moral judgment capable of [having] determinate constitutive principles, but its possibility *depends* on our basing the[se] maxims on those principles and their universality.

The common understanding also habitually bears this analogy in

354

---

[40] [Sensibility is the *lower* cognitive power (cf. the *Anthropology*, §40, Ak. VII, 196) and as such is passive (whereas the higher cognitive powers are active). In the *Critique of Pure Reason* (A 19 = B 33), Kant calls sensibility a capacity (*Fähigkeit*), rather than a *power* (*Vermögen*). But elsewhere in the work it becomes clear that Kant intends the two terms to be synonymous: see *ibid.*, A 51 = B 75, and cf. above, Ak. 177.]

mind, and beautiful objects of nature or of art are often called by names that seem to presuppose that we are judging [these objects] morally. We call buildings or trees majestic and magnificent, or landscapes cheerful and gay; even colors are called innocent, humble, or tender, because they arouse sensations in us that are somehow analogous to the consciousness we have in a mental state produced by moral judgments. Taste enables us, as it were, to make the transition from sensible charm to a habitual moral interest without making too violent a leap; for taste presents the imagination as admitting, even in its freedom, of determination that is purposive for the understanding, and it teaches us to like even objects of sense freely, even apart from sensible charm.

§ 60

APPENDIX
On Methodology
Concerning Taste

A critique that precedes a science is divided into elementology and methodology. But this division is not applicable to a critique of taste, since there neither is, nor can be, a science of the beautiful, and a judgment of taste cannot be determined by means of principles. It is true that in every art there is a scientific [element] whose concern is that the object of this art be exhibited [or rendered] *truthfully,* and which is indeed the indispensable condition (*conditio sine qua non*) of fine art, though it is not itself fine art. So in fine art there is only *manner* (*modus*), not *method* (*methodus*):[41] the master must show by his example [*vormachen*] what the student is to produce, and how. He may in the end bring his procedure under universal rules, but these are more likely to be useful to the student as occasional reminders

355

---

[41] [Cf. the *Logic.* §94, Ak. IX, 139: "All cognition, and a whole of cognition, must conform to a rule. (A lack of rules is also a lack of reason.) This rule is either *manner* (which is free) or *method* (which is constraint)." Cf. also above, § 49, Ak. 318–19.]

of what the main features of that procedure are, than as prescriptions of these features. And yet the artist must bear in mind a certain ideal; art must keep this ideal in view even though in practice it never achieves it in full. The master must stimulate the student's imagination until it becomes commensurate with a given concept; he must inform the student if the latter has not adequately expressed the idea, the idea that even the concept cannot reach because the idea is aesthetic; and he must provide the student with sharp criticism. For only in this way can the master keep the student from immediately treating the examples offered him as if they were archetypes, models that he should imitate as if they were not subject to a still higher standard and to his own judgment, [an attitude] which would stifle his genius, and along with it would stifle also the freedom that his imagination has even in its lawfulness, the freedom without which there can be no fine art, indeed not even a correct taste of one's own by which to judge such art.

It seems that for all fine art, insofar as we aim at its highest degree of perfection, the propaedeutic does not consist in [following] precepts but in cultivating our mental powers by exposing ourselves beforehand to what we call *humaniora;*[42] they are called that presumably because *humanity* [*Humanität*] means both the universal *feeling of sympathy,* and the ability to engage universally in very intimate *communication.* When these two qualities are combined, they constitute the sociability that befits [our] humanity [*Menschheit*] and distinguishes it from the limitation [characteristic] of animals. There were peoples during one age whose strong urge to have sociability *under laws,* through which a people becomes a lasting commonwealth, wrestled with the great problems that surround the difficult task of combining freedom (and hence also equality) with some constraint (a constraint based more on respect and submission from duty than on fear). A people in such an age had to begin by discovering the art of reciprocal communication of ideas between its most educated and its cruder segments, and by discovering how to make the improvement and refinement of the first harmonize with the natural simplicity and originality of the second, finding in this way that mean between higher culture and an undemanding nature constituting the

356

---

[42] [The humanities.]

right standard, unstatable in any universal rules, even for taste, which is the universal human sense.

It is not likely that peoples of any future age will make those models dispensable, for these peoples will be ever more remote from nature. Ultimately, since they will have no enduring examples of nature, they will hardly be able to form a concept of the happy combination (in one and the same people)[43] of the law-governed constraint coming from highest culture [*Kultur*] with the force and rightness of a free nature that feels its own value.

However, taste is basically an ability to judge the [way in which] moral ideas are made sensible ([it judges this] by means of a certain analogy in our reflection about [these ideas and their renderings in sensibility]); the pleasure that taste declares valid for mankind as such and not just for each person's private feeling must indeed derive from[44] this [link] and from the resulting increase in our receptivity for the feeling that arises from moral ideas (and is called moral feeling). Plainly, then, the propaedeutic that will truly establish our taste consists in developing our moral ideas and in cultivating [*Kultur*] moral feeling; for only when sensibility is made to harmonize with this feeling can genuine taste take on a definite, unchangeable form.

[43] [Parentheses added.]

[44] [On the force of this "derivativeness," see the Translator's Introduction, *lxiii* and *lxv–lxvi*.]

PART II

CRITIQUE OF
TELEOLOGICAL JUDGMENT

§ 61

On Objective
Purposiveness of Nature

Transcendental principles do provide us with a good basis for assuming that nature in its particular laws is *subjectively*[1] purposive for the ability of human judgment[2] to take [it] in, making it possible to connect the particular experiences to [form] a system of nature;[3] and we can then expect that the many natural products in such a system might include some that, as if adapted quite expressly to our judgment, contain certain specific forms: forms that are commensurate with our judgment because, as it were, their diversity and unity allow them to serve to invigorate and entertain our mental powers (which are in play when we engage in judging) and hence are called *beautiful* forms.

But the universal idea of nature as the sum total of sense objects[4] gives us no basis whatever [for assuming] that things of nature serve one another as means to purposes,[5] and that even their possibility cannot adequately be understood except [as arising] through a causality in terms of purposes. For in the case of beautiful forms we were dealing with the presentation[6] of things, which is something in ourselves, and hence it was readily conceivable, even a priori, how such a presentation could be fit and suitable for attuning our cognitive powers in a way that is purposive within [us]; but we have no a priori basis whatever for the following presumption: how purposes that are not ours, and that we also cannot attribute to nature (since we do not assume nature to be an intelligent being), yet are to

---

[1] [Emphasis added.]

[2] [*Urteilskraft*, in this case. Cf. Ak. 167 br. n. 4.]

[3] [Cf. the Introduction, IV–V, Ak. 179–86.]

[4] [This idea is what the mentioned transcendental principles spell out.]

[5] [Cf. Ak. 194, *On Using Teleologicul Principles in Philosophy* (1788), Ak. VIII, 182.]

[6] [*Vorstellung*, traditionally rendered as 'representation.' See Ak. 175 br. n. 17 and Ak. 203 br. n. 4.]

360

constitute, or could constitute, a special kind of causality, or at least a quite distinct lawfulness of nature. Not only [do we have no a priori basis for such a presumption,] but even experience cannot prove that there actually are such purposes, unless we first do some subtle reasoning and merely slip the concept of a purpose into the nature of things rather than take it from objects and our empirical cognition[7] of them, so that we would not so much cognize nature from objective bases as use the concept of a subjective basis on which we connect presentations within us, namely, the concept of a purpose, so that we can grasp nature by analogy with that subjective basis.

Moreover, so far is objective purposiveness, as a principle for the possibility of things of nature, from being connected *necessarily* with the concept of nature that it is rather this very purposiveness to which we primarily appeal in order to prove that it (nature) and its form are contingent. For when we point, for example, to the structure of birds regarding how their bones are hollow, how their wings are positioned to produce motion and their tails to permit steering, and so on, we are saying that all of this is utterly contingent if we go by the mere *nexus effectivus* in nature and do not yet resort to a special kind of causality, viz., the causality of purposes (the *nexus finalis*[8]); in other words, we are saying that nature, considered as mere mechanism, could have structured itself differently in a thousand ways without hitting on precisely the unity in terms of a principle of purposes, and so we cannot hope to find a priori the slightest basis for that unity unless we seek it beyond the concept of nature rather than in it.

Yet we are right to bring teleological judging[9] into our investigation of nature, at least problematically, but only if we do this so as to bring nature under principles of observation and investigation by *analogy* with the causality in terms of purposes, without presuming to *explain* it in terms of that causality. Hence teleological judging is reflective, not determinative. Yet the concept of connections and natural forms in terms of purposes does at least serve us as *one more principle* for bringing nature's appearances under rules in those cases

---

[7] [*Erkenntnis*. Cf. Ak. 167 br. n. 2.]

[8] [The distinction is between causal connection in terms of efficient causes (*nexus effectivus*) and in terms of final causes (*nexus finalis*).]

[9] [*Beurteilung*. On Kant's attempt to make a terminological distinction between '*beurteilen*' and '*urteilen*,' see Ak. 169 br. n. 9.]

where the causal laws of nature's mere mechanism are not sufficient to allow us to do so.[10] For we adduce a teleological basis when we attribute to the concept of an object—just as if that concept were in nature (not in us)—a causality concerning [the production of] an object, or, rather, when we conceive of the object's possibility by analogy with such a causality (which we find in ourselves) and so think nature as *technical*[11] in what it itself can do. If, on the other hand, we did not attribute to it such a way of operating, we would have to present its causality as blind mechanism. Suppose, alternatively, that we attributed to nature causes that act *intentionally*, and thereby based teleology not merely on a *regulative* principle for merely judging appearances, a principle to which[12] we could think nature as being subject in its particular laws, but based teleology also on a *constitutive* principle [that would allow us] to derive nature's products from their causes. On this alternative, the concept of a natural purpose would belong no longer to reflective but to determinative judgment. But then it would in fact not be judgment's own concept (as is the concept of beauty, i.e., of formal subjective purposiveness); instead it would be a rational concept[13] and hence would introduce a new causality into natural science, even though in fact we only borrow this causality from ourselves and attribute it to other beings without wishing to assume that they and we are of the same kind.

361

---

[10] [Cf. *The Only Possible Basis of Proof for Demonstrating the Existence of God*, Ak. II, 114.]

[11] [In the sense derived from the Greek τέχνη (téchnē), i.e., 'art' in the sense that includes craft.]

[12] [Reading '*dem*' for '*denen*.']

[13] [Or "concept of reason."]

DIVISION I

ANALYTIC OF
TELEOLOGICAL
JUDGMENT

§ 62

On Merely Formal, as
Distinguished from
Material, Objective
Purposiveness

All geometric figures drawn on a principle display a diverse objective purposiveness, often admired: they are useful for solving many problems by a single principle, and each of them presumably in an infinite variety of ways. This purposiveness is obviously objective and intellectual, and not merely subjective and aesthetic; for it means that the figure is suitable for the production of many shapes that serve purposes, and we cognize this purposiveness through reason. And yet this purposiveness does not make the concept of the [geometric] object itself possible, i.e., we do not regard the concept's [i.e., the figure's] possibility as depending on that use.

A figure that is as simple as the circle allows us to solve a multitude of problems that, if we tried to solve them individually, would require considerable apparatus; and this solution, one of the infinitely many splendid properties of this figure, arises spontaneously, as it were. For example, suppose we are to construct a triangle, and are given the

239

base and the vertical angle: this problem is indeterminate, i.e., it can be solved in an infinite variety of ways; and yet the circle encompasses them all, since it is the geometric locus for all triangles satisfying that [given] condition. Or suppose two lines are to intersect so that the rectangle under the two parts of the one line will be equal to the rectangle under the two parts of the other: solving this problem seems very difficult; but in fact all lines that intersect within a circle and are bounded by its circumference divide automatically in this proportion. The other curves in turn provide us with other purposive solutions that we did not think of at all in [thinking] the rule for their construction. All conic sections, whether by themselves or when compared with one another, and no matter how simple it may be to explicate their concept, are fertile in principles for solving a multitude of possible problems. It is a true joy to see how eagerly the ancient geometers[14] investigated these properties of such lines, not letting themselves be disconcerted if asked by narrow minds of what use such knowledge might be. Thus they investigated the properties of the parabola without knowing the law of terrestrial gravitation, which would have allowed them to apply the parabola to the trajectory of heavy bodies (whose motion has a gravitational direction that may be regarded as parallel to a parabola). Again, they investigated the properties of the ellipse without suspecting that celestial bodies too had gravity, and without knowing the law that governs gravity at varying distances from the point of attraction and makes these bodies describe that curve when they are in free motion. While these geometers were thus unwittingly working for posterity, they took delight in a purposiveness which, though it belonged to the nature [*Wesen*] of things, could still be exhibited completely a priori in its necessity. Plato, himself a master of this science, was overcome by enthusiasm [when he saw] that the original character of things is such that it can be discovered without any experience whatever, and that the mind is able to derive the harmony of beings from their supersensible principle; (to [these beings] we must add the properties of numbers, with which the mind plays in music). It was this enthusiasm that lifted Plato above empirical concepts to ideas that he thought could be explained only by an intellectual community [between ourselves and] the origin of all

363

[14] [Including Plato, who is about to be mentioned; cf. *On* [*the*] *Dignified Tone Recently Adopted in Philosophy*, Ak. VIII, 391.]

beings. No wonder he turned away from his school everyone who was ignorant of geometry; for what Anaxagoras inferred from objects of experience and their connection in terms of purposes, Plato meant to derive from the pure intuition residing within the human intellect [*Geist*[15]]. For there is a necessity in what is purposive and of such a character [that it seems] as if it had intentionally been so arranged for our use, while yet it also seems to belong to the original nature [*Wesen*] of things, without any concern as to [how] we might use it; and this necessity is the basis for our great admiration of nature [*Natur*], not so much nature outside us as nature in our own reason. Surely it is pardonable if, as the result of a misunderstanding, this admiration gradually increased to the point of fanaticism.[16]

This intellectual [*intellektuell*] purposiveness is indeed objective (rather than subjective, like aesthetic purposiveness); but, as to how it is possible, we can readily grasp this purposiveness, though only in a universal way, as being merely formal (rather than real [i.e., material]), that is, as a purposiveness that does not have to be regarded as based on a purpose and hence does not require teleology. A circular figure is an intuition that the understanding has determined according to a principle; I choose to assume this principle, presupposing it as a concept, and apply it to a form of intuition (space) that is also within me, a priori, as a mere presentation: and the unity of this principle allows us to grasp the unity of many rules which result from constructing that concept and which are purposive for all sorts of aims we might have, even though we are not entitled to regard this purposiveness as based on a *purpose* or on anything else whatsoever. This is different from cases where I find order and regularity in an aggregate, enclosed within certain boundaries, of *things* outside me: e.g., in a garden, order and regularity among trees, flower beds, walks, etc. For in these cases I cannot hope to infer a priori this order and regularity from the way I have bounded a space in accordance with this or that rule. For these are existing things that must be given empirically if they are to be cognized and are not a mere presentation

364

---

[15] [Cf. Ak. 335 br. n. 76.]

[16] ["Plato . . . was . . . the father of all fanaticism [aroused] *by means of philosophy*": *On [the] Dignified Tone Recently Adopted in Philosophy*, Ak. VIII, 398. (All translations given in footnotes are my own, and this fact is not indicated in each such footnote individually.)]

in myself determined according to an a priori principle. Hence the latter (empirical) purposiveness is [not formal but] *real,* and hence is dependent on the concept of a purpose.

But we can also easily see why it is that we admire, and rightly so, a purposiveness that we perceive, though perceive in the nature [*Wesen*] of things (insofar as their concepts can be constructed): The diverse rules whose unity (which is based on a principle) arouses this admiration are one and all synthetic and do not follow from a *concept* of the object, e.g., that of a circle, but [finding] these rules require[s] that this object is given in intuition. But that makes it seem as if the rules of this unity had an empirical basis outside us and distinct from our presentational power,[17] and hence as if the harmony [*Übereinstimmung*] of the object with our understanding's need for rules were in itself contingent and hence possible only through a purpose that aimed expressly at this harmony. And yet this harmony [*Harmonie*], despite all that purposiveness, is cognized a priori rather than empirically, and that fact alone should make us realize that the space to which I had to give determination (by means of imagination in conformity with a concept) so as to make the object possible is not a characteristic of things outside me but a mere way of presenting [them] within me; I should realize, therefore, that when I draw a figure *in accordance with a concept,* I *introduce* the *purposiveness into* the figure, i.e., into my own way of presenting something that is given to me from outside, whatever it may be in itself, rather than this something's instructing me empirically about that purposiveness, and hence should realize that I need no special purpose outside me in the object [to account] for that purposive harmony. On the other hand, this consideration already requires a critical use of reason and hence cannot already be contained in my very judging of the object concerning its properties; and hence this judging [itself] provides me with nothing directly except unification of heterogeneous [*heterogen*] rules in a principle (even with respect to what is heterogeneous [*ungleichartig*] about them)—a principle whose truth I cognize a priori, without any need for a special basis beyond my concept, or beyond my a priori presentation in general. Now [the admiration here must be distinguished from amazement.] *Amazement* [*Verwunderung*] consists in the mind's being struck by the fact that a presentation, and the rule it

365

[17] [For my use of 'power,' rather than 'faculty,' see Ak. 167 br. n. 3.]

provides, cannot be reconciled with the principles that the mind already presupposes, so that we begin to doubt whether we saw or judged correctly. *Admiration* [*Bewunderung*], on the other hand, is an amazement that keeps returning even after that doubt is gone.[18] Hence admiration is an entirely *natural* [*natürlich*] effect of that purposiveness observed in the nature [*Wesen*] of things (as appearances), and to that extent there is also nothing wrong with such admiration. For not only are we unable to explain the agreement [*Vereinbarung*] of that form of sensible intuition (called space) with our power of concepts (the understanding), [inasmuch] as it is precisely this [viz., purposive] agreement rather than some other, but this agreement also expands the mind; it makes it suspect, as it were, that there is something else above and beyond those presentations of sense, something which, although we do not know it, might hold the ultimate basis for that [agreement or] harmony [*Einstimmung*]. It is true that we also have no need to know this basis when we are dealing merely with formal [even though formal objective] purposiveness of our a priori presentations; but even just being forced to look in that direction inspires in us at the same time an admiration for the object that makes us do so.

The mentioned properties of geometric figures, and presumably of numbers as well, are commonly called [their] *beauty*,[19] because they have a certain a priori purposiveness for all sorts of cognitive uses which is unexpected in view of how simple it is to construct these figures. For example, people will speak of this or that *beautiful* property of the circle, discovered in one way or another. Yet it is not by an aesthetic judging that we find such a property purposive, not by a judging without a concept, a judging that reveals to us a mere *subjective* purposiveness in the free play of our cognitive powers; rather, it is by an intellectual judging, according to concepts, and this judging reveals distinctly an objective purposiveness, i.e., a suitability for all sorts of purposes (of infinite diversity). Instead of calling such a property of a mathematical figure its beauty, it would be better to call it the figure's *relative perfection.* It would also be quite improper to

366

---

[18] [On amazement and admiration, cf. Ak. 272.]
[19] [Cf. Ak. 241–42.]

call it *intellectual* beauty,[20] since then the word beauty would lose all definite meaning, or intellectual liking[21] would lose all superiority over the liking of sense. It would be more plausible to call a *demonstration* of such properties beautiful, since such a demonstration makes understanding and imagination, the powers of concepts and of their a priori exhibition,[22] respectively, feel invigorated, so that here at least the liking is subjective, even though based on concepts, whereas perfection carries with it an objective liking. (That [invigoration of understanding and imagination], when it is combined with the precision that reason introduces, is called the demonstration's elegance.)

§ 63

On Relative, as Distinguished from Intrinsic, Purposiveness of Nature

Only in one case does experience lead our power of judgment to the concept of a purposiveness that is both objective and material [or real], i.e., to the concept of a purpose of nature—namely, when we have to judge a relation of cause to effect[23] which is such that we can see it as law-governed only if we regard the cause's action as based on the idea of the effect, with this idea as the underlying condition under which the cause itself can produce that effect. We can do this in two ways: we may regard the effect either as directly the product of art, or as only the material that other possible natural beings employ in their

367

---

[20] [Cf. Ak. 271.]

[21] [*Wohlgefallen*; see Ak. 207 br. n. 14.]

[22] [*Darstellung*, traditionally rendered as 'presentation.' See Ak. 232 br. n. 51.]

[23] Since pure mathematics cannot deal with the existence of things but can deal only with their possibility, i.e., with an intuition corresponding to their concept, it cannot at all deal with cause and effect. Hence all purposiveness taken note of there must be regarded as merely formal, never as a natural purpose.

art; in other words, we may regard the effect either as a purpose, or as a means that other causes employ purposively. The second purposiveness is called either usefulness (for human beings) or benefit (for any other creature), and this second purposiveness is merely relative, whereas the first is an intrinsic purposiveness of the natural being.

For example, rivers carry along all sorts of soil on which plants can grow. Sometimes they deposit it inland, but often also at their mouths. On some coasts the high tide carries this mud over the land, or deposits it along the shore. And if the low tide is kept, above all by people, from carrying the mud off again, then the fertile land expands and the vegetable kingdom takes over where fish and crustaceans used to live. Probably in most cases it is nature itself that extended the land in this way, and is doing so still, even if slowly. Here the question arises whether we should judge this [process] to be a purpose of nature, since it is useful to human beings. (That it is useful for the vegetable kingdom itself does not count, since the sea creatures lose as much as the land gains.)[24]

An example of how certain natural things benefit other creatures as a means (if we presuppose that these creatures are purposes) is the following: There is no better soil for spruces than a sandy soil. Now as the ancient sea withdrew from the land, it left behind so many tracts of sand in these northern regions that this soil, so useless for any cultivation otherwise, enabled extensive spruce forests to establish themselves, for whose unreasonable destruction we often blame our ancestors. And so we may ask: did nature pursue a purpose in depositing these very ancient layers of sand, namely, to make spruce forests possible there? This much is clear: if we assume that the spruce forests are a purpose of nature, then we must also grant that the sand is a purpose, though only a relative one, for which in turn the beach and the withdrawal [of the ancient sea] were the means. For in the series of mutually subordinated links in a connection of purposes, each intermediate link must be regarded as a purpose (though, by the same token, not as a final purpose), and its proximate cause is the means to it. Thus if there were to be cattle, sheep, horses, etc. in the world one day, then grass had to grow on the earth. And alkaline plants [*Salzkräuter*] had to grow in the deserts if camels were to

368

---

[24] [Parentheses added.]

thrive. Again, camels and other herbivorous animals had to abound if there were to be wolves, tigers, and lions. Hence objective purposiveness that is based on benefit is not an objective purposiveness of things themselves; for in that case it would have to be impossible for us to grasp how the sand, considered by itself, could be an effect caused by the sea without our regarding the sea as having acted on a purpose, and without our regarding the sand—its effect—as a work of art. Rather, it is a purposiveness that is merely relative and that the thing to which we attribute this purposiveness has merely contingently; and although, among the examples just mentioned, the various kinds of grass, considered by themselves, must be judged as organized products of nature and hence as artistic, nevertheless in relation to the animals that feed on them they [must] be regarded as mere raw material.

But man, because of the freedom he has in his causality, seems to consider all natural things beneficial: many of them for foolish aims (such as colorful bird feathers to adorn his clothes, or colored earths or plant juices for makeup), but others for reasonable aims, such as horses for riding, oxen and—in Minorca—even donkeys and pigs for plowing. Yet in these cases we cannot even assume a relative purpose of nature (directed to these uses). For man's own reason knows how to make things harmonize with the notions[25] [*Einfälle*] that were his own choice, notions to which even nature did not predestine him. Only *if* we assume that human beings were [meant] to live on the earth, then there had to be at least the means without which they could not subsist as animals, or even as (to however low a degree) rational animals. In that case, however, those natural things that would be indispensable for this would also have to be regarded as natural purposes.

We can easily see from this that extrinsic purposiveness (a thing's being beneficial to others) can be regarded as an extrinsic natural purpose only under the condition that the existence of what it benefits proximately or remotely is a purpose of nature in its own right. This, however, we can never tell by merely examining nature; and hence it follows that, although relative purposiveness points hypothetically to natural purposes, it does not justify any absolute teleological judgment.

369

[25] [Not in the technical sense of 'notion' found in the *Critique of Pure Reason*, A 320 = B 377.]

In cold lands,[26] snow protects crops from the frost. It makes it easier for people to get together (by means of sleighs). In Lapland, the people find animals (reindeer) that they use to get together. These animals find adequate nourishment in a dry moss that they have to scrape out for themselves from under the snow. But they are also easily tamed, and willingly permit people to deprive them of their freedom even though they could easily support themselves on their own. For other peoples in the same frigid zone, the sea holds rich supplies of animals that provide them not only with food and clothing, and with timber that the sea floats to them, as it were, as building material for their homes, but also with fuel for heating their huts. So here we have an admirable collection of cases where nature relates to a purpose; that purpose is the Greenlander, the Lapp, the Samoyed, the Yakut, etc. And yet it is not clear why people should have to live in those regions at all. Therefore it would be hazardous and arbitrary indeed if we judged that vapors fall from the air as snow, that currents in the sea bring timber grown in warmer lands, and that large marine animals replete with oil are there *because* the cause providing all these natural products acts on the idea of an advantage for certain wretched creatures. For even if there were none of that natural utility, we would find that natural causes are fully adequate to make [things] come out this way; rather, we ourselves would then consider it impudent and rash even to. demand that there be such a predisposition and to require nature to pursue such a purpose (on the ground that otherwise only people's extreme inability to get along with one another could have scattered them all the way to such inhospitable regions).

[26] [On this entire paragraph, cf. *Perpetual Peace,* Ak. VIII, 363–65.]

§ 64

On the Character
Peculiar to Things
[Considered]
as Natural Purposes

To say that a thing is possible only as a purpose is to say that the causality that gave rise to it must be sought, not in the mechanism of nature, but in a cause whose ability to act is determined by concepts. And seeing that a thing is possible only as a purpose requires that the thing's form could not have arisen according to mere natural laws, laws we can cognize by understanding alone as applied to objects of sense, but requires that even empirical cognition of this form in terms of its cause and effect presupposes concepts of reason. [Therefore] the form of such a thing is, as far as reason is concerned, *contingent* in terms of all empirical laws.[27] But reason, even if it tries to gain insight only into the conditions attached to the production of a natural product, must always cognize not only the product's form but the form's necessity as well. And yet in that given form it cannot assume that necessity. Hence that very contingency of the thing's form is a basis for regarding the product as if it had come about through a causality that only reason can have. Such a causality would be the ability to act according to purposes (i.e., a will), and in presenting an object as possible only through such an ability we would be presenting it as possible only as a purpose.

Suppose that someone coming to a seemingly uninhabited country perceived a geometric figure, say a regular hexagon, traced in the sand. As he reflected on this figure, working out a concept for it, reason would make him aware, even if obscurely, of the unity of the principle [required] for producing this concept. And so, following reason, he would not judge that such a figure is made possible by the sand, the adjoining sea, the wind, or even animals that leave footprints familiar to him, or by any other nonrational cause; for it would

370

[27] [Cf. *The Only Possible Basis of Proof*, Ak. II, 107.]

248

seem to him that coming across such a concept [a regular hexagon], one that is possible only in reason, is so infinitely contingent that there might as well be no natural law for it at all, and hence that such an effect could also not have been caused by anything in nature, which operates merely mechanically, but could have been caused only by the concept of such an object, a concept that only reason can provide and compare the object with. It would seem to him therefore that, although this effect [the figure] can be considered a purpose, it cannot be considered a natural purpose, but can be considered only a product of *art* (*vestigium hominis video*[28]).

If, on the other hand, we cognize something as a natural product and yet are to judge it to be a purpose, and hence a *natural purpose* —unless perhaps the very [thought] is contradictory—then we need more [than the above example provided]. I would say, provisionally, that a thing exists as a natural purpose if it is *both cause and effect of itself* (although [*of itself*] in two different senses). For this involves a causality which is such that we cannot connect it with the mere concept of a nature without regarding nature as acting from a purpose; and even then, though we can think this causality, we cannot grasp it. Before we analyze this idea of a natural purpose in full, let me elucidate its meaning by [the] example [of a tree].[29]

In the first place, a tree generates another tree according to a familiar natural law. But the tree it produces is of the same species [*Gattung*[30]]. Hence with regard to its *species* the tree produces itself: within its species, it is both cause and effect, both generating itself and being generated by itself ceaselessly, thus preserving itself as a species.

371

---

[28] ["I see the trace of a man." The allusion is to the *De Architectura* (*On Architecture*) by Vitruvius (Marcus Vitruvius Pollio), architect and engineer in early imperial Rome (the beginning of the preface to book vi): *Aristippus philosophus Socraticus, naufragio cum eiectus ad Rhodiensium litus animadvertisset geometrica schemata descripta, exclamavisse ad comites ita dicitur: Bene speremus, hominum enim vestigia video.* (Aristippus, the Socratic philosopher (c. 435–366 B.C., founder of the Cyrenaic school], was shipwrecked but reached the shore of Rhodes. There he noticed geometric figures drawn [in the sand], and is said to have shouted to his companions: There is hope, for I see traces of men.)]

[29] [Cf. *The Only Possible Basis of Proof*, Ak. II, 114–15.]

[30] The literal meaning of the term is 'genus,' but to render it so would make it come out, in contexts like this, rather more technical than is intended in the original term.]

Second, a tree also produces itself as an *individual*. It is true that this sort of causation is called merely growth; but this growth must be understood in a sense that distinguishes it completely from any increase in size according to mechanical laws: it must be considered to be equivalent to generation, though called by another name. [For] the matter that the tree assimilates is first processed by it until the matter has the quality peculiar to the species, a quality that the natural mechanism outside the plant cannot supply, and the tree continues to develop itself by means of a material that in its composition is the tree's own product. For though in terms of the ingredients that the tree receives from nature outside it we have to consider it to be only an educt,[31] still the separation and recombination of this raw material show that these natural beings have a separating and forming ability of very great originality; all our art finds itself infinitely outdistanced if it tries to reconstruct those products of the vegetable kingdom from the elements we obtain by dissecting them, or for that matter from the material that nature supplies for their nourishment.

Third, part of the tree also produces itself inasmuch as there is a mutual dependence between the preservation of one part and that of the others. If an eye is taken from the leaf of one tree and set into the branch of another, it produces in the alien stock a plant of its own species, and so does a scion grafted onto the trunk of another tree. Hence even in one and the same tree we may regard each branch or leaf as merely set into or grafted onto it, and hence as an independent tree that only attaches itself to another one and nourishes itself parasitically. The leaves, too, though produced by the tree, also sustain it in turn; for repeated defoliation would kill it, and its growth depends on their effect on the trunk. There are other examples that I shall mention only in passing, even though they are among the most marvelous properties of organized creatures: if such beings are injured, nature aids itself, and the loss of a part that was needed to sustain [*erhalten*] adjoining ones is made up by the rest; if birth defects occur, or deformities come about during growth, certain parts, on account of their deficiencies or impediments, form in an entirely new

372

---

[31] [Rather than a product. To produce (which means, even literally, to "bring forth") something includes giving it its form; to educe something is merely to "bring out" something that already has a (predetermined) form. Cf. Ak. 423–24.]

way so as to preserve [*erhalten*] what is there, and so produce an anomalous creature.

§ 65
Things [Considered]
as Natural Purposes
Are Organized Beings

We said in the preceding section that if a thing is a natural product but yet we are to cognize it as possible only as a natural purpose, then it must have this character: it must relate to itself in such a way that it is both cause and effect of itself. But this description is not quite appropriate and determinate and still needs to be derived from a determinate concept.

A causal connection, as our mere understanding thinks it, is one that always constitutes a descending series (of causes and effects): the things that are the effects, and that hence presuppose others as their causes, cannot themselves in turn be causes of these others. This kind of causal connection is called that of efficient causes (*nexus effectivus*). But we can also conceive of a causal connection [*Verbindung*] in terms of a concept of reason (the concept of purposes). Such a connection, considered as a series, would carry with it dependence both as it ascends and as it descends: here we could call a thing the effect of something and still be entitled to call it, as the series ascends, the cause of that something as well. This sort of causal connection [*Verknüpfung*] is easily found in the practical sphere (namely, in art). For example, although a house is the cause of the money received for rent, yet, conversely, the presentation [we formed] of this possible income also caused the house to be constructed.[32] This kind of causal connection is called that of final causes (*nexus finalis*). Perhaps it would be more appropriate to call the former causal connec-

---

[32] [Hence the *income itself* is the *final* cause (purpose) of the house (or of the house's being constructed).]

373

tion that of real causes, the latter that of ideal causes, since these terms would make it clear at the same time that there cannot be more than these two kinds of causality.

Now in order for a thing to be a natural purpose, it must meet two requirements. *First,* the possibility of its parts (as concerns both their existence and their form) must depend on their relation to the whole. For since the thing itself is a purpose, it is covered [*befaßt*] by a concept or idea that must determine a priori everything that the thing is to contain. But if we think of a thing as possible only in *that*[33] way, then it is merely a work of art. For it is then the product of a rational cause distinct from the matter of the thing ([i.e.,] distinct from the thing's parts), [a cause which is] determined to exercise its causality (in procuring and combining the parts) by the idea of a whole that is possible through that idea (and [which] therefore [is] not [a cause (viz., the product's matter, i.e., its parts) determined to exercise its causality] by *nature*[34] outside the product).

A *second* requirement must be met if a thing that is a product of nature is yet to have, within itself and its inner possibility, reference to purposes, i.e., if it is to be possible only as a natural purpose, without the causality of concepts, which rational beings outside it have. This second requirement is that the parts of the thing combine into the unity of a whole because they are reciprocally cause and effect of their form. For only in this way is it possible that the idea of the whole should conversely (reciprocally) determine the form and combination of all the parts, not as cause—for then the whole would be a product of art—but as the basis on which someone judging this whole cognizes the systematic unity in the form and combination of all the manifold contained in the given matter.

Therefore in order for us to judge a body as being, in itself and in its inner possibility, a natural purpose, what is needed is that all its parts, through their own causality, produce one another as regards both their form and combination, and that in this way they produce a whole whose concept ([if present] in a being possessing the causality in terms of concepts that would be adequate for such a product) could, conversely, be the cause of this body according to a principle,

---

[33] [Emphasis added.]
[34] [Emphasis added.]

so that the connection of *efficient causes* could at the same time be judged to be a *causation through final causes.*

In such a product of nature, just as each part exists only *as a result* of all the rest, so we also think of each part as existing *for the sake* of the others and of the whole, i.e., as an instrument (organ). But that is not enough (for the part could also be an instrument of art, in which case we would be presenting its possibility as depending on a purpose as such [but not yet on a natural purpose]). Rather, we must think of each part as an organ that *produces* the other parts (so that each reciprocally produces the other). Something like this cannot be an instrument of art, but can be an instrument only of nature, which supplies all material for instruments (even for those of art). Only if a product meets that condition [as well], and only because of this, will it be both an *organized* and a *self-organizing* being, which therefore can be called a *natural purpose.*

In a watch, one part is the instrument that makes the others move, but one gear is not the efficient cause that produces another gear; [and hence] even though one part is there for the sake of another, the former part is not there as a result of the latter. That is also the reason why the cause that produced the watch and its form does not lie in nature (the nature of this material), but lies outside nature and in a being who can act according to the ideas of a whole that he can produce through his causality. It is also the reason why one gear in the watch does not produce another; still less does one watch produce other watches, [by] using (and organizing) other matter for this [production]. It is also the reason why, if parts are removed from the watch, it does not replace them on its own; nor, if parts were missing from it when it was first built, does it compensate for this [lack] by having the other parts help out, let alone repair itself on its own when out of order: yet all of this we can expect organized nature to do. Hence an organized being is not a mere machine. For a machine has only *motive* force. But an organized being has within it *formative* force, and a formative force that this being imparts to the kinds of matter that lack it (thereby organizing them). This force is therefore a formative force that propagates itself—a force that a mere ability [of one thing] to move [another][35] (i.e., mechanism) cannot explain.

In considering nature and the ability it displays in organized products,

[35] [Cf. the *Metaphysical Foundations of Natural Science*, Ak. IV, 530.]

we say far too little if we call this an *analogue* of *art,* for in that case we think of an artist (a rational being) apart from nature. Rather, nature organizes itself, and it does so within each species of its organized products; for though the pattern that nature follows is the same overall, that pattern also includes deviations useful for self-preservation as required by circumstances. We might be closer if we call this inscrutable property of nature an *analogue of life.* But in that case we must either endow matter, as mere matter, with a [kind of] property ([viz., the property of life, as] hylozoism [does][36]) that conflicts with its nature [*Wesen*]. Or else we must supplement matter with an alien principle (a soul) *conjoined* to it. But [that also will not work. For] if an organized product is to be a natural product, then we cannot make this soul the artificer that constructed it, since that would remove the product from (corporeal) nature. And yet the only alternative would be to say that this soul uses as its instrument organized matter;[37] but if we presuppose organized matter, we do not make it a whit more intelligible. Strictly speaking, therefore, the organization of nature has nothing analogous to any causality known to us.[38] Beauty in nature may rightly be called an analogue of art, since we attribute it to objects only in relation to our reflection on our *external* intuition of them, and hence only on account of the form of their surface. But *intrinsic natural perfection,* as possessed by those things that are possible only as *natural purposes* and that are hence called organized beings, is not conceivable or explicable on any analogy to any known physical ability, i.e., ability of nature, not even—since we too belong to nature in the broadest sense—on a precisely fitting analogy to human art.

[36] [See Ak. 392 and 394–95.]

[37] [Cf. Ak. 424.]

[38] On the other hand, the analogy of these direct natural purposes can serve to elucidate a certain [kind of] association [among people], though one found more often as an idea than in actuality: in speaking of the complete transformation of a large people into a state, which took place recently,[39] the word *organization* was frequently and very aptly applied to the establishment of legal authorities, etc., and even to the entire body politic. For each member in such a whole should indeed be not merely a means, but also a purpose; and while each member contributes to making the whole possible, the idea of that whole should in turn determine the member's position and function.

[39] [The allusion is probably to the formation of the United States of America.]

Hence the concept of a thing as in itself a natural purpose is not a constitutive concept either of understanding or of reason. But it can still be a regulative concept for reflective judgment, allowing us to use a remote analogy with our own causality in terms of purposes generally, to guide our investigation of organized objects and to meditate regarding their supreme basis—a meditation not for the sake of gaining knowledge either of nature or of that original basis of nature, but rather for the sake of [assisting] that same practical power in us [viz., our reason] by analogy with which we were considering the cause of the purposiveness in organized objects.

Hence organized beings are the only beings in nature that, even when considered by themselves and apart from any relation to other things, must still be thought of as possible only as purposes of nature. It is these beings, therefore, which first give objective reality to the concept of a *purpose* that is a purpose *of nature* rather than a practical one, and which hence give natural science the basis for a teleology, i.e., for judging its objects in terms of a special principle that otherwise we simply would not be justified in introducing into natural science (since we have no a priori insight whatever into the possibility of such a causality).

376

§ 66

On the Principle for Judging Intrinsic Purposiveness in Organized Beings

This principle, which is also the definition of organized beings, is: *An organized product of nature is one in which everything is a purpose and reciprocally also a means.*[40] In such a product nothing is gratuitous, purposeless, or to be attributed to a blind natural mechanism.

---

[40] [Cf. *On Using Teleological Principles in Philosophy* (1788), Ak. VIII, 179–81.]

Now in a way this principle must be derived from experience: experience must prompt us to [adopt] it, namely, the kind of experience in which we engage methodically and which we call observation. But because of the universality and necessity which that principle claims [*aussagen*] for such purposiveness, it cannot rest merely on empirical bases but must be based on some a priori principle, even if this principle turns out to be merely regulative and those purposes turn out to reside merely in the idea of the judging person and in no efficient cause. Hence we may call the above principle a *maxim* for judging the intrinsic purposiveness of organized beings.

It is a familiar fact that those who dissect plants and animals in order to investigate their structure and gain insight into the reasons why and to what end these plants and animals were given those very parts, their position and combination, and were given precisely that internal form assume this maxim as inescapably necessary—i.e., the maxim that nothing in such a creature is *gratuitous*. They appeal to it just as they appeal to the principle of universal natural science—viz., that *nothing* happens *by chance*. Indeed, they can no more give up that teleological principle than they can this universal physical principle. For just as abandoning this physical principle would leave them without any experience whatsoever, so would abandoning that teleological principle leave them without anything for guidance in observing the kind of natural things that have once been thought teleologically, under the concept of natural purposes.

377

For the concept of natural purposes leads reason into an order of things that is wholly different from that of a mere natural mechanism, which we no longer find adequate when we deal with such natural products. And hence the possibility of such a product is to be based on an idea. But an idea is an absolute unity of presentation, whereas matter is a plurality of things that cannot itself supply a determinate unity for its combination. Therefore if the unity of the idea is to serve as the very basis that determines a priori a natural law of the causality [responsible] for a product with such a form in its combination, then the purpose [the idea] of nature has to be extended to *everything* that is in this product of nature. For once we take such an effect *as a whole* beyond the blind mechanism of nature and refer it to a supersensible basis as determining it, then we must also judge this effect wholly in terms of that principle. There would be no basis for assuming that the form of such a thing still depends in part on blind mechanism, since we would then be mixing heterogeneous principles and hence be left without any safe rule by which to judge.

Now it is entirely possible that some parts in (say) an animal body (such as skin, bone, or hair) could be grasped as accumulations governed by merely mechanical laws. Still the cause that procures the appropriate matter, that modifies and forms it in that way, and that deposits it in the pertinent locations must always be judged teleologically. Hence everything in such a body must be regarded as organized; and everything, in a certain relation to the thing itself, is also an organ in turn.

§ 67

On the Principle by Which We Teleologically Judge Nature in General as a System of Purposes

We said above that *extrinsic* purposiveness of natural things does not give us adequate justification for also considering them to be purposes of nature so as to explain their existence, and for treating—in thought—their contingently purposive effects as the bases [responsible] for their existence in terms of the principle of final causes. For example, though *rivers* further communication among peoples who live inland, that does not yet entitle us to regard them as natural purposes; nor may we so regard *mountains* because they contain the sources of these rivers and the supply of snow required to sustain them during rainless periods; nor again the *slope* of the land, which carries that water away and allows the land to dry. For although these features of the earth's surface were very necessary in order that the vegetable and animal kingdoms could arise and be sustained, still there is nothing about these features that forces us to assume a causality in terms of purposes so as to account for their possibility. The same holds for plants that man employs for his needs or his

378

enjoyment; it also holds for animals, such as camels, cattle, horses, dogs, etc., for which man has such varied uses, sometimes as food and sometimes to do work for him, that for the most part he finds them quite indispensable. If things are such that we have no cause to regard any of them as itself a purpose, then the extrinsic relation between them can be judged purposive only hypothetically.

Judging a thing to be a natural purpose on account of its intrinsic form is something quite different from considering the existence of that thing to be a purpose of [i.e., pursued by] nature.[41] To make the latter assertion we would need more than the concept of a possible purpose; we would have to cognize the final purpose (*scopus*) of nature. To do that, we would have to refer nature to something supersensible, for the purpose of the existence of nature itself must be sought beyond nature; and yet referring nature to something supersensible far surpasses all our teleological cognition of nature. The internal form of a mere blade of grass suffices to prove to our human judging ability that the blade can have originated only under the rule of purposes. But we arrive at no categorical [but only at a hypothetical] purpose if we disregard the internal form and organization, and consider instead extrinsic purposive relations as to what use other natural beings make of the grass: how cattle need grass, and how people need cattle as a means for their existence. We cannot arrive at a categorical purpose in this way because, after all, we cannot see why people should have to exist (a question it might not be so easy to answer if we have in mind, say, the New Hollanders or the Fuegians); rather, each such purposive relation rests on a condition that we have to keep putting off: this condition (namely, the existence of a thing as a final purpose) is unconditioned and hence lies wholly outside a physicoteleological consideration of the world. But such a thing is also not a natural purpose, since it (or its entire species) is not to be regarded as a natural product.

Hence only as far as matter is organized does it necessarily carry with it the concept of it as a natural purpose, because the specific [purposive] form it has is at the same time a product of nature. But this concept of a natural purpose leads us necessarily to the idea of all of nature as a system in terms of the rule of purposes, and we must

379

---

[41] [But Kant sometimes uses 'purpose of nature' where he should say 'natural purpose,' and this inconsistency has been left intact in the translation.]

subordinate all mechanism of nature to this idea according to principles of reason (at least in order to test nature's appearance against this idea). The principle of reason applies to this idea only subjectively, namely, as this maxim: Everything in the world is good for something or other; nothing in it is gratuitous; and the example that nature offers us in its organic products justifies us, indeed calls upon us, to expect nothing from it and its laws except what is purposive in [relation to] the whole.

It goes without saying that this principle [for judging nature teleologically] holds only for reflective but not for determinative judgment, that it is regulative and not constitutive. It only serves us as a guide that allows us to consider natural things in terms of a new law-governed order by referring them to an already given basis [a purpose] as that which determines them. Thus we expand natural science [*Naturkunde*] in terms of a different principle, that of final causes, yet without detracting from the principle of mechanism in the causality of nature. That is all the principle does; it does not in any way allow us to decide whether anything we judge in terms of it is an *intentional* purpose of nature: whether grass is there for cattle or sheep, and these and all other natural things are there for man. It is helpful to consider from this point of view even things that we find disagreeable and contrapurposive in particular respects. For example, we might say that the vermin that plague people in their clothes, hair, or beds are there by a wise provision of nature, namely, as an incentive to keep clean, which even by itself is an important means for preserving our health. Or we might say that the mosquitoes and other stinging insects that make the wilderness areas of America so troublesome for the savages are so many prods to stir these primitive people to action, such as draining the marshes and clearing the dense forests that inhibit the flow of air, so that in this way, as well as by tilling the soil, they will also make the place where they live healthier. There are features in man's internal organization that seem to us to be contrary to nature; but even these, if dealt with in this manner, provide an entertaining and sometimes also instructive outlook into a teleological order of things to which we would not be led if we used no such principle as this but considered them merely in physical terms. Some say that when people or animals have a tapeworm, they were given it to compensate, as it were, for some deficiency in their vital organs. I

380   would ask, similarly, whether dreams[42] (there is no sleep without dreams, even though we rarely remember them) might not be a purposive arrangement made by nature. For when all the motive forces of the bodily kind relax, dreams serve to thoroughly agitate the vital organs by means of imagination and its great activity (which in dreams usually reaches the level of an affect). Imagination frequently does the same when we have gone to sleep with an overloaded stomach; we then need this agitation all the more, and the imagination's play is all the more lively. Therefore if no such force moved us inwardly and made us restless and tired, for which we then blame the dreams (though in fact these consequences of them may be conducive to our health), sleep would even in a healthy person probably be a complete extinction of life.

Moreover, once nature has been judged teleologically, and the natural purposes that we find in organized beings have entitled us to the idea of a vast system of purposes of nature, then even beauty in nature, i.e., nature's harmony with the free play of our cognitive powers as we apprehend and judge its appearance, can similarly be considered an objective purposiveness, namely, of the whole of nature [regarded] as a system that includes man as a member. We may regard nature as having held us in favor[43] when it distributed not only useful things but a wealth of beauty and charms as well; and we may love it for this, just as its immensity may lead us to contemplate it with respect and to feel that we ourselves are ennobled in this contemplation—just as if nature had erected and decorated its splendid stage quite expressly with that aim.

The only point I want to make in this section is this: that once we have discovered that nature is able to make products that can be thought of only in terms of the concept of final causes, we are then

---

[42] [For this account of dreams, cf. the *Anthropology*, § 37, Ak. VII, 189–90.]

[43] We said in the aesthetic part[44] that we *regard beautiful nature with favor* when we like its form quite freely (without interest). For we are then making a mere judgment of taste, in which we do not at all take into account for what purpose these natural beauties exist: whether they have the purpose of arousing a pleasure in us, or whether they do not at all refer to us as purposes. But in a teleological judgment we pay attention also to this reference; and hence we may *regard as a favor of nature* [the fact] that it decided to further our culture by displaying so many beautiful shapes.

[44] [See Ak. 350, and cf. Ak. 210.]

entitled to go further; we may thereupon judge products as belonging to a system of purposes even if they (or the relation between them, though [perhaps] purposive) do not require us, [so as to account] for their possibility, to look for a different principle beyond the mechanism of blind efficient causes. For the idea of nature as a system of nature already leads us, as concerns its basis, beyond the world of sense, so that the unity of the supersensible principle must be considered valid not merely for certain species of natural beings, but just as much for the whole of nature as a system.

381

NATURAL PURPOSES

§ 68
On the Principle of Teleology as a Principle Inherent in Natural Science

Principles of a science are either inherent in it and are called indigenous (*principia domestica*); or they are based on concepts that can have their place only outside the science, in which case they are *foreign* principles (*principia peregrina*). Sciences containing foreign principles base their doctrines on auxiliary propositions (*lemmata*), i.e., they borrow some concept from another science and use it as a basis for their own arrangement.

Every science is a system in its own right. It is not enough that in building [something] in the science we follow principles and so proceed technically; we must also set to work with the science architectonically,[45] treating it as a whole and independent building, not as an annex or part of another building, though we may later construct, starting from either building, a passage connecting the one to the other.

Thus if we introduce the concept of God into the context of

---

[45] [On this distinction, cf. the *Critique of Pure Reason,* A 832–51 = B 860–79.]

natural science in order to make the purposiveness in nature explicable, and then in turn use this purposiveness to prove that there is a God, then neither natural science nor theology is intrinsically firm; a vicious circle makes both uncertain, because they have allowed their boundaries to overlap.

But the very expression, purpose of nature, is sufficient to guard against this confusion [between those two sciences]. It keeps us from mingling natural science, and the occasion it gives us to judge its objects *teleologically,* with our contemplation of God and hence with a *theological* derivation [of these objects]. We must not consider it unimportant whether the expression, purpose of nature, is interchanged with that of a divine purpose in the arrangement of nature, let alone whether the latter is passed off as more appropriate and more fitting for a pious soul, on the ground that surely in the end we cannot get around deriving those purposive forms in nature from a wise author of the world. Rather, we must carefully and modestly restrict ourselves to the expression that says no more than we know—viz., purpose of nature. For even before we inquire into the cause of nature itself, we find that nature contains such products and engages in their production. They are produced there in accordance with known empirical laws; it is in terms of these laws that natural science must judge its objects. And hence the causality in terms of the rule of purposes [that is responsible] for those objects must also be sought within natural science. Hence natural science must not leap over its boundary in order to absorb, as an indigenous principle, something to whose concept no experience whatever can be adequate and which we are not entitled to dare approach until we have completed natural science.

Natural characteristics that can be demonstrated a priori, and whose possibility we can therefore see from universal principles without any aid from experience, are absolutely necessary. Hence, even if such characteristics carry with them technical purposiveness, they still cannot at all be included in the teleology of nature, which is a method that belongs to physics and that we use to solve problems of physics. Arithmetic analogies or geometric ones, or also universal mechanical laws, no matter how strange and admirable may seem to us [the ability] to unify in one principle [their] different and seemingly quite independent rules, still cannot on that

382

account claim that they can serve as bases for teleological explanations in physics. Even if they too deserve to be considered in the
universal theory of the purposiveness of natural things generally,
still that theory would belong elsewhere, namely, to metaphysics,
and would not constitute an inherent principle of natural science.
In the case of the empirical laws of natural purposes in organized
beings, on the other hand, it is presumably not only permissible,
but also unavoidable, to use the teleological *way of judging* as a
principle of natural science when dealing with a special class of its
objects.

Now in order to keep physics strictly within its bounds, we there
abstract entirely from the question as to whether natural purposes are
purposes *intentionally* or *unintentionally,* since otherwise we would
be meddling in extraneous affairs (namely, those of metaphysics). We
settle for regarding natural purposes as objects that are *explicable*
solely in terms of natural laws that must be conceived of by using the
idea of purposes as principle, and that are even internally *cognizable*
only in this way as regards their intrinsic form. Therefore we must
avoid any suspicion, in physics, that we might presume to mix something in with our bases of cognition that does not belong to physics at
all—viz., a supernatural cause. That is why, when in teleology we
speak of nature as if the purposiveness in it were intentional, we do so
in such a way that we attribute this intention to nature, i.e., to matter.
This serves to indicate that this term refers here only to a principle of
reflective, rather than of determinative, judgment. (It indicates this
inasmuch as no one would attribute to lifeless material an intention in
the proper sense of the term, and so no misunderstanding can arise.)
It indicates, therefore, that we are not trying to introduce [into
physics] a special causal basis, but are trying to introduce only another
method for our use of reason in investigation—a method different
from the one in terms of mechanical laws—in order to compensate
for the inadequacy we find in the latter method when we search even
empirically for all the particular laws of nature. Thus, when we
apply teleology to physics, we do quite rightly speak of nature's
wisdom, parsimony, foresight, or beneficence. But in speaking this
way we do not turn nature into an intelligent [*verständig*] being (since
that would be absurd), nor are we so bold as to posit a different,
intelligent being above nature as its architect, since that would be

presumptuous.[46] Rather, we use these terms only to designate a kind of causality of nature by analogy with the causality we have in the technical use of reason, since that helps us to keep in view the rule we must follow in investigating certain products of nature.

Why, then, does teleology usually not constitute a distinct part of theoretical natural science, but is employed by theology as a propaedeutic or transition? This is done so that, when we study nature in terms of its mechanism, we keep to what we can observe or experiment on in such a way that we could produce it as nature does, at least in terms of similar laws; for we have complete insight only into what we can ourselves make and accomplish according to concepts. But organization, as an intrinsic purpose of nature, infinitely surpasses all our ability to exhibit anything similar through art. As for extrinsic natural arrangements that we consider purposive (such as wind, rain, and so on), physics does indeed examine the mechanism in them; but it is quite unable to exhibit their reference to purposes insofar as this reference is to be a condition that attaches to the cause necessarily, since that necessity in the [causal] connection concerns nothing but the connection of our concepts, and does not concern the character of things.

[46] The German word *vermessen* [presumptuous, but literally *mismeasured*] is a good word, full of meaning. A judgment in which we forget to estimate the extent of our powers (of understanding) may at times sound very humble, and yet it makes vast claims and is very presumptuous. Of that sort are most of those judgments in which we purport to exalt divine wisdom, by attributing the works of creation and preservation to divine intentions that are actually meant to give credit to the wisdom of the very person who does this subtle reasoning.

DIVISION II

DIALECTIC OF TELEOLOGICAL JUDGMENT

§ 69

What an Antinomy of Judgment Is

When judgment *determines,* it has no principles of its own that form the basis for *concepts of objects.* It is not autonomous; for it only *subsumes* under laws or concepts that are given it as principles. By the same token, it is exposed to no danger of having an antinomy of its own and is exposed to no conflict in its principles. Thus [we found that] transcendental judgment, which contains the conditions under which we can subsume under categories, is not itself *nomothetic;* it only specifies the conditions of sensible intuition under which a given concept, a law of the understanding, can be given reality (i.e., application),[1] and it could never come to be at variance with itself about that (at least not in terms of its principles).

When judgment *reflects,* on the other hand, it has to subsume under a law that is not yet given, and hence must subsume under a law that is in fact only a principle of reflection on [certain] objects for which we have no objective law at all, no concept of the object adequate as a principle for the cases that occur. But since it is not

---

[1] [Cf. the *Critique of Pure Reason,* A 131–36 = B 170–75.]

265

permissible to use the cognitive powers without principles, reflective judgment will in those cases have to serve itself as a principle. Since this principle is not objective and cannot provide an objectively adequate basis for cognizing the object, it has to serve as a merely subjective principle governing the purposive use of our cognitive powers—i.e., our reflection on a [certain] kind of objects. So reflective judgment has maxims for cases involving such objects. These maxims are necessary in order that we may cognize natural laws in experience. For these maxims allow us to arrive at concepts, even if these were to be concepts of reason; and reflective judgment needs such concepts whenever it seeks so much as to get to know nature in terms of its empirical laws. Now between these necessary maxims of reflective judgment a conflict may arise, and hence an antinomy; and this antinomy forms the basis for a dialectic. If two conflicting maxims both have their basis in the nature of our cognitive powers, then this dialectic may be called a natural one, an unavoidable illusion that we must expose and resolve in the critique so that it will not deceive us.

§ 70

Presentation of That Antinomy

Insofar as reason deals with nature as the sum total of objects of outer senses, it can use laws as a basis: in part understanding itself prescribes these laws a priori to nature, in part it can expand them indefinitely by means of the empirical attributes that occur in experience. To apply the first kind of laws, the *universal* laws of material nature in general, judgment does not need a special principle of reflection; for here it is determinative, since the understanding has given it an objective principle. But [judgment does need a special principle of reflection] for the particular laws, the laws that only experience can reveal to us, and so in their case judgment must serve itself as a principle. For the particular laws of nature can be so very diverse and heterogeneous that, without such a principle to guide it, judgment could not even search for and spot a law in the appearances of nature, and so could not even hope to reach a coherent empirical cognition based on a thorough lawfulness of nature, i.e., on the unity of nature in terms of empirical laws. Now when [we find] such a contingent unity of particular laws, it may happen that judgment presupposes two maxims as it reflects [on this unity]: one of these the understanding gives it a priori; the other it is prompted to [adopt] by special experiences, experiences that bring reason into play so that we may judge corporeal nature and its laws in terms of a special principle. When judgment reflects on the basis of these two maxims, it may happen that they do not seem quite compatible, so that a dialectic arises that leaves judgment perplexed as to what principle [it should follow] in its reflection.

387

The first maxim of judgment is this *thesis:* All production of material things and their forms must be judged to be possible in terms of merely mechanical laws.

The second maxim is this *antithesis:* Some products of material nature cannot be judged to be possible in terms of merely mechanical laws. (Judging them requires a quite different causal law—viz., that of final causes.)

These maxims are regulative principles for our investigation [of nature]. If we converted them into constitutive principles concerning the possibility of the objects themselves, they would read:

Thesis: All production of material things is possible in terms of merely mechanical laws.

Antithesis: Some production of material things is not possible in terms of merely mechanical laws.

In this latter form, as objective principles for determinative judgment, the two propositions would contradict each other, so that one of them would have to be false; and so an antinomy would result. But this antinomy would not be one of judgment, but instead would be a conflict within the legislation of reason. Reason, however, cannot prove either of these two principles, because we cannot have a determinative a priori principle for the possibility of things in terms of merely empirical laws of nature.

But if we consider instead the two maxims of a power of judgment that reflects [i.e., the first thesis and antithesis above], the first of those two maxims does in fact not contradict [the second] at all. For if I say that I must *judge* all events in material nature, and hence also all the forms that are its products, in terms of merely mechanical laws as to [how] they are possible, then I am not saying that they *are possible* in terms of mechanical laws *alone* (i.e., even if no other kind of causality comes in). Rather, I am only pointing out that I *ought* always to *reflect* on these events and forms *in terms of the principle* of the mere mechanism of nature, and hence ought to investigate this principle as far as I can, because unless we presuppose it in our investigation [of nature] we can have no cognition of nature at all in the proper sense of the term. But none of this goes against the second maxim—that on certain occasions, in dealing with certain natural forms (and, on their prompting, even with all of nature), we should

388

probe these and reflect on them in terms of a principle that differs entirely from an explanation in terms of the mechanism of nature: the principle of final causes. For doing so does not void reflection in terms of the first maxim; rather, we are told to follow it as far as we can.[2] Nor does the second maxim say that those forms would not be possible in terms of the mechanism of nature.[3] It asserts only that *human reason,* if it obeys the first maxim and acts accordingly, will never be able to discover the slightest basis for what is specific in a natural purpose, though it may acquire other cognitions of natural laws. And this assertion leaves it undecided whether in the inner basis of nature itself, which we do not know, the physical-mechanical connection and the connection in terms of purposes may not, in the same things, be linked in one principle. It is only that our reason is incapable of reconciling them in such a principle; therefore, when judgment *reflects* (on a subjective basis), rather than determines (in which case it follows an objective principle of the possibility of things themselves), then in the case of certain forms in nature it has to think of their possibility as based on a principle that differs from that of natural mechanism.

---

[2] ["More than is commonly done": *The Only Possible Basis of Proof* (1763), Ak. II, 115 and 126. Cf. also the *Critique of Pure Reason,* A 691 = B 719, *On Using Teleological Principles in Philosophy* (1788), Ak. VIII, 159–60, and the *Universal Natural History and Theory of the Heavens* (1755), Ak. I, 331–47. See also below, § 81, Ak. 421–22 incl. br. n. 8.]

[3] [Compare and contrast *The Only Possible Basis of Proof,* Ak. II, 114.]

§ 71

Preliminary to the Solution
of the Above Antinomy

We are quite unable to prove that organized natural products cannot be produced through the mere mechanism of nature. For we have no insight into the first inner basis (responsible) for the endless diversity of the particular natural laws, because they are contingent for us since we cognize them only empirically; and so we cannot possibly reach the inner and completely sufficient principle of the possibility of nature (this principle lies in the supersensible). Hence our reason, whose concept of causality is greatly restricted if reason has to specify it a priori, cannot possibly tell us whether nature's productive ability, which is quite adequate for whatever seems to require merely that nature be like a machine, is not just as adequate for [things] that we judge to be formed or combined in terms of the idea of purposes, [or] whether things [considered] to be actual natural purposes (which is what we must necessarily judge them to be) are in fact based on a wholly different kind of original causality, namely, an architectonic understanding, which cannot at all lie in material nature nor in its intelligible substrate. On the other hand, it is just as indubitably certain that the mere mechanism of nature cannot provide our cognitive power with a basis on which we could explain the production of organized beings. Hence the following principle is entirely correct *for reflective judgment,* however rash and unprovable it would be *for determinative judgment:* that [to account] for the very manifest connection of things in terms of final causes we must think a causality distinct from mechanism—viz., the causality of an (intelligent) world cause that acts according to purposes. Applied to reflection, this principle is a mere maxim of judgment; and the concept of that causality is a mere idea. We make no claim that this idea has reality, but only use it as a guide for reflection, which meanwhile continues to remain open to [the discovery of] any basis for a mechanical explanation and never strays from the world of sense. On the other hand, if the principle were determinative, it would be an objective principle prescribed by reason; and judgment, to determine [anything], would

389

269

have to subject itself to it. But if it does so, then it strays beyond the world of sense and into the transcendent, and perhaps will be misled.

Hence all semblance of an antinomy between the maxims of strictly physical (mechanical) and teleological (technical) explanation rests on our confusing a principle of reflective judgment with one of determinative judgment, and on our confusing the *autonomy* of reflective judgment (which holds merely subjectively for our use of reason regarding the particular empirical laws) with the *heteronomy* of determinative judgment, which must conform to the laws (universal or particular) that are given by understanding.[4]

§ 72

On the Various
Systems Concerning
the Purposiveness of Nature

No one has ever doubted the correctness of the principle [which says] that we must judge certain things in nature (organized beings) and their possibility in terms of the concept of final causes, even if we demand [to use] this principle only as a guide for observing these things so as to become acquainted with their character, without presuming to investigate their first origin. Therefore, the only possible question is whether this principle is merely subjectively valid, merely a maxim of our judgment, or whether it is an objective principle of nature that says that nature has not only its mechanism (governed by mere laws of motion), but also another kind of causality, that of final causes, with the mechanical causes (the motive forces) [functioning] as mere intermediate causes that are subject to the final causes.

Now we could leave this speculative question or problem quite

390

---

[4] [This paragraph seems to suggest that the solution of the antinomy of teleological judgment is already complete. But in fact this paragraph is only *preliminary* to that solution, as the heading of this section indicates. On this problem, and on the actual solution of the antinomy, see the Translator's Introduction, *lxxxviii–xciii* incl. n. 90.]

undecided and unsolved. For if we settle for speculating[5] within the bounds of mere cognition of nature, the above maxims [mechanistic and teleological] are sufficient for us to study nature to the extent of our human powers, and to probe its most hidden secrets. So [if in fact we try to do more than this,] it must be that reason has a certain suspicion, or that nature gives us a hint, as it were, that if we use the concept of final causes we could perhaps reach beyond nature and connect nature itself to the highest point in the series of causes. Why not stop our investigation of nature (even though we have not yet advanced far in it), or at least suspend it for a while, and try first to find out where that stranger in natural science, the concept of natural purposes, may lead us?

At this point, however, the undisputed maxim above should be turned into a problem, a problem that opens up a wide field for controversy: Does the connection in terms of purposes in nature *prove* that nature has a special kind of causality? Or is it, rather, that this connection, considered in itself and according to objective principles, is identical with the mechanism of nature, or rests on one and the same basis? Perhaps, on the latter alternative, it is just that in many natural products this basis is often too deeply hidden for our investigation, and so we try a subjective principle instead, the principle of art, i.e., of causality in terms of ideas, attributing this causality to nature by analogy. This expedient does in fact succeed in many cases, though in some it seems to fail; but in any case it does not entitle us to introduce a kind of causation into natural science that is distinct from the causality in terms of merely mechanical laws of nature. Given that we find something purposelike in nature's products, let us call nature's procedure (causality) a technic, and let us then divide this technic into an *intentional* and an *unintentional* one (*technica intentionalis* and *technica naturalis*). By an intentional technic I mean that nature's ability to produce [things] in terms of final causes must be considered a special kind of causality; by an unintentional technic I mean that this ability is basically quite identical with the mechanism of nature, and that we have falsely interpreted the contingent agreement of that ability with our concepts and rules of art, namely, as a special kind of natural production, whereas in fact

391

[5] [On speculating and theorizing, see Ak. 454 br. n. 51.]

it is merely [the result of] a subjective condition under which we judge that ability.

Now as we talk about the systems that try to explain nature as concerns final causes, we must note carefully that the dispute among all of them is dogmatic—i.e., the dispute is about objective principles concerning the possibility of things, whether through causes that act intentionally or only [*lauter*] those that act unintentionally, and by no means is the dispute about the subjective maxim as to what mere judgment we should make concerning the cause of such purposive products. On the latter alternative the principles, though *disparate,* might well still be reconcilable; on the former, the principles are *opposed as contradictories,* so that they are incompatible and annul each other.

The systems that deal with the technic of nature, i.e., with nature's power to produce [things] in terms of the rule of purposes, are of two kinds: one interprets natural purposes *idealistically,* the other *realistically.* The idealistic interpretation maintains that all purposiveness of nature is *unintentional;* the realistic interpretation maintains that some of this purposiveness (the purposiveness in organized beings) is *intentional,* from which we could then infer, as a hypothesis, the consequence that the technic of nature is intentional, i.e., a purpose, even as concerns all other products of nature in their relation to the whole of nature.

(1) The *idealistic* interpretation of purposiveness (I always mean objective purposiveness here) then interprets the natural determination [that gives rise] to the purposive form of its products either as *casualistic* or as *fatalistic.* The casualistic principle refers matter to the physical basis [responsible] for its form—the laws of motion; the fatalistic principle refers it to the *hyperphysical* basis of matter and of all of nature. The system that espouses the *casualistic* interpretation— it is attributed to Epicurus or Democritus—is so manifestly absurd, if taken literally, that we must not let it detain us. But it is not so easy to refute the system that espouses the fatalistic interpretation. (Its author is said to be Spinoza, even though it is to all appearances much older than that.) This system appeals to something supersensible, which therefore our insight cannot reach. What makes the refutation of this system so difficult is the fact that its concept of the original being is quite unintelligible. But this much is clear: in this system the connection in terms of purposes in the world must be considered uninten-

tional (for though the system derives the connection from an original being, it derives it not from that being's understanding, and hence not from its intention, but from the necessity of its nature and from the unity in the world that stems from that nature). Hence the fatalistic interpretation of purposiveness is also idealistic.

(2) The *realistic* interpretation of the purposiveness of nature is also either physical or hyperphysical. The *physical* version regards the purposes in nature as based on the analogue of a [mental] power that acts according to intentions—the *life of matter* (where that life is either in the matter, or due to an inner animating principle, viz., a world soul); this view is called *hylozoism*. The *hyperphysical* version derives the purposes in nature from the original basis of the universe, namely, an intelligent being (endowed with life originally) that produces according to intentions; this view is theism.[6]

§ 73

None of the Above Systems Accomplishes What It Alleges to Accomplish

What do all those systems try to do? They try to explain our teleological judgments about nature, and they go about this in two different ways: some of them deny that these judgments are true and hence declare them to constitute an idealistic interpretation of nature (presented as art); the others acknowledge them as true and promise

---

[6] This shows that, in most of the speculative matters of pure reason, and as far as dogmatic assertions are concerned, the schools of philosophy have usually tried all the solutions that are possible for a certain problem. Thus, on [the problem of] the purposiveness of nature, some have tried *lifeless matter* or a *lifeless God*, others a *living matter* or else a *living God*. For us there is no alternative except, if necessary, to drop all these *objective assertions*, and instead to weigh our judgment *critically* merely in its relation to our cognitive powers, so as to provide the principle of that purposiveness with a validity that, if not dogmatic, is yet the validity of a maxim and is sufficient for the safe use of reason.

to establish [how] a nature is possible in terms of the idea of final causes.

(1) The systems that defend the idealistic interpretation of final causes in nature are of two types. Some of them, while granting the principle of these final causes a causality in terms of laws of motion (where this causality is responsible for the purposive existence of natural things), deny that it follows *intentions:* they deny that intentions determine it to produce [things] purposively, i.e., that a purpose is the cause. This is how Epicurus explains [the purposiveness in nature]. He completely denies the distinction of a technic of nature from mere mechanism. Instead he adopts blind chance to explain not only [nature's] technic, i.e., why [nature's] products harmonize with our concepts of a purpose, but even nature's mechanism, i.e., how the causes of this production are determined to this [production] according to laws of motion. Hence nothing has been explained, not even the illusion in our ideological judgments, so that the alleged idealism in them has by no means been established.

Spinoza, on the other hand, wants to relieve us of [any need to] inquire into the basis that makes purposes of nature possible, and wants to deprive the idea of this basis of all reality. He does this by refusing to count them as products at all. Instead he regards them as accidents that inhere in an original being; and he attributes to this being, the substrate of those natural things, not causality regarding these things, but merely subsistence. Thus Spinoza does indeed provide natural forms with something that all purposiveness requires— viz., unity in their basis. (For the original being is unconditionally necessary, and so are all natural things, which inhere in it as accidents.) But the *unity of a purpose,* [which is also required for such purposiveness,) cannot be thought unless the natural forms are also contingent; and yet Spinoza has taken this contingency away from them and has thus also deprived these forms of everything *intentional,* and has deprived the original basis of natural things of all understanding.

[Thus] Spinozism does not accomplish what it tries to accomplish. It tries to offer a basis that will explain why things of nature are connected in terms of purposes (which it does not deny), but all it points to is the unity of the subject in which they all inhere. But even if Spinozism be granted [the claim] that the beings of the world exist in this way, this does not yet make the [resulting] ontological unity the *unity of a purpose,* and certainly does not allow us to grasp the latter

393

unity. For the unity of a purpose is a very special kind of unity. It does not follow at all from a connection of things (beings of the world) in one subject (the original being), but always carries with it reference to a *cause* that has understanding. Rather, even if we were to unite all these things in a simple subject, the unity will amount to reference to a purpose only if we also think of these things, first, as inner *effects* of the substance as a *cause,* and, second, as having been caused by this substance *through its understanding.* Unless these formal conditions are met, all unity is mere natural necessity; and if we nevertheless attribute it to things that we present as external to one another, then it is blind necessity. Of course we could use the expression, purposiveness of nature, for what the schoolmen call the transcendental perfection of things (relative to their own essence), which means [merely] that all things have in them everything that is required for being a thing of that kind rather than being a thing of some other kind. But [to make this move] is to play a childish game with words in the place of concepts. For on this view we must think of all things as purposes, so that being a thing and being a purpose are one and the same, and so basically there is nothing that especially deserves to be presented as a purpose.

394

So when Spinoza reduced our concepts of purposive [things] in nature to the consciousness that [these things and] we ourselves are within an all-encompassing (though at the same time simple) being, and sought that purposive form merely in the unity of that being, he clearly must have intended to interpret the purposiveness of that form merely idealistically rather than realistically. But even that he was unable to do, because the mere presentation of the unity of the substrate cannot give rise to the idea of even so much as an unintentional purposiveness.

(2) As for the *realistic* interpretation of natural purposes, there are those who not only assert this realism but also think they are explaining it. They believe they have insight into at least the possibility of a special kind of causality, the kind [found] in causes that act intentionally; for if they did not believe they had this insight, then they could not even attempt to explain those natural purposes. For even if we are to make a hypothesis that [we acknowledge to] be very daring, we must have *certainty* that the basis we have assumed for it is at least *possible,* [so that we] can be sure that the concept of that basis has objective reality.

And yet we cannot even think of living[7] matter [as postulated by one form of hylozoism[8]] as possible. (The [very] concept of it involves a contradiction, since the essential character of matter is lifelessness, [in Latin] *inertia.*) Is it possible that [as the other form of hylozoism says] there is a matter endowed with life [by something else], and that nature as a whole is [thus] an animal? This possibility must be used only as far as experience manifests such matter in the organization [of beings] within [*im Kleinen*] nature, and [even then] only with great caution (if we are trying to support a hypothesis about purposiveness in nature as a whole [*im Großen*]). But we certainly have no a priori insight into whether such matter is possible. But this means that our explanation can only move in a circle: we try to derive the natural purposiveness in organized beings from the life of matter, while yet we are familiar with this life only in organized beings and hence cannot form a concept of the possibility of this purposiveness unless we have experienced such beings. Hence hylozoism does not accomplish what it promises.[9]

395

That leaves *theism.* It too cannot dogmatically provide a basis that accounts for the possibility of natural purposes, and so provide a key to teleology. But it does have one advantage over all [other] bases [that have been offered] to explain these purposes—viz., theism is best able to rescue the purposiveness of nature from idealism; for it attributes an understanding to the original being and [so] introduces an intentional causality [to account] for the production of natural purposes.

For [theism to succeed in its explanation,] we would first of all have to prove, adequately for determinative judgment, that the unity of a purpose, which we find in matter, could not possibly result from the mere mechanism of nature. Only such a proof would entitle us to postulate determinately that the basis of this unity lies beyond nature.

---

[7] [In the *Critique of Practical Reason* (Ak. V, 9 n.), *life* is defined (narrowly) as "the ability of a being to act according to laws of the power of desire." In the *Metaphysics of Morals* (Ak. VI, 211), Kant defines it similarly as "the ability of a being to act in conformity with its presentations." Cf. also above, § 72, Ak. 392.]

[8] ["*Hylozoism* endows everything with life, whereas *materialism*, strictly considered, kills everything": *Dreams of a Spirit-Seer,* Ak. II, 330.]

[9] [Hylozoism "would be the death of all natural philosophy": *Metaphysical Foundations of Natural Science,* Ak. IV, 544.]

But in fact all we can make out is that the character and limits of our cognitive powers (which give us no insight into the first, inner basis of even this mechanism) force us to give up any attempt to find in matter a principle [that implies] determinate references [of this matter] to a purpose, so that we are left with no other way of judging nature's production of things as natural purposes than in terms of a supreme understanding as cause of the world. That basis, however, [holds] only for reflective and not for determinative judgment, and is absolutely incapable of justifying any objective assertion.

§ 74

The Reason Why It Is Impossible to Treat the Concept of a Technic of Nature Dogmatically Is That a Natural Purpose Is Inexplicable

We treat a concept (even an empirically conditioned one) dogmatically if we consider it as contained under, and determine it in accordance with, another concept of the object such that this other concept amounts to a principle of reason. We treat a concept merely critically if we consider it only in relation to our cognitive power, and hence in relation to the subjective conditions under which we think it, without venturing to decide anything about its object. Hence dogmatic treatment of a concept has the force of law for determinative judgment, critical treatment merely for reflective judgment.

Now the concept of a thing as a natural purpose is one that subsumes nature under a causality that is conceivable only [as exercised] by reason; this subsumption then allows us to use that [causal] principle in order to judge what experience gives us of that object. But in order to use the concept of a thing as a natural purpose

396

dogmatically, for determinative judgment, we would first have to be sure that it has objective reality, since otherwise we could not subsume any natural thing under it. Now it is true that the concept of a thing as a natural purpose is empirically conditioned, i.e., a concept that is possible only under certain conditions given in experience.[10] Yet it is a concept that cannot be abstracted from experience but is possible only in terms of a rational principle [that we use] in judging the object. Since this is the sort of principle it is, we have no way of seeing and establishing dogmatically that it has objective reality (i.e., that an object conforming to it is possible). [Therefore,] we do not know whether the concept is an objectively empty one that [we use] merely [for] reasoning (*conceptus ratiocinans*), or is a rational concept, a concept that is a basis for cognition and is confirmed by reason (*conceptus ratiocinatus*).[11] Hence we cannot treat this concept dogmatically, for determinative judgment—i.e., not only are we unable to tell whether or not things of nature considered as natural purposes require for their production a causality of a very special kind (a causality in terms of intentions), but we cannot even ask the question. For reason is quite unable to prove the concept of a natural purpose, i.e., that it has objective reality. (In other words, the concept is not constitutive for determinative judgment, but merely regulative for reflective judgment.)

That [the objective reality of] the concept of a thing as a natural purpose cannot be proved by reason is clear from this: as concept of a *natural product* it contains natural necessity; and yet, as concept of that same thing as a purpose, it contains at the same time a contingency (relative to mere laws of nature) of the form of the object. Hence, if this is not to be contradictory, then the concept must contain not only a natural basis that makes the thing possible, but also a basis that makes possible nature itself and its reference to something that is not empirically cognizable nature (but is supersensible) and hence is not cognizable for us at all, [a reference] by which we can judge the [object of the] concept in terms of a causality other than that of natural mechanism when we try to decide on its possibility. Hence the concept of a thing as a natural purpose is transcendent for *determinative judgment* if we consider the object through reason

[10] [And to that extent it might seem that it must have objective reality.]

[11] [Cf. Ak. 337 br. n. 2.]

(even though for reflective judgment it may be immanent as concerns objects of experience), and hence we cannot provide it with the objective reality [needed] for determinative judgments. This explains why all the systems that might be devised to treat dogmatically the concept of natural purposes and the concept of nature as a whole having coherence in terms of final causes cannot decide anything whatsoever by way of either objective affirmation or objective negation. For if we subsume things under a concept that is merely problematic, then we do not know whether we are judging about something or nothing, and hence the synthetic predicates of the concept (here, e.g., whether it is an intentional or an unintentional purpose of nature that, in thought, we add to the production of the things) can yield only problematic judgments, whether affirmative or negative, about the object. The concept of a causality through purposes ([i.e., the concept] of art) does indeed have objective reality, as does also the concept of a causality in terms of the mechanism of nature. But the concept of a natural causality in terms of the rule of purposes—and even more so the concept of a being which is the original basis of nature, viz., a being such as cannot at all be given us in experience—while thinkable without contradiction, is nevertheless inadequate for [making] dogmatic determinations. For we cannot derive such a concept from experience, nor is it required to make experience possible; and hence we have nothing that could assure us that the concept has objective reality. But suppose even that we could get this assurance: Once I have determinately stated that certain things are products of divine art, how can I still include them among products of nature, when it was precisely because nature cannot produce such things in terms of its [own] laws that I had to appeal to a cause distinct from it?

397

§ 75

The Concept of an Objective Purposiveness of Nature Is a Critical Principle of Reason for Our Reflective Judgment

There is clearly a big difference between saying that certain things of nature, or even all of nature, could be produced only by a cause that follows intentions in determining itself to action, and saying that *the peculiar character of my cognitive powers* is such that the only way I can judge [how] those things are possible and produced is by conceiving, [to account] for this production, a cause that acts according to intentions, and hence a being that produces (things) in a way analogous to the causality of an understanding. If I say the first, I am trying to decide something about the object, and am obliged to establish that a concept I have assumed has objective reality. If I say the second, reason determines only [how I must] use my cognitive powers commensurately with their peculiarity and with the essential conditions [imposed by] both their range and their limits. Hence the first is an *objective* principle for determinative judgment, the second a subjective principle for merely reflective judgment and hence a maxim imposed on it by reason.

For if we want to investigate the organized products of nature by continued observation, we find it completely unavoidable to apply [*unterlegen*] to nature the concept of an intention, so that even for our empirical use of reason this concept is an absolutely necessary maxim. Now, obviously, once we have adopted such a guide for studying nature and found that it works, we must at least try this maxim of judgment on the whole of nature too, since this maxim may well allow us to discover many further laws of nature that would otherwise remain hidden to us since our insights into the inner [nature] of its mechanism is so limited. But while that maxim of judgment is useful when applied to the whole of nature, it is not indispensable there, since the whole of nature is not given us as organized (in the strictest sense of *organized* as given above[12]). But when we deal with those products of nature that we can judge only as having intentionally been formed in just this way rather than some other, then we need that maxim of reflective judgment essentially, if we are to acquire so much as an empirical cognition of the intrinsic character of these products. For we cannot even think them as organized things without also thinking that they were produced intentionally.

Now if we present the existence or form of a thing as possible [only] under the condition [that there is] a purpose, then the concept of the thing is inseparably connected with the concept that the thing is contingent (in terms of natural laws). That is also why those natural things that we find possible only as purposes constitute the foremost proof that the world as a whole is contingent, and are the sole basis for a proof that holds both for common understanding and for the philosopher: that this whole depends on and has its origin in a being that exists apart from the world and (given how purposive these forms are) is moreover intelligent. Hence these things are the sole basis for proving that teleology cannot find final [*Vollendung*] answers to its inquiries except in a theology.[13]

But what does even the most complete teleology of all prove in the end? Does it prove, say, that such an intelligent being[14] exists? No; all it proves is that, given the character of our cognitive powers, i.e., in connecting experience with the supreme principles of reason, we are absolutely unable to form a concept of [how] such a world is possible except by thinking of it as brought about by a supreme cause that *acts intentionally.* Hence we cannot objectively establish the proposition: There is an intelligent original being; we can do so only subjectively, for the use of our judgment as it reflects on the purposes in nature, which are unthinkable on any principle other than that of an intentional causality of a supreme cause.

If we tried, from teleological bases, to establish dogmatically the proposition that such an intelligent being exists, we would get entangled in difficulties from which we could not extricate ourselves. For

399

---

[12] [See §§ 65–66, Ak. 372–77.]

[13] [Cf.§ 85, Ak. 436–42.]

[14] [As to why expressions such as this are not capitalized in this translation, see above, Ak. 273 br. n.43.]

such inferences would have to presuppose the proposition that the organized beings in the world are impossible except through a cause that acts intentionally. This means that we would have to be willing to assert that, [merely] because we need the idea of purposes in order to study these things in their causal connection and to cognize the lawfulness in that connection, we are also justified in presupposing that every thinking and cognizing being is subject to the same need as a necessary condition, and hence that this condition attaches to the object rather than merely to our[selves, as] subject[s]. But there is no way that such an assertion can be upheld. For purposes in nature are not given to us by the object: we do not actually *observe* purposes in nature as intentional ones, but merely add this concept [to nature's products] in our *thought,* as a guide for judgment in reflecting on these products. [And] an a priori justification for accepting such a concept, as having objective reality, is even impossible for us. Hence there is absolutely no proposition left us except one that rests on subjective conditions only, the conditions under which judgment reflects commensurately with our cognitive powers. This proposition, if expressed as holding objectively and dogmatically, would read: There is a God. But in fact the proposition entitles us human beings only to this restricted formula: The purposiveness that we must presuppose even for cognizing the inner possibility of many natural things is quite unthinkable to us and is beyond our grasp unless we think of it, and of the world as such, as a product of an intelligent cause (a God).

400

Now if this proposition, which is based on an indispensable [and] necessary maxim of our judgment, is perfectly satisfactory for all speculative and practical uses of our reason from every *human* point of view, then indeed I would like to know just what we have lost if we cannot also prove it valid for higher beings, i.e., prove it from pure objective bases (to which unfortunately our powers do not extend). For it is quite certain that in terms of merely mechanical principles of nature we cannot even adequately become familiar with, much less explain, organized beings and how they are internally possible. So certain is this that we may boldly state that it is absurd for human beings even to attempt it, or to hope that perhaps some day another Newton might arise who would explain to us, in terms of natural laws unordered by any intention, how even a mere blade of grass is produced.[15] Rather, we must absolutely deny that human beings have such insight. On the other hand, it would also be too presumptuous for us to judge that, supposing we could penetrate to the principle in terms of which nature made the familiar universal laws of nature specific, there simply *could* not be in nature a hidden basis adequate to make organized beings possible without an underlying intention (but through the mere mechanism of nature). For where would we have obtained such knowledge? Probabilities are quite irrelevant here, since we are concerned with judgments of pure reason. Hence we can make no objective judgment whatever, whether affirmative or negative, about the proposition as to whether there is a being who acts according to intentions and who, as cause (and hence author) of the world, is the basis of the beings we rightly call natural purposes. Only this much is certain: If at any rate we are to judge by what our own nature grants us to see (subject to the conditions and bounds of our reason), then we are absolutely unable [to account] for the possibility of those natural purposes except by regarding them as based on an intelligent being. This is all that conforms to the maxim of our reflective judgment and so to a basis that, though in the subject, attaches inescapably to the human race.

401

§ 76

Comment

The following contemplation would greatly deserve elaborate treatment in transcendental philosophy;[16] but here I insert it only as a digression intended for elucidation (not as a proof of what I have set forth here).

Reason is a power of principles, and its ultimate demand [for principles] aims at the unconditioned. Understanding, on the other hand, always serves reason only under a certain condition, one that must

---

[15] [Cf. the *Universal Natural History and Theory of the Heavens* (1755), Ak. I, 230; also above, Ak. 378, and below, Ak. 409.]

[16] [See above, Ak. 213 br. n. 25.]

be given [to us]. But without concepts of the understanding, to which objective reality must be given, reason cannot make objective (synthetic) judgments at all. As theoretical reason it has absolutely no constitutive principles of its own, but merely regulative ones. Two points emerge from this. First, if reason advances to where understanding cannot follow, it becomes transcendent, displaying itself not in objectively valid concepts, but instead in ideas, though these do have a basis (as regulative principles). But, second, since the understanding cannot keep pace with reason, while yet it would be needed to make [ideas] valid for objects, it restricts the validity of those ideas of reason to just the subject, yet in a universal way, i.e., [as a validity] for all subjects of our species. In other words, understanding restricts the validity of these ideas to this condition: that, given the nature of our (human) cognitive ability, or even given any concept *we can form* of the ability of a finite rational being as such, all thinking must be like this and cannot be otherwise—though we are not asserting that such a judgment has its basis in the object. Let me [illustrate my point by] some examples. I am not urging the reader to accept these examples immediately as proved propositions; they are both too important and too difficult for that. But they may still provide him with food for meditation, and serve to elucidate what is our proper task here.

It is indispensable [and] necessary for human understanding to distinguish between the possibility and the actuality of things, and this fact has its basis in the subject and in the nature of his cognitive powers.[17] For if the exercise of these powers did not require two quite heterogeneous components, understanding to provide concepts, and sensible intuition to provide objects corresponding to these, then there would be no such distinction (between the possible and the actual). If our understanding were intuitive [rather than discursive, i.e., conceptual] it would have no objects except actual [ones].[18] [For] we would then be without concepts (and these deal with the mere possibility of an object) and also be without sensible intuitions (which do give us something [actual], yet without allowing us to

402

---

[17] [See also the *Critique of Pure Reason*, A 218–26 = B 265–74.]

[18] [This is discussed more fully in the next section, § 77, Ak. 405–10.]

cognize it as an object).[19] But our entire distinction between the merely possible and the actual rests on this: in saying that a thing is possible we are positing only the presentation of it with respect to our concept and to our thinking ability in general; but in saying that a thing is actual we are positing the thing itself [*an sich selbst*][20] (apart from that concept). Hence the distinction between possible and actual things holds merely subjectively, for human understanding. For even if something does not exist, we can still have it in our thoughts; or we can present something as given, even though we have as yet no concept of it. Hence the two propositions, that things can be possible without being actual, and that consequently one cannot at all infer actuality from mere possibility, do indeed hold for human reason. And yet this does not prove that the distinction lies in things themselves [*selbst*]; there clearly is no such implication. It is true that those two propositions also hold for objects insofar as our cognitive power, which is conditioned by the sensible, deals also with objects of sense; but they do not hold for things in general [i.e., even for things in themselves]. That this is so is evident from the fact that reason forever demands that we assume something or other (the original basis) as existing with unconditioned necessity, something in which there is no longer to be any distinction between possibility and actuality; and for this idea our understanding has absolutely no concept, i.e., it cannot find a way to present such a thing and its way of existing. For if the understanding *thinks* it (no matter how), then we are merely presenting the thing as possible. If the understanding is conscious of it as given in intuition, then it is actual, and no thought of possibility comes in. Hence the concept of an absolutely necessary being, though an indispensable idea of reason, is for human understanding an unattainable problematic concept. This concept does hold for the use we [humans] make of our cognitive powers in accordance with their peculiar character; but by the same token it does not hold for the object, and hence for every cognizing being. For I cannot presuppose that thought and intuition are two distinct conditions for the exercise of the cognitive powers of every such cognizing

[19] [So while neither concepts nor sensible intuitions (alone) can give us *actual objects*, an intuitive understanding would do only that.]

[20] [Thing *in itself*, literally, yet no *noumenon* seems to be intended *here*, as the next two sentences indicate.]

being, and hence for the possibility and actuality of things. An understanding to which this distinction did not apply would mean: All objects cognized by me *are* (exist);[21] such a being could have no presentation whatever of the possibility that some objects might not exist after all, i.e., of the contingency of those that do exist, nor, consequently, of the necessity to be distinguished from that contingency. What makes it so difficult for our understanding with its concepts to match reason here is merely this: that there is something which for it, as human understanding, is transcendent (i.e., impossible in view of the subjective conditions of its cognition), but which reason nevertheless treats as belonging to the object and turns into a principle. Now in this [kind of case] the following maxim always holds: where cognizing [certain] objects is beyond the ability of our understanding, we must think them in accordance with the subjective conditions for exercising [our] powers, conditions that attach necessarily to our (i.e., human) nature. And if the judgments we make in this way cannot be constitutive principles that determine the character of the object (as is indeed inevitable where the concepts are transcendent), they can still be regulative principles, safe and immanent in their employment and commensurate with the human point of view.

[We said that] reason, when it considers nature theoretically, has to assume the idea that the original basis of nature has unconditioned necessity. But when it considers nature practically, it similarly presupposes its own causality as unconditioned (as far as nature is concerned), i.e., its own freedom, since it is conscious of its [own] moral command. Here, however, the objective necessity of the action, in other words, duty, is being opposed to the necessity that the action would have if it were a [mere] event with its basis in nature rather than in freedom (i.e., the causality of reason); and the action that morally is absolutely necessary is regarded as quite contingent physically (i.e., [we see] that what *ought* necessarily to happen still fails to happen on occasion. It is clear, therefore, that only because of the subjective character of our practical ability do we have to present moral laws as commands (and the actions conforming to them as duties) and does reason

---

[21] [Cf. the *Critique of Pure Reason*, B 139 (and cf. B 135), where Kant describes an intuitive understanding as "an understanding through whose [spontaneous] presentation the objects of this presentation would at the same time exist. . . ." For a fuller discussion of an intuitive understanding, see the next section, § 77, Ak. 405–10.]

express this necessity not by *is* (i.e., happens) but by *ought to be*.[22]
This would not be the case if we considered reason, regarding its
causality, as being without sensibility (the subjective condition for
applying reason to objects of nature), and hence as being a cause in
an intelligible world that harmonized throughout with the moral law.
For in such a world there would be no difference between obligation
and action, between a practical law that says what is possible through
our doing, and the theoretical law that says what is actual through
our doing. It is true that an intelligible world in which everything
would be actual just because it is (both good and) possible—and,
along with this world, even freedom, its formal condition—is for us
a transcendent concept that is inadequate for a constitutive principle
for determining an object and its objective reality. Yet [the concept
of] freedom serves us as a universal *regulative* principle because of
the (in part sensible) character of our nature and ability, and the same
applies to all rational beings connected with the world of sense, insofar as our reason is capable of forming a presentation of them. That
principle does not objectively determine the character of freedom as
a form of causality; rather, and with no less validity than if it did do
that, it makes the rule [that we ought] to act according to that idea a
command for everyone.

404

Similarly, regarding the case before us, we may grant that, unless
we had the kind of understanding that has to proceed from the universal to the particular, we would find no distinction between natural
mechanism and the technic of nature, i.e., connection in it in terms of
purposes. For the fact that our understanding has to proceed from the
universal to the particular has the following consequence: In terms
of the universal [supplied by the understanding] the particular, as
such, contains something contingent. And yet reason requires that
even the particular laws of nature be combined in a unified and hence
lawful way. (This lawfulness of the contingent is called purposiveness.)
Therefore, unless the power of judgment has [its own] universal law
under which it can subsume that particular, it cannot recognize any
purposiveness in it and hence cannot make any determinative judgment about it. [Differently put:] It is impossible to derive the particular laws, as regards what is contingent in them, a priori from the
universal ones [supplied by the understanding], [i.e.,] by determining

---

[22] [Emphasis added.]

the concept of the object. Hence the concept of the purposiveness that nature displays in its products must be one that, while not pertaining to the determination of objects themselves, is nevertheless a subjective principle that reason has for our judgment, since this principle is necessary for human judgment in dealing with nature. The principle is regulative (not constitutive), but it holds just as necessarily for our *human judgment* as it would if it were an objective principle.

405

§ 77

On the Peculiarity of the Human Understanding That Makes the Concept of a Natural Purpose Possible for Us

In the preceding Comment[23] we mentioned peculiarities of our cognitive power (even of the higher one), and how we are easily misled into transferring these peculiarities to things themselves as [if they were] objective predicates. But in fact these peculiarities concern ideas, to which no commensurate object can be given in experience, so that they can serve us only as regulative principles in the pursuit of experience.[24] Now the same applies to the concept of a natural purpose as regards the cause that makes it possible [to apply] such a predicate: that cause [we] can [find] only in [our] idea [of it]. And yet here the result which conforms to that idea (i.e., the product itself) is given in nature. [Hence] the concept of a causality of nature which implies that nature is a being acting according to purposes seems to turn the idea of a natural purpose into a principle that is constitutive of the natural purpose. In this respect this idea is distinguished from all others.

---

[23] [§76, Ak. 401–04.]

[24] [See the *Critique of Pure Reason*, A 642–68 = B 670–96.]

But [in fact] the distinguishing feature consists [merely] in this: the idea in question is a principle of reason for the power of judgment, not for the understanding. Hence it is a principle [that helps us] merely to apply understanding generally to possible objects of experience, namely, in those cases where we cannot judge determinatively but can judge merely reflectively. Therefore, even though in those cases the object can be given in experience, yet we cannot even *determinately judge* it in conformity with the idea (let alone do so with complete adequacy) but can only reflect on it.

Hence this distinguishing feature of the idea of a natural purpose concerns a peculiarity of *our* (human) understanding in relation to the power of judgment and its reflection on things of nature. But if that is so, then we must here be presupposing the idea of some possible understanding different from the human one (just as, in the *Critique of Pure Reason,* we had to have in mind a possible different intuition if we wanted to consider ours as a special kind, namely, as an intuition for which objects count only as appearances).[25] Only by presupposing this idea can we say that because of the special charac- ter of our understanding *must we consider* certain natural products, as to [how] they are possible, as having been produced intentionally and as purposes. [And we do say this,] though without implying that there must actually be a special cause that determines [objects] on

---

[25] [The "different understanding" and the "different intuition" turn out to be (almost) the same thing: an intuitive understanding (or "intuitive intellect") is a power of intellectual intuition. Its intuitions would (like understanding itself) be *spontaneous,* whereas our intuitions consist of two forms (space, time) and (if empirical) sensations that we *receive.* In the *Critique of Pure Reason* (B 72), Kant says that our intuition "is called sensible *because it is not original,* i.e., not one through [the spontaneous presentationsof]whichtheveryexistenceof*the*intuition'sobjectisgiven[asnoumenon, thing in itself: see B 307–09] (an intuition that, as far as we can see, only the original being can have); rather, our intuition is dependent on the existence of the object [in itself, as noumenal ground of our sensation), and hence is possible only inasmuch as the subject's capacity to present is affected by that object. . . . [Our intuition] is derivative (*intuitus derivativus*), not original (*intuitus originarius*), hence not an intellectual intuition." (Cf. also B 68, B 135, and esp. B 139.) So while, as Kant says here, for our intuition (as connected with our understanding) objects "count only as appearances," for an intellectual intuition an object would count as a thing in itself (*Critique of Pure Reason,* B 307–09), which would then be the thing we "regard . . . as based on a corresponding intellectual intuition. . . ." (See below, Ak. 409. Cf. also the Translator's Introduction, *xci–xcii.*]

406   the basis of the presentation of a purpose, i.e., without implying that
the basis that makes such products of nature possible could not be
found, even by an understanding different from (higher than) the
human one, in the very mechanism of nature, i.e., in a causal connection that does not necessarily [*ausschließungsweise*] presuppose an
understanding as cause.

So what matters here is how *our* understanding relates to judgment:
we must find in this relation a certain contingency in the character of
our understanding, so that we can take note of this peculiarity as
what distinguishes our understanding from other possible ones.

We find this contingency quite naturally in the *particular* that
judgment has to bring under the *universal* supplied by the concepts of
the understanding. For the universal supplied by *our* (human) understanding does not determine the particular; therefore even if different
things agree in a common characteristic, the variety of ways in which
they may come before our perception is contingent. For our understanding is a power of concepts, i.e., a discursive understanding, so
that it must indeed be contingent for it as to what the character and
all the variety of the particular may be that can be given to it in nature
and that can be brought under its concepts. Now [all] cognition
requires [not only understanding] but also intuition; and a power of
complete spontaneity [as opposed to *receptivity*] *of intuition* would
be a cognitive power different from, and wholly independent of, sensibility: thus a power of complete spontaneity of intuition would be
an understanding in the most general sense of the term. Hence we
can conceive of an *intuitive* understanding as well (negatively, merely
as one that is not discursive[26]), which, [unlike ours,] does not (by
means of concepts) proceed from the universal to the particular and
thus to the individual. For such an understanding there would not be
that contingency in the way nature's products harmonize with the

_____

[26] [We say "how this [intellectual] intuition of the object is *not*." (*Critique of Pure
Reason,* B 149.) We can similarly characterize the (noumenal) *object* of this intuition
negatively: "So if we suppose an object of *nonsensible* intuition as given, we can
indeed conceive of it by all those predicates that lie in the very presupposition,
[namely,] that *it has nothing that belongs to sensible intuition,* i.e., that it is not
extended, i.e., not in space, that its continuance is not [in] time, that no change
occurs in it (no succession of states in time), etc.î (*Ibid.,* B 149.) Cf. also *ibid.,* B
307, where a noumenon in the *negative* sense is characterized as "a thing *insofar as
it is not an object of our sensible intuition*; but in the *positive* sense, as "an *object* of
a *nonsensible intuition*, . . . namely, an intellectual intuition. . . ."]

understanding in terms of *particular* laws. It is this contingency that makes it so difficult for our understanding to unify the manifold in nature so as to [give rise to] cognition. This task, which an intuitive understanding does not need to perform, can be accomplished by our understanding only through a harmony between natural characteristics and our power of concepts; and this harmony is very contingent.

Therefore our understanding has this peculiarity as regards judgment: when cognition occurs through our understanding, the particular is not determined by the universal and therefore cannot be derived from it alone. And yet this particular in nature's diversity must (through concepts and laws) harmonize with the universal in order that the particular can be subsumed under the universal. But, under these circumstances, this harmony must be very contingent, and must lack a determinate principle as far as the power of judgment is concerned.

How then can we at least conceive of the possibility of such a harmony—one that is presented as contingent and hence as possible only through a purpose that aims at it—between the things of nature and our judgment? To do this, we must at the same time conceive of a different understanding: without as yet attributing any [concept of a] purpose to this understanding, we can then present this harmony between the [particular] natural laws and our judgment as *necessary* relative to that understanding, [even though] our own understanding can conceive of this harmony only as mediated by purposes.

The point is this: Our understanding has the peculiarity that when it cognizes, e.g., the cause of a product, it must proceed from the *analytically universal* to the particular (i.e., from concepts to the empirical intuition that is given); consequently, in this process our understanding determines nothing regarding the diversity of the particular. Instead (under the supposition that the object is a natural product) our understanding must wait until the subsumption of the empirical intuition under the concept provides this determination for the power of judgment. But we can also conceive of an understanding that, unlike ours, is not discursive but intuitive, and hence proceeds from the *synthetically universal* (the intuition of a whole as a whole) to the particular, i.e., from the whole to the parts. Hence such an understanding as well as its presentation of the whole has no *contingency* in the combination of the parts in order to make a determinate form of the whole possible. Our understanding, on the other hand, requires this contingency, because it must start from the parts

407

taken as bases—which are thought of as universal—for different possible forms that are to be subsumed under these bases as consequences. [We,] given the character of our understanding, can regard a real whole of nature only as the joint effect of the motive forces of the parts. Let us suppose, then, that we try to present, not the possibility of the whole as dependent on the parts (which would conform to our discursive understanding), but the possibility of the parts, in their character and combination, as dependent on the whole, so that we would be following the standard set by intuitive (archetypal) understanding. If we try to do this, then, in view of that same peculiarity of our understanding, we cannot do it by having the whole contain the basis that makes the connection of the parts possible (since in the discursive kind of cognition this would be a contradiction). The only way that we can present the possibility of the parts as dependent on the whole is by having the *presentation* of [the] whole contain the basis that makes possible the form of that whole as well as the connection of the parts required to [make] this [form possible]. Hence such a whole would be an effect, a *product,* the *presentation* of which is regarded as the *cause* that makes the product possible. But the product of a cause that determines its effect merely on the basis of the presentation of that effect is called a purpose. It follows from this that the fact that we present [certain] products of nature as possible only in terms of a kind of causality that differs from the causality of the natural laws pertaining to matter, namely, the causality of purposes and final causes, is merely a consequence of the special character of our understanding. Therefore, this principle [of the causality in terms of final causes] does not pertain to [how] such things themselves are possible through this kind of production (not even if we consider them as phenomena), but pertains only to the way our understanding is able to judge them. This clarifies at the same time why we are far from satisfied in natural science if we can explain the products of nature through a causality in terms of purposes: the reason for this is that all we demand in such an explanation is that natural production be judged in a way commensurate with our ability for judging such production, i.e., in a way commensurate with reflective judgment, rather than with the things themselves and for the sake of determinative judgment. And [to make these points] we do not have to prove that such an *intellectus archetypus* is possible. Rather, we must prove only that the contrast [between such an intellect and] our discursive understanding—an understanding which requires images (it is an *intellectus ectypus*)[27]—and the contingency of its having this character lead us to that idea (of an *intellectus archetypus*), and we must prove that this idea does not involve a contradiction.

When we consider a material whole as being, in terms of its form, a product of its parts and of their forces and powers for combining on their own (to which we must add other matter that the parts supply to one another), then our presentation is of a whole produced mechanically. But we get no concept of a whole as a purpose in this way; the inner possibility of a whole as a purpose always presupposes that there is an idea of this whole and presupposes that what these parts are like and how they operate depend on that idea, which is just how we have to present an organized body. But, as I have shown, it does not follow from this that it is impossible for such a body to be produced mechanically. For that would be tantamount to saying that it is impossible (contradictory) *for any understanding* to present such a unity in the combination of [a thing's] manifold without also [thinking of] the idea of that unity as causing it, in other words, without [thinking of] the production as intentional. But this consequence [that an organized body cannot be produced mechanically] would in fact follow if we were entitled to regard material beings as things in themselves. For then the unity that is the basis on which natural formations are possible would be only the unity of space, and yet space is not a basis [responsible] for the reality of products but is only their formal condition; space merely resembles the basis we are seeking inasmuch as no part in space can be determined except in relation to the whole (so that [in its case too] the possibility of the parts is based on the presentation of the whole). But in fact it is at least possible to consider the material world as mere appearance, and to think something as [its] substrate, as thing in itself (which is not appearance), and to regard this thing in itself as based on a corresponding intellectual intuition (even though not ours). In that way there would be for nature, which includes us as well, a supersensible basis of its reality, though we could not cognize this basis. Hence we would consider in terms of mechanical laws whatever is necessary in

409

---

[27] [The "archetypal" understanding would present *originals* (things in themselves); our "ectypal" understanding, with the help of "images" (perceptions) gained from our intuition, presents *derivatives* (things as appearances) of those originals.]

nature as an object of sense; but the harmony and unity of the particular laws of nature and of the forms based on them are contingent in terms of mechanical laws, and [so] this harmony and unity, as objects of reason, we would at the same time consider in terms of teleological laws (as, indeed, we would consider the whole of nature as a system). So we would judge nature in terms of two kinds of principles, and the mechanical kind of explanation would not be excluded by the teleological as if they contradicted each other.

This also allows us to see what we could otherwise have suspected, but could hardly have asserted with certainty and have proved: that although the principle of a mechanical derivation of purposive natural products is compatible with the teleological principle, the mechanical one could certainly not make the teleological one dispensable. In other words, when we deal with a thing that we must judge to be a natural purpose (i.e., when we deal with an organized being), though we can try on it all the laws of mechanical production that we know or may yet discover, and though we may indeed hope to make good progress with such mechanical laws, yet we can never [account] for the possibility of such a product without appealing to a basis for its production that is wholly distinct from the mechanical one, namely, a causality through purposes. Indeed, absolutely no human reason (nor any finite reason similar to ours in quality, no matter how much it may surpass ours in degree) can hope to understand, in terms of nothing but mechanical causes, how so much as a mere blade of grass is produced. For it seems that [*wenn*] judgment is quite unable to study, even if it restricts itself to experience as its guide, [how] such objects are possible, without [using] the teleological connection of causes and effects. [Yet] it also seems that for external objects as appearances we cannot possibly find an adequate basis that refers to purposes, but it seems instead that, even though this basis also lies in nature, we must still search for it only in nature's supersensible substrate, even though all possible insight into that substrate is cut off from us: hence it seems [(German) *so*] that there is absolutely no possibility for us to obtain, from nature itself, bases with which to explain combinations in terms of purposes; rather, the character of the human cognitive power forces us to seek the supreme basis for such combinations in an original understanding, as cause of the world.

410

§ 78

How the Principle of the Universal Mechanism of Matter and the Teleological Principle Can Be Reconciled in the Technic of Nature

Reason is tremendously concerned not to abandon the mechanism nature [employs] in its products, and not to pass over it in explaining them, since without mechanism we cannot gain insight into the nature of things. Even if it were granted that a supreme architect directly created the forms of nature as they have always been, or that he predetermined the ones that in the course of nature keep developing according to the same model, still none of this advances our cognition of nature in the least; for we do not know at all how that being acts, and what its ideas are that are supposed to contain the principles by which natural beings are possible, and [so] we cannot explain nature by starting from that being, i.e., by descending (in other words, a priori) [from that being to nature]. Or suppose we try to explain by ascending (in other words, a posteriori), i.e., we start from the forms of objects of experience because we think they display purposiveness, and then, to explain this purposiveness, we appeal to a cause that acts according to purposes: in that case our explanation would be quite tautologous and we would deceive reason with [mere] words—not to mention that with this kind of explanation we stray into the transcendent, where our cognition of nature cannot follow us and where reason is seduced to poetic raving, even though reason's foremost vocation is to prevent precisely that.

On the other hand, it is just as necessary a maxim of reason that it not pass over the principle of purposes in [dealing with] the products of nature. For though this principle does indeed not help us grasp how these products originate, yet it is a heuristic principle for investigating the particular laws of nature. It would serve for this even if we did not

411

295

try, by searching beyond nature for the basis on which these products are possible, to use it to explain nature itself, but continued in the meantime to call these products natural purposes only, even though they plainly display the intentional unity [that characterizes] a purpose. But since the question of how these products are possible must be raised in the end, it is just as necessary for reason to think a special kind of causality that cannot be found in nature, as it is necessary for the mechanism of natural causes to have its own causality. For if we are to indicate a basis that makes those forms possible, then we need more than this mechanism, since matter can receive more and other forms than it can get through mechanism: we need in addition a cause that has spontaneity (which, as such, cannot be matter). Of course, before reason takes this step, it must proceed cautiously; it must not try to explain as teleological every technic of nature, i.e., every power of nature to produce [things] with a shape that manifests purposiveness for our mere apprehension (as in the case of bodies [of] regular [shape]), but reason must continue meanwhile to regard such technic as possible by mere mechanism. But reason must not carry this attempt to explain things in mechanical terms to the point of excluding the teleological principle, i.e., to the point of insisting on following mere mechanism even in cases where natural forms are purposive [or specially suitable] for rational investigation into how their causes make them possible and where this purposiveness manifests itself quite undeniably as a reference to a different kind of causality. For [going to the extreme of explaining everything only mechanically] must make reason fantasize and wander among chimeras of natural powers that are quite inconceivable, just as much as a merely teleological kind of explanation that takes no account whatever of the mechanism of nature made reason rave.

As applied to one and the same natural thing, we cannot link or reconcile the mechanical and the teleological principle [if we regard them] as principles for explaining (deducing) one thing from another, i.e., [regard them] as dogmatic and constitutive principles [of] determinative judgment for [gaining] insight into nature. For example, if I assume that a maggot should be regarded as a product of the mere mechanism of matter (i.e., of the restructuring that matter does on its own, once its elements are set free by putrefaction), I cannot then go on to derive the same product from the same matter [now regarded] as a causality that acts in terms of purposes. Conversely, if I assume

412

that the maggot is a natural purpose, then I cannot count on there being a mechanical way of producing it and cannot assume this as a constitutive principle for judging how the maggot is possible. We cannot reconcile the two principles in this way. For the two kinds of explanation exclude each other, even on the supposition that objectively both these bases for the possibility of such a product rested [in turn] on a single one, though one that we left out of account. [Rather,] if we are to have a principle that makes it possible to reconcile the mechanical and the teleological principles by which we judge nature, then we must posit this further principle in something that lies beyond both (and hence also beyond any possible empirical presentation of nature), but that nonetheless contains the basis of nature, namely, we must posit it in the supersensible, to which we must refer both kinds of explanation. On the other hand, we can have no concept of the supersensible except the indeterminate concept of a basis that makes it possible for us to judge nature in terms of empirical laws; but we cannot determine this basis any further by any predicate. It follows from this that we cannot reconcile the two principles on a basis that would allow *explanation* (explication), on the part of *determinative* judgment, of how a product is possible in terms of given laws, but only on a basis that allows *examination* [*Erörterung*] (exposition) of this possibility, on the part of reflective judgment. For to explain [something] means to derive [it] from a principle, and hence we must be able to cognize and state this principle distinctly. Now it is true that the principle of the mechanism of nature and the principle of nature's causality in terms of purposes, as both are applied to one and the same natural product, must be linked in a single higher principle and flow from it together [*gemeinschaftlich*], since otherwise we could not consistently use both in considering nature. And the fact that the two principles [or maxims] have this higher one objectively in common [*gemeinschaftlich*] also establishes the fact that the maxim[s] of natural investigation that depend on it [belong] together. But if this principle is of such a kind that we can only point to it, but can never cognize it determinately and state it distinctly so as to apply it to the cases that occur, then we cannot use it to explain, i.e., derive distinctly and determinately, how there can be a natural product that is possible in terms of both of those hetergeneous principles. Now the principle that mechanical and teleological derivation have in common is the *supersensible,* which we must regard as the basis of nature as phenomenon. But of the supersensible we cannot, from a theoretical point of view, form the slightest determinate and positive concept. Hence there is no way we can explain how, under the supersensible as principle, nature (in terms of its particular laws) constitutes for us a system that can be cognized as possible in terms of two principles: that of production from physical and that of [production from] final causes. All we can do is this: if we happen to find natural objects whose possibility is inconceivable to us in terms merely of the principle of mechanism (which in the case of a natural being always has a claim [to being applied]) so that we must rely also on teleological principles, then we can presume that we may confidently investigate natural laws in accordance with both principles (once our understanding is able to cognize [how] the natural product is possible on the basis of one or the other principle), without our being troubled by the seeming conflict that arises between the two principles for judging that product. For we are assured that it is at least possible that objectively, too, both these principles might be reconcilable in one principle (since they concern appearances, which presuppose a supersensible basis).

Hence it may be that, regarding one and the same product and its possibility, both the mechanism and the teleological (intentional) technic of nature are subject to a common higher principle of nature in its particular laws. But even if they are subject to such a higher principle, inasmuch as this principle is *transcendent* and our understanding is so limited, we still cannot reconcile the two principles *in an explanation* of the same natural product, even where (as in the case of organized kinds of matter) the inner possibility of the product is *understandable* only through a causality in terms of purposes. Hence we must keep to the above principle of teleology—viz., the principle that, in view of the character of human understanding, the only cause that can be assumed [in order to account] for the possibility of organic beings in nature is a cause that acts intentionally, and that the mere mechanism of nature cannot at all suffice to explain these products of nature. But we are not trying to use this principle to decide anything about how such things themselves are possible.

Consequently, this principle is only a maxim of reflective rather than of determinative judgment; and hence it holds only subjectively, i.e., for us, rather than objectively, i.e., for the possibility of this kind of things themselves (where the two types of production might well be linked in one and the same basis). Moreover, if we did not supplement the production that we think of as teleological with any concept of a mechanism of nature as also involved [*anzutreffen*] in that production, then we could not judge such a product to be a product of nature at all. Hence the above maxim also carries with it the necessity of reconciling the two principles when we judge things as natural purposes, but not with the aim of putting one type of production, wholly or in part, in the place of the other. For we cannot assume mechanism in the place of something that is thought of (at least by us) as possible only according to an intention; furthermore, in the place of something that is cognized as necessary in terms of mechanism we cannot assume a contingency that would require a purpose as the basis determining [the thing]. All we can do is subordinate the one type of production (mechanism) to the other (an intentional technic); the transcendental principle of the purposiveness of nature certainly permits that.

414

For where we think purposes as bases that make certain things possible, we must also assume means whose causal law does not *itself* require anything that presupposes a purpose, so that this law can be mechanical and yet also a subordinate cause of intentional effects. Hence even if we consider no more than the organic products of nature—but above all if their endless multitude prompts us to go on and adopt (at least as a permissible hypothesis) the intentional [element] that natural causal connection has in terms of particular laws as a *universal principle* of reflective judgment for the whole of nature (i.e., the world)—then we can easily conceive of a common [*große*] or even universal connection between mechanical and teleological laws in the products of nature. Moreover, we can do this without confusing the two principles for judging these products and putting one in the place of the other. For even where we teleologically judge that the form which the matter assumes is possible only through an intention, the matter may still also be subordinated, according to mechanical laws as its own nature requires [*nach*], as a means to that conceived purpose. On the other hand, since the basis for this reconcilability lies in what is neither the one nor the other (neither mechanism nor connection in terms of purposes), but is nature's supersensible substrate that we cannot cognize at all, [it follows that] our (human) reason cannot fuse these two ways of conceiving how such objects are possible. We can only judge them as based, in terms of the connection of final causes, on a supreme understanding, so that nothing is taken away from the teleological kind of explanation.

It is however quite undetermined, and for our reason forever undeterminable, how much the mechanism of nature does as a means toward each final intention in nature. Moreover, because of the above-mentioned intelligible principle for the possibility of a nature as such, we may even assume that nature is possible throughout in terms of both kinds of law (physical laws and laws [in terms] of final causes) [operating] in universal harmony, even though we have no insight whatever into how this happens. Hence we also do not know how far we may get with the mechanical kind of explanation that is possible for us. Only this much is certain: no matter how far it will take us, yet it must always be inadequate for things that we have once recognized as natural purposes, so that the character of our under-standing forces us to subordinate all those mechanical bases to a teleological principle.

Because of this we are authorized to adopt the following procedure, and [indeed], since the study of nature in terms of the principle of mechanism is so very important for the theoretical use of our reason, we are also called upon to adopt this procedure: we are to explain all products and events of nature, even the most purposive ones, in mechanical terms as far as we possibly can (we cannot tell what are the limits of our ability for this way of investigating); yet, in doing so, we are never to lose sight of the fact that, as regards those natural products that we cannot even begin to investigate except under the concept of a purpose of reason, the essential character of our reason will still force us to subordinate such products ultimately, regardless of those mechanical causes, to the causality in terms of purposes.

Appendix

Methodology of Teleolgical Judgment

§ 79

Whether Teleology Must Be Given Treatment as a Part of Natural Science

Every science must have its definite position in the encyclopaedia of all the sciences. If the science is philosophical, we must assign it either to the theoretical or to the practical part of that encyclopaedia. If its place is in the theoretical part, we must assign it either to natural science, namely, to the extent that it examines whatever can be an object of experience (and so we must assign it either to the science of bodies, or to psychology, or to universal cosmology), or else to theology (which deals with the original basis of the world as the sum total of all objects of experience).

So the question arises: What is the proper position for teleology? Does it belong to natural science (in the proper sense of the term), or to theology? It has to belong to one or the other, since no science can belong to the transition between the two, because a transition only articulates or organizes the system and [does] not [have] a place within it.

Now although teleology is useful to theology in very important

301

302   PART II.   CRITIQUE OF TELEOLOGICAL JUDGMENT

ways, it quite obviously does not belong to theology as a part of it. For it deals with natural products and their cause; and though it points to this cause as a basis that lies beyond and above nature (namely, a divine author), it does this not for determinative judgment, but merely for reflective judgment in its contemplation of nature (so that the idea of this divine author may serve us as a regulative principle that will guide us in judging the things in the world in a way appropriate to our human understanding).

417

But teleology also does not seem to belong to natural science. For natural science requires determinative and not merely reflective principles in order to indicate objective bases for natural effects. Indeed, since the theory of nature explains natural phenomena in mechanical terms, through their efficient causes, there would be no advantage for it if we considered them according to their relations [in terms] of purposes. Actually, positing purposes of nature in natural products insofar as these form a system in terms of teleological concepts is only part of describing nature, namely, by using a special guide. It is true that in such descriptions reason performs a splendid and instructive task that is purposive for a variety of aims, but it gives us no information whatever about the origin and inner possibility of these forms, while that is exactly what theoretical natural science is concerned with.

So teleology as a science does not belong to any doctrine, but belongs only to critique: the critique of a special cognitive power, namely, judgment. But teleology does contain a priori principles, and to that extent it can and must indicate by what method we must judge nature in terms of the principle of final causes. Hence the methodology [the study of the method] of teleology has at least a negative influence on how we must proceed in theoretical natural science, and also on how this science can, in metaphysics, serve as a propaedeutic in relation to theology.

§ 80

On the Necessary Subordination of the Principle of Mechanism to the Teleological Principle in Explaining a Thing [Considered] as a Natural Purpose

Our *authority to try* to explain all natural products in merely mechanical terms is intrinsically quite unlimited. But, in view of the character of our understanding, our *ability to make do* with such an explanation alone, when dealing with things [considered] as natural purposes, is not only very limited, but has distinct bounds. [These consist in the fact that] there is a principle of judgment according to which we cannot accomplish anything by way of explaining such things if we proceed in mechanical terms alone, and hence our judging of such products must always be subordinated to a teleological principle as well.

Therefore, it is reasonable, even praiseworthy, to try to explain natural products in terms of natural mechanism as long as there is some probability of success. Indeed, if we give up this attempt, we must do so not on the ground that it is *intrinsically* impossible to find the purposiveness of nature by following this route, but only on the ground that it is impossible *for us* as human beings: for, [it might be argued, in order to find nature's purposiveness by this route,] we would have to have an intuition other than our sensible one, and [through it[1]] a determinate cognition of the intelligible substrate of nature which would enable us to indicate a basis even for the mechanism of appearances as governed by particular laws, and that quite surpasses all our ability.

So if in investigating nature we are to avoid working for nothing at

---

[1] [Cf. Ak. 405 br. n. 25.]

all, then, in judging things whose concept as natural purposes does undoubtedly have a basis (i.e., in judging organized beings), we must always presuppose some original organization that itself uses mechanism, either to produce other organized forms or to develop the thing's own organized form into new shapes (though these shapes too always result from the purpose and conform to it).

It is commendable to do comparative anatomy and go through the vast creation of organized beings in nature, in order to see if we cannot discover in it something like a system, namely, as regards the principle of their production. We do not have to settle for the mere principle for judging them (it tells us nothing that would give us insight into how they are produced), and do not have to abandon all hope for a claim to *insight into nature* in this area. For there are [some facts in this area] that offer the mind a ray of hope, however faint, that in their case at least we may be able to accomplish something with the principle of natural mechanism, without which there can be no natural science at all: So many genera of animals share a certain common schema on which not only their bone structure but also the arrangement of their other parts seems to be based; the basic outline is admirably simple but yet was able to produce this great diversity of species, by shortening some parts and lengthening others, by the involution of some and the evolution of others. Despite all the variety among these forms, they seem to have been produced according to a common archetype, and this analogy among them reinforces our suspicion that they are actually akin, produced by a common original mother. For the different animal genera approach one another gradually: from the genus where the principle of purposes seems to be borne out most, namely, man, all the way to the polyp, and from it even to mosses and lichens and finally to the lowest stage of nature discernible to us, crude matter. From this matter, and its forces governed by mechanical laws (like those it follows in crystal formations[2]), seems to stem all the technic that nature displays in organized beings and that we find so far beyond our grasp that we believe that we have to think a different principle [to account] for it.

When the archaeologist[3] of nature considers these points, he is free to have that large family of creatures (for that is how we must

419

[2] [Cf. Ak. 348–49.]

[3] [Emphasis removed.]

conceive of them if that thoroughly coherent kinship among them is to have a basis) arise from the traces that remain of nature's most ancient revolutions, and to have it do so according to all the natural mechanism he knows or suspects. He can make mother earth (like a large animal, as it were) emerge from her state of chaos, and make her lap promptly give birth initially to creatures of a less purposive form, with these then giving birth to others that became better adapted to their place of origin and to their relations to one another, until in the end this womb itself rigidified, ossified, and confined itself to bearing definite species that would no longer degenerate, so that the diversity remained as it had turned out when that fertile formative force ceased to operate.[4] And yet, in giving this account, the archaeologist of nature will have to attribute to this universal mother an organization that purposively aimed at all these creatures, since otherwise it is quite inconceivable [how] the purposive form is possible that we find in the products of the animal and plant kingdoms.[5] But if he attributes such an organization to her, then he has only put off the basis for his explanation and cannot pretend to have made the production of those two kingdoms independent of the condition of [requiring] final causes.

420

Even [some of] the changes that certain individuals of the organized genera undergo accidentally [have to be judged in this way.] If

---

[4] [In the *Anthropology* (Ak. VII, the n. on 327–28), Kant wonders whether, in one of nature's later epochs, the organs that an orangutan or a chimpanzee uses to walk, feel objects, or talk might have developed into human structures, the inmost of which contained an organ that understanding could use and that gradually developed through social culture.]

[5] A hypothesis like this may be called a daring adventure of reason, and one that has probably entered, on occasion, even the minds of virtually all the most acute natural scientists. For at least this [kind of generation] is not absurd, as is a *generatio aequivoca*, which is the production of an organized being by the mechanics of crude, unorganized matter. Rather, this generation would still be a *generatio univoca* in the most general sense of the word, because anything organic would be produced only from something else that is also organic, even though different in kind from it among beings of that type, as when, e.g., certain aquatic animals developed gradually into marsh animals and from these, after several generations, into land animals. This is not inconsistent a priori, in the judgment of mere reason. Experience however does not show an example of it. The only generation we know from experience is a generatio that is not only *univoca*—as opposed to *aequivoca*, from unorganized material—but also *homonyma*, where the product shares even the organization of what produced it. As far as our empirical knowledge of nature goes, we do not find anywhere a *generatio heteronyma*.

we find that the altered character of these individuals becomes heredi-
tary and is taken up into their generative force, then the only proper
way to judge it is as the development, on [a given] occasion, of a
purposive predisposition that was originally present in the species and
that serves the preservation of the kind. For in an organized being,
with its thorough intrinsic purposiveness that makes it a system of
purposes, the fact that it generates others of the same kind is closely
connected with the condition that nothing is to be taken up into the
generative force that does not already belong to one of the being's
undeveloped original predispositions.[6] For if we depart from this
principle, then we cannot [even] be certain as to whether some of
the other features we now find in a species did not have an equally
accidental and purposeless origin. And so we could no longer with
any reliability apply the principle of teleology: the principle of judging nothing in an organized being as unpurposive if it is preserved in
the being's propagation. The principle's validity would then be restricted
to the original stock (back to which, however, our knowledge does
not reach).

Hume raises an objection against those who find it necessary to
assume a teleological principle for judging all such natural purposes,
i.e., an architectonic understanding. It would be equally legitimate,
he says, to ask how such an understanding is possible, i.e., how the
various powers and properties that are needed to make possible an
understanding that also has executive might, could have met so
purposively in one being.[7] This objection, however, is idle. For the
whole difficulty about how a thing that has purposes within itself
and can be grasped only through them was first produced, rests on
this question: What is the unity of the basis [that accounts] for the
combination, in this product, of the manifold [elements] *extrinsic
to one another?* But this question, as far as it is teleological, is

---

[6] [Cf. *On the Various Races of Human Beings*, Ak. II, 435.]

[7] [Actually, Hume's concern (in the passage to which Kant seems to be alluding) is
with a causal explanation of the *existence*, not just the possibility, of such a postulated
intelligent being. In the *Dialogues Concerning Natural Religion* (Pt. IV, pars. 6–9),
Philo says: "We are still obliged to mount higher in order to find the cause of this
cause. . . . [A] mental world or universe of ideas requires a cause as much as does a
material world. . . . Have we not the same reason to trace that ideal world into
another ideal world or new intelligent principle? . . . If the material world rests upon
a similar ideal world, this ideal world must rest upon some other, and so on without
end."]

answered sufficiently if we posit that basis in the understanding of a
producing cause that is a simple substance. If, on the other hand, we
seek the cause merely in matter, as an aggregate of many substances
extrinsic to one another, then we have no principle whatever [to
account] for the unity in the intrinsically purposive form of its
structure. And to speak of *autocracy* of matter in products that our
understanding can grasp only as purposes is to use a word without
meaning.

That is why those who seek a supreme basis [to account] for the
possibility of objectively purposive forms of matter, yet without granting
it an understanding, do make a point of satisfying this condition of all
purposiveness: that there be *unity* in its basis. And so they like to
make the world whole a single all-encompassing substance (this is
pantheism), or the sum total of many attributes inhering in a single
simple substance (this is Spinozism, which is only a more determinate
version of pantheism). In making this move, these people do in fact
satisfy *one* condition of the problem: that in such forms there be
unity in their reference to a purpose; they satisfy this condition by
means of the merely ontological concept of a simple substance. But
they offer nothing to satisfy the *other* condition: that the consequence
of this substance be related to it as its *purpose;* and yet it is this relation that is to make that ontological basis more determinate so that
we can answer the question [how objects with intrinsically purposive
form are possible]. So these people do not by any means answer
the *whole* question. And the question remains absolutely unanswer-
able (for our reason) unless we treat it as follows: we must think
of that original basis of things as a simple *substance;* the quality
that enables this substance to give rise to the specific character of the
natural forms based on it, namely, their unity of a purpose, we must
think of as its intelligence; and the relation of this substance to those
natural forms we must think of as a *causality* (because of the contingency we find in everything that we think possible only as a purpose).

§ 81

On Conjoining Mechanism to the Teleological Principle in Explaining Natural Purposes [Considered] as Natural Products

422

We saw in the preceding section that the mechanism of nature alone is insufficient to allow us to conceive of how organized beings are possible, but that (at least in view of the character of our cognitive power) we must regard mechanism as originally subordinated to a cause that acts intentionally. But if we are to consider and judge such beings as also products of nature, then appealing on their behalf to a teleological basis alone is equally insufficient, but we must conjoin to this teleological basis the mechanism of nature—as the instrument, as it were, of a cause that acts intentionally—but with nature and its mechanical laws subordinated to the purpose pursued by that cause. It is beyond our reason's grasp how this reconciliation of two wholly different kinds of causality is possible: the causality of nature in its universal lawfulness, with [the causality of] an idea that confines nature to a particular form for which nature itself contains no basis whatsoever. The possibility of this reconciliation lies in the supersensible substrate of nature, about which we cannot determine anything affirmatively, except that it is the being in itself of which we know merely the appearance. But the fact [that it is beyond our reason's grasp how this reconciliation of the two kinds of causality is possible] does not diminish the force of this principle: that everything we assume to belong to this nature (as phenomenon) and assume to be its product must also be thought of as connected with it in terms of mechanical laws; for without this kind of causality, organized beings, while purposes of nature, would not be natural products.

Now if we assume (as we inevitably must) the teleological principle for the production of these beings, we may attribute their intrinsically purposive form to their cause either in terms of *occasionalism* or in terms of the *theory of preestablished harmony.* According to occasionalism the supreme cause of the world would, in conformity with its idea and on the occasion of every copulation, directly give the mingling matter its organic structure. According to the theory of preestablished harmony, the supreme cause would have imparted to the initial products of its wisdom only the predisposition by means of which an organic being produces another of its kind and the species perpetuates itself; and while nature works toward the destruction of individuals, it also continually compensates for their disappearance. If we assume occasionalism for the production of organized beings, then all nature in this production is lost entirely,[8] and along with it all [our ability] to judge by reason how such products are possible. Hence we may assume that anyone who is at all concerned to do philosophy will not adopt this system.

The *theory of preestablished harmony* can in turn proceed in two ways: any organic being generated by another of its kind is considered by this theory to be either the *educt* or the *product*[9] of that other being. The system that considers the generated beings as mere educts is called the system of *individual preformation,* or the *theory of evolution.* The system that considers them as products is called the system of *epigenesis.* We may also call it the system of *generic preformation,* since the productive power of the generating beings, and therefore the form of the species, was still preformed *virtualiter*[10] in the intrinsic purposive predispositions imparted to the stock. Accordingly it might also be better if we called the opposing theory of individual preformation the *theory of involution* [rather than of evolution] (or of encapsulation).[11]

Therefore, even though the advocates of the *theory of evolution*

423

---

[8] [This view is already discernible in Kant's earliest published work (written when he was still a student), *Thoughts on the True Estimation of Living Forces* (1747), Ak. I, 23–25.]

[9] [For this distinction, see Ak. 371 br. n. 31.]

[10] [As a power (*virtus*).]

[11] [I.e., if we characterize these theories by reference to (the kind of) *preformation,* the first theory is better characterized in terms of the initial "enfolding" (involution) of the preformed individuals than in terms of the later "unfolding" (evolution). (The theory is of course utterly different from Darwin's.)]

denied the formative force of nature to all individuals, so as to have them come directly from the hand of the creator, they still were reluctant to allow this to happen in terms of the hypothesis of occasionalism; on that hypothesis copulation would be a mere formality, and in each case of copulation a supreme [and] intelligent cause of the world would have resolved to form a fruit (i.e., offspring] directly, leaving to the mother only [the task of] developing[12] and nourishing it. Instead the advocates of the theory of evolution opted for preformation, as if it made a difference whether they had these forms of supernatural origin come about at the beginning of the world or in the course of it.[13] In fact, creation on [individual] occasions would eliminate the need for very many supernatural arrangements that preformation would require in order that an embryo formed at the beginning of the world might be kept uninjured and safe from the destructive forces of nature during the long interval between its creation and its development. Similarly, whereas preformation would require a vastly greater number of such preformed beings than of beings ever to be developed, occasionalism would make that greater number, and along with it as many acts of creation, unnecessary and purposeless. And yet the evolutionists did want to avoid lapsing into an utter hyperphysics that can dispense with all natural explanation, and so they did leave something in this process to nature: On the one hand, they continued to adhere to hyperphysics, even to the point of holding that freak births (which cannot possibly be considered purposes of nature) manifested an admirable [hyperphysical, i.e., supernatural] purposiveness, even if one whose only aim was that one day an anatomist might be bothered by its being a purposeless purposiveness and feel an admiration mixed with dejection. On the other hand, there was one thing they simply could not fit into their system of preformation: the production of hybrids. In cases where the whole product is produced by two creatures of the same species, they had granted neither of these two a formative force, granting the seed of male creatures nothing but the mechanical qualification to serve as the embryo's first food. In the case of hybrids, however, they had to grant the male seed a purposively formative force as well.

Consider, on the other hand, *epigenesis*. Even if we were unaware

424

---

[12] ["Unfolding," in effect. Cf. the etymology of 'develop' and 'evolve.']

[13] [Cf. *The Only Possible Basis of Proof,* Ak. II, 115.]

how much easier it is to defend this theory, rather than the theory of evolution, as far as proving it from empirical bases is concerned, still reason would from the start be greatly in favor of the kind of explanation [it offers]. For in considering those things whose origin can be conceived only in terms of a causality of purposes, this theory, at least as far as propagation is concerned, regards nature as itself producing them rather than as merely developing them; and so it minimizes appeal to the supernatural, [and] after the first beginning leaves everything to nature. (But it does not determine anything about this first beginning, on which physics founders in general, even if it tries to use a chain of causes, of whatever kind).

No one has done more by way of proving this theory of epigenesis than Privy Councilor *Blumenbach*,[14] and by way of establishing correct [*echt*] principles for applying it, which he did in part by avoiding too rash a use of it. Whenever he explains any of these structures physically he starts from organized matter. For he rightly declares it contrary to reason that crude matter on its own should have structured itself originally in terms of mechanical laws, that life could have sprung from the nature of what is lifeless, and that matter could have molded itself on its own into the form of a self-preserving purposiveness. Yet by appealing to this principle of an original *organization,* a principle that is inscrutable to us,[15] he leaves an indeterminable and yet unmistakable share to natural mechanism. The ability of the matter in an organized body to [take on] this organization he calls *a formative impulse.* (It is distinguished from the merely mechanical *formative force* that all matter has, [but] stands under the higher guidance and direction, as it were, of that formative force.)

---

[14] [Johann Friedrich Blumenbach (1752–1848), German anatomist, physiologist, anthropologist, and zoologist at Göttingen. He is the author of several works, in particular *Über den Bildungstrieb* (*On the Formative Impulse*, 1781), from which Kant is about to draw. See also Kant's *On Using Teleological Principles in Philosophy*, Ak. VIII, 180, first n.]

[15] [Cf. Ak. 374–75.]

§ 82

On the Teleological System in the Extrinsic Relations among Organized Beings

By extrinsic purposiveness I mean a purposiveness where one thing of nature serves another as a means to a purpose. Now things that have no intrinsic purposiveness and whose possibility does not presuppose one—e.g., earth, air, water, etc.—may still be very purposive extrinsically, i.e., in relation to other beings. But these latter beings must always be organized ones, i.e., natural purposes, since otherwise we could not judge the former to be means [to them]. Thus we cannot regard water, air, and earth as means for the accretion of mountains, because there is in fact nothing whatever in mountains that would require that their possibility have a basis in terms of purposes, and hence we never have any purposes here to which we could refer in order to present the cause of the mountains under the predicate of a means (useful for making the mountains possible).

The concept of extrinsic purposiveness is quite different from that of intrinsic purposiveness. Intrinsic purposiveness has to do with the possibility of an object regardless of whether or not the object's actuality is itself a purpose. About an organized being we can [always] go on to ask: What is it there for? But we cannot readily ask that question about things in which we recognize nothing but the effect of the mechanism of nature. For in presenting organized beings we are already presenting, [to account] for their inner possibility, a causality in terms of purposes, a creative understanding, an active power, and are relating it to the basis that determines it, its intention. There is only one [case where] extrinsic purposiveness is connected with the intrinsic purposiveness of organization. This [case] is the organization of the two sexes as related to each other to propagate their species. Here, although we must not ask what is the end for which the being had to exist [as] so organized, [that being] still serves as a means extrinsically related to a purpose. For here, just as in the case of an

312

individual, we can always go on to ask: Why did such a pair have to exist? The answer is: This pair is what first amounts to an *organizing* whole, even if not to an organized whole in a single body.

Now if someone asks what a thing is there for, then there are two possible answers. One is that the thing's production and existence do not refer at all to a cause that acts in terms of intentions, and in that case we always mean that the production and existence of the thing are due to the mechanism of nature. The other possible answer is that (the thing is a contingent natural being and so) its existence has some intentional basis. It is hard to separate this [latter] thought from the concept of an organized thing. For, in view of the fact that we have to regard the inner possibility of an organized thing as based on a causality in terms of final causes and on the idea underlying that causality, the only way we can conceive of the existence of this product is as a purpose; for a presented effect is called a *purpose* if the presentation of it is also the basis that determines the intelligent efficient cause to produce this effect. Therefore, if we say that the existence of the thing has some intentional basis, we can proceed in two ways again: We can say that the purpose of the existence of such a natural being is in that thing itself, i.e., the thing is not merely a purpose but also a *final purpose.* Or we can say that the final purpose is outside the thing and in other natural beings, i.e., that although the thing exists purposively it is not a final purpose: rather, it is necessarily a means as well.

But even if we go through all of nature, we still do not find in it, as nature, any being that could claim the distinction of being the final purpose of creation. We can even prove a priori that what might perhaps be an *ultimate purpose* for nature can still, insofar as it is a natural thing, never be a *final purpose,* even if we endowed it with all conceivable [natural] attributes and properties.

If we look at the vegetable kingdom and the immense fertility with which it spreads over almost any soil, we might initially be led to think of it as merely the product of the [same] mechanism that nature displays in the formations of the mineral kingdom.[16] But a closer acquaintance with the indescribably wise organization in the vegetable kingdom prompts us to abandon that thought and ask instead: What are these creatures there for? We might answer: For the animal

426

---

[16] [See Ak. 348–49.]

kingdom, in order to supply it with food, so that it could spread over the earth in the diversity of species it displays. But here the same question arises again: What then are these herbivores there for? The answer might be: For the predators, who can feed only on what has life.[17] Finally the question is: What are the predators good for, along with the other natural kingdoms? For man, for the diverse uses to which his understanding teaches him to put all those creatures; man is the ultimate purpose of creation here on earth, because he is the only being on earth who can form a concept of purposes and use his reason to turn an aggregate of purposively structured things into a system of purposes.

427

We could, alternatively, join Chevalier Linné[18] in taking the seemingly reverse route, and say: The herbivores are there to moderate the opulent growth in the plant kingdom, which would otherwise choke many species of plants; the predators are there to limit the voracity of the herbivores; finally, man is there to hunt the predators in order to diminish their numbers and so establish a certain equilibrium between the productive and the destructive forces of nature. On this alternative, though man might in a certain respect have the dignity of being a purpose, in a different respect he would hold only the rank of a means.

Once we adopt the principle that there is an objective purposiveness in the diverse species of creatures on earth and in their extrinsic relation[s] to one another as purposively structured beings, it is reasonable to think of the[se] relation[s] as having a certain organization in turn, and as [forming] a system, of all the natural kingdoms, in terms of final causes. And yet it seems that experience flatly contradicts such a maxim of reason, especially [the implication] that there is an ultimate purpose of nature. An ultimate purpose of nature is certainly required for such a system to be possible, and we cannot posit it anywhere but in man: But man too is one of the many animal species, and nature has in no way exempted him from its destructive forces any more than from its productive forces,[19]

---

[17] [For Kant's narrow definition of *life*, see Ak. 394 br. n. 7.]

[18] [Carl von Linné, Latinized *Linnaeus*, (1707–78), Swedish botanist and explorer and author of a large number of works. He is best known for his systematic classification of the three kingdoms of nature.]

[19] [Cf. the *Universal Natural History and Theory of the Heavens*, Ak. I, 318.]

but has subjected everything to a natural mechanism without a purpose.

If the natural beings on earth formed a purposively ordered whole, the first intentional arrangement would presumably have to be their habitat, the ground or [other] element on [or] in which they were to thrive, [since] that is the foundation of all organic production. But as we become better acquainted with what that foundation is like, we find that it points to no causes other than those that act wholly unintentionally, causes that are more likely to be devastating than to foster production, order, and purposes. Land and sea contain memorials of mighty devastations that long ago befell them and all creatures living on or in them. Indeed, their entire structure, the strata of the land and the boundaries of the sea, look quite like the product of savage, all-powerful forces of a nature working in a state of chaos. The shape of the land, its structure and its slope, may now seem very purposively arranged: to receive water from the air, to feed the water veins between diverse kinds of layers of soil (each [suitable] for all sorts of products), and to direct the rivers. But a closer investigation of them proves that they are in fact merely the result of eruptions, either of fire or of water, or of upheavals of the ocean. This is how this shape was first produced, but especially also how it was later restructured, a restructuring that brought along with it the destruction of the first organic products on the earth.[20] So the habitat of all these creatures, the native soil (of the land) and the lap (of the sea), provides no indication of having been produced by any but a wholly unintentional mechanism. But, if that is so, how can we, and what right do we have, to demand and assert that those creatures have a

428

[20] We have come to apply the name *natural history* to the description of nature[21] [as it is at present]. If we want to keep using it in that sense, then the [subject] to which [the term] natural history refers literally, namely, an exposition of the earth's former, *ancient* state, could be called instead the *archaeology of nature*, as distinguished from [the archaeology of] *art*. We do in fact have good grounds for venturing conjectures about that ancient state, though we must not hope for certainty. Such an archaeology of nature would cover, for example, petrifactions, just as cut stones, etc. are covered by [the archaeology of] art. We are in fact constantly working—even if slowly, as is proper—in this archaeology (which we call theory of the earth), and so we would be giving the name archaeology of nature not to a merely imaginary investigation of nature, but to one that nature itself invites and summons us to.

[21] [Cf. *On Using Teleological Principles in Philosophy*, Ak. VIII, 161–62, and *On the Various Races of Human Beings*, Ak. II, 434n.]

different origin? [And that holds even for man. For] although a meticulous examination of the traces of those natural devastations seems to prove (in Camper's[22] judgment) that man was not included in those revolutions, yet he is so dependent on the other creatures on earth that, once we grant that a natural mechanism holds sway over the others universally, man too must be considered subject to it, even though his understanding was able to rescue him (for the most part, at least) from those devastations.

This argument, however, seems to prove more than it was intended to prove: not merely that man cannot be an ultimate purpose of nature, and that by the same token the aggregate of organized natural things on earth cannot be a system of purposes, but even that the natural products we earlier considered natural purposes originate from nothing but the mechanism of nature.

429

But [we must not forget] the above solution of the antinomy between the principles of the mechanical and the teleological kind of production of organic natural beings. There we saw that, as far as nature's construction in terms of particular laws is concerned (for whose systematic coherence we do not have the key), those principles pertain merely to reflective judgment: they do not determine the actual [*an sich*] origin of these beings, but only say that the character of our understanding and of our reason is such that the only way we can conceive of the origin of such beings is in terms of final causes. And hence we are certainly permitted to strive as hard and even as boldly as possible to explain such beings mechanically. Indeed, reason calls on us to make this attempt, even though we know that there are subjective grounds why we can never make do with a mechanical explanation, grounds that have to do with the particular kind and limitation of our understanding (and not with any intrinsic contradiction between a mechanical production and an origin in terms of purposes). Finally we saw, in the solution of the antinomy, that the possibility of reconciling the two ways of presenting [how] nature is possible may very well lie in the supersensible principle of nature (nature outside as well as within us). For presentation in terms of final causes is only a subjective condition of the use of our reason, [which applies] when reason wants us to judge certain objects not merely as appearances but insists on

[22] [See Ak. 304 br. n. 34.]

referring these appearances themselves, along with their principles, to the supersensible substrate. Reason insists on making that reference so that it can consider as possible that there be certain laws unifying those appearances, laws that reason can conceive of only as arising from purposes (since [our] reason too has supersensible purposes).

§ 83

On the Ultimate Purpose
That Nature Has
as a Teleological System

We have shown in the preceding section that [certain] principles of reason give us sufficient grounds for judging man—though reflectively rather than determinatively—to be not merely a natural purpose, which we may judge all organized beings to be, but also to be the *ultimate* purpose of nature here on earth, the purpose by reference to which all other natural things constitute a system of purposes. Therefore our next question must be: what is it, within man himself, that is a purpose and that he is to further through his connection with nature? This purpose must either be such as can be fulfilled by nature itself in its beneficence, or else [must] be man's aptitude and skill for [pursuing] various purposes for which he can use nature (outside or within him). On the first alternative the purpose of nature would be man's *happiness,* on the second his *culture.*

430

The concept of happiness is not one that man abstracts (say) from his instincts and hence gets from himself as animal. Rather, it is a mere *idea:* the idea of a state of his, an idea to which he tries to make that state adequate under merely empirical conditions (which is impossible). Man himself formulates this idea; and since his understanding is tied to imagination and the senses, he formulates the idea so diversely and even changes the concept so often that nature, even if it were subjected completely to man's choice, still could not possibly adopt a definite and fixed universal law that would [keep] it in harmony with that wavering concept and so with the purpose that each person chooses to set himself.[23] Even if we restricted the concept of happiness to the true natural needs shared by our entire species, or if instead we maximized man's skill for accomplishing the purposes he imagines, he would still never reach what he means by happiness, and reach what is in fact his own ultimate natural purpose (as distinguished from [*nicht*] the purpose of freedom): for it is not his nature to stop possessing and enjoying at some point and be satisfied. Nature, on the other hand, is very far from having adopted him as its special darling and benefited him in preference to the other animals, but has in fact spared him no more than any other animal from its destructive workings: plague, famine, flood, frost, or attacks from other animals large or small, and so on. What is more, man's own absurd *natural predispositions*[24] land him in further troubles that he thinks up himself, and [make him] put others of his own species in great misery through oppressive domination, barbaric wars, etc., and [so] man himself does all he can to work for the destruction of his own species. Hence even if nature outside us were utterly beneficent, its purpose would not be achieved in a system of nature on earth if that purpose aimed at the happiness of our species, because nature within us is not receptive to it. Therefore, in the chain of natural purposes man is never more than a link: There are indeed many purposes for which he seems to have been determined by nature's predisposition, and with regard to these man is a principle by making himself that; but he is also a means for preserving the purposiveness in the mechanism of the other links. Man is indeed the only being on earth that has understanding and hence an ability to set himself purposes of his own choice, and in this respect he holds the title of lord of nature; and if we regard nature as a teleological system, then it is man's vocation to be the ultimate purpose of nature, but always subject to a condition: he must have the understanding and the will to give both nature and himself reference to a purpose that can be independent of nature, self-sufficient, and a final purpose. The final purpose, however, we must not seek within nature at all.

431

But where in man must we posit at least that *ultimate purpose* of nature? To discover this, we must find out what nature can accomplish in order to prepare man for what he himself must do in order to be a final

[23] [Cf. the *Foundations of the Metaphysics of Morals,* Ak. IV, 395–96, but esp. 418–19. Cf. also the *Critique of Practical Reason,* Ak. 25–26 and 36.]

[24] [To certain affects and inclinations, especially passions. Cf. the *Anthropology,* Ak. VII, 251–82, esp. 265–75. See also *Religion within the Bounds of Reason Alone,* Ak. VI, 19–53.]

purpose, and [then] separate that from all those purposes whose achievability rests on conditions that we can expect nature to fulfill alone.
[Now the] latter kind of purpose is man's happiness on earth, by which
I mean [the achievement of] the sum total of all those of his purposes
that can [be achieved] through nature outside and within him; this is the
matter of all his purposes on earth, and if he makes it his whole purpose
it makes him unable to set a final purpose for his own existence and to
harmonize with this final purpose. Hence among all of his purposes in
nature there remains only this [one], as that which nature can accomplish with a view to the final purpose outside of nature, and this [one]
may therefore be regarded as nature's ultimate purpose: It is a formal
and subjective condition, namely, man's aptitude in general for setting
himself purposes, and for using nature (independently of [the element
of] nature in man's determination of purposes) as a means [for achieving
them] in conformity with the maxims of his free purposes generally.
Producing in a rational being an aptitude for purposes generally (hence
[in a way that leaves] that being free) is *culture*. Hence only culture can
be the ultimate purpose that we have cause to attribute to nature with
respect to the human species. (It cannot be man's own happiness on
earth, let alone [the goal of making] him merely the foremost instrument
for establishing order and accord in nonrational nature outside him).

But not just any culture is adequate for this ultimate purpose of
nature. The culture of *skill* is indeed the foremost subjective condition
for an aptitude to promote [*befördern*] purposes generally; but it is
not adequate to assist [*befördern*] the *will* in the determination and
selection of its purposes, while yet the will's determination and selection of its purposes is surely an essential part of our entire aptitude for
purposes], and is the other condition, besides skill, of this aptitude].
This other condition could be called the culture of discipline [*Zucht
(Disziplin)*]. It is negative and consists in the liberation of the will
from the despotism of desires, a despotism that rivets us to certain
natural things and renders us unable to do our own selecting; we allow
ourselves to be fettered by the impulses that nature gave us only as
guides so that we would not neglect or even injure our animal characteristics, whereas in fact we are free enough to tighten or to slacken, to
lengthen or to shorten them, as the purposes of reason require.

[As for the culture of skill:] It is hard to develop skill in the human
species except by means of inequality among people. The majority
take care, mechanically as it were and without particularly needing
art for this, of the necessities of life for others, who thus have the ease

432

and leisure to work in science and art, the less necessary ingredients in culture. These others keep the majority in a state of oppression, hard labor, and little enjoyment, even though some of the culture of the higher class does gradually spread to the lower also. But on both sides trouble increases with equal vigor as culture progresses. (The height of this progress, when people's propensity to [strive for] what is dispensable begins to interfere with what is indispensable, is called luxury.) For the lower class the trouble results from violence from without, for the higher from insatiability within. And yet this shining misery has to do with the development of man's natural predispositions, and [so] nature still achieves its own purpose, even if that purpose is not ours. The formal condition under which nature can alone achieve this final aim is that constitution of human relations where the impairment to freedom which results from the mutually conflicting freedom [of the individuals] is countered by lawful authority within a whole called *civil society*. For only in this constitution of human relations can our natural predispositions develop maximally. But this constitution requires something further,[25] even if human beings were intelligent enough to discover it and wise enough to submit voluntarily to its constraint: a *cosmopolitan* whole, a system of all states that are in danger of affecting one another detrimentally. Without such a whole—and given how the very possibility of such a scheme is hindered by people's ambition, lust for power, and greed,[26] especially on the part of those in authority—there will inevitably be *war* (in which some states dissolve and split up into smaller ones, while other states unite with smaller ones and try to form a larger whole). Though war is an unintentional human endeavor (incited by our unbridled passions), yet it is also a deeply hidden and perhaps intentional endeavor of the supreme wisdom, if not to establish, then at least to prepare the way for lawfulness along with the freedom of states, and thereby for a unified system of them with a moral basis. Despite the terrible tribulations that war inflicts on the human race, and the perhaps even greater tribulations that oppress us in time of peace because [then] we are constantly preparing for war, still war is one more incentive for us to develop to the utmost all the talents that serve culture (while the

[25] [For a more elaborate discussion of the difficulties involved in achieving a civil society, in particular the dependence of civil society on a cosmopolitan whole, see the *Idea for a Universal History from a Cosmopolitan Point of View* (1784), Ak. VIII, 15–31.]

[26] [For this triad, cf. the *Anthropology*, Ak. VII, 271–74.]

hope for a permanent happiness of the people continues to recede).[27]

As for the discipline of our inclinations: Though our natural predisposition is quite purposive[ly adapted] to [the satisfaction of] our inclinations pertaining to our animal characteristics, the inclinations interfere very much with the development of our humanity, and [so] their discipline is the second requirement for our culture. But in this regard too we find nature acting purposively, for it strives to give us an education that makes us receptive to purposes higher than those that nature itself can provide. Now I cannot dispute the preponderance of evils that the refinement of our taste to the point of its idealization, and even the luxury of [treating] sciences as food for our vanity, shower on us by producing in us so many insatiable inclinations. But we also cannot fail to notice that nature [within us] pursues the purpose of making room for the development of our humanity, namely, by making ever more headway against the crudeness and vehemence of those inclinations that belong to us primarily as animals and that interfere most with our education for our higher vocation (namely, the inclinations [to] enjoyment). [For we have] the fine art[s] and the sciences, which involve a universally communicable pleasure as well as elegance and refinement, and through these they make man, not indeed morally [*sittlich*] better for [life in] society, but still civilized [*gesittet*] for it:[28] they make great headway against the tyranny of man's propensity to the senses, and so prepare him for a sovereignty in which reason alone is to dominate; and the evils that either nature or our quarrelsomeness and selfishness visit on us do also summon, increase, and steel the soul's forces to keep them from succumbing to those evils, and so let us feel a hidden aptitude within us for higher purposes.[29]

434

---

[27] [On this whole topic, cf. the *Idea for a Universal History*, Ak. VIII, 15–31, as well as *Perpetual Peace* (1795), Ak. VIII, 341–86, and *Religion within the Bounds of Reason Alone*, Ak. VI, 19–53.]

[28] [On this contrast, cf. the *Anthropology*, Ak. VII, 244.]

[29] If the value that life has for us is assessed merely in terms of *what we enjoy* (i.e., happiness, the natural purpose of the sum of all our inclinations), then the answer is easy: that value falls below zero. For who indeed would want to start life over under the same conditions, or even under a plan that he had devised himself (though in conformity with the course of nature) but that also aimed merely at enjoyment? We have shown above what value life has on account of its content if we lead it according to the purpose that nature pursues with us; that content consists in *what we do* (not just enjoy), though we are in this never more than a means to an undetermined final purpose. So presumably the only value that remains is the value that we ourselves give our lives through what we not only do, but do purposively and do so independently of nature that even the existence of nature can be a purpose only under this condition [of our acting this way].

§ 84

On the Final Purpose
of the Existence
of a World, i.e.,
of Creation Itself

A *final purpose* is a purpose that requires no other purpose as a condition of its possibility.

If we assume the mere mechanism of nature as our basis for explaining nature's purposiveness, then we cannot ask: What are things in the world there for? For in such an idealistic system the only issue is the physical possibility of things (and if we thought of things as purposes we would merely be reasoning without any object). Whether we interpreted the purposive form of things as an accident or as blind necessity, in either case the question, What are those things there for, would be pointless. On the other hand, if we assume that the connection in terms of purposes in the world is real, and we assume a special kind of causality for it, namely, that of a cause *that acts intentionally,* then we cannot stop at the question: For what [end] do things in the world (organized beings) have the form they have, for what [end] has nature put them into just these relations toward one another? Rather, once we think an understanding that we must regard as the cause that makes such forms possible, forms that we actually find in things, we must also ask what objective basis within this productive understanding could have determined it to [produce] an effect of this kind; and that basis will be the final purpose for which such things are there.

I said above that the final purpose is unconditioned, and that nature would therefore be incapable of achieving it and producing it in accordance with the idea of this purpose. For nothing in nature (considered as a being of sense) has, within nature itself, a basis determining it that is not always conditioned in turn. This holds not merely for nature outside us (material nature) but also for nature within us (thinking nature), though it must be understood here that I am considering within me only what is nature. But a thing that, on account of its objective character, is to exist necessarily as the final

435

purpose of an intelligent cause must be of such a kind that in the order of purposes it depends on no condition other than just the idea of it.

Now in this world of ours there is only one kind of beings with a causality that is teleological, i.e., directed to purposes, but also so constituted that the law in terms of which these beings must determine their purposes is presented by these very beings as unconditioned and independent of conditions in nature, and yet necessary in itself. That being is man, but man considered as noumenon. Man is the only natural being in whom we can nonetheless cognize, as part of his own constitution, a supersensible ability (*freedom*), and even cognize the law and the object of this causality, the object that this being can set before itself as its highest purpose (the highest good in the world).

Now about man, as a moral being, (and so about any other rational being in the world), we cannot go on to ask: For what [end] (*quem in finem*) does he exist? His existence itself has the highest purpose within it; and to this purpose he can subject all of nature as far as he is able, or at least he must not consider himself subjected to any influence of nature in opposition to that purpose. Now if things in the world, which are dependent beings with regard to their existence, require a supreme cause that acts in terms of purposes, then man is the final purpose of creation. For without man the chain of mutually subordinated purposes would not have a complete basis. Only in man, and even in him only as moral subject, do we find unconditioned legislation regarding purposes. It is this legislation, therefore, which alone enables man to be a final purpose to which all of nature is ideologically subordinated.[30]

436

---

[30] It would be possible for the happiness of rational beings in the world to be a purpose of nature, and in that case it would also be its *ultimate* purpose. At least we cannot see a priori why nature could not be so arranged, since this effect, at least as far as we can see, could certainly be brought about by nature's mechanism. But morality and a causality in terms of purposes that is subordinated to it is absolutely impossible through natural causes. For the moral principle that determines us to action is supersensible. Hence it is the only possible [thing] in the order of purposes that is absolutely unconditioned as concerns nature, and hence alone qualifies man, the subject of morality, to be the final purpose of creation to which all of nature is subordinated. Happiness, on the other hand, as the preceding section showed by the testimony of experience, is not even a purpose of nature directed to human beings in preference to other creatures, much less a final purpose of creation. Let human beings forever make it their ultimate subjective purpose; but if I inquire after the final purpose of creation:

§ 85

On Physicotheology[31]

PHYSICOTHEOLOGY is reason's attempt to infer the supreme cause of nature, and the properties of this cause, from the *purposes* of nature (which we can cognize only empirically). A MORAL THEOLOGY (ethicotheology) would be the attempt to infer that cause and its properties from the moral purpose of rational beings in nature (a purpose that we can cognize a priori).

It is natural for physicotheology to come before moral theology. For if we want to infer a world cause *teleologically* from the things in the world, then we must first be given purposes of nature, for which we must then try to find a final purpose, and then for this final purpose the principle of the causality of that supreme cause.

437

We certainly can, and must, follow the teleological principle in many of our investigations of nature, without needing to inquire into the basis for the possibility of purposive causation, a possibility we find [actualized] in various products of nature. But if we do want to have a concept of that basis, then [we find that] we have absolutely no insight into it beyond the mere maxim of reflective judgment: that our cognitive power is of such a character that, if but a single organic product of nature were to be given us, the only basis we can conceive it to have is one that is a cause of nature itself (whether of all

---

For what [end] did human beings have to exist? then I am talking about a supreme objective purpose, such as the highest reason would require for its creation. Now if someone replies: So that beings may exist to whom that supreme cause can be beneficent, then he is contradicting the condition to which man's reason subjects even his most heartfelt wish for happiness (namely, harmony with his own inner moral legislation). This proves that happiness can be only a conditioned purpose, so that it is only as a moral being that man can be the final purpose of creation, with man's state of happiness connected with that [final] purpose only as its consequence, and as dependent on the degree to which man is in harmony with that purpose, the purpose of his existence.

[31] [For other places where Kant gives extended and similar discussions of physicotheology, see *The Only Possible Basis of Proof* (1763), Ak. II, esp. 116–37, and the *Critique of Pure Reason,* esp. A 620–30 = B 648–58.]

of nature or of just this component of it) and is able to cause that product by virtue of [its] understanding. Although this maxim is [only] a principle for judging [things] and in no way helps us to explain natural things and their origin, it does allow us to look beyond nature with some prospect that perhaps we can determine the concept of an original being more closely, a concept that is so unfruitful otherwise.

Now I say that, no matter how far we take physicotheology, it still cannot reveal to us anything about a *final purpose* of creation, for it does not even reach the question about such a purpose. It can indeed justify the concept of an intelligent cause of the world, [by showing that it is] for us the only suitable concept—i.e., suitable for the character of our cognitive power—of the possibility of those things that we can understand [only] in terms of purposes. But physicotheology cannot determine this concept any further, whether from a theoretical or a practical point of view, and [so] it fails to accomplish what it intends: to provide a basis for theology. It remains forever only a physical teleology: for it always considers, and must consider, any reference to purposes as having its conditions within nature, so that it cannot even inquire into the purpose for which nature itself exists ([since] the basis for the existence of nature must be sought outside nature); and yet it is on the determinate idea of this purpose that the determinate concept of that supreme intelligent cause of the world depends, and hence also the possibility of a theology.

A teleological consideration of the world does quite splendidly in certain areas: Of what use are the things in the world to one another? What good is the manifold in a thing to that thing itself? Indeed, we even seem to have grounds for assuming that nothing in the world is gratuitous, but that—on condition that certain things were [meant] to exist (as purposes)—everything is good for something or other *in nature,* so that here the only principle our reason can offer judgment, [to account] for the possibility of the object that it cannot avoid judging teleologically, is to subordinate the mechanism of nature to the architectonic of an intelligent author of the world. It is extremely admirable how well a teleological consideration of the world does in all of this. But since the data, and hence the principles, [that it uses] to *determine* the concept of an intelligent world cause (as supreme artist) are merely empirical, they do not allow us to infer any other

438

properties [of this cause] than those that experience manifests to us in the effects of that cause;[32] and since experience can never encompass all of nature as a system, it must often encounter bases of proof that (seem to) conflict with the concept of that cause and with one another. But even if we could have an empirical overview of the whole system, insofar as it involves mere nature, still experience could never raise us above nature, to the purpose of nature's own existence, and so to the determinate concept of that supreme intelligence.

There is a way to make it seem easy to solve the problem that a physicotheology tries to solve: we can make the problem small. We might squander the concept of a *deity* on every—and there could be one or more of these—intelligent being that we think of as having both many and very great properties, and yet not quite [*überhaupt*] all the properties needed to found a nature that harmonizes with the greatest possible purpose. Again, we might regard it as a trifle to supplement arbitrarily a theory for a deficiency in its bases for proving [the existence of a deity], e.g., if we felt entitled to assume *all possible* perfection where we have only a basis for assuming *much* perfection.[33] (And what is much for us?) [If] physical teleology [takes

---

[32] [On this and the next paragraph, cf. Hume: "When we infer any particular cause from an effect, we must proportion the one to the other, and can never be allowed to ascribe to the cause any qualities, but what are exactly sufficient to produce the effect.... [I]f we ascribe to it further qualities, or affirm it capable of producing other effects, we can only indulge the license of conjecture, and arbitrarily suppose the existence of qualities and energies, without reason or authority." (*Enquiry*, XI, par. 12.)]

[33] [Cf. Hume again: "The Deity is known to us only by his productions. . . . As the universe shews wisdom and goodness, we infer wisdom and goodness. As it shews a particular degree of these perfections, we infer a particular degree of them, precisely adapted to the effect which we examine. But further attributes or further degrees of the same attributes, we can never infer or suppose, by any rules of just reasoning." (Enquiry, XI, 5th par. from the end.) And in the *Dialogues*, Philo says to Cleanthes: "*First*, by this method of reasoning, you renounce all claim to infinity in any of the attributes of the Deity. For, as the cause ought only to be proportioned to the effect, and the effect, so far as it falls under our cognizance, is not infinite, what pretensions have we, upon your suppositions, to ascribe that attribute to the Divine Being? . . . *Secondly*, you have no reason, on your theory, for ascribing perfection to the Deity, even in his finite capacity, or for supposing him free of error, mistake, or incoherence, in his undertakings." (Pt. V, pars. 5–6.) Cf. also below, Ak. 455 incl. br. n. 49.]

such liberties,] then [it] makes weighty claims to the distinction of providing the basis for a theology. But what if we are told to indicate what impels and even justifies us in making those supplementations? In vain would we try to base our justification on the principles of the theoretical use of reason, since that use always requires us to attribute to [the] object of experience that we are trying to explain only properties for which we have empirical data as to their possibility. On closer examination we would see that in fact we have within us a priori an underlying idea of a supreme being, an idea which rests on an entirely different (namely, the practical) use of reason, and that this idea impels us to supplement the deficient presentation (as provided by physical teleology)[34] of the original basis of the purposes in nature until it becomes the concept of a deity. And, [in view of this,] we would not falsely imagine that we had brought about this idea, and with it a theology, by applying reason theoretically to our physical knowledge of the world, much less that we had proved the reality of this idea.

439

One cannot blame the ancients so very much for thinking of all their gods, including even the chief god, as still limited in the way human beings are, despite the considerable diversity in the powers or intentions and preferences they attributed to them. For, on the one hand, when the ancients considered the order and course of things in nature, they found sufficient grounds for assuming that these things were caused by something that was more than mechanical, and for suspecting behind the machinery of this world the intentions of certain higher causes that they could conceive of only as superhuman. But, on the other hand, they also found that—at least as far as we can see—in this world good and bad, purposive and contrapurposive are thoroughly mixed; and they could not take the liberty of nonetheless secretly assuming underlying wise and beneficent purposes, of which after all they saw no proof, for the sake of [supporting] the arbitrary idea of a supremely perfect author [of the world]. Hence the ancients' judgment about the supreme cause of the world could hardly have turned out other than it did, since in terms of maxims of the merely theoretical use of reason they proceeded quite consistently. Others, who were physicists but wanted also to be theologians, tried to satisfy

---

[34] [Parentheses added.]

reason's demand for absolute unity in the principle of natural things by getting this unity from the idea of a being in which, as the sole substance, all those natural things would only inhere as [its] attributes. Though this substance would not be the cause of the world through [its] understanding, it would still be the subject containing all the understanding that the beings of the world have. Hence, though this being would not produce anything in accordance with purposes, yet all things, because of the unity of the subject whose mere attributes they are, must still of necessity relate purposively to one another, even without there being a purpose [or] intention. And so these people introduced [an] idealism concerning final causes: for instead of [making] the unity—which it is so difficult to obtain—of a multitude of purposively connected substances a unity of causal dependence *on one* substance, they turned it into a unity of inherence *in one* substance. This system, considered from the side of the inhering world beings, then became *pantheism;* and considered from the side of the sole subsisting subject, the original being, it (later) became *Spinozism.*[35] Rather than solving the problem concerning the first basis of the purposiveness of nature, this system instead denied it; for the concept of that first basis, deprived of all its reality, had been turned into a mere misinterpretation of [the] universal ontological concept of a thing as such.

440

Hence, if the concept of a deity is to be adequate for our teleological judging of nature, we can never obtain it by following principles of the merely theoretical use of our reason ([and yet] physicotheology is based on these principles alone). For [we are then left with these two alternatives:] On the one alternative, we assert that all teleology is mere deception of the power of judgment as it judges the causal connection among things; we say that the unity of the substance, whose mere manifold of attributes [*Bestimmungen*] nature is, merely makes it seem to us as if there were a universal reference to purposes in nature, and hence we seek refuge with mere mechanism as the sole principle of nature, thereby adopting an idealism concerning final causes. On the other alternative, we may wish to hold on to the realistic principle concerning this special kind of causality, and then regard natural purposes as based either on many intelligent original beings or on only a single one. But once we have nothing left as a

[35] [Cf. Ak. 421 and 393–94.]

basis for the concept of this original being except empirical principles, taken from what actual connections in terms of purposes [are found] in the world[, we face two consequences]: first, we are at a loss about the discordance, as far as the unity of a purpose is concerned, displayed by nature in many examples; second, the concept of a single intelligent cause, as this concept is if justified by mere experience, will never be determinate [*bestimmt*] enough for any theology that is to be of any (theoretical or practical) use whatsoever.

Physical teleology does induce us to look for a theology; but it cannot produce one, no matter how far we take our empirical investigation of nature and use ideas of reason to help [us with] whatever connections in terms of purposes we discover there. (For physical problems, these ideas must be theoretical.) There is no point, we may rightly complain, in basing all these arrangements [in nature] on [the theoretical idea of] a great and to us unfathomable understanding, and in having that understanding order this world according to intentions. For that still leaves us without the final intention, about which nature does not tell us anything, nor ever will, while yet, apart from this final intention, we can form no common reference point for all these natural purposes, no adequate teleological principle: no principle that would allow us to cognize all the purposes [as united] in a system, and also to form a concept of the supreme understanding, as cause of such a [systematic] nature, that our power of judgment could use as a standard for its teleological reflection on that nature. Therefore, we would still not have [arrived at] a *wisdom* to [provide] a final purpose, but only [at] an *artistic understanding* to [provide] sporadic purposes, even though the basis determining that understanding must actually be in that final purpose. Only pure reason can provide a priori a final purpose (because all the purposes in the world are empirically conditioned and [hence] cannot contain what is good absolutely, but only what is good for this or that, i.e., for some contingent aim). And only a final purpose would instruct me how I must conceive of the supreme cause of nature in order to judge nature as a teleological system: [i.e.,] what properties this supreme cause must have, in what degree it must have them, and what its relation must be [to nature]. Without a final purpose, the only concept I have of that original understanding is the very limited one that I am able to derive from my scant knowledge of the world: the concept of that original being's might to actualize its ideas, of its will

441

to do so, and so on. What then would give me the ability and the right to expand this concept arbitrarily and supplement it until it becomes the idea of an all-wise [and] infinite being? In order to do this theoretically, I myself would have to be omniscient, so that I could have insight into the purposes of nature in their overall coherence, and could be able moreover to conceive of all possible alternative designs, so that by a comparison with these I could have grounds for judging the present one to be best. For without such perfect knowledge of the effect I cannot infer a determinate concept of the supreme cause—which has to be the concept of a deity, i.e., an intelligence that is infinite in all respects—and [so] produce a foundation for theology.

Hence, even if we expand physical teleology as far as possible, we must surely keep to the principle we stated above: that, in view of the character and principles of our cognitive power, the only way we can conceive nature as regards what purposive arrangements we have come to know in it is by conceiving nature as the product of an understanding to which it is subjected. But as to whether this understanding might also have pursued a final intention with the whole of nature and the production of that whole (in which case this intention would not lie in nature as the world of sense): this [is something that] a theoretical investigation of nature can never reveal to us. Rather, no amount of knowledge of nature [will] allow us to decide whether it is indeed [through] a final purpose that the supreme cause is nature's original basis, rather than [merely] through an understanding whose very nature necessarily determines it to produce certain forms (by analogy with what we call artistic instinct in animals), in which case there would be no need for us to attribute even wisdom to it, let alone supreme wisdom combined with all the other properties that are required to make its product perfect.

Hence physicotheology is physical teleology misunderstood. It is of no use to theology except as a preliminary (a propaedeutic). But [even] for that aim it is adequate not by itself, as its name tries to suggest, but only if we supplement it by a further principle for its support.

442

§ 86

On Ethicotheology[36]

There is a judgment that even the commonest understanding cannot escape when it meditates about the existence of the things in the world and of the world itself. It is the judgment that all these diverse creatures would exist for nothing if they did not include human beings (or some kind of [*überhaupt*] rational beings), no matter how artfully devised these creatures may be, and how diversely, coherently, and purposively interrelated, and the judgment that even the whole of all the systems of these, which we incorrectly call worlds, would then exist for nothing. In other words, it is the judgment that without man all of creation would be a mere wasteland, gratuitous and without a final purpose. On the other hand, it is not by reference to man's cognitive power (theoretical reason) that the existence of everything else in the world first gets its value, i.e., it is not [because] (say) there is someone *to contemplate* the world. For if all this contemplation offered to man's presentation nothing but things without a final purpose, then the fact that the world is cognized cannot make its existence valuable; only if we presupposed that the world has a final purpose, could its contemplation itself have a value by reference to that purpose. Nor do we think of creation as [having been] given a final purpose with reference to the feeling of pleasure, and to the sum of that pleasure; in other words, we do not assess the absolute value of the existence of the world by reference to [man's] well-being, or enjoyment (whether bodily or intellectual)—in a word, happiness. For the fact that man, once he exists, makes happiness his own final intention gives us no concept [that tells us] for what [end] he exists at all, and what his own value is, on account of which his existence should be made agreeable to him. Therefore, we must already presuppose that man is the final purpose of creation, if we are to have a rational basis as to why nature, considered as an absolute whole in terms of prin-

[36] [For other places where Kant gives extended and similar discussions of moral theology, see the *Critique of Pure Reason,* A 632–42 = B 660–70 and A 804–19 = B 832–47; the *Critique of Practical Reason,* Ak. V, 124–48; and *Religion within the Bounds of Reason Alone,* Ak. VI, 137–47.]

ciples of purposes, should have to harmonize with [the goal of achieving] his happiness. Hence the only [thing] which can give man's existence an absolute value, and by reference to which the existence of the world can have a *final purpose,* is the power of desire. But I do not mean here that power of desire which makes man dependent on nature (through impulses of sense), i.e., not the one according to which the value of man's existence depends on what he receives and enjoys. I mean the value that he can only give himself, and that consists in what he does, how and on what principles he acts, not as a link in nature, but in the *freedom* of his power of desire; in other words, I mean a good will.

In fact, even the commonest judgment of sound human reason, once it has been led to address the question and been prompted to try a judgment on it, agrees completely with this view, that it is only as a moral being that man can be a final purpose of creation. People will say: If this person does not possess a good will, what point is there in his having all this talent, assuming even that he applies it very much in action and thereby exerts a useful influence on his community, so that he is very valuable in relation both to his own state of happiness and to the benefit of others? If we consider what this person is like inwardly, then he is an object worthy of contempt; and if creation is indeed to have a final purpose, then the only way for this person's existence to be consistent with that final purpose is on this condition: while as a human being he is [of course] a member of creation, as an evil human being in a world subject to moral laws he still must, in accordance with these laws, forfeit his subjective purpose (i.e., happiness).

Therefore, if we find in the world arrangements in terms of purposes, and we follow reason's inevitable demand to subordinate these merely conditioned purposes to a supreme unconditioned one, i.e., a final purpose, then, to begin with, we are obviously not concerned with a purpose of (i.e., within) nature, so far as nature [already] exists, but with the purpose of the [very] existence of nature and all its arrangements. In other words, we are then concerned with the ultimate *purpose of creation,* and actually, within that purpose, with the supreme condition under which alone there can be a final purpose (where this final purpose is the basis that determines a supreme understanding to produce the beings of the world).

Therefore, it is only as a moral being that we acknowledge man to be   444
the purpose of creation. Thus we now have, in the first place, a basis,
or at least the primary condition, for regarding the world as a whole
that coheres in terms of purposes, and as a *system* of final causes.
But above all, in referring natural purposes to an intelligent world
cause, as the character of our reason forces us to do, we now have *a*
principle that allows us to conceive of the nature and properties of
this first cause, i.e., the supreme basis of the kingdom of purposes,
and hence allows us to give determination to the concept of this
cause. Physical teleology was unable to do this; all it could do was
to give rise to concepts of this supreme basis that were indeterminate
and on that very account were inadequate for both theoretical and
practical use.

Determining the principle of the causality of the original being in this
way has the following consequences: We shall have to think of this
being not merely as an intelligence and as legislating to nature, but
also as the legislating sovereign in a moral kingdom of purposes. In
reference to the *highest good*—possible solely under the reign of this
being—namely, the existence of rational beings under moral laws,
we shall think of this original being as *omniscient,* so that even our
inmost attitudes (in which the proper moral value of the acts of rational world beings consists) will not be hidden from it. We shall think
of it as *omnipotent,* so that it can make all of nature accord with that
highest purpose. We shall think of it as *omnibenevolent* as well as *just,*
because these two properties (which together constitute *wisdom*)
are the conditions under which a supreme cause of the world can
be the cause of the world [taken] as the highest good under moral
laws. And we shall similarly have to think of this being as having
all the remaining transcendental properties (for goodness and justice
are moral properties), such as *eternity, omnipresence,* etc., which
[achieving] such a final purpose presupposes. In this way *moral* teleology compensates for the deficiency of *physical* teleology and for
the first time supplies a basis for a *theology.* For physical teleology
on its own, if it proceeded consistently instead of borrowing, unnoticed, from moral teleology, could not provide a basis for anything
but a *demonology,* which is incapable of [providing] a determinate
concept [of the deity].

But the principle that [allows us to] refer the world to a supreme
cause, as deity, because some of the beings in it are morally destined

for a purpose, does not do this by merely supplementing the physicoteleological basis for proving [the existence of this deity], in which case it would necessarily presuppose that basis. Rather, it is sufficient even *by itself* to provide this reference (and it [even assists physical teleology by) directing our attention to the purposes of nature and by [inviting us] to investigate the unfathomably great art that lies hidden behind nature's forms, so that the ideas that pure practical reason supplies may find incidental confirmation in natural purposes).[37] For the concept of world beings under moral laws is an a priori principle, by which man must necessarily judge himself. Moreover, there is another principle that reason regards a priori as necessary[,] for judging the existence of things teleologically: the principle that, if there is indeed a world cause that acts intentionally and aims at a purpose, then the possibility of a creation requires [*Bedingung*] the mentioned moral relation [of the world to a supreme cause *as deity*] just as necessarily as it requires the relation [to a supreme cause] in terms of physical laws. (The moral relation is required if that intelligent cause pursues [not just a purpose but] a final purpose as well.) What matters, then, is whether we do have a basis, sufficient for reason (whether speculative or practical), for attributing a *final purpose* to the supreme cause acting in terms of purposes. For [even] a priori we may then consider as certain, given the subjective character of our reason, or given even that of the reason of other beings no matter how such reason might be conceived, that this final purpose can only be *man under moral laws.* On the other hand, we are quite unable to cognize a priori the purposes of nature in the physical order; above all we have no insight of any kind [that tells us] that a nature could not exist without such purposes.

445

Comment

Consider a human being at those moments when his mind is attuned to moral feeling: If, surrounded by a beautiful nature, he finds himself calmly and serenely enjoying his existence, he will feel within him a

---

[37] [Parentheses added.]

need to be grateful for this to someone. Or suppose that, at another time [but] in the same frame of mind, he finds himself under the pressure of many duties that he is willing to perform and can perform only through voluntary sacrifice: he will feel within him a need that in performing them he will also have carried out something commanded, and have obeyed some sovereign. Again, suppose that perhaps he has unthinkingly violated his duty, yet without having made himself answerable to [other] people: still, within him he will sternly reprimand himself in words that sound as if they were spoken by a judge to whom he had to account for his action. In a word: he has a need for a moral intelligence, because he exists for a purpose and needs a being that caused both him and the world in conformity with that purpose. There would be no point in artful attempts to find incentives behind these feelings, for they are linked directly to the purest moral attitude: *gratitude, obedience,* and *humiliation* (submission to deserved punishment) are special attunements of the mind to duty. Rather, in such cases the mind has the inclination to expand its moral attitude, and voluntarily thinks an object that is not in the world, so that it may possibly do its duty to that [being] as well. Therefore, it is at least possible—and the moral way of thinking even contains a basis for it—to form a presentation of a pure moral need for the existence of a being under which our morality gains either in fortitude or (at least according to our presentation) in range, namely, by gaining a new object to which we can apply it. In other words, it is at least possible to assume a being [that exists] apart from the world, and that legislates morally, and to make this assumption without any concern about theoretical proof, let alone selfish interest, but on a basis that (while indeed only subjective) is purely moral and free from all foreign influence: on the mere recommendation of a practical reason that legislates only to itself. Suppose even that such an attunement of the mind occurred rarely, or that it did not persist but passed swiftly and without lasting effect, or without inducing us to meditate a little about the object presented in such a shadowy image and to attempt to bring it under distinct concepts: yet the basis for this mental attunement is unmistakable, i.e., its basis is the moral predisposition within us, as the subjective principle not to settle for considering the world in terms of the purposiveness it has through natural causes, but to regard the world [itself] as based on a supreme cause that rules nature in terms of moral principles. Add to this the fact that we feel urged by

446

the moral law to strive toward a universal highest purpose, while yet we feel that we and all of nature are incapable of achieving it. Add also the fact that it is only insofar as we strive toward that purpose, that we may judge ourselves as conforming to the final purpose of an intelligent world cause (if there be such a cause). And so practical reason gives us a pure moral basis for assuming this cause (since we can do so without contradiction), even if only for the sake of avoiding the risk of [having to] regard that striving as wholly futile in its effects and of therefore allowing it to flag.

447   By all of this I wish to convey only the following: First, while *fear* was first able to give rise to *gods* (i.e., demons), it is *reason* that, by means of its moral principles, was first able to give rise to the concept of *God* (and it did so despite the fact that people were usually very ignorant in the teleology of nature, or had serious doubts about it because it is so difficult to [find] a sufficiently established principle that will reconcile those appearances [of nature] that contradict one another in teleological terms). Second, the inner *moral* destination of man's existence for a purpose has compensated for the deficiency in our knowledge of nature, by directing us to add something to the final purpose of the existence of all things, a purpose whose principle satisfies reason only *ethically:* to add, [namely,] the thought of the supreme cause (as a *deity,* i.e.,) as having properties that enable it to subject all of nature to that single intention (with nature merely as the instrument for achieving this intention).

§ 87

On the Moral Proof of the Existence of God

There is a *physical teleology;* it provides us with a basis that gives us sufficient proof, for theoretically reflective judgment, for assuming the existence of an intelligent cause of the world. But we also find in ourselves, and even more so in the general concept of a rational being endowed with freedom (of its causality), a *moral teleology.* But our reference to a purpose, and with it the law that governs it, can be determined a priori within ourselves, and hence can be cognized as necessary; hence for *this*[38] [reference to a purpose] moral teleology does not require an intelligent cause outside us [to account] for that inner lawfulness, just as the purposive[ness] we find in the geometric properties of figures (namely, for various possible uses of them by art) does not entitle us to look beyond them to a supreme understanding that imparts it to them. On the other hand, this moral teleology does deal with us as beings of the world and hence as beings connected with other things in the world; and those same moral laws enjoin us to direct our judging to those other things [regarded] either as purposes or as objects for which we ourselves are the final purpose. This moral teleology, then, deals with the reference [*Beziehung*] of our own causality to purposes, and even to a final purpose at which we must aim in the world, and also with the reciprocal relation [*Beziehung*] the world has with that moral purpose and with how we can, as far as external [nature] is concerned, carry it out (for which a physical teleology cannot give us any guidance). Now this moral teleology [does] raise this necessary question: Does this moral teleology compel [us in] our rational judging to go beyond the world and seek an intelligent supreme principle [so as to account] for that relation of nature to what is moral in us, in order that we may form a presentation of nature as purposive also in relation to our inner moral legislation and to how we can carry it out? Hence there is indeed a moral teleology. It is connected with the *nomothetic* of freedom on the one hand and with that of nature on the other, [and it is so connected] just as necessarily as civil legislation is connected with the question of where we must seek executive authority, and as there is connection in everything generally where reason has to state a principle [to account] for the actuality of a certain lawful order of things that is possible only in terms of ideas. Let me begin by stating how from that moral teleology and its relation to physical teleology reason advances to *theology*. After that I shall make some observations about the possibility and cogency of this kind of inference.

448

If we assume that the existence of certain things (or even only of certain forms of things) is contingent and hence possible only through something else as its cause, then we can seek the supreme basis of this

---

[38] [Emphasis added.]

causality, and hence the unconditioned basis for what is conditioned, either in the physical or in the teleological order (i.e., in terms of the *nexus effectivus* or the *nexus finalis*). In other words, we may ask either: What is the supreme producing cause? or: What is the supreme (i.e., absolutely unconditioned) purpose that this cause pursues, i.e., the final purpose for which it produces these or all of its products? In the second question we are of course presupposing that this cause is capable of forming a presentation of purposes, and hence that it is an intelligent being, or at least that we must conceive of it as acting according to the laws of such a being.

Now, supposing we follow the teleological order, there is a *principle* to which even the commonest human reason is obliged to give immediate assent: that if there is indeed to be *a final purpose* that reason has to indicate a priori, then it can only be *man* (or any rational being in the world) *under moral laws*.[39] For (so we all judge) if the world consisted only of lifeless beings, or if it included living beings that

449

---

[39] I say deliberately: *under* moral laws. The final purpose of creation is not man [acting] *in accordance with* moral laws, i.e., a man whose behavior conforms to them. For the[se] latter expression[s] would say more than we know, namely, that an author of the world has the power to ensure that man will at all times behave in accordance with the moral laws. To [know] that, we would need a concept of freedom and of nature (only for nature is an external author conceivable) that implied that we had insight both into the supersensible substrate of nature and into the identity of this substrate with what the causality [that acts] through freedom makes possible in the world; but such insight far surpasses that of our reason. Only of *man under moral laws* can we say, without overstepping the limits of our insight, that his existence is the final purpose of the world. And this [view] agrees perfectly with the judgment that human reason makes when it reflects morally on the course of the world. Even in evil [deeds] we believe we perceive the traces of a wise reference to a purpose, provided we see that the wanton villain does not die until he has suffered the punishment he deserves for his misdeeds. According to our concepts of free causality, whether our conduct is good or evil depends on ourselves; but the highest wisdom in the government of the world we posit in this [arrangement]: that the opportunity for good conduct, but the consequence of both good and bad conduct, is ordained according to moral laws. In the latter [part of the arrangement] consists, properly speaking, the glory of God, and hence it is not unfitting if theologians call it the ultimate purpose of creation. I should add that in speaking of creation I mean no more than I have said here, namely, the cause of the *existence of a world*, or of the things in it (the substances); that is in fact what the proper concept of the word conveys (*actuatio substantiae est creatio*[40]), so that this [definition] does not already presuppose a freely acting and hence intelligent cause (whose existence we first of all want to prove).

[40] [Creation is the actualization of a substance.]

were, however, nonrational, the existence of such a world would have no value whatever, because there would exist in it no being that had the slightest concept of a value. But suppose even there were rational beings [in the world], but that their reason were able only to posit the value of the existence of things in nature's relation to these beings (their well-being), but not able to procure that value originally [and] on its own (in its freedom): then there would indeed be purposes in the world (relative ones), but no final (i.e., absolute) purpose, because the existence of such rational beings would still always be purposeless. Moral laws, on the other hand, have this peculiar characteristic: they prescribe something to reason and they prescribe it as a purpose not subject to a condition, and hence just as the concept of a final purpose requires; therefore, this kind of reason is one that in [its] relation to purpose[s] can be its own supreme law. Hence the only conceivable final purpose of the existence of a world is the existence of this kind of reason, in other words, the existence of rational beings under moral laws. But if this is not so,[41] then the existence of the world is either based on no purpose at all in the cause, or only on purposes without a final purpose.

450

The moral law is reason's formal condition for the use of our freedom and hence obligates us all by itself, independently of any purpose whatever as material condition. But it also determines for us, and a priori, a final purpose, and makes it obligatory for us to strive toward [achieving] it; and that purpose is the *highest good in the world* that we can achieve through freedom.

The subjective condition under which man (and, as far as we can conceive, any [other] rational [and] finite being as well) can set himself a final purpose under the above law, is happiness. Hence the highest physical good we can [achieve] in the world is *happiness,* and this is what we are to further as the final purpose as far as we can, [though] subject to the objective condition that man be in harmony with the law of *morality,*[42] [since] our worthiness to be happy consists in that harmony.

Hence there are two requirements [we must fulfill in order to

[41] [I.e., if the existence of rational beings under moral laws is not the final purpose, while yet no other final purpose is conceivable.]

[42] [Cf., above all, the *Critique of Pure Reason,* A 804–19 = B 832–47, and the *Critique of Practical Reason,* Ak. V, 107–13, but also the *Anthropology,* Ak. VII, 277.]

achieve] the final purpose that the moral law enjoins on us.[43] Yet all our rational powers still do not enable us to form a presentation of these two requirements [considered fulfilled] as *connected* through mere natural causes and [yet] as commensurate with the idea of that final purpose. Hence the concept of the *practical necessity* of [achieving] such a purpose by applying our forces does not harmonize with the theoretical concept of the *physical possibility* of its being achieved, if the causality of nature is the only causality (of a means [for achieving it]) that we connect with our freedom.

Hence in order to set ourselves a final purpose in conformity with the moral law, we must assume a moral cause of the world (an author of the world); and to the extent that setting ourselves a final purpose is necessary, to that extent (i.e., to the same degree and on the same ground) it is also necessary that we assume [that there is] a moral cause of the world: in other words, that there is a God.[44]

451

This proof, to which we could easily give the form of logical precision, is not trying to say that it is as necessary to assume that God exists as it is to acknowledge that the moral law is valid,[45] so that anyone who cannot convince himself that God exists may judge himself released from the obligations that the moral law imposes. No! All we would have to give up [if we could not convince ourselves that God exists] is our *aiming* at that final purpose that we are to achieve in the world by complying with the moral law (in other words, our aiming at the highest good in the world: a happiness of rational beings that harmoniously accompanies their compliance with moral laws); every rational being would still have to cognize himself as strictly

---

[43] [Man's happiness, but as conditional on his harmony with the moral law.]

[44] This moral argument is not meant to provide an *objectively* valid proof of the existence of God. It is not meant to prove to the skeptic that there is a God, but that he *must adopt* the assumption of this proposition as one of the maxims of his practical reason if he wants to think consistently in morality. Nor is the argument meant to say that it is necessary *for morality* [*Sittlichkeit*] that we assume that the happiness of all rational beings in the world is [to be] proportionate [*gemäß*] to their morality [*Moralität*], but rather that *morality makes* it necessary for us to make this assumption. Hence this argument is sufficient *subjectively*, for moral beings.

[45] [Cf. the *Critique of Practical Reason*, Ak. V, 125–26, and *Religion within the Bounds of Reason Alone*, Ak. VI, 3–4.]

bound by what morality prescribes, because the moral laws are formal and command unconditionally, without regard to purposes (which are the matter of volition). On the other hand, one of the requirements of the final purpose, as practical reason prescribes it to the beings of the world, is a purpose that is irresistible and is put into these beings by their nature (as finite beings); [but] all that reason insists upon concerning this purpose [happiness] is that [our achieving] it be subject to the moral law *as* its inviolable *condition,* or that it[s attainment] be made universal only in accordance with that law, so that what reason makes the final purpose is the furtherance of happiness in harmony with morality. Now the moral law commands us to further that final purpose (with regard to the beings of the world) as far as we can, whatever may be the result of our endeavor. Fulfillment of duty consists in the form of the earnest will, not in the intermediate causes [responsible] for success.

Suppose, then, that a person, partly because all the highly praised speculative arguments [for the existence of God] are so weak, and partly because he finds many irregularities both in nature and in the world of morals, became persuaded of the proposition: There is no God.[46] Still, if because of this he regarded the laws of duty as merely imaginary, invalid, nonobligatory, and decided to violate them boldly, he would in his own eyes be a worthless human being. Indeed, even if such a person could later overcome his initial doubts and convince himself that there is a God after all, still with his way of thinking he would forever remain a worthless human being. For while he might fulfill his duty ever so punctiliously as far as effects are concerned, he would be doing so from fear, or for reward, rather than with an attitude of reverence for duty. Conversely, if he believed [in the existence of God] and complied with his duty sincerely and unselfishly according to his conscience, and yet immediately considered himself free from all moral obligation every time he experimentally posited that he might some day become convinced that there is no God, his inner moral attitude would indeed have to be in bad shape.

Therefore, let us consider the case of a righteous man (Spinoza, for

452

---

[46] [Cf. *On the Failure of All Philosophical Endeavors in Theodicy* (1791), Ak. VIII, 253–71.]

example) who actively reveres the moral law [but] who remains firmly persuaded that there is no God and (since, as far as [achieving] the object of morality is concerned, the consequence is the same) that there is also no future life: How will he judge his own inner destination to a purpose, [imposed] by the moral law? He does not require that complying with that law should bring him an advantage, either in this world or in another; rather, he is unselfish and wants only to bring about the good to which that sacred law directs all his forces. Yet his effort [encounters] limits: For while he can expect that nature will now and then cooperate contingently with the purpose of his that he feels so obligated and impelled to achieve, he can never expect nature to harmonize with it in a way governed by laws and permanent rules (such as his inner maxims are and must be). Deceit, violence, and envy will always be rife around him, even though he himself is honest, peaceable, and benevolent. Moreover, as concerns the other righteous people he meets: no matter how worthy of happiness they may be, nature, which pays no attention to that, will still subject them to all the evils of deprivation, disease, and untimely death, just like all the other animals on the earth. And they will stay subjected to these evils always, until one vast tomb engulfs them one and all (honest or not, that makes no difference here) and hurls them, who managed to believe they were the final purpose of creation, back into the abyss of the purposeless chaos of matter from which they were taken. And so this well-meaning person would indeed have to give up as impossible the purpose that the moral laws obligated him to have before his eyes, and that in compliance with them he did have before his eyes. Alternatively, suppose that, regarding this [purpose] too, he wants to continue to adhere to the call of his inner moral vocation, and that he does not want his respect for the moral law, by which this law directly inspires him to obey it, to be weakened, as would result from the nullity of the one ideal final purpose that is adequate to this respect's high demand (such weakening of his respect would inevitably impair his moral attitude): In that case he must—from a practical point of view, i.e., so that he can at least form a concept of the possibility of [achieving] the final purpose that is morally prescribed to him— assume the existence of a *moral* author of the world, i.e., the existence of a God; and he can indeed make this assumption, since it is at least not intrinsically contradictory.

453

§ 88

Restriction of the Validity
of the Moral Proof

Pure reason is [not only a theoretical but also] a practical power: our power to determine the free use of our causality by means of ideas (pure rational concepts). It contains a principle that regulates our acts, namely, the moral law, and through this [law] it provides us in addition with a principle that is subjectively constitutive: the concept of an object that only reason can think [the final purpose] and that we are to actualize in the world through our acts. Hence the idea of a final purpose [that we are to pursue] in using our freedom according to moral laws has subjective *practical* reality: reason determines us a priori to strive to the utmost to further the highest good in the world. This highest good in the world consists in the combination of universal happiness, i.e., the greatest welfare of the rational beings in the world, with the supreme condition of their being good, namely, that they be moral in maximal conformity with the [moral] law. Therefore, the final purpose has two components: our happiness and our morality. Now as regards our morality, we are free from the effects that nature contributes, and [hence] it is established a priori and dogmatically that our morality is possible. But the possibility of the other component of the final purpose, our happiness, has an empirical condition, for it depends on how nature is constituted (i.e., on whether or not nature harmonizes with that final purpose), and [hence] it is problematic from a theoretical point of view. Therefore, in order for the concept of the final purpose of rational beings in the world to have objective theoretical reality, not only must a [moral] final purpose be set before us a priori, but creation, i.e., the world itself, must also have a final purpose for its existence; for if indeed creation has a final purpose, then we have to conceive of it as harmonizing with the moral final purpose ([since] only the moral final purpose makes the concept of a[ny] purpose [of creation] possible). If we could prove a priori that the existence of the world has a final purpose, then the final purpose [of rational beings in the world] would have not only subjective but also objective reality.

454

[But can we?] It is true that we find purposes in the world, and physical teleology exhibits them on such a scale that, if we judge by reason, we are ultimately justified in assuming, as a principle for investigating nature, that nothing whatever in nature is without a purpose. Yet if we seek the final purpose of nature, we seek it in vain if we look for it within nature itself. Hence, just as the idea of that final purpose resides only in reason, so we can and must seek that purpose itself only in rational beings: [only there] is this purpose objectively possible. But the practical reason of these beings does more than indicate that final purpose: it also determines this concept by [stating] what conditions [must be met] if [achieving] a final purpose of creation is to be conceivable for us.

Here a question arises: can we not establish the objective reality of the concept of a final purpose of creation in a way that would satisfy pure reason's theoretical demands? Even if we could not do this apodeictically, for determinative judgment, could we not do it in a way that would be adequate for the maxims that judgment uses in reflecting theoretically? [Surely] this much at least we may require of speculative[47] philosophy, which undertakes to connect the moral purpose with the natural purposes by means of the idea of a single purpose. Yet even this, little though it is, is far more than speculative philosophy can ever accomplish.

If we followed the principle of theoretically reflective judgment, what we would say is: If [in order to account] for the purposive products of nature we have a basis for assuming a supreme cause of nature, whose causality in actualizing (creating) nature we must think of as different in kind from the one that nature's mechanism requires, namely, as the causality of an understanding, then presumably we also have a sufficient basis for thinking of this original being as pursuing not merely purposes [manifested] everywhere in nature, but as pursuing also a final purpose. And though this [reasoning] would not establish the existence of such a being, it would at least suffice (as we saw in physical teleology) to convince us that, if we are to grasp the possibility of such a world, we cannot do this in terms of

---

[47] [For Kant's distinction between 'speculative' and 'theoretical,' see below, Ak. 456 br. n. 51.]

mere purposes, but must base its existence on a final purpose as well.

And yet [the concept of a] final purpose is merely a concept of our practical reason; we cannot infer it from any data of experience, so as to judge nature theoretically [in terms of it], nor can we apply it to cognition of nature. There is no other possible use for this concept except for [our employment of] practical reason according to moral laws; and the final purpose of creation is [nothing other than] that constitution of the world which harmonizes with the only [thing that, by way of a final purpose,] we can indicate determinately according to laws: the final purpose that our pure practical reason has, namely, insofar as it is to be practical. Now since the final purpose of pure practical reason is enjoined on us by the moral law, this law provides us—from a practical point of view, namely, so that we shall apply our forces toward achieving that final purpose—with a basis for assuming that this final purpose is possible, that it can be achieved,[48] and hence also that the nature of things is such that it harmonizes with that [aim] (since we could not achieve the final purpose if nature did not help us by fulfilling a condition of that possibility that is not within our power). Hence we have a moral basis for thinking that, since there is a world, there also is a final purpose of creation.

This is not yet the inference from moral teleology to a theology, i.e., to the existence of a moral author of the world, but only to a final purpose of creation that we make determinate in this way. It is a second inference [if we conclude] that this creation, i.e., the existence of things in conformity with a *final purpose,* requires us to make two assumptions: first, that there is, as author of the world, an intelligent being (this was required in order for those things of nature to be possible that we had to judge to *be purposes*); but, second, that [this] being is not merely intelligent but also *moral,* and hence a

[48] [Cf. *Perpetual Peace*, Ak. VIII, 370: "Morality, as such, is practical [*Praxis*] in an objective sense of this term, for it is the sum total of laws that command unconditionally how we *ought* to act; and it is obviously absurd to grant the authority of this concept of duty and then go on to claim that yet we *cannot* [do our duty], since in that case this concept would automatically drop out of morality ([since] *ultra posse nemo obligatur* [no one has an obligation to do more than he can]). . . ."]

455

God.[49] We can see from the character of this second inference that we make it only for [the use of] judgment in accordance with concepts of practical reason, and hence for reflective rather than determinative judgment. For though in us [human beings] morally practical reason differs essentially in its principles from technically practical reason,[50] we cannot claim to see that the same must hold for the supreme cause of the world once we assume it as an intelligence; [i.e.,] we cannot claim to see that the final purpose requires that this cause has a special kind of causality that differs from the one it must have to [produce] mere purposes of nature; and hence we cannot claim that our final purpose provides us not merely with a *moral basis* for assuming a final purpose of creation ([with creation] as [its] effect), but also with a *moral being* as the original basis of creation. What we can say, however, is this: that *the character of our power of reason is such* that we cannot at all grasp how such a purposiveness as there is in this final purpose is possible, namely, a purposiveness that has reference to *the moral law* and its object, unless we assume an author and ruler of the world who is also a moral legislator.

456

Hence it is merely *for the practical use* of our reason that we have established sufficiently the actuality of a supreme author who legislates morally, and we have not determined anything theoretically regarding the existence of this author. For even without this [theoretical determination], reason's own legislation enjoins on us a purpose, and the possibility of [achieving] this purpose requires that reason has an idea that removes (sufficiently for reflective judgment) the obstacle

---

[49] [Cf. Hume, who, in the *Dialogues* (Pt. V, next to last paragraph), has Philo say: "In a word, Cleanthes, a man who follows your hypothesis [that a God is needed to account for the order in the world] is able, perhaps, to assert or conjecture that the universe sometime arose from something like design; but beyond that position he cannot ascertain one single circumstance, and is left afterwards to fix every point of his theology [including the *moral* properties of the deity] by the utmost license of fancy and hypothesis." Even later on (Pt. XII), after Philo *seems* to have reversed himself on his assessment of the argument from design (the standard view is to discount this "reversal," as well as a similar position in the *Natural History of Religion,* on various evidence, both internal and external), he accepts the argument (Pt. XII, par. 8) only for the *natural* attributes of the deity, not for the *moral* attributes, adding merely (and independently from the argument) that "the Supreme Being is *allowed* to be absolutely and entirely perfect." (Emphasis added.)]

[50] [For this distinction, cf. above, Ak. 171–73.]

that arises from our inability to comply with that legislation if we adhere merely to the natural concept of the world. And from this [i.e., from the fact that achievability of that final purpose requires that reason has such an idea] that idea gets practical reality, even though [we] have no means whatever of providing it with reality from a theoretical point of view, i.e., for explaining nature and determining the supreme cause, and [hence] for speculative cognition.[51] For theoretically reflective judgment, physical teleology sufficiently proved, from the purposes of nature, [the existence of] an intelligent cause. Moral teleology proves this [existence] for practical [reflective] judgment, namely, through the concept of a final purpose that moral teleology is compelled to attribute to creation from a practical point of view. Now the objective reality of the idea of God, as moral author of the world, cannot be established by [appeal to] physical purposes *alone.* Yet if we combine our cognition of physical purposes with that of the moral purpose, then, because of pure reason's maxim to strive to unify principles as much as we can, physical purposes are very important, since they support the practical reality of the idea of God by the reality that from a theoretical point of view it already has for judgment.

Two crucial comments are needed here, in order to prevent a misunderstanding that might easily arise. First, we can *think* these properties of the supreme being only by an analogy.[52] For how could we investigate its nature, in view of the fact that experience can show us nothing similar? Second, this analogy allows us only to think the supreme being, not to *cognize* it [theoretically[53]] and perhaps attribute these properties to it theoretically; for that we would do for determinative judgment, from a speculative point of view of our reason, namely, to have insight into what the supreme cause of the world is *in itself.* Here our only concern is this: Since even without presupposing the existence of such a being, pure practical reason enjoins us a priori

---

[51] [In the *Critique of Pure Reason* (A634–35=B662–63), Kant distinguishes *speculative* cognition from *theoretical* cognition (generally) as follows: "Theoretical cognition is *speculative* if it concerns [such] an object, or such concepts of an object, as we cannot reach in any experience. It is contrasted with *cognition of nature*, which concerns only those objects or predicates of objects which can be given in a possible experience."]

[52] [By analogy with ourselves (cf. above, Ak. 455), we think of God as having not only technically practical but also *morally* practical reason.]

[53] [We do *cognize* it *practically* by this analogy: see below, Ak. 484–85.]

to strive to the utmost to achieve a [final] purpose: what concept must we form of this supreme cause in view of the character of our cognitive powers, and must we assume the existence of this cause, in order to provide that purpose with a reality that is also only [*nur*] practical, i.e., in order that we can at least [*nur*] think that [the] effect we intend is possible? The concept of that supreme cause may indeed be transcendent for speculative reason; and the properties we attribute to the being that we think through that concept may indeed involve a concealed anthropomorphism if we use them objectively.[54] But we do not in fact intend to use them in an attempt to determine that being's nature, which is inaccessible to us, but to determine ourselves and our will. When we name a cause after the concept we have of its effect (though only with regard to the relation it has to this effect), we are not trying to determine intrinsically the inner character of this cause, by the properties that we can know solely from such causes and that experience must give us.[55] For example, one of the forces we attribute to the soul is a *vis locomotiva,* because bodily movements do actually arise whose cause lies in the soul's presentations; but we do this without trying to attribute to the soul the one manner in which we know motive forces (namely, through attraction, pressure, impact, and hence motion, all of which always presuppose an extended being). Now in the same way we shall have to assume *something* that contains the basis for the possibility and practical reality, i.e., achievability, of a necessary moral final purpose. But, in view of the character of the effect we expect from this something, we can think of it as a wise being ruling the world according to moral laws; and, according to the character of our cognitive powers, we must think of it as a cause of things that is distinct from nature. We must think of it in this way only in order to express the *relation* that this being, which

457

[54] [Cf. Ak. 353 and 459. Anthropomorphism, Kant says elsewhere, is the "source of superstition" (*Critique of Practical Reason,* Ak. V, 135, and cf. 137–38, as well as *Religion within the Bounds of Reason Alone,* Ak. VI, 65n). On the other hand, in the *Prolegomena* (Ak. IV, 357), he rejects *dogmatic* anthropomorphism, which attributes human properties to God as he is in himself, but permits *symbolic* anthropomorphism, which "concerns only our language, not the object itself." This is the "subtler" anthropomorphism which is also permitted in the *Critique of Pure Reason* (A 700 = B 728), and which "merely assists a certain regulative principle" (A 697 = B 725).]

[55] [Cf. "symbolic hypotyposis," i.e., exhibition by analogy: Ak. 351–54 incl. br. n. 31; see also below, Ak. 482–85.]

surpasses all our cognitive powers, has to the object of *our* practical reason. And we are not thereby trying to attribute to it theoretically the only causality of this kind familiar to us: an understanding and a will. We are not even trying to make an objective distinction, within this being itself, between the causality we conceive it to have with regard to what is *for us* [a] final purpose, and the causality with regard to nature (and all the attributes nature has in terms of purposes). We can assume this distinction only as subjectively necessary for the character of our cognitive power, and as valid for reflective but not for determinative judgment. And yet, when we are concerned with the practical sphere, such a *regulative* principle (of prudence or wisdom)—namely, to act in conformity with something, as a purpose, that in view of the character of our cognitive powers we can conceive of as possible only in a certain manner—is also *constitutive,* i.e., determinative practically. But the same principle, [construed] as a principle for judging the objective possibility of things (namely, that the object too is restricted to the one kind of possibility to which our ability to think is restricted), is in no way theoretically determinative but is merely a *regulative* principle for reflective judgment.

458

Comment

This moral proof by no means [offers] a newly discovered basis for proving [the existence of God], but at most a new elucidation of that basis. For it resided in man's power of reason even before that power first began to germinate; after that it only developed more and more as the culture of reason progressed. Once people began to reflect on right and wrong—at a time when they were still indifferent to and ignored the purposiveness of nature, taking advantage of it without seeing in it more than the familiar course of nature—they inevitably had to arrive at this judgment: that in the end it must make a difference whether a person has acted honestly or deceitfully, fairly or violently, even if to the end of his life he has received no good fortune for his virtues and no punishment for his crimes, at least none that we could see. It is as if they heard an inner voice that said:

This[56] is not how it should be. Hence they must also have had a lurking conception, even if an obscure one, of something toward which they felt obligated to strive and with which such a result cannot be made to agree, or with which they could not reconcile that inner destination of their minds to a purpose once they regarded the course of the world as the only order of things. Now they might form all sorts of conceptions, however crude, as to how an irregularity of this sort [i.e., in the moral sphere] could be straightened out (a sort of irregularity that must be far more upsetting to the human mind than blind chance, which some have even sought to use as a principle by which to judge nature); but the only principle they were ever able to devise in order to be able to reconcile nature with the moral law within them was a supreme cause that rules the world according to moral laws: because there [would] be a contradiction between an inner final purpose that is set them as a duty, and an external nature in which that final purpose is to be actualized but which itself has no final purpose whatever. It is true that they hatched a lot of nonsense about the intrinsic constitution of that cause of the world, but that moral relation in its government of the world always remained the same; it is a relation that everyone can grasp, even the most uncultivated reason, provided it considers itself as practical reason, with which speculative reason cannot even remotely keep pace. Indeed, it was in all probability through this moral interest that people first became attentive to the beauty and the purposes of nature. And this attentiveness was in turn superbly suited to reinforce that idea [of a moral cause and ruler of the world], even though it could not provide a basis for it, let alone make the moral interest dispensable: for only by reference to the final purpose does even our investigation of the purposes of nature acquire that immediate interest that manifests itself to so great an extent when we admire nature without any concern about an expected advantage.

459

---

[56] [I.e., receiving no good fortune for one's virtues and no punishment for one's crimes.]

§ 89

On the Benefit of the
Moral Argument

Restricting reason, as regards all our ideas of the supersensible, to the conditions of its practical employment, has an unmistakable benefit concerning the idea of God. For it keeps *theology* from soaring to the heights of a THEOSOPHY (in which transcendent concepts confuse reason), and from sinking to the depths of a DEMONOLOGY (which is an anthropomorphic way of conceiving the supreme being); and it keeps *religion* from lapsing either into *theurgy* (a fanatical delusion that we can receive a feeling from, and in turn influence, other supersensible beings) or into *idolatry* [*Idolatrie*] (a superstitious delusion that we can make ourselves pleasing to the supreme being by means other than a moral attitude).[57]

For once we allow that reasoning, whether from vanity or impudence, about what lies beyond the world of sense is able to determine anything whatsoever theoretically (and in a way that expands cognition), [or] if we permit [people] to boast of having insight into the existence and constitution of divine nature, his understanding and will, the laws of these and the properties to which they give rise in the world: then I would surely like to know where and at what point they are going to restrict the pretensions of reason. After all, whatever the source of these insights, we might expect it to yield still more (if only, so these people suppose, we meditate hard enough). Now in restricting such claims we must surely follow some principle; we must not do it (say) merely because we have found that so far all tests of these claims have failed, since that in no way proves that a better result is impossible. But the only possible principle [for restricting those claims] is one of

460

[57] Any religion still remains idolatry [*Abgötterei*], in a practical sense of the term, if it conceives of the supreme being as having properties that allow something else besides morality to be, of itself, a sufficient condition for man's conforming, in what he is capable of doing, to that being's will. For no matter how pure and free from images of sense such a concept of the supreme being may be from a theoretical point of view, practically the being is still conceived of as an *idol*, i.e., it is conceived of anthropomorphically in what its will is like.

these two assumptions: either that (except in only a negative way) we can determine absolutely nothing theoretically about the supersensible, or that our reason holds a trove, still unused, [of] expansive[58] knowledge that is of unknown magnitude and is stored there for us and our descendants. But as far as religion is concerned, i.e., morality in relation to God as legislator, [the benefit of restricting reason's theoretical claims is this]: if we had to cognize God before [having morality], then morality would have to be governed by theology: not only would we have to replace an inner [and] necessary legislation of reason by an introduced external and arbitrary legislation of a supreme being, but all the deficiencies in our insight into the nature of this being would have to affect the ethical precept[s] in this legislation and so pervert religion and make it immoral.

As far as our hope for a future life is concerned, we have a guide for reason's judgment about our vocation: the final purpose that the moral law enjoins us to achieve ourselves (so that we regard this judgment as necessary or worthy of acceptance in a practical respect only). If we replace this guide and consult instead our theoretical cognitive power, [we find that] psychology offers us on the present question, just as theology did on the one above,[59] only a negative concept of our[selves as] thinking being[s];[60] this concept tells us no more than that none of the acts and none of the appearances of the inner sense of these beings can be explained in materialistic terms, so that our entire theoretical cognitive power cannot possibly make a determinative [and] expansive judgment, from speculative bases, concerning the separate nature of these [beings] and the continuance or discontinuance of their personality after death. Hence this entire [question] is left to the teleological judgment we make about our existence from a necessary [but] practical point of view, and to our assumption of our continued [life after death] as the condition that must be met [in order] for [us to achieve] the final purpose that reason enjoins on us absolutely. [Restricting the question to the

[58] [Or *ampliative* (*erweiternd*). I prefer 'expansive' because the corresponding verb, *erweitern*, is rendered less misleadingly by 'expand' than by 'amplify' (which might, to some contemporary readers, suggest increase in *force*).]

[59] [Concerning the supersensible in the case of divine nature.]

[60] [On the remainder of this section, cf. the *Critique of Pure Reason*, On the Paralogisms of Pure Reason, A 341–405 = B 399–432.]

practical sphere] shows us a benefit at once (though at first glance it seems a loss): For we see that, just as theology can never become theosophy for us, so rational *psychology* can never become *pneumatology,* which would be a science that expands [our knowledge]; nor, on the other hand, does rational psychology run the risk of lapsing into a *materialism.* Rather, we see that it is merely an anthropology of the inner sense, i.e., knowledge of our thinking self [as it is] *in life;* and since it is theoretical cognition, it also remains merely empirical. On the other hand, as far as the question of our eternal existence is concerned, rational psychology is not a theoretical science at all, but rests on a single inference of moral teleology; and indeed it is necessary for us to use it merely because of moral teleology, [i.e., because of] our practical vocation.

461

§ 90

On What Kind of Assent There Is in a Teleological Proof of the Existence of God

We can prove by exhibiting directly and empirically what is to be proved (e.g., if we prove something by observing the object, or by experimenting), or we can prove a priori from principles [and] by reason. But all proofs must, in the first place, not [merely] *persuade* but *convince,*[61] or at least tend to convince. In other words, the basis of the proof, or the inference, must not be a basis, determining us to approve, that is merely subjective (aesthetic, [and so] a mere seeming [*Schein*]), but it must be objectively valid and a logical basis of cognition; for otherwise the understanding is beguiled, but not won over. An example of such an illusory [*Schein-*] proof is the one that people offer in natural theology; their intention may be good, but

---

[61] [Cf. the *Logic*, Ak. IX, 73.]

they do deliberately conceal the weakness of the proof. For when they point to the large amount of evidence [which suggests] that natural things originated in terms of the principle of purposes, they take advantage of [a] merely subjective basis in human reason, a propensity peculiar to it: Human reason thinks a single principle, rather than several, wherever it can do so without contradiction; and if it finds that the principle contains just some [of the features] that are needed to determine a concept, or perhaps many [but not all], it adds the remaining ones in thought so as to perfect the concept of the thing by choosing to supplement it. Indeed: If we find so many properties in nature that seem to us to point to an intelligent cause, why should we not think a single such cause rather than many? And why should we not think of it as having, (say), not merely great understanding and might, etc., but instead omniscience and omnipotence, in a word: why should we not think of it as a cause that contains [a] basis, for such properties [as we find in those products], that would suffice for [producing] all possible things? And why should we not also attribute to this single all-powerful original being, not merely understanding, [which it must have] for the natural laws and products, but also the supreme ethical and practical reason [it needs] as a moral cause of the world? For perfecting the concept in this way gives us a principle that is sufficient both for insight into nature and for moral wisdom, and no objection that has any basis at all can be brought against the possibility of such an idea. Now if in addition the moral springs of the mind are set in motion, and this motion is supplemented by a lively interest through the use of oratorical force (of which these moral springs are indeed worthy), then the result is a persuasion that the proof is adequate objectively, and an illusion (a wholesome one in most cases where this proof is used) [in] which [the person who offers the proof] exempts [him]self completely from any examination of its logical rigor, and even has a loathing for and aversion from such examination, as if it were based on sacrilegious doubt. Now I suppose there is nothing to be said against [any of] this if our express concern is with how useful the proof is to the public. And yet this cannot and must not keep us from distinguishing in it the two heterogeneous components contained in the argument, one of which belongs to physical and the other to moral teleology. For if we fuse the two, we can no longer tell where the actual nerve of the proof lies, and how and on what part we would have to work on [the proof]

462

so that we could guarantee it to be valid under the most rigorous examination (even if concerning some part we had to acknowledge the weakness of our reason's insight). Hence a philosopher has the duty (assuming he leaves out of account [the risk in following] the demand to be sincere) to expose the illusion, no matter how wholesome it is, that such mingling can produce. He must separate what pertains merely to persuasion from what leads to conviction (two forms of approval that differ not merely in degree but also in kind), so that he can exhibit openly and very clearly what frame of mind this proof involves, and subject the proof candidly to the strictest examination.

Now proofs that try to convince are, in turn, of two kinds. Such a proof may be intended to decide what the object is *in itself,* or what it is *for us* (human beings as such) according to the principles of reason that we must follow in judging it. (In other words, the proof may be κατ᾽ ἀλήθειαν or κατ᾽ ἄνθρωπον,[62] with the last word taken in a universal sense, for human beings as such). A proof of the first kind is based on principles sufficient for determinative judgment, a proof of the second kind on principles sufficient merely for reflective judgment. If a proof of the second kind rests on merely theoretical principles, then it cannot ever tend to convince. But if it is based on a practical principle of reason (which therefore holds universally and necessarily), then it may indeed claim to convince sufficiently from a pure practical point of view, that is, morally. But a proof *tends to convince,* rather than already convinces, if [its only deficiency is that] it is [still] on the way toward conviction, i.e.: it does contain objective bases for conviction, and, though they are not yet sufficient to [produce] certainty, they are still of a kind that are not merely subjective bases of the judgment, which would accordingly serve merely to persuade.

All theoretical bases of proof are sufficient either (1) for proof by logically rigorous *syllogistic inferences;* or, if not that, (2) for *inference* by *analogy;* or, if that too does not apply, then at any rate (3) for *probable opinion;* or, finally, which is least, (4) for a *hypothesis,* i.e., for assuming a merely possible basis for an explanation. Now I say that none of the bases of proof that tend toward theoretical conviction can produce an assent of this kind, from the highest degree to the lowest, if what is to be proved is the proposition about the existence

463

[62] [Kat' alētheian or kat' ánthrōpon: according to the truth or according to man.]

of an original being who is a God in the full sense of that concept, namely, a *moral* author of the world, so that the concept also indicates the final purpose of creation.

(1) As far as the *logically correct* proof is concerned, which proceeds from the universal to the particular, it was dealt with in the *Critique [of Pure Reason],*[63] which sufficiently established the following: Since it is impossible for us to have an intuition that would correspond to the concept of a being that we must seek beyond nature, the very concept of this being, as far as we try to determine it theoretically by synthetic predicates, always remains problematic for us. Hence we have absolutely no cognition of this being (that would in the least expand the range of our theoretical knowledge), and cannot at all subsume the particular concept of a supersensible being under the universal principles of the nature of things, so as to infer this being from them; for these principles hold solely for nature as an object of sense.

(2) [As for an inference by analogy:] It is true that even if two things are heterogeneous, we can still *conceive* of the one by an *analogy*[64] with the other, and on the very point of their heterogeneity.

464

---

[63] [See A 631–42 = B 659–70.]

[64] *Analogy* (in a qualitative sense[65]) is the identity of the relation between bases and consequences (causes and effects) insofar as it is present despite what difference in kind [*spezifisch*] there is between the things themselves (i.e., considered apart from that relation), or between those properties themselves that contain the basis of similar consequences. Thus when we compare the artful acts of animals with those of man, we do not know what basis in these animals gives rise to such effects, but we do know what basis gives rise to similar effects in the case of man (namely, reason); and hence we conceive of the basis for such acts in animals by means of the basis of such acts in man: i.e., we conceive of the former basis as an analogue of reason. In doing so we wish to indicate at the same time that the basis of the artistic power in animals, called instinct, while indeed different in kind from reason, still has a similar relation to its effect (for example, if we compare the construction[s] of beavers with th[ose] of human beings). But that does not entitle me to infer that because man needs *reason* in order to construct [things], beavers too must have it, and to call this an inference by analogy.[66] What we can quite correctly infer *by analogy*, from the similarity between animal behavior [*Wirkung*] (whose basis we cannot perceive directly) and man's behavior (of whose basis we are conscious directly), is that animals too act according to *presentations* (rather than being machines, as Descartes would have it), and that regardless of the

---

[65] [Philosophical, rather than mathematical, analogy; cf. the *Critique of Pure Reason*, A 179–81 = B 222–24. See also above, Ak. 351 br. n. 31, and below, Ak. 483–85.]

[66] [Cf. *Religion within the Bounds of Reason Alone*, Ak. VI, the n. on 64–65.]

But from that in which they are heterogeneous we cannot by analogy draw an *inference* from the one to the other, i.e., transfer that mark of the difference in kind between them from one to the other. Thus, by analogy with the law that action and reaction are equal when bodies attract or repel one another, I can also conceive of the community between the members of a commonwealth that is governed by rules of law. But I cannot transfer those specific characteristics (the material attraction or repulsion) to this community, and attribute them to the citizens so that these will form a system called a state. Similarly, we may indeed conceive of the original being's causality, concerning the things [regarded] as natural purposes [we find] in the world, by analogy with an understanding, i.e., with the basis [that accounts] for the forms of certain products that we call works of art (for we do this only in order to assist our cognitive power in dealing with natural things in the world, because we need that concept [of the original being's causality] when we apply our cognitive power to these things, theoretically and practically, according to a certain [viz., teleological] principle). But from the fact that in the case of beings of the world we must attribute understanding to the cause of an effect that we judge to be artificial, we can in no way infer by analogy that the same causality that we perceive in man can also be ascribed to the being that is wholly distinct from nature, with nature itself as [its effect]. For that concerns precisely the point of heterogeneity that, in contrasting the supersensible original being with a cause who[se

465

---

difference in specific kind [*spezifisch*] between them and man, they are still of the same general kind [*Gattung*] (namely, as living beings). The principle that authorizes us to make this inference is this: with respect to the characteristic in question, the basis on which we here include animals in the same general kind as human beings is the same as the basis on which we include [different] human beings in the same general kind when we compare them with one another outwardly, by their acts. In other words, in this case we do have *par ratio* [the same grounds].[67] Similarly, though I can conceive of the causality of the supreme world cause when I compare its purposive products in the world with the works of art of man, by analogy with an understanding, I cannot by analogy infer that it has these [same] properties: for in this case the principle that authorizes such an inference is just what is lacking, i.e., we do not have *paritas rationis* [sameness of grounds] for including the supreme being in one and the same general kind as man (as regards their respective causalities). The causality of world beings (which includes the causality through understanding) is always conditioned by the sensible, [and so] cannot be transferred to a being that has no generic [*Gattungs-*] concept in common with them except that of a thing as such.

[67] [Cf. the *Logic*, Ak. IX, 132–33.]

production of] its effects has [a] condition in the sensible, we think in the very concept of that being and hence cannot transfer to that concept. The very fact that I am to think of divine causality only by analogy with an understanding (a power we do not know in any being other than man,[68] who has [a] condition in the sensible) forbids me to attribute to this being an understanding in the proper sense of the term.[69]

(3) As far as *opinion* is concerned, it has no place whatever in a priori judgments: through them either we cognize something as completely certain, or else we cognize nothing at all. But even if in our proof we start from bases [or grounds] that are given us empirically (as, in the present case, the purposes in the world), they still do not allow us to form an opinion about anything beyond the world of sense and to grant such hazardous judgments the slightest claim to probability. For probability[70] is part of a certainty that is achievable [*möglich*] in a series of grounds (in this series the grounds for probability compare to the sufficient ground as parts to a whole), [so that] it must be possible to supplement that insufficient ground until [the series of] these grounds [is] complete. But since they are grounds that determine the certainty of one and the same judgment, they must be of the same kind, since otherwise they would not jointly form a magnitude (and certainty is a magnitude), and so it cannot be that some of them lie within the bounds of possible experience and others beyond all possible experience. Hence, since merely empirical bases [or grounds] cannot lead our proof to anything supersensible, and since there is nothing with which we could supplement them to make up for the deficiency in their series, the attempt to get from them to the supersensible and to a cognition of it does not result in even the slightest approximation; and so a judgment we make about the supersensible will also have no probability if we base it on arguments that rely on experience.

466

---

[68] [Cf. the *Critique of Pure Reason*, A 626 = B 654.]

[69] This does not result in the slightest loss to our presentation of that being's relation to the world, neither in the theoretical nor in the practical consequences of that concept. To try to investigate what that being is in itself shows an inquisitiveness that is as purposeless as it is doomed.

[70] [On probability, cf. the *Logic*, Ak. IX, 81–82.]

(4) If something is to serve as a *hypothesis*[71] to explain how a given phenomenon is possible, then at least the possibility of this something must be completely certain. All I have to waive if I make a hypothesis is [the claim that I am] cognizing actuality. (In an opinion that we offer as probable this claim is still made.) More than that I cannot give up: at least the possibility of what serves as the basis for my explanation must not be open to any doubt, since otherwise there would be no end to empty chimeras. But we would be making a completely baseless presupposition if we assumed that a supersensible being, as determined in terms of certain concepts, is possible. For in the case of this assumption, none of the conditions are given that a cognition requires insofar as it rests partly on intuition, and hence the only criterion we have left for this being's possibility is the mere principle of contradiction (which however can prove only the possibility of conceiving the object, not the possibility of the conceived object itself[72]).

The result of this is as follows: For human reason it is absolutely impossible, from a theoretical point of view, to prove the existence of the original being as a deity, or of the soul as an immortal spirit, and to produce even the slightest degree of assent. And we can readily grasp why this is so: we have no material whatever for determining the ideas of the supersensible, since we would have to get this material from things in the world of sense, and yet such material is absolutely inadequate for that [supersensible] object. Hence, since we cannot at all determine these ideas, we are left with nothing more than the concept of a nonsensible something that contains the ultimate basis of the world of sense, and that concept does not yet amount to cognition (which [in this case would] be[73] an expansion of the concept) of that thing's intrinsic constitution.

---

[71] [On hypothesis, cf. the *Logic*, Ak. IX, 84–86, and the *Critique of Pure Reason*, A 769–82 = B 797–810.]

[72] [I.e., it can prove only the thing's logical possibility, not its real possibility.]

[73] [I.e., in the case of an indeterminate concept. Cf. the Translator's Introduction, *xxxiv–xxxv, xl.*]

§ 91

On What Kind of
Assent Results
from a Practical Faith

If we look merely to the way in which (in view of the subjective character of our presentational powers) something can be an object of cognition (*res cognoscibilis*) *for us,* then we are not comparing concepts with objects but are comparing them merely with our cognitive powers and with the (theoretical or practical) use that these can make of the given presentation. [Hence] the question whether something is a cognizable being or not is not a question concerning the possibility of things themselves but concerning the possibility of our cognizing them.

There are three kinds of *cognizable* things: *matters*[74] *of opinion (opinabilia), matters of fact (scibilia),* and *matters of faith (mere credibilia).*[75]

(1) Objects of the mere ideas of reason cannot be exhibited at all in any possible experience, so as to give rise to theoretical cognition [for us], and to that extent such objects are also not *cognizable* things at all. Hence about them we cannot even *have an opinion.* Indeed, the very expression, a priori opinion, is absurd and invites all sorts of chimeras; and hence either our a priori proposition is certain, or there is nothing whatever in it to assent to. Hence *matters of opinion* are always objects of an empirical cognition that is at least intrinsically

---

[74] [*Sachen*: the term does also mean 'things.']

[75] [Respectively, things opinable, knowable, or merely believable. For extended discussions of opinion, knowledge, and (belief or) faith, see the *Critique of Pure Reason,* A 820–31 = B 848–59 (cf. also B xxx), and the *Logic,* Ak. IX, 65–73. Cf. also *Religion within the Bounds of Reason Alone,* Ak. VI, the n. on 153–54; *What Does It Mean: to Orient Oneself in [One's] Thought,* Ak. VIII, 140–47; and *On [the] Dignified Tone Recently Adopted in Philosophy,* Ak. VIII, the n. on 395–97. My main reason for rendering Kant's Glaube (usually) as 'faith' rather than as 'belief' is that 'faith' tends to suggest, rather more readily than does 'belief,' the mutual exclusiveness of Glaube (properly so called, i.e., practical *Glaube*) and *Wissen* (knowledge) that Kant emphasizes so frequently: see, e.g., Ak. 471–72 (and cf. 470); the *Critique of Pure Reason,* B xxx; and the Logic, Ak. IX, 67–70, esp. 68–69.]

possible (i.e., they are objects of the world of sense) even though that cognition is impossible *for us* because our cognitive power is so weak. For example, the aether that the more recent physicists have discussed, an elastic fluid that permeates all other kinds of matter [*Materie*] (it is thoroughly mingled with them), is a mere matter [-*sache*] of opinion. But it is still such that we could perceive it if our outer senses were made maximally acute, even if in fact it can never be exhibited in observation or [through] experiment. If we assume rational inhabitants on other planets,[76] this is a matter of opinion. For if we could get closer to these planets, which is intrinsically possible, then we could decide by experience whether or not these beings exist. But we shall in fact never get that close to them, and hence we cannot get beyond opinion here. On the other hand, if we hold the opinion that there are pure spirits in the material universe, spirits that think but have no bodies,[77] then we engage in fiction (provided we dismiss, as we should, certain actual phenomena that have been passed off as spirits). For this is not at all a matter of opinion, but is a mere idea that remains if we take away from a thinking being everything material and yet suppose that it retains thought: [for] we cannot tell whether thought remains in that case (since we know it only in man, [where it is] connected with a body). A thing like this spirit is a *being of [our] reasoning* (*ens rationis ratiocinantis*), not a *being of reason* (*ens rationis ratiocinatae*);[78] for in the case of a being of reason we can sufficiently establish that its concept has objective reality, at least for the practical use of reason, since that use has its own and apodeictically certain a priori principles and does in fact demand (*postulare* [*postuliert*]) that concept.

    (2) Objects of concepts whose objective reality can be proved are *matters of fact* (*res facti*).[79] (This may be done by pure reason or by

468

---

[76] [In his *Universal Natural History and Theory of the Heavens* (1755), Kant speculated elaborately about such inhabitants of other planets (Ak. I, 349–68).]

[77] [On this topic, cf. *Dreams of a Spirit-Seer* (1766), Ak. II, 315–83.]

[78] [See the *Critique of Pure Reason*, A 669 = B 697 and A 681 = B 709, and cf. above, Ak. 337 n. 1 and br. n. 2, and Ak. 396.]

[79] I here expand, rightly I think, the concept of a matter of fact beyond the ordinary meaning of the word. For it is neither necessary nor even feasible, when we are speaking of the relation of things to our cognitive powers, to confine this expression to actual experience, because a merely possible experience is sufficient in order to speak of these things merely as objects of a certain way of cognizing.

experience, and in the former case either from theoretical or from practical data of reason; but in all cases it must be done by means of an intuition corresponding to these data.) Examples of matters of fact are the mathematical properties of magnitudes (in geometry), since they admit of a priori *exhibition* for the theoretical use of reason.[80] Matters of fact also include things or characteristics of things that can be established by experience (whether our own or that of other people, through their testimony). It is very remarkable, however, that even a rational idea is to be found among the matters of fact (even though it is intrinsically impossible to exhibit rational ideas in intuition, and hence also intrinsically impossible to prove theoretically that they are possible): the idea of *freedom;* the reality of this idea, as [the idea of] a special kind of causality (the concept of which would be transcendent if we considered it theoretically), can be established through practical laws of pure reason and, [if we act] in conformity with these, in actual acts, and hence in experience. Among all the ideas of pure reason this is the only one whose object is a matter of fact and must be included among the *scibilia.*

469

(3) As for objects that we have to think a priori (either as consequences or as grounds) in reference to our practical use of reason in conformity with duty, but that are transcendent for the theoretical use of reason: they are mere *matters of faith.* One such object is the *highest good* in the world that we are to achieve through freedom. We cannot prove the concept of this good, as to whether it has objective reality, in any experience that is possible for us, and hence adequately for the theoretical use of reason. But since practical pure reason commands us to use this concept in order to achieve that purpose [the highest good in the world] as best we can, we must assume it as possible [to realize]. This commanded effect, *together with the sole conditions conceivable by us under which [achieving] that effect is possible,* namely, the existence of God and the immortality of the soul, are *matters of faith* (*res fidei*), and they are moreover the only objects whatsoever that can be called matters of faith.[81] It is true

---

[80] [Cf. Ak. 232 br. n.51.]

[81] If something is a matter of faith, that does not yet make it an *article of faith*, if we mean by this those matters of faith to which we can become obligated to *confess*[82] (inwardly or outwardly) and which therefore do not form part of natural theology. For as matters of faith they cannot (as matters of fact can) be based on theoretical proofs. Hence assent to them is free, and only as such is it compatible with the subject's being a moral subject.

[82] [Cf. *Religion within the Bounds of Reason Alone*, Ak. VI, 165.]

that something that we can learn only from the experience of others, through their *testimony,* is something in which we must have faith, but it is not yet on that account itself a matter of faith ([but only a case of] historical faith), because for *one* of those witnesses it was after all his own experience and a matter of fact, or [we] presuppose that it was that. Moreover, by following the path of historical faith it must [always] be possible to arrive at knowledge; and [hence] the objects of history and geography, and everything whatever that in view of the character of our cognitive powers it is at least possible for us to know, are not matters of faith but matters of fact. Only objects of pure reason can be matters of faith at all; but not if they are merely objects of pure theoretical reason, for in that case it is not even certain that we can number them among the matters, i.e., objects of [a] cognition that is possible for us. [Rather,] they are ideas, i.e., concepts of whose objective reality we cannot have theoretical assurance. On the other hand, the highest final purpose which we are to achieve, that which alone can make us worthy of being, ourselves, the final purpose of creation, is an idea that has objective reality for us in a practical respect, and hence is a matter [i.e., an object of a cognition that is possible for us].[83] But since we cannot provide this concept with reality from a theoretical point of view, this final purpose is a mere matter of faith [for] pure reason; but along with it so are God and immortality, which are the conditions under which alone, given the character of our (human) reason, we can conceive of the possibility of [achieving] the effect [the final purpose] of the lawful use of our freedom. But assent in matters of faith is an assent from a pure practical point of view, i.e., it is a moral faith that proves nothing for theoretical pure rational cognition, but only for pure practical cognition[84] that aims at [our] complying with [our] duties; it does not at all expand our speculation, nor our practical rules of prudence governed by the principle of self-love. If the supreme principle of all moral laws is a postulate, then the possibility of [achieving] their highest object [the final purpose], and hence also the condition[s: God and immortality of the soul] under which [alone] we can conceive of that possibility, [are] postulated with it at the same time.[85] But that does not make our cognition of that possibility either

470

[83] [On practical cognition, cf. below, Ak. 475 incl. br. n. 96.]
[84] [Cf. Ak. 467 br. n.74.]
[85] [Cf. the *Critique of Pure Reason,* A 805–19 = B 833–47.]

knowledge or opinion[86] of the existence and character of these conditions [God and immortality of the soul], which would be a theoretical way of cognizing them; but it is merely an assumption that we make and are commanded to make in a practical respect: for the moral use of our reason.

If it seemed to us that the purposes of nature that physical teleology displays to us on such a lavish scale could after all be used to support a *determinate* concept of an intelligent cause of the world, that would still not make the existence of this being a matter of faith. For I would be assuming the existence of this being only in order to explain nature, rather than in order to perform my duty, and hence it would merely be the opinion or hypothesis most commensurate with my reason. But in fact physical teleology does not at all lead to a determinate concept of God. Such a concept can be found only in the concept of a moral author of the world; for this concept alone indicates the final purpose, the purpose which includes us only insofar as our conduct conforms to what the moral law enjoins on us as the final purpose and hence imposes on us as a duty. Hence the only way in which the concept of God acquires the distinction of counting, for our assent, as a matter of faith is through [its] reference to the object of our duty [i.e., the final purpose], as the condition under which [alone] it is possible for us to attain the final purpose [enjoined on us by the moral law]. And yet this same concept cannot claim its object as a matter of fact: for though the necessity of duty is indeed clear to practical reason, our attainment of the final purpose it enjoins on us is not wholly in our power and hence we merely assume it for the sake of our practical reason, so that our attainment of that final purpose is not practically necessary as duty itself is.[87]

471

[86] [On (some) practical cognition as involving faith but not knowledge, see below, Ak. 475 br, n. 96.]

[87] The final purpose that the moral law enjoins us to further is not the basis of duty. For that basis lies in the moral law, which is a practical principle that is formal and hence directs categorically, without regard to the objects of the power of desire (which are the matter of volition) and hence without regard to any purpose [= the matter] whatever. This formal character of my acts (their subordination under the principle of universal validity), in which alone their intrinsic moral value consists, is wholly in my power; and I certainly can abstract from whether the purposes that this law obligates me to further are possible or unachievable, (because they constitute only the extrinsic value of my acts,) since that is never completely in my power, in order to look only to what I can do. And yet that law of duty does enjoin us to aim at furthering the final

Faith (as *habitus,* not as *actus*[88]) is reason's moral way of thinking in assenting to [*Fürwahrhalten*[89]] what is not accessible to theoretical cognition. It is the mind's steadfast principle to assume as true [*wahr*] what we must necessarily presuppose as a condition for the possibility of [achieving] the highest moral final purpose, and to assume this because of our obligation to this final purpose,[90] and despite the fact that we have no insight into whether [achieving] this purpose is possible, or for that matter whether this is impossible. To have faith (simply so called) is to have confidence that we shall reach an aim that we have a duty to further, without our having *insight* into whether achieving it is possible (nor, consequently, into whether the conditions are possible under which alone we can conceive of achieving that aim). Therefore, a wholly moral faith is one that refers to special objects that are not objects of possible knowledge or opinion (otherwise, above all in the case of history, it would have to be called credulity [*Leichtgläubigkeit*] rather than faith [*Glaube*]. Faith is free assent, not to something for which we can find dogmatic proofs for theoretically determinative judgment, nor to something to which we consider ourselves obligated, but to something that we assume for some aim and in accordance with laws of freedom. Yet faith is not

472

---

purpose of all rational beings (happiness insofar as it is possible in harmony with duty). But speculative reason has no insight whatever into the possibility of achieving that aim (neither as far as our own physical ability nor as far as the cooperation of nature is concerned). Rather, as far as we can rationally judge, speculative reason must consider it a baseless and idle—even if well-meant—expectation to assume that such merely natural causes (within and outside us), without God and immortality [of the soul], will make our good conduct have such a result. Indeed, if speculative reason could have complete certainty on that assumption [*Urteil*] it would have to regard the moral law itself as a mere deception of our reason in a practical respect. But since speculative reason convinces itself completely that such deception can never occur, while those ideas whose object lies beyond nature can be thought without contradiction, it will in a moral respect, i.e., for its own practical law and the task this law enjoins on us, have to acknowledge those ideas as real, so as not to fall into contradiction with itself.

[88] [As an attitude, not as an act.]

[89] ["Considering true," literally.]

[90] Faith is a confidence in the promise [*Verheißung*] of the moral law; but the moral law does not contain this promise: it is I who put it there, and on a morally sufficient basis. For no law of reason can command [us to pursue] a final purpose unless reason also promises [*versprechen*], even if not with certainty, that this final purpose is achievable, and hence also justifies us in assenting to the conditions under which alone our reason can conceive of that achievability. In fact the word *fides* [faith] already

without an adequate basis, as, e.g., an opinion is, but has a basis in reason *that is adequate for the aim of reason* (although that aim is only practical): For without faith the moral way of thinking lacks firm steadfastness whenever it fails to fulfill theoretical reason's demand for proof (that the object of morality is possible), but vacillates between practical commands and theoretical doubts. To be *incredulous [ungläubisch]* means to cling to the maxim not to believe in people's testimony at all. But an *unbelieving [ungläubig]* person is one who denies all validity to those rational ideas [of God and immortality of the soul] because there is no *theoretical* foundation for their reality. Hence such a person judges dogmatically. A dogmatic *unbelief* in a person is incompatible with his having a moral maxim prevail in his way of thinking (since reason cannot command us to pursue a purpose that we cognize as being nothing but a chimera). *Skepticism [Zweifelglaube[92]]*, on the other hand, is quite compatible with having a moral maxim prevail in one's way of thinking, because for skepticism the lack of conviction from bases of speculative reason is only an obstacle, and a critical insight into the limits of speculative reason can keep our conduct from being influenced by this obstacle and provide this skepticism with a stronger practical assent as a substitute.

473

If, in the place of certain unsuccessful attempts in philosophy, we wish to introduce a different principle and make it influential, it is very helpful to see how and why those attempts had to fail.

God, freedom, and *immortality of the soul* are the problems at

---

472

expresses this,[91] and it must seem dubious how this term and this special idea have made their way into moral philosophy: for they were first introduced with Christianity, and it might seem as if their acceptance [by moral philosophy] is perhaps only a fawning imitation of the language of Christianity. But this is not the only case where this wondrous religion has in the greatest simplicity of its statement enriched philosophy with far more determinate and pure concepts of morality than philosophy had until then been able to supply, but which, once they are there, reason sanctions *freely* and accepts as concepts that it surely could and should itself have hit upon and introduced.

[91] [Cf. the *Logic*. Ak. IX, the n. on 67–69.]

[92] [The literal meaning of this term is roughly 'faith (or belief) mixed with doubt.']

whose solution all the apparatus of metaphysics aims as its ultimate and sole purpose.[93] Now, people believed that the doctrine of freedom was needed for practical philosophy only as a negative condition, whereas the doctrine of God and of the nature [Beschaffenheit] of the soul belong[ed] to theoretical philosophy and must be established separately and on its own. [Only] then were the two [God and immortality of the soul] to be linked with what the moral law (which is possible only under the condition of freedom) commands, so as to give rise to a religion. But we can readily see that these attempts had to fail. For [if we form] a concept of an original being [and do this] from mere ontological concepts of things as such, or from the existence of a necessary being, [then we] cannot possibly determine this concept by predicates that can be given in experience and hence could serve for cognition. On the other hand, the concept that people based on experience of the physical purposiveness of nature was in its turn unable to yield a proof adequate for morality and hence for cognizing a God. In the same way, the knowledge we have of the soul through experience (in which we engage only in this life) cannot provide us with a concept of its spiritual and immortal nature [*Natur*] and hence with a concept adequate for morality. *Theology* and *pneumatology,* [regarded] as problems for the sciences of a speculative reason, cannot be established by means of any empirical data and predicates, because their concepts are transcendent for all our cognitive powers. The only way to determine these two concepts, of God and the (immortal) soul, is through predicates that, though they themselves are possible only on the basis of [something] supersensible, must yet prove in experience that they have reality: for only in this way can these concepts make cognition of wholly supersensible beings possible. Now the only such concept to be found in human reason is that of man's freedom under moral laws, together with the final purpose that reason[94] prescribes through these laws. The moral laws enable us to attribute to the author of nature, and the final purpose

474

---

[93] [Cf. the *Critique of Pure Reason,* B 7, B 395n, A 798 = B 826. In *The Only Possible Basis of Proof* (Ak. II, 65), Kant says that our most important cognition is "There is a God." In another place, Kant suggests a kind of "syllogistic" relation between God, freedom, and immortality of the soul: *Announcement That a Treatise on Perpetual Peace in Philosophy Is Nearly Completed,* Ak. VIII, 418.]

[94] [Or perhaps freedom.]

enables us to attribute to man, the properties[95] that [are] necessary acondition[s] for the possibility of [carrying out] both of them [the moral laws and the final purpose]. Hence it is from this same idea of freedom that we can infer the existence and the nature [*Beschaffenheit*] of these beings [God and soul] that are otherwise wholly hidden from us.

Therefore, the attempt to prove God and immortality by the merely theoretical route had to fail because by this route (of concepts of nature) no cognition whatever of the supersensible is possible. That the attempt succeeds by the moral route (of the concept of freedom) is due to this: not only does the supersensible that underlies [the proof] in this case (namely, freedom) provide us, through a determinate law of causality to which it gives rise, with material for cognizing the other supersensible (the moral final purpose and the conditions for its achievability); but it is also a matter of fact [and hence] establishes its [own] reality in [our] acts. Precisely because of that, however, the only basis it can provide for proving [God and immortality of the soul] is one that is valid from a practical point of view. (That, however, is the only point of view that religion requires.)

What always remains very remarkable about this is that among the three pure ideas of reason, *God, freedom,* and *immortality,* that of freedom is the only concept of the supersensible which (by means of the causality that we think in it) proves in nature that it has objective reality, by the effects it can produce in it. It is this that makes it possible to connect the other two ideas with nature, and to connect all three with one another to form a religion. Therefore, we have in us a principle that can determine the idea of the supersensible within us, and through this also the idea of the supersensible outside us, so as to give rise to cognition [of them], even though one that is possible only from a practical point of view; and that is something of which merely speculative philosophy (which could provide also merely a negative concept of freedom) had to despair. Hence the concept of freedom (the concept underlying all unconditioned practical laws) can expand reason beyond those bounds within which any concept of nature (i.e., theoretical concept) would have to remain hopelessly confined.

[95] [Morality in the case of God, immortality of the soul in the case of man.]

General Comment
on Teleology

The moral argument proves the existence of God only as a matter of faith, for practical pure reason. If we ask how it ranks, in philosophy, with the other arguments [the theoretical arguments for the existence of God], we can easily assess all [those] that philosophy possesses. If we do this, we find that there is nothing to select here, but that theoretical philosophy is so [limited] in ability that it must on its own give up all claims [to those theoretical arguments] if faced by an impartial critique.

In the first place, all assent in philosophy must be based on [some] matter of fact, if it is not to be completely baseless. Hence the only difference that can arise between proofs is whether we can base on this matter of fact an assent (to the conclusion drawn from it) that is *knowledge,* for theoretical cognition, or merely *faith,* for practical cognition.[96] All matters of fact pertain either to the [a priori] *concept of nature,* which proves its reality in the objects of sense that are (or can be) given prior to all [empirical] concepts of nature, or to the *concept of freedom,* which sufficiently establishes its reality through the causality that reason has by being able to [produce] certain effects in the world of sense and that it irrefutably postulates in the moral law. Now the concept of nature (which pertains merely to theoretical cognition) is either metaphysical and completely a priori; or it is physical, i.e., a posteriori and of necessity conceivable only [as arising] through determinate experience. The metaphysical concept of nature (which does not presuppose any determinate experience) is therefore ontological.

Now *the ontological proof* tries to prove the existence of God from the concept of an original being, and has two variants. One of these starts from ontological predicates that alone allow us to think this being completely determinately, and from these infers its absolutely

---

[96] [On practical cognition, cf. the *Critique of Pure Reason,* A 633 = B 661, the *Critique of Practical Reason,* Ak. V, 137; the *Logic,* Ak. IX, 86–87; and above, Ak. 174–76. For the relation between practical cognition and knowledge, see the references at Ak. 467 br. n. 75; the *Prolegomena,* Ak. IV, 278; and the Translator's Introduction, *xl–xlii.*]

necessary existence. The other variant starts from the absolute necessity of the existence of some thing or other, no matter what, and from
that infers the predicates of the original being. For in order for the
original being not to be [a] derived [being], the concept of it must
include the unconditioned necessity of the being's existence, and
(so that we can conceive of that necessity) the being must be completely determined by its [very] concept. Now it was believed that
both these requirements were fulfilled by this concept: the ontological idea of a *supremely real being*. And so two metaphysical proofs
arose.

The first of these proofs is based on a merely metaphysical concept
of nature (and is called ontological proper). It starts from the concept
of the supremely real being, and infers from this that being's absolutely
necessary existence; for (we are told) if it did not exist, then it would
lack one reality: existence. The other ontological proof (which is also
called the metaphysical-*cosmological* proof) starts from the necessity of the existence of some thing or other (which must certainly be
granted, since an existence is given me in self-consciousness [but
could not be there unless some thing or other existed necessarily[97]]),
and infers from this the complete determination of it as the supremely
real being. For, [we are told,] though everything that exists must be
completely determined,[98] what is absolutely necessary (i.e., what we
are to cognize as being so, and hence cognize a priori) must be completely determined *by its concept;* but the only concept [adequate] for
this [i.e., completely determining something absolutely necessary]
is that of a supremely real thing. I do not need to expose here the
sophistry in both inferences, since I have already done so elsewhere.[99]

476

---

[97] [Cf. the *Critique of Pure Reason*, A 604 = B 632: "If anything exists, then an
absolutely necessary being must also exist. Now at least I myself exist. Therefore
an absolutely necessary being exists." Cf. also *The Only Possible Basis of Proof*,
Ak. II, 157–58.]

[98] [Cf. *Thoughts on the True Estimation of Living Forces* (1747), Ak. I, 27.]

[99] [*Critique of Pure Reason*, A 583–620 = B 611–48. See also *The Only Possible
Basis of Proof*, Ak. II, 155–63 and cf. 72–77. Kant himself had tried to infer the
existence of God from the *real possibility* (rather than the existence) of things. The
real (as distinguished from the merely *logical*) possibility of things, he had argued,
must be derived from, or be the consequence of, an existent being that has *all* realities
(logically independent affirmative attributes). See *The Only Possible Basis of Proof*,
Ak. II, 70–92, and the *Principiorum primorum cognitionis metaphysicae nova
dilucidatio* (*New Elucidation of the First Principles of Cognition in Metaphysics*,
1755), Ak. I, 385–416.]

All I need to point out is that, even if such proofs could be defended with a lot of dialectical subtlety, they still could never reach beyond the school and have the slightest influence on mere sound understanding in the community.

The proof that is based on a concept of nature that can only be empirical and yet is to lead us beyond the bounds of nature as the sum total of objects of sense, can only be the proof [that starts] from the *purposes* of nature. Although the concept of these purposes cannot be given a priori but must be given through experience, it still promises us, among all thinkable concepts of the original basis of nature, the only one that is such as befits the supersensible: the concept of a highest understanding [*Verstand*] as cause of the world. And this the proof does accomplish perfectly, as concerns principles of reflective judgment, i.e., the character of our (human) cognitive power. But the question arises whether the concept that this proof is able to derive from these data is not only that of a *supreme* being, i.e., an independent intelligent [*verständig*] being, but also that of a God, i.e., author of a world under moral laws, and hence a concept that is sufficiently determinate to [involve] the idea of a final purpose of the existence of the world. On this question everything hinges, whether we demand a theoretically sufficient concept of the original being for the sake of [completing] our entire knowledge of nature, or a practical concept for religion.

This argument, taken from physical teleology, is a venerable one. It is just as effective in convincing common understanding as in convincing the subtlest thinker; and a *Reimarus*[100] has acquired immortal merit through his still unsurpassed work, where, with the thoroughness and clarity peculiar to him, he elaborately puts forth this basis for proving [the existence of God]. And yet what is it that gives this proof its powerful influence on the mind, inducing in it calm and utterly yielding agreement, above all if we are judging by means of cool

477

[100] [Hermann Samuel Reimarus (1694–1768), German philosopher (with views similar to those of Christian Wolff [1679–1754]) and man of letters. He is the author of several works and is particularly known through his *Abhandlungen von den vornehmsten Wahrheiten der natürlichen Religionen* (*Treatises on the Foremost Truths of Natural Religions*, 1754) and especially his *Apologie oder Schutzschrift für die vernünftigen Verehrer Gottes* (*Defense or Vindication for Those Who Revere God Rationally*), a work cautiously held back during his lifetime and then published in excerpts by Gotthold Ephraim Lessing (1729–81).]

reason (since if the mind is moved and elevated by the wonders of nature, this could be counted as persuasion)? It is not the fact that the physical purposes all point to an unfathomable understanding in the world cause. They are not sufficient to give the proof this influence, because they fail to satisfy the need[s] of inquiring reason: for, (reason inquires,) what are all those artistic natural things for? What is man himself for, with whom we have to stop because he is the ultimate purpose of nature conceivable to us? What is all this nature there for, and what is the final purpose of this great and varied art? It cannot satisfy reason [to be told] that the ultimate final purpose for which the world and man himself are there and were created is so that [man can] enjoy [the world], or so that [he can] behold, contemplate, and admire [it] (which, if that is all we do, is also nothing more than enjoyment of a particular kind). For reason presupposes a personal value, one that man can only give himself, as the condition under which alone he and his existence can be [a] final purpose. In the absence of such a value (which alone admits of a determinate concept) the purposes of nature fail to satisfy [man in] his inquiry, above all because they cannot provide a *determinate concept* of the supreme being as an all-sufficient (and precisely because of this single and in the proper sense *supreme*) being and of the laws in terms of which its understanding is cause of the world.

This shows that while the physicoteleological proof convinces, just as if it were also a theological proof, it does not do so because it uses the ideas of purposes of nature as so many empirical bases for proving a *supreme* understanding. Rather, the moral basis for proving [the existence of God], the basis which dwells in every human being and moves him so very deeply, is inadvertently mingled with the inference. It is on this basis that we attribute to that being, which manifests itself with such unfathomable artistry in the purposes of nature, a final purpose as well, and hence wisdom (even though our perception of the purposes of nature does not justify this [addition]); and hence we choose to supplement the physicoteleological argument to make up for the deficiency it still has. In fact, therefore, only the moral basis for proving [the existence of God] gives rise to our conviction, and that only from a moral point of view, with which everyone feels deep agreement. The only merit that the physicoteleological proof has is that it leads the mind, in its contemplation of the world, onto the path of purposes, and through this to an *intelligent* author of the world;

478

and at that point [our] moral reference to purposes, and [our] idea of a moral legislator and author of the world, an idea that is a theological concept, seems to develop on its own from the physicoteleological basis for proving [the existence of God], even though it is nothing but an addition.

There is also no need to change this situation as far as *stating* [the proof] under ordinary circumstances is concerned; for when common sound understanding mingles different and heterogeneous principles, from only one of which it is in fact inferring, and moreover inferring correctly; then it usually finds it difficult to separate them, if doing so requires much meditation. Actually the moral basis for proving the existence of God does not merely *supplement* the physicoteleological one and make it a complete proof. Rather, it is a special proof that *makes up* for the failure of the physicoteleological proof to convince. For in fact the latter proof can accomplish only one thing: as reason judges the basis of nature and the basis of nature's contingent but admirable order that we come to know only through experience, this proof directs it and draws its attention to the causality of a cause on which nature and its contingent order are based in terms of purposes (a cause that, given the character of our cognitive powers, we have to think of as intelligent); and through this the proof makes reason more receptive to the moral proof. [But] what this latter concept requires [the qualification *moral,* as added to the concept of that intelligent cause,] is so essentially different from anything that concepts of nature can contain and teach us, that we need a special proof, and basis for it, completely independent of physicoteleological ones, in order to state the concept of the original being in a way that suffices for a theology, and to infer that this being exists. Hence the moral proof (which admittedly proves the existence of God from a point of view of reason that is only practical, though also indispensable [*unnachlaßlich*]) would still retain its force if the world offered us no material at all, or only ambiguous material, for physical teleology. We can conceive of rational beings finding themselves surrounded by a nature that showed no distinct trace of organization, but only the effects of a mere mechanism of crude matter. If [they considered] that nature, and how changeable the merely contingently purposive forms and relations are that occasionally occur in it, it would seem to them that there is no basis for inferring an intelligent author, and nothing would prompt them to [try] a physical teleology. And yet

479

reason, which would get no instruction from concepts of nature, would still find in the concept of freedom, and in the moral ideas based on it, a practically sufficient basis for postulating the concept of the original being as adequate to these ideas, i.e., as a deity, and for postulating nature (even our own existence) as a final purpose that conforms to [the concept] and the laws of freedom, [with both of these postulations made] in response [*Rücksicht*] to the insistent [*unnachlaßlich*] command of practical reason. On the other hand, the fact that the actual world offers the rational beings in it a wealth of material for physical teleology (which indeed would not have to be so) does serve the moral argument as welcome confirmation, as far as nature is able to offer something analogous to the (moral) ideas or reason. For this [confirmation] provides the concept of a supreme cause that has understanding (though this [qualification, that the supreme cause has understanding] is far from sufficient for a theology) with sufficient reality for reflective judgment. But this concept is not required as a basis for the moral proof. Nor does the moral proof serve the physicoteleological proof, which by itself does not point to morality at all, as a supplement to form *one* proof by a continued inference in terms of a single principle; [for] two such heterogeneous principles as nature and freedom can only yield two different kinds of proof, and we find that the attempt to start the proof from nature is insufficient for what is to be proved.

If the physicoteleological basis were sufficient for the desired proof [of the existence of a moral author of the world], speculative reason would be greatly satisfied. For then we could hope to produce a theosophy (which is the appropriate term for a theoretical cognition of divine nature and [God's] existence that would suffice to explain both the character of the world and the vocation of the moral laws). Similarly, if psychology were sufficient for reaching cognition of the immortality of the soul, it would make possible a pneumatology that would be equally welcome to speculative reason. But in fact, no matter how dear a theosophy and pneumatology would be to our conceit [and] desire for knowledge [*Wissen*], neither fulfills the wish of reason as far as theory is concerned, which would have to be based on a knowledge [*Kenntnis*] of the nature of things. Perhaps they would fulfill their objective final aim better if we based both of them—the first as theology, the second as anthropology—on the moral principle, i.e., the principle of freedom, so that they would have a basis adequate for the practical use of reason; but that is a different question that we need not here pursue further.

That the physicoteleological basis for proving [the existence of God] is insufficient for theology is due to the fact that it does not, and cannot, provide a sufficiently determinate concept of the original being. Rather, we must get such a concept from a quite different [source], or compensate for the deficiency in the concept by choosing to supplement it. You infer, from the great purposiveness in natural forms and in their relations, a world cause with understanding; but what degree of this understanding? Doubtless you cannot presume to infer the highest possible understanding; for that would require that you can see that a greater understanding than the one for which you perceive evidence in the world is inconceivable, which would amount to attributing omniscience to yourselves. You similarly infer, from the magnitude of the world, that its author has very great might. But you will agree that this has meaning only by comparison to your grasp, and agree that, since you do not cognize everything that is possible and hence cannot compare it with the world's magnitude that you know, you are using too small a standard to infer that its author has omnipotence; and so on.[101] You cannot in this way arrive at a determinate concept of an original being—such a concept as would be suitable for a theology. For this concept can be found only in that of the totality of perfections united with an understanding, and merely *empirical* data can in no way help you arrive at such a concept. But without such a determinate concept you also cannot infer a *single* intelligent original being, but can only assume it (for whatever aim [*Behuf*]). It is true that we may readily allow you to choose to make an addition (since reason has no well-founded objection against it): that where we find so much perfection we may surely assume all perfection as united in a single cause of the world, since reason manages better, theoretically and practically, with so determinate a principle. But then you surely cannot extol this concept of the original being as one you have proved, since you have only assumed it to assist you in using reason. Hence all lamentation and impotent rage about the alleged crime [we commit] in casting doubt on the cogency

[margin] 480

---

[101] [For similar points, see the *Critique of Pure Reason*, A 622–28 = B 650–56, and the *Critique of Practical Reason*, Ak. V, 138–39.]

of your chain of inference is idle swagger; [you] would like for the doubt we freely express about your argument to be considered doubt about sacred truth, so that under this cover the shallowness of your argument may escape [us].

Moral teleology, on the other hand, whose basis is no less firm than that of physical teleology, even deserves to be preferred to it, because it rests a priori on principles inseparable from our reason and leads us to what is required to make a theology possible: a determinate *concept* of the supreme cause as cause of the world according to moral laws, and hence of a cause that satisfies our moral final purpose. And this requires that this cause has, as properties of its nature, nothing less than omniscience, omnipotence, omnipresence, etc.; [for] we must think these properties as connected with, and hence as adequate to, the moral final purpose, and that purpose is infinite. Thus moral teleology alone can provide us with the concept of a *single* author of the world suitable for a theology.

In this way theology also leads directly to *religion,* as the *cognition*[102] *of our duties as divine commands;*[103] for the cognition of our duty, and of the final purpose reason enjoins on us in this duty, is what was first able to produce a determinate concept of God, so that in its very origin this concept is inseparable from our obligation to that being.[104] On the other hand, if we could find a determinate concept of the original being along the merely theoretical route (namely, the concept of this being as mere cause of nature), even then it would still be very difficult and perhaps even impossible, without choosing to interpolate, to [find] careful proofs [that would entitle us] to attribute to this being a causality in terms of moral laws, while without such a causality that allegedly theological concept [of the original being] cannot form a foundation for religion. Even if we could give religion a basis following this theoretical route, such a

---

[102] [Or *recognition.*]

[103] [Cf. the *Critique of Pure Reason,* A 818–19 = B 846–47; the *Critique of Practical Reason,* Ak. V, 129; *Religion within the Bounds of Reason Alone,* Ak. VI, 153; and the *Dispute among the [University's] Schools [Fakultäten],* Ak. VII, 36.]

[104] [According to the *Metaphysics of Morals* (Ak. VI, 486–88), the duties we have *toward God* are distinct from the duties we have *toward man*; the latter (presumably inasmuch as we cognize them as divine commands) are duties (merely) "with respect to" God, or "actually with respect to the idea we form of such a being."]

religion would actually differ from one in which the concept of God and the (practical) conviction of his existence arise from basic moral ideas: it would differ from it as far as attitude is concerned (yet that is what is essential in it). For if we had to presuppose the omnipotence and omniscience, etc. of an author of the world, as concepts given us from elsewhere, so as only then to apply our concepts of duties to our relation to this being, then the concepts of these duties would have to carry with them a very strong tincture of compulsion and forced submission. On the other hand, if our deep respect for the moral law, quite freely [and] in accordance with what our own reason prescribes, [makes us] conceive of the final purpose of our vocation, then there is the truest reverence, which is wholly different from pathological fear, in our accepting and including in our moral perspectives a cause that   482 is in harmony with the final purpose and with [the possibility of] achieving it, and in our submitting to this cause willingly.[105]

Why are we concerned to have a theology at all? Obviously we do not need it in order to expand or correct our knowledge of nature, or in fact any theory whatever. We need it solely for a subjective aim: for religion, i.e., for the practical—specifically, the moral—use of reason. Now if it turns out that the only argument that leads us to a determinate concept of the object of theology is itself a moral argument, not only shall we not have misgivings about confessing that such an argument establishes the existence of God sufficiently only for a practical aim, our moral vocation, and that in such an argument our speculation neither proves its strength in any way nor extends the range of its domain: confessing this will also not make us find the assent, arising from this basis for proving [the existence of God], insufficient in any way for its final aim. We might also have misgivings about, or find an alleged contradiction between, the assertion made here that a theology is possible, and what the critique of speculative reason said about the categories, namely, that they can give rise to

---

[105] The admiration for [the] beauty [of nature], as well as the emotion aroused by the so diverse purposes of nature, that a meditative mind is able to feel even before it has a clear conception of an intelligent author of the world, have something about them similar to a *religious* feeling. Hence, when they inspire in us that admiration which is connected with far more interest than mere theoretical contemplation can arouse, they initially seem to affect the moral feeling (of gratitude and veneration toward the cause we do not know), because we [then] judge [nature] in a way analogous to the moral way, and therefore they seem to affect the mind by arousing moral ideas.

cognition only if they are applied to objects of sense, but not at all if they are applied to the supersensible. But these misgivings and this alleged contradiction will disappear once we see that, though we here use the categories for a cognition of God, we do so solely from a practical and not from a theoretical point of view (as to what the nature of God, which is inscrutable for us, is in itself). Let me take this opportunity to put an end to the misinterpretation of that doctrine of the *Critique* [*of Pure Reason*] which, although very necessary, does also relegate reason to its [proper] bounds, to the vexation of the blind dogmatist. To this end, I shall here add the following elucidation of that doctrine.

483

If I attribute to a body *motive force,* and hence think it by means of the category of *causality,* then as a result I *cognize* the body at the same time, i.e., I determine the concept of it, as an object as such, by means of what (as [the] condition that makes that [causal] relation possible) this object itself must have as an object of sense. For if the motive force that I attribute to it is a repulsive one, then (even if I do not yet posit another object next to it against which it exerts this force) the object [must have all of the following]: it must have a place in space; it must also have extension, i.e., space within the object itself, and this space must moreover be permeated by the repulsive force of the parts of the object; finally, [there must be] the law that governs this permeation (namely, that the basis for the repulsion of the parts must decrease in the same proportion as the body's extension—and the space that the parts occupy as a result of that force—increases). By contrast, if I think a supersensible being as the *first mover,* and hence think it by means of the category of causality, since [I find] that same attribute [*Bestimmung*] in the world (namely, the motion of matter), then I must not think this being as having some place or other in space, nor as extended; indeed, I must not even think it as existing in time and simultaneously with other beings. Hence I have no determinations [or attributes: *Bestimmungen*] whatever for this being that could allow me to understand under what condition it is possible for it to be [the] basis for motion. Therefore, [using] the predicate of cause does not in the least allow me to cognize this being itself (as first mover). All I have is the presentation of a something that contains the basis of the motions in the world; and the relation that this being has to these motions, as their cause, gives me no further [information] about the character of the thing that is this cause, and therefore leaves the concept of it quite empty. This is because, while predicates whose object[s] are found only in the world of sense allow me to proceed to the existence of something that must contain the basis of the world of sense, they do not allow me to determine [*Bestimmung*] the concept of this something as a supersensible being, since that concept excludes all those predicates. Hence if I determine the category of causality by means of the concept of a *first mover,* then this category does not in the least allow me to cognize what God is. But what if I [start] from the order in the world: perhaps I shall be more successful [in my attempt] not merely to *think* the causality of that being as the causality of a supreme *understanding,* but also to *cognize* that being by determining the concept [of a first mover] in this way [i.e., as involving understanding], since then the irksome condition of space and extension does not come in. Now the great purposiveness in the world does indeed compel us to *think* a supreme cause for that world, and as one having a causality [that it exercises] through an understanding. But that does not at all authorize us to *attribute* this understanding to that cause. (Similarly, we have to think, e.g., the eternity of God as existence in all time, because we can form no other concept of mere existence as a magnitude, i.e., as duration.[106] Again, we have to think divine omnipresence as existence in all places, so that we can grasp God's direct presence to all things that are external to one another. But we are not entitled to attribute any of these determinations to God as something we have cognized in him.) If I determine the causality of man, in view of certain products that are explicable only [as arising] through an intentional purposiveness, by thinking this causality as an understanding in man, then I need not stop there [i.e., at the mere thought] but can attribute this predicate to him as a very familiar property of his and cognize him through it. For I know that intuitions are given to the senses of man, and that his understanding brings them under a concept and hence under a rule. I know that this concept contains only the common characteristic[s] (and omits the particular) and hence is discursive, and that the rules for bringing given presentations under a consciousness as such are given by the understanding even prior to those intuitions, etc. Hence I attribute this property to man as

484

---

[106] [Cf. *Dreams of a Spirit-Seer,* Ak. II, 339, and *The End of All Things* (1794), Ak. VIII, 327–28.]

a property through which I *cognize* him. Now if I want to *think* a supersensible being (God) as an intelligence, then for a certain point of view in my use of reason this is not only permitted but also unavoidable. But I am in no way entitled to flatter myself that I [can] attribute [an] understanding to this being and *cognize* this being through it as through a property. For in the case of God I have to omit all those conditions under which alone I am familiar with an understanding; and hence this predicate, which serves to determine only man, cannot at all be applied to a supersensible object, and therefore through a causality determined in this way we cannot at all cognize what God is. And thus it is with all the categories; they cannot have any significance whatever for cognition from a theoretical point of view if they are not applied to objects of a possible experience. But from a certain different point of view, I certainly can, indeed must, use the analogy with an understanding to think even a supersensible being, yet without trying to cognize it through this theoretically: I must do so when this attribute [viz., understanding] of its causality concerns an effect [to be achieved] in the world which involves an aim that is morally necessary, but impossible for beings of sense to achieve. For then we can have, through properties and attributes of God's causality that we think in him merely by analogy, a cognition of God and his existence[107] (a theology) that has all the reality required for a practical point of view [*Beziehung*] but it also has it *only with respect to this* (the moral) *point of view.* Hence an ethicotheology is indeed possible. For although morality with its rule can subsist without theology, morality with the final aim [or intention] that this same rule enjoins on us cannot subsist without theology, but reason would in that case be at a loss concerning that aim. On the other hand, a theological ethics (of pure reason) is impossible; for if laws are not

485

---

[107] [Cf. above, Ak. 351–52. On "cognition by analogy," see also the *Prolegomena*, §§ 57–59, Ak. IV, 357–62; the *Anthropology*, Ak. VII, 191; *On [the] Dignified Tone Recently Adopted in Philosophy*. Ak. VIII, the n. on 399–401; and *On the Progress of Metaphysics since Leibniz and Wolff.* Ak. XX, 280: "In this way [as described in the quote given above, Ak. 351 br. n. 31] I can have a cognition of the supersensible, e.g., of God, not actually a theoretical cognition, but still one by analogy, an analogy, moreover, which it is necessary for reason to think. At the basis of this [cognition] lie the categories, because they belong necessarily to the form of [all] thought, whether this thought is directed to the sensible or to the supersensible, even though—and precisely because—the categories on their own do not yet determine any object, [i.e.,] they do not yet amount to any cognition."]

originally given by reason, and compliance with them brought about by it as a pure practical power, they cannot be moral [laws]. A theological physics would be a similar absurdity, because it would put forth not natural laws, but orders of a supreme will. On the other hand, a physical (properly speaking, physicoteleological) theology can at least serve as a propaedeutic to theology proper: for it finds a wealth of material in natural purposes, and contemplating these prompts in us the idea of a final purpose, a purpose that nature cannot offer; and so it can allow us to feel the need for a theology that would determine the concept of God sufficiently for the highest practical use of reason, even though it cannot produce such a theology and have an adequate basis for it in the evidence to which it appeals.

TRANSLATOR'S SUPPLEMENT

FIRST INTRODUCTION TO THE CRITIQUE OF JUDGMENT

INTRODUCTION

I

On Philosophy as a System

If philosophy is the *system* of rational [*Vernunft-*] cognition[1] through concepts, this [characterization] already suffices to distinguish it from a critique of pure reason [*Vernunft*]. For though a critique of pure reason contains a philosophical inquiry into the possibility of such cognition, it does not belong to a system of philosophy as a part of it, but outlines and examines the very idea of such a system in the first place.

If we divide this system, we must start by dividing it into its formal and its material part. The formal part (logic) encompasses merely the form of thought in a system of rules, while the material (or real) part considers systematically the objects we think about, insofar as we can have rational cognition of them from concepts.

Now this real system of philosophy, in turn, can be divided only into *theoretical* and *practical* philosophy. This is because the [respective] objects [of these two parts of philosophy] are distinct originally, and because, as a consequence, the [respective] principles of a science that includes these objects differ essentially. This division of the real system of philosophy into a theoretical and a practical part must be such that the one part [is] the philosophy of nature, the other that of morals. The philosophy of nature can include empirical principles, but the philosophy of morals must contain no principles other than pure a priori ones (since freedom cannot possibly be an object of experience).

There is however a prevailing [and] serious misunderstanding about what [objects, or areas] should be considered *practical* in such a sense of the term that [they] deserve to be included in a *practical*

---

[1] [*Erkenntnis*. Cf. above, Ak. 167 br. n. 2.]

philosophy, a misunderstanding that is quite detrimental to the very way the science [is to] deal [with these areas]. People have thought they could include in practical philosophy [such areas as] statesmanship, political economy, rules of household management as well as of etiquette, precepts for the well-being and hygiene of both soul and body (indeed, why not all professions and arts?), since all of them do contain a set [*Inbegriff*] of practical propositions. Now practical propositions do differ from theoretical ones, which deal with [*enthalten*] the possibility of things and with their attributes; they differ from them in the way we present[2] [this possibility and these attributes]. But that does not mean that they differ from them in content; the only practical propositions that differ from theoretical ones in content are those that concern *freedom* under laws. All other practical propositions are nothing more than the theory of what belongs to the nature of things, except that here this theory is applied to the way we can produce these things according to a principle, i.e., here we present [how] they are possible through a voluntary [*willkürlich*] act (and such acts are included among natural causes). Consider, for example, this problem in mechanics: to find, for a given force that is to be in equilibrium with a given weight, the proportion [or ratio] of the respective lever arms. Though the solution of this problem is expressed as a practical formula, this formula contains no more than the theoretical proposition that the length of the lever arms is inversely proportional to that force and that weight when these are in equilibrium, except that here we present this proportion, as far as its origin is concerned, as possible through a cause [which is such that] the basis determining it [to act] is the *presentation* of that proportion. (This cause is our power of choice [*Willkür*].) The same holds for all practical propositions that concern merely the production of objects. Suppose that we are offered precepts for furthering our happiness, and that, e.g., all they talk about is what we must do about our own person to [make ourselves] receptive to happiness. All we present in such precepts is the conditions within [us] under which this happiness is possible, such as modesty, moderation of our inclinations to keep them from becoming passion[s], etc.: we present these conditions as belonging to the nature of the subject, and we also present the way we

196'

[2] [*Vorstellen*, traditionally rendered as 'to represent.' See above, Ak. 175 br. n. 17 and Ak. 203 br. n. 4.]

[can] produce this equilibrium [within us], namely we present it as a causality that we ourselves can [exercise], and so we present everything as [a] direct consequence of the theory of the object [happiness, in this case] as related to the theory of our own nature ([i.e., of³] ourselves as cause). Hence, while this practical precept differs from a theoretical [proposition] in formula[tion], it does not differ from it in content, and hence [we] do not need a special kind of philosophy in order to gain insight into this connection between [those] bases [or grounds] and their consequences. In a word: all practical propositions which derive something that nature can contain from our power⁴ of choice as cause belong to theoretical philosophy, i.e., to cognition of nature; only those practical propositions that legislate to freedom are different in kind from theoretical propositions in terms of their content. The first type of practical propositions may be said to constitute the practical part of a *philosophy of nature,* but the second type alone [may be said to] form the basis of a special *practical philosophy.*

197'

Comment

It is very important to define philosophy precisely, as to its parts; hence we must not include something as a [distinct] member in the division of philosophy as a system, if it is only a consequence or an application of philosophy to given cases and [hence] requires no special principles.

We distinguish [*werden unterschieden*] practical propositions from theoretical ones either by their principles or by their consequences. If we distinguish them by their consequences, then they do not form a special part of the science [to which they pertain] but belong to the theoretical part, as a special kind of consequences [drawn] from the science. Now the possibility of things in terms of natural laws differs [*ist unterschieden*], in its principles, essentially from the possibility of things in terms of laws of freedom. But this difference does not

³ [Deleting the comma between '*Natur*' and '*(uns selbst als Ursache).*']
⁴ [On my use of 'power,' rather than 'faculty,' see Ak. 167 br. n. 3.)

consist in [the fact] that in the case of the possibility of things in terms of laws of freedom we posit the cause in a will, while in the case of their possibility in terms of natural laws we posit the cause outside the will, in the things themselves. For suppose the will obeys no other principles than those about which the understanding [can] see that in terms of them, as mere natural laws, the object is possible: in that case, though the proposition concerning the object's possibility through the causality of our power of choice may be called a practical proposition, yet in its principle it does not differ at all from theoretical propositions about the nature of things; rather, it must borrow its principle from the nature of things in order to exhibit[5] an object's presentation as actualized.

198'

Hence practical propositions that in their content deal merely with the possibility of a presented object (through voluntary action) are only applications of a complete theoretical cognition and cannot form a special part of a science. A practical geometry as a separate science [of geometry] is an absurdity, no matter how many practical propositions the pure science [of geometry] contains, most of which are problems [for] whose solution [we] need special instruction[s]. The problem of constructing a square by means of a given line and a given right angle is a practical proposition, but [is nevertheless] purely a consequence [drawn] from theory. Similarly, the art of surveying ([ars] agrimensoria) can in no way claim the title of practical geometry, and be called a special part of geometry in general; rather, it belongs to the scholia of geometry, concerning the application of this science to [various] tasks.[6]

[5] [Darstellen, traditionally rendered as 'to present.' See above, Ak. 232 br. n. 51.]

[6] This pure and, precisely because of that purity, sublime, science of geometry seems to compromise some of its dignity if it confesses that on its elementary level it needs instruments to construct its concepts, even if only two: compass and ruler.[7] These constructions alone are called geometric, while those of higher geometry are called mechanical, because to construct the concepts of higher geometry we need more complex machines. Yet even when we call compass [Zirkel] and ruler [Lineal] (circinus et regula) instruments, we mean not the actual instruments, which could never produce those figures [circle and (straight) line] with mathematical precision, but only the simplest ways [these figures can] be exhibited by our a priori imagination, [a power] that no instrument can equal.

[7] [See the Preface to Isaac Newton's Mathematical Principles of Natural Philosophy, and cf. Kant's Metaphysical Foundations of Natural Science, Ak. IV, 478.]

Consider even a natural science insofar as it rests on empirical principles, i.e., physics proper: even here the practical arrangements, called experimental physics, that we make in order to discover hidden natural laws, can in no way justify our calling this [experimental physics] a practical physics (another absurdity, just like [a practical geometry]), as a [distinct] part of natural philosophy. For the principles we follow in performing experiments must themselves always be obtained from our knowledge [*Kenntnis*] of nature, and hence from theory. The same holds for the practical precepts concerning the voluntary production in us of a certain state of mind (e.g., the state of stirring or restraining our imagination, pacifying or abating our inclinations). There is no practical *psychology* as a special part of the philosophy of human nature. For the principles of [how we] can [produce a certain mental] state by means of art must be borrowed from those of [how our] attributes can [arise] from what our nature is like, and although they consist of practical propositions, they still do not form a practical part of empirical psychology but belong merely to its scholia, because they have no special principles.

199'

In general, practical propositions (whether purely a priori or empirical) that directly [*unmittelbar*] assert the possibility of an object through our power of choice, always belong to our knowledge of nature and to the theoretical part of philosophy. [They must be distinguished from] those practical propositions that directly [*direkt*] express [*darstellen*], as necessary, the determination of [our power of choice to] an act by the mere presentation of the act's form (in terms of laws as such), without regard to the means [used] to achieve the act's object: only these latter practical propositions can and must have their own principles (namely, in the idea of freedom); and although those propositions base on these same principles the concept of an object of the will (the highest good), yet this object belongs to that practical precept (which is then called [a] moral [precept]) only indirectly, as consequence. Also, our knowledge of nature (i.e., theory) gives us no insight into the possibility of this object [the highest good]. Hence these practical propositions alone belong to a special part of a system of rational cognitions, a part called practical philosophy.

All other propositions of performance, with whatever science they

200′

may be affiliated, we might call *technical*[8] rather than practical, if we are worried about ambiguity. For they belong to the *art* of bringing about something that we want to exist [*sein*], and in a complete theory this art is never more than a consequence of it, not an independent part with whatever kind of injunctions. Hence all precepts of skill belong, as consequences, to the *technic*[9] of nature, and hence to our theoretical knowledge of nature. But I shall henceforth use the term technic in other cases too, namely, where we merely *judge* [certain] objects of nature *as if* they were made possible through art. In those cases the judgments are neither theoretical nor practical (in the [proper] sense just discussed), because they *determine*

201′

nothing about the character of the object, nor about how to produce it; rather, in them we judge nature itself, though merely by analogy with an art, in its subjective relation to our cognitive power, rather than in its objective [*objektiv*] relation to objects [*Gegenstände*] Now I shall not here call the[se] judgments themselves technical, but I shall call technical the power of judgment[11] on whose laws they are

---

[8] [In the sense derived from the Greek τέχνη (téchnē), i.e., 'art' in the sense that includes craft.]

[9] This is the place to correct a mistake I made in the *Foundations of the Metaphysics of Morals*: having said there that imperatives of skill command only conditionally[10]— namely, under the condition of merely possible, i.e., *problematic*, purposes—I called such practical precepts problematic imperatives. But in fact this expression is contradictory. I should have called them *technical*, i.e., imperatives of art. Now it is true that *pragmatic* imperatives, i.e., rules of prudence, which command under the condition of an *actual* and even subjectively necessary purpose [happiness], are also [usually] included under the technical imperatives. (For what is prudence but the skill of using free human beings—and in particular one's own natural predispositions and inclinations—for one's [own] aims?) Yet we are justified in giving these [so-called] technical imperatives a special name [viz., *pragmatic*, thus confining the term 'technical' to (ordinary) imperatives of skill]. For in the case of technical imperatives as such [*allgemein*], the task is merely how [we are] to achieve a [certain] purpose, and what this purpose itself consists in must be presupposed as known. But in the case of pragmatic imperatives the purpose we attribute to ourselves and others is not just some purpose or other, but is one's own happiness, so that here we have the additional task of determining what this purpose itself (happiness) consists in [, not just how (we are) to achieve it].

[10] [The reference is to Ak. IV, 414–17. The conditional imperatives (there called "hypothetical") are there said to be of two kinds: *problematic* and *assertoric*. But *there too*, contrary to what Kant goes on to say here, the same distinction is also made using the terms 'technical' and 'pragmatic.']

[11] [*Urteilskraft*, rendered either as 'power of judgment' or simply as 'judgment'; see above, Ak. 167 br. n. 4.]

based, as well as nature [as judged] in accordance with that power. Since this technic contains no propositions that are determinative objectively, it also forms no part of doctrinal philosophy, but only a part of the critique of our cognitive powers.

II

On the System of the Higher Cognitive Powers Which Lies at the Basis of Philosophy

[Now] suppose we are concerned with dividing, not a *philosophy,* but our *ability* [or *power: Vermögen*] to *cognize a priori through concepts* (our higher cognitive power), i.e., suppose we are concerned with [dividing] a critique of pure reason, but of pure reason as regards only its ability to think (i.e., leaving out of account [even] pure intuition): then the systematic presentation of our ability to think turns out to have three parts. The first part is *understanding,* the ability to cognize the *universal* (i.e., rules); the second is *judgment,* the ability to *subsume the particular* under the universal; and the third is *reason,* i.e., the ability to *determine* the particular through the universal (i.e., to derive [the particular] from principles).

The critique of pure *theoretical* reason was devoted to the sources of all a priori cognition (hence including the sources of what, in this cognition,[12] belongs to intuition), and it provided us with the laws of *nature,* while the critique of *practical* reason provided us with the law of *freedom;* and so it seems as if we have already completed our treatment of the a priori principles of all philosophy.

On the other hand, if understanding provides us a priori with laws

202′

---

12 [Reading '*ihm*' for '*ihr*']

of nature, [and] reason with laws of freedom, then surely it is to be expected by analogy that judgment, which mediates the connection [*Zusammenhang*] between understanding and reason, will similarly provide its own a priori principles for this [mediation], and that perhaps it will lay the basis for a special part of philosophy, even though philosophy as a system can have only two parts.

Yet judgment is a very special cognitive power, not at all independent: it gives us neither concepts nor ideas of any object whatever, whereas understanding does give us such concepts, and reason such ideas. For judgment is merely an ability to subsume under concepts given from elsewhere. So if there is to be a concept or rule that arises originally from the power of judgment, it would have to be a concept of things of *nature insofar as nature conforms to our power of judgment,* and hence a concept of a [special] character of nature: the only concept we could form of this character is that [nature's] arrangement conforms to the ability we have to subsume the particular laws, which are given, under more universal laws, even though [*doch*] these are not given. In other words, this concept would have to be that of a purposiveness of nature for the sake of our ability to cognize nature, insofar as this ability requires that we be able to judge the particular as contained under the universal and to subsume it under the concept of a nature.

203'

Now a concept of this sort is the concept of experience *as a system in terms of empirical laws.* For although experience forms a system in terms of *transcendental* laws, which comprise the condition under which experience as such is possible, yet empirical laws might be so *infinitely diverse,* and *the forms* of nature which pertain to particular experience *so very heterogeneous,* that the concept [*Begriff*] of a system in terms of these (empirical) laws must be quite alien to the understanding, and that the possibility—let alone the necessity—of such a whole is beyond [our] grasp [*begriffen*]. And yet for particular experience to cohere thoroughly in terms of fixed principles, it must have this systematic coherence of empirical laws as well; for only then can judgment subsume the particular under what is universal though still always empirical, and so on until [it arrives at] the highest empirical laws and the natural forms conforming to them, and hence only then can it consider the *aggregate* of particular experiences as a *system* of them. For unless this [systematic coherence of empirical laws] is presupposed, particular experiences cannot have thoroughly lawful coherence,[13] i.e., empirical unity.

This [systematicity is a] lawfulness [that] intrinsically [*an sich*] is contingent (in terms of all concepts of the understanding). Judgment (only for its own benefit) presupposes it in nature, as a presumption. This lawfulness is a formal purposiveness of nature that we simply *assume* in it; it provides no basis for a theoretical cognition of nature, nor for a practical principle of freedom, but it does give us a principle for judging and investigating nature: a principle by which to seek, for particular experiences, the universal [empirical] laws we must follow in engaging in such experiences in order to bring out that systematic connection [of them] which [we] need for coherent experience and which we have grounds to assume a priori.

Hence the concept that arises originally from judgment, as its own concept, is the concept of nature as *art;* in other words, it is the concept of the *technic of nature* regarding its *particular* [*besonder*] laws. This concept provides no basis for any theory, and it does not contain cognition of objects and their character any more than logic does; it gives us only a principle by which we [can] proceed in terms of empirical laws, which makes it possible for us to investigate nature.

204'

205'

[13] The possibility of experience as such is the possibility of empirical cognitions, which are [*als*] synthetic judgments. Hence we cannot (as is commonly supposed) derive [*ziehen*] this possibility *analytically*[,] from [a] mere compar[ison of] perceptions; for the connection of two different perceptions in the concept of an object (to yield a cognition of the object) is a *synthesis*, and the only way in which this synthesis makes empirical *cognition* possible, in other words, experience, is in terms of principles [*Prinzipien*] of the synthetic unity of appearances, i.e., in terms of principles [*Grundsätze*] by which they are brought under the categories. Now these empirical cognitions [with the synthetic unity that each has] do [in turn] form an analytic unity of all experience, [namely,] in terms of what they necessarily have in common (the transcendental laws of nature I just mentioned [which are the principles of the synthetic unity of every appearance]); but they do not form that synthetic unity, of experience as a system, that connects the empirical laws under a principle even in terms of that in which they differ (and where the[ir] diversity can be infinite). Now what a category is for [*in Ansehung*] every particular experience [giving it its synthetic unity], this the purposiveness or appropriateness of nature (even in its particular laws) [for our power of judgment] is for [*zu*] that power [in judging nature, as experienced, in terms of the synthetic unity of a system]. In terms of [the concept of] this purposiveness or appropriateness of nature, we present nature not merely as mechanical [as we do under the categories], but also as technical; and though it is true that this concept does not objectively determine [this] synthetic unity, as a category does [for every particular experience], yet it provides us with subjective principles [of judgment] that serve us as a guide in investigating nature.

204'

But this [concept of the technic of nature] does not enrich our knowledge of nature with a special [*besonder*] objective law, but only serves judgment as the basis for a maxim by which we [can] observe nature and to which we [can] hold up [and compare] nature's forms.

Now [using] this [concept of the technic of nature] does not add a new part to philosophy as a doctrinal system of our cognition of nature and of freedom: for our presentation of nature as art is a mere idea that serves as a principle for our investigation of nature, and hence merely for [us] subjects, so that we may possibly introduce into the aggregate of empirical laws, as empirical laws, the coherence that a system has, by attributing to nature a reference to this our need [for systematicity]. On the other hand, our concept of a technic of nature, as a heuristic principle for judging nature, will belong to the critique of our cognitive power, [the part of this critique] which indicates what cause we have for presenting nature in this way, where this idea originates and whether it is to be found in an a priori source, and also what the range and the limit of its use are. In a word, such an inquiry will belong, as a part, to the system of the critique of pure reason, but not to the system of doctrinal philosophy.[14]

III

On the System of
All the Powers
of the Human Mind

We can reduce all the powers of the human mind, without exception, to these three: the *cognitive power,* the *feeling of pleasure and displeasure,* and the *power of desire.* It is true that philosophers who otherwise deserve unlimited praise for the thoroughness in their way of thinking have asserted that this distinction is only illusory, and have tried to bring all powers under nothing but the cognitive power. Yet it is quite easy to establish, and has in fact been realized for some

206'

[14] [Cf. Ak. 170 incl. br. n. 11.]

time, that this attempt to bring unity into that diversity of powers, though otherwise undertaken in the genuine philosophic spirit, is futile. For there is always a great difference between presentations insofar as, on the one hand, they belong to [theoretical] cognition, when they are referred merely to the object and to the unity of consciousness these presentations [contain]—or, similarly, insofar as they have objective reference when they are considered at the same time as cause of the actuality of this object and are included with the power of desire [a power that can give rise to practical cognition]—and, on the other hand, presentations insofar as they are referred merely to the subject: for here the presentations themselves are bases merely for preserving their own existence in the subject, and in so far are considered [merely] in relation to the feeling of pleasure; but this feeling neither is nor provides any cognition at all, though it may presuppose cognition as a basis that determines it.

Now the[re is a] connection between the cognition of an object and the feeling of pleasure [or] displeasure in the object's existence, [and in this connection consists] the determination, of the power of desire, to produce the object. But while this link is knowable enough empirically, it is not based on any a priori principle; and hence to that extent the mental powers form no system, but only an *aggregate*. It is true that we can show [the following] a priori connection between the feeling of pleasure and the other two powers [of cognition and of desire]. We can connect a [certain] a priori cognition, namely, reason's concept of freedom, with the power of desire, as the basis determining this power, and can then find in this objective determination [something] subjective as well: a feeling of pleasure contained in the determination of the will. But if this is how the cognitive power and the power of desire are connected, then they are not connected *by means of* pleasure or displeasure; for then the pleasure or displeasure does not precede [the determination of] the power of desire, but either only [*allererst*] follows it, or perhaps is nothing other than our sensation of this very ability of the will to be determined by reason, in which case it is no special feeling and separate [*eigentümlich*] receptivity at all that would need [to occupy] a special division among the properties of the mind. On the other hand, an analysis of the mental powers in general yields incontestably a[nother] feeling of pleasure[, one] that is independent of the determination of the power of desire and can even serve as a basis determining it. But in order for this

207'

feeling of pleasure to be connected with the other two powers in a system, this feeling must, as these other two powers do, also rest not on merely empirical bases but on a priori principles. Hence for the idea of philosophy as a system we also need *a critique* (even if not a doctrine) *of the feeling of pleasure and displeasure* insofar as its basis is not empirical.

Now the *power of cognition* according to concepts has its a priori principles in pure understanding (in its concept of nature), and the *power of desire* has its a priori principles in pure reason (in its concept of freedom). That leaves, among the general properties of the mind, an intermediate power or receptivity, the *feeling of pleasure and displeasure,* just as judgment is left as an intermediate power between the [other] higher cognitive powers [understanding and reason]. What is more natural than to suspect that judgment will also contain a priori principles[,] for the feeling of pleasure and displeasure?

Even before we decide anything about the possibility of this connection, we can already [see] a certain unmistakable appropriateness of the power of judgment to the feeling of pleasure, an appropriateness either for serving the feeling of pleasure as [a] basis that determines it, or for finding in the feeling of pleasure [a] basis that determines the power of judgment. For, in the *division of our power of cognition through concepts,* while understanding and reason refer their presentations to objects in order to acquire concepts of them, judgment refers solely to the subject and does not on its own produce any concepts of objects. Similarly, while in the general *division of all the mental powers* both the cognitive power and the power of desire [have] an *objective* reference in the presentations, the feeling of pleasure and displeasure is only the subject's receptivity to a [certain] state [*Bestimmung*]. Therefore, if the power of judgment is indeed to determine [*bestimmen*] anything on its own, then presumably this can only be the feeling of pleasure; and, conversely, if the feeling of pleasure is indeed to have an a priori principle, then presumably we can find it only in the power of judgment.

208'

IV

On Experience as a System for the Power of Judgment

We saw in the *Critique of Pure Reason* that nature as a whole, as the sum total of all objects of experience, constitutes a system in terms of transcendental laws, those that the understanding itself gives a priori (to appearances insofar as, connected in one consciousness, they are to constitute experience). That is why experience too, considered objectively, i.e., in the way experience as such is possible (ideally), must constitute a system of possible empirical cognitions, and it must do so in terms of both universal and particular laws: for the unity of nature [which is implicit in the concept of nature[15] as spelled out by those transcendental laws[16]] requires [that intrinsically experience form] such [a system, one] in terms of a principle of the thorough connection of everything contained in that sum total of all appearances. To this extent, then, experience as such must be regarded, according to transcendental laws of the understanding, as a system and not as a mere aggregate.[17]

209'

But it does not follow from this that nature is, even in terms of [its] *empirical laws,* a system which the human cognitive power *can grasp* [*fassen*], and that the thorough systematic coherence of its appearances in an experience, and hence experience itself as a system, is possible for human beings. For the empirical laws might be so diverse and heterogeneous that, though we might on occasion discover particular laws in terms of which we could connect some perceptions to [form] an experience, we could never bring these empirical laws themselves under a common principle [and so] to the unity [characteristic] of kinship. We would be unable to do this if—as is surely

---

[15] [See above, Ak. 180.]

[16] [Cf. above, Ak. 359.]

[17] [Cf. below, Ak. 232'–33'. Though understanding asserts *that there is* (this system in terms of) such a principle, it *does not know* this principle (cf. *ibid.*), i.e., it does not know *what sort* of thorough connection there is among all appearances. It is judgment which fills this gap by *presupposing* a principle of its own. Cf. above, Ak. 203'–04'.]

possible intrinsically (at least insofar as the understanding can tell a priori)—these laws, as well as the natural forms conforming to them, were infinitely diverse and heterogeneous and manifested themselves to us as a crude chaotic aggregate without the slightest trace of a system. Yet, according to transcendental laws, we must presuppose such a system [even as one that can be manifested to us, i.e., a system of experience].

For *unity of nature in time and space,* and unity of the experience possible for us, are one and the same, since nature is a sum total [*Inbegriff*] of mere appearances (ways [we] present [things]), [a concept (*Begriff*) which] can have its objective reality solely in experience; [hence,] if we think of nature as a system (as indeed we must), then experience [too] must be possible [for us] as a system even in terms of empirical laws. Therefore it is subjectively necessary [for us to make the] transcendental *presupposition* that nature [as experience possible for us] does not have this disturbing boundless heterogeneity [*Ungleichartigkeit*] of empirical laws and heterogeneity [*Heterogeneität*] of natural forms, but that, rather, through the affinity of its particular laws under more general ones it takes on the quality of experience as an empirical system.

Now this presupposition is the transcendental principle of judgment. For judgment is not merely an ability to subsume the particular under the universal (whose concept is given), but also, the other way round, an ability to find the universal for the particular. But [the principle it needs for this cannot come from the understanding. For] the understanding, in its transcendental *legislation* to nature, considers only the conditions under which experience as such is possible as far as its form is concerned, [i.e.,] the understanding abstracts from all the diversity of possible empirical laws, and hence this principle of the affinity of the particular natural laws cannot be in the understanding. But since judgment does have to bring the particular laws under higher—though still always empirical—laws, even with regard to what is different about them in terms of the universal [a priori] laws, it is judgment [itself] which must [here] lay such a principle at the basis of its procedure. For suppose judgment [could only] grope about among natural forms: though [it might still find] them harmonizing with one another to [form certain] higher—though [still] empirical—laws they had in common, it would yet have to regard this harmony as quite contingent; and the contingency would be even greater if *particular*

210'

perceptions ever happened to take on the quality of an empirical law; but the contingency would be far greater [yet] if diverse empirical laws were fit, *in their overall coherence,* to [give rise to] the systematic unity of a cognition of nature in a possible experience, unless [judgment] presupposed such a form in nature by means of an a priori principle.

Consider all these formulas that have come to be in vogue: Nature takes the shortest way; *Nature does nothing in vain; Nature makes no leap in the diversity of its forms (continuum formarum*[18]*); Nature is rich in species and yet parsimonious in genera;* and so on. These formulas are nothing but that same transcendental utterance of judgment [by which] it stipulates to itself a principle for [considering] experience as a system, and hence for its own needs. Neither understanding nor reason can provide a priori a basis for such a natural law. For although our insight can tell us that nature in its merely formal laws (the laws through which it is object of experience as such) conforms to our understanding, yet in its particular laws, their diversity and heterogeneity, nature is free from all restrictions [imposed] by our legislative cognitive power. Rather, the basis of that principle is a mere presupposition that judgment makes for its own use, for the sake of unifying empirical laws, so that it can always ascend from what is empirical [and] particular, to what is more general [even if] also empirical. Experience, too, can in no way be credited with [offering us] such a principle, because only by presupposing this principle can we engage in experiences in a systematic way.

211'

V

On Reflective Judgment

Judgment can be regarded either as mere[ly] an ability to *reflect,* in terms of a certain principle, on a given presentation so as to [make] a concept possible, or as an ability to *determine* an underlying concept by means of a given empirical presentation. In the first case it is the

---

[18] [Continuum of forms.]

reflective, in the second the *determinative, power of judgment.* To *reflect* (or consider [*überlegen*])[19] is to hold given presentations up to, and compare them with, either other presentations or one's cognitive power [itself], in reference to a concept that this [comparison] makes possible. The reflective power of judgment [*Urteil*] is the one we also call the power of judging [*Beurteilung*] (*facultas diiudicandi*).[20]

When we *reflect* (even animals reflect, though only instinctively, i.e., in reference not to acquiring a concept, but to—say—determining an inclination), we need a principle just as much as we do when we determine, where the underlying concept of the object prescribes the rule to judgment and so takes the place of the principle.

The principle by which we reflect on given objects of nature is this: that for all natural things *concepts* can be found that are determined empirically.[21] This means that we can always presuppose nature's products to have a form that is possible in terms of universal laws which we can cognize. For if we were not allowed to presuppose this,

212'

---

[19] [Cf. the *Critique of Pure Reason*, A 260 = B 316.]

[20] [On Kant's difficulty with this terminological distinction, see above, Ak. 169 br. n. 9.]

[21] At first glance this principle does not look at all like a synthetic and transcendental proposition, but seems rather to be tautologous and to belong to mere logic. For logic teaches how we can compare a given presentation with others, and form a concept by extracting, as a characteristic for general use, what this presentation has in common with different ones. Yet logic teaches us nothing about whether, for each object, nature can offer us, for comparison, many more objects with a somewhat similar form, which is [the] condition under which it is possible to apply logic to nature. Rather, this condition is a principle by which we present nature as a system for our judgment, a system in which dividing the diverse into genera and species enables us, by making comparisons, to bring all the forms we find in nature to (more or less general) concepts. It is true that even pure understanding teaches us (though it too does so by means of synthetic principles) to think all things of nature as contained in a transcendental *system in terms of* a priori *concepts* (the categories). Yet (reflective) judgment, which seeks concepts even for empirical presentations, *qua* empirical, must make for this [end] this further assumption: it must assume that nature, with its boundless diversity, has hit upon a division of this diversity (into genera and species)[22] that enables our judgment to find accordance among the natural forms it compares, and [so] enables it to arrive at empirical concepts, as well as at coherence among these by ascending to concepts that are more general [though] also empirical. In other words, judgment presupposes a system of nature even in terms of empirical laws, and it does so a priori and hence by means of a transcendental principle.

212'

[22] [Parentheses added.]

and did not base our treatment of empirical presentations on this principle, then all our reflection would be performed merely haphazardly and blindly, and hence without our having a basis for expecting that this [reflection] is in agreement with nature.

With regard to the universal concepts of nature, which first make possible a concept of experience at all (apart from the particular determination[, which it gets empirically]), judgment requires no special principle by which to reflect: the instruction for this reflection is already [contained] in the concept of a nature as such, i.e., in the understanding, and judgment *schematizes* a priori and applies these schemata to each empirical synthesis, [the synthesis] without which no empirical judgment whatever would be possible. Here judgment not only reflects but also determines, and its transcendental schematism also provides it with a rule under which it subsumes given empirical intuitions.

But for concepts that must first be found for given empirical intuitions, and that presuppose a special [*besonder*] natural law in terms of which alone *particular* [*besonder*] experience is possible, judgment needs for its reflection a principle of its own, a principle that is also transcendental; and we cannot refer it to other [*wiederum*], already familiar, empirical laws and turn reflection into mere comparison with empirical forms for which we already have concepts. For this question arises: How could we hope that comparing perceptions would allow us to arrive at empirical concepts of what different natural forms have in common, if nature, because of the great variety in its empirical laws, had made these forms (as is surely conceivable) exceedingly heterogeneous, so heterogeneous that comparing [them], so as to discover among them an accordance and a hierarchy of species and genera, would be completely—or almost completely—futile? Surely something is presupposed whenever we compare empirical presentations in order to cognize, in natural things, empirical laws and *specific* forms that conform to them, [and] in order to cognize, by comparing these [forms] with others, even forms that *harmonize generically:* what is presupposed is that nature, even in its empirical laws, has adhered to a certain parsimony suitable for our judgment, and adhered to a uniformity we can grasp; and this presupposition must precede all comparison, as a priori principle of judgment.

So when reflective judgment tries to bring given appearances under empirical concepts of determinate natural things, it deals with

213'

them *technically* rather than schematically. In other words, it does not deal with them mechanically, as it were, like an instrument, guided by the understanding and the senses; it deals with them *artistically,* in terms of a principle that is universal but also indeterminate: the principle of a purposive arrangement of nature in a system—an arrangement [made], as it were, for the benefit of our judgment—by which the particular natural laws (about which the understanding says nothing) are [made] suitable for the possibility of experience as a system, as we must presuppose if we are to have any hope of finding our way in [the] labyrinth [resulting] from the diversity of possible particular laws. Hence judgment itself makes a priori the *technic of nature* [a] principle for its reflection. But it can neither explain this technic nor determine it more closely; nor does it have for this [adoption of that principle] an objective basis ([derived] from a cognition of things in themselves) determining the universal concepts of nature. Rather, judgment makes this technic its principle only so that it can, according to its need[s], reflect in terms of its own subjective law, and yet in a way that also harmonizes with natural laws in general.

But the principle of reflective judgment, by which we think nature as a system in terms of empirical laws, is merely a principle *for the logical use of judgment.* Though in its origin it is a transcendental principle, it allows us only to regard nature a priori as having in its diversity the quality of a *logical system* under empirical laws.

The logical form of a system consists merely in the division of given universal concepts (here the concept of a nature as such); [we make this division] by thinking, in terms of a certain principle, the particular (here the empirical) in its diversity as contained under the universal. In order to do this we must, if we proceed empirically and ascend from the particular to the universal, *classify* the diverse, i.e., compare several classes, each falling under a definite concept; and, when these classes are complete[ly enumerated] in terms of the[ir] common characteristic, we must subsume them under higher classes (genera), until we reach the concept containing the principle of the entire classification (and constituting the highest genus). On the other hand, if we start from the universal concept, so as to descend to the particular by a complete division, we perform what is called the *specification* of the diverse under a given concept, since we proceed from the highest genus to low genera (subgenera or species) and from species to subspecies. Instead of saying (as we do in ordinary speech) that we must make specific the particular that falls under a universal, it would be more correct to say, rather, that we *make the universal concept specific* by indicating the diverse [that falls] under it. For the genus is (logically considered) as it were the matter, or the crude [*roh*] substrate, that nature processes into particular species and subspecies by determining it multiply; and so we can say that *nature makes itself specific* in terms of a certain principle (or in terms of the idea of a system), by analogy with how teachers of law use this term when they talk about the specification of certain raw [*roh*] material [*Materien*].[23]

Now it is clear that reflective judgment, by its nature, cannot undertake to *classify* all of nature in terms of its empirical variety unless it presupposes that nature itself *makes* its transcendental laws *specific* in terms of some principle. Now this principle can only be that of [nature's] appropriateness for the power of judgment itself, [i.e., for judgment's attempt] to find among things, [despite] their immense diversity in terms of [all the] possible empirical laws, sufficient kinship to be able to bring them under empirical concepts (classes), and bring these under more general laws (higher genera), and so arrive at an empirical system of nature. Now this kind of classification is not [derived from] ordinary empirical cognition, but is artificial; by the same token, so far as we think of nature as making itself specific in terms of such a principle, we regard nature as *art*. Hence judgment necessarily carries within itself a priori a principle of the *technic* of nature; this technic differs from the *nomothetic* of nature, in terms of transcendental laws of the understanding, in that the nomothetic can assert [*geltend machen*] its principle as a law, while the technic can assert its principle only as a necessary presupposition.[24]

Hence judgment's own principle is: *Nature, for the sake of the*   216'

---

[23] The Aristotelian school too called the *genus* matter, but the *specific difference* the form.

[24] One may wonder whether Linnaeus[25] could have hoped to design a system of nature   216'
if he had had to worry that a stone which he found, and which he called granite, might differ in its inner character from any other stone even if it looked the same, so that all he could ever hope to find would be single things—isolated, as it were, for the understanding—but never a class of them that could be brought under concepts of genera and species.

[25] [See above, Ak. 427 incl. br. n. 17.]

power of judgment, makes its universal laws specific [and] into empirical ones, according to the form of a logical system.

This is where the concept of a *purposiveness* of nature arises. This concept belongs to reflective judgment, not to reason, because the purpose is not posited in the object at all, but is posited solely in the subject: in the subject's mere power to reflect. For we call something purposive if its existence seems to presuppose a presentation of that same thing; [and] natural laws that are constituted, and related to one another, as if judgment had designed them for its own need[s] are [indeed] similar to [the cases where] the possibility of [certain] things presupposes that these things are based on a presentation of them. Hence judgment, by means of its principle, thinks of nature as purposive, in [the way] nature makes its forms specific through empirical laws.

But in thinking of nature as purposive in this way, what we think of as purposive is not these forms themselves but only their relation to one another, as well as the suitability which, despite their great diversity, they have for a logical system of empirical concepts. Now if nature showed us no more than this logical purposiveness, we would indeed already have cause to admire it for that [purposiveness], since we cannot indicate a basis for it in terms of the universal laws of the understanding. Yet hardly anyone but perhaps a transcendental philosopher would be capable of this admiration, and even he could not point to a definite case that proved this purposiveness *in concreto,* but would have to think it only in a universal way.

VI

On the Purposiveness
That [Certain Individual]
Natural Forms Have as
So Many Particular Systems

There is a logical purposiveness in the [overall] form of nature, inasmuch as nature in its empirical laws makes itself specific as is required to make experience possible *as one system* of empirical cognition. This purposiveness [lies in] nature's harmonizing with what the subjective conditions of judgment are under which empirical concepts can cohere to [form] a whole of experience. But this [purposiveness] does not allow us to infer that nature is capable [*tauglich*] of [having] a real purposiveness within its products, i.e., capable of producing individual [*einzeln*] things that have the form of systems. For these things might well be—as far as [our] intuition can tell—mere aggregates, even if aggregates that are possible [only] in terms of empirical laws that together with others cohere in a system *of logical division,* [so that] we would not be entitled to assume, as the condition of the possibility of these particular things, a concept expressly directed to it, and hence a purposiveness of nature as underlying this possibility. Thus we see that earths, stones, minerals, and so on have no purposive form whatever [but] are mere aggregates, and yet are so akin in their inner character, and in the bases on which we cognize their possibility, that they are suitable for a classification of things under empirical laws in a system of nature, even though they do not *individually* [*an ihnen selbst*] manifest the form of a system.

So in saying that [certain] natural forms have an *absolute purposiveness,* I mean that their shape or inner structure is of such a character that we must, in our power of judgment, base their possibility on an idea. [We must do so] because purposiveness is a lawfulness that [something] contingent [may] have [insofar] as [it] is contingent. Insofar as nature's products are aggregates, nature proceeds *mechanically, as mere nature;* but insofar as its products are systems—e.g., crystal formations, various shapes of flowers, or the inner structure of plants

405

and animals—nature proceeds *technically,* i.e., it proceeds also as *art.* The distinction between these two ways of judging natural beings is made merely by *reflective* judgment. [Making this distinction is] something that *determinative* judgment did not (under principles of reason) allow it [to do], as regards the possibility of things themselves, wishing perhaps to have everything reduced to a mechanical kind of explanation. [But] reflective judgment certainly can, and perhaps must, permit [*geschehen lassen*] this distinction. For there is no inconsistency whatever between a *mechanical explanation* of an appearance, which is a task that reason performs in terms of objective principles, [and] a *technical* rule for *judging* that same object in terms of subjective principles of reflection on [such an] object.

So, on the one hand, it is true that judgment's principle of the purposiveness of nature in the specification of its universal laws by no means extends far enough for us to infer from it the production of *natural forms that are themselves purposive* (for even without such forms it is possible for nature to [form] this system in terms of empirical laws, and it is for the postulation of this alone that judgment had a basis), and [so] these forms must be given solely through experience. On the other hand, since we do have a basis for regarding nature in its particular laws as based on a principle of purposiveness, it always remains *possible* and permissible for us, if experience shows us purposive forms in nature's products, to ascribe such purposive forms to the same basis on which the first purposiveness may rest.

It may even be that this basis itself lies in the supersensible, and beyond the sphere of what insights into nature are possible for us; still we have already gained something even by having ready, in our power of judgment, a transcendental principle of the purposiveness of nature, a principle for [dealing with] whatever purposiveness experience [may] show us in natural forms. Though this principle is not adequate to explain how such forms are possible, it does at least give us permission to apply to nature and its lawfulness a very special concept, the concept of purposiveness, even though this concept cannot be an objective concept of nature, but is taken merely from the subjective relation of nature to a power of the mind.

VII

On the Technic of
Judgment as the Basis
of the Idea of a
Technic of Nature

As we have shown above, judgment first makes it possible, indeed necessary, for us to think of nature as having not only a mechanical necessity but also a purposiveness; if we did not presuppose this purposiveness, there could not be systematic unity in the thorough classification of particular forms in terms of empirical laws. We showed initially that this principle of purposiveness does not determine anything regarding the forms of natural products, since it is only a subjective principle of the division and specification of nature. So [to that extent] this purposiveness would remain merely conceptual: while it would supply us, to assist us in using reason in regard to nature's objects, with a maxim on which to base the logical use of judgment in experience (the maxim of the unity of nature in terms of its empirical laws),[26] yet no natural objects would be given us as products that in their [own] form correspond to that special kind of systematic unity, the systematic unity in terms of the presentation of a purpose. Now nature's *causality* regarding the form that its products have as purposes I would call the *technic* of nature. It contrasts with the mechanism of nature, which consists in the causality nature has insofar as it connects the diverse without (there being) a concept underlying the manner of this unification, roughly as when we call certain lifting devices—e.g., a lever or an inclined plane—machines but not works of art, since they can produce their purpose-directed effect even without [there being] an underlying idea; for while these devices can be used for purposes, their [own] possibility does not require a reference to purposes.

The first question that arises here is this: How can the technic of nature be *perceived* in nature's products? The concept of purposiveness

---

[26] [Parentheses added.]

407

220'

is not at all a constitutive concept of experience; it is not [a concept that can] determine an appearance [and so] belong to an empirical *concept* of the object, for it is not a category. [Rather,] we perceive purposiveness in our power of judgment insofar as it merely reflects on a given object, whether it reflects on the object's empirical intuition so as to bring it to some concept or other (which concept this is being indeterminate), or on the empirical concept itself so as to bring the laws it contains under common principles. So it is actually the *power of judgment* that is technical; nature is presented as technical only insofar as it harmonizes with, and [so] necessitates, that [technical] procedure of judgment. I shall show presently how the concept of reflective judgment, which enables us to perceive inwardly a purposiveness of our presentations, can also be applied to the presentation of the object [itself] as falling under this concept.[27]

Every empirical concept requires three acts of the spontaneous cognitive power: (1) *apprehension* (*apprehensio*) of the manifold of intuition; (2) *comprehension*[28] of this manifold, i.e., synthetic unity of the consciousness of this manifold, in the concept of an object (*apperceptio comprehensiva*); (3) exhibition (*exhibitio*), in intuition, of the object corresponding to this concept.[29] For the first of these acts we need imagination; for the second, understanding; for the third, judgment, which would be determinative judgment if we are dealing with an empirical concept.

But when we merely reflect on a perception we are not dealing with a determinate concept, but are dealing only with the general rule for reflecting on a perception for the sake of understanding, as a power of concepts. Clearly, then, in a merely reflective judgment imagination and understanding are considered as they must relate in general in the power of judgment, as compared with how they actually relate in the case of a given perception.

So if the form of an object given in empirical intuition is of such a character that the *apprehension,* in the imagination, of the object's manifold agrees with the *exhibition* of a concept of the understanding (which concept this is being indeterminate), then imagination and

221'

---

[27] We say that we put final causes into things, rather than, as it were, lifting them out of our perception of things.

[28] [*Zusammenfassung*; see above, Ak. 251 br. n. 14.]

[29] [Cf. the *Critique of Pure Reason*, A 98–110.]

understanding are—in mere reflection—in mutual harmony, a harmony that furthers the task of these powers; and the object is perceived as purposive, [though] purposive merely for judgment. Hence we then consider the purposiveness itself[30] as merely subjective; by the same token, this [purposiveness] neither requires nor produces a determinate concept of the object, and the judgment itself is not a cognitive one. Such a judgment is called an AESTHETIC *judgment of reflection.*

On the other hand, if empirical concepts and empirical laws, conforming to the mechanism of nature, are already given, judgment may compare such a concept of the understanding with reason and its principle concerning the possibility of a system; and if we then find this [systematic] form in the object, we judge th[is] purposiveness *objectively* and call the thing a *natural purpose,* whereas above we judged things only as indeterminately purposive *natural forms.* A judgment about the objective purposiveness of nature is called TELEOLOGICAL. It is a *cognitive judgment,* yet it belongs only to reflective and not to determinative judgment. For nature's technic as such, whether it is merely *formal* or *real,* is only a relation of things to our power of judgment. In this power alone can we find the idea of a purposiveness of nature, and only in relation to this power do we attribute this purposiveness to nature.

VIII

On the Aesthetic of
the Power of Judging

The expression, aesthetic *way of presenting,* is quite unambiguous if we mean by it that the presentation is referred to an object, as appearance, to [give rise to] cognition of that object. For here the term *aesthetic* means that the form of sensibility ([i.e.,] how the subject is affected) attaches necessarily to the presentation, so that

[30] [As distinguished from the object that manifests it.]

222'

this form is inevitably transferred to the object (though to the object only as phenomenon). That is why it was possible to have a transcendental aesthetic, as a science pertaining to the cognitive power. However, for a long time now it has become customary to call a way of presenting aesthetic,[31] i.e., sensible, in a different meaning of the term as well, where this means that the presentation is referred, not to the cognitive power, but to the feeling of pleasure and displeasure. Now it is true that (in line with this meaning of the term aesthetic) we are in the habit of calling this feeling too a sense (a modification of our state), since we have no other term for it. Yet this feeling is not an objective sense, not a sense the determination of which we would use to *cognize* an object, but a sense that contributes nothing whatever to our cognition of objects. (For to intuit, or otherwise cognize, something with pleasure is not merely to refer the presentation to the object, but is a receptivity of the subject.) Precisely because all determinations of feeling have only subjective significance, there cannot be, as a science, an aesthetic of feeling as there is, say, an aesthetic of the cognitive power. Hence the expression, aesthetic way of presenting, always retains an inevitable ambiguity, if sometimes we mean by it a way of presenting that arouses the feeling of pleasure and displeasure, but sometimes a way of presenting that concerns merely the cognitive power insofar as we find in it sensible intuition that allows us to cognize objects, [though] only as appearances.

But we can remove this ambiguity if we apply the term aesthetic not to intuition, let alone to presentations of the understanding, but solely to the acts of the *power of judgment.* [For to speak of] an *aesthetic judgment,* if [this were interpreted as meaning a judgment] to be used for objective determination, would be so strikingly contradictory that we would have sufficient assurance against [such a] misinterpretation. For while intuitions can be sensible, *judging* pertains to absolutely nothing but the understanding (in the broader meaning of that term); and aesthetic or sensible *judging,* where this is [meant] to be *cognition* of an object, is contradictory even in cases where sensibility meddles in the task of the understanding and (by a *vitium subreptionis*[32]) points the understanding in a false direction; rather, an *objective* judgment is always made only by the understanding, and

---

[31] [From Greek αἰσθέσθαι (aisthésthai), 'to sense.']
[32] [Fallacy of subreption. Cf. above, Ak. 257 br. n. 22.]

in so far cannot be called aesthetic. Hence our transcendental aesthetic of the cognitive power was indeed able to talk about sensible intuitions, but not at all about aesthetic judgments; for since it deals only with cognitive judgments, which determine the object, its judgments must all be logical. Therefore, in calling a judgment about an object aesthetic, we indicate immediately that, while a given presentation is being referred to an object, by judgment we mean here not the determination of the object, but the determination of the subject and of his feeling.[33] For in the power of judgment we consider understanding and imagination as they relate to each other, [and we can do this in two ways:] We can consider that relation objectively (as was done in the transcendental schematism of judgment),[34] as belonging to cognition; but we can also consider this same relation between [those] two cognitive powers merely subjectively, [namely,] insofar as one of these powers furthers or hinders the other in one and the same presentation and thereby affects one's *mental state,* so that here we consider this relation as one that *can be sensed* (as does not happen in the case of the separate use of any cognitive power other [than judgment]). Now although this sensation [*Empfindung*] is not a sensible [*sinnlich*] presentation of an object,[35] it is connected subjectively with judgment['s general activity of] making concepts of the understanding sensible, and hence may be included with sensibility, namely,

---

[33] [Here, and in some of the occurrences below, 'feeling' refers to the receptivity, which is one of our mental powers; in other occurrences below, it refers to a *state* of that receptivity, i.e., to an *individual* feeling. Also, whereas here Kant equates an aesthetic judgment with the determination—later (Ak. 229') he will also say that an aesthetic judgment "determines"—of the subject and his feeling (the receptivity), he is about to talk about an (individual) feeling as the basis determining something. Does the individual feeling determine the feeling as receptivity? In some cases Kant seems to have meant this, even though one would have expected him, in that case, to *distinguish* the two senses of 'feeling.' But in other cases below (identified, where possible, with bracketed insertions) it seems more plausible to interpret him as switching to the terminology he adopted in the work itself, where he says (explicitly, e.g., above, Ak. 221) that what the feeling determines is an aesthetic *judgment.* The only other alternative for the translation (too unhelpful, it seems, in the case of this terminology) would have been to *leave* the ambiguity and speak merely of the "determining basis of" an aesthetic judgment.]

[34] [See the *Critique of Pure Reason,* A 137–47 = B 176–87.]

[35] [But a *feeling.* On the ambiguity of both '*Empfindung*' and 'sensation,' see also above, Ak. 291–92 incl. br. n. 19.]

as a sensible presentation of the state of the subject who is affected by an act of that power [of judgment]. We may include this [kind of] sensation with sensibility, and call a judgment aesthetic, i.e., sensible (as regards the subjective effect [the feeling, as effect of the harmony between the two cognitive powers[36]], not as regards the [whole[37]] basis determining [the judgment]), even though judging is (objectively) an act of the understanding (i.e., of one of the [*überhaupt*] higher cognitive power[s]), not an act of sensibility.

Every *determinative* judgment is *logical,* because its predicate is a given objective concept. But a merely *reflective* judgment about a given individual object *can be aesthetic;* [it is aesthetic] if (before we attend to a comparison of the object with others) the power of judgment, having no concept ready for the given intuition, holds [for the sake of comparison] the imagination [itself] (as it merely apprehends the object) up to the understanding [itself] ([so that] a concept as such[38] is exhibited) and perceives a [certain] relation between the two cognitive powers, a relation that constitutes the condition, which we can only sense, under which [alone] we can use the power of judgment objectively (namely, the mutual harmony of imagination and understanding). But there can also be an aesthetic judgment of sense [rather than of reflection]; [such a judgment occurs] if the predicate of the judgment *cannot be* a concept of an object at all, because it does not belong to the cognitive power at all—as, e.g., in the judgment: The wine is agreeable—so that the predicate expresses that a presentation is referred directly to the feeling of pleasure and not to the cognitive power.

224′

Hence we may define an aesthetic judgment in general as one whose predicate can never be cognition (i.e., concept of an object, though it may contain the subjective conditions for cognition as such). In such a judgment, the basis determining [it] is sensation. There is, however, only one so-called sensation that can never

---

[36] [Kant is so far talking only about aesthetic judgments *of reflection*, but is here beginning to distinguish them from aesthetic judgments *of sense.* See the Translator's Introduction, *lv–lvi.*]

[37] [The basis determining aesthetic judgments of reflection, Kant will tell us shortly, includes not only a feeling but also a certain *rule.*]

[38] [Rather than any individual concept.]

become a concept of an object: the feeling of pleasure and displeasure. This sensation is merely subjective, whereas all other sensation can be used for cognition. Hence an aesthetic judgment is one
in which the basis determining [it] lies in a sensation that is connected directly with the feeling of pleasure and displeasure.[39] In an
aesthetic judgment of sense the basis determining [it] is the sensation that is produced directly by the empirical intuition of the object.
In an aesthetic judgment of reflection, on the other hand, the basis
determining [it] is the sensation brought about, in the subject, by the
harmonious play of the two cognitive powers [involved] in the power
of judgment, imagination and understanding; [they are in harmonious play] when, in the given presentation, the imagination's ability to apprehend, and the understanding's ability to exhibit, further
each other. In such a case this relation between them brings about,
through its mere form, a sensation; and this sensation is the basis
determining a judgment, which is therefore called aesthetic, and
amounts to [*als*][40] subjective purposiveness (without a concept) and
hence is connected with the feeling of pleasure.

An aesthetic judgment of sense contains material purposiveness;
an aesthetic judgment of reflection, formal purposiveness. But since
an aesthetic judgment of sense does not refer to the cognitive power
at all but refers—through sense—directly to the feeling of pleasure,
only an aesthetic judgment of reflection is to be regarded as based on
the power of judgment's own principles. For if reflection on a given
presentation precedes the feeling of pleasure (where this feeling is
the basis determining the judgment), then we *think* the subjective
purposiveness before we *sense* it [by] its effect, and to this extent an
aesthetic judgment belongs—as far as its principles are concerned—   225'

[39] [A moment ago the sensation was said to be this feeling. One might wonder if Kant
is now talking about an "objective" sensation (cf. above, Ak. 206)—i.e., the kind that
can enter into cognition of an object—as "connected with" the feeling. Yet this same
sensation will now be said to be *produced* either by an empirical intuition (which
already *includes* "objective" sensation) or by the harmonious play of imagination
and understanding (and the "sensation" that this produces is *feeling*). So clearly the
sensation in question must indeed *be* the feeling; and since this feeling is an *individual*
one, we may take Kant to be saying that it is "connected with" the *receptivity* which
he also calls 'feeling.']

[40] [Inserting a comma after '*heißt*.']

to the higher cognitive power, specifically, the power of judgment, under whose subjective, and yet universal, conditions[41] the presentation of the object is subsumed. But since a merely subjective condition of a judgment permits no determinate concept of the basis determining this judgment, that basis can only be given [us] in the feeling of pleasure. Yet [it must be given us] in such a way that the aesthetic judgment is always a judgment of reflection; the aesthetic judgment must not be one of sense, which is an aesthetic judgment that does not presuppose a comparison of the presentation with the cognitive powers that work in unison in the power of judgment, [though] it too refers a given presentation to the feeling of pleasure (but not by means of the power of judgment and its principle). The mark by which we can tell this difference [between the two kinds of aesthetic judgment] cannot be stated [in full] until we get to the treatise itself. It consists in the claim of the [aesthetic] judgment [of reflection] to universal validity and necessity. For if an aesthetic judgment carries such a claim with it, it also claims that the basis determining [it] must lie *not merely in the feeling* of pleasure and displeasure by itself, but *also in a rule* of the higher cognitive powers, specifically, in the power of judgment, which thus legislates a priori as regards the conditions of reflection, and [hence] proves that it has AUTONOMY. This autonomy, however, is not valid objectively (as is the autonomy of the understanding in regard to the theoretical laws of nature, or as is that of reason in practical laws of freedom); i.e., it is not valid through concepts of things or of possible acts. It is valid merely subjectively, for the judgment based on [*aus*] feeling, [a feeling] which, if it can claim universal validity, proves that it originates on the basis of a priori principles. We should actually call this legislation *heautonomy:* for judgment legislates neither to nature nor to freedom, but solely to itself; and it is not a power to produce concepts of objects, but a power only to compare occurring cases with concepts given it from elsewhere, and to state a priori the subjective conditions under which this connection is possible.

This also allows us to understand why judgment, in an act that it performs for itself, as merely reflective judgment (without presupposing a concept of the object), instead of referring the given presentation to this power's own rule, while being conscious of this [rule], directly

---

[41] [The harmonious relation between imagination and understanding.]

refers the reflection only to sensation, which like all sensations is   226'
always accompanied by[42] pleasure or displeasure. (None of the other
higher cognitive powers does this.) This is because that rule itself
is only subjective, and agreement with it can be recognized only
in something that also expresses a reference merely to the subject,
namely, in sensation, as the mark of the judgment and as the basis
determining [it], which is also why the judgment is called aesthetic.
Hence all our judgments can be divided, in terms of the order of
the higher cognitive powers, into *theoretical, aesthetic,* and *practical*
ones; but by the aesthetic ones I mean [here] only aesthetic judgments of reflection, which alone refer to a principle of the power of
judgment, as a higher cognitive power, whereas aesthetic judgments
of sense directly concern only the relation of presentations to the
inner sense, insofar as that sense is feeling.

Comment

It is very important here that we examine the explication [that some
people give] of pleasure, namely, as the sensible presentation of an
object's *perfection.* According to this explication an aesthetic judgment of sense or of reflection would always be a cognitive judgment
about the object, because perfection is an attribute [*Bestimmung*] that
presupposes a concept of the object. Hence a judgment ascribing [this
alleged] perfection to an object [would] in no way be distinguished
from other logical judgments, except perhaps by the confusedness
which—as [those] people allege—this concept has [in this kind of
judgment] (and which they presume to call sensibility). But in fact
such confusedness cannot possibly constitute a difference in kind
between judgments; for otherwise an endless multitude of [further]
judgments, not only of understanding but even of reason, would also
have to be called aesthetic [i.e., sensible], because in them [too] an
object is determined [*bestimmt*] by a confused concept, e.g., judgments

---

[42] [Kant must mean that the sensation in question is the (feeling of) pleasure or
displeasure, and it is only the other, viz., "objective," sensations which are always
"accompanied by" pleasure or displeasure.]

227'

about right and wrong, since most people (even most philosophers) do not have a distinct concept of what right is.[43] [The expression] sensible presentation of perfection is an explicit contradiction, and if the harmony of [something] manifold to [form] a unity is to be called perfection, then we must present it through a concept; otherwise we must not give it the name perfection. If pleasure and displeasure are to be nothing but mere cognitions of things through the understanding (except that the understanding is not conscious of its concepts) and are only to seem to us to be mere sensations, then any judging of things by pleasure or displeasure would have to be called intellectual, not aesthetic (i.e., sensible), and senses would basically be nothing but a judging understanding (though this understanding would be judging without being adequately conscious of its own acts), so that the aesthetic way of presenting would not differ in kind from the logical; hence the boundary between the two could not possibly be drawn in a determinate way, so that it would be quite pointless to give them different names. (Not to mention [the problems with] this mystical way of presenting the things of the world, which rules out a sensible intuition that differs from concepts as such and so presumably reduces to nothing but an intuiting understanding.)

A further question might be raised: Does not our concept of a purposiveness of nature mean exactly the same as what the concept of *perfection* says, and is not therefore the empirical consciousness of subjective purposiveness (i.e., the feeling of pleasure in certain

---

[43] We may say in general that we must never consider things as *differing in kind* by virtue of a quality that passes into some other quality by a mere increase or decrease in its degree. Now in the case of the difference between the distinctness and confusedness of concepts, the difference does lie solely in the degree to which we are conscious of the characteristics, which depends on how much attention we direct to them; and so to this extent the two ways of presenting [i.e., the distinct and the confused way] do not differ in kind. But intuition and concept do differ in kind; for they do not pass into each other, no matter how much our consciousness of the two and of their characteristics increases or diminishes. For the greatest lack of distinctness in the conceptual way of presenting (e.g., if the concept is that of right) still leaves what is different in kind about that way of presenting and has to do with the fact that it originates in the understanding; and the greatest distinctness of intuition does not in the least bring it closer to concepts, since intuition resides in sensibility. Moreover, logical distinctness and aesthetic distinctness are as different as day and night [*himmelweit*], and aesthetic distinctness [may] occur even if we do not present the object through concepts at all, i.e., even if our presentation is an intuition and hence sensible.

227'

objects)[44] the sensible intuition of a perfection, as some would explicate pleasure as such?

I reply: *Perfection,* [construed] as mere completeness of the many insofar as [they] together constitute a unity, is an ontological concept; it is identical with the concept of the totality [*Totalität (Allheit)*] of something composite ([the totality which results] if the manifold [elements] in an aggregate are coordinated, or simultaneously subordinated [to one another] in a series as grounds and consequences) and has nothing whatever to do with the feeling of pleasure and displeasure. The perfection a thing has in the reference of its manifold to a concept of that thing is only formal. But if I speak of *a* perfection ([so that] a thing may, under the same concept of it, have many perfections), then I always presuppose the concept of something as a purpose, to which [purpose] I apply that ontological concept of the harmony of the manifold to [form] a unity. This purpose need not always be a practical one, which does presuppose or imply a pleasure in the object's existence; it may also pertain to technic, and hence concerns merely the possibility of things and is the *lawfulness of an intrinsically contingent connection of the manifold* in the object. As an example let me mention the purposiveness that we necessarily think when we think [how] a regular hexagon is possible, since it is quite contingent that six equal lines in a plane should happen to [*gerade*] meet at nothing but equal angles, which is a lawful connection and [so] presupposes a concept [that serves] as the principle making this connection possible.[45] This kind of objective purposiveness, which we observe in things of nature (above all in organized beings), we think as objective and material, and it carries with it necessarily the concept of a purpose of nature (either actual or ascribed to it fictitiously) by reference to which we also attribute perfection to things. A judgment about this purposiveness is called teleological; it carries with it no feeling of pleasure whatever, as, in general, pleasure must not be sought at all in judgments about mere causal connection.

So [it holds] in general [that] the concept of perfection as objective

228′

---

[44] [Parentheses added.]

[45] [Kant means a regular hexagon we find drawn somewhere: cf. above, Ak. 370, where a regular hexagon is found traced in the sand on some beach. That is why this purposiveness is about to be called "objective and material," whereas that of geometric figures *as such* is objective and *formal*: see above, Ak. 362–66.]

purposiveness and the feeling of pleasure have nothing whatever to do with each other. To judge perfection we must have a *concept* of the object, whereas we need no concept to judge by pleasure, [but] can get pleasure through mere empirical intuition. In contrast, the presentation of a subjective purposiveness in an object [not only has something to do with but] is even identical with the feeling of pleasure (nor do we need for this [feeling of pleasure] an abstracted concept of a relation to a purpose). [So] there is a very great gulf between subjective and objective purposiveness. For in order to [decide] whether something that is subjectively purposive is also objectively purposive we must usually engage in fairly extensive investigation, one that not only [deals with] practical philosophy but also [looks into] the technic of either nature or art. In other words, to find perfection in a thing we need reason, to find agreeableness in it we need mere sense, and to find beauty in it we need nothing but mere reflection (without any concept whatever) on a given presentation.

Hence our aesthetic power of reflection judges only the subjective purposiveness of an object (not its perfection); and so the question arises whether this judgment is made only *by means of* the pleasure or displeasure we sense, or whether perhaps it even is a judgment *about* this pleasure or displeasure, in which case it would also determine that this presentation of the object *must* be connected with pleasure or displeasure.

As I have already mentioned, this question cannot yet be decided adequately here. We shall have to wait for the exposition of this kind of judgments in the treatise, to tell us whether these judgments carry with them a universality and necessity that qualifies them for derivation from an a priori basis determining [the subject and his feeling[46]]. If so, [such] a judgment would indeed determine something by means of the sensation[47] of pleasure or displeasure, yet it would also determine a priori—through the cognitive power (specifically the power of judgment)—something about the universality of the rule for connecting this sensation with a given presentation. On the other hand, should these judgments contain nothing but the relation between the presentation and the feeling [of pleasure or displeasure] (without mediation by a cognitive principle), as is the case with aesthetic judgments of

[46] [The *receptivity*.]
[47] [The *individual* feeling.]

sense (which are neither cognitive nor reflective), then all aesthetic judgments would belong merely to the empirical realm.

For now, we may make this further comment: that from cognition to the feeling of pleasure and displeasure there is no transition *through concepts* of objects (insofar as these [objects] are to relate to that [feeling]). Hence we must not expect to determine a priori [what] influence a given presentation [will] have on the mind. Similarly, in the *Critique of Practical Reason,*[48] while we noted that the presentation of a universal lawfulness in volition must—as a law contained, a priori, in our moral judgments—also determine the will and thereby must also arouse the feeling of respect, we were nonetheless unable to derive this feeling from concepts. In the same way our analysis of aesthetic judgments of reflection will show that they contain the concept, which rests on an a priori principle, of the formal but subjective purposiveness of objects, a[n indeterminate] concept that is basically identical with the feeling of pleasure but cannot be derived from any [determinate] concepts, even though it is to the possibility of concepts as such that our presentational power refers when it affects the mind in reflecting on an object.

230'

A definition of this feeling in general [terms], *without considering the distinction as to whether it accompanies sensation proper [Sinnesempfindung]*[49] *or accompanies reflection, or the determination of the will,* must be transcendental.[50] It may read: *Pleasure* is

---

[48] [See Ak. V, 71–89.]

[49] [I.e., sensation that involves a sense (in the ordinary meaning of this term), as distinguished from *feeling*: see above, Ak. 291 br. n. 19.]

[50] If concepts are used as empirical principles and there is cause to suppose that there is a kinship between them and the pure a priori cognitive power, then it is useful to attempt to give a transcendental definition of them. We then proceed like the mathematician, who makes it much easier to solve his problem by leaving the empirical data in it undetermined and bringing the mere synthesis of them under the expressions of pure arithmetic. I followed that procedure when (in the *Kritik der praktischen Vernunft,* p. 16, in the Preface[51]) I explicated the power of desire as *the power of being the cause, through one's presentations, of the actuality of the objects of these presentations.* But against this it was objected that the power of desire cannot be defined in this way, because—so the objection goes—mere wishes are desires too, and yet each of us knows that they [alone] cannot produce their objects. But in fact this proves nothing more than that the power of desire can also be determined in such a way that it contradicts itself. This phenomenon is certainly important for empirical psychology

[51] [Of the first edition (1788) of the *Critique of Practical Reason,* Ak. V, 9 n.]

a mental *state* in which a presentation is in harmony with itself [and] which is the basis either for merely preserving this state itself (for the state in which mental powers further one another in a presentation preserves itself) or for producing the object of this presentation. On the first alternative the judgment about the given presentation is an aesthetic judgment of reflection; on the second, a pathological aesthetic judgment or a practical aesthetic judgment. We can easily see from [all of] this: that, since pleasure [and] displeasure are not ways of cognizing, they cannot at all be explicated on their own; that we cannot have insight into them but can only feel them; and that consequently we can explicate them only in a meager way, by the influence that a presentation has by means of this feeling on the activity of the mental powers.

(as, e.g., it is important for logic to note the influence that prejudices have on the understanding); but it must not influence how we define the power of desire considered objectively, i.e., as to what it is in itself before anything at all interferes with [*ablenken*] its being determined [in a certain way]. In fact man can desire something most fervently and persistently even though he is convinced that he cannot achieve it, or that it is perhaps even [something] absolutely impossible, e.g., if his wish is to undo what is done, or if his desire [and] longing is that a certain bothersome interval should pass faster, etc. And it is indeed an important article for morality to warn us emphatically against such empty and fanciful desires, which are often nourished by novels and sometimes also by mystical presentations, similar to novels, of superhuman perfections and fanatical bliss. But some empty desires and longings, which [alternately] expand the heart and make it languid [*welk*], do have their effect on the mind: they make it languish [*schmachten*] by exhausting its forces; and even that effect [already] proves sufficiently that these forces are indeed repeatedly made tense by presentations so as to actualize their object, but that each time they allow the mind to relapse into the consciousness of its impotence. It is indeed a not unimportant problem for anthropology to investigate why it is that nature has given us the predisposition to such fruitless expenditure of our forces as [we see in] empty wishes and longings (which certainly play a large role in human life). It seems to me that here, as in all else, nature has made wise provisions. For if we had to assure ourselves that we can in fact produce the object, before the presentation of it could determine us to apply our forces, our forces would presumably remain largely unused. For usually we do not come to know what forces we have except by trying them out. So nature has provided for the connection between the determination of our forces and the presentation of the object [to be there] even before we know what ability we have, and it is often precisely this effort, which to that very mind seemed at first an empty wish, that produces that ability in the first place. Now wisdom is obligated to set limits to that instinct, but wisdom will never succeed in eradicating it, or [rather] it will never even demand its eradication.

IX

On Teleological Judging

By a *formal* technic of nature I meant the purposiveness that nature has in intuition; by *real* technic I mean the purposiveness it has in terms of concepts.[52] The formal technic of nature provides shapes that are purposive for the power of judgment, i.e., the [kind of] form where, as we present it, imagination and understanding harmonize with each other on their own to make a concept possible. The real technic of nature [involves] the concept of things as natural purposes, i.e., as things whose inner possibility presupposes a purpose and hence a concept that is the underlying condition of the causality [responsible] for their production.

As far as purposive forms [in] intuition are concerned, judgment itself can indicate and construct these a priori, namely if it finds [*erfindet*] them to be such in [*für*] apprehension that they are suitable for exhibiting a concept. But purposes, i.e., presentations that themselves are regarded as conditions of the causality [responsible] for their objects (their effects), must always [*überhaupt*] be given from somewhere before judgment [can] concern itself with the conditions under which the manifold [will] harmonize with these purposes; and if these purposes are to be natural purposes, then we must be able to consider certain natural things as if they were products of a cause whose causality could be determined [to its action] only by a *presentation* of the object. But we cannot determine a priori how and in what variety of ways things are possible through their causes; for that we need empirical laws.

A judgment about the [kind of] purposiveness in things of nature that we consider the basis for their possibility (as natural purposes) is called a *teleological judgment.* Now in the case of aesthetic judgments, although they themselves are not possible a priori, yet a priori principles are given [us] in the necessary idea of experience as a system,[53] and these principles contain the concept of a formal purposiveness of

---

[52] [The distinction, in these terms, was made above, Ak. 221'.]

[53] [Cf. above, Ak. 208'–09'.]

233'   nature for our judgment and [so] reveal a priori the possibility of aesthetic judgments of reflection as judgments based on a priori principles. [For] not only does nature in its transcendental laws harmonize necessarily with our *understanding:* in addition, nature in its empirical laws harmonizes necessarily with *judgment* and its ability to exhibit nature when the imagination apprehends nature's forms empirically; [but] this harmony of nature with our judgment [is there] merely for the sake of [systematizing] experience, and so nature's formal purposiveness as regards this harmony (with judgment) can still be established as necessary. But now nature, as object of our teleological judging, is to be thought as harmonizing, in its causality, with *reason* as well, as harmonizing with it in terms of the concept reason forms of a purpose. That is more than we can require of judgment alone; for all that judgment can do, as a separate cognitive power, is to consider the relation, prior to any concept, in which two powers—imagination and understanding—are in a presentation, and thereby perceive, as the object is apprehended (by imagination), the object's subjective purposiveness for the cognitive powers. Hence, while judgment can indeed have a priori principles of its own for the form of intuition, yet it cannot have a priori principles of its own for the concepts [concerning] the production of things, and so the concept of a real *natural purpose* lies completely beyond the realm of the power of judgment, considered by itself. Hence in [dealing with] the teleological purposiveness things have as natural purposes, a purposiveness that can be presented only through concepts, judgment will have to put the understanding in a relation to reason ([while] reason is not needed at all for experience) in order to present things as natural purposes.

In judging natural forms aesthetically, we were able to find, without presupposing a concept of the object, that certain objects which occur in nature are purposive in the mere empirical apprehension [of them in] intuition, namely, purposive merely in relation to the subjective conditions of the power of judgment. So when we judged aesthetically, no concept of the object was needed, nor was one produced. By the same token, there we did not make an objective judgment and declare these objects *natural purposes,* but declared them only *purposive* in relation to the subject, namely, for his presentational power; we may call this purposiveness of forms *figurative* purposiveness, and similarly for nature's technic concerning it (*technica speciosa*[54]).

In a teleological judgment, on the other hand, we presuppose a concept of the object, and judge [how] the object is possible in terms of a law about the connection of causes and effects. Hence this technic of nature could be called *plastic,* if that word were not already in vogue in a more general sense, as including not only natural intentions but natural beauty as well. So perhaps we could call it the *organic technic* of nature, since this expression does stand for the concept of [a] purposiveness for the possibility of things themselves, not merely [a] purposiveness for the way we present [them].

But I suppose that what is most essential and important for this section is this: It is the proof that the concept of *final causes* in nature—which separates the teleological judging of nature from a judging of it in terms of universal, [i.e.,] mechanical, laws—is a concept that belongs merely to judgment, not to understanding or reason. In other words, it is the proof that, while we could use the concept of natural purposes in an objective sense too, i.e., as [meaning] *natural intention,* this use would already [involve] reasoning, and so could not possibly be based on experience. For though experience can show us purposes, nothing in it can prove that these purposes are also intentions. So whenever we encounter, in experience, something belonging to teleology, it refers objects of experience solely to judgment, namely, to a principle of this power by which, as reflective judgment, it legislates to itself (not to nature).

It is true that the concept of purposes and of purposiveness is a concept of reason insofar as we attribute to reason the basis that makes an object possible. But [the concept of the] purposiveness of nature, or even the concept of things as natural purposes, relates reason, as cause, to things where no experience informs us that reason is [in fact] the basis that makes them possible. For only in *products of art* can we become conscious of reason's causality [as giving rise to] objects, which are therefore called purposive or purposes; and to call reason technical with regard to products of art is in keeping with the experience we have of the causality of our own power [of reason]. But to present nature as technical like a reason

---

[54] [Technic regarding shape (or perhaps regarding appearance [to the subject]).]

235'   (and so attribute purposiveness and even purposes *to nature*) is [to use] a special concept that we cannot find in experience; it is a concept that judgment only puts into its reflection on objects, so as to let this concept direct it as it engages in experience in terms of particular laws, those that have to do with the possibility of a system.

For all purposiveness of nature can be regarded either as *natural* (*forma finalis naturae spontanea*) or as *intentional* (*[forma finalis naturae] intentionalis*[55]). Mere experience justifies only the first way of presenting [the purposiveness of nature]; the second way of presenting [it] is a hypothetical way of explaining [certain things] which is an addition to the above concept of things as natural purposes. The first concept of things, as natural purposes, belongs originally to *reflective* judgment (though to judgment reflecting not aesthetically but logically); the second concept [i.e., of things as *intentional* natural purposes, i.e., as purposes of nature] belongs originally to *determinative* judgment. For the first concept too we need reason, but here we need it only in order to engage in experience in terms of principles (hence this is reason in its *immanent* use); but for the second concept reason would have to stray into what is excessive [for it] (hence this would be reason in its transcendent use).

In our empirical investigation of nature in its causal connection, we can and should endeavor to [proceed] in terms of nature's merely mechanical laws as far as we can, for in these laws lie the true physical bases for [an] explanation [of nature, the bases] which [in their] coherence constitute what scientific knowledge of nature we have through reason. On the other hand, we find among the products of nature some special and very widespread genera, in which the efficient causes are connected in such a way that we must base this connection on the concept of a purpose, if we want so much as to experience [these natural products], i.e., observe [them] in terms of a principle appropriate to their inner possibility. Suppose we tried to judge their form and its possibility merely in terms of mechanical laws, where it is not the idea of the effect which is regarded as the basis that makes [it] possible [for] the cause [to be the cause] of this effect, but the other way round [the cause is regarded as the basis that makes the effect possible]: if we tried this, we could not acquire

---

[55] [The distinction, as expressed in the Latin, is between spontaneous and intentional purposive form of nature.]

regarding the specific form of these natural things even so much as an empirical concept that would enable us to get from their intrinsic predisposition, as cause, to the effect. For the effect we see in these machines is caused by their parts not insofar as each part on its own contains a separate basis, but only insofar as all of them together contain a joint basis making these machines possible. But it is quite contrary to the nature of physical-mechanical causes that the whole should be the cause that makes possible the causality of the parts; rather, here the parts must be given [us] first in order for us to grasp from them the possibility of a whole. Moreover, when the special presentation of a whole precedes the possibility of the parts, then it is a mere idea; and when this idea is regarded as the basis of the causality, it is called a purpose. Clearly, then, if there are such products of nature, we cannot even investigate their character and its cause in experience (let alone explain them by reason) without presenting them, their form and causality, as determined according to a principle of purposes.

236′

Now, it is clear that in such cases the concept of an objective purposiveness of nature serves [us] merely *for reflecting* on the object, not for *determining* the object through the concept of a purpose, and that the ideological judgment about the inner possibility of a natural product is a merely reflective and not a determinative judgment. For example, if we say that the crystal lens in the eye has the *purpose* of bringing about by means of a second refraction of the light rays [the result] that the light rays emanating from one point will be reunited in one point on the retina of the eye, all we are saying is that our thought of the causality nature [exercised] in producing an eye includes the thought of the presentation of a purpose, because such an idea serves us as a principle by which we can guide our investigation of the eye as far as its lens is concerned, and also because thinking the presentation of a purpose here might [help] us devise means to further that effect [if the natural lens does not do so adequately]. But in talking this way we do not yet attribute to nature a cause that acts in terms of the presentation of purposes, i.e., *intentionally;* if we did, we would be making a determinative teleological judgment, and hence a transcendent judgment, inasmuch as it [would] suggest a causality that lies beyond the bounds of nature.

Hence the concept of natural purposes is a concept solely of reflective judgment, a concept [it must use] solely for its own sake in pursuing the causal connection in objects of experience. In [using] a teleological principle for explaining the inner possibility of certain natural forms, we leave undetermined whether their purposiveness is *intentional* or *unintentional.* If a judgment asserted either of these alternatives, it would no longer be merely reflective but would be determinative; and the concept of a natural purpose would also no longer be a mere *concept of the power of judgment,* for immanent use (i.e., use in experience), but would be connected with a *concept of reason:* the concept of a cause that we posit beyond nature and that acts intentionally, a concept that is transcendent, whether we are in this case judging affirmatively or negatively.

237'

X

On the Inquiry into a Principle of Technical Judgment

If for something that happens we are to find merely the basis that explains it, this basis may be either an empirical principle, or an a priori principle, or a combination of both, as we can see in the physical-mechanical explanations of events in the corporeal world, which find their principles partly in universal (rational) natural science, and partly in the natural science that contains the empirical laws of motion. The situation is similar if we try to find psychological bases that explain what goes on in our minds. The only difference here is that, as far as I am aware, in the case of mental events the principles [of explanation] are one and all empirical, with just one exception: the principle of the *continuity* of all changes. (This principle is an exception because time, which has only one dimension, is the formal condition of inner intuition.)[56] But although this principle lies a priori at the basis of these perceptions, it is virtually useless for explanation, because the universal theory [*Lehre*[57]] of time, unlike the pure theory of space (geometry), does not provide us with enough material for a whole science.

[56] [See the *Critique of Pure Reason*, A 30–49 = B 46–73.]
[57] [On *Lehre* as *theory*; see above, Ak. 172 br. n. 15.]

Hence if our concern were to explain how what we call taste first arose among people, how these objects [objects of taste] came to occupy taste much more than others and induced people to make judgments about beauty under varying local and societal circumstances, what cause enabled taste to grow into a luxury, and so on, we would have to seek the principles of such an explanation largely in psychology. (In all cases like this, only empirical psychology is meant.) Thus moralists demand that psychologists explain to them the strange phenomenon of greed, where [people] posit an absolute value in the mere possession of the means for living well (or the means for any other aim), and yet [are] also resolved never to use them; or the desire for distinction [*Ehrbegierde*] where [people] think [they] find this distinction in mere reputation, without [having] any further aim. The moralists demand this explanation so that they can adjust their precepts accordingly, not the precepts of the moral laws themselves, but those concerning the removal of the obstacles that interfere with the influence of the moral laws. Yet we must concede that psychological explanations are in very sad shape compared to physical ones, that they are forever hypothetical, and that for any three different bases explaining [a mental event] we can easily think up a fourth that is equally plausible. And so we have a multitude of alleged psychologists like this, who can tell us the causes of every mental response [*Affektion*] or agitation aroused by plays, presentations of poetry, or objects of nature—and will even call this ingenuity of theirs philosophy—[but] who fail to show not only the knowledge, but perhaps even the capacity for [acquiring] it, that is needed to explain scientifically the most ordinary natural event in the corporeal world. Empirical psychology will hardly ever be able to claim the rank of a philosophical science, and probably its only true obligation is to make psychological observations (as Burke does in his work on the beautiful and sublime[58]), and hence to gather material for future empirical rules that are to be connected systematically, yet to do so without trying to grasp these rules.

Suppose, on the other hand, a judgment offers itself as universally valid and hence claims *necessity* for what it asserts, whether this alleged necessity rests on a priori concepts of the object, or on subjective conditions underlying a priori [our acquisition of] concepts.

238'

[58] [See above, Ak. 277–78.]

If we grant this sort of claim to such a judgment, it would be absurd if we justified it by explaining the origin of the judgment psychologically, since we would then be acting against our own aim: if the attempted explanation were perfectly successful, it would prove that the judgment cannot possibly claim necessity, precisely because we can prove that its origin is empirical.

Now aesthetic reflective judgments (which we shall later analyze under the name of judgments of taste) are of the kind just mentioned: they claim necessity; they do not say that everyone judges like that—in which case the task of explaining them would fall to empirical psychology—but say that we *ought* to judge like that, which amounts to saying that they have for themselves an a priori principle. If these judgments, in claiming necessity, did not contain a reference to such a principle, we would have to assume it legitimate to assert that the judgment ought to hold universally because observation proves that it actually holds universally, and to assert, conversely, that from the fact that everyone judges a certain way it follows that he also *ought* to judge that way. But that is obviously absurd.

It is true that aesthetic judgments of reflection manifest the difficulty that they are never based on concepts and hence cannot be derived from a determinate principle, because then they would be logical; [and] the subjective presentation of purposiveness is in no way to be a concept of a purpose. And yet, when a judgment claims necessity, there still can and must always be a *reference* to an a priori principle. This claim, and the possibility of such a claim, is all that is at issue here; but the same claim prompts a rational critique to search for the underlying principle itself, even if that principle is indeterminate. That critique may in fact succeed in finding this principle, and succeed in acknowledging it as one that underlies the judgment subjectively and a priori, even though this principle can never provide a determinate concept of the object.

[As we just did for aesthetic reflective judgments,] we must concede that teleological judgments [too] are based on an a priori principle, and are impossible without one, even though in such judgments we discover the purpose of nature solely through experience, and without experience could not cognize that things of this kind are so much as possible. For teleological judgments too, like aesthetic reflective judgments, are always only reflective, even though (unlike them) they connect with the presentation of the object a determinate concept of a purpose and regard the possibility of the object as based on that concept. Teleological judgments in no way presume to assert that, in this objective purposiveness, nature (or some other being [acting] through nature) in fact proceeds *intentionally*, i.e., that the causality of nature or of nature's cause is determined [to its action] by the thought of a purpose. All they assert is that we must use the mechanical laws of nature in accordance with this analogy (relations of causes and effects), if we are to cognize [how] such objects are possible, and to acquire a concept of them that can provide those mechanical laws with a coherence [that will allow us] to engage in experience systematically.

A teleological judgment compares [two] concept[s] of a natural product; it compares what [the product] is with what it *is* [*meant*] *to be*. Here our judging of the object's possibility is based on a concept (of a purpose) that precedes a priori [that possibility]. In products of art we do not find it difficult to conceive of the possibility of objects in this way. But if we think that a product of nature *was* [*meant*] *to be* something, and judge the product as to whether it actually is [that], then we are already presupposing a principle that we cannot have derived from experience (which teaches us only what things are).

That our eyes allow us to see, this we experience directly, and we also experience directly their outer structure and their inner structure, which contain the conditions that make it possible to use them in this way, and so we experience directly the causality [our eyes involve] in terms of mechanical laws. Now if I use a stone to smash something on it, or to build [something] on it, etc., I can [regard] these effects too as purposes [and] refer them to their causes; but that does not entitle me to say that the stone was [meant] to serve for building. Only about the eye do I make the judgment that it *was* [*meant*] *to* be suitable for sight; and though its shape, the character of its parts and their combination is quite contingent for my power of judgment if [it] judges them in terms of merely mechanical laws of nature, yet I think a necessity in this form and structure of the eye: [the] necessity of being built a certain way, namely, in terms of a concept which precedes [the action of] the causes that build this organ, and without which (unlike in the case of that stone) no mechanical law of nature will allow me to grasp the possibility of that natural product. Now this is-to-be contains a necessity that differs distinctly from the physical-mechanical necessity under which a thing is possible in terms of mere laws of efficient causes (without a prior idea of the thing), and it cannot be defined [*bestimmt*] through merely physical (empirical) laws any more than the necessity of an aesthetic judgment can through psychological laws; rather, it requires an a priori principle of its own in the power of judgment insofar as that power is reflective, a principle under which teleological judgments fall and by which we must also define their validity and limitation.

Hence all judgments about the purposiveness of nature, whether they are aesthetic or teleological, fall under a priori principles: a priori principles that belong exclusively to the power of judgment, as its own principles, because these judgments are merely reflective and not determinative. That is also why they belong to the critique of pure reason (in the most general sense of that expression). Teleological judgments need this critique more than aesthetic judgments do. For teleological judgments, if left to themselves, invite reason to inferences that may stray into the transcendent. Aesthetic judgments, on the other hand, require laborious investigation in order to keep them from limiting themselves—even as regards their principle—to just the empirical, and hence to keep them from destroying their claims to necessary validity for everyone.

241'

XI

Encyclopaedic Introduction [Introduktion] of the Critique of Judgment into the System of the Critique of Pure Reason

Any introduction [*Einleitung*] of a discourse either introduces [us] to a proposed doctrine [*Lehre*], or introduces the doctrine itself into a system to which it belongs as a part. The first kind of introduction precedes the doctrine. The second kind should properly form only the conclusion of the doctrine; there it should, in terms of principles, assign the doctrine its place within the body of the doctrines to which it is connected by common principles. The first kind of introduction is *a propaedeutic* one, the second may be called *encyclopaedic*.

Propaedeutic introductions are the usual ones. They prepare us for a doctrine about to be offered; for they point to whatever prior cognition, from other doctrines or sciences already available, is needed for this doctrine, and hence such introductions allow us to make the transition. If they aim at distinguishing carefully the newly offered doctrine's own principles ([*principia*] *domestica*) from those belonging to another doctrine ([*principia*] *peregrina*), then they serve to determine the boundaries of the sciences—a precaution that can never be recommended too much, since without it we cannot hope for thoroughness, especially not in philosophical cognition.

What an encyclopaedic introduction presupposes, on the other hand, is not a doctrine akin and preparatory to the newly announced one, but the idea of a system that this doctrine will first render complete. Now we cannot arrive at a system if we [merely] pick up and gather together the diverse [items] we have found along the path of investigation, but can do so only if we can indicate completely the subjective or objective sources of a certain kind of cognitions. For this we need the formal concept of a whole, a concept that also contains a priori the principle for a complete division [of that whole]. Hence we can

431

easily grasp why encyclopaedic introductions, however useful they
would be, are yet so unusual.

Now the power whose own principle we are here trying to discover
and discuss—the power of judgment—is of a very special kind: it
does not on its own produce any cognition at all (whether theoretical
or practical); and regardless of its a priori principle it does not supply a part [of] transcendental philosophy as an objective doctrine,
but constitutes only the connection [*Verband*] of two other higher
cognitive powers (understanding and reason). Therefore, as I determine the principles of such a power—one that is fit not for a doctrine
but merely for a critique—I may be permitted to depart from the
order that is indeed necessary elsewhere, and to begin [rather than
conclude] with a brief encyclopaedic introduction of judgment. I
shall introduce this power not into the system of the *sciences* of pure
reason, but merely into the *critique* of all the powers of the mind
that can be determined a priori, insofar as together they constitute
a system in the mind. In this way I shall combine the propaedeutic
introduction with the encyclopaedic one.

The introduction of judgment into the system of the pure powers
of cognition through concepts rests on that power's own transcendental principle: the principle that nature, in the specification of the
transcendental laws of understanding (the principles of nature's possi-
243'   bility as a nature as such), i.e., in the diversity of its empirical laws,
proceeds in terms of the idea of a system for dividing nature, so as to
make experience possible as an empirical system. This principle is
what first provides us, a priori, with the concept of a lawfulness that
is contingent objectively but necessary subjectively (for our cognitive power)—the concept of a purposiveness of nature. Although this
principle determines nothing regarding the particular natural forms,
[and] their purposiveness must always be given [us] empirically, still
the judgment about these forms, as a merely reflective judgment,
acquires a claim to universal validity and necessity. It does so because
in it the subjective purposiveness that a given presentation has for
judgment is referred to that a priori principle of judgment, the principle of the purposiveness nature [displays] in its empirical lawfulness
in general. Hence we shall be able to regard aesthetic reflective judgments as resting on an a priori principle (even if not on a determinative one), and the power of judgment will, regarding these judgments,

find itself entitled to a place in the critique of the higher pure powers of cognition.

However, if the concept of a purposiveness of nature (as a technical purposiveness that differs essentially from practical purposiveness) is not to be a mere fraudulent replacement of *what nature is* by *what we turn it into,* then this concept lies outside of all dogmatic philosophy (both theoretical and practical): its sole basis is that principle of judgment, which precedes empirical laws and first allows them to harmonize to [form] the unity of a system. This shows that, of the two ways (aesthetic and teleological) of using the reflective power of judgment, the judgment that precedes any concept of the object, and hence the aesthetic reflective judgment, is the only one in which the basis determining [it] lies solely in the power of judgment, unmixed with an[y] other cognitive power. Teleological judgments, on the other hand, are judgments about the concept of a natural purpose; and although in these judgments themselves we use this concept only as a principle of the reflective rather than of the determinative power of judgment, yet we can make these judgments only by connecting reason with empirical concepts. Hence it is easy to show the possibility of teleological judgments about nature, without our being entitled to regard them as based on a special principle of the power of judgment, since [here] judgment merely follows the principle of reason. By contrast, [in order to show] the possibility of a judgment of taste, i.e., a judgment of mere reflection that is aesthetic and yet based on an a priori principle, we certainly do need a critique of the power of judgment as a power having (like understanding and reason) its own transcendental principles, if it can be proved that an aesthetic reflective judgment is in fact justified in claiming universal validity. Only such a critique [can] qualify this [power of] judgment for acceptance into the system of the pure cognitive powers. This is because, while aesthetic judgments attribute purposiveness to their object, and do so with universal validity, yet they do this without presupposing a concept of that object; and hence the principle for this [attribution] must lie in the power of judgment itself. Teleological judgments, on the other hand, do presuppose a concept of the object, a concept that reason brings under the principle of connection in terms of purposes, and the only [special feature of these judgments] is that the power of judgment uses this concept of a natural purpose in a merely reflective and not in a determinative judgment.

244'

So it is actually only in taste, and in taste concerning objects of nature [rather than of art], that judgment reveals itself as a power that has its own principle and hence is justified—which in the case of this power might come as a surprise—in claiming a place in the general critique of the higher cognitive powers. But once judgment's ability to set itself principles a priori is given, we must also determine the range of that ability; and in order thus to complete the critique we must cognize judgment's aesthetic ability, together with its ideological ability, as contained in one ability and resting on the same principle, since ideological judgments about things of nature belong to the reflective (and not the determinative) power of judgment just as much as aesthetic ones do.

Critique of taste, in other [contexts], is used only to improve or solidify taste itself. But if the treatment of it has a transcendental aim, then this critique fills a gap in the system of our cognitive powers, and hence opens up a striking and—I think—most promising prospect [for] a complete system of all the mental powers, insofar as in being determined they are referred not just to the sensible but also to the supersensible, though referred to it without any shifting of the boundary stones that a strict critique has laid down for such use of these powers. To help the reader gain an overview of how the upcoming inquiries cohere, it may be useful if I sketch even now an outline of this systematic connection, even though its proper place, as indeed that of this entire section, would be at the end of the treatise.

245'

All the powers of the mind can be reduced to the following three:

cognitive power

feeling of pleasure and displeasure

power of desire

But employment of all three of these powers is always based on the cognitive power, even if not always on cognition (since a presentation can belong to the cognitive power and yet be [only] an intuition, pure or empirical, without concepts). Hence, insofar as what we deal with is the power of cognition according to principles, the following higher mental powers take their place next to the mental powers in general:

congintive power	*understanding*
feeling of pleasure and displeasure	*judgment*
power of desire	*reason*

It turns out that understanding has its own a priori principles for the cognitive power, judgment only for the feeling of pleasure and displeasure, and reason merely for the power of desire. These formal principles [righthand column, below] are the basis of a necessity. Some of this necessity is objective, some subjective, but some by being subjective is objectively valid too, [the alternative] depending on [which] higher power it is, next to them [in the middle column], through which these principles determine the [general] mental powers [left column] corresponding to these:

cognitive power	*understanding*	*lawfulness*
feeling of pleasure and displeasure	*judgment*	*purposiveness*
power of desire	*reason*	purposiveness that is also law (*obligation*)

Finally, these a priori bases for the possibility of forms are joined by the following forms, their products: 246′

POWERS OF THE MIND	HIGHER COGNITIVE POWERS	A PRIORI PRINCIPLES	PRODUCTS
cognitive power	*understanding*	*lawfulness*	*nature*
feeling of pleasure and displeasure	*judgment*	*purposiveness*	*art*
power of desire	*reason*	purposiveness that is also law (*obliga-tion*)	*morals*

So NATURE bases its *lawfulness* on *a priori principles of the understanding* as a *cognitive power;* ART is governed a priori in its *purposiveness* by *judgment* in reference to *the feeling of pleasure and displeasure;* finally, MORALS (as product of freedom) fall under the idea of such a form of *purposiveness* as is qualified to be universal law, as a basis by which *reason* determines the *power of desire.* The judgments that arise in this way from a priori principles belonging to each basic power of the mind are *theoretical, aesthetic,* and *practical* judgments.

Thus we find a system of the mental powers in their relation to nature and to freedom, each having its own *determinative* a priori principles and hence constituting the two parts of philosophy (theoretical and practical) as a doctrinal system, as well as a transition by means of judgment, which connects the two parts through a principle of its own. This transition is from the *sensible* substrate of theoretical philosophy to the *intelligible* substrate of practical philosophy; [it is made] through the critique of a power (judgment) that serves only for [making this] connection. Hence this power cannot on its own provide any cognition or contribute anything whatever to doctrine; but its judgments—called *aesthetic* judgments (whose principles are merely 247′   subjective), since they differ from all those that are called *logical,* i.e., from those (whether theoretical or practical) whose principles must be objective—are of so special a kind that they refer sensible intuitions to an idea of nature in which [nature's] lawfulness is beyond [our] understanding unless [we] relate nature to a supersensible substrate. The proof of this is in the treatise itself.

Rather than calling the critique of this power, with regard to its aesthetic judgments, [an] *aesthetic* (doctrine of sense, as it were), we shall call it *critique of aesthetic judgment.*[59] This is because the first expression has too broad a meaning, since it could also mean the sensibility of *intuition,* which belongs to theoretical cognition and provides the material for logical (objective) judgments; that is why we have already defined the expression, [an] aesthetic, exclusively as [having to do with] the predicate which in cognitive judgments belongs to intuition. But we need not worry about being misinterpreted if we call a power of judgment aesthetic because it does not refer the presentation of an object to concepts and hence does not refer the judgment to cognition (in other words, because it is not determinative at all but only reflective). This is because for the logical power of judgment intuitions, despite being sensible (aesthetic), must first be

---

[59] [In fact, Kant does not always adhere to this stipulation.]

raised to [the level of] concepts, so that they can serve for cognition of the object; but this is not the case with the aesthetic power of judgment.

XII

Division of the Critique of Judgment

Dividing [the] range of a certain kind of cognitions, so that we can conceive of it as a system, is more important than people realize, but is also more difficult. If the parts of such a possible whole are regarded as already completely given, the division is performed *mechanically,* according to mere comparison, and the whole becomes an *aggregate* (roughly as cities become if land is divided among applicant settlers according to the intentions of each and without concern for policy). But if before determining the parts we can, and are to, presuppose the idea of a whole in terms of a certain principle, then we must perform the division *scientifically;* and only in this way does the whole become a system. The latter [procedure] is required whenever we are dealing with a range of a priori cognition (which together with its principles rests on a special legislative power of the subject), since here the range within which these laws [can] be used is determined a priori by the particular character of this power, but through this is also determined the number of the parts and their relation by means of which they form a whole of cognition. But one cannot make a justified division without also *making* the whole itself and exhibiting it completely beforehand in all its parts, even if only according to the rule of [a] *critique.* In order, thereafter, to put this whole into the systematic form of a *doctrine* (insofar as, in view of the nature of this cognitive power, there can indeed be a doctrine), nothing more is needed than to add *elaborateness* [in the] application [of the division] to the particular, and the elegance of *precision.*

Now in order to divide a critique of judgment (this power, even though based on a priori principles, is indeed one that can never

248'

provide the material for a doctrine), we must presuppose the distinction [between determinative judgment and reflective judgment, which I shall now spell out). It is not determinative judgment, but merely reflective judgment, that has a priori principles of its own. Determinative judgment proceeds only *schematically,* under laws of another power (the understanding), and reflective judgment alone proceeds *technically* (according to laws of its own). This technical procedure is based on a principle of the technic of nature, and hence on the concept of a purposiveness, a purposiveness we must presuppose a priori in nature. Judgment, in accordance with the principle of reflective judgment, presupposes this purposiveness necessarily [but] only as subjective, i.e., judgment presupposes it only in relation to this power itself, even though this purposiveness does also carry with it the concept of a *possible* objective purposiveness, i.e., of a lawfulness of things of nature as natural purposes.

A purposiveness which is judged merely subjectively, [and] which therefore neither is based on a concept nor, insofar as it is judged merely subjectively, can be based on one, is the reference [of something] to the feeling of pleasure and displeasure; and a judgment about such a purposiveness is *aesthetic* (and this is moreover the only possible way to judge aesthetically). However, [first,] if this feeling accompanies merely the sensible presentation of the object, i.e., the sensation of it, the aesthetic judgment is empirical and [hence] requires no special power of judgment, but only a special receptivity. Moreover, [second,] if we assume this power as determinative, [the judgment] would have to be based on a concept of [a] purpose, so that the purposiveness would be objective and hence would have to be judged logically, not aesthetically. Hence we must [adopt the third alternative and] regard aesthetic judgment, [considered] as a special power, as necessarily *reflective judgment;* and we must regard the feeling of pleasure (which is identical with the presentation of *subjective purposiveness*) as attaching neither to the sensation in an empirical presentation of the object, nor to the concept of that object, but consequently as attaching to—and as connected with, in terms of an a priori principle—nothing but the reflection and its form ([i.e., with] judgment's own act), [the reflection] by which judgment endeavors [to proceed] from empirical intuitions to concepts as such. Hence the *aesthetic* of reflective judgment will occupy one part of the critique of this power, while the *logic* of reflective judgment constitutes,

249′

under the name of *teleology,* the other part of that critique. In both, however, nature itself is regarded as technical, i.e., as purposive in its products: in the aesthetic case we regard nature as purposive sub- jectively, mere[ly] with reference to the subject's way of presenting [something]; in the teleological case we regard nature as purposive objectively, by reference to the possibility of the object itself. We shall see later that the purposiveness that [a] form has in appearance is *beauty,* and that our ability to judge it is *taste.* It might seem to follow from this that the division of the critique of judgment into aesthetic and teleological must comprise merely the *theory [Lehre] of taste* and the *theory of physical purposes* (i.e., of our judging of things of the world as natural purposes).

And yet all *purposiveness,* whether subjective or objective, can be divided into *intrinsic* and *relative.* Intrinsic purposiveness has its basis in the presentation of the object itself, relative purposiveness merely in the contingent *use* of this presentation. Accordingly, [to start with subjective purposiveness, there is,] *first,* [the case of beauty, intrinsic subjective purposiveness,] where the form of an object even on its own, i.e., in mere intuition [and] without concepts, is perceived as purposive for reflective judgment, and here we attribute the subjective purposiveness to the thing and to nature itself; *second,* [there is the case of sublimity, relative subjective purposiveness:] even assuming that the object, when we perceive it, has nothing for our reflection that [would] be purposive for a[ny] determination of its form, yet [here] the presentation of it, applied to a purposiveness lying a priori in the subject (such as the supersensible vocation of the subject's mental powers) and [so] arousing a feeling of this purposiveness, is the basis of a [different] aesthetic judgment: this aesthetic judgment also refers to an a priori principle (though this principle is only sub- jective), but—unlike the first kind of aesthetic judgment—it refers not to *a purposiveness of nature* concerning the subject, but only to a possible purposive *use* which, by means of merely reflective judg- ment, [we can make] of certain sensible intuitions as far as their form is concerned. If, then, the first kind of aesthetic judgment attributes *beauty* to objects of nature, while the second attributes *sublimity,* but with both judgments doing so merely aesthetically (reflectively), without concepts of the object, but merely in regard to subjective purposiveness, still the latter kind of aesthetic judgment would not require us to presuppose a special technic of nature; for all that

250'

matters in that judgment is a contingent use [we make] of the presentation, not for the sake of cognizing the object but for the sake of a different feeling [different from the feeling involved in beauty]—the feeling of the inner purposiveness in the predisposition of our mental powers. Yet, on the other hand, the judgment about the sublime in nature could not [on that account] be excluded from the division of the aesthetic of reflective judgment, because it too expresses a subjective purposiveness that does not rest on a concept of the object.

The same [distinction, between intrinsic (*inner*) and relative,] applies also to objective purposiveness of nature, i.e., to the possibility of things as natural purposes, which we judge, in a judgment called teleological, only in terms of concepts of these [natural purposes], and hence not aesthetically (in reference to the feeling of pleasure or displeasure) but logically. Objective purposiveness is the purposiveness on which we base either the inner [*inner*] possibility of the object or the relative possibility of its outward consequences. In the first case the teleological judgment considers the *perfection* of a thing in terms of a purpose that lies in that thing itself (where the manifold [elements] in it relate to one another as purpose[s] and means); in the second case the teleological judgment about a natural object deals only with its *usefulness,* i.e., with [whether] the object harmonizes with a purpose that lies in other things.

Accordingly, the critique of aesthetic judgment contains, first, the critique of *taste* (the ability to judge the beautiful); second, the critique of *intellectual feeling,*[60] which is what I provisionally call the ability to present a sublimity in objects. Since the teleological power of judgment refers its presentation of purposiveness to the object not by means of feelings but rather through concepts, [i.e.,] since it refers its reflection always to reason (not to feeling), we do not need special names in order to distinguish the abilities it contains, [as pertaining, respectively, to] intrinsic and relative [purposiveness] (though in both cases the purposiveness is objective).

A further comment is needed: It is not the causality of man's presentational powers, which is called *art* (in the proper sense of that term), but rather the technic in nature, concerning which we are here investigating purposiveness as a regulative concept of judgment; and

251′

---

[60] [*Geistesgefühl*; see above, Ak. 335 br. n. 76.]

we are not here inquiring into the principle of artistic beauty or of an artistic perfection, even though, when we consider nature as technical (or plastic), because we must present its causality by an analogy with art, we may call nature technical in its procedure, i.e., as it were, artistic. For we are dealing with the principle of merely reflective and not of determinative judgment (determinative judgment underlies all human works of art), and in the case of reflective judgment the purposiveness is to be considered *unintentional* and hence can belong only to nature [but not to art]. Our judging of artistic beauty will have to be considered, afterwards, as a mere consequence of the same principles that underlie judgments about natural beauty.

Hence the critique of reflective judgment regarding nature will consist of two parts: the critique of our *aesthetic* and the critique of our *teleological ability to judge* things of nature.

The first part will contain two books: the first will be the critique of *taste,* or of our judging of the *beautiful,* the second the critique of *intellectual feeling* (in mere reflection on an object) or of our judging of the *sublime.*

The second part also contains two books: the first will bring under principles our judging of things as natural purposes as regards their *inner possibility,* the other judgments about their *relative purposiveness.*

Each of these books will contain two divisions, an *analytic* and a *dialectic* of the ability to judge.

The analytic will seek to accomplish, again in two chapters, first the *exposition* and then the *deduction* of the concept of a purposiveness of nature.

SELECTED
BIBLIOGRAPHY

A. EDITIONS OF THE GERMAN TEXT

1. Original Editions

Critik der Urtheilskraft von Immanuel Kant. Berlin and Libau: Lagarde und Friederich, 1790.
Critik der Urtheilskraft von Immanuel Kant. 2d ed. Berlin: F. T. Lagarde, 1793.
Critik der Urtheilskraft von Immanuel Kant. 3d ed. Berlin: F. T. Lagarde, 1799.

2. Contemporary Editions

Akademie edition*: Kants gesammelte Schriften.* Königlich Preußische Akademie der Wissenschaften. Berlin: Walter de Gruyter & Co. and Predecessors, 1902–. The third *Critique,* ed. Wilhelm Windelband, is in vol. 5 (1908); the First Introduction, ed. Gerhard Lehmann, is in vol. 20 (1942).
Philosophische Bibliothek edition*: Kants sämtliche Werke.* Leipzig: Felix Meiner Verlag, 1921–40. The third *Critique,* ed. Karl Vorländer, is in vol. 39a (1924); the First Introduction, ed. Gerhard Lehmann, is in vol. 39b (1927). Second edition of the First Introduction: *Erste Einleitung in die Kritik der Urteilskraft; nach der Handschrift.* Ed. Gerhard Lehmann. Hamburg: Felix Meiner Verlag, 1970.
Cassirer edition: *Immanuel Kants Werke.* Ed. Ernst Cassirer. Berlin: Bruno Cassirer, 1912–22. The third Critique as well as the First Introduction, both edited by Otto Buek, are in vol. 5 (1914).
Further edition of the First Introduction: *Faksimiledruck der Ersten Einleitung in die Kritik der Urteilskraft.* Ed., with an introduction, by Norbert Hinske et al. Stuttgart: Fromman-Holzboog, 1965.

B. PREVIOUS ENGLISH TRANSLATIONS

Critique of Judgment. Trans., with an introduction, by J. H. Bernard. London: Macmillan & Co., 1892. 2d ed., rev., 1914.
The Critique of Aesthetic Judgment. Trans., with seven introductory essays, notes, and analytical index, by James Creed Meredith. Oxford: Clarendon Press, 1911.
The Critique of Teleological Judgment. Trans., with introduction, notes, and

analytical index, by James Creed Meredith. Oxford: Clarendon Press, 1928.

The Critique of Judgment. Trans., with analytical indexes, by James Creed Meredith. Oxford: Clarendon Press, 1952. (Reprint of the above two editions without the introductions and notes.)

Analytic of the Beautiful from the Critique of Judgment, with Excerpts from Anthropology from a Pragmatic Point of View. Trans., with an introduction, comments, and notes, by Walter Cerf. Indianapolis: The Bobbs-Merrill Company, Inc., 1963.

First Introduction to the Critique of Judgment. Trans. James Haden. Indianapolis: The Bobbs-Merrill Company, Inc., 1965.

Immanuel Kant on Philosophy in General. (Translation of the First Introduction.) Trans., with four essays, by Humayun Kabir. Calcutta: The University Press, 1935.

C. OTHER WORKS BY KANT
CITED IN THIS TRANSLATION

Volume and page numbers refer to the original texts in the *Akademie* edition. The index lists these works under their English titles, as given here.

Announcement That a Treatise on Perpetual Peace in Philosophy Is Nearly Completed (Verkündigung des nahen Abschlusses eines Traktats zum ewigen Frieden in der Philosophie). Vol. 8, 411–22.

Anthropology from a Pragmatic Point of View (Anthropologie in pragmatischer Hinsicht). Vol. 7, 117–333.

Brief Outline of Some Reflections Concerning Fire (Meditationum quarundam de igne succincta delineatio). Vol. 1, 369–84.

Critique of Practical Reason (Kritik der praktischen Vernunft). Vol. 5, 1–163.

Critique of Pure Reason (Kritik der reinen Vernunft). Vol. 3; vol. 4, 1–252.

Dispute Among the University's Schools (Streit der Fakultäten). Vol. 7, 1–116.

Dreams of a Spirit-Seer (Träume eines Geistersehers). Vol. 2, 315–73.

The End of All Things (Das Ende aller Dinge). Vol. 8, 325–39.

Foundations of the Metaphysics of Morals (Grundlegung zur Metaphysik der Sitten). Vol. 4, 385–463.

Idea for a Universal History from a Cosmopolitan Point of View (Idee zu einer allgemeinen Geschichte in weltbürgerlicher Absicht). Vol. 8, 15–31.

Logic (Logik). Vol. 9, 1–150.

Metaphysical Foundations of Natural Science (Metaphysische Anfangsgründe der Naturwissenschaften). Vol. 4, 465–565.

Metaphysics of Morals (Metaphysik der Sitten). Vol. 6, 203–493.

New Elucidation of the First Principles of Cognition in Metaphysics (Principorum primorum cognitionis metaphysicae nova dilucidatio). Vol. 1, 385–416.

Observations on the Feeling of the Beautiful and Sublime (Beobachtungen über das Gefühl des Schönen und Erhabenen). Vol. 2, 205–56.

On a Discovery According to Which Any New Critique of Pure Reason Has Been Made Superfluous by an Earlier One (Über eine Entdeckung, nach der alle Kritik der reinen Vernunft durch eine ältere entbehrlich gemacht werden soll). Vol. 8, 185–251.

The Only Possible Basis of Proof for Demonstrating the Existence of God (Der einzig mögliche Beweisgrund zu einer Demonstration des Daseins Gottes). Vol. 2, 63–163.

On Medicine of the Body, as far as This Discipline Belongs to Philosophy (De medicina corporis, quae philosophorum est). Vol. 15, 939–53.

On the Dignified Tone Recently Adopted in Philosophy (Von einem neuerdings erhobenen vornehmen Ton in der Philosophie). Vol. 8, 387–406.

On the Failure of All Philosophical Endeavors in Theodicy (Über das Mißlingen alter philosophischen Versuche in der Theodizee). Vol. 8, 253–71.

On the Form and Principles of the Sensible and Intelligible World (De mundi sensibilis atque intelligibilis forma et principiis). Vol. 2, 385–419.

On the Progress of Metaphysics since Leibniz and Wolff (Über die Fortschritte der Metaphysik seit Leibniz' und Wolffs Zeiten). Vol. 20, 253–351.

On the Saying: That May Be Correct in Theory but Is Inadequate for Practice (Über den Gemeinspruch: Das mag in der Theorie richtig sein, taugt aber nicht fur die Praxis). Vol. 8, 273–313.

On the Various Races of Human Beings (Von den verschiedenen Rassen der Menschen). Vol. 2, 427–43.

On Using Teleological Principles in Philosophy (Über den Gebrauch teleologischer Prinzipien in der Philosophie). Vol. 8, 157–84.

Perpetual Peace (Zum ewigen Frieden). Vol. 8, 341–86.

Prolegomena to Any Future Metaphysics (Prolegomena zu einer jeden künftigen Metaphysik . . .). Vol. 4, 253–383.

Religion within the Bounds of Reason Alone (Die Religion innerhalb der Grenzen der bloßen Vernunft). Vol. 6, 1–202.

Thoughts on the True Estimation of Living Forces (Gedanken von der wahren Schätzung der lebendigen Kräfte). Vol. 1, 1–181.

Universal Natural History and Theory of the Heavens (Allgemeine Naturgeschichte und Theorie des Himmels). Vol. 1, 215–368.

What Does It Mean: to Orient Oneself in One's Thought? (Was heißt: sich im Denken orientieren?) Vol. 8, 131–47.

D. EIGHTEENTH CENTURY BACKGROUND WORKS CITED IN THIS TRANSLATION

Further works of the eighteenth-century German, British, and French background are listed in the bibliography of Cohen & Guyer (see F below), 310–12.

Baumgarten, Alexander Gottlieb. *Aesthetica.* 2 vols. Frankfurt an der Oder, 1750–58. Reprint. Hildesheim: Georg Holms Verlagsbuchhandlung, 1961.

Burke, Edmund. *A Philosophical Enquiry Into the Origin of Our Ideas of the Sublime and Beautiful.* London: R. & J. Dodsley, 1757. Modern edition. Ed., with an introduction and notes, by James T. Boulton. London: Routledge & Kegan Paul, 1958.

Hume, David. *Dialogues Concerning Natural Religion.* Ed., with commentary, by Nelson Pike. Indianapolis: The Bobbs-Merrill Company, 1970.

——. *An Enquiry Concerning Human Understanding.* Ed., with an introduction, by Eugene Freeman. La Salle: Open Court Publishing Company, 1907 (2d ed., 1966).

——. *Essays, Moral and Political.* Edinburgh, 1741–42.

——. *Of the Standard of Taste and Other Essays.* Ed. John W. Lenz. Indianapolis: The Bobbs-Merrill Company, 1965.

——. *A Treatise of Human Nature.* Ed., with an analytical index, by L. A. Selby-Bigge. 2d ed. Oxford: Clarendon Press, 1888.

Hutcheson, Francis. *An Inquiry Concerning Beauty, Order, Harmony, Design.* Ed., with an introduction and notes, by Peter Kivy. The Hague: Martinus Nijhoff, 1973.

Locke, John. *An Essay Concerning Human Understanding.* Ed. J. W. Yolton. 2 vols. New York: E. P. Dutton Company, 1961.

Meier, Georg Friedrich. *Anfangsgründe aller schönen Wissenschaften.* Halle im Magdeburgischen, 1754. Modern edition. Hildesheim and New York: Georg Holms Verlag, 1976.

Mendelssohn, Moses. *Über das Erhabene und Naïve in den schönen Wissenschaften.* 1758. In Moses Mendelssohn, Ästhetische Schriften in Auswahl. Ed. Otto F. Best. Darmstadt: Wissenschaftliche Buchgesellschaft, 1974.

E. SECONDARY SOURCES
CITED IN THIS TRANSLATION

Allison, Henry E. *Kant's Transcendental Idealism.* New Haven: Yale University Press, 1983.

Beck, Lewis White. *A Commentary on Kant's Critique of Practical Reason.* Chicago: The University of Chicago Press, 1960.

——. "A Prussian Hume and a Scottish Kant." In *Essays on Kant and Hume,* 111–29. New Haven: Yale University Press, 1978.

——. *Early German Philosophy: Kant and His Predecessors.* Cambridge, Mass.: The Belknap Press of Harvard University Press, 1969.

Butts, Robert E. *Kant and the Double Government Methodology.* Dordrecht, Boston, Lancaster: D. Reidel Publishing Company, 1984.

Cohen, Ted. "Why Beauty Is a Symbol of Morality." In *Essays in Kant's Aesthetics.* Ed. Ted Cohen and Paul Guyer, 221–36. Chicago: The University of Chicago Press, 1982.

Cramer, Konrad. "Non-Pure Synthetic A Priori Judgments in the 'Critique of Pure Reason.'" *Proceedings of the Third International Kant Congress,* 246–54. Dordrecht: D. Reidel Publishing Company, 1972.

Crawford, Donald W. *Kant's Aesthetic Theory.* Madison: The University of
Wisconsin Press, 1974.
Ellington, James W. Translator's Introduction to Kant's *Prolegomena.* In
Immanuel Kant, Philosophy of Material Nature, ix–xix. Indianapolis:
Hackett Publishing Company, 1985.
Guyer, Paul. *Kant and the Claims of Taste.* Cambridge, Mass. and London:
Harvard University Press, 1979.
McFarland, John D. *Kant's Concept of Teleology.* Edinburgh: Edinburgh
University Press, 1970.
Pluhar, Werner S. "How to Render Zweckmäßigkeit in Kant's Third Critique."
In *Interpreting Kant.* Ed. Moltke S. Gram, 85–98. Iowa City: University of
Iowa Press, 1982.
Wallace, William. *Kant.* Philadelphia: J. B. Lippincott Company, no date.

F.   SOME FURTHER MAJOR AND
CONTEMPORARY SECONDARY SOURCES
IN ENGLISH

Additional book-length studies, besides those included in E above,
are listed in the bibliography of Cohen & Guyer (see below, in this
section), 312–16.

Cassirer, Heinrich Walter. *A Commentary on Kant's Critique of Judgment.*
London: Methuen & Co., 1938. Reprint. London and New York: Methuen
& Co. and Barnes & Noble, 1970.
Cohen, Ted, and Paul Guyer, ed. *Essays in Kant's Aesthetics.* Chicago: The
University of Chicago Press, 1982.
Coleman, Francis X. J. *The Harmony of Reason: A Study in Kant's Aesthetics.*
Pittsburgh: University of Pittsburgh Press, 1974.
Schaper, Eva. *Studies in Kant's Aesthetics.* Edinburgh: Edinburgh University
Press, 1979.
Uehling, Theodore E., Jr. *The Notion of Form in Kant's Critique of Aesthetic
Judgment.* De Proprietatibus Litterarum, Series Minor, 5. The Hague:
Mouton & Co., 1971.

G.   FURTHER SECONDARY SOURCES IN ENGLISH
AND SELECTED FOREIGN LANGUAGES

This list supplements, updates, and broadens the excellent one in
Cohen & Guyer (see F above), 312–23. In particular, it *excludes* works
dealing specifically with aesthetics that are already listed in Cohen &
Guyer, whose bibliography heavily (and appropriately) emphasizes
aesthetics. See also Anthony C. Genova, "Selected Bibliography:

Kant's Critique of Judgment," *Philosophy Research Archives,* 5 (1979). Since the list below is again dominated somewhat by aesthetics, works focusing expressly on other major subjects are marked, for convenience, enclosed in square brackets, as follows:

> T = (physical) teleology, including physical theology
> M = moral teleology, including moral theology and rational faith in the existence of God and in immortality
> U = unity of the critical system

M   Adams, Robert Merrihew. "Moral Arguments for Theistic Belief." In *Rationality and Religious Belief.* Ed. C. F. Delaney. Notre Dame: University of Notre Dame Press, 1979, 116–40.

T   Adickes, Erich. *Kant als Naturforscher.* Berlin, 1924–25.

Agich, George J. "Lewis White Beck's Proposal of Meta-Critique and the 'Critique of Judgment.'" *Kant-Studien,* 74 (1983), 261–70.

Ameriks, Karl. "How to Save Kant's Deduction of Taste." *Journal of Value Inquiry,* 16 (1982), 295–302.

———. "Kant and the Objectivity of Taste." *British Journal of Aesthetics,* 23 (1983), 3–17.

———. *Kant's Theory of Mind.* Oxford: Clarendon Press, 1982.

T   Andersen, Svend. *Ideal und Singularität: Über die Funktion des Gottesbegriffs in Kants theoretischer Philosophie.* Berlin: Walter de Gruyter & Co., 1983.

Aquila, Richard E. "A New Look at Kant's Aesthetic Judgment." *Kant-Studien,* 70 (1979), 17–34.

M   Auxter, Thomas. *Kant's Moral Teleology.* Macon: Mercer University Press, 1982.

Baeumler, Alfred. *Das Irrationalitätsproblem in der Ästhetik und Logik des 18. Jahrhunderts: Kants Kritik der Urteilskraft. Ihre Geschichte und Systematik. Vol.* 1 (the only volume published). Halle: Max Niemeyer, 1923. Reprint. Darmstadt: Wissenschaftliche Buchgesellschaft, 1967.

———. *Das Problem der Allgemeingültigkeit in Kants Ästhetik.* Munich, 1915.

Barker, Stephen. "Kant on Experiencing Beauty." In *Essays on Aesthetics.* Ed. John Fisher. Philadelphia: Temple University Press, 1983, 69–85.

Bartuschat, Wolfgang. "Neuere Arbeiten zu Kants Kritik der Urteilskraft." *Philosophische Rundschau,* 18(1972), 161–89.

U   ———. *Zum systematischen Ort von Kants Kritik der Urteilskraft.* Philosophische Abhandlungen, 43. Frankfurt am Main: Vittorio Klostermann, 1972.

Bauch, Bruno. *Immanuel Kant.* Berlin and Leipzig: Vereinigung wissenschaftlicher Verleger, 1921 (1917).

T   Baumanns, Peter. *Das Problem der organischen Zweckmäßigkeit.* Bonn, 1965.

M   Baumer, William H. "Kant and 'God Is': A Reply to Mr. Engel." *Kant-Studien,* 55 (1964), 498–504.

Baumgart, Hermann. "Über Kants Kritik der aesthetischen Urteilskraft." *Altpreußische Monatsschrift,* 23 (1886), 258–82.

Beardsley, Monroe C. *Aesthetics from Classical Greece to the Present,*

209–25. New York: Macmillan Publishing Co., 1966.
Beck, Lewis White. "Kant on the Uniformity of Nature." *Synthèse,* 47 (1981), 449–64.
———. "Was haben wir von Kant gelernt?" *Kant-Studien,* 72 (1981), 1–10.
Benedikt, Michael. *Bestimmende und reflektierende Urteilskraft.* Reihe Referate 4 der Klagenfurter Beiträge zur Philosophie. Ed. J. Huber and Thomas Macho. Vienna: Verlag des Verbandes der wissenschaftlichen Gesellschaften Österreichs, 1981.
Bolzano, Bernard. "Über den Begriff des Schönen. Eine philosophische Abhandlung." Prague, 1843. In Bernard Bolzano, *Untersuchungen zur Grundlegung der Ästhetik.* Frankfurt am Main, 1972.
Bommersheim, Paul. "Der Begriff der organischen Selbstregulation in Kants Kritik der Urteilskraft." *Kant-Studien,* 23 (1919).   T
———. "Der vierfache Sinn der inneren Zweckmäßigkeit in Kants Philosophie des Organischen." *Kant-Studien* 32 (1927), 290–309.   T
Bröcker, Walter. *Kants Kritik der ästhetischen Urteilskraft.* Marburg, 1928.
Bubner, Rüdiger. "Über einige Bedingungen gegenwärtiger Asthetik." *Neue Hefte für Philosophie,* 5 (1973), 38–73.
Buchdahl, Gerd. "Der Begriff der Gesetzmäßigkeit in Kants Philosophie der Naturwissenschaft." In *Zur Kantforschung der Gegenwart.* Ed. Peter Heintel und Ludwig Nagl. Darmstadt, 1981, 90–121.   T
Büttner, Manfred. "Kant and the Physico-theological Consideration of the Geographical Facts." *Organon,* 1975, 231–49.   T
Butts, Robert E. "Hypothesis and Explanation in Kant's Philosophy of Science." *Archiv für Geschichte der Philosophie,* 43 (1961), 153–70.   T
———. "Kant on Hypothesis in the 'Doctrine of Method' and the Logik." *Archiv für Geschichte der Philosophie,* 44(1962), 185–203.   T
Byrne, Peter. "Kant's Moral Proof of the Existence of God." *Scottish Journal of Theology,* 32 (1979), 333–43.   M
Caird, Edward. *The Critical Philosophy of Immanuel Kant.* Glasgow, 1889.
Carchia, Gianni. "Le rovine della rappresentazione. Letture della *Critica del Giudizio.*" Rivista di Estetica (Padua), 21 (1981), 57–84.
Carritt, E. F. "The Sources and Effects in England of Kant's Philosophy of Beauty." *Monist,* 35 (1925), 315–28.
Chung-Yuan, Chang. "Kant's Aesthetics and the East." *Journal of Chinese Philosophy,* 3 (1976), 399–411.
Collins, James. "Functions of Kant's Philosophy of Religion." *Monist,* 60 (1977), 157–80.   M
Copleston, Frederick. "Aesthetics and Teleology." In his *A History of Philosophy,* v. 6. New York: Doubleday, Image Books, 1964.
Cortina Orts, Adela. *Dios en la filosofía trascendental de Kant.* Biblioteca Salmanticensis, Studios 36. Salamanca: Universidad Pontifica, 1981.   M,U
———. "Los intereses de la razón en el criticismo kantiano." *Estudios de Metafísica,* 4 (1974), 81–95.   M,U
———. "El lugar de Dios en el sistema trascendental kantiano." *Pensamiento,* 37 (1981), 401–16.   M,U

M,U   ——. "La teología trascendental, el más elevado punto de vista de la filosofía trascendental kantiana." *Annales del Seminario de Metafísica,* 13 (1978), 47–66.

U   Cox, J. Gray. "The Single Power Thesis in Kant's Theory of the Faculties." *Man and World,* 16 (1983), 315–33.

Crawford, Donald W. "Kant's Principles of Judgment and Taste." *Proceedings of the Sixth International Kant Congress.* Forthcoming.

——. "The Place of the Sublime in Kant's Aesthetic Theory." In *The Philosophy of Immanuel Kant.* Ed. Richard Kennington. Washington: Catholic University of America Press, 1985, 161–83.

U   ——. "The Unity of Kant's Three Critiques." *The Heraclitean Society. The Heritage of Kant,* 1 (1974), 309–26.

Crowther, Paul. "Fundamental Ontology and Transcendental Beauty: An Approach to Kant's Aesthetics." *Kant-Studien,* 76 (1985), 55–71.

——. "Kant and Greenberg's Varieties of Aesthetic Formalism." *The Journal of Aesthetics and Art Criticism,* 42 (1984), 442–45.

Danzel, Theodor Wilhelm. "Über den gegenwärtigen Zustand der Philosophie der Kunst und ihre nächste Aufgabe." In his *Gesammelte Aufsätze.* Ed. Otto Jahn. Leipzig, 1855.

T   Debrock, G. "Enkele Beschouwingen over de Status van teleologische Bewerungen." *Algemeen Nederlands Tijdschrift voor Wijsbegeerte,* 73(1981), 151–67.

T   Debru, Claude. "L'introduction du concept d'organisme dans la philosophie kantienne." *Archives de Philosophie,* 43 (1980), 487–517.

U   Deleuze, Gilles. *Kant's Critical Philosophy: The Doctrine of the Faculties.* Trans. Hugh Tomlinson and Barbara Habberjam. Minneapolis: University of Minnesota Press, 1984.

Dissanayake, Ellen. "Aesthetic Experience and Human Evolution." *The Journal of Aesthetics and Art Criticism,* 41 (1982), 145–55.

Dobrileit-Helmich, Margitta. "Ästhetik bei Kant und Schopenhauer." *Schopenhauer Jahrbuch,* 64 (1983), 125–37.

U   Donaldson, Th. J. "Connecting Nature and Freedom in Kant's Third Critique." *Auslegung,* 1–2 (1973–75), 98–107.

T   Driesch, Hans. "Kant und das Ganze." *Kant-Studien,* 29 (1924).

T   Duque, Félix. "Teleologie und Leiblichkeit beim späten Kant." *Kant-Studien,* 75 (1984), 381–97.

T   Düsing, Klaus. *Die Teleologie in Kants Weltbegriff.* Kantstudien Ergänzungshefte, 96. Bonn: H. Bouvier Verlag, 1968.

T   Engfer, Hans-Jürgen. "Über die Unabdingbarkeit teleologischen Denkens. Zum Stellenwert der reflektierenden Urteilskraft in Kants kritischer Philosophie." In *Formen teleologischen Denkens. Philosophische und wissenschaftshistorische Analysen. Kolloquium an der Technischen Universität Berlin WS 1980/81.* Ed. Hans Poser. Berlin, 1981, 119–160.

Erdmann, Johann Eduard. *Geschichte der neuern Philosophie.* Vol. 3, 1. Leipzig, 1848.

Falk, Barrie. "The Communicability of Feeling." In *Pleasure, Preference and Value: Studies in Philosophical Aesthetics.* Ed. Eva Schaper. Cambridge: Cambridge University Press, 1983, 57–85.

Ferreira, M. Jamie. "Kant's Postulate: The Possibility or the Existence of   M
God?" *Kant-Studien,* 74 (1983), 75–80.
Flach, Werner, "Zu Kants Lehre von der symbolischen Darstellung." *Kant-Studien,* 73 (1982), 452–62.
Fontan, Pierre. "L'unité du kantisme." *Revue Thomiste,* 76 (1976), 576–90.   U
Forrest, William. "Philosophical Anthropology and the Critique of Aesthetic
Judgment." *Kant-Studien,* 46 (1954–55).
Freudenberg, G. *Die Rolle von Schönheit und Kunst im System der Transzen-*   U
dentalphilosophie. Meisenheim am Glan: A. Hain, 1960.
Frost, Walter. "Kants Teleologie." *Kant-Studien,* 11 (1906).   T
Funke, Gerhard. "Logik, Systematik, Architektonik in der Transzendental-   U
philosophie Kants." In *Überlieferung und Aufgabe. Festschrift für Erich*
Heintelzum 70. Geburtstag. Ed. Herta Nagl-Docekal. Vol. 1. Vienna, 1982,
23–34.
Gadamer, Hans-Georg. "On the Problematic Character of Aesthetic Con-
sciousness." *Graduate Faculty Philosophy Journal,* 9 (1982), 31–40.
Gambazzi, Paolo. *Sensibilità, immaginazione e bellezza. Introduzione alla*
dimensione estetica nelle tre Critiche di Kant. Verona, 1981.
Gauthier, David. "The Unity of Reason: A Subversive Reinterpretation of   U
Kant." *Ethics,* 96 (1985), 74–88.
Genova, Anthony C. "Aesthetic Justification and Systematic Unity in Kant's   U
Third Critique." *Proceedings of the Sixth International Kant Congress.*
Forthcoming.
———. "Kant's Complex Problem of Reflective Judgment." *Review of Meta-*
physics, 23 (1970), 452–80.
———. "Kant's Three Critiques: A Suggested Analytical Framework." *Kant-*   U
Studien, 60 (1968–69), 135–46.
———. "The Purposive Unity of Kant's Critical Idealism." *Idealistic Studies,* 5   U
(1975), 177–89.
Gilbert, Kathryn, and Helmut Kuhn. *A History of Esthetics.* Ch. 11. New
York: Macmillan Publishing Co., 1939.
Gilead, Amihud. "Restless and Impelling Reason: On the Architectonic of   U
Human Reason, According to Kant." *Idealistic Studies,* 15 (1985), 137–50.
———. "Teleological Time: A Variation on a Kantian Theme." *Review of*   T
Metaphysics, 38 (1985), 529–62.
Gniffke, Franz. "Über den Geschmack kann man streiten. Ästhetisches Urteil
und Genie bei Kant." In *Die Kunst gibt zu denken. Über das Verhältnis von*
Philosophie und Kunst. Eds. Ursula Franke and Volker Gerhardt. Münster,
1981, 32–53.
Gomez Caffarena, José. "Fé racional y existencia de dios." *Revista de Filosofía.*   M
Ser. 2, vol. 4 (1981), 179–95.
Gordon, Kate. "Criticism of Two of Kant's Criteria of the Aesthetic." In
Essays in Honor of John Dewey. New York: Henry Holt, 1929, 148–55.
Gram, Moltke S. "Intellectual Intuition: The Continuity Thesis." *Journal of*
the History of Ideas, 42 (1981), 287–304.
Graubner, Hans. "Kant (1724–1804)." In *Klassiker der Literaturtheorie. Von*
Boileau bis Barthes. Ed. Horst Turk. Munich, 1979, 35–61.
Gregor, Mary J. "Aesthetic Form and Sensory Content in the *Critique of*

Judgment." In *The Philosophy of Immanuel Kant.* Ed. Richard Kennington. Washington: Catholic University of America Press, 1985, 185–99.

Groot, Ger, and Charo Crego. "Pierre Bourdieu en de Filosofische Esthetica." *Algemeen Nederlands Tijdschrift voor Wijsbegeerte,* 77 (1985), 21–35.

Guanti, Giovanni. *Romanticismo e musica. L'estetica musicale da Kant a Nietzsche.* Turin, 1981.

M   Guérin, M. "Kant et l'ontologie analogique." *Revue de Métaphysique et de Morale,* 79 (1974), 516–48.

Guillermit, Louis. "Esthétique et Critique." In *Sinnlichkeit und Verstand in der deutschen und französischen Philosophie von Kant bis Hegel.* Ed. Hans Wagner. Bonn, 1976, 124–40.

Gulyga, A. V. "The Beautiful: Its Principles." *Soviet Studies in Philosophy,* 22 (1983–84), 49–67.

Guyer, Paul. "Autonomy and Integrity in Kant's Aesthetics." *Monist,* 66 (1983), 167–88.

———. "Kant's Distinction between the Beautiful and the Sublime." *Review of Metaphysics,* 35 (1982), 753–84.

Hancock, Robert. "A Note on Kant's Third Critique." *Philosophical Quarterly,* 8 (1958), 261–65.

Harrell, Jean G. "Kant's A Priori in the Critique of Judgment." *The Journal of Aesthetics and Art Criticism,* 39 (1980), 198–200.

Hattingh, J. P. "The Problem of Art and Morality in the Context of Kant's Aesthetics" (in Dutch). *South African Journal of Philosophy,* 4 (1985), 8–15.

M   Hegel, Georg Wilhelm Friedrich. *Glauben und Wissen (Faith and Knowledge).* Trans. and ed. Walter Cerf and H. S. Harris. Albany: State University of New York Press, 1977.

T   Heintel, Erich. "Naturzwecke und Wesensbegriff." In *Zur Kantforschung der Gegenwart.* Ed. Peter Heintel and Ludwig Nagl. Darmstadt, 1981, 271–97.

U   Heintel, Peter. *Die Bedeutung der Kritik der ästhetischen Urteilskraft für die transzendentale Systematik.* Kantstudien Ergänzungshefte, 99. Bonn: H. Bouvier Verlag, 1970.

Henckmann, Wolfhart. "Das Problem der ästhetischen Wahrnehmung in Kants Ästhetik." *Philosophisches Jahrbuch,* 78 (1971).

T   Hermann, István. *Kants Teleologie.* Budapest: Akadémiai Kiadó, 1972.

U   Horkheimer, Max. *Über Kants Kritik der Urteilskraft als Bindeglied zwischen theoretischer und praktischer Philosophie.* Frankfurt am Main, 1925.

Hund, William B. "Kant and A. Lazaroff on the Sublime." *Kant-Studien,* 73 (1982), 351–55.

M   ———. "The Sublime and God in Kant's 'Critique of Judgment.'" *The New Scholasticism,* 57 (1983), 42–70.

Imbert, Claude. "La philosophie critique et l'énigme du jugement de goût (Kant, Husserl et Heidegger)." In *Les fins de l'homme à partir du travail de Jacques Derrida.* Paris, 1981, 619–35.

Jacoby, Günther. *Herders und Kants Ästhetik.* Leipzig: Dürr, 1907.

Jergius, Holger. *Subjektive Allgemeinheit. Untersuchungen im Anschluß an Kant.* Freiburg: Verlag K. Alber, 1984.

Jordan, Elijah. *The Constitutive and Regulative Principles in Kant.* Chicago: University of Chicago Press, 1912.

Kalinnikov, L.A. "What Sense is Concealed in the Postulates of Practical Reason?" *Proceedings of the Sixth International Kant Congress.* Forthcoming.   M

Kaulbauch, Friedrich. *Ästhetische Welterkenntnis bei Kant.* Würzburg: Verlag Königshausen & Neumann, 1984.

——. "Der Zusammenhang zwischen Naturphilosophie und Geschichtsphilosophie bei Kant." *Kant-Studien,* 56 (1965).   T

Kemal, Salim. "Aesthetic Necessity, Culture and Epistemology." *Kant-Studien,* 74 (1983), 176–205.

——. "The Importance of Artistic Beauty." *Kant-Studien,* 71 (1980), 488–507.

——. "Kant and the Production of Fine Art." *Proceedings of the Sixth International Kant Congress.* Forthcoming.

Kim, Jong Doo. "Wissen und Glauben bei I. Kant und H. Dooeyweerd." *Philosophia Reformata,* 48 (1983), 1–144.   M

Kirchmann, Johann Heinrich. *Erläuterungen zu Kants Kritik der Urteilskraft.* Heidelberg, 1888 (Leipzig, 1882).

Kirschner, Gilbert. "Schelling et Kant: Finalité et organisme." *Studi Urbinati,* 1977, 191–215.   T

Kitcher, Philip. "Kant's Philosophy of Science." *Midwest Studies in Philosophy,* 8 (1983), 387–407.   T

Konhardt, Klaus. *Die Einheit der Vernunft. Zum Verhältnis von theoretischer und praktischer Vernunft in der Philosophie Kants.* Meisenheim-Königstein, 1979.   U

Körner, Stephan. "Kant's Theory of Aesthetic Taste." In his *Kant.* Ch. 8. New Haven: Yale University Press, 1982 (Baltimore: Penguin Books, 1955).

Kraft, Michael. "Kant's Theory of Teleology." *International Philosophical Quarterly,* 22 (1982), 41–50.   T

——. "The Moral Interest in Aesthetics." *Zeitschrift für philosophische Forschung,* 37 (1983), 588–98.

——. "Thinking the Physico-Teleological Proof." *International Journal for Philosophy of Religion,* 12 (1981), 65–74.   T

Krämling, Gerhard. *Die systembildende Rolle von Ästhetik und Kulturphilosophie bei Kant.* Freiburg: Verlag K. Alber, 1985.   U

Kroner, Richard. *Von Kant bis Hegel.* Vol. 1, 224–302. Tubingen, 1921.

Kuehn, Manfred. "Kant's Transcendental Deduction of God's Existence as a Postulate of Pure Practical Reason." *Kant-Studien,* 76 (1985), 152–69.   M

Kulenkampff, Jens, ed. *Materialien zu Kants 'Kritik der Urteilskraft.'* Frankfurt am Main: Suhrkamp Verlag, 1974.

Kuypers, Karel. *Kants Kunsttheorie und die Einheit der Kritik der Urteilskraft.* Verhandelingen der Koninklijke Nederlandse Akademie van Wetenschapen, Afd. Letterkunde. Nieuwe Reeks, Vol. 77, no. 3. Amsterdam: North-Holland Publishing Co., 1972.

Laermann, Klaus. "Kants Theorie des Geschmacks." In *Litteraturwissenschaft und Geschichtsphilosophie. Festschrift für Wilhelm Emrich.* Eds. H. Arntzen et al. Berlin and New York, 1975, 96–108.

Lamacchia, Ada. "Cognitio symbolica: un problema de la hermenéutica kantiana." *Cuadernos de Filosofia,* 13 (1973), 371–411.   M

Lebrun, Gérard. *Kant et la fin de la métaphysique.* Paris, 1970.

M ———. "La Troisième 'Critique' ou la théologie retrouvée." *Proceedings of the Ottawa Congress on Kant in the Anglo-American and Continental Traditions.* Eds. Pierre Laberge, Francois Duchesneau, and Bryan E. Morrisey. Ottawa: University of Ottawa Press, 1976, 297–317.

T Lehmann, Gerhard. "Hypothetischer Vernunftgebrauch und Gesetzmäßigkeit des Besonderen in Kants Philosophie." In his *Kants Tugenden: Neue Beiträge zur Geschichte und Interpretation der Philosophie Kants.* Berlin and New York: Walter de Gruyter & Co., 1980, 5–26.

———. "Kants Nachlaßwerk und die Kritik der Urteilskraft." In his *Beiträge zur Geschichte und Interpretation der Philosophie Kants.* Berlin: Walter de Gruyter & Co., 1968, 295–373.

U ———. "System und Geschichte in Kants Philosophie." *Ibid.,* 152–70.

T ———. "Die Technik der Natur." *Ibid.,* 289–94.

T Lieber, Hans Joachim. "Kants Philosophie des Organischen und die Biologie seiner Zeit." *Philosophia Naturalis,* 1 (1950).

Liedtke, Max. "Der Begriff der Reflexion bei Kant." *Archiv für Geschichte der Philosophie,* 48 (1966), 207–16.

Lindsay, A. D. *Kant.* Oxford: Oxford University Press, 1934.

U Long, David. "Critique and the Completion." *Proceedings of the Fifth International Kant Congress.* Ed. Gerhard Funke. Bonn, 1981, I. 2, 737–42.

Lopez Molina, Antonio Miguel. "Sentido y funciones de la facultad de juzgar en la reflexion kantiana sobre la naturaleza." *Annales del Seminario de Metafísica,* 13 (1978), 47–66.

Lories, Danielle. "Kant et la liberté esthétique." *Revue Philosophique de Louvain,* 79 (1981), 484–512.

Lotze, Hermann. *Geschichte der Ästhetik in Deutschland.* Munich, 1868.

Lüthe, Rudolf. "Kants Lehre von den ästhetischen Ideen." *Kant-Studien,* 75 (1984), 65–73.

M Macintosh, J. J. "The Impossibility of Kantian Immortality." *Dialogue* (Canada), 19 (1980), 219–34.

M Mackinnon, D.M. "Kant's Philosophy of Religion." *Philosophy,* 50 (1975), 131–44.

MacMillan, Claude. "Kant's Deduction of Pure Aesthetic Judgments." *Kant-Studien,* 76 (1985), 43–54.

U Macmillan, R. A. C. *The Crowning Phase of the Critical Philosophy.* London: Macmillan & Co., 1912. Reprint. New York: Garland Publishing, 1976.

Makkreel, Rudolf A. "Imagination and Temporality in Kant's Theory of the Sublime." *The Journal of Aesthetics and Art Criticism,* 42 (1984), 303–16.

———. "The Role of Synthesis in the Critique of Judgment." *Proceedings of the Sixth International Kant Congress.* Forthcoming.

Malter, Rudolf. "Vom Zeichencharakter ästhetischer Lust. Bemerkungen zu Kants Kritik der Urteilskraft." In *Alte Fragen und neue Wege des Denkens.* Festschrift für Josef Stallmach. 1977, 190–200.

———. "Reflexionsbegriffe." *Philosophia Naturalis,* 19 (1982), 124–49.

Marc-Wogau, Konrad. *Vier Studien zu Kants "Kritik der Urteilskraft."* Uppsala Universitets Arsskrift 1938, 2. Uppsala: A.-b. Lundequistka Bokhandeln, 1938.

McLaughlin, Peter. "What Is an Antinomy of Judgment?" *Proceedings of the Sixth International Kant Congress*. Forthcoming.

McRae, Robert. "Kant's Conception of the Unity of the Sciences." *Philosophy and Phenomenological Research*, 1957–58, 1–17. U

Menzer, Paul. *Kants Lehre von der Entwicklung in Natur and Geschichte*. Berlin, 1911. T

Mertens, Helga. *Kommentar zur ersten Einleitung zu Kants Kritik der Urteilskraft: zur systematischen Funktion der Kritik der Urteilskraft für das System der Vernunftkritik*. Epimelea, 25. Munich: Berchmann, 1975. U

Michaelson, G. E. *The Historical Dimensions of a Rational Faith: The Role of History in Kant's Religious Thought*. Washington: University Press of America, 1979. M

Mitias, Michael H. "Kant and Art Object." *The Pakistan Philosophical Journal*, 13 (1974), 1–9.

Mothersill, Mary. *Beauty Restored*. Oxford: Clarendon Press, 1984.

Müller, U. "Objektivität und Fiktionalität. Einige Überlegungen zu Kants Kritik der ästhetischen Urteilskraft." *Kant-Studien*, 77 (1986), 203–23.

Muyskens, James L. "Kant's Moral Argument." *Southern Journal of Philosophy*, 12 (1974), 425–34. M

Nelson, Leonard. *Fortschritte und Rückschritte der Philosophie*. Frankfurt am Main, 1962.

Nivelle, Armand. *Les théories esthétiques en Allemagne de Baumgarten à Kant*. Paris: Société d'Edition "Les Belles Lettres," 1955.

O'Farrell, Francis. "Kant's Concern in Philosophy of Religion." *Gregorianum*, 58 (1977), 471–522. M

———. "Kant's Treatment of the Teleological Principle." *Gregorianum*, 56 (1975), 639–80. T

———. "Problems of Kant's Aesthetics." *Gregorianum*, 57 (1976), 409–58.

———. "System and Reason for Kant." *Gregorianum*, 62 (1981), 5–49. U

Oppell, Baron von. "Beauty in Shakespeare and Kant." *Hibbert Journal*, 40 (1942).

Pagano, Giacomo Maria. "Il concetto di 'Erhabene' nel pensiero di E. Kant." *Rivista di Filosofia Neo-Scolastica*, 67 (1975), 267–87.

———. "Il problema dell'immortalità in Kant." *Rivista Rosmiana de Filosofia* (Stresa), 73 (1979), 172–80. M

Palmquist, Stephen. "Faith as Kant's Key to the Justification of Transcendental Reflection." *Heythrop Journal*, 25 (1984), 442–55. M

Paul, Gregor. "Der Begriff des interesselosen Wohlgefallens als systematische Konsequenz Kantischer Transzendentalphilosophie. Eine Notiz zum systematischen Charakter der Kritik der reinen Vernunft." *Proceedings of the Fifth International Kant Congress*. Ed. Gerhard Funke. Bonn, 1981, I. 2, 839–51. U

Philonenko, A. "L'antinomie du jugement téléologique chez Kant." *Revue de Métaphysique et de Morale*, 82 (1977), 13–37. T

Plat, J. "Fysische Teleologie bij Immanuel Kant." *Wijsgerig Perspectief op Maatschappij en Wetenschap*, 21 (1980), 17–24. T

Plessner, Helmut. "Ein Newton des Grashalms." In *Argumentationen; Festschrift für Josef König*. Göttingen, 1964. T

———. "Kants Kunstsystem der enzyklopädischen Propädeutik." In *Der* U

Idealismus und seine Gegenwart. Festschrift für Werner Marx zum 65. Geburtstag. Ed. Helmut Plessner. Hamburg, 1976, 349–60.

——. "Untersuchungen zu einer Kritik der philosophischen Urteilskraft." In his *Gesammelte Schriften.* V. 2. Frankfurt am Main: Suhrkamp Verlag, 1981, 7–321.

U   Prauss, Gerold. "Kants Problem der Einheit theoretischer und praktischer Vernunft." *Kant-Studien,* 72 (1981), 286–303.

——. "Kants Theorie der ästhetischen Einstellung." *Dialectica,* 35 (1981), 265–81.

Reed, Arden. "The Debt of Disinterest: Kant's Critique of Music." *Modern Language Notes, 95* (1980), 563–84.

Reibenschuh, Gernot. "Über Ordnung." *Proceedings of the Fifth International Kant Congress.* Ed. Gerhard Funke. Bonn, 1981, I. 2, 1168–75.

U,T   Riedel, Manfred. "System der Vernunft und Natursystem: Kants Überwindung der neuzeitlichen Wissenschaftsidee." *Proceedings of the Sixth International Kant Congress.* Forthcoming.

U   Rogers, Wiley Kim. "On a Comprehensive Principle in the Kantian Critiques." *Kant-Studien,* 52 (1960–61), 448–51.

Rogerson, Kenneth F. "The Meaning of Universal Validity in Kant's Aesthetics." *The Journal of Aesthetics and Art Criticism,* 40 (1981), 301–08.

T   Roque, Alicia Juarrero. "Self-Organization: Kant's Concept of Teleology and Modern Chemistry." *Review of Metaphysics,* 39 (1985), 107–35.

T   Roretz, Karl. *Zur Analyse von Kants Philosophie des Organischen.* Vienna, 1922.

Rotenstreich, Nathan. *Experience and Its Systematization: Studies in Kant.* The Hague: Martinus Nijhoff, 1972.

——. "The Problem of the Critique of Judgment and Solomon Maimon's Scepticism." In H. A Wolfson *Jubilee Volume on the occasion of his seventy-fifth birthday.* Jerusalem: American Academy for Jewish Research, 1965, 677–702.

——. "The Scepticism of the Critique of Judgment." In *Experience and Its Systematization.* 2d ed. The Hague: Martinus Nijhoff, 1972, 88–110.

M   Salvo, Gloria di. *Cristianesimo e fede razionale in Kant.* Milan, 1981.

Savile, Anthony. "Objectivity in Aesthetic Judgment: Eva Schaper on Kant." *British Journal of Aesthetics,* 21 (1981), 363–69.

——. "What Is a Judgment of Taste?" *Proceedings of the Sixth International Kant Congress.* Forthcoming.

Scarre, Geoffrey. "Kant on Free and Dependent Beauty." *British Journal of Aesthetics,* 21 (1981), 351–62.

Schaper, Eva. "The Kantian 'as-if' and Its Relevance for Aesthetics." *Proceedings of the Aristotelian Society,* 65 (1964–65), 219–34.

——. "Kant on Imagination." *Philosophical Forum (*Boston), 2 (1971), 430–45.

——. "The Pleasures of Taste." In *Pleasure, Preference and Value: Studies in Philosophical Aesthetics.* Ed. Eva Schaper. Cambridge: Cambridge University Press, 1983, 39–56.

Schasler, Max. *Kritische Geschichte der Asthetik von Plato bis auf die Gegenwart.* Berlin, 1872.

Schrader, George. "The Status of Teleological Judgment in the Critical   T
Philosophy." *Kant-Studien, 45* (1953–54), 204–35.
Schubert, Giselher. "Zur Musikästhetik in Kants 'Kritik der Urteilskraft.'"
Archiv für Musikwissenschaft, 32(1975), 12–25.
Schüßler, Ingeborg. "Wissenschaftliche und ästhetische Wahrnehmung: Kants
Lehre von der Wahrnehmung." *Revue de Métaphysique et de Morale,* 86
(1981), 180–92.
Sessions, William Lad. "Kant and Religious Belief." *Kant-Studien,* 71 (1980),   M
455–68.
Sichirollo, Livio. "Fede e sapere. Giobbe e gli amici. Reflessioni in tema di   M
filosofia, religione e filosofia della religione in Kant e Hegel." In *Hegel
interprete di Kant.* Ed. Valerio Verra. Naples, 1981, 219–66.
Silber, John. "The Ethical Significance of Kant's Religion." Introductory   M
essay in *Kant's Religion Within the Limits of Reason Alone.* Trans. T. M.
Greene and H. H. Hudson. New York: Harper & Row, 1960, lxxix–cxxxvii.
Simon, Josef. "Teleologisches Reflektieren und kausales Bestimmen."   T
Zeitschrift für philosophische Forschung, 30 (1976), 369–88.
Softer, Walter. "Kant on the Tutelage of God and Nature." *Thomist,* 45 (1981),   M,U
26–40.
Souriau, Michel. *Le jugement réfléchissant dans la philosophie critique de
Kant.* Paris: Librairie Félix Alcan, 1926.
Stadler, August. *Kants Teleologie und ihre erkenntnistheoretische Bedeutung.*   T
Berlin, 1912 (1874).
Stallknecht, Newton P. "Kant's Concept of the Aesthetic Idea and the Appre-
ciation of Modern Art." *Review of International Philosophy,* 29 (1975),
175–86.
Stout, Jeffrey. *The Flight from Authority: Religion, Morality and the Quest*   M
for Autonomy. Notre Dame: University of Notre Dame Press, 1981.
Strube, Werner. "Burkes und Kants Theorie des Schönen." *Kant-Studien,* 73
(1982), 55–62.
Taminiaux, Jacques. "Des interpretations de la 'Critique de la Faculté
de juger.'" *Proceedings of the Ottawa Congress on Kant in the Anglo-
American and Continental Traditions.* Eds. Pierre Laberge, Francois
Duchesneau, and Bryan E. Morrisey. Ottawa: University of Ottawa Press,
1976, 124–42.
Tonelli, Giorgio. "La formazione del testo della Kritik der Urteilskraft.'"
Revue Internationale de Philosophie, 8 (1954), 423–48.
——. "Kant, dall'estetica metafisica all'estetica psicoempirica." *Memorie
dell'Academia delle Scienze di Torino.* Ser. 3, vol. 3, pt. 2 (1955).
——. "Von den verschiedenen Bedeutungen des Wortes 'Zweckmäßigkeit' in
der Kritik der Urteilskraft." *Kant-Studien,* 49 (1957–58), 154–66.
Trede, Johann Heinrich. "Ästhetik und Logik: Zum systematischen Problem   U
in Kants Kritik der Urteilskraft." In *Das Problem der Sprache: VIII.
Deutscher Kongress der Philosophie.* Ed. Hans-Georg Gadamer. Munich:
Wilhelm Fink Verlag, 1967, 169–82.
——. *Die Differenz von theoretischem und praktischem Vernunftgebrauch*   U
und dessen Einheit innerhalb der Kritik der Urteilskraft. Heidelberg,
1965.

T   Tufts, J. H. *The Sources and Development of Kant's Teleology.* Chicago, 1892.

T,M   Vanni Rovighi, Sofia. "Ricerche sull'evidenza dei principi della teologia naturale e della morale." *Atti del Convegno di Saint-Vincent 25/27 marzo 1981.* Rome, 1981, 111 ff.

Velkley, Richard L. "Gadamer and Kant: The Critique of Modern Aesthetic Consciousness." *Truth and Method. Interpretation,* 9 (1980–81), 353–64.

Verra, Valerio. "Immaginazione trascendentale e intelletto intuitivo." In *Hegel interprete di Kant.* Ed. Valerio Verra. Naples, 1981, 67–89.

M   Vieira Jordão, Francisco. "Criticismo Kantiano e pressupostos racionais de fé religiosa." *Revista Portuguesa de Filosofia,* 37 (1981), 249–86.

Vorländer, Karl. *Immanuel Kant. Der Mann und das Werk.* Vol. 1, 343–405. Leipzig, 1924.

Vuillemin, Jules. "La conception kantienne des beaux-arts comme exemple d'esthétique intuitionniste." *Proceedings of the Sixth International Kant Congress.* Forthcoming.

M   Wagner, Hans. "Moralität und Religion bei Kant." In his *Kritische Philosophie. Systematische und historische Abhandlungen.* Eds. Karl Bärthlein and Werner Flach. Würzburg, 1980, 339–48.

M   ——. "Die vier großen Probleme Immanuel Kants: Wissen—Sittlichkeit—Recht—Religion." *Ibid.,* 290–301.

Weiler, Gershon. "Kant's 'Indeterminate Concept' and the Concept of Man." *Revue Internationale de Philosophie,* 16 (1962), 432–46.

U   Werkmeister, W. H. *Kant: The Architectonic and Development of His Philosophy.* London: Open Court Publishing Company, 1980.

Wettstein, Ronald Harri. *Kants Prinzip der Urteilskraft.* Forum Academicum, 1981.

U   White, David A. "On Bridging the Gulf between Nature and Morality in the Critique of Judgment." *The Journal of Aesthetics and Art Criticism,* 38 (1979), 179–88.

M   Wiebe, Don. "The Ambiguous Revolution: Kant and the Nature of Faith." *Scottish Journal of Theology,* 6 (1980), 515–32.

M   Winter, Alois. "Gebet und Gottesdienst bei Kant: nicht 'Gunstwerbung,' sondern 'Form aller Handlungen.'" *Theologie und Philosophie,* 52 (1977), 341–77.

M   ——. "Theologische Hintergründe der Philosophie Kants." *Theologie und Philosophie,* 51 (1976), 1–51.

Wolandt, Gerd. "Überlegungen zu Kants Erfahrungsbegriff." *Kant-Studien,* 69 (1978), 46–57.

Wolff, E. "La structure du monde intelligible." *Archives de Philosophie,* 31 (1968), 464–67.

M   Wood, Allen W. "The Immorality of Moral Faith." *Proceedings of the Sixth International Kant Congress.* Forthcoming.

M   ——. *Kant's Moral Religion.* Ithaca: Cornell University Press, 1970.

M   ——. *Kant's Rational Theology.* Ithaca: Cornell University Press, 1978.

Zeldin, Mary-Barbara. "Formal Purposiveness and the Continuity of Kant's Argument in the Critique of Judgment." *Kant-Studien,* 74 (1983), 45–55.

——. *Freedom and the Critical Undertaking: Essays on Kant's Later Critiques.* Ann Arbor: UMI Monographs, 1980.

Zimmermann, Robert. *Geschichte der Ästhetik als philosophischer Wissenschaft.* Vienna, 1858.

Zocher, Rudolf. *Kants Grundlehre.* Erlangen, 1959.

Zumbach, Clark. "Kant's Argument for the Autonomy of Biology." *Nature and System,* 3 (1981), 67–79.   T

——. *The Transcendental Science: Kant's Conception of Biological Methodology.* Boston: Martinus Nijhoff, 1984.   T

GLOSSARY

(The German terms are given in their modern spellings, in order to facilitate finding them in a modern German dictionary.)

A

Abänderung	alteration
Abbruch tun	impair
Aberglaube	superstition
abgeschmackt	insipid
Abgötterei	idolatry
Abgrund	abyss
ableiten	derive
Abschnitt	division
Absicht	intention, aim, point of view
Absonderung	isolation, separation
abstammen	originate from, stem from
abstoßend	repulsive
Abteilung	division
abweichen	deviate
Achtung	respect
Affekt	affect
Akzidenz	accident
Algebra	algebra
Allegorie	allegory
allerrealst	supremely real
allgemein	universal
Allgemeingültigkeit	universal validity
Allgemeinheit	universality
Allheit	totality
allmächtig	omnipotent
allweise	all-wise
Allweisheit	omniscience
allwissend	omniscient
Alten, die	the ancients
Analogie	analogy
analytisch	analytic
Anatomie	anatomy
anbeten	worship
Andachtsübung	prayer
anerkennen	acknowledge
angemessen	commensurate, adequate, fitting
angenehm	agreeable
Anlage	predisposition
anmutig	graceful
annehmen	assume, accept, adopt
Anordnung	arrangement
Anreiz	stimulus
anschauend	intuitive
Anschauung	intuition
an sich	in itself, intrinsically, in principle

ansinnen	require	ausmachen	establish, tell, constitute
Anstrengung	effort		
Anthropologie	anthropology	ausnehmen	exempt
Anthropo-morphismus	anthropomorphism	ausrichten	accomplish, carry out
Anthropophobie	anthropophobia	aussagen	predicate, assert
Antinomie	antinomy	Ausschlag	result
Antipathie	antipathy	äußer	outer, extrinsic, external
antreiben	impel		
Anwendung	application	Äußerung	manifestation
anzeigen	indicate, point out	Aussicht	prospect
anziehend	attractive	auswärtig	foreign
apodiktisch	apodeictic	Auswicklung	evolution
Architekt	architect	Autokratie	autocracy
Architektonik	architectonic	Autonomie	autonomy
architektonisch	architectonic		
Arithmetik	arithmetic	**B**	
Art	kind, way, manner, species	Bastard	hybrid
		Bau	structure, construction
Artikel	article		
Artikulation	articulation	Baukunst	architecture
Assoziation	association	Baum	tree
Ästhetik	aesthetics, aesthetic	Bauwerk	edifice, work of architecture
ästhetisch	aesthetic	Bedauern	regret
Äther	aether	Bedeutung	meaning, sense
Attribut	attribute	bedingt	conditioned
Aufenthalt	residence	Bedingung	condition
auferlegen	enjoin	Bedürfnis	need
Auffassung	apprehension	Befehl	command
auffinden	discover	befördern	further, promote
Aufgabe	problem	Begehrung	desire
aufheben	cancel	Begehrungsver-mögen	power of desire
Aufklärung	enlightenment		
auflösen	solve, resolve	Begeisterung	enthusiasm
aufnehmen	receive, adopt, take up	Begierde	desire
		begreifen	grasp
Aufopferung	sacrifice	begrenzt	bounded
aufrichtig	sincere	Begriff	concept
Aufschluß	disclosure	behaglich	appealing
aufsuchen	look for, discover, locate	Beifall	approval, assent
		beilegen	attribute
Aufwand	expenditure	Beispiel	example
augenscheinlich	obvious	Beistimmung	assent
Ausdruck	expression, term	Beitritt	cooperation, agreement
ausführen	carry out, achieve		
auslegen	construe	bekommen	acquire, receive

beleben	arouse, animate, quicken
belebt	animate, vivid
Belege	support
beliebig	this or that
Bemühung	endeavor
Beobachtung	observation
berechtigt	entitled
Beredsamkeit	oratory
Beredtheit	rhetorical power
beruhen	rest
Beschaffenheit	characteristic, character, constitution
Beschäftigung	occupation, activity
Beschauung	contemplation
Beschränkung	restriction
beseelt	animate
besonder	particular, special, separate
beständig	permanent, constant
Bestandstück	constituent
Bestandteil	constituent
bestärken	reinforce
bestimmen	determine
bestimmend	determinative
Bestimmung	attribute, determination, vocation, destination
Bestimmungs-grund	determining basis
Bestrebung	effort
bestreiten	dispute
Betrachtung	contemplation
Betrübnis	grief
Betrug	deceit
beurteilen	judge
Beurteilung	judging, judgment
bewegend	motive
Bewegung	agitation, motion, movement
Beweis	proof
Beweisgrund	basis of proof
Beweistum	manifestation
bewirken	bring about, effect

Bewunderung	admiration
Bewußtsein	consciousness, awareness
bezeichnen	designate, mark
Beziehung	reference, relation, respect
Bild	image, effigy
bilden	mold, construct
bildende Kunst	visual art
Bildhauerkunst	(art of) sculpture
Bildungen	formations
Bildungskraft	formative force
Bildungstrieb	formative impulse
Bildwerk	work of sculpture
billigen	approve, endorse
Blume	flower
Boden	territory, soil
borniert	narrow-minded
böse	evil
brauchbar	useful
bündig	cogent
bürgerlich	civil

C

Chaos	chaos
Charakterismus	characterization
Chemie	chemistry
Chiffreschrift	cipher
Christentum	Christianity

D

Dämonologie	demonology
darlegen	set forth
darstellen	exhibit
Darstellung	exhibition
dartun	establish
Dasein	existence
Dauer	duration, continuance
Deduktion	deduction
Definition	definition
Deismus	deism
Dekadik	decadic system
Demonstration	demonstration
Demut	humility
Denken	thought, thinking
Denkungsart	way of thinking
deutlich	distinct

Dialektik	dialectic
Diallele	circle
Diätetik	hygiene
dichten	engage in fiction
Dichter	poet
Dichtkunst	(art of) poetry
Ding	thing
Ding an sich	thing in itself
diskursiv	discursive
disputieren	dispute
Disziplin	discipline
dogmatisch	dogmatic
Doktrin	doctrine
Drangsal	tribulation
Dummkopf	fool
Dünkel	conceit
durchdringen	permeate
durchgängig	throughout
dynamisch	dynamical

E

echt	genuine
edel	noble, lofty
Edukt	educt
Ehrfurcht	reverence
Eifer	zeal
eigentümlich	peculiar, own
Einbildung	imagination
Einbildungskraft	imagination
Eindrücke	impressions
einfach	simple
Einfalt	simplicity
Einfluß	influence
Eingebung	inspiration
einheimisch	indigenous
Einheit	unity, unit
Einhelligkeit	accordance
Einleitung	introduction
Einöde	wasteland
einräumen	grant, concede
einrichten	arrange
Einschachtelung	encapsulation
einschließen	imply
einschmeicheln	ingratiate
einschränken	restrict, confine, limit
einsehen	see
Einsicht	insight

Einstimmigkeit	agreement
Einstimmung	harmony, agreement
Einteilung	division
Eintracht	concord
Einwicklung	involution
Einwurf	objection
einzeln	singular, individual
einzig	single
Ekel	disgust
Ektypon	ectype
Eleganz	elegance
Element	component, element, ingredient
Elementarlehre	elementology
Elend	misery
Empfänglichkeit	receptivity
Empfindelei	sentimentality
empfindsam	sensitive
Empfindung	sensation
empirisch	empirical
Empirismus	empiricism
Endabsicht	final intention, final aim
Ende	end
Endursache	final cause
Endzweck	final purpose
entdecken	discover
enthalten	contain, comprise
Enthusiasmus	enthusiasm
entrüstet	indignant
entspringen	arise, originate, spring, result
entwerfen	sketch
entwickeln	develop, unfold
Enzyklopädie	encyclopaedia
Epigenesis	epigenesis
Erbauung	edification
Erde	earth
erdichtet	fictitious
Ereignis	event
Erfahrung	experience
Erfahrungs-	empirical, of experience
erforschen	explore
erfreulich	gladdening
ergötzen	delight, amuse
erhaben	sublime

erhalten	maintain, sustain, preserve, obtain	Fleiß	diligence
erheben	elevate, raise, lift, exalt	Flüssigkeit	fluid
		Folge	consequence, result
erheischen	demand	Folgerung	consequence
erkennen	cognize, recognize	fordern	demand
Erkenntnis	cognition, recognition	fördern	further, promote
		Form	form
Erkenntnis-	cognitive, of cognition	formal	formal
		formlos	formless
erklären	explain, explicate, declare	Forschung	investigation, research
erläutern	elucidate	Fortpflanzung	procreation
Erörterung	discussion, examination	Fortschritt	progress
		Frage	question, issue
erreichen	reach, attain, achieve	Freiheit	freedom
		Freude	joy
Erscheinung	appearance	Frevel	sacrilege
erwecken	awaken, arouse	frevelhaft	wanton
erweitern	expand, extend	Friede	peace
erweiternd	expansive	fröhlich	cheerful
erwerben	acquire	Frohsein	gladness
erzeugen	produce	fühlen	feel
Ethik	ethics	Furcht	fear
Ethikotheologie	ethicotheology	furchtbar	fearful
Evolution	evolution	fürchten	be afraid
exemplarisch	exemplary	Fürwahrhalten	assent
Existenz	existence		
Experiment	experiment		
exponieren	expound		
Exposition	exposition		

G

Ganzes	whole
Garten	garden
Gartenkunst	horticulture
Gattung	genus, race, species

F

fähig	capable, able, fit
falsch	wrong, incorrect, false
Familie	family
Farbe	color
fassen	take in, grasp
Fatalismus	fatalism
Fatalität	fatalism
Fehler	defect
fein	refined, delicate
Feld	realm
Feldherr	general
Feldmeßkunst	art of land surveying
Figur	figure

Gebärdung	gesture
Gebet	prayer
Gebiet	domain
Gebot	command
Gebrauch	use, employment
Gedanke	thought
gedeihen	prosper
Gedicht	poem
gefallen	be liked
gefällig	likable
Gefühl	feeling
Gegend	region
Gegenstand	object

gehen auf	concern, apply to, aim at	Gewißheit	certainty
gehören	belong, pertain	gewöhnlich	usual
Gehorsam	obedience	geziemen	befit
Geist	spirit, intellect	Glaube	faith, belief
Geistes-	intellectual	Glaubenssache	matter of faith
geistreich	inspired	gleichartig	of the same kind, homogeneous
Gelegenheit	occasion, opportunity, context	gleichförmig	uniform
		Gleichheit	equality
		gleichsam	as it were
Gelehrigkeit	teachability	Glück	fortune
gemein	common, general	Glückseligkeit	happiness
Gemeinschaft	community, getting together	Gott	God
		Götter	gods
Gemeinsinn	common sense	Gotteslehre	theology
Gemeinwesen	commonwealth	Gottheit	God, deity
Gemüt	mind	göttlich	divine
Gemüts-	mental, of (the) mind	Gram	grief
		Grammatik	grammar
general	general	Gras	grass
Genie	genius	gräßlich	horrible, horrid
Genuß	enjoyment	Grenze	bounds, boundary
Geographie	geography	groß	large, great
Geometrie	geometry	Größe	magnitude
gesamt	total, entire	Größtes	maximum
Gesang	song	grotesk	grotesque
Geschäft	task, occupation, business	Grund	basis, ground, reason
Geschichte	history	gründen	establish, supply a basis for
Geschicklichkeit	skill		
Geschlechter	sexes	Grundlage	foundation
Geschmack	taste	gründlich	careful, solid
Geselligkeit	sociability	Grundsatz	principle
Gesellschaft	society	Gültigkeit	validity
Gesetz	law	Gunst	favor
gesetzgebend	legislative	gut	good
Gesetzgebung	legislation	gutmütig	well-meaning
Gesetzlichkeit	lawfulness		
Gesetzmäßigkeit	lawfulness	**H**	
Gesicht	face, sight	Handlung	action
Gesinnung	attitude	Handwerk	craft
gesittet	civilized	Hang	propensity
Gestalt	shape	Harmonie	harmony
Gestikulation	gesticulation	häßlich	ugly, odious
gesund	sound, healthy	Hauptstück	chapter
Gesundheit	health	Heautonomie	heautonomy
gewagt	hazardous	heilig	holy, sacred
Gewalt	dominance, authority	herrschen	reign, prevail

hervorbringen	produce, bring forth, give rise to
Heterogeneität	heterogeneity
Heteronomie	heteronomy
heuristisch	heuristic
Hindernis	obstacle, hindrance, impediment
hinreichend	sufficient
hinzudenken	add in thought
Hirngespinst	chimera
Hochachtung	deep respect
Hochschätzung	esteem
höchst	supreme, highest
höher	higher
humaniora	humanities
Humanität	humanity
Hylozoismus	hylozoism
Hyperphysik	hyperphysics
Hypothese	hypothesis
Hypotypose	hypotyposis

I

Ideal	ideal
idealisch	ideal
Idealismus	idealism
Idee	idea
Idol	idol
Idolatrie	idolatry
immanent	immanent
Imperativ	imperative
Inbegriff	sum total, sum, set
inner	inner, intrinsic, internal
innerst	inmost
innig	intense, deep, intimate
Instinkt	instinct
intellektuell	intellectual
Intelligenz	intelligence
intelligibel	intelligible
Interesse	interest
Introduktion	introduction
intuitiv	intuitive
Involution	involution
irren	err

J

jedermann	everyone
Jude	Jew

K

Karikatur	caricature
Kasualität	casualism
Kategorie	category
kategorisch	categorical
Kausal-	causal
Kausalität	causality
kennen	be acquainted with, know
Kenntnis(se)	acquaintance, knowledge
Kennzeichen	mark
klar	clear
Klasse	class
Klassifikation	classification
klassisch	classical
klein	small, little, slight
Kluft	gulf
Klugheit	prudence
kolossal	colossal
Kompetent	competitor
Komplazenz	approbation
Komposition	composition
können	be able to, can
konstitutiv	constitutive
Konstruktion	construction
Kontemplation	contemplation
Kontinuität	continuity
Körper	body
körperlich	bodily, corporeal
kosmologisch	cosmological
Kraft	power, force
kriechen	grovel
Krieg	war
Kristallisation	crystallization
Kritik	critique
krumm	curved
Kultur	culture, cultivation
künftig	future
Kunst	art
Kunst-	artistic
künstlich	artistic, artificial
kunstreich	artistic, artful

L

Lachen	laughter
lästig	irksome
launig	whimsical
launisch	moody
Leben	life
lebendig	alive
Lebens-	vital, of life
Lebenswandel	conduct
lebhaft	lively, vivid
leblos	lifeless
Legitimation	legitimation
Lehrart	method
Lehre	doctrine, science, theory
Lehrgedicht	didactic poem
leichtgläubig	credulous
Leidenschaft	passion
leisten	accomplish
leiten	guide
Leitfaden	guide
letzter Zweck	ultimate purpose
Liberalität	liberality
Liebe	love
lieblich	lovely
Liebling	darling
liefern	supply
liegen	lie, reside
Logik	logic
Lohn-	mercenary
Lust	pleasure
Lustgärtnerei	landscape gardening
lustig	cheerful, joyful
Luxus	luxury

M

Macht	might, power
Made	maggot
Malerei	painting
mangelhaft	deficient
Manier	manner
Manierieren	mannerism
mannigfaltig	diverse, manifold
Mannigfaltigkeit	diversity, variety
Maschine	machine
Maschinenwerk	machinery
Maß	measure
Maßstab	scale, measure
material	material
Materialismus	materialism
Materie	matter
materiell	material
Mathematik	mathematics
Maxime	maxim
Maximum	maximum
Mechanik	mechanism
Mechanismus	mechanism
Meinung	opinion
Meinungssache	matter of opinion
Meister	master
Melodie	melody
Mensch	human being, man
Menschenscheu	fear of people
Menschheit	humanity, mankind
messen	measure
Meßkunst	geometry
Metaphysik	metaphysics
Methode	method
Methodenlehre	methodology
Mikroskop	microscope
Milchstraße	Milky Way
Mimik	mime
mischen	mix, mingle
Mißfallen	dislike
Mißgeburt	freak birth
Mißhelligkeit	discordance
mißlingen	fail
Mitleid	sympathy
Mitteilbarkeit	communicability
Mittel	means, average
Mittel-	mediating
mittelbar	indirect
Mitwirkung	cooperation
Modalität	modality
Modulation	modulation
Möglichkeit	possibility
Mohammedanis-mus	Islam
Momente	moments
monarchischer Staat	monarchy
Moral	morals, morality
moralisch	moral
Moralität	morality
Motion	inner motion

Musik	music
Muster	model
mystisch	mystical

N

nach	according to, in accordance with, in terms of
nachäffen	ape
nachahmen	imitate
Nachbild	derivative image
nachdenken	meditate
Nachdruck	emphasis
Nachfolge	following
nachforschen	investigate
Nachfrage	inquiry
nachmachen	copy
nachteilig	detrimental
Nahrungs-	nutritive
Naïvität	naiveté
Natur	nature
Natur-	natural, of nature
Nebenvorstellung	supplementary presentation
negativ	negative
Neigung	inclination
nichtig	idle
Nichtigkeit	nullity
nichts	nothing
Nomothetik	nomothetic
Normalidee	standard idea
nötigen	compel
Notwendigkeit	necessity
Noumenon	noumenon
Nutzbarkeit	usefulness
Nützlichkeit	utility

O

ober	higher
Oberhaupt	sovereign
Oberherr	overlord
Obersatz	major premise
oberst	supreme
Objekt	object
objektiv	objective
Obliegenheit	obligation
Ohnmacht	impotence
Okkasionalismus	occasionalism

ontologisch	ontological
Oper	opera
Oratorium	oratorio
Ordnung	order
Organ	organ
organisiert	organized
Originalität	originality
Ort	place, locus
Ozean	ocean

P

Pantheismus	pantheism
Paragraph	section
parteilich	partial
pathologisch	pathological
peinlich	painstaking
Pflicht	duty
Phänomen	phenomenon
Phantasie	fantasy, fancy
pharisäisch	Pharisaical
Philosophie	philosophy
Physik	physics
Physikoteleologie	physicoteleology
Physikotheologie	physicotheology
Physiologie	physiology
Planet	planet
Plastik	plastic art
Pneumatologie	pneumatology
Poesie	poetry
positiv	positive
Postulat	postulate
prachtvoll	magnificent, splendid
prädeterminiert	predetermined
Prädikat	predicate
Präformation	preformation
praktisch	practical
Prästabilismus	theory of preestablished harmony
Predigt	sermon
preziös	precious
Prinzip	principle
problematisch	problematic
Produkt	product
Progressus	progression
Propädeutik	propaedeutic
Proportion	ratio, proportion
Prüfung	examination

Psychologie	psychology	Rührung	emotion
pünktlich	punctilious	rüstig	vigorous
Putz(werk)	adornment		
Pyramide	pyramid	**S**	
		Sache	thing, matter
Q		St.-Peterskirche	St. Peter's Basilica
Qualität	quality	Satz	proposition
Quantität	quantity	Säulengang	colonnade
Quelle	source	schaffen	create
		schal	insipid
R		scharfsinnig	acute
Rahmen	frame	schätzen	estimate
Rationalismus	rationalism	Schauer	thrill
Raum	space	Schauspiel	play, drama
Raumlehre	geometry	Schein-	illusory, seeming
real	real	scheitern	founder
Realismus	realism	Schema	schema
Realität	reality	Scherz	jest
Recht	rights, law, justice	schicklich	fitting
recht	right	Schicksal	fate
rechtfertigen	justify	Schlaf	sleep
rechtmäßig	legitimate, rightful	schlechthin	absolutely
	proper	schlechtweg	simply
rechtschaffen	righteous	Schlund	abyss
Rede(n)	speech	Schluß	inference
redlich	upright	schmelzend	languid, tender
Rednerkunst	oratory	Schmerz	pain, grief
reflektierend	reflective	Schmuck	finery, decoration
Reflexion	reflection	Schmückung	decoration
Regel	rule	schön	beautiful, fine
regelmäßig	regular, orderly	schöne Kunst	fine art
Regierung	government	schöne	
Regressus	regression	Wissenschaft	fine science
regulativ	regulative	Schönheit	beauty
Reich	kingdom, realm	schöpferisch	creative
rein	pure	Schöpfung	creation
Reiz	charm, stimulus	Schranke	limit, barrier
Relation	relation	Schul-	academic
Religion	religion	Schule	school
Revolutionen	revolutions	Schüler	pupil
Rhapsodie	rhapsody	schwärmen	rave
Rhetorik	rhetoric	Schwärmerei	fanaticism
Richtmaß	standard	Schwere	gravitation
Robinsonaden	Robinsonades	Schwung	momentum
roh	crude	Seele	soul
Roman	novel	Seelenlehre	psychology
Rücksicht	respect, concern	Sein	is
ruhig	restful	selbst	self

selbständig	independent	studiert	studied
Selbstsucht	selfishness	Studium	endeavor
Selbsttätigkeit	spontaneous activity	Stufenordnung	hierarchy
		Stümper	bungler
Serie	series	stürmisch	impetuous
setzen	posit, consider, set	Subjekt	subject
Silbenmaß	meter	subjektiv	subjective
Sinn	sense	Subreption	subreption
Sinnesemp-		Subsistenz	subsistence
findung	sensation proper	Substanz	substance
Sinnlichkeit	sensibility	Substrat	substrate
sinnreich	ingenious	Subsumption	subsumption
Sitten	morals	Superstition	superstition
Sitten-	moral	Symbol	symbol
Sittenlehrer	moralist	Symmetric	symmetry
sittlich	moral	Sympathie	sympathy
Sittlichkeit	morality	synthetisch	synthetic
Skeptizismus	skepticism	System	system
sofort	immediately		
soll	ought, is (meant) to	**T**	
		Talent	talent
Sophisterei	sophistry	Tanz	dance
Sparsamkeit	parsimony	Tätigkeit	activity
Spaß	joke	Tatsache	matter of fact
Spekulation	speculation	tauglich	suitable, fitting
Spezies	species	täuschendes	
Spezifikation	specification	Diallele	vicious circle
spezifisch		tautologisch	tautologous
unterschieden	distinct in kind	Technik	technic
spezifisch		technisch	technical
verschieden	different in kind	Technizismus	technic
spezifizieren	make specific	Teil	part
Spiel	play, game	Teilnehmungs-	feeling of sympathy
spielend	at play	gefühl	
Spontaneität	spontaneity	Teleologie	teleology
Sprache	language, speech	teleologisch	teleological
Sprechen	speech	Teleskop	telescope
Staat	state	Tetraktik	tetradic system
Staatsmann	statesman	Theismus	theism
standhaftig	steadfast	Thema	topic, theme
Stärke	strength, fortitude	Theologie	theology
Stimme	voice	theoretisch	theoretical
Stimmung	attunement	Theorie	theory
Stoff	material, matter	Theosophie	theosophy
streben	strive	Theurgie	theurgy
streiten	quarrel, contend	Tier	animal
streng	strict, stern	tierisch	animal
Stück	component	Ton	tone

Tonkunst	music	unbestimmt	indeterminate, undetermined
Totalität	totality		
transzendent	transcendent	Unding	absurdity
transzendental	transcendental	unendlich	infinite
Trauerspiel	tragedy	unerfindlich	inscrutable
Traum	dream	unergründlich	unfathomable
Traurigkeit	sadness	ungeheuer	monstrous
Trichotomie	trichotomy	Ungenügsamkeit	insatiability
Trieb	impulse, urge	ungestalt	unshapely
Triebfeder	incentive, spring	ungestüm	vehement
trügen	be deceptive	ungesucht	unstudied
Tugend	virtue	Unglaube	unbelief
tun	do	ungläubisch	incredulous
tunlich	practicable	ungleichartig	heterogeneous
		Unlust	displeasure
U		unmittelbar	direct
übel	evil, unwell	unmöglich	impossible
übereinkommen	agree	unrecht	wrong
Übereinstim- mung	harmony, agreement	Unsterblichkeit	immortality
		untauglich	unsuitable, unfit
Übergang	transition	unterhalten	entertain, sustain
überhaupt	in general, as such, at all	Unterordnung	subordination
		unterscheiden	distinguish
überlegen	consider, deliberate	unterschieden	distinct, different
		Untersuchung	inquiry
Überlegenheit	superiority	Unterweisung	instruction
übermenschlich	superhuman	unterworfen	subject, subjected
übernatürlich	supernatural	untunlich	impracticable
überreden	persuade	unverkenntlich	unmistakable
überschwenglich	transcendent, excessive, high- flown	unzählig	innumerable
		unzulänglich	insufficient
		unzweckmäßig	unpurposive
übersinnlich	supersensible	Urbanität	urbanity
übersteigen	exceed, surpass	Urbild	archetype, original image
übertreffen	surpass		
überzeugen	convince	Urheber	author
üblich	customary	Urmutter	original mother
Uhr	watch	Ursache	cause
Umriß	outline	Ursprung	origin
umsonst	gratuitous	Urteil	judgment
unabsehlich	immense	Urteilskraft	(power of) judgment
unangemessen	incommensurate, inadequate		
unaussprechlich	unspeakable	**V**	
unbedingt	unconditioned, unconditionally	vague	vague
		Veränderung	change, variation
unbegrenzt	unbounded	veranlassen	prompt, occasion

verantwortlich	answerable, responsible	verteidigen	defend
Verbindlichkeit	obligation	verwandeln	transform
Verbindung	connection, link, combination	Verwandtschaft	kinship, affinity
		Verwechslung	confusion
Verbindungs-	mediating	Verweis	reprimand
verborgen	hidden, concealed	verwerflich	reprehensible
verbrämt	veiled	Verworrenheit	confusedness
verdienen	deserve	Verwunderung	amazement
verehren	venerate	verzagt	despondent
Vereinbarkeit	reconcilability, compatibility, unifiability	Verzierung	ornament, decoration
		Verzweiflung	desperation
verfehlt	miscarried	Vielheit	multiplicity
Verfeinerung	refinement	Virtuosi	virtuosi
vergeblich	futile, vain	vollführen	accomplish
Vergnügen	gratification	völlig	completely, fully
Verhältnis	relation(ship)	Vollkommenheit	perfection
verhängen	ordain	Vollständigkeit	completeness
Verknüpfung	connection	voraussetzen	presuppose
verkündigen	proclaim	vorgeblich	alleged
verlangen	demand	vorläufig	provisional
Vermittlung	mediation	Vorsatz	resolve
Vermögen	power, ability	vorschreiben	prescribe, enjoin
vermuten	suppose, presume, conjecture	Vorschrift	precept
		vorstellen	present
Vernunft	reason	Vorstellung	presentation
Vernunft-	rational, of reason	Vorstellungsart	way of presenting
Vernünfteln	reasoning, subtle reasoning	Vorurteil	prejudice
		Vorzüglichkeit	excellence, primacy, distinction, priority
vernünftelnd	reasoning		
Vernunftschluß	syllogistic inference		
verrichten	accomplish, perform	**W**	
		wacker	vigorous
verschaffen	provide, procure	wagen	venture
verschieden	different, various	wählen	choose, select
verschönern	embellish	Wahn	delusion
verschwenden	squander	Wahnsinn	madness
verschwende-		Wahnwitz	mania
risch	extravagant	Wahrheit	truth
versinnlichen	make sensible	Wahrnehmung	perception
Verstand	understanding	Wahrscheinlich-	
verständig	intelligent, with understanding	keit	probability
		Wärmematerie	caloric
verstärken	reinforce, increase	wechselseitig	reciprocal
Verstellung	dissimulation	weilen	linger
versuchen	endeavor, try	Weisheit	wisdom

Welt	world	zerstreut	sporadic
Welt-	of the world	zeugen	engender, generate
Weltbestes	highest good in the world	Zeugnis	testimony
		Zierat	ornament
weltbürgerlich	cosmopolitan	Zivilisierung	civilization
weltlich	worldly	Zorn	anger
Weltwissenschaft	cosmology	Zucht	discipline
Werkzeug	instrument	Zufall	accident, chance
Wert	value	Zufälligkeit	contingency
Wesen	being, nature	zufrieden	content
Widerspruch	contradiction	zügellos	unbridled
Widerstand	resistance	zugestehen	concede
Widerstreit	conflict	Zugleichsein	simultaneity
Wille	will	zugrunde legen	presuppose, lay at the basis, regard as basis
Willensmeinung	preference		
Willkür	power of choice		
willkürlich	chosen, arbitrary	zukommen	belong to, apply to
Wirklichkeit	actuality		
Wirkung	effect, action, operation, causation	zulangen	suffice
		zulassen	admit
		zuletzt	ultimately
Wissen	knowledge	zumuten	require
Wissenschaft	science	zureichend	sufficient
wissenschaftlich	scientific	Zusammenfas-sung	comprehension
Wohl	welfare		
Wohlbefinden	well-being	zusammengesetzt	composite
wohldenkend	upright	Zusammenhang	coherence
Wohlgefallen	liking	Zusammenset-zung	combination
wohlgesinnt	well-meaning		
Wohlredenheit	excellence of speech	Zusammenstim-mung	harmony, agreement
Wohlsein	well-being		
Wohlwollen	benevolence	zusammentreffen	concur, coincide
wollen	will	Zuschauer	beholder, spectator
Wollen	volition		
Wunsch	wish	Zustand	state, condition
Würde	dignity	Zuträglichkeit	benefit
Würdigkeit	worthiness	Zwang	constraint
Wüste	wasteland, wilderness, desert	Zweck	purpose
		zweckähnlich	purposelike
		Zweckbestim-mung	destination for a purpose
Z			
Zahl	number	Zweckbeziehung	reference to a purpose
zählen	number, class, include		
		Zweckeinheit	unity of a purpose, unity in terms of purposes
Zeichen	sign		
Zeichnung	design	Zweckform	purposive form
Zeit	time, period, age	zweckmäßig	purposive

Zweckverbindung	connection in terms of purposes	Zweifel	doubt
		Zweifelglaube	skepticism
zweckwidrig	contrapurposive	zwingen	compel, force

INDEX

The *roman* numerals refer to the materials that precede the Kantian text: Foreword, Preface, and Introduction. All references in *arabic* numerals are to the pagination along the margin of the text, which is the pagination from the *Akademie* edition on which this translation is based. The unprimed numbers refer to volume 5 of that edition, which contains the *Critique of Judgment* that Kant published; the primed numbers refer to volume 20, containing the First Introduction, which is included here as the Translator's Supplement. Although the headings are arranged alphabetically, the material underneath any one heading is ordered by affinity of topics, not by alphabetical or page sequence. Works by Kant are indexed by their English titles; references to other authors are given under these authors' names.

God (*continued*)
479, 481, 484–85, *see also*
Determination, Reality, Analogy;
idea of, not as he is in himself but
as he relates to the final purpose,
lxxxv, 456–58, 463, 465 n. 69,
482–84, cf. 351 br. n. 31, 438, 456,
459, 466, 481; as needed to make
nature cooperate with practical
reason's aim, xlvi, lxiii, ci, 452,
453, 455, 471 n. 87, cf. lxxxviii,
196, 346, 353, 444, *see also* Final
purpose; we have practical (a priori)
cognition of, xli–xlii, xlvi, lxxxiv,
167 br. n. 2, 456, 472, 474, 482,
484–85, cf. xli n. 23, 438, 450–51,
455, 470, 473 br. n. 93, 478, 485
br. n. 107, *see also* Cognition
(practical); our cognition of, is
symbolic, 353, cf. 351 br. n. 31 (*see
also* Symbol), i.e., it is cognition by
analogy, 353 br. n. 35, 484–85, 485
br. n. 107, cf. lxxxiv–lxxxv, 351 br.
n. 31, 437, 456, 456 br. n. 52, 457
br. n. 54, 464 n. 64, 465, 473–74,
479, 481, *see also* Analogy; we do
not have knowledge of, xlii, xlvi,
lxxxiv, 167 br. n. 2, cf. xli n. 23,
351 br. n. 31, 467, 470, 472, 475,
see also Knowledge; is a matter of
(rational) faith, xlii, xlvi, lxxxiv,
469, 470, 475, cf. 467 br. n. 75,
471–72, *see also* Faith; existence
of, as a postulate, *see* Postulate;
moral proof for the existence of,
lxxxiv, 436, 442–85, cf. xlvi, *see
also* Final purpose; moral proof for
the existence of, is independent of
the teleological proof, 444, 477–79,
cf. 446, 447; moral proof for the
existence of, preparation for it, ci,
477–78, *see also* Propaedeutic (to
theology), Teleology (its relation
to theology); moral proof for the
existence of, what kind of validity it
has, 450 n. 44, 453–58, cf. 461, 482,
and what its benefit is, 459–61, cf.
451–52; nonexistence of, effects of
believing in it, 451–52, cf.

459–61; fear of, 263, 264,
contrasted with his fearfulness
(and sublimity), 260–64, *see also*
Fear; fitting mental attunement and
behavior regarding, 263, cf. 273,
see also Religion; our obligation
to, 481, cf. 446, 481 br. n. 104, *see
also* Duty

Good—the (*das Gute*), knowing it is
identical with willing it, according
to Wolff, xlii, xlviii; is that to which
we attribute an objective value,
210, cf. 215, 226; holds for every
rational being as such, 210, *see also*
Rational; involves the concept of
a (determinate) purpose, 207–08,
221, 226, cf. 214, 244, *see also*
Perfection, Purpose; judgments
about it are cognitive, 215, 228,
cf. 209, 221, and not free, 210; is
the object of the will, 208, 209,
cf. 201, *see also* Will; judgments
about it determine our liking for
(pleasure in) an object, 215, *see
also* Determination, Pleasure; is
what (by means of reason) we
like through its mere concept,
207, 241, cf. 213, 244, 346, *see
also* Reason (practical); our liking
for (pleasure in) it is interested,
207–10, cf. 222, 230, 241, 228', *see
also* Interest, Desire—power of;
our liking for it is a pure practical
liking, 209 (*see also* Pleasure), and
has an intellectual basis, 222, viz.,
a concept, 214; is presented as the
object of a universal liking, 213, *see
also* Presentation; judgments about
it have logical universality, 215, cf.
213, *see also* Validity; contrasted
with the agreeable, 207–10, 213,
266–67, cf. 222, 292 (*see also*
Agreeable—the, Pleasure), and
with the beautiful (and sublime),
207–10, 213–15, 221–22, 226–28,
241, 266–67, 346, cf. liv, *see
also* Perfection, Beautiful—the,
Pleasure; as united with the

Perfection (*continued*)
ideal of, nothing in the world but
our humanity admits of it, 233;
superhuman, 230' n. 50; of God,
see God

Perpetual Peace (*Zum ewigen
Frieden*), xxix, 172 br. n. 15, 263
br. n. 28, 369 br. n. 26, 433 br. n.
27, 455 br. n. 48

Perpetual Peace in Philosophy, *see*
Announcement . . .

Persuasion (*Überredung*), contrasted
with conviction, 461–63, 477; art
of, 327, cf. 462, *see also* Oratory

Pharisaical (*pharisäisch*), 330 n. 69

Phenomenon (*Phänomen*), nature or
the world as (or as phenomenal),
xxviii, xxxii–xxxiii incl. n. 10,
xxxviii, xlviii, cvi n. 107, 268, 412,
422, cf. 277, 408, 417; means the
same as 'appearance,' xxxii, xxxiii,
cf. 422, *hence see* Appearances

Philosophy (*Philosophie*), is the
system of rational cognition
(cognition in terms of principles)
through concepts, 195', cf.
168, 174, 197', 242', *see also*
Metaphysics, Rational, Cognition;
pure, divisions in it almost always
turn out tripartite, 197 n. 43; divides
into formal (viz., formal logic)
and material (real), 195'; material,
contains principles for the rational
cognition (cognition in terms
of principles) of things through
concepts, 171, 195', cf. 174, 422; as
(insofar as material) the doctrinal
system of our cognition of nature
and of freedom, 205', cf. 207', 242',
see also Doctrine, Metaphysics (of
nature and of morals); all assent
in it must be based on matters
of fact, 475, *see also* Assent
(Fürwahrhalten)] its only parts
are theoretical and practical, 168,
170–74, 177, 179, 195'–97', 202',
246', cf. 416 (*see also* Cognition),

i.e., natural and moral, 171, 195'–
201', cf. 172, 471 n. 90, 205', *see
also* Metaphysics (of nature and of
morals); theoretical and practical,
mediation of the transition between
the two, *see* Judgment—power
of (as mediating the transition
between understanding and
reason), Transition; distinguished
from critique, 168, 195', 242',
cf. 207', *see also* Critique;
transcendental, 213 br. n. 25, 289,
341, 401, 242', cf. 170, 216' (*see
also* Transcendental), its general
problem, 289; speculative, 454,
474, cf. 451, 456 br. n. 51; pure,
can prove propositions from
a priori grounds, but cannot
demonstrate (exhibit) them, 343,
see also Proofs, Demonstration,
Exhibition; its entire possession
of theoretical arguments for
the existence of God, 475, *see
also* God; its duty to separate
what convinces from what
merely persuades, 462, *see also*
Conviction, Persuasion; schools
of, have usually tried all the
dogmatic solutions possible for a
certain problem, 392 n. 6, *see also*
Dogmatic; enriched by Christianity
with moral concepts, 471 n. 90

Physical (*physisch*), equated with
natural, 375; strictly, equated
with mechanical, 389, *see also*
Mechanical; -mechanical, 388,
240'; equated with empirical, 241';
contrasted with metaphysical, 475,
cf. 382, *see also* Metaphysical;
contrasted with psychological,
238', cf. 277, *see also*
Psychological; contrasted with
ideological, 448, cf. 377, 379,
413, 434, *see also* Teleological;
contrasted with moral, 445, *see
also* Moral, Metaphysics; and
moral teleology, *see* Teleology;

‎‎